Uncle John's *UNSINKABLE* BATHROOM *READER®*

By the
Bathroom Readers'
Institute

Bathroom Readers' Press
Ashland, Oregon

OUR "REGULAR" READERS RAVE!

"I just wanted to say I love *Uncle John's Bathroom Reader*! I have learned more from them than in school (ha!). I hope to collect all of them."

—**Andrea**

"Just a note to say I love your books. I read them from cover to cover, over and over. I dazzle people with my seemingly bottomless well of useless information. Thanks so much for that!"

—**Jenny**

"Keep 'em coming! I am totally addicted to your books, currently owning 14. I was a teacher for 30 years, and am now a reference librarian. I suggested to my supervisor that we order your books for our local library collection, as they are the most consistently fascinating series on facts and trivia that I have ever come across. I have sung your praises to our librarian patrons on numerous occasions, so hopefully I have helped spawn a new generation of BR fanatics!"

—**Jack**

"I love your books and have read and reread and reread the *Bathroom Readers* I have. My wife tells me I am a warehouse of useless information, thanks in part to you guys."

—**Ben**

"As a former teacher who used trivia as the main source of inspiring students, I have enjoyed all 15 books that I have read. The ones directed at children were spectacular and I used them in my daily routine. Keep up the great effort as there is always another fact or detail to be uncovered!"

—**Marty**

"I love your book so much. One day, I brought it to school and my friend went all crazy about it. He won't give it back!"

—**Peter**

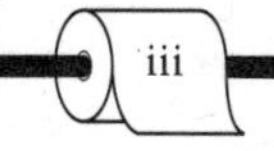

For Richard Farnsworth Staples

UNCLE JOHN'S UNSINKABLE BATHROOM READER®

For information, write:
The Bathroom Readers' Institute, P.O. Box 1117, Ashland, OR 97520
www.bathroomreader.com • 888-488-4642

Cover design by Michael Brunsfeld, San Rafael, CA (*Brunsfeldo@comcast.net*)
BRI "technician" on the back cover: Larry Kelp

Printed on Rolland Enviro100 Book, which contains 100% post-consumer fiber, is Environmental Choice, Processed Chlorine Free, and manufactured in Québec by Cascades using biogas energy.

By using 500,000 lb. of Rolland Enviro100 Book instead of virgin-fiber paper in the printing of this book, we saved:
4,250 trees, 155,333 gallons of water, 270,066 lb. of solid waste, 616,000 cubic feet of natural gas, and 593,043 lb. of air emissions (equivalent to the emissions of 53 cars for one year).

ISBN-13: 978-1-59223-916-0 / ISBN-10: 1-59223-916-1

Library of Congress Cataloging-in-Publication Data

Uncle John's unsinkable bathroom reader / [by the Bathroom Readers' Institute].
p. cm.
ISBN 978-1-59223-916-0 (pbk.)
1. American wit and humor. 2. Curiosities and wonders. I. Bathroom Readers' Institute (Ashland, Or.)
PN6165.U56 2008
814'.54—dc22

2008018111

Printed in Canada
First Printing
1 2 3 4 5 6 7 8 9 12 11 10 09 08

Hiya, Sophie! Hiya, Jesse!

THANK YOU!

The Bathroom Readers' Institute sincerely thanks the people whose advice and assistance made this book possible.

Gordon Javna
John Dollison
Thom Little
Brian Boone
Jay Newman
Amy Miller
Kait Fairchild
Julia Papps
Lorraine Bodger
Michael Brunsfeld
Angela Kern
Jeff Altemus
Jolly Jeff Cheek
Jef Fretwell
Megan Todd
Nephew Dave Fitzpatrick
Kyle Coroneos
Sue Steiner
Viola Rose
Christine DeGueron
Scarab Media
Elise Gochberg
Julie Bégin
Claudia Bauer
Claire Breen
Sydney Stanley
JoAnn Padgett
Melinda Allman
Lisa Meyers
Amy Ly
Amelia & Greta
Ginger Winters
Monica Maestas
Maggie Javna
(Mr.) Mustard Press
Steven Style Group
Eddie Deezen
Jeffrey Assisi
Publishers Group West
Raincoast Books
Porter the Wonder Dog
Thomas Crapper

* * *

I YAM NOT KIDDING

The people of Kiriwana, New Guinea, have a unique way of resolving disputes peacefully: Opponents meet in front of witnesses, then go search for a yam. Whoever finds the biggest yam wins.

CONTENTS

Because the BRI understands your reading needs, we've divided the contents by length as well as subject.

Short—a quick read

Medium—2 to 3 pages

Long—for those extended visits, when something a little more involved is required

* **Extended**—for those leg-numbing experiences

* * *

WHAT'S IN A (OW!) NAME?

In October 2007, Jacqueline Holmes of West Palm Beach, Florida, filed a lawsuit against a local nightclub after its disco ball fell from the ceiling and hit her on the head. (She was not badly injured.) The name of the nightclub: the Coco Bongo.

INTRO-DUCK-TION

Welcome back! Here we are again with our 21st edition, *Uncle John's Unsinkable Bathroom Reader*! As I sit here writing this intro in my office—surrounded by a gallery of 1950s kitsch and a flock of rubber duckies—our incredible team of editors, writers, researchers, and designers is downstairs at the Bathroom Readers' Institute, putting the finishing touches on yet another amazing book. And I realize just how fortunate I am (and you are) to have such a dedicated staff of kooks and assorted nuts putting their hearts and souls into this job.

And what does that mean for you, our equally dedicated readers? A book like no other on the market. Some examples:

• **History that never came to be.** A rocket powered by hundreds of atomic bombs, the Russians' plans to land a man on the Moon, and the secret plot to overthrow the U.S. government (it failed).

• **History you didn't know.** The car designer who was more influential than Henry Ford, the forgotten American colony, and the legendary silver mine that gave and gave...and then took it all back.

• **The answers to life's most persistent questions:** Why are snooze buttons always set to nine minutes? Whatever happened to milkmen? And is "either" pronounced "ee-ther" or "ay-ther"?

• **Foodstuffs.** Many things have been described as "the best thing since sliced bread." Now you'll know who's responsible for sliced bread! Plus, the spirited history of cocktails, famous cookbooks, and for you junk-food fanatics—a recipe for sushi Twinkies.

• **Pop Science:** All about constellations and meteors, getting to know your knuckles, self-cleaning underwear, the baby girl that was born twice, and a porky page of pig facts.

• **Wordplay, wordplay, wordplay!** Bumper stickers, idioms in other languages, flubbed headlines, and one of our weirdest pages ever: "Leave Ready Zagromyhat to Us!" (or, what happens when a bored writer has too much fun on Internet translation sites).

• **Speaking of weird,** there's "Vrillon of the Ashtar Galactic Command," Communist Smurfs, the tapeworm diet, people who drill holes in their heads, and the great sport of mullet tossing.

• **Lots of great how-to tips.** Increase the flow (of ch'i) in your bathroom and increase the flow of gas in your car's tank. How to wash your washing machine, how to shop at (and have) a yard sale, and how to make a $200-million movie.

• **Calling all nerds!** (Or is the correct term "geeks"?) We've got a lot about comic books and superheros (my favorite: an Indonesian Aquaman who shoots rainbows from his belt). And you'll find the origins of World of Warcraft and Dungeons & Dragons.

It all starts on the very next page...but before we get on with the show, I'd like to give a big THANK YOU to the great BRI staff:

• To Amy. Her patience, organizational prowess, and artistic eye has led to yet another book formatted to perfection.

• To Brian, Thom, Jay, and JD, our in-house outhouse writers who are (still) busy finishing up articles they've been working on for months. Great job!

• To Julia, our production manager for many years, and Kait, our new production manager. (Welcome to the family, Kait!)

• To our cuckoo cover designer, Michael B. Every year, he surprises us with something new...such as an unsinkable commode, floating in the vast ocean.

• To Angie, who runs in every few days with a few dozen running feet (those facts at the bottom of the page). And Jeff, our formatter-at-large extraordinaire.

• And to our fantastic crew of freelance writers—Lorrie, Jolly Jeff Cheek, Sue, Megan, Kyle, Jef F., Viola, and Nephew Dave.

And finally, a sad farewell to our old friend, Richard Staples, who shared with us his razor-sharp wit and left us a legacy of humor. Thank you, Richard. We'll miss you.

What gets all of us through life is the ability to laugh and the desire to learn something today that we didn't know yesterday. Both are waiting for you on the pages ahead, so have fun! And as always...

Keep on going with the Flow!

—Uncle John, the BRI Staff, and Porter the Wonderdog

YOU'RE MY INSPIRATION

It's always interesting to find out where the architects of pop culture get their ideas. These may surprise you.

THE T-1000. The idea for the liquid metal robot that tries to assassinate Arnold Schwarzenegger's character in 1991's *Terminator 2: Judgment Day* came to director James Cameron while he was eating a hot fudge sundae. He told his effects team that the robot had to look like a "spoon going into hot fudge; it dimples down, then flows up over and closes."

DOES SHE...OR DOESN'T SHE? After Clairol introduced this ad campaign in 1956, the number of American women who colored their hair rose from 7 percent to 50 percent, earning it a spot in *Advertising Age's* "Top 10 Taglines of the 20th Century." The line, which ends with "only her hairdresser knows for sure," came from advertising legend Shirley Polykoff. When she returned from her own hairdresser with blond hair, her disapproving mother-in-law asked that same question to Polykoff's husband...in Yiddish.

THE OAKLAND RAIDERS LOGO. The pirate's stern face—drawn in silver and gray, sporting an eye patch and old style football helmet (with two crossed swords behind him)—wasn't based on a pirate. It was modeled after Hollywood Western star Randolph Scott, who appeared in more than 100 movies in the 1950s.

"OCTOPUS'S GARDEN" On a boat trip in Sardinia in 1968, Ringo Starr turned down the octopus he was served for lunch. That sparked a conversation about octopuses. According to the Beatles' drummer, "The captain told me how they go 'round the sea bed and pick up stones and shiny objects to build gardens. I thought, 'How fabulous!'"

THE NIGHTMARE BEFORE CHRISTMAS. Tim Burton was walking by a storefront one day as workers were removing the Halloween display and setting up for Christmas. Seeing the ghouls and goblins next to Santa and his reindeer got Burton thinking: What would happen if these two worlds collided?

South Africa's national anthem is sung in five languages.

LET'S DO A STUDY

If you're worried that the really important things in life aren't being researched by our scientists...keep worrying.

• Have you ever been around someone who yawned...and you suddenly had to yawn, too? It's common in humans (no one knows why), but scientists at Birkbeck College in England discovered that dogs can "catch" yawns from people, too. A 29-dog study found that after they made eye contact with a yawning person, 21 of the dogs yawned as well.

• University of London doctoral students Sarah Carter and Kristina Aström discovered that as male college professors ascend the academic ladder—from lecturer to senior lecturer to tenured professor—they are more likely to grow beards.

• In 2005 linguists from the University of Barcelona discovered that rats have difficulty telling the difference between Japanese spoken backward and Dutch spoken backward.

• A joint study conducted by the Gloucestershire Royal Foundation Trust and the Sword Swallowers Association International (really) concluded that sword swallowers were at high risk for sore throats, cuts in the esophagus, and internal bleeding, especially if they were distracted while swallowing swords.

• In the 2004 study "Fragmentation of Rods by Cascading Cracks," French physicists Basile Audoly and Sebastien Neukirch looked into why when dry spaghetti is bent, it breaks into lots of smaller pieces, instead of cleanly in half.

• Food scientists at Leeds University in England tested more than 700 combinations of cooking temperatures and ingredients in order to determine the formula for the perfect bacon sandwich. Their finding: thin, crunchy bacon works best.

• Cognitive psychologist Daniel Oppenheimer of Princeton wrote a study arguing that short, simple words make writers seem more intelligent than long words do. The name of Oppenheimer's study: "Consequences of Erudite Vernacular Utilized Irrespective of Necessity."

There are more English-speaking people living in India than in the U.S., U.K., and Canada combined.

HATS INCREDIBLE

Three origins to keep the sun out of your eyes.

THE STETSON (COWBOY) HAT. Before the Stetson, ranchers and cowboys wore whatever hats they had, from top hats to sailor caps. During a hunting trip in the late 1850s, John B. Stetson made himself a hat (he knew what he was doing—his father was a hatmaker) with what he considered to be a comically large brim, but soon realized that it was big enough to keep the sun (and rain) off of his head and neck. In 1865 Stetson decided to start making the hats professionally. He rented a room in Houston, Texas, bought some tools and $10 worth of fur, and founded the Stetson Hat Company. Twenty years later, the company employed more than 1,100 people and manufactured hundreds of hats every day. Stetson died in 1906, but the company continued until it shut down in 1971, when it licensed the Stetson name to other hatmakers.

THE SOMBRERO. Nineteenth-century farmers in the scorching hot farmlands of northern Mexico wove whatever grass or hay they had on hand to make hats big enough to provide protection from the sun on their heads, necks, shoulders, and arms. They called the hats *sombreros*, which comes from *sombra*, the Spanish word for "shade." Mexican cowboys (*vaqueros*) adopted the hat, but made theirs out of felt or velvet with embroidery, gold thread, and other adornments. Today, the traditional sombrero is mostly worn by mariachi bands and as part of cultural celebrations.

THE FEDORA. Exactly who invented the fedora is lost to history, but it got its name from the 1882 play *Fedora*. Sarah Bernhardt played Princess Fedora, a European royal who wore the now-familiar soft felt hat with a narrow brim, a crease on top, and a pinch on each side. The fedora became the everyday hat of the 20th century (back when men commonly wore hats) but is most associated with movie tough guys like Humphrey Bogart in *Casablanca*, or real-life tough guys like gangster Al Capone. Men don't wear formal hats much anymore, but the fedora is still the bestseller in the United States.

In Spain, they call the sombrero a *sombrero mexicano*.

PRO-NUN-CI-A-TION

What are the correct pronunciations for the words below? The answers might surprise you. If you pronounce them differently, don't worry—many people do. But here's how they were originally meant to be pronounced 50, 100, or 200 years ago—and, according to the dictionary, still should be.

STATUS: "stay-tus"

TRANSIENT: It has two syllables not three, so it's "tran-shent," not "tran-zee-ent."

APPLICABLE: The first syllable is the one that should be emphasized, as in *app*-lic-able, rather than app-*lic*-able.

VALET: It's not a French word, so pronouncing the last syllable as "ay" is incorrect. It should be sounded as "val-it." (Another fake French word: foyer, which is pronounced "foy-ur," not "foy-ay.")

SPHERICAL: "sferr-i-kal," not "sfeer-i-kal."

EITHER: "Eee-thur" or "aye-thur"? "Eee-thur" is the preferred way. (And so is "nee-thur.")

PRELUDE: "pray-lood" is incorrect; the proper pronunciation is "prel-yood."

FORTE: If you're discussing someone's "forte," as in a strength, the "e" is silent. "For-tay" is correct only if you're using it as a musical term.

DECREASE: If you're using it as a noun, it's *de*-crease. If you're using it as a verb, it's de-*crease*.

ERR: Rhymes with "hair?" No, it rhymes with "her."

CARAMEL: "Kah-ruh-mull" is the original way and still the preferred way, although "kar-mull," which was once a Midwestern regional pronunciation, is also acceptable.

GALA: "gay-luh"

MAUVE: It once rhymed with "stove," but now the "au" is sounded as "aw."

REGIME: The first syllable is sounded as "ray."

JOUST: In the 13th century, it was pronounced (and spelled) like the word "just."

LONG-LIVED: Today we say the "lived" as "livd," but until the 20th century, it was pronounced "lyved."

QUASI: Today it's often pronounced "kwah-zee," but it's more correct to say "kway–zi."

A first-class ticket for the *Titanic* cost more than a typical crew member would earn in 18 years.

OOPS!

Everyone's amused by tales of outrageous blunders—probably because it's comforting to know that someone else is screwing up even worse than we are. So go ahead and feel superior for a few minutes.

BIKELAHOMA

In 2001 a German bicyclist named Gerhard Brunger set out from Quebec in an attempt to cycle all the way across Canada. But he never made it. Somehow, despite numerous border checkpoints, Brunger unknowingly crossed the border into the United States and got all the way to Oklahoma—about 1,000 miles from the Canadian border—before he realized where he was.

LOOKS FISHY

One night in 2008, a taxi driver named Shen in Huaninan, China, picked up a passenger who was carrying a load of boxes, bags, and appliances. Curiously, he was also carrying a frozen fish. "I thought how much it looked like the fish in my freezer at home," Shen later said. After dropping the man off at his apartment, Shen returned to his own home, where he discovered that most of his possessions—including his frozen fish—had been stolen.

YO SOY ESTUPIDO

While running for president in March 2007, former Massachusetts governor Mitt Romney gave a speech in Florida to a group of fiercely anti-Communist, anti-Castro Cuban-Americans. He ended the speech with a phrase delivered in Spanish: "*Patria o muerte, venceremos!*" Romney's Spanish was impeccable, but the phrase was poorly chosen. It translates to "Fatherland or death, we shall overcome!" It's the Communist rallying cry routinely used since the 1950s by Cuban dictator Fidel Castro at the end of speeches.

THE STRAIGHT STORY

In June 2008, at the U.S. Olympics trials in Eugene, Oregon, sprinter Tyson Gay won the 100-meter event. OneNewsNow.com—a news service run by the conservative American Family Association—reported the story, but because they use computerized word

Q: You may know that Roy Kroc founded McDonald's. Who founded Dairy Queen? A: Sherb Noble.

replacement filters that substitute "family-friendly" words for ones they find objectionable, readers were told that the 100 meters was won by "Tyson Homosexual."

YOU OKAY, DADDY?

At 6'2", 238 pounds, David Kidwell is one of the biggest and toughest guys in Australia's National Rugby League. On Easter 2007, he suffered an injury that benched him for the rest of the season: He tore a knee ligament tripping over his two-year-old daughter.

YOU GOT IT WRONG, SONNY

In March 2008, a man called in to Howard Stern's satellite radio show to report that he thought he'd almost met the radio host a few days earlier. While on Rodeo Drive in Beverly Hills, the man spotted a tall person with long, dark hair getting out of a limo. Believing it to be Stern, the man rushed over, yelling "Yo, Howard, I am such a huge fan!" When the person turned around, the man saw that it wasn't Stern—it was Cher. "You thought I was Howard Stern?" Cher reportedly yelled back. "What did you have for breakfast this morning, a bowl of stupid?"

BEE PREPARED

Joshua Mullen of Mobile, Alabama, spotted a swarm of bees in his utility shed. Trying to kill them, or at least make them go away, Mullen dumped a can of gasoline onto the pile of rags where the bees were congregating, then ran away. A few minutes later the pilot light from a nearby water heater ignited the gas fumes. The shed burned down and the fire spread to Mullen's house, ultimately causing $80,000 in damage. "Looking at all this, there might have been a better way," said Mullen.

OOPSS

It's fairly common for newspapers to make typographical errors, but the New Hampshire *Valley News* managed to make an especially boneheaded one—the paper misspelled their own name. The front-page banner of the July 21, 2008, edition called it the "*Valley Newss*." "Given that we routinely call on other institutions to hold themselves accountable," an editor's note the next day read, "let us say for the record, we sure feel silly."

Lowest temperature ever recorded at the North Pole: –59°F.

IN HOG WE TRUST

Pigs are where bacon comes from. They also have curly tails and say "oink." For more complex facts, keep reading.

• Pig squeals have been recorded as loud as 130 decibels, only 10 decibels less than a supersonic jet taking off.

• According to behavioral scientists, the pig is the smartest farm animal, and one of the smartest on Earth after humans, primates, whales, dolphins, and elephants.

• World's largest pig: Big Norm. He's 8 feet long, 4 feet high, and weighs 1,600 pounds.

• Pig lingo: Females are called *sows*, adult males are *boars*. A pregnant pig is a *farrow*, a female that's never been pregnant is a *gilt*, and a neutered male is a *barrow*.

• Pigs have four toes on each hoof, but use only two to walk, giving the appearance that they walk on their tiptoes.

• A pig's natural lifespan: 15–20 years.

• Pigs have such thick skin that fleas and ticks generally leave them alone—the insects can't get through to the pig's blood.

• Synthetics are mostly used today, but at one time paintbrush bristles were made out of pig hair.

• A litter of piglets most commonly numbers between 8 and 12. All-time record for a single litter: 37.

• Although a group of pigs is called a *herd*, pigs don't need to be herded. They come when called.

• Smallest breed of pig: the Mini Maialino. They reach a top weight of only 20 pounds.

• Myth-conception: If you "sweat like a pig," you sweat profusely. The truth: If you sweat like a pig, you don't sweat at all, because pigs don't have sweat glands. They keep cool by staying in the shade or, occasionally, rolling in mud.

• Worldwide population of domesticated pigs: around 940 million.

• Pigs have an excellent sense of smell. In India, they're used by police departments to sniff out illegal drugs.

FLUBBED HEADLINES

Unintentionally naughty or just plain bizarre—but they're all real.

Joint Chiefs Head Will Be Replaced

CASKETS FOUND AS WORKERS DEMOLISH MAUSOLEUM

U.S., France Agree to Mideast Truce

Butts Swiped Toilet Paper From Court

Man Battles to Prove He's Not Dead

Hearings to Be Held on Statue of Liberty's Crown

College Drinking Games Lead to Higher Blood Alcohol Levels

Helping Hurt Children Is Reward Enough

Man Stabbed With Fish

DOE to do NEPA's EIS on BNFL's AMWTP at INEEL after SRA protest

MAN SOUGHT FOR LEWD ACT

Breast Augmentation Available at Moundview

Sadness Is No. 1 Reason Men And Women Cry

YANKEES TAKE A WALK TO TIE STORE

2 States May See Delegates Halved

Governor, Legislators Disagree About When They Might Agree

MEAT HEAD RESIGNS

SCHOOLS CAN EXPECT MORE STUDENTS THAN THOUGHT

Clinton Apologizes to Syphilis Victims

0.10 INCHES OF RAIN PUMMELS COUNTY

Man Shot In Groin Area On Love Lane

Volunteers Search for Old Civil War Planes

Prisoner Serving 2,000-Year Sentence Could Face More Time

Meeting on Open Meeting Is Closed

The nape of your neck is also called the *niddick*.

THE BEST DEAL IN $PORT$ HISTORY

When you hear about how much money sports generates for players, owners, and agents, it can make you feel sick—even fed up with the whole sports establishment. But, for some reason, these guys make us smile.

THE A-B-AWAY

In 1974 textile tycoons Ozzie and Dan Silna paid about $1 million for the struggling Carolina Cougars of the American Basketball Association and moved the team to Missouri, where they renamed it the Spirits of St. Louis. Why did they buy the team? Oddly enough, because they knew the league would be going out of business soon. The ABA, just seven years old at the time, was in terrible shape: They couldn't compete with the growing and much more popular National Basketball Association (NBA), and ABA teams were losing money or folding altogether. The Silna brothers felt that a merger between the two leagues was probably in the cards, and that some of the more successful ABA teams would become NBA teams, a potentially lucrative opportunity. So they beefed up the Spirits with great young players—Moses Malone and Don Chaney among them—and waited for the league to collapse. In 1976 it did, and the NBA moved in. One problem: they didn't want the Spirits.

THE DEAL

The ABA was down to just six teams by this point (the NBA had 18), but the bigger league wanted only four of them—the Denver Rockets (later the Nuggets), the Indiana Pacers, the New York (later New Jersey) Nets, and the San Antonio Spurs. The two they didn't want: the Kentucky Colonels and the Spirits. Luckily, that didn't leave the Silnas and the Colonels' owners John Y. Brown powerless: For the merger to go through, every owner had to agree with whatever deal was hammered out. The NBA dealt with the Colonels by offering them a $3.3 million "buyout"—and they took it. They offered the same to the Silnas...but they declined. They had other ideas.

On top of the $3.3 million, the Silnas, along with their bulldog of an attorney, Donald Schupak, demanded one-seventh of future television revenues generated by the four former ABA teams. At the time, television revenues for pro basketball games were relatively miniscule—the league had terrible ratings compared to pro baseball and football. So the NBA, after negotiating the lump-sum payment down to $2.2 million, agreed. It was a mistake that they regret to this day.

SPIRITS IN THE MATERIAL WORLD

For the first few years, the Silnas made less than $100,000 per year from the TV deal. That's not bad for doing nothing, but it was about to get a lot better. The legendary rivalry between Larry Bird's Boston Celtics and Magic Johnson's Los Angeles Lakers, starting in 1980, fueled a huge growth in the NBA's popularity—and in TV revenues. By 1982 the Silnas were making almost $200,000 a year. The league offered the brothers $5 million to buy out their contract. They said they'd take $8 million, but the NBA refused—which was probably a dumber move than when it made the original deal. In 1984 Michael Jordan entered the league; by 1988 the Silnas were getting nearly $1 million a year. In 1992 the league offered them $18 million to end the contract. No way. By 1994 their earnings were up to around $4 million annually. And it gets still better.

SLAM DUNK

Business experts have called the Silna brothers' 1976 contract possibly the best in history—and not just in sports, but in all business. And the most significant clause in it: "The right to receive such revenues shall continue for as long as the NBA or its successors continue in its existence."

As of 2008, the former owners of the former team known as the Spirits of St. Louis have raked in about $180 million in total. Over the next eight years, based on the NBA's latest contracts with ABC, TNT, and ESPN, they'll be getting around $130 million *more*. That'll bring their total up to more than $320 million…for an initial investment of about $5 million. "I would have loved to have an NBA team," says 73-year-old Ozzie Silna. "But if I look at it retrospectively over what I would have gotten, versus what I've received now—then I'm a happy camper."

HISTORY'S LAST STANDS

What happens when a few brave warriors refuse to quit, even when the cause seems lost? Victory...or doom.

THE BATTLE OF THERMOPYLAE

Defenders: 2,300 Greeks

Background: In 480 B.C. Persia's King Xerxes I sought to add Greece to his already enormous empire and invaded with an army of 80,000 soldiers. In a rare display of unity (and out of desperation), several Greek city-states banded together to stop them. Led by King Leonidas of Sparta, an initial force of about 5,000 soldiers awaited the Persians at a narrow mountain pass near the northern town of Thermopylae. Xerxes was informed of the size of the Greek army and sent a message to them: Surrender your weapons and you will live. Leonidas replied, "Come and get them." Xerxes sent thousands of soldiers into the pass. They were repelled and suffered heavy losses. He sent thousands more; they were stopped again. This went on repeatedly for two days...at which point a Greek local told Xerxes about another pass—one that would allow the Persians to encircle their outnumbered foes.

The Stand: When the Greeks learned of the betrayal, Leonidas ordered most of his army to retreat and gather more forces for a battle farther south. He, his 300 best Spartan fighters, and about 2,000 other Greeks remained to hold off the Persians long enough to give the retreating army time to escape. Attacked by the main force from the pass—and now by 10,000 more from the rear—the Greeks fought with spear, sword, hands, and teeth until every last one of them was dead, including Leonidas. Xerxes had his head cut off and his body raised on a stake. Despite winning, the Persians lost nearly 20,000 soldiers in the battle. A year later, they were crushed by the Greeks in the Battle of Plataea and the Greco-Persian Wars were over.

THE BATTLE OF NUMANTIA

Defenders: 6,000 Celtiberians (ancient Celtic peoples who had settled in Spain)

Background: In 135 B.C., the Roman senate sent their greatest general, Scipio Africanus, to finish off the Celtiberian tribes in present-day Spain. Scipio decided to avoid fighting the notoriously aggressive Celts and ordered his army of 60,000 to surround their largest town, Numantia, instead. They completely cut off every possible supply route...and waited for the 6,000 people trapped inside the town to surrender.

The Stand: They waited...and waited...and waited. Six months later the surviving residents of Numantia were living on rats and dead bodies—having resorted to cannibalism—and still refused to give up. After another three months, they opened peace talks: Scipio demanded unconditional surrender, the Celtiberians refused, and most of those remaining killed themselves instead. After nine months, Scipio's 60,000 soldiers had finally taken a town of 6,000 (which he then ordered completely destroyed).

THE BATTLE OF EGER

Defenders: 2,000 Hungarians

Background: In 1520 Turkish sultan Suleiman the Magnificent sought to expand his Ottoman Empire eastward into Europe. In 1552, after more than 30 years of war and advances, a Turkish force of approximately 80,000 soldiers attacked a castle fortress in the town of Eger, one of the Kingdom of Hungary's last strongholds. Roughly 2,000 people, including 1,500 soldiers, defended it.

The Stand: The Turks had more than 150 pieces of artillery, including 15 huge cannons. They fired at the castle from every direction for days, and then for weeks...and couldn't get inside. They made repeated attempts to storm the castle, shot flaming arrows over the sides, even dug under the walls and planted bombs...and they still couldn't get inside. Finally, after 39 days, during which roughly a third of the Hungarians inside were killed, the Turks just gave up and left. The Hungarians, outnumbered almost 50 to 1, had won.

THE BATTLE OF SZIGETVÁR

Defenders: 2,300 Croatians and Hungarians

Background: In 1566 Suleiman the Magnificent was back at it. The now 72-year-old sultan himself led a force of 100,000 men against a fortress in Szigetvár, Hungary. The enormous procession

Australia's tallest mountain, Mt. Kosciuszko, and largest city, Sydney,...

left Constantinople on May 1, 1566, and arrived on August 6.

The Stand: For a month the Turks attacked; for a month they were repelled. In September they made an offer to the leader of the Croatian defenders, Nikola Zrinski: If he agreed to surrender, they would make him ruler of Croatia. He refused. On September 7 Suleiman died, apparently of natural causes, and the following day the Turks bombarded the fortress until it was almost completely destroyed. Zrinski, now commanding just 600 men, made his last stand against tens of thousands of storming Turks. They fought until only seven Croatian soldiers were left alive, Zrinski not among them. Estimates put the Turkish losses at more than 20,000.

OTHER NOTABLE LAST STANDS

The Sicarii: In 72 A.D., in the midst of the First Jewish-Roman War, about 1,000 Jewish extremists known as the Sicarii ("dagger" in Latin) were holed up in the Masada, a massive stone fortress at the top of an isolated plateau. An army of 10,000 Roman soldiers surrounded it and spent nine months building a ramp to the top. Then they dragged up huge battering rams and slammed the 12-foot-thick walls over and over until they finally breached it. They put on their armor and prepared for battle...but found every man, woman, and child inside dead. The night before they had all committed suicide rather than be taken alive.

Admiral Yi Sunsin: On October 26, 1597, a Korean force of 13 ships met 133 Japanese warships and 200 more smaller ships in Myeongnyang Strait at the southwest tip of Korea. When the day-long battle was over, Korean admiral Yi Sunsin had masterminded one of the most successful naval stands in history, losing no ships while sinking 31 Japanese ships and damaging 92 more.

Los Niños Héroes: On September 12, 1847, an American force of 13,000 led by General Winfield Scott attacked Chapultepec Castle in Mexico City in one of the last battles of the Mexican-American War. Near the end of the following day, Mexican General Nicolás Bravo finally ordered retreat, but six military cadets—between 13 and 19 years old—refused. They stayed and faced the American onslaught, going down one by one to rifle fire or bayonet wounds. Legend says the last one wrapped himself in a Mexican flag and threw himself off the castle. Los Niños Héroes—the Boy Heroes—are among Mexico's most admired historical figures.

...are both named for men who never visited Australia.

LAUGH LINES

Where sit-down readers salute stand-up comedians.

"When people blow their noses, they always look into their hankies to see what came out. What do they expect to find?"

—**Billy Connolly**

"I love to sleep. It's the best of both worlds—you get to be alive...and unconscious."

—**Rita Rudner**

"The sign said, 'This door to remain closed at all times.' Correct me if I'm wrong, but doesn't that defeat the purpose of a door?"

—**Danny McCrossan**

"Who invented the brush they leave next to the toilet? That thing hurts!"

—**Andy Andrews**

"Is it fair to say that there'd be less litter if blind people were given pointy sticks?"

—**Adam Bloom**

"I've always wanted to give birth...to kittens. It would hurt less, and when you're done, you'd have kittens!"

—**Betsy Salkind**

"My love life is like a fairy tale. Grimm."

—**Wendy Liebman**

"I realized I was dyslexic when I went to a toga party dressed as a goat."

—**Marcus Brigstocke**

"I wish I could play Little League now. I'd be way better than before."

—**Mitch Hedberg**

"I went to a bookstore and asked the saleswoman, 'Where's the self-help section?' She said if she told me, it would defeat the purpose."

—**George Carlin**

"I joined Gamblers Anonymous. They gave me two-to-one odds I wouldn't make it."

—**Rodney Dangerfield**

"Fortunately my parents were intelligent, enlightened people. They accepted me for what I was: a punishment from God."

—**David Steinberg**

"If I ever had twins, I'd use one for parts."

—**Steven Wright**

One out of every 200 American 30-year-olds is still in high school.

BEHIND THE HITS

Ever wonder what inspired your favorite songs? Here are a few inside stories about some legendary hit tunes.

The Artist: Elton John

The Song: "Bennie and the Jets"

The Story: John's lyricist Bernie Taupin wrote the song about a fictional glam rock band—it was a satire of the cocaine-fueled excesses of the 1970s music industry. But after recording the song, John and his band thought the song was bland, so producer Gus Dudgeon added in applause, whistles, and handclaps to make it sound more like a "live" performance. Released on John's 1973 album *Goodbye Yellow Brick Road,* it wasn't intended to be a single, but when an R&B station in Detroit surprisingly started playing "Bennie and the Jets," MCA Records decided to release it. John thought the song was too weird and predicted it would flop. He was wrong—it went to #1 on the pop chart.

The Artist: The Go-Go's

The Song: "Our Lips Are Sealed"

The Story: In 1980 the British band the Specials asked the Go-Go's, who had not yet made a record and were still basically unknowns, to be the opening act on their American tour. Specials singer Terry Hall and Go-Go's guitarist Jane Wiedlin struck up a romance on the road, but a few weeks after the tour ended, Hall sent Wiedlin a "dear John" note explaining that they had to break up because he had a girlfriend back in England. Wiedlin turned the letter into the bouncy pop song, "Our Lips Are Sealed," which became the Go-Go's first single and first hit in 1981, reaching the Billboard Top 20. (Hall got a co-writing credit.)

The Artist: AC/DC

The Song: "You Shook Me All Night Long"

The Story: AC/DC was one of the most popular hard rock bands of the late 1970s. In 1980 lead singer Bon Scott died of alcohol poisoning and the band, as well as its fans, didn't think it should—or could—continue. But they had an album's worth of

Since 1990 the average length of a wedding engagement has grown from 11 months to 16 months.

songs already written when Scott died, so they went into the recording studio to record them with a new singer, Brian Johnson. One day while they were working on the new album, Johnson was staring out the window watching cars go by and had a thought that cars and women were similar. "They go fast and then they let you down," he said. He immediately came up with the line "She was a fast machine / She kept her motor clean" and then wrote "You Shook Me All Night Long," which became AC/DC's first pop hit in the United States. Not only was the band able to carry on without Scott, it was more successful than ever. The album, *Back in Black*, sold 42 million copies worldwide.

The Artist: Tracy Chapman

The Song: "Give Me One Reason"

The Story: The singer was discovered in a Boston coffeehouse in 1988, and her first single "Fast Car," a melancholy acoustic-guitar driven folk song, went to #5 on the chart. Chapman won the Grammy for Best New Artist but had no more hit singles. Then in late 1995, she quietly released her album *New Beginnings*. It included an old-fashioned acoustic blues song she'd written called "Give Me One Reason," which she had been playing live in clubs for years. Despite the fact that the dominant musical styles of the day were alternative rock and gangsta rap, and Chapman was considered a has-been, the song went to #3 on *Billboard*, making it an even bigger hit than "Fast Car."

The Artist: Marty Robbins

The Song: "El Paso"

The Story: In 1959 Robbins, a country music star, recorded an album of cowboy songs called *Gunfighter Ballads and Trail Songs*, inspired by stories he'd heard as a child from his grandfather Bob Heckle, who had been a Texas Ranger. The standout song was "El Paso," a first-person story of a cowboy who falls in love with a Mexican dancer, kills his romantic rival, goes back for the girl, gets shot, and dies in her arms. Columbia Records refused to release it as a single—at five minutes long, it was nearly twice as long as the average hit song. But *Gunfighter Ballads* was selling briskly and radio stations were playing "El Paso." Columbia relented and made it a single, and it went to #1 on both the pop and country charts.

Only 35% of blind people were born blind.

CITY OF SUPERLATIVES

The Big Apple isn't the only big-city nickname. For instance, there's...

• **Chicago, the City of Big Shoulders:** You may know it as the "Windy City" (which refers to blustery politicians, not the weather), but it's also called the "City of Big Shoulders," taken from a line in Carl Sandburg's 1916 poem "Chicago."

• **Seattle, the Emerald City:** This was the winning entry in a 1982 contest held by the Seattle-King County Convention and Visitors Bureau.

• **Charlotte, the Queen City:** Settlers named the North Carolina city after the wife of King George III of England, Queen Charlotte.

• **Philadelphia, the City of Brotherly Love:** A reflection of the state of Pennsylvania's founding by the peaceful religious sect known as the Quakers, *Philadelphia* in Greek translates literally to "city of brotherly love."

• **Rochester, New York, the Flour City:** Flour milling was the biggest industry in the city in the late 19th century.

• **Milwaukee, the Cream City:** It has nothing to do with the dairy industry for which the rest of the state is famous. Red lacustrine clay is found in nearby lakes, and when it's fired, it turns from red to cream-colored. Since the late 1800s, these cream-colored bricks have been a popular building material in the Milwaukee area.

• **Houston, the Magnolia City:** First coined in the 1870s. Parts of the city occupy what used to be large forests of magnolia trees.

• **New Orleans, the Big Easy:** There are two versions of the origin, both from the early 1900s. Theory #1: Musicians called it "the Big Easy" because it was so easy to find work in one of the city's many nightclubs. Theory #2: There were too few cops in New Orleans to enforce Prohibition, so there were a lot of illegal bars—so many that the city earned the nickname the "Big Speakeasy," or the "Big Easy," for short.

45% of Americans believe in the Devil...but only 13% of Brits do.

• **Miami, the Magic City:** The term was coined by a reporter in the 1910s after the city's population exploded, as if by magic, from 300 in 1896 to 12,000 by 1910.

• **Dallas, the Big D:** The name was used as early as the 1930s but was popularized by the 1956 musical *The Most Happy Fella*. A character sings "Big D" about Dallas, which includes the lyric "Big D, little *a*, double *l*, *a-s*."

• **Nashville, the Athens of the South:** The city has been called that since the 1850s. Like the ancient Greek city, Nashville was a center of education, hosting four colleges. It was also the first Southern city with a public school system. (Nashville is also known as "Music City, USA," because it's the hub of the country music industry.)

• **San Francisco, Baghdad by the Bay:** *San Francisco Chronicle* columnist Herb Caen invented the phrase in the 1940s in honor of the city's multicultural population.

• **Indianapolis, the Circle City:** Unlike most cities, which are arranged in a rectangular grid, Indianapolis was originally built as a series of concentric circles, with a circular commons at the center.

• **Portland, the City of Roses:** The city's wet climate makes it well suited for growing roses. The International Rose Test Garden is located there; there's been an annual Rose Festival since 1905.

• **Boston, the Cradle of Liberty:** Two major events that directly led to the American Revolution occurred in Boston: the Boston Massacre and the Boston Tea Party.

• **Washington, D.C., the Chocolate City:** It may not be politically correct, but Washington disc jockeys coined the term in the 1970s to affectionately refer to the city's predominantly African-American population. It was popularized when the funk band Parliament released an album called *Chocolate City* in 1975.

* * *

"I have an affection for a great city. I feel safe in the neighborhood of man, and enjoy the sweet security of the streets."

—**Henry Wadsworth Longfellow**

In a single day, the average person takes about 18,000 steps.

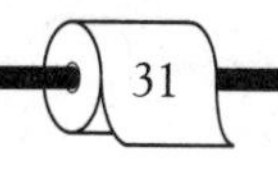

DON'T MAKE THEM ANGRY

Tales of humans and animals getting their dander up.

DON'T MAKE THE BUNNY ANGRY
Linda Mellberg of Vaasa, Finland, heard a ruckus in her farmyard in June 2008, and looked outside to see three crows harassing a hare. The hare responded by catching one of the crows by the neck and killing it. Mellberg grabbed her camera and filmed the rest of the battle, during which the two remaining crows screeched and dive-bombed the hare repeatedly while it thrashed their dead friend. Mellberg told reporters she thought the crows may have angered the hare by attacking its litter of babies.

DON'T MAKE THE PUFFER FISH ANGRY
A 13-year-old Cambodian boy was fishing with his father in May 2008 when a poisonous puffer fish became trapped in his net. After he waded into the water and freed the fish, it swam straight for the boy's testicles and bit them several times. Luckily the boy wasn't stung by the fish's spines (they're the poisonous parts), but he did require hospitalization...for his very personal fish story.

DON'T MAKE THE EX-GIRLFRIEND ANGRY
In 2007 Timothy Mortimore of Torquay, England, broke up with his girlfriend, Lee Armor, after a six-month relationship. The woman was pregnant...and so upset that Mortimore was leaving that she let him know in a text message. Then she sent another one...and another...and another. Over the next two months she sent him 10,843 text messages. That's an average of one every eight seconds. She also made angry phone calls, sent angry video messages, and made angry visits to his home. Mortimore finally called police, and Armor was ultimately fined £200 (about $400) to cover court costs and banned from any further contact with Mortimore. (It was later determined that he was not the father of Armor's child.)

The Chinese words for "crisis" and "opportunity" are the same.

DON'T MAKE THE DAY TRADER ANGRY

Wall Street stockbroker Christopher Carter, 44, was in Manhattan's exclusive Equinox gym in August 2007, taking a "spinning" class (i.e., riding stationary bikes). The guy two bikes down from him, investment banker Stuart Sugarman, 48, was a loud and exuberant participant, and often grunted, whooped, and yelled things like "You go girl!" That, apparently, got on Carter's nerves. He told Sugarman to "Shut the %#@* up," then ran over, grabbed the front of Sugarman's bike, and flipped it (and Sugarman) into a wall. Sugarman suffered a concussion and six injured vertebrae, and was in the hospital for two weeks. Carter was charged with assault, for which he could have spent a year in prison, but he was found not guilty. (Jurors later said that they would have been annoyed, too.)

DON'T MAKE THE BRIDE ANGRY

Adrienne Samen of Manchester, Connecticut, got married in 2003. The reception was held at The Mill on the River restaurant and, by all accounts, she had a good time. At the end of the evening the bar closed, which apparently upset the bride. Samen, who, at 18, was too young to drink anyway, proceeded to throw anything and everything she could find, including bottles, glasses, silverware, chairs, tables, wedding gifts, and even the wedding cake. Police were called and had no trouble identifying the drunken woman in the wedding dress walking down the road. Still angry, she bit one of the officers on the arm while they were trying to get her in the car. She was convicted on charges of criminal mischief and fined $90. "This behavior," the judge told her in court, "does not bode well for the well-being of your marriage."

* * *

I'M GIVING UP UNDERWEAR FOR LINT

Contrary to the long-held scientific belief that belly-button lint accumulates downward from the upper body, researchers at Sydney University in Australia now believe that lint moves upward from the underwear.

Where are the Mount of Jupiter and the Girdle of Venus located? On the palm of your hand.

THE WORD FARM

Here's a crop of common words that have farm-related origins.

DELIRIUM
Meaning: Mental disturbance
Origin: The Latin root of this word is *deliriare*, meaning "to go off the furrow," or to not plow in a straight line.

BALK
Meaning: To hesitate
Origin: From the Middle English noun *balca*, referring to a ridge of unplowed land between two fields. The modern verb came about because horses approaching such a ridge would often hesitate.

THRESHOLD
Meaning: A door sill or any kind of boundary, real or imagined
Origin: The Old English word for the stone or timber at the floor of an entryway was *þrescold*, from *þrescan*—meaning "thresh," to trample grain.

HACK
Meaning: Someone hired for low-quality work
Origin: It came to modern English in about 1700 from the Middle English word *hackney*, which meant "an ordinary horse."

MARSHAL
Meaning: A high ministerial official or law officer
Origin: Appearing in the 1300s, from the Old High German *marahscalc*, and combination of *marah*, meaning "horse," and *scalc*, meaning "servant." It referred to a servant in charge of stables.

VILLAIN
Meaning: A scoundrel or criminal
Origin: Its root is the Middle Latin word *villanus*, or "farmhand." (A *villa* is a farm or country estate.) The word entered the English language around 1300 meaning "lowborn," which evolved over the centuries into a person who commits crimes or ill deeds.

The longest known alligator was 19'2". It was found in Louisiana in the early 1900s.

WORLD'S LARGEST...

Dozens of American towns have special claims to fame: They have the "world's largest" something. Here are some examples.

• **LOON (Virginia, Minnesota).** Sitting on Silver Lake is this steel and fiberglass bird, which measures 20 feet across. It's been tethered to the bottom of the lake since 1982. (The original loon was stolen in 1979.)

• **BALL OF STRING (Weston, Missouri).** This 19-foot-wide, 3,712-pound ball of string was made by a farmer in the 1950s. It now it sits on a red, white, and blue platform in a local bar.

• **BASEBALL BAT (Louisville, Kentucky).** This 120-foot, 34-ton, hollow steel bat rests against the Louisville Slugger Museum.

• **TIME CAPSULE (Seward, Nebraska).** It's not just a box in the ground—it's a 45-ton vault, buried in 1975. There are more than 5,000 items from the 1970s inside, including a leisure suit and a Chevy Vega. (It's scheduled to be opened in 2025.)

• **GOLD NUGGET (Las Vegas, Nevada).** It was discovered in Australia in 1980 and purchased by the Golden Nugget casino for $1 million. It weighs 62 pounds and it's the size of a cat.

• **THERMOMETER (Baker, California).** At the gateway to Death Valley, one of the hottest places on Earth, stands this working thermometer, which is 134 feet tall to commemorate the highest temperature ever recorded at Death Valley: 134°F (1913).

• **FISHING BOBBER (Pequot Lakes, Minnesota).** It's called "Paul Bunyan's Fishing Bobber" (but it's really just the town water tower painted red and white to resemble a piece of tackle).

• **COWBOY BOOTS (San Antonio, Texas).** They're white and brown, and 40 feet tall. They sit outside Saks Fifth Avenue.

• **CHEST OF DRAWERS (High Point, North Carolina).** Honoring the region's furniture industry is this 80-foot-tall chest, built by the Furnitureland Store.

The quartz crystal in a wristwatch vibrates at a rate of 32,768 times per second.

CLASSROOM FILMS

Anyone who grew up in the 1950s or '60s probably remembers the "mental hygiene" and "good citizenship" films that were shown in school, featuring important information on topics like health, nutrition, and dating. Here are some memorable ones. (And they're all real.)

ARE MANNERS IMPORTANT? (Encyclopedia Brittanica Films, 1954). Mickey is a rude little boy who thinks that "manners are just for grown-ups." He realizes he's wrong and starts to be more polite when nobody will sit with him at lunch, and when he has a nightmare in which he imagines he's president, he abolishes manners, and the entire world attacks him.

BEGINNING TO DATE (Encyclopedia Brittanica Films, 1953). George wants to take Mildred to the Winter Frolic at the community center, but he's never dated before and doesn't know how. He asks his swim coach, who gives him advice like "keep trying" and possible conversation topics, such as Mildred's new dog.

CINDY GOES TO A PARTY (Young America Films, 1955). Cindy is a 12-year-old tomboy, and because of that, doesn't get invited to a birthday party. She goes to bed sobbing, but is awakened by her fairy godmother who gives her a frilly dress and takes her to the party. At the party, the fairy waves her wand and party etiquette rules appear on the screen. Samples: "Don't break things" and "Leave on time."

HEALTHY FEET (Coronet Instructional Films, 1958). Tom is a popular teenager. Why? Because he takes good care of his feet. He always dries between his toes, checks for fungus, and cuts his nails evenly so as not to contract foot problems such as bunions, blisters, and ingrown toenails (all graphically illustrated).

IT'S ALL IN KNOWING HOW (Chicago Film Studios, 1954). Bob's life is a mess—his girlfriend thinks he's boring and his football playing isn't what it used to be. Bob's coach tells him how to fix it: Eat the right foods, like three pats of butter and two quarts

The first known use of separate men's and women's bathrooms was at a Parisian ball in 1739.

of milk every day. (The film was co-produced by the National Dairy Council.)

WARNING FROM OUTER SPACE (Professional Arts, 1967). Aliens from the Galaxy Zeta are flying past Earth in their spaceship when their video screen picks up images of humans smoking. Alarmed, the aliens kidnap five human smokers and warn them that if they don't all stop smoking, they will end up like the Zetas—nearly eradicated. All the dialogue is spoken in rhyming couplets.

GOING STEADY (Coronet Instructional Films, 1951). Jeff and Marie are two teenagers seeing each other exclusively. They learn from the adults around them why this is wrong—getting too attached may make them give in to their "urges."

BODY CARE AND GROOMING (Audio Productions, 1947). Rather than watch pretty girls walk by, a teenage boy prefers to sit outside on a nice day and read a book. But he's not the one with the problem—it's the sloppily dressed girl who doesn't get his attention. The girl gets a magic makeover (her socks get pulled up and her skirt gets ironed). The boy finally notices her, throws down his book, and chases after her. The film also includes grooming tips such as "wear deodorant" and "cut your fingernails."

ARE YOU POPULAR? (Coronet Instructional Films, 1947). The audience is shown two girls: Caroline, "the kind of girl you'd like to know," is popular because "there's no scandal about her." Ginny, meanwhile, "dates all the boys." Despite the fact that Ginny is clearly more popular (at least with boys), the film argues that Caroline is actually the one more people like because she's a "good girl."

IT'S WONDERFUL BEING A GIRL (Audio Productions, 1966). A 12-year-old girl named Libby dreads menstruation and is worried that she "won't like it." Her mother relieves her fears by bringing home a wide range of feminine hygiene products. (The film was sponsored by Modess, a manufacturer of feminine hygiene products.) By the end, Libby is excited about menstruation and proud that she's growing up.

The Ottoman Empire once had seven emperors in seven months.

STRANGE COINCIDENCES

Do you think that's a clever title for this article? That's amazing! So do we!

DREAM A LITTLE E-S-P

On the night of Friday the 13th in June 2008, Tony Nutbrown of Carlisle, England, had a dream in which he won the Lotto grand prize. The 54-year-old had played every week for 13 years, but had very little to show for it. Still, the next morning he went to the shop where he always bought his tickets, bought one...and that night won the £3 million ($5.9 million) grand prize. But the really weird part is what happened when Nutbrown called his daughter, Claire, who owns a beauty salon in Hull, 170 miles away. When he told her he'd won the lottery, she said that a woman she didn't know had come into the shop that day and predicted that someone in her family was going to win the lottery. "She said this peculiar thing," Nutbrown told the London *Mail*, "and then left without another word. Then, that night, I won the jackpot."

IS THERE A DOCTOR IN THE OCEAN?

In 2002 Michelle Glen, 41, was scuba diving off the Turks and Caicos Islands in the Caribbean when she was attacked by a shark. The seven-foot Caribbean reef shark bit her arm, back, and shoulder, leaving her with shredded muscles and a severed major artery. With her that day were her husband and a friend. Her husband is an orthopedic surgeon; the friend is a vascular surgeon—who specializes in damaged arteries. He was able to reach into Glen's shredded shoulder, find the severed artery, and halt the bleeding until emergency crews arrived and flew her to Miami's Ryder Trauma Center. Doctors there said it was the "worst shark bite" they'd ever seen, and that Glen probably wouldn't have made it if the two doctors, especially the friend, hadn't been with her.

BROKEN HEARTS

In 1995 Terry Cottle, 33, of Charleston, South Carolina, shot himself. He died in the hospital, but not before his heart could be

Cities take up 2% of the Earth's surface, but consume 75% of the resources.

transplanted into 56-year-old Sonny Sugarman, who was suffering from congestive heart failure. Thirteen years later, Sugarman shot and killed *him*self. Worse than that: Cheryl Cottle, the widow of the first victim, had married Sugarman after meeting him through the organ donor program. Both of her husbands—who had the same heart in their bodies—had shot and killed themselves.

THE WREST IS HISTORY

In 2004 alternative-country singer Neko Case was asked to perform on the soundtrack to a documentary about women on the professional wrestling circuit in the 1940s and '50s. Director Ruth Leitman gave Case some rough video footage to view for inspiration. In an interview, one of the "lady wrestlers," Ella Waldek, mentioned that her original last name was Shevchenko. Case yelled at the TV—"Hey! That's my name!" Waldek went on to say that she was born in Custer, Washington. That's where Case was from, too! She got on the phone to her grandmother, and, sure enough, Ella Waldek was Case's aunt. The two met later that year and have been friends ever since. "I always thought there must be some tough ladies in the family hiding somewhere," she told *Entertainment Weekly*. "I felt so proud."

WORTH A THOUSAND WORDS

In August 2007, Londoner Michael Dick went to the nearby town of Sudbury to find his daughter, Lisa, who had moved there with her mother when she was a baby. Dick had seen her only occasionally as she grew up; the last time was a decade earlier. After searching the city's election records without success, he went to the local newspaper, the *Free Press*, and asked for their help. The paper's photographer took him outside and snapped a shot of him, and Dick went home to London. A couple of hours after the paper hit the streets, Dick got a call. It was Lisa. She had seen the photo of her dad—and she had seen herself and her mother *in the photo*, too. They happened to be across the street from where her father was photographed, and ended up in the photo. "I was completely shocked," she said. "We'd been standing in that exact place where the picture was taken about a minute earlier, and you can see us in the picture. It is incredible." She met up with her dad later that night. "He's promised to keep in touch," she said.

MODERN WISDOM

Some present-day philosophers chime in on the human condition.

"No matter what happens, somebody will find a way to take it too seriously."

—Dave Barry

"What we dwell on is who we become."

—Oprah Winfrey

"As you get older, the pickings get slimmer, but the people don't."

—Carrie Fisher

"If you're going to be able to look back on something and laugh about it, you might as well laugh about it now."

—Marie Osmond

"Oppressed groups are not, generally speaking, people who stand firmly together. No, sadly, they subdivide among themselves and fight like hell."

—J. K. Rowling

"Most things I worry about never happen anyway."

—Tom Petty

"Bad taste is simply saying the truth before it should be said."

—Mel Brooks

"The true measure of an individual is how he treats a person who can do him absolutely no good."

—Ann Landers

"The less secure a man is, the more likely he is to have extreme prejudices."

—Clint Eastwood

"It's all right letting yourself go as long as you can get yourself back."

—Mick Jagger

"The most important things happen when you stop looking for them."

—Phil Donahue

"The most common way people give up their power is by thinking they don't have any."

—Alice Walker

"If everything is under control, you are going too slow."

—Mario Andretti

"The difference between reality and fiction? Fiction has to make sense."

—Tom Clancy

Just going through a spell? *Harry Potter* author J. K. Rowling doesn't believe in witchcraft.

GAMES PEOPLE PLAY

In past Bathroom Readers, *we've written about bog snorkeling, cheese rolling, and pooh sticking. Here's this year's crop of crazy sports.*

MULLET TOSSING

Where It Originated: The Florida/Alabama border

How It's Played: Every April, several thousand participants pay $18 each to throw a mullet (the fish, not the haircut) from a 10-foot circle on a beach in Alabama across the state line into Pensacola, Florida. "Most people take the fish and roll it up like a baseball, tight as they can," explains Barbara Burns, a bartender at the FloraBama Package & Lounge, which has hosted the charity event—followed by a big party—since 1984. The record holder: Josh Serotum, who threw a mullet 189'8" in 2004. (After the competition, pelicans swoop in and eat all of the mullets.)

PROFESSIONAL PILLOW FIGHTING

Where It Originated: Toronto, Canada

How It's Played: It's kind of like the sleepover variety of the game...only much more brutal. The Pillow Fight League (PFL) consists solely of women and resembles pro wrestling—except these fights aren't staged, and the combatants hit each other with pillows. Wearing bizarre costumes (as well as mouth guards, knee pads, and elbow pads), fighters with names like "Betty Clock'er," "Polly Esther," "Mickey Dismantle," and "Lady Die" duke it out in front of hundreds of spectators at clubs and ballrooms across the United States and Canada. If a five-minute bout ends without one fighter successfully pinning her opponent's shoulders down (with a pillow), then a panel of three PFL judges chooses the winner based on "style, stamina, and the Eye of the Tiger."

SEPAK TAKRAW

Where It Originated: Malaysia

How It's Played: The word *sepak* means "kick" in Malay; *takraw* means "ball" in Thai. And this 500-year-old kickball game is arguably the most difficult sport in the world to master. Resembling a combination of volleyball, soccer, and Cirque du Soleil, two teams of three players each face off on a court with a net in the middle. Like volleyball, they have to keep a ball in the air, scoring a point when the other team lets it hit the ground. Unlike volleyball, players may use only their heads, legs, and bodies—no hands. So at breakneck speeds they do front flips, backflips, and an array of amazing bodily contortions, just to get to the softball-size ball and keep it in the air. It's a major sport in southeast Asia, and is becoming more popular in the Western world each year.

BA'

Where It Originated: Kirkwall, in Scotland's Orkney Islands

How It's Played: Ba' matches have taken place on Christmas and New Year's Day every year since the 1600s. Starting from the center of town, 300 men divide into the "Uppies," from the north side, who try to get the three-pound leather ball—or ba'—a mile away to a designated wall while the "Doonies," from the south side, try to get it into the frigid sea. The jumble of men, called a *scrum* (taken from rugby), shove, punch, and kick each other until someone wins—often battling well into the night. There are no rules and no referees, and no such thing as "out of bounds." The sport is so destructive that townies board up their doors and windows beforehand, as past scrums have laid waste to everything from cars to spectators to cemeteries. The winner hosts a giant party for both teams at his house (with beer donated by the local grocer) and gets to display the ba' in his living-room window for the rest of his life.

ZORBING

Where It Originated: Auckland, New Zealand

How It's Played: This isn't exactly a sport, just a dizzying outdoor activity. A person (the "Zorbonaut") is strapped into a harness inside a 10-foot inflatable clear plastic sphere (the Zorb), which is then released from the top of a hill. The Zorb rolls and rolls until the green grass and blue sky meld into a blue-green blur. After reaching speeds of nearly 30 mph, the big ball gently rolls to a stop at the bottom of the ½-mile-long course, more of which are popping up around the world. As stomach-turning as the sport may seem, according to Zorb inventors Dwayne van der Sluis and Andrew Akers, out of the 100,000 Zorb rides they've witnessed over the past 15 years, no one's ever thrown up…*inside* the ball.

...to remove all references to alcohol, including the fact that Jesus drank wine.

COURT TRANSQUIPS

The verdict is in! Court transquips make for some of the best bathroom reading there is. These were actually spoken, word for word, in a court of law.

Defense: Your Honor, I have a short witness.

Judge: How short?

Defense: It's Mr. Long.

Judge: Put Long on.

Prosecutor: As long as he's short.

Lawyer: Where was the officer in relation to you when you were struck by the car?

Witness: To my left.

Lawyer: How far to your left?

Witness: I don't really remember. I was getting run over at the time.

Clerk: Please state your name and spell your last name.

Judge: She has already been sworn.

Clerk: I am sorry, Your Honor. She looks different.

Witness: I ate.

Q: Do you drink alcohol?

A: No, sir.

Q: Are you a teetotaler?

A: Not really. Just coffee once in a while.

Lawyer: Were you the lone ranger on duty that night?

Witness: I was a park ranger on duty that night.

Lawyer: I mean the only one, the lone—

Witness: You mean alone?

Lawyer: Alone.

Witness: Yes, I was.

Q: I notice from the rehabilitation reports that you were recently in Mexico, correct?

A: I did not go to Mexico. I went to Tijuana.

Lawyer: Did your son tell you what day it was?

Witness: No, he didn't tell me, but I myself knew.

Lawyer: Did your granddaughter talk to you about it?

Witness: No, sometimes when I'm sober and working around the house, I remember these things.

Federal judge: This seems like a fairly simple problem. Let's not make a federal case out of it.

Sports quiz: Who made the very first Super Bowl touchdown? Max McGee (Green Bay Packers).

CHEESEY DOES IT

Random facts about the world's favorite milk product.

• Cheese is popular in most parts of the world. A notable exception: China. Invading Tatars and Mongols ate dairy products, so the Chinese associated cheese with the enemy.

• Most-consumed cheese worldwide: Cheddar.

• Six cheeses named after the European cities where they were first made: Parmesan (Parma, Italy), Romano (Rome), Gouda (Netherlands), Edam (Netherlands), Cheddar (England), and Camembert (France).

• Cheddar is naturally white. It's dyed orange with annatto seed, which comes from the tropical bixa tree.

• At cheese tastings, testers freshen and neutralize their mouths with gingerbread.

• According to the USDA, there are only 18 basic kinds of cheese: Brick, Edam, Whey, Camembert, Cheddar, Gouda, Cottage, Cream, Neufchatel, Hand, Limburger, Roquefort, Trappist, Romano, Parmesan, Swiss, Provolone, and Sapsago.

• Cheese can be made from the milk of most mammals, including reindeer, buffalo, camels, llamas, horses, donkeys, zebras, and yak.

• In 2007 a Dutch cheesemaker created the largest cheese wheel in history. It was six feet wide and weighed 1,323 pounds.

• What causes milk to harden and form into cheese: rennet, an enzyme extracted from the abomasum, the cow's fourth stomach.

• The red wax casing used on Gouda cheese in the U.S. was invented by the grandfather of 1980s pop star Huey Lewis.

• "Real" certified Brie cheese is made only in the Brie region of France and only by two companies: Brie de Meaux and Brie de Melun.

• Hard cheeses, like cheddar, have less moisture than soft cheeses, like brie. Result: Hard cheeses have more fat.

• The blue stuff in blue cheese is a mold that's actually a form of penicillin.

That's a lot of gobbling: The biggest turkey on record weighed 86 pounds.

LOST ARTS

Whether they were burned, disintegrated, stolen, blown to smithereens, or simply lost, countless works of art from ancient Greece, Shakespeare, and even the 20th century have been lost forever.

ANCIENT GREEK DRAMA

• Historians consider Aeschylus (525–456 B.C.) the "father of tragedy" because he invented that basic theatrical form and, thereby, all of Western theater. More than that, he wrote about Greek gods, Greek history, and Greek life. In fact, much of what we know about that era comes from Aeschylus's plays. But we could have known even more. Records suggest that Aeschylus wrote between 70 and 90 plays. While we know the titles, only the scripts for seven of those plays survive. Three of those (*Agamemnon*, *The Libation Bearers*, and *The Eumenides*) form *The Oresteia*, the only Greek tragic trilogy still in existence.

• Aeschylus wasn't the only Greek playwright whose work was lost. His successor as the leading playwright and documentarian of Athens, Sophocles, (496–406 B.C.), wrote 123 plays, but only seven still exist today, including *Antigone*, *Oedipus Rex*, and *Electra*. *His* successor was Euripides (480–406 B.C.). Historical records indicate that he wrote as many as 80 tragedies, but the scripts of only 18 survive, including *Medea*, *The Trojan Women*, and *The Bacchae*.

SHAKESPEARE

William Shakespeare (1564–1616) is widely regarded as history's finest playwright, if not the most acclaimed writer in the entire English language. When Shakespeare wrote his plays in the late 16th and early 17th centuries, he wrote them quickly and in fragments, handing scraps of paper to the actors to memorize. The publication of his plays didn't occur until after his death, and they were based on those script fragments. How many plays? A total of 36. But historians think there may have been two *more* Shakespeare plays.

• ***Love's Labor's Won.*** In 1598 English author Francis Meres wrote one of the first books about Shakespeare, *Palladis Tamia*. It lists nearly all of Shakespeare's known 36 plays...along with one called *Love's Labour's Won*, a sequel to *Love's Labour's Lost*. But Meres failed to include *The Taming of the Shrew*, leading scholars to believe for nearly 400 years that *Shrew* and *Won* were the same play. They were wrong. In 1953 a 1600-era list of Shakespeare's plays was discovered that listed both *The Taming of the Shrew* and *Love's Labour's Won*.

• ***Cardenio.*** Shakespeare often built his plays on previously existing works. For example, *Hamlet* is based on *The Spanish Tragedy* by playwright Thomas Kyd. *Cardenio* was an adaptation of Miguel de Cervantes's 1605 novel *Don Quixote*. There is a record of the play being produced in 1613 by The King's Men, Shakespeare's theater troupe. The script has never been found.

MOVIES

Today, hundreds of thousands of films are archived, many of them stored digitally, but it turns out that almost as many have been lost as have been saved. There are many reasons. From the birth of cinema in the 1890s until the late 1940s, the standard film stock was made of a nitrate base, which gave black-and-white movies sharp contrast and crisp images. But nitrate is highly combustible. What's worse, it disintegrates quickly if it's not stored in a special low-oxygen, low-humidity, climate-controlled vault. But that's an incredibly expensive storage system for films that, when they were made, weren't considered to have any lasting value—they were worth more for their raw materials. Low-budget movie producers (and Universal Studios in a 1948 vault-clearing measure) melted down their old movies for their silver content.

Another reason films were lost: Every major studio experienced vault fires, most of them started by the very same combustible nitrate films, which in turn burned thousands of other films. More than 95% of Fox's silent films were destroyed in a 1937 warehouse fire. The Film Preservation Foundation estimates that 80% of *all* silent-era films are gone for good. With the advent of television in the late 1940s, studios realized that their old movies could be a lucrative source of TV programming. By the 1960s, the major stu-

Which basketball star fought Arnold Schwarzenegger in *Conan the Destroyer*? Wilt Chamberlain.

dios used safer, more fireproof vaults and the standard film stock had changed to a less-combustible acetate base.

Here are some of the movies that are gone forever:

• ***The Fairylogue and Radio-Plays*** (1908). The first-ever adaptation of L. Frank Baum's *Oz* books, it starred Baum interacting with drawings of his characters. The single print was in Baum's possession, but it disintegrated and was thrown out by his heirs.

• ***The Werewolf*** (1913). The first werewolf film, it was destroyed in a 1924 fire.

• ***Cleopatra*** (1917). It starred silent-film icon Theda Bara in the title role and had a then huge budget of $500,000. All but 45 seconds were destroyed in a Fox Studio vault fire.

• ***The Gulf Between*** (1917). The first full-length color film made in America. Only a few frames are left.

• ***El Apostol*** (1917). Made in Argentina by Italian filmmaker Quirino Cristiani, this was the first-ever full-length animated movie. All copies were destroyed in a fire in 1926. Cristiani's other major work was *Peludópolis* (1931), the first animated feature with sound. All copies of that movie were lost in a 1961 fire.

• ***Humor Risk*** (1921). The first Marx Brothers movie. Harpo plays a detective chasing Groucho. It had a single screening, the audience hated it, and the Marxes destroyed the only print.

• ***The Great Gatsby*** (1926). Only a trailer remains of the first movie version of the classic novel.

• ***Hats Off*** (1927). Laurel and Hardy's first hit. There was only one print, and it was misplaced after the movie's theatrical run.

• ***The Way of All Flesh*** (1927). Emil Jennings won the first Oscar for Best Actor, but only five minutes of footage remains. It's the only lost Academy Award–winning performance.

• ***For the Love of Mike*** (1927). It was directed by Frank Capra (*It's a Wonderful Life*) and marked the screen debut of Claudette Colbert.

• ***King Kong Appears in Edo*** (1938). One of the first Japanese "giant monster" movies, it was destroyed during World War II.

Plays and films aren't the only artworks that get lost to time. Turn to page 382 for paintings, books, and even TV shows that have vanished forever.

Harry Houdini was buried in the coffin he used in his magic act.

THE COMSTOCK LODE, PT. I

Practically everybody has daydreamed about prospecting for gold and striking it rich. But what happens after the big strike? Here's the amazing tale of one of the biggest bonanzas in U.S. history.

KILLING TIME

In January 1848, gold was discovered at Sutter's Mill, California, sparking the Gold Rush that brought more than 300,000 people to the territory. In the spring of 1850, some prospectors heading for the California gold fields stopped at the foot of the Sierra Nevada mountains about 20 miles outside of modern-day Reno, Nevada, to wait for the snow to melt before they continued over the mountains. Why not look for gold while they waited? They fanned out along the Carson River's edge and up a stream that fed into the river from a nearby canyon. And sure enough, they did manage to find some gold...but not enough to justify staying put. So after the snow melted a few weeks later, they moved on to California. Before they left, though, they named the spot "Gold Canyon."

PAY DIRT

Word of the discovery at Gold Canyon spread, and each spring as a new wave of settlers and prospectors headed to California along the same route, many stopped there long enough to pan for gold. As the years passed and the original deposits were played out, prospectors started exploring farther afield. In January 1859, a prospector named James "Old Virginny" Finney and three friends took advantage of some good weather and went prospecting on top of a low hill in Gold Canyon where the dirt was yellower than in the surrounding lowlands. Old Virginny thought that was a good sign. When they started testing the soil, each pan yielded about 15¢ worth of gold. Not exactly Sutter's Mill, but it was enough to justify staking a claim and exploring the area further.

In those days, tradition and mining law dictated that no miner could stake a claim larger than he could work himself. Old Virginny and his associates each filed a claim for a 50-by-400-foot area, and over the next few days some other miners filed adjacent claims. Many more made trips to the site to look around, but for

In Caracas, Venezuela, the streets are blocked off on Christmas so people can roller-skate to church.

most of them, 15¢ a pan wasn't enough gold to make them abandon the claims they were already working.

DOWNS AND UPS

When Old Virginny and the others finished washing all the surface dirt through their "rockers"—mining equipment resembling baby cradles that rocked back and forth to separate out the gold—they dug deeper. As they did, the amount of gold steadily increased, first to $5 per day for each miner, then $12, and for a time as high as $20, at a time when gold sold for $13.50 an ounce.

So why isn't the Comstock Lode known as the Finney Lode or the Old Virginny Lode? Because as the months passed and the miners dug deeper, they eventually hit a deposit of difficult-to-work clay that had very little gold in it. Most deposits of gold are small, so when the miners ran out of the easy diggings they assumed they'd found all there was. That's what happened to Old Virginny: the gold ran out, so he moved on.

That June, just a mile down the hill, two miners named Peter O'Riley and Pat McLaughlin struggled to make a profit on a 900-foot-long claim they'd staked for themselves. The claim was yielding only one or two dollars' worth of gold a day, and the men had heard about richer claims near the West Walker River, about 25 miles away. But they decided to stick around a little longer, probably until they made enough money to pay for the move.

It takes water to sift gold out of sand and dirt, and the closest water source was a tiny spring that the men decided to dam up with some strange bluish sand they'd uncovered nearby. Almost on a whim, they tossed some of the odd sand into the rocker to see if it contained any gold. It was heavy and difficult to work with, but when they cleared it away they were stunned to see that the entire bottom of the rocker was covered in a layer of shimmering gold. Where Old Virginny had recovered gold by the ounce, O'Riley and McLaughlin were mining it by the *pound*.

RANCHO COMSTOCKO

So why isn't the Comstock Lode known as the O'Riley Lode or the McLaughlin Lode? Because later that same day, another miner, Henry "Old Pancake" Comstock, happened to ride by while the men were celebrating their good fortune. When Comstock saw

The term "taken aback" comes from sailing: a gust of wind can catch the sails and stop the ship.

the gold, he hopped off his pony and told the two men that they were prospecting on land that he and a partner had already claimed for a ranch. In those days, you could claim unoccupied land for a ranch just as easily as you could stake a mining claim. Comstock told the "trespassers" that if they would let him and his partner, Emmanuel Penrod, become equal partners in the claim, he wouldn't take them to court. Furthermore, if he and Penrod were given 100 feet of the claim to work by themselves, he'd even let them use the water from "his" stream.

DEAL OR NO DEAL

Nearly 150 years have passed since then, and in all that time no record of a ranch claim by Comstock has ever been found. But O'Riley and McLaughlin didn't know that, and in those days it was common to settle mining disputes quickly without resorting to lawsuits—why waste money on lawyers when nobody knew how long the gold would last? Even the best claims might peter out after a month or two.

O'Riley and McLaughlin took the deal...and Comstock started getting credit for their discovery. Comstock "was the man who did all the heavy talking," Dan DeQuille wrote in his 1876 book *A History of The Big Bonanza*. "He made himself so conspicuous on every occasion that he soon came to be considered not only the discoverer but almost the father of the lode. People began to speak of the vein as Comstock's mine, Comstock's lode...while the names of O'Riley and McLaughlin, the real discoverers, are seldom heard."

THE BAD WITH THE GOOD

Beneath the crumbly blue dirt was a firmer, compacted blue stone that yielded even more gold. On good days, the men pulled more than $1,000 worth of gold from the earth, more than 5½ pounds of gold a day. When the men hit a *really* rich patch, they might collect $150 worth in a single pan of dirt. The only frustration was the fact that the strange blue dirt clogged the rockers and other mining equipment terribly. "For weeks they let it go to waste," DeQuille wrote, "throwing it anywhere to get it out of the way. They not only did not try to save it, but constantly cursed it. It was the great drawback."

Hey, who said life was fair? ***Part II of the story is on page 222.***

First known phobia to be described: Hydrophobia, a fear of water, in the mid-1500s.

LAW AND ORDER: SPECIAL PANTS UNIT

Why, yes—those are *lobster tails in my pants. Why do you ask?*

In May 2008, a liquor store manager in Fort Pierce, Florida, told a man with what newspaper accounts called "a very large bulge" in his pants to hand over whatever it was he had "down there." The man reached into his pants, pulled out two bottles of Hennessy cognac, gave them to the manager…and then ran out the door with the other two bottles he still had in his pants. (He wasn't caught.)

• **Keith Miller**, 51, was arrested at Sydney Airport in Australia in 2004. He was a rare-animal smuggler, and had 23 birds' eggs in his underwear. Miller was later sentenced to two years in prison.

• **Giraldo Wong** of Hialeah, Florida, was arrested in 2005 at Miami International Airport. He was also a rare-animal smuggler, and had two live Cuban songbirds in his underwear.

• **Workers at Junior's** Restaurant in Brooklyn called 911 in June 2008 to report the theft of 15 lobster tails from their walk-in freezer. Police found them in the cook's pants.

• **A man in Michigan** should have listened to his mother when she said, "Don't run with sharp things in your hands! Or in your pants!" The man went to a Meijer superstore in Grand Rapids and stuffed about $300 worth of hunting knives in his pants. When security tried to stop him a scuffle broke out, and the man fell and stabbed himself. He was treated at a local hospital…and then arrested.

• **Police in Sweetwater**, Tennessee, pulled into a church parking lot in the middle of the night in early 2008 after getting a report of a suspicious car there. A woman walked out from behind the church, saying she'd been going to the bathroom. Then a crowbar fell out of her pants. She was arrested for possession of burglary tools.

• **Ignacio Gueta**, 22, was booked into the Santa Clara County Jail in California in June 2008 for violating parole. A search of Gueta found a 4'2" machete in his pants. Gueta said he had it "for protection."

All hornets are wasps; not all wasps are hornets.

MEDICAL MIRACLES

Do you believe in miracles? These folks do.

DO THE WALK OF LIFE

Eugene Stolowski, 33, and five other firefighters were searching for people trapped in a burning apartment building in the Bronx, New York, in January 2005 when the room they were in became engulfed in flames. The only way out was the window—and they were on the fourth floor. They all jumped. Tragically, two were killed on impact; three others survived with various injuries. But Stolowski suffered a freak injury: His spine became detached from his skull in what doctors called an "internal decapitation." The only thing holding his head to his spine was the spinal cord—which is jellylike in consistency—so the slightest movement of his head could have paralyzed or even killed him. Doctors gave him a 5% chance of surviving emergency surgery. He beat those odds. After the first two weeks, during which he underwent *nine* surgeries, he was given a 30% chance of survival. He beat those odds, too, and four months later sat in a wheelchair next to his wife as she gave birth to their twin daughters. Nine months later he slowly shuffled—on his feet and without assistance—out the hospital door. And in November 2007, Stolowski went back to work for the New York City Fire Department—not as a firefighter, but back on the force—and can walk just fine today.

Extra heroics: Of the three others who jumped and survived, Jeff Cool and Joey DiBernardo Jr. both retired. The third, Brendan Cawley, was just a month into the job when he had to jump that day...except that he didn't actually jump—Stolowski threw him out the window to save his life, then jumped himself. After his recovery, Cawley was able to return to full duty as a firefighter.

MY BIRTHDAY IS IN FEBRUARY...AND MAY

Macie Hope McCartney was born in February 2008. But then the doctors put her back in her mom's womb...and she was born again on May 3, her official birthday. The explanation: A routine ultrasound during the sixth month of pregnancy revealed a tumor growing from the region of Macie's tailbone. It was noncancerous, but it was huge—about as big as a grapefruit, which was larger than the baby herself at the time. And it was full of veins, so it was robbing the baby of her blood supply. Doctors decided the only thing to do was to operate, so mother Keri McCartney was very deeply anaesthetized—necessary to completely relax the uterus, doctors explained—then the surgical team cut open the uterus, pulled the fetus mostly out (feet first), removed the tumor, put her back inside, and sewed up the uterus very carefully so that it would still hold the amniotic fluid. Ten weeks later Macie Hope was "born again," a perfectly healthy little girl.

BATS IN THE BELFRY

Jeanna Giese of Fond du Lac, Wisconsin, was 15 in 2004 when she went to the hospital with tremors and difficulty walking. Doctors couldn't figure out what was wrong, and she was getting worse, so she was transferred to Children's Hospital of Wisconsin (CHW) in Milwaukee. Doctors there suspected rabies, and Jeanna then told them that she'd been bitten by a bat that she had picked up at church...more than 40 days earlier. A test for the virus confirmed that she had it, which was very, very bad—people infected with the rabies virus who don't get vaccine shots immediately—before the onset of symptoms—don't live. Nobody in history had been known to recover from such a situation. That meant Jeanna, whose brain was already swelling, was in grave danger. The doctors at CHW searched in vain for a treatment plan; there wasn't one. So they had to invent one: With her parents' approval, they gave Jeanna drugs to protect her nervous system, then put her in a coma and hoped her immune system would "learn" to fight the virus, build up, and eventually win. They tested her spinal fluid to see how she was progressing, and a week later brought her out of the coma...because her immune system had *eradicated* the virus. She spent the next month in intensive care, followed by therapy to get her brain and muscles back in shape, and within a year she was back in school and even able to drive. She is the first unvaccinated person in history known to have had full-blown rabies and fully recovered. She's now being studied by some of the world's leading neurologists, who want to know just how she did it. Asked if she'd ever pick up a live bat again, the ardent animal lover answered, "I would."

About 25 million meteors hit Earth's atmosphere every day.

THY WILL BE DONE

There are famous last words, and then there are the last words of the famous. Here are some odd bequests made in the wills of well-known people.

BOB FOSSE. The choreographer and Oscar-winning director of *Cabaret* died in 1987 and left exactly $378.79 each to 66 people so they could "go out and have dinner on me." Recipients included Dustin Hoffman, Liza Minelli, Melanie Griffith, and Roy Scheider (who portrayed Fosse in *All That Jazz*).

GEORGE BERNARD SHAW. When the playwright (*Pygmalion*) died in 1950, he left more than £300,000 to develop a new, more precise English alphabet of 40 letters to replace the current one. (Someone created it, but it never caught on.)

GENE RODDENBERRY. The creator of *Star Trek*, who died in 1991, arranged for his cremated remains to be scattered in space. And in 1997, they were shot out into space from a Spanish satellite (along with the ashes of 23 other people).

WILLIAM SHAKESPEARE. It's been widely reported that when Shakespeare died he willed his wife, Anne Hathaway, his "second-best bed." Some scholars say it was an insult that he didn't leave her his *best* bed. But in the 17th century, a home's best bed was reserved for guests; a husband and wife slept in the second-best. The note in the will was a sentimental gesture.

HARRY HOUDINI. The famous magician bequeathed his collection of books on magic to the American Society for Psychical Research...on condition that J. Malcolm Bird, an ASPR official whom Houdini hated, resign. Bird refused, so the books went to the Library of Congress. Houdini also had a bronze bust of himself placed on his tomb to guide him back from "the other side."

DUSTY SPRINGFIELD. The 1960s singer ("Son of a Preacher Man"), who died in 1999, set aside a large sum to purchase a supply of baby food, the favorite meal of her cat, Nicholas. She also directed the executor to line Nicholas's bed with her old nightgowns and play her songs each night as Nicholas went to sleep.

McDonald's restaurants will buy 54,000,000 pounds of fresh apples this year.

UNSEEN TV

Ever wondered what the network geniuses do behind closed doors? Here are some TV shows that they approved and produced...but never broadcast.

SHOW: *Manchester Prep*

STORY: For fall 1999, the Fox network planned a TV series version of the racy teen film *Cruel Intentions*. The movie had a lot of sex scenes, a lesbian kiss, and even incest between two main characters, and the show was just as graphic—too graphic for TV. Fox chairman Rupert Murdoch personally told producers to cut a horseback sex scene. They refused, and the show was cancelled. But rather than let it sit on the shelf, producers reassembled the cast and filmed new footage—sex scenes with full nudity—and added it to the two episodes of *Manchester Prep* already produced, and released it as a straight-to-video movie called *Cruel Intentions 2*.

SHOW: *The Young Astronauts*

STORY: In early 1986, the United States was in the middle of a "space craze" not seen since the 1960s. Reason: the upcoming launch of the Space Shuttle *Challenger*, which would have civilians on board for the first time ever. To play into the excitement, CBS produced *The Young Astronauts*, a Saturday morning cartoon about teenage space travelers, to air in February 1986. When the *Challenger* tragically exploded shortly after liftoff, killing everyone on board, CBS immediately cancelled the unaired series.

SHOW: *Babylon Fields*

STORY: Like *Desperate Housewives*, *Babylon Fields* was part comedy and part drama, and set in an upscale suburb. Except that in this suburb (for reasons unknown), hundreds of people had risen from the dead and were now zombies, trying to resume their lives. *Babylon Fields* was supposed to deal with the kind of problems a new zombie might face, such as rotting flesh, rigor mortis, and soothing the emotions of loved ones who'd mourned their deaths and were trying to move on. CBS actually picked up the show for fall 2007, but at the last second (reportedly because of ABC's raising the dead-themed *Pushing Daisies*), killed it.

SHOW: *Aquaman* (also known as *Mercy Reef)*
STORY: In 2006 producers of the Superman-based *Smallville* introduced another superhero, Aquaman (played by Justin Hartley) into an episode, intending to spin him off into his own series. A pilot was filmed (also starring Ving Rhames and Lou Diamond Phillips), which TV insiders and entertainment writers called one of the best of the year. But when the fall 2006 schedule was announced, there was no *Aquaman*. Why? The WB was merging with UPN, another network, and in consolidating their programming, they left a lot of shows on the sidelines, including *Aquaman*. Later that year, the pilot was quietly put up for sale on iTunes, and became the online store's most-downloaded TV show. It still never became a series.

SHOW: *Snip*
STORY: In 1976 NBC gave comedian David Brenner his own sitcom. The premise: Brenner played a divorced hairdresser whose ex-wife moves back in with him. It looked like a surefire hit. Brenner was one of the most popular comedians of the time, and the show was created by James Komack (who also made *Chico and the Man* and *Welcome Back, Kotter*). Seven episodes were filmed, but at the last minute, some NBC executives got nervous and pulled the plug. Why? The network feared controversy over another character—a openly gay hairdresser. Brenner bitterly quipped to a reporter, "Apparently, in 1976 there were no gay people in America."

SHOW: *Mr. Dugan*
STORY: In 1978 the title character of *Maude* got elected to Congress and moved to Washington, but after two episodes, star Bea Arthur got bored with the concept and quit. Producer Norman Lear quickly reworked the show to make it about James Dugan, a freshman African-American congressman, starring Cleavon Little (*Blazing Saddles*) in the title role. A few weeks before the show's heavily advertised 1979 debut, Lear screened the show for black members of Congress. They hated it, finding it to be full of stereotypes. One member called it "demeaning" and threatened to organize a boycott of CBS. Lear promptly ended production on *Mr. Dugan*.

...Kareem Abdul-Jabbar, Wilt Chamberlain, Karl Malone, and Charles Barkley.

SINCERELY, STEVEN

Take martial arts, add explosions, gunplay, ridiculous dialog, and some watered-down Eastern philosophy...and what do you have? The films of Steven Seagal.

Senator Trent: You can take that to the bank!

Mason Storm (Seagal): I'm gonna take you to the bank, Senator. To the blood bank!

—Hard to Kill

Monkey: Want some blow?

John Hatcher (Seagal): Yeah, I want some blow. Put your hands where I can see 'em or I'm gonna blow your head off!

—Marked for Death

Hatch: What the hell are you doing here?

Jack Taggert (Seagal): Well, I was just out taking a Sunday stroll. But I guess maybe it's not Sunday.

—Fire Down Below

"Love is eternal, and that's a long time."

—Ticker

"I guess it doesn't really matter since I kind of blew up all the evidence."

—On Deadly Ground

"I'm gonna cut off your feet and throw them in that basket there. Cute, huh?"

—Above the Law

"I love giving away all my possessions. It makes me feel real spiritual."

—Marked for Death

George: Did you really beat a suspect unconscious with a dead cat?

Orin (Seagal): No. The cat wasn't dead.

—Exit Wounds

"I want to kill you so bad, I can hardly contain myself."

—Hard to Kill

"If your daddy knew exactly how stupid you were, he'd trade you in for a pet monkey."

—Fire Down Below

"One thought he was invincible, the other thought he could fly. They were both wrong."

—Marked for Death

Jordan: I hate being alone.

Casey Ryback (Seagal): Do you hate being dead?

—Under Siege

"What am I doing? Oh, I'm making a bomb."

—Under Siege 2

John *wej:jav'maH*: Besides Klingon, the Bible is also available in Vulcan and Romulan.

THE LEGO SPILL OF '97

Oil spills get all the press—but what about Legos? Sneakers? TNT? It turns out that a lot of strange things end up in our oceans.

THE SS *TOKIO EXPRESS*

Lost Cargo: Toys

What Happened: In February 1997, a rogue wave struck the *Tokio Express* off Lands End, England, knocking several cargo containers into the sea. Inside the containers: 4,756,940 Legos, including tiny frying pans, witch hats, and countless Lego scuba tanks, life preservers, rafts, spear guns, and other sea-themed Legos. Some of the toys washed up on the shores of England; others drifted all the way Florida. Those Legos are not alone: Shipping containers fall into the sea all the time. During the stormy winter season it's not uncommon for as many as 500 containers to fall off the world's ships *every month*, and many of them burst open when they hit the water. If the cargo inside is buoyant, it can float for months or even years before washing ashore somewhere in the world.

THE SS *RICHARD MONTGOMERY*

Lost Cargo: Bombs

What Happened: In August 1944, this American cargo ship ran aground and broke in two in the Thames Estuary in southeast England. It was carrying 6,127 tons of explosives—including more than 13,000 bombs weighing 250 pounds each—bound for U.S. military forces in France. About half the deadly cargo was salvaged in the weeks that followed. The rest, including more than 1,400 tons of TNT, remain on or near the wreck today, in water so shallow that parts of the ship can be seen poking out of the water.

Whether the passage of time has made the wreck more or less likely to explode is debatable. Opinions are similarly divided over whether the wreck should be cleaned up, detonated, "contained" inside a massive concrete barrier, or just left alone. When an attempt was made in 1967 to remove munitions from a similarly laden Polish ship that sank in the English Channel in 1946, the wreck exploded with a force equivalent to an earthquake measuring 4.5 on the Richter scale. If the *Richard Montgomery* ever blew

At latitude 60° south, it is possible to sail around the world without reaching land.

up, it's estimated that the blast and resulting tsunami would do $1.8 billion worth of damage to nearby coastal communities. The British government says the risk of such an explosion is "remote," but it has established a 24-hour guard to keep divers and pleasure boaters away...just in case.

THE *HANSA CARRIER*

Lost Cargo: Sneakers

What Happened: In May 1990, the freighter was traveling from South Korea to the United States when it encountered a violent storm off the Alaskan Peninsula. By the time the storm passed, 21 cargo containers had been washed off the deck and into the sea, including five containers holding an estimated 80,000 Nike sneakers and work boots. When the soggy but still wearable shoes began washing up along the coasts of Washington and Oregon, local residents used the serial numbers to match left and right shoes and created pairs that could be worn or sold. "Meet and Match" days were even organized for people to get together and swap shoes.

THE *TRICOLOR*

Lost Cargo: Automobiles

What Happened: In 2002 the Norwegian *Tricolor* sank after colliding with another cargo ship while both were trying to avoid a third ship in heavy fog. The *Tricolor* was carrying 2,862 brand new luxury cars, including BMWs, Volvos, and Saabs. Because it sank in shallow water in one of the busiest sea lanes in the world, the *Tricolor* could not be left where it was; instead, it was cut into nine sections that were recovered one by one in a salvage operation that took 15 months. The cars were recovered, too, but they had to be written off as a total loss. Estimated retail value: $105 million, making this arguably the biggest "car wreck" in history.

OTHER SPILLS O' STUFF

- **The *Hyundai Seattle* (1994):** 34,000 hockey gloves, chest protectors, and shin guards.
- **The *Hengtong 320* (1997):** 480,000 cans of Chinese beer.
- **The Diamond Knot (1946):** Seven million cans of salmon, or roughly 10% of Alaska's salmon catch for the year. Half of the cans were later "vacuumed" up from the wreck and salvaged.

Beaver Cleaver's address: 211 Pine St., Mayfield, USA.

DUCK...DUCK...GOOSE!

These vintage kids' games don't involve TVs or high-tech computers—just a bunch of kids who want to have fun. If you've got a few bored youngsters hanging around, teach them how to play...and maybe even join in yourself.

GAME: Follow the Leader
HOW IT'S PLAYED: A "leader" is chosen by drawing straws, or by consensus. Everyone else forms a line behind that person. The leader then leads the procession around the room, and each follower must mimic the leader's actions (like twirling around three times, jumping in the air, and shouting "Potatoes!") as closely as possible. Those who don't mimic the leader correctly are out of the game, and the last person standing is the next leader.

GAME: I Spy
HOW IT'S PLAYED: One kid looks around a room or yard and gives a clue about a chosen object, such as "I spy, with my little eye, something beginning with the letter *W*. The rest of the kids have to guess what it is; if nobody can, the spy continues with more clues until someone guesses what it is. The correct guesser becomes the next leader. (The object in the example: a Wurlitzer.)

GAME: Indian Wrestling
HOW IT'S PLAYED: This was taken, so the story goes, from an actual game played by Native Americans (although the tribe has never been identified). In any case it's a fun game: Two players lie on their backs next to each other, head to toe, and lock arms. They each raise one leg—the one closest to the other player—straight up three times, counting "one, two, three" as they do. On the third lift they quickly interlock their legs and, like arm wrestling, they each attempt to pull the other player's leg over and touch their opponent's foot to the ground.

GAME: Memory
HOW IT'S PLAYED: Place 10 to 15 small items—a pencil, a

paper clip, a key, and so on—on a tray. One person is the "monitor," and makes a list of all the items. The rest of the players sit in a circle, and the monitor places the tray—with a towel over it—in the middle of the circle. The monitor takes the towel off, and the kids get to look at the items for a specific length of time (20 to 60 seconds), after which the towel is replaced. Then the kids, in order around the circle, attempt to name one item on the tray. When an item is named, the monitor crosses it off the list. If a player can't name an object—no repeats—they're out. Last person in wins.

GAME: Statues

HOW IT'S PLAYED: One player—often called "grandmother" or "grandfather"—stands at the end of a room facing away from the other players. She yells "Go!" and the others race toward her. The first person to tag her wins...but there's a catch: Grandmother may turn around suddenly any time she likes, at which time the other players must stand stock still...like a statue. If grandmother sees you moving, you're out!

GAME: Duck, Duck, Goose

HOW IT'S PLAYED: A group of kids sit in a circle, facing inward. One kid—the "goose"—walks around the circle tapping each sitting child on the head, saying "duck" each time, until she decides to say "goose." The "goosed" child jumps up and chases the goose around the circle, trying to tag her before she can reach and sit in the empty spot. If the goose is caught, she's still the goose. If not, the goosed duck is the new goose.

GAME: Sardines

HOW IT'S PLAYED: This version of "Hide and Seek" was (and presumably still is) more popular in the U.K. and Canada than in the United States. A group of players close their eyes and count to an agreed upon number (50 or 100 or whatever) while one player goes and hides. When the number is reached, the seekers split up and search for the player. If a seeker finds the hider, the seeker hides, too, as close to that person as possible. The game goes on until only one player is still looking for the seeker, and the hiders are all packed together...like sardines.

The board game Risk has released *Star Wars, Lord of the Rings, Narnia,* and *Transformers* editions.

WEIRD CANADA

Crystal lakes, snow-capped mountains, hockey, Mounties, universal health care, bilingual traffic signs...and some really, really weird news stories.

NEWS JUNKIE

In 2007 the *Edmonton Sun* interviewed a 70-year-old woman identified only as "Maggie" who claimed she devoured the *Edmonton Sun* every day—literally. For the previous seven years, she'd cut the newspaper into strips and eaten it because, she said, it "tastes good." The woman decided to come forward after doctors removed a massive ball of paper that was lodged in her esophagus.

THESE BANK FEES ARE CRIMINAL

In 2007 Christopher Emmorey tried to rob a bank in Peterborough, Ontario. Instead of asking a teller for all the money, for some reason Emmorey demanded just $5,000. The teller replied that she had only $200 on hand, adding that because he wasn't a customer of that bank, he'd have to pay a $5 withdrawal fee. Emmorey waited while the clerk did the paperwork—which he signed—and gave him $195. He was arrested an hour later.

ICE DANCING WINS

In 2002 a group of softball players met in a Calgary park for a late-night game. At the next field over, a group of croquet players were also playing a late-night game. A few hours later, six players from both groups were in the hospital (two were seriously injured)—the result of a brawl over which sport was the "manliest."

WHO MOVED THE CHEESE?

La Fromagerie Boivin, one of Quebec's largest cheese manufacturers, dropped about a ton of cheese into the Saguenay River in 2004. They thought that aging the cheese underwater for twelve months would give it extra moisture and improve its taste and texture. Did it work? We may never know. In October 2005, the cheesemaker announced that despite the use of thousands of dol-

Glenn Close and Brooke Shields are second cousins.

lars in high-tech locating equipment, divers were unable to find the 2,000 pounds of lost cheese.

TATTOO YOU

Lane Jensen, an Alberta tattoo artist, has a tattoo of a large-breasted cowgirl on his left leg. In 2007 he decided his cowgirl didn't look buxom enough. So his tattoo got "breast" implants—dime-sized bags of silicone inserted into his leg under the tattoo. Two weeks later, Jensen lost a liter of lymphatic fluid from his leg—his body had rejected the implants. "I guess my girl wasn't meant to have 3-D breasts," he said.

WHAT GOES AROUND...

In 2007 a 15-year-old in Hamilton, Ontario, was sledding one night and decided he wanted to tag a local bridge with some graffiti. He left his gloves and cell phone in the sled and rappelled down the side of the bridge. Suddenly the rope shifted and the boy panicked. He tried to scurry back up but somehow ended up hanging by his feet, upside down. As he tried to wiggle free, his shirt came off. And it was February. And it was –5°F. He was there for two hours before someone finally heard his screams for help and saved him.

THE SMOKING GUN

Keep It Simple, a bar in Edmonton, was in danger of being closed in 2003 when officials found out it was not abiding by the city-wide smoking ban. The only place smoking is legal is in liquor-licensed bars. But Keep It Simple is a bar for recovering alcoholics—it doesn't serve alcohol. It does allow smoking, which helps many alcoholics not to drink. But because it didn't have a liquor license, it was illegal for people to smoke there. So in order to let its non-drinking customers smoke, Keep It Simple applied for and received a liquor license, which it doesn't use, because it doesn't sell liquor.

* * *

"Everything is funny as long as it's happening to someone else."

—Will Rogers

THE MYSTERIOUS EEL

And we mean reely, reely, mysterious.

WHAT ARE THEY?

Eels have been one of the aquatic world's great mysteries for for more than 2,000 years. It wasn't until relatively modern times that scientists discovered that they were a type of fish—specifically members of the class *Actinopterygii*, the "ray-finned" fishes, making them relatives of herring, anchovies, salmon, and goldfish. Like all fish, eels are cold-blooded, they obtain oxygen via gills, and they have fins. Beyond that they are completely unique.

Eels make up their own fish order—the *Anguilliformes* (from "snake-shaped" in Latin). They all have long, tubular bodies, and instead of having separate fins on their backs, tails, and bellies like most other fish, they have one long, continuous fin that goes down the back, around the tail, and up the belly. Another unique characteristic: they're "naked." Almost all species of eel have no scales, and those that do have them embedded in their skin. What do they have instead of protective scales? Slime. Eels produce a thick, mucuslike substance that protects their naked skin, and, of course, makes them very slippery.

SEA EELS

There are more than 600 different eel species and a tremendous variety of shapes, color, and sizes. Most, by far, are marine—they live exclusively in saltwater oceans and seas. Some standouts:

• There are about 200 species of Moray eels living in tropical reefs in all the world's oceans. Some are small, just several inches long; some are huge. Giant Morays, for example, can reach 13 feet in length. Morays have canine-like snouts and large mouths with very sharp teeth. Bonus: They also have an extra set of jaws inside their throats that lunge forward to help swallow prey (just like the creature in the *Alien* films).

• Conger eels have pectoral fins—the pair of fins found on the sides of fishes near the head—and big puffy "lips." Giant Congers are the most massive eels, growing to more than 10 feet long and

The first Harley-Davidson motorcycle, built in 1903, used a tomato can for a carburetor.

weighing as much as 240 pounds. If you've ever eaten *anago* at a sushi restaurant—you've eaten Conger eel.

• Snipe eels can be found from about 1,300 to 13,000 feet deep, and they look like eel-birds. The upper part of their long, pointy, beaklike jaws curves upward and the lower part curves downward—like the beaks of the wading birds known as snipes.

RIVER EELS

There are only about 16 species of *freshwater* eels—but that's deceiving. Although they're found in lakes, rivers, and streams around the world, they're all *catadromous*: They're actually born in the oceans, spend most of their lives in freshwater, and eventually go back to the sea to spawn and die. Some standouts:

• European eels can be found throughout Europe, from Scandinavia to Greece. They grow to about 40 inches in length, and can weigh up to 20 pounds. They have been eaten, and even farmed, for millennia: The ancient Romans kept eels in elaborate garden ponds, and some even kept them for pets.

• American eels look similar to European eels (though females can grow to five feet long). They're found in the eastern Americas from northern Canada to Brazil, and as far inland as the Great Lakes. They're the only freshwater eels in the Western Hemisphere.

• American eels were a dietary staple to many Native Americans tribes: to the *Mi'kmaq* people of New England and eastern Canada they were called *kat*, and they were prepared in many different ways—from raw to steamed to stewed—and their skins were used for making belts, decorations, and even medicine.

• Japanese eels are found in freshwaters in Japan, Korea, and the Philippines. In the sushi world, they're *unagi*.

A LONG, STRANGE EEL

The life cycle of freshwater eels is one of the wonders of nature and ones of its ongoing mysteries. The first person known to study them: 4th century B.C. Greek scholar Aristotle. After being unable to find pregnant females carrying eggs, or witness eels mating, he concluded that eels do not procreate—they simply sprout up from "putrefying" mud. That was incorrect, of course, but it took more than 2,000 years to prove him wrong.

The wad of cotton on the end of a Q-tip is called the *bud*.

In 1896 several small, transparent, willow-leaf-shaped fish were discovered in the Mediterranean Sea. They were deemed a new fish species and named *leptocephalus*, meaning "small head." Then two Italian biologists captured and raised some in aquariums, and watched—in amazement—as the leptocephali slowly turned into eels. This was the first big clue that eels, even freshwater varieties, were born in the ocean. But where?

In 1905 Danish oceanographer Johannes Schmidt started searching the Atlantic for the smallest leptocephali he could find. The smaller they were, naturally, the closer he'd be to their place of birth. Fifteen years later, he finally narrowed it down to the Sargasso Sea—a 2,000-mile-long, warm section of the Atlantic Ocean, running roughly from Bermuda to the Azore Islands off Portugal.

EEL LIFE

The Sargasso Sea is where all European and American eels (and many marine species, as well) go to spawn. According to scientists, it's one of the world's most remarkable animal migrations.

- Eel eggs hatch somewhere in the Sargasso Sea.
- The young leptocephali spend about a year being carried many thousands of miles by ocean currents to estuaries and river mouths all over western Europe and the eastern Americas.
- Once near freshwater, they begin to change into young eels, or *elvers*. As they grow, they make their way up rivers and streams, some for many hundreds of miles, eventually becoming adults and making homes in muddy-bottomed streams and lakes. There they feed on prey such as insects, fish, crabs, worms, and frogs.
- After 10 to as many as 40 years, they make their way back downstream to the Atlantic and swim back to the Sargasso. There, in the depths, the females each lay millions of eggs, males fertilize them, and then both adults die. And it all starts all over again.

* * *

"If dandelions were difficult to grow, they would be welcome on any lawn."

—**Andrew Mason**

ROBOTS IN THE NEWS

Uncle John bought one of those cool robot vacuums this year. His house is much cleaner now, but he can't find Porter the Wonder Dog anywhere.

CROWD CONTROL–BOT

The Advanced Telecommunications Research Institute of Osaka, Japan, has created a friendly robot that monitors large groups of people and helps anyone it thinks might be lost. On a trial run at a local shopping mall, the robot gathered information from 16 cameras and several range finders to monitor 20 people and categorize their behavior (such as walking fast, running, wandering, waiting, or "suspicious"). If it spots someone who looks "lost," the robot—about the size of a toddler—wheels up and asks if they need assistance. If the robot is wrong and the person is just loitering, it recommends shops and restaurants.

LOVE-BOT

David Levy, an expert on artificial intelligence, theorizes in his book *Love and Sex with Robots: The Evolution of Human-Robot Relationships*, that by the year 2025 humans will be able to engage in realistic romantic situations with robots. Levy believes that intimate relations with ultrarealistic, humanoid-looking robots will be commonplace by then, perfect for anyone who might have difficulties attracting a mate (such as the authors of books about sex with robots).

COP-BOT

Rufus Terrill, of Atlanta, an engineer, bar owner, and 2006 candidate for lieutenant governor of Georgia, got tired of the high rate of crime in his neighborhood. So he mounted a meat smoker to a three-wheeled scooter; added a spotlight, a loudspeaker, and an infrared camera; and made a remote-controlled crime-fighting robot. Each night, Terrill stands on a corner and guides the robot to a nearby daycare center where drug dealers and vagrants gather. He flashes the spotlight at them, informs them (through the robot's speaker) that they are "trespassing," and then shoots them

What do Angelina Jolie, George W. Bush, and Morgan Freeman have in common? They're all pilots.

with the robot's on-board high-powered squirt gun. "The city lacks the ability to control crime in the area," he said. "I'm doing what I have to do."

COP-BOT II

The city of Perm, Russia, spent a fortune on a crime-fighting robot designed to patrol streets and beam video to police stations, alerting officers to crimes in progress. After just three hours on the job, the six-foot-tall, egg-shaped robot broke down. Reason: It was raining, which shorted out the robot's electrical system.

KEVORKIAN-BOT

An 81-year-old man from Australia's Gold Coast was upset about his relatives' plans to move him into a nursing home. Unwilling to live in an institutional facility, he decided he'd lived long enough, and searched on the Internet to find a way to kill himself. Using various information he collected, he made a robot...with a remote control and a .22-caliber handgun attached. When the man activated the robot, it pulled the trigger, killing him instantly.

BOT BITS

• **Dancer-Bot.** To address growing concerns in Japan that with rapid modernization, many of its ancient traditions will be lost, Tokyo scientists created *wa*, 14-inch-tall robots that visit schools and teach school-age children traditional Japanese dances. (The robots even wear tiny kimonos.)

• **Sneeze-Bot.** Scientists at Weathernews, a Japanese weather news service, plan to install 200 beach ball–size robotic spheres around the country. The mission of the robo-balls will be to monitor pollen levels in the air. Passersby can then glance at the robots' "eyes" to see the pollen levels. White eyes means low pollen, green means medium pollen, and blue indicates high pollen levels.

• **Gas-Bot.** "Tankpitstop," the creation of Dutch inventor Nico van Staveren, is a robotic arm that can fill a car's gas tank. Attached to a regular gas pump, Tankpitstop uses multiple sensors that recognize the make of the car, locate and open the car's gas tank, and fill it up. Van Staveren says he got the idea after seeing a robotic arm used to milk a cow.

Good news? Astronauts cannot burp in zero gravity, but they can still fart.

ATOM BOMBS AWAY!

Both the United States and the USSR experimented with a lot of crazy ideas during the Cold War, but Project Pluto may be one of the strangest of them all.

WHAT GOES UP

If you're a history buff, you probably already know that the space race between the United States and the Soviet Union officially began on October 4, 1957, when the Soviets beat out the Americans by launching the first satellite, *Sputnik*, into orbit. Rockets that could lift satellites into space could also be used to launch nuclear warheads—in fact, the R-7 rocket that launched *Sputnik* into orbit was originally designed to carry nuclear warheads. The fear of falling behind the Soviets in this critical technology is what led the United States to create the National Aeronautics and Space Administration (NASA) in 1958, and put the country on a course to the Moon in the early 1960s.

But back then, who knew for sure whether the United States would ever catch up to the Soviet Union in missile technology? What if the Russians pulled so far ahead that they developed missiles capable of shooting down American missiles? If the United States lacked the ability to retaliate against a Soviet first strike, wouldn't that make a first strike that much more likely?

LOW BLOW

American military planners decided that they had to have another type of weapon available if the Soviets ever developed the means to shoot down intercontinental ballistic missiles (ICBMs).

When ICBMs are launched, they leave the Earth's atmosphere for a time and then re-enter it at a point high above the target. Because of this, any Soviet anti-missile defense systems would be aimed skyward to detect incoming missiles. One way to beat such a system would be to use a weapon that entered Soviet airspace at a very *low* altitude—treetop level, if possible. It would also have to fly so fast that the Soviets couldn't shoot it down even if they did manage to detect it. The effort to come up with such a "supersonic low-altitude missile" (SLAM) became known as Project Pluto.

William Shatner, Leonard Nimoy, and James Doohan have all appeared on *The Twilight Zone*.

GRAND SLAM

Weapon designers came up with an 85-foot-long missile carrying anywhere from 14 to 26 nuclear warheads, and a ramjet engine powered by an unshielded nuclear reactor powerful enough to generate 500 million watts of electricity.

Ramjets are designed to operate at three to five times the speed of sound. Their name comes from the fact that at those speeds the air is literally *rammed* into the engine as it travels through the atmosphere. As the air enters the engine, it is compressed; then the nuclear reactor heats the compressed air and causes it to expand. The expanding air is exhausted out the rear of the engine, creating thrust.

Because ramjets work only at very high speeds, the SLAM would have been launched with conventional rocket boosters; the ramjet reactor would have been activated when the missile accelerated to three times the speed of sound. Once it was fired up, the nuclear reactor would have given the missile nearly unlimited range. It could have remained aloft at 35,000 feet in a holding pattern for weeks or even months on end, waiting for the command to proceed with (or abort) the attack.

If the attack order was given, the SLAM would have descended to 1,000 feet and proceeded to its first target. When it arrived at the target, it would have ejected one of its warheads through a hatch on top of the missile, like a giant flying toaster. In the time it took the warhead to fall to earth and detonate, the SLAM would have cleared the blast zone and been on its way to the next target, and then the next, and so on, until it ran out of warheads.

EASIER SAID THAN DONE

That was how the SLAM worked on paper; whether such a missile could ever really be built is questionable. Traveling three to five times the speed of sound in all weather, at low altitudes where the air is thickest, would have exposed the missile to very high temperatures and atmospheric pressures. The unshielded nuclear reactor would have pushed temperatures even higher, to about 2,500°F, well past the point where materials used in most jet and rocket engines would have melted. Even the special high-temperature materials the engineers did plan on using auto-ignited at just 150°F above the reactor's expected operating temperature, so if the SLAM ran even slightly hotter than expected, the missile could have burst into flames and disintegrated in midflight, showering highly radioactive material over a very wide area.

DIRTY BOMB

But a SLAM could be lethal without launching a single warhead. Traveling at three times the speed of sound at 1,000 feet would have produced a sonic boom strong enough to destroy buildings and kill people on the ground, and the unshielded nuclear reactor would have spewed deadly radiation over the surrounding region—no small consideration when it was expected that the SLAM would have to pass over countries allied with the United States on its way to the Soviet Union. The SLAM was a flying Chernobyl—so deadly, in fact, that the designers considered leaving the nuclear warheads out entirely. After months of flying around in Soviet airspace, the radiation and sonic boom would have killed more people than the warheads would have.

TOO DEADLY

How would you even test something as deadly as a SLAM? There was no test site big enough to contain it, especially if it went out of control during flight. Even when the engineers tested the ramjet engine on the ground in 1961, they had to build the disassembly building two miles away from the test stand and operate both by remote control—the ramjet engine became so radioactive after firing that it would have killed anyone who got near it. The building where the engineers monitored the tests by closed-circuit cameras was even farther away and included a nuclear fallout shelter stocked with a two-week supply of food and water in case radiation levels rose so high that immediate rescue was impossible.

The logic behind the SLAM concept was probably flawed from the beginning. Its success depended on using it in a surprise attack, but once it was launched and spewing sonic booms and giant clouds of radiation in its wake, how long could it possibly have remained undetected? Lucky for us, for the Russians, and probably for everyone else on Earth, the United States pulled ahead of the Soviet Union in missile technology in the mid-1960s and scrapped the SLAM project before it ever got off the drawing board.

In 2004 an elementary-school book report written by Britney Spears sold for $1,900 at auction.

(NOT) COMING TO A THEATER NEAR YOU

You'd be surprised by how many films in Hollywood are started... but not finished. Here's a look at a few fascinating could-have-beens and almost-wases that never were.

STAR WARS: EPISODES VII, VIII, IX

While making *The Empire Strikes Back* in 1979, *Star Wars* creator George Lucas told a reporter that he ultimately planned on making nine movies in the series, a project that would take more than 30 years. (He even asked actor Mark Hamill if he'd be available for filming the ninth film, which he planned to start in 2011.) Lucas said that the original three movies (*Star Wars, The Empire Strikes Back,* and *Return of the Jedi*) were actually episodes four, five, and six in the saga; episodes seven, eight, and nine would depict Luke Skywalker defeating the Empire and establishing peace throughout the galaxy. Lucas did eventually make the first three episodes, but abandoned the final three. What happened? Insiders say that Lucas never wrote a script, or anything beyond a vague outline, for movies seven, eight, and nine, and what he did write was incorporated into *Return of the Jedi*.

BIKER HEAVEN (1983)

Easy Rider (1969) was written, produced, and directed by the movie's stars, Peter Fonda and Dennis Hopper. The film, a celebration of 1960s counterculture, follows two hippie bikers who travel from Los Angeles to New Orleans to search for the "real" America, a journey that amounts to taking lots of drugs, partying at Mardi Gras, and getting hassled by small-town rednecks. By 1982 America had changed so much that Fonda decided to make a sequel. The countercultural movement was out, Reagan and yuppies were in. He wanted to show the death of the '60s ethic, so he and former *Saturday Night Live* writer Michael O'Donoghue concocted *Biker Heaven*. The plot: After a nuclear apocalypse, "Biker God" brings Fonda and Hopper's characters back to life in order to find a magical American flag that will resurrect all the

Why is it called a *carpenter frog*? Its croak sounds like a hammer.

dead. They snort the ground-up skull of Chief Crazy Horse, find the flag, and return to "Biker Heaven." No movie studios were interested in *Biker Heaven*. Why? Because Fonda was considered a has-been and Hopper couldn't work because of a substance-abuse problem (and probably because the story was too "far out").

NAPOLEON (1972)

Filmmaker Stanley Kubrick was a perfectionist who researched project for years before he began filming it. In 1968 he set aside four years to make a movie about Napoleon. He read dozens of books, organized his research into thousands of index cards, wrote the script over the course of a year, and scouted locations in France, Italy, Romania, and Czechoslovakia. He also hired 75,000 extras to play soldiers, ordered 20,000 gallons of fake blood and commissioned 4,000 costumes for the main cast, making it one of the largest productions ever. (Kubrick's choice for the title role: Jack Nicholson.) But while he was doing research, another Napoleon movie—*Waterloo*, starring Rod Steiger—beat him to theaters in 1970. When *Waterloo* bombed at the box office, Kubrick's financial backers got cold feet and pulled out of the project, forcing Kubrick to scrap *Napoleon* altogether. He made *A Clockwork Orange* instead.

NIGHT SKIES (1982)

In 1979 Columbia Pictures asked Steven Spielberg to produce a sequel to *Close Encounters of the Third Kind*. Doing a sequel didn't interest him, so he came up with an idea for a different movie: *Night Skies*, based on the real-life story of a Kentucky family who claimed that a group of aliens visited their farm in 1955 and tried to kill them. Spielberg hired John Sayles (*Eight Men Out*) to flesh out a screenplay. Sayles added a subplot: One of the aliens is kind and gentle, and befriends the family's son. In 1980, while Spielberg was in Tunisia filming *Raiders of the Lost Ark*, Melissa Mathison, a novice screenwriter, came to the set to visit her fiancé, Harrison Ford. Spielberg read her the *Night Skies* script and they both realized the only good part was the benevolent alien and his relationship with the little boy. Spielberg cancelled *Night Skies* and instead directed the movie Mathison wrote based on their conversation: *E.T.: The Extra-Terrestrial*. (The plot about the terrorized suburban family became the basis for *Poltergeist*.)

The Goodfellows insurance company sells policies that protect against damages from alien abduction.

CAUGHT IN THE ACT

There are a lot of dishonest scams out there. From insurance fraud to phony advertising, no matter how smart you are, you're still a potential victim. That's why it's so satisfying when these tricksters get found out.

CULPRIT: Saratoga Spa State Park, in upstate New York
GRAND SCHEME: For only $20, visitors to the public resort are invited to soak in warm, pure mineral water. The park opened in 1835, but for the last 25 years, the mineral water has been mixed with regular tap water. Why? An underwater boiler had been heating the mineral water, but when it broke in 1983, park officials found it was less expensive to mix in already-heated tap water—only they kept on telling their patrons it was *pure* mineral water.
EXPOSED! When a new state governor took over at the beginning of 2007, the New York parks department was overhauled and the new director discovered the ruse. Then the press found out and the story spread. "They're lying to the public. It's the state committing fraud," complained former Saratoga Springs Mayor Raymond Watkin. The state placed the blame on the Colorado-based company that runs the park.
OUTCOME: Today, the park is slowly transitioning back to heating the spring water pools with actual heaters—so far they've completed two of them. The rest of the pools still use tap water (with full disclosure), and it still costs $20 to take a bath.

CULPRIT: Hospitals in Hangzhou, in China's Zhejiang province
GRAND SCHEME: The hospitals routinely encourage people to take urine tests to find out if there's anything wrong with them. If so, then the hospitals are there to help.
EXPOSED! Sensing that the hospitals might be cheating patients for extra revenue, a few Chinese reporters went undercover and submitted urine tests to the hospitals—but instead of urine, the vials were filled with tea. While four of the ten hospitals told the reporters that there was tea in their urine samples, the other six (four of which are state-owned) prescribed medication for various disorders that cost up to 400 yuan ($50). Said

Charles Addams, creator of *The Addams Family*, got married in a pet cemetery.

one of the reporters, "It makes one shiver all over even though it's not cold."

OUTCOME: Activists are pushing the Chinese government to overhaul the health-care system, but so far little progress has been made.

CULPRIT: Federal Emergency Management Agency (FEMA)

GRAND SCHEME: Still reeling from their heavily criticized response to Hurricanes Katrina and Rita in 2005, FEMA knew that all eyes were upon them during the 2007 wildfire season and wanted to reassure California citizens that they had everything under control. So on the afternoon of October 23, 2007, the agency informed the major news outlets of a press conference at their Washington, D.C., office…in 15 minutes. Reporters were also given a number to call, but it was a "listen only" line. During the conference (broadcast live on several cable news outlets), reporters asked deputy director Harvey Johnson, "Are you happy with FEMA's response so far?" He replied, "I'm very happy with FEMA's response so far." Another asked, "Do you think FEMA has learned its lesson since Katrina?" Again, Johnson answered positively. That was the way the entire briefing went—not a single tough question, such as the reports of formaldehyde being present in trailers used to shelter those who'd lost their homes.

EXPOSED! Many *actual* reporters smelled a rat, and it didn't take much digging to discover that the press conference was staffed by FEMA employees posing as reporters. When the story broke, Johnson explained that his staff had to pull the ruse because no real reporters showed up (even though they were only given 15 minutes' advance notice). Plus, he said, "We pulled questions from those we had been getting from reporters earlier in the day."

OUTCOME: Everyone from the White House to major media outlets was furious with FEMA's tactics. Homeland Security Chief Michael Chertoff said, "I think it was one of the dumbest and most inappropriate things I've seen since I've been in government. I have made unambiguously clear, in Anglo-Saxon prose, that it is not to ever happen again, and there will be appropriate disciplinary action taken against those people who exhibited what I regard as extraordinarily poor judgment." In the end, a few reprimands were given, but no one was fired.

Alaska is the only state whose name can be typed on a single keyboard row.

POLITICAL ANIMALS

Think your elected representative is a turkey? You're not alone. From ancient to modern times, all kinds of critters have entered politics. And some have had been more popular than their human counterparts.

INCITATUS

The brief reign of Roman emperor Caligula (37–41 A.D.) was marked by eccentric behavior (some historians call it insanity), some of which involved Incitatus, his prize stallion. Caligula was a passionate racing fan, and Incitatus was the fastest horse in the Roman Empire. Caligula came to believe that his horse was victorious because he possessed not only speed, but also a high intelligence. The Emperor provided a house, furniture, and servants for Incitatus so that the horse could meet and entertain dignitaries. Sitting at Incitatus's table, senators and nobles were forced to toast his health and respectfully speak to him about state business. Declared a full citizen of Rome, Incitatus was even given the title of Deputy High Priest. The horse got a hefty salary for "supervising" temples built in honor of the Emperor. The steed was even appointed senator, and he was in line for more high honors when real senators—tired of their emperor's horsing around—helped assassinate Caligula in 41 A.D. Most historians say that Caligula's appointment of a horse to public office was a sign of his progressive mental illness, but others believe Caligula was just humiliating his enemies in the Senate.

PIGASUS

During the 1968 presidential election, the United States was deeply divided over the war in Vietnam. That August thousands of antiwar activists gathered at the Democratic National Convention in Chicago to protest. Among them were members of the Youth International Party, or "Yippies." They bought a young boar at a local farm (folk singer Phil Ochs paid for it), named him Pigasus the Immortal, and made him their candidate for president. On August 23, with great media fanfare, Yippie leader Jerry Rubin stood in front of the Chicago Civic Center and announced Pigasus's candidacy. Along with the nomination, Rubin was about to announce the pig's first press conference, where (according to Rubin) Pigasus would not only answer reporter's questions but also demand a White House foreign policy briefing. But before Rubin could say anything, Chicago cops converged on the news conference and arrested him and his friends on charges of disorderly conduct and bringing livestock into the city. As for Pigasus, photos show policemen surrounding the captured candidate—right before they took him to the local humane society. (He was later adopted by members of the commune known as the Hog Farm.)

CACARECO

The saying that politicians need to be thick-skinned might explain why this female rhinoceros won Sao Paulo, Brazil's 1958 city council election in a landslide. With a population of well over three million, the city suffered from such problems as unpaved streets, open sewers, food shortages, and rampant inflation, but officials had ignored them for years. When the city council elections were held, local college students decided to run a protest campaign and picked Cacareco, who lived in the Sao Paulo Zoo, as their candidate. (Part of the attraction might have been that her name means "garbage" in Portuguese.) In all, 540 candidates—including many well-known incumbents—participated in the election, but voters were so eager to embarrass the failed city government that Cacareco won easily with a spectacular 100,000 votes. And even though the city hastily disqualified her from serving, Cacareco's win made news around the world. "Better a rhinoceros than an ass," a voter explained, and the quote made *Time* magazine. Cacareco's election left a legacy: Today in Brazil, a protest vote is still known as a *voto Cacareco*.

* * *

WHAT'S IN *YOUR* LIPSTICK?

In 2006 the U.S. Food and Drug Administration revised its rules for the manufacture of beauty products such as hairspray and lipstick. From now on, beauty companies are forbidden to use any cow brains in their products...at least from older cattle. The brain parts taken from younger cows, however, are still allowed.

Bolivia's 4,000-man navy has never patrolled the Bolivian coastline. (Bolivia doesn't have a coast.)

AFTER THE OLYMPICS

The Olympics can turn an unknown athlete into an international star overnight. But then what? For most, there are no professional leagues to join. So what do they do?

Athlete: Mark Spitz
Event: Swimming (1972)
Story: Spitz won two gold medals in the 1968 Olympics, but going into the 1972 Games, he told a reporter he planned on winning *six more* golds. He didn't—he won *seven*, a single-Games record that stood until 2008. Not only that, but all of his winning times in those seven swimming events (100m and 200m freestyle, 100m and 200m butterfly, and three four-man relays) were new world records.
After: The 22-year-old swimmer became an overnight sensation—he appeared on magazine covers, posters, and advertisements, often striking risqué poses while clad in only his Speedo (and mustache). Then he went into show business, playing a paramedic on the medical drama *Emergency!* and reportedly making the short list to host the 1973 Academy Awards, despite the fact that he had never made a movie (or hosted a live TV show). There was even speculation that he might be the next James Bond. In 1974 Spitz decided he didn't like acting and started a successful motivational speaking company. In 1992 he attempted to make the U.S. swim team for the Olympics in Barcelona, Spain…and almost did. At age 42, his times in the trials were actually *better* than they'd been in the 1972 trials. But the level of competition had increased so much in the previous 20 years that Spitz wasn't fast enough to make the team. Still, he was the last swimmer cut.

Athlete: Bruce Jenner
Event: Decathlon (1976)
Story: Jenner played football in college, but switched to track and field because he felt that football was too physically draining. His event: the decathlon, which consists of 10 individual events: 100m, 400m, and 1500m runs, 110m hurdles, javelin, pole vault, discus, high jump, long jump, and shot put. Jenner

won the gold medal at the 1976 Olympics, setting a record high score, and as he ran a victory lap, he carried an American flag handed to him by a fan. It became one of American sports' most iconic images.

After: Completely dominating what is considered one of the most grueling and difficult sporting events made Jenner an instant celebrity. Helping matters were Jenner's movie-star good looks, which he took, naturally, to Hollywood. It didn't go so well—after turning down a chance to star in the movie version of *Superman*, he co-starred with the Village People in the musical *Can't Stop the Music* (considered by many critics to be one of the worst movies of all time) and spent half a season on the TV police drama *CHiPs* filling in for Erik Estrada, who was in a contract dispute. More recently, Jenner has become a regular on TV reality shows and game show "celebrity" editions, including *Skating with Celebrities*, *Family Feud*, *I'm a Celebrity…Get Me Out of Here*, and *The Weakest Link*. He currently co-stars on *Keeping Up With the Kardashians*, which follows Jenner, his second wife Kris Kardashian, and his children and stepchildren.

Athlete: Dick Fosbury

Event: High jump (1968)

Story: Before Fosbury, the usual method of performing the high jump was to run straight to the bar, then jump over it, with legs spread, either front-to-back or side-to-side. Fosbury found that he was too tall to successfully execute it, so he worked on a new method. When Fosbury went up, he ran to the bar at a curve, then jumped over the bar backwards, landing on his back. The curved run allowed for more power and leverage in the jump, and the backwards landing let him focus all of his energy on the jump because he didn't have to worry about a soft landing. He won the gold medal.

After: Not many athletes can say they completely revolutionized their sport. Today, his method—nicknamed the "Fosbury Flop" by a sportswriter—is the *only* way athletes attempt the high jump.

Athlete: Nadia Comaneci

Event: Gymnastics (1976)

Story: The 14-year-old Romanian was the first gymnast ever to score a perfect 10.0 from all seven judges. She won three gold medals in 1976. (She came in second in the individual all-around in 1980, by less than one-tenth of a point.) She won golds on the beam (1976 & '80) and floor exercise (1980), for a career medal count of five gold, three silver, and one bronze.

After: Comaneci returned to Romania and trained Olympic hopefuls. But in 1989 she defected to the United States and in 1996 married gymnast Bart Conner. Comenaci now coaches gymnastics in Norman, Oklahoma, writes for *International Gymnast*, and provides commentary during gymnastics TV broadcasts.

Bonus: Comaneci was so popular that she inspired a hit song. ABC used the theme song from *The Young and the Restless* as music for showing much-repeated montages of her perfect routine. It was renamed "Nadia's Theme" and became a Top 10 hit in late 1976.

Athlete: Greg Louganis

Event: Diving (1988)

Story: Louganis first competed in the 1976 Games at age 16, winning a silver medal in 10m platform diving. The U.S. boycotted the 1980 Games (held in the communist USSR), but Louganis returned in 1984 with record-setting scores in both the 10m platform dive and 3m springboard dive. Amazingly, he won the gold medal again in both events at the 1988 Games in South Korea with even better scores than before. But what really made Louganis famous was a slipup: During a dive in a preliminary round, he leapt off the board, did a midair flip, came back down...and smashed his head on the diving board. Louganis suffered a concussion, but still won the gold medal.

After: Louganis retired from diving after the 1988 games and became a spokesman for several nonprofit groups, raising awareness of depression and domestic violence, both of which he'd suffered. In 1994 Louganis made news with the announcement that he was homosexual. The following year he wrote his autobiography, *Breaking the Surface*, a #1 bestseller for five weeks. The book created a controversy with the revelation that Louganis was HIV positive, and had been so during his Olympics accident—which had spilled some of his blood into the pool. (None of his competitors became infected as a result.) Since then, he's been a TV announcer at diving events, acted in the Broadway play *Jeffrey*, and competed with his Jack Russell Terriers in dog agility competitions.

...into his mouth, they are engaged to be married.

DOING A RATNER

Ever had one of those moments when you realize, immediately after you've said something, that you just said exactly the wrong thing? It's a terrible feeling. But when the CEO of a big company does it...it's hilarious.

THE £500 MILLION MAN

Founded in 1949, Ratners became one of Great Britain's top jewelry chains by selling bargain-priced rings, watches, and glassware. Gerald Ratner was the company's 42-year-old CEO in 1991, having joined the family business when he was 18. Under him, Ratners grew into one of Britain's largest chains and acquired numerous other jewelry chains, including Kay Jewelers in the United States. Life was good for Gerald Ratner...until April 1991, when he gave a speech at the Institute of Directors (a kind of a CEO think tank) and said this:

> "We do cut-glass sherry decanters complete with six glasses on a silver-plated tray, all for £4.95. People say, 'How can you sell this for such a low price?' I say, because it's total crap."

He went on to say that Ratners earrings were "cheaper than a prawn sandwich, but probably won't last as long." Ratner was obviously joking—and he didn't know any media would be covering the event. But they were, and the speech was widely reported in the British media. The self-inflicted wound so damaged the Ratners brand name that in less than a year the company plunged in value from £1 billion to £500 million. Ratner was fired; the company changed its name to the Signet Group. Since then, when executives get caught saying something stupid about their own company, the corporate world has a special phrase to describe it: They're said to be "doing a Ratner"—and it happens a lot.

RATNER: Allen Roses, the vice president in charge of genetics for pharmaceutical giant GlaxoSmithKline addressed a medical convention in 2003. "Over 90% of drugs only work on 30 to 50% of people," he said. Media analysts pointed out Roses' implication that most of GlaxoSmithKline's products don't work for most people.
RESULT: The corporation responded that Roses' remarks "were misinterpreted."

Squeezeboxer: The accordion was patented by Albert Faas of Philadelphia in 1854.

RATNER: Matt Barrett, the CEO of Barclays Bank, a British financial services company, was called to testify at a 2003 Parliament hearing about interest rates (Barclays was charging 17.9%—double that of their competitors). Barrett was asked if he himself uses credit cards. His answer: No, he doesn't, because "it's too expensive." Not only does Barrett not use them, but he admitted that he actively warns his own family not to use them. "I have four young children. I give them advice not to pile up debts on their credit cards."
RESULT: Barrett was reprimanded by Barclays, right? No, he was promoted to chairman.

RATNER: An Orlando man known only as "James" missed a concert in Atlanta because his Spirit Airlines flight was delayed. He wrote a letter to several Spirit employees asking to be reimbursed $377 for the cost of the flight, parking, hotel, and concert tickets. No one responded, so James wrote directly to CEO Ben Baldanza (and cc'ed his other contacts at the company). Seeing all the names on the e-mail, Baldanza assumed that it was an internal company memo and hit "reply all" with this message, which went to James: "We owe him nothing. Let him tell the world how bad we are. He will be back when we save him a penny."
RESULT: Despite a firestorm of bad publicity, Baldanza managed to remain head of Spirit Airlines.

RATNER: Anders Dahlvig, the president of IKEA furniture stores, told the *Financial Times* in 2001 that one of its biggest corporate struggles was the "appalling service" at its stores on weekends.
RESULT: Dahlvig quickly amended his remarks to say that he wasn't criticizing the company—he meant that IKEA is so successful that it has crowded stores, which keeps its employees very busy.

RATNER: In July 2001, David Shepherd, head of the suit manufacturer TopMan, gave an interview to the trade journal *Menswear*. The reporter asked Shepherd to describe TopMan's customer base. Shepherd's response: "Hooligans, or whatever. Very few of our customers have to wear suits for work. [Our suits] will be for his first interview or first court case."
RESULT: The company's stock only dropped a few points, then rebounded. (Their customer base apparently wasn't offended.)

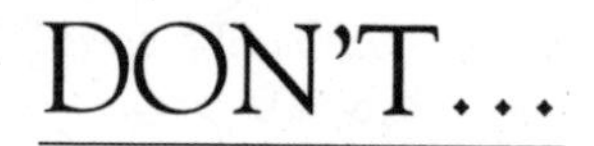

DON'T...

"Don't even think about skipping this page." —Uncle John

"Don't ask the barber whether you need a haircut."

—Daniel Greenberg

"Don't take advice from people with missing fingers."

—Henry Beard

Don't approach a goat from the front, a horse from the back, or a fool from any side.

—Yiddish proverb

"Don't tell fish stories where the people know you; but particularly, don't tell them where they know the fish."

—Mark Twain

"Don't stay in bed...unless you can make money in bed."

—George Burns

"Don't do what you would undo if caught."

—Leah Arendt

"Don't take any class where you have to read *Beowulf*."

—Woody Allen

"Don't worry that children never listen to you; worry that they're always watching you."

—Robert Fulghum

"Don't ever confuse the two—your life and your work."

—Anna Quindlen

"Don't think. Thinking is the enemy of creativity."

—Ray Bradbury

"Don't lose your head. It's the best part of your body."

—Jimmy Snyder

"Don't do what you want—do what you don't want. Do the things that scare you the most."

—Chuck Palahniuk

"Don't worry. Being eaten by a crocodile is just like going to sleep. In a giant blender."

—Homer Simpson

"Don't trust a sane person."

—Lyle Alzado

"Don't ever write anything you don't like yourself and if you do like it, don't take anyone's advice about changing it. They just don't know."

—Raymond Chandler

"You were born an original. Don't die a copy."

—John Mason

The *Yale Book of Quotations'* most memorable quote of 2007: "Don't tase me, bro!"

THE BIG BROTHER FILES

It seems like the government intrudes into our lives more and more. Thank goodness there's still one room in the house where you can shut the door and feel that your privacy is secure (for now, anyway).

WAKE-UP CALL

In June 2008, police in Lakeville, Minnesota, walked into a house at 3 a.m., went upstairs to the homeowner's bedroom, woke him up—and told him that he had left his front door unlocked and his garage door open. The officers had been walking the streets, putting notices on people's doors reminding them to lock their doors so strangers couldn't break into their houses...and just let themselves in when they found the door unlocked. The homeowner, Troy Molde, whose two sons were also in the house, was outraged, telling reporters that he felt violated. The officers said they were performing a "public service."

FREE PRESS?

On May 15, 2006, veteran ABC News reporters Richard Esposito and Brian Ross reported on ABC's "The Blotter" Web site that they'd received a call from a senior federal law enforcement official. The official, who requested anonymity, said, "It's time for you to get new cell phones, quick." Why? The government was tracking their calls. The CIA and the FBI, the reporters said, were upset about stories they had done and were trying to determine if any of their sources were from inside either of the two organizations.

BEAT YOUR CHILDREN WELL

A 14-year-old girl was in court with her parents in Brownsville, Texas, in April 2008. The judge, Gustavo Garza, told the girl's father, Daniel Zurita, that he was going to find the girl guilty of criminal truancy and fine her $500...unless Zurita spanked his daughter with a large, heavy paddle that the judge kept nearby—right there in the courtroom. Zurita thought he didn't have a choice, so he hit the girl on the butt with the paddle. The judge told him he hadn't hit her hard enough, so he paddled her again. The Zuritas later filed a lawsuit against the judge. (But another judge ruled that Garza was immune from lawsuits.)

In 874 King Charles the Bald granted independence to Barcelona under Count Wilfred the Hairy.

THE EYE ON THE POLE

In 2006 the United Kingdom instituted an "Automatic Number Plate Recognition" (ANPR) program, a massive surveillance system consisting of cameras on the nation's roads. Cameras able to register the license plates of passing cars at the rate of one per second were placed every 400 yards on all of Britain's major motorways. They record how fast the cars drive and whether the vehicles are registered. In addition, they can find people who are wanted by the law—and keep track of the driving habits of ordinary people who are driving perfectly legally. The ANPR includes the compilation of a "24x7 national vehicle movement database," a log of the movement of every single vehicle on the U.K.'s major roads, which is kept in the database for two years (so they say).

THE THIN BLUE LINE

In 2006 the University of Chicago performed a study that looked into reports of police abuse in the city. Findings: Between 2002 and 2004, more than 10,000 abuse claims had been filed by citizens against Chicago police officers, but only 19 had resulted in what the report called "meaningful disciplinary action," meaning a suspension of at least seven days. Possible reason: Police abuse claims are investigated...by the police department. "If the CPD investigated civilian crime in the same way it investigates police abuse," said law professor Craig Futterman, who headed the study, "they'd never solve a case." Police spokesman Patrick Camden said, "We don't respond to studies."

THE NAME POLICE

An Italian court ruled in December 2007 that a couple in the city of Genoa had to change their 15-month-old son's name from *Venerdi*, the Italian word for "Friday," to "Gregory." Italian law stipulates that odd names must be reported by city officials to the federal government, and they ruled that the name Venerdi was "ridiculous" and "shameful." Why "Gregory?" Because the boy was born on the day of the Feast of St. Gregory. (Italy is 90 percent Catholic.) The parents later appealed the case—but lost. "My son was born Friday, baptized Friday, will call himself Friday, we will call him Friday, but when he gets older he will have to sign his name Gregory," said the boy's mother. "I am livid about this!"

Smallest rodent: the African pygmy mouse (7g). Largest: the South American capybara (100 lb.).

BATHROOM NEWS

All the latest from the news stream...

HOUSTON, WE HAVE A *REALLY BIG* PROBLEM

What do the residents of the *International Space Station* do when their only toilet breaks? They improvise. Fortunately, it was only the urinal (the "#2" unit still worked). After the fan that sucks away the urine malfunctioned (Ewww!), the *ISS* team had to improvise a manual flushing system that took two crewmembers about 10 minutes per flush to perform. Luckily, the Space Shuttle *Discovery* was only two weeks away from launching when the malfunction occurred in May 2008, so the new crew brought an extra pump unit along with them. When the toilet was finally fixed, the occupants were relieved. "Like any home anywhere, the importance of having a working bathroom is obvious," said a NASA spokesman.

A SENSORLESS CRIME

A Taiwanese car mechanic named Wang Chi-sheng was arrested after he was caught breaking into a gas station bathroom to steal the automatic hands-free urinal sensor. He told the police that he had planned to use the sensor to "improve" his Mercedes-Benz. According to press reports, the officers laughed at him. And just in case anyone else wants to try the same thing, a Mercedes official stated that "the probability of successfully using a sensor from a public urinal to replace special factory-made sensors is zero." He added that an improperly installed urinal sensor could—in the worst-case scenario—cause the car to explode.

IT'S IN THE BAG

According to complaints made to their union, 25 male field technicians for Qwest, a telecommunications company in the western United States, were told by a supervisor in Montrose, Colorado, to bring "urine bags" out to the job to cut down on "lengthy bathroom breaks" (the workers generally go all the way back to the garage to do their business). The union claims the workers were ordered to use the bags; the company counters that there's no set

In Japan, you can buy Stick-on Belly-Button Cleaners. A box of six sells for $6.15.

policy—the bags are simply provided for the workers' convenience, should they need them.

DOWN THE DRAIN

When the euro took over as Europe's official currency in 2002, many people believed—incorrectly—that their old money would be worthless. A man in Berlin, Germany, believed it...and flushed 60,000 Deutsche marks down his toilet. When informed that he could have exchanged the cash for about 30,000 euros ($37,000 U.S.), the man (his name was withheld—wouldn't you want yours withheld if you were him?) called the city public works department and begged them to retrieve his money for him. The workers had to go out to the man's street anyway...because the sewer line was clogged with his money. After working for hours, they were able to pull some of the man's cash from the sewage, which he then painstakingly dried and cleaned before exchanging it.

JUST PLANE RUDE

In February 2008, as a JetBlue red-eye flight from San Diego to New York was boarding, a standby passenger named Gokhan Mutlu was informed that the plane was full. But a flight attendant offered to let him sit in her assigned seat; she would sit in the "jump seat," which folds down from the inside wall of the plane. So Mutlu settled into seat 2E and was happily on his way. But about 90 minutes in, the pilot called the dozing passenger to the front and informed him that the flight attendant was uncomfortable in the jump seat. She needed 2E. And because it was against regulations for a *passenger* to sit in the jump seat, Mutlu would have to sit in the bathroom...for the rest of the flight. Mutlu protested but (according to him) the captain said, "This is my plane, under my command, and you should be grateful for being on board." (Mutlu also claimed that while they argued, the flight attendant sat in his seat pretending to be asleep.) So what could Mutlu do? He spent the remaining three hours in the bathroom, with no way to strap himself in during turbulence. As he was deplaning, he says the pilot told him, "I don't think you appreciate what I did for you." Mutlu replied, "You locked me in the bathroom." To which the pilot said, "I brought you home." At last report, Mutlu was suing JetBlue for $2 million.

The okapi is the only known relative of the giraffe (its neck is much shorter).

FAMILIAR PHRASES

Here's one of our regular features—the origins of some common phrases.

APPLE OF MY EYE

Meaning: One's beloved

Origin: "It was once believed that the pupil was a vital spot in the human anatomy. Early healers thought it was apple-shaped, and so it became known as the 'apple of the eye.' Because the pupil was considered as vital as life itself, it became customary to call the object of one's affection 'the apple of my eye.'" (From *Common Phrases and Where They Come From*, by Myron Korach)

SPITTING IMAGE

Meaning: A lookalike or exact replica

Origin: "Long ago the phrase referred to a son who looked so much like his father, it was said that the boy had been 'spit from his father's mouth.' Over time, the expression was altered and modified to 'spit and image' and then to 'spitting image.'" (From *Cat Got Your Tongue*, by Daniel J. Porter)

WHAT THE DICKENS?

Meaning: "What the heck?"

Origin: "It has nothing to do with English novelist Charles Dickens—Shakespeare had made use of the phrase much earlier in *The Merry Wives of Windsor*. (Mrs. Page says of Falstaff, 'I cannot tell what the dickens his name is.') In those times the word 'dickens' was used in preference to 'devil,' which was considered impolite." (From *Everyday Phrases*, by Neil Ewart)

TONGUE IN CHEEK

Meaning: Being facetious or knowingly ironic

Origin: "A contemptuous gesture common from at least the 18th century involved poking your tongue in your cheek. But because it was impossible to understand someone who spoke with their tongue in their cheek, 'to put one's tongue' in one's cheek came to

An erupting volcano can shoot ash as high as 30 miles into the atmosphere.

mean 'to speak insincerely.'" (From *The Real McCoy: The True Stories Behind Our Everyday Phrases*, by Georgia Hole)

TO HAVE A CRUSH

Meaning: To be in (what at least feels like) love

Origin: "It's a distortion of the French word *crèche*, meaning 'crib.' To be 'in a *crèche*,' or to 'have one's own *crèche*,' in 17th century France, meant you were so smitten with love that you were as helpless and irresponsible as an infant, or were crib-bound." (From *The Cat's Pajamas*, by Tad Tuleja)

NO PAIN, NO GAIN

Meaning: To improve, one must work hard

Origin: "This dictum, long uttered by athletic coaches urging players to train harder, is far more ancient than most of them probably realize. Indeed, 'Without pains, no gains,' was in John Ray's proverb collection of 1670. Some versions reinforce it by adding, 'No sweat, no sweet.'" (From *Southpaws and Sunday Punches*, by Christine Ammer)

PIPE DOWN

Meaning: "Be quiet!"

Origin: "In Britain's Royal Navy, this was the last call of the day through the bosun's pipe, a ship's signaling whistle played by the bosun, or petty officer. There were numerous standard signals, and the one for lights-out and silence was called 'pipe down.' In 'navalese' the phrase became a forceful suggestion to the noisy or argumentative that they should shut up and be quiet." (From *To Coin a Phrase*, by Edwin Radford and Alan Smith)

STRAIGHT FROM THE HORSE'S MOUTH

Meaning: Verifiably accurate information

Origin: "It has nothing to do with a horse speaking, of course. A horse's age can more accurately be judged by looking at its teeth (which grow according to a strict system). So, if you were buying the horse, you would do better to look at the horse's mouth than rely on any information about its age that the vendor might give you." (From *Why Do We Say...?*, by Nigel Rees)

Ammonia gets its name from the Egyptian god Amun.

PARK ON AN ANGEL

What's the difference between good and evil? Proofreading. The following are excerpts from real church bulletins.

"The church office will be closed until opening. It will remain closed after opening. It will reopen Monday."

"When parking on the north side of the church, please remember to park on an angel."

"The cost for attending the Fasting and Prayer conference includes meals."

"Irving Benson and Jessie Carter were married on October 24 in the church. So ends a friendship that began in their school days."

"Please place your donation in the envelope along with the deceased person you want remembered."

"There is a sign-up sheet for anyone wishing to be baptized on the table in the foyer."

"Please join us as we show our support for Amy and Alan in preparing for the girth of their first child."

"The third verse of 'Blessed Assurance' will be sung without musical accomplishment."

"The sermon this morning: 'Jesus Walks on the Water.' The sermon tonight: 'Searching for Jesus.'"

"The concert held in Fellowship Hall was a great success. Special thanks are due to the minister's daughter, who labored the whole evening at the piano, which as usual fell upon her."

"The visiting monster today is Rev. Jack Bains."

"The Sunday Night Men's Glee Club will meet on Saturday at the park, unless it rains. In that case they will meet at their regular Tuesday evening time."

"The class on prophecy has been cancelled due to unforeseen circumstances."

"Jean will be leading a weight-management series Wednesday nights. She's used the program herself and has been growing like crazy!"

"Next Thursday there will be tryouts for the choir. They need all the help they can get."

In 2004 the Russian Orthodox Church officially ruled that playing chess is not a sin.

TEQUILA MOCKINGBIRD

Real—and really punny—names of restaurants in the U.S. and Europe.

Snacks Fifth Avenue

Pony Espresso

Lawrence of Oregano

Pulp Kitchen

Wiener Take All

Chez When

Relish the Thought

Eaton Gogh

The Hearty Boys

Jonathan Livingston Seafood

Boogie Woogie Bagel Boy

Thai Foon

Ein Stein

Just for the Halibut

Grill from Ipanema

The Frying Dutchman

Syriandipity

Brew Ha Ha

Adams Rib

Crepevine

Barnum and Bagel

Latte Da

Sacred Chow

Miso Hapi

Debbie Does Donuts

Sea Señor

Seoul Man

Wok Around the Clock

What Ales You

The Wieners Circle

Brewed Awakenings

Legal Grounds

Aesop's Tables

Men at Wok

Lord of the Fries

Dine One One

The Codfather

ThaiTanic

Mustard's Last Stand

Custard's Last Stand

Pizza the Action

Tequila Mockingbird

Franks for the Memories

Auntie Pastos

Lox, Stock and Bagel

Just Falafs

The Boston Sea Party

Peking Inn

Pizza My Heart

Nin Com Soup

Pita Pan

Marquis de Salade

The bookkeeping terms "in the red" & "in the black" come from the colors of 12th-century abacuses.

THE WISDOM OF THE GYPSIES

"Gypsies," or Roma, *as many prefer to be called, are an ethnic group that originates from India, though for centuries Europeans assumed they were from Egypt (hence the name "gypsy," from the latin word for "Egyptian"). In the late 19th century a writer named Charles Godfrey Leland formed a group called the Gypsy Lore Society. Their mission: to collect Roma folklore before the pressures of the rapidly modernizing world caused them to disappear forever. Here's a sample of the information they collected.*

HEALTH TIPS

• **How to Cure the Common Cold:** Take the dried, powdered lungs and livers of three frogs and stir them into a glass of alcohol (Uncle John recommends rum, tequila, or some other alcoholic spirit strong enough to mask the taste of the frog). Drink the alcohol, and when you're finished, recite the following chant: "Frogs in my belly, devour what is bad! Frogs in my belly, show the evil the way out!"

• **Cure for a Fever:** Go to a stream or creek before sunrise and dig a hole in the bank, using a shovel that has never been used before. Pee into the hole; then fill it with dirt while saying, "Fever stay here! Do not come to me! Dry up in dust, come unto me when no water is in the river."

• **Cure for the Toothaches of Children:** Save whatever teeth fall out during your child's seventh year. Then, whenever he or she has a toothache, throw one of the teeth into a stream to cure it.

• **Cure for Backaches:** "He who turns three somersaults at the first sound of a thunderstorm will be free from back pains for twelve months."

HAIR DO'S (AND DON'TS)

• If you see a strand of human hair lying in your path, step over or around it but not on it! If the hair is from a lunatic, you too will go insane.

New England is larger than England; New York is larger than York; New Jersey is larger than Jersey.

• To ensure an easy childbirth, put some red hair in a small pouch and wear it on the belly against the skin during pregnancy. The red hair brings good luck.

• If you're having nightmares involving a dead person, sew some of your hair into an old shoe and then give the shoe to a beggar. That will keep the dead person's spirit away from you. (No word on what happens to the beggar.)

HAIR AND RELATIONSHIPS

• If a woman wants to win the heart of the young man she desires, she must steal a strand of his hair and mix it with dirt taken from one of the young man's footsteps. Then she must burn both to powder and somehow trick the young man into eating the ashes.

• For a woman to obtain *complete* mastery over a man, more-drastic steps are necessary. She must strip naked and sneak into his room while he's asleep. If she can snip off a lock of his hair and retreat from the room without awakening him, he will be under her spell. The woman must wear the lock of hair on her person, perhaps in a small bag or in a ring. One caveat: If the man catches her with it, the spell will turn against her.

FAMILY PLANNING

• If a woman who wants children is having trouble conceiving, she should eat grass growing atop the grave of a woman who died during pregnancy. Another solution: the husband should poke a tiny hole in each end of a raw egg and then blow the contents into his wife's mouth, and she must eat them.

• How to tell if you're pregnant: Take an axe or a hammer to a place where two roads cross, and stand there nine nights in a row. On the ninth night, pee on the implement and bury it there. Wait nine days and then dig it up again. If the implement is rusty, you're pregnant.

• To ensure that her children are healthy and strong, the expectant mother must wear a necklace made of bear claws and children's teeth. Avoid eating fish and snails during pregnancy; otherwise, the child will be as stupid as a fish and as slow as a snail.

• Avoid cemeteries during pregnancy. If the shadow of a cross on a grave falls on a pregnant woman, she will have a miscarriage.

Snails breathe through their feet.

(Note: The wishes of any naughty gypsy who "anticipated the privileges of matrimony" notwithstanding, this is not an effective means of contraception.)

MISCELLANEOUS ADVICE

• If your child is born during the light of the full moon, it will go on to have a happy marriage.

• If you are the victim of a burglary or a robbery, buy a black hen and fast with the hen for nine Fridays in a row. If the thief does not return your property, he will die.

• Avoid dustdevils and whirlwinds. They are signs that the devil is dancing with a witch, and if you approach too close you can be carried away, body and soul, straight to the depths of hell.

• If your cow wanders away and gets lost, jam a pair of scissors into the crossbeam running across the living room ceiling, if it has one. This will protect the cow from witches.

• If a cow "makes water" (pees) while being milked, she is bewitched.

• It is bad luck to meet up with a priest or a nun, especially if they're the first person you meet in the morning. Conversely, it is very lucky to meet with a woman "of easy virtue—the easier, the better."

* * *

STRANGE SPORT: MOUNTAIN UNICYCLING

Where It Originated: Seward, Alaska

How You Do It: Called MUni for short, mountain unicycling was invented in the mid-1980s by a local judge named George Peck, who customized his unicycle with a bigger tire. A mountain unicycle can go anywhere a mountain bike can, but it's much safer because it can turn sharp corners and its "direct drive" prevents you from coasting down steep hills at high speeds. Still, competitive MUni riders fall frequently and are required to wear helmets at tournaments, which take place in North America, Europe, and Australia. Carefully maneuvering a unicycle down a mountainside, Peck explains, is "not exactly exhilarating…but it is a series of little joys."

Andorra has the world's lowest unemployment rate (0%) & the highest life expectancy (83.48 yrs.).

HEEERE'S BABY!

Millions of babies are born every day, but only a select few of these births are weird enough to make it into a Bathroom Reader.

STRINGS ATTACHED

In December 2006, Sharon Taylor was rushing into the hospital in West Yorkshire, England—she could feel her baby coming and wasn't sure she could "hold it" until she reached the delivery room. She couldn't. Once inside the doors, the newborn "shot out" of Taylor so fast that her boyfriend tried to catch it. He couldn't. According to reports, baby Ashleigh landed on the floor and skidded a few feet, but then—thanks to the umbilical cord—was retracted right back up into her mommy's arms.

JACKPOT!

While playing the slot machines at an Atlantic City, New Jersey, casino, Nyree Thompson started going into labor, even though her baby wasn't due for another month. She alerted a security guard, but he didn't believe her...until her water broke. With Thompson lying on the floor of the crowded casino, a guard yelled, "Don't push!" Thompson replied, "Forget you! This baby is coming right now!" And she was right. The baby boy, who she named Qualeem, was wrapped up in a casino jacket and placed in his mother's arms. Casino spokesman Steve Callender told reporters, "We've had people die here, but this is the first time we've had people born here."

LIFE IN THE FAST LANE

At 3 a.m. on a March night in 2007, Lisa Tauer, a 28-year-old retail manager from Hurley, Wisconsin, started feeling contractions. They were only 10 minutes apart, so she and her husband Jereme *thought* they had plenty of time. But as their Dodge Neon sped down Highway 2, the contractions got much closer. "You need to get us there, like now!" Lisa said from the passenger seat. As the speedometer wavered between 90 and 100 mph on the empty highway, Jereme turned on the interior light and saw his baby boy's head crowning. "So he was holding onto the head, while I was trying to push," recalled Lisa. She was scooted so far back on the reclined seat that

Poll results: Americans in their thirties are 26% less likely to make a New Year's resolution...

Jereme Jr. landed right on the seat cushion. Jereme Sr. recalled, "I just kind of cradled him as he came out, and watched him, watched the road, watched him, watched the road." Shortly after, the couple found a police car that escorted them to the hospital, where Jereme Jr. was reported to be in excellent condition.

BIG THINGS DO COME IN SMALL PACKAGES

Due to a genetic bone disorder, 33-year-old Stacey Herald is only 2'4" tall. "My whole life, I've been told that I wasn't able to have children, that the baby would grow up underneath my lungs and smother out my heart, and we would both die. Something inside me just didn't believe that." So Stacey and her husband Wil convinced their doctor to let her try. First, the couple had Katira, born with the same small stature as her mother. But when Stacey became pregnant again, there were no signs of the defect; it was going to be the size of a regular baby, growing inside the frame of a very small woman. "If I laid down, I looked like a snail. That's how big my belly was. I looked like an Idaho potato with arms and legs. I couldn't see my feet." In February 2008, baby Makaia, measuring 18 inches, was born successfully to Stacey, who measures 28 inches. (To put it in perspective, it's equivalent to a 5'8" woman giving birth to a 4' baby.)

ROCK-A-BYE BABY, IN THE TREETOP

As floodwaters raged through Mozambique in 2000, 23-year-old expectant mother Cecilia Chirindza and her family took refuge on a makeshift platform in the top of a tree for three days. There was no sign of rescue...and Cecilia went into labor. Only an hour after baby Rositha was born, a military helicopter arrived. As news cameras rolled, a rescuer lowered himself down and cut the baby's umbilical cord before pulling the family to safety one by one. The footage made Cecilia and Rositha the faces of the disaster.

Four months later, mother and child were flown around the world as part of an appeal for aid to the poor country still reeling from the floods that left two million people homeless. Cecilia told reporters she hoped the attention would not only help her people, but also give her child an opportunity to one day become a "great leader."

...than people in their twenties, but are 26% more likely to keep it.

LET'S GO STREAKING

Uncle John has mentioned Elvis Presley in 21 consecutive Bathroom Readers. *Here are some more notable streaks.*

• **Most Consecutive Academy Award Nominations:** Walt Disney was nominated for Best Animated Short Subject every year from 1942 to 1963—a span of 22 years. He won four times.

• **Most Consecutive Seasons Without Winning a World Series:** The Chicago Cubs hold baseball's longest futility streak—100 seasons without a championship (and counting).

• **Most Consecutive Emmy nominations Without a Win:** Susan Lucci was nominated for a Daytime Emmy for her role as Erica Kane on *All My Children* 13 years in a row, from 1981 to 1993. On her 19th (nonconsecutive) nomination in 1999, she finally won.

• **Most Consecutive Razzie Award Nominations:** The Razzies are the Oscars of bad movies. Sylvester Stallone was nominated for Worst Actor 13 years in a row (1985–1997). He won five times.

• **Most Consecutive #1 Songs by a Single Artist:** From 1985 to 1988, Whitney Houston had seven straight singles reach #1. They were: "Saving All My Love for You," "How Will I Know," "Greatest Love of All," "I Wanna Dance With Somebody," "Didn't We Almost Have It All," "So Emotional," and "Where Do Broken Hearts Go."

• **Most Consecutive Nominations for U.S. President:** Eugene Debs was the Socialist candidate in 1900, 1904, 1908, and 1912. (How'd he do? Have you ever heard of President Eugene Debs?)

• **Most Consecutive Games Started in the NFL:** Green Bay Packers quarterback Brett Favre started 253 straight games from 1992 to 2008. His closest rival is the Colts' Peyton Manning, with 160 consecutive starts over nine years.

• **Most Consecutive Blockbuster Movies:** Tom Hanks starred in 10 consecutive movies that made more than $100 million at

On the island of Cyprus, the archbishop is the only person allowed to write with purple ink.

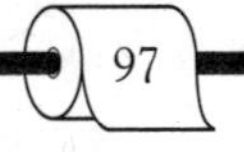

the box office. They were *Forrest Gump*, *Apollo 13*, *Toy Story* (voice only), *Saving Private Ryan*, *You've Got Mail*, *Toy Story 2* (voice only), *The Green Mile*, *Cast Away*, *Road to Perdition*, and *Catch Me If You Can*.

• **Most Consecutive Postseason Bowl Game Appearances:** The University of Michigan football team (the Wolverines) has played for 32 straight seasons.

• **Most Consecutive Years of Drought:** Geologists have determined that in the "four corners" region of the United States (where Colorado, New Mexico, Arizona, and Utah meet), there was no rainfall between 1276 and 1299, making that 23-year period the longest drought in "American" history.

• **Most Consecutive "Most Points Scored" Titles in the NBA:** Michael Jordan scored more points than anyone else for 10 consecutive seasons (not including a two-year hiatus to play baseball), from 1987 to 1998. The streak ended when he retired.

• **Most Consecutive Years in Primetime:** *Gunsmoke* aired first-run shows on television for 20 years straight, from 1955 to 1975.

• **Most Consecutive Sellouts:** The Portland Trail Blazers of the NBA sold out 814 straight home games between 1976 and 1996.

• **Most Consecutive Years With a Hit Song:** Each year from 1970 to 2000, Elton John charted at least one single on the Billboard Hot 100—a period of 31 years. (The first: "Border Song." The last: "Someday Out of the Blue.")

• **Most Consecutive Sports Broadcasts:** Chick Hearn started calling Los Angeles Lakers basketball games on the radio in 1961. Between November 1965 and December 2001, he never missed a single game. Grand total: 3,338 games.

• **Most Consecutive Emmy Award Wins:** The Oustanding Reality-Competition Series award was created in 2002. As of 2007, the only program to ever win the award—a total of five times—is *The Amazing Race*.

No streak: Ray Stevens's song "The Streak" spent one consecutive week at #1, in 1974.

TOM SWIFTIES

This classic style of pun was originally invented in the 1920s. They're atrocious and corny...so of course we couldn't resist them.

"I'm taller than I was yesterday," said Tom gruesomely.

"Well, that certainly took the wind out of my sails," said Tom disgustedly.

"I'm waiting to see the doctor," said Tom patiently.

"I have no idea," said Tom thoughtlessly.

"I have diamonds, clubs, and spades," said Tom heartlessly.

"I can't walk. My leg hurts too much," reported Tom lamely.

"I wonder if there's a number between seven and nine," said Tom considerately.

"I'm the butcher's assistant," said Tom cuttingly.

"Don't you have any oranges?" Tom asked fruitlessly.

"Someday, I want to teach at a university," Tom professed.

"I can't remember anything from the last 24 hours," said Tom lackadaisically.

"Your Honor, you're crazy!" said Tom judgmentally.

"Elvis is dead," said Tom expressly.

"I can take photographs if I want to!" Tom snapped.

"Congratulations, you graduated," said Tom diplomatically.

"I love mustard on my hot dogs," said Tom with relish.

"I hate this Chardonnay," Tom whined.

"Has my magazine arrived?" Tom asked periodically.

"Stop, horse! Stop!" cried Tom woefully.

"I think that wasp is in pain," Tom bemoaned.

"Look! Here comes a big black bird," Tom crowed.

"I love the taste of orange peels," said Tom zestfully.

"I've only enough carpet for the hall and landing," said Tom with a blank stare.

50% of lingerie purchases are returned to the store.

CABLE PIONEERS

Uncle John's grandpa had a motto for success in business: Find a need and fill it. That's more difficult than it sounds, because you have to be in the right place at the right time...but as these folks prove, it does work.

ON THE AIR

Today, almost 90% of American viewers get their television signal by paying for a subscription service—either cable or satellite. The days of rabbit ears and rooftop antennas are nearly gone. Cable TV has become a $75 billion a year business, but it started out as the hobby of small-town tinkerers and entrepreneurs.

Back in the late 1940s, television was the latest technological marvel. In those days, TV sets had to be within 50 or 75 miles of a broadcast station in order to receive a clear signal. Since there were so few stations—just 98 in the entire country in 1950—the only people who could watch TV were those who lived in and around major cities. That also meant they were the only people who had a reason to buy a TV.

Small-town appliance dealers hoping to get in on the lucrative new business became the pioneers who brought television to rural America. They created the first cable systems in the late 1940s and early '50s, calling them "Community Antenna TV," or CATV. Though cable TV appears to have been developed simultaneously by several different people in several different places, the story of John Walson of Mahanoy City, Pennsylvania, exemplifies the experience.

OVER THE WIRE

Walson started out working for Pennsylvania Power & Light (PP&L), running electrical cables from utility poles into people's houses and repairing electrical appliances—which, in those days, were leased from the power company. When PP&L decided to get out of the appliance business, Walson saw an opportunity and took advantage of it by opening an appliance store and showroom in Mahanoy City.

He began carrying television sets in 1947, but didn't sell very

What's a *scroggling*? A small, runty apple left on the tree after a harvest.

many at first. The problem: The nearest broadcast stations were 80 miles away in Philadelphia, and Mahanoy City, located in a valley and surrounded by mountains, just couldn't get any reception. He did have potential customers—the nearby towns of Frackville, Volcan, and Hazeton were built on mountaintops and could tune in a few stations, but those people wanted to see the product demonstrated before they were willing to shell out $500 for a brand-new 12½" black-and-white TV.

So Walson bought a piece of property on top of a local mountain, where he fixed an antenna to the end of a 70-foot utility pole. If a customer was serious about purchasing a set, Walson would drive them up the hill and show them how well it worked by plugging it into his giant antenna. This was better than nothing, but what he really wanted was TV reception in his showroom. There was only one thing he could do to get it.

THE MOTHER OF INVENTION

First Walson bought a mile of U.S. Army surplus cable and a bunch of set-top amplifiers designed to boost television signals. Then, in the summer of 1948, he set out to connect his store to the mountaintop antenna. He had to modify the amplifiers and insert them into the line every 500 feet to maintain the strength of the signal, but when he was done, he had all three Philadelphia stations playing in his store window—with speakers wired up outside so that locals could stand out on the sidewalk and fully enjoy the first television reception in town.

People soon asked him to run the cable to their houses—and it was obviously in his best interest to do so: If they could get channels, they would buy TVs. So he designed a new signal amplifier and began making improvements to the system. (One early problem: Walson's customers lost their signal whenever it rained. He solved that by upgrading his original army surplus cable.)

THE FUTURE OF TV

Walson soon had hundreds of customers in Mahanoy City and the surrounding communities. His original subscription rate: $2.00 a month (plus a onetime $100 installation fee). Over the years, he continued to build his business, expanding into other towns and improving his antenna technology to capture more stations. His company, Service Electric Cable, is still in business and is now run by his children. Among their claims to fame: In 1972 they were the first cable system in the United States to carry HBO.

OTHER CABLE PIONEERS

• **Ed Parsons:** A radio technician who sold and serviced ship-to-shore systems in the port town of Astoria, Oregon, Parsons began building his CATV system when his wife announced that she wanted to be able to watch television. He managed to tune in a Seattle station on Thanksgiving Day 1948 by placing an antenna on the roof of the tallest hotel in downtown Astoria. By 1950 he had over 100 customers. Rate: $3.00 a month with a $125 installation fee.

• **Robert Tarlton:** Pennsylvania was the early center of CATV. Not far from where John Walson built his system in Mahanoy City, Tarlton organized several appliance dealers into an investment group to form the Panther Valley Television Company in 1950. Two years later, Tarlton was among the group of CATV operators that formed the National Community Television Council in nearby Pottsville.

• **John Campbell:** A movie theater projectionist who learned electronics in the U.S. Navy, Campbell brought CATV to Texas after reading an article on the Pennsylvania systems in 1951. Since he didn't have enough money to travel to Pennsylvania and study the existing CATV facilities, he simply designed and built his own from scratch. He charged a $95 installation fee and $3.00 a month for service. The installation fee became his seed money: "We would wire up one block, hook up five people, get the $95 each, and go buy some more cable."

• **Bill Daniels:** To bring CATV to Casper, Wyoming, Daniels had to become the first cable operator in the United States to use microwave transmitters. His system went on the air in 1953 and carried four Denver stations across 230 miles of mountain ranges. The added technological difficulties translated to higher costs: $7.50 a month. It also meant less expansive service. Even though the system brought in four stations, it could transmit only one at a time. So how did Daniels decide what to show? He mailed ballots to his customers every month so they could vote on which channels they wanted to watch at what times.

The Monopoly character locked behind bars: Jake the Jailbird. (Policeman: Officer Edgar Mallory.)

HOLLYWOOD SPEAK

The entertainment industry trade journal Variety *has a "slanguage" all its own. To assist the "aud," here's a glossary to help make sense of words like..."aud."*

CRIX. The collective term for critics

MELLER. Melodrama

CLICK. A movie that does good B.O. (box office)

SPROCKET OPERA. Film festival

BLURB. TV commercial

PERF. Acting performance

TUBTHUMP. Promote heavily

AYEM. Morning

ANKLE. To quit or be dismissed from a job, without necessarily specifying which

MOUSE. The Walt Disney Co. (also called Mouse House)

LENSE. To shoot a movie

AUD. Audience

PERCENTER. An agent

BIRD. Satellite

KUDOCAST. Awards show

DISKERY. A record company

ZITCOM. A sitcom aimed at teens

FEEVEE. Pay TV

DUCATS. Movie or concert tickets

HOOFER. Dancer (also called a **terper**)

KIDVID. Children's TV show

SOCKO. Very good, as in "socko B.O."

OFF-NET. Network TV series reruns sold into syndication

N.S.G. Not So Good, usually bad reviews or poor B.O.

NABE. Neighborhood theater

NET. TV network—the **Eye** (CBS), the **Peacock** (NBC), or the **Alphabet** (ABC)

AD-PUB. The advertising and publicity department of a movie studio

CLEFFER. Songwriter

PREEM. A movie premiere

SCRIBBLER. TV writer. (A screenwriter is a **scripter**.)

MITTING. When the aud applauds

Slow hand: How fast does the hour hand travel on a wristwatch? .00000275 mph.

REGIONAL TREATS

You've probably had a Philadelphia cheesesteak or a Chicago deep-dish pizza. You might even have had them in Chicago or Philadelphia. Here are some local delicacies rarely found outside their home territory.

FOOD: Garbage Plate
FOUND IN: Rochester, New York
DESCRIPTION: Diner owner Nick Tahou (of Nick Tahou Hots) invented this dish in the late 1940s when some college students asked him for a plate with "all the garbage on it." The Plate starts with home fries and macaroni salad mixed together. It's then topped with two hamburger patties, onions, mustard, ketchup, and hot sauce. You can replace the hamburger patties with cheeseburgers, a steak, hot dogs, Italian sausages, link sausages, ham, or fried fish. The entrée is served at other Rochester restaurants, but since Tahou trademarked "Garbage Plate," it's usually listed on rival menus as the "Dumpster Plate."

FOOD: St. Paul Sandwich
FOUND IN: Chinese restaurants in St. Louis, Missouri
DESCRIPTION: It's a sandwich that consists of an egg foo yung patty on white bread with lettuce, tomato, bean sprouts, onions, dill pickle, and lots of mayonnaise. The origins of the sandwich—and its name—are unknown.

FOOD: Runza
FOUND IN: Nebraska and Kansas
DESCRIPTION: German and Russian immigrants settled there in the late 1800s and developed this dish—a stuffed bread pocket, filled with minced beef, pork, sauerkraut, and onions. If you get one in Nebraska, it will be rectangular. A Kansas runza is usually round.

FOOD: Scrapple
FOUND IN: Philadelphia and Delaware
DESCRIPTION: Created by German butchers, scrapple is

He who says it cannot be done should not interrupt the person doing it. —Chinese proverb

believed to be the first pork dish that originated in the United States. The main ingredient is pork bits left over from butchering, including the head, liver, and heart. The meat is boiled off the bone, chopped, and added with spices to a cornmeal mush. It's gelled into loaves, cut into slices, and pan-fried. It's served as a breakfast food, topped with maple syrup.

FOOD: Slinger

FOUND IN: St. Louis, Missouri

DESCRIPTION: A mountain of food similar to the Garbage Plate. The Slinger consists of two eggs topped with hash browns and a hamburger patty. The whole thing is then covered in chili, topped with cheese and onions, and served with bacon or sausage. (Ugh!)

FOOD: Horseshoe Sandwich

FOUND IN: Springfield, Illinois

DESCRIPTION: It's an open-faced sandwich of thick sourdough toast topped with ham, french fries, and a cheese sauce. It was invented at the Leland Hotel in 1928 by cooks Joe Schweska and Steve Tomko. Local legend says it was created to honor local horseshoe makers who frequently dined at the Leland. It was originally served on a hot metal platter (to represent an anvil); the ham looked like a horseshoe, and the fries resembled nails.

FOOD: Hot Brown

FOUND IN: Louisville, Kentucky

DESCRIPTION: It's named after the place where it was created in 1926: the Brown Hotel. The most popular dish on the menu was ham and eggs, but chef Fred Schmidt became bored with making it. So he came up with this sandwich as an alternative: an open-faced sandwich of turkey, bacon, and Mornay sauce (a basic cheese sauce), cooked under a broiler. It quickly gained popularity because sliced turkey was a novelty at the time—it was rare to see turkey when it wasn't Thanksgiving. Result: within a year, the Hot Brown was being ordered by 95 percent of Brown Hotel customers.

Your chances of dying by drowning are about 1 in 900.

NETWORDS

Hey! There's a new invention out there called the "Internet."

"The Internet is the first thing that humanity has built that humanity doesn't understand. It's the largest experiment in anarchy that we've ever had."

—Eric Schmidt

"Getting information off the Internet is like taking a drink from a fire hydrant."

—Mitchell Kapor

"The Internet is just a world passing around notes in a classroom."

—Jon Stewart

"There's a statistical theory that if you gave a million monkeys typewriters and set them to work, they'd eventually come up with the complete works of Shakespeare. Thanks to the Internet, we now know this isn't true."

—Ian Hart

"I've just found out there are pages on the Internet dedicated to whether I'm gay or not."

—Matthew Perry

"National borders aren't even speed bumps on the information superhighway."

—Tim May

"The Internet is the most powerful stupidity amplifier ever invented. It's like TV without the TV part."

—James "Kibo" Parry

"First we thought the PC was a calculator. Then we found out how to turn numbers into letters with ASCII—and we thought it was a typewriter. Then we discovered graphics, and we thought it was a television. With the World Wide Web, we've realized it's a brochure."

—Douglas Adams

"My favorite thing is that you get to go into the private world of real creeps without having to smell them."

—Penn Jillette

"Sometimes I think the Web is a big plot to keep people like me away from normal society."

—Scott Adams

"Looking at the proliferation of personal Web pages on the Net, it looks like very soon everyone on Earth will have 15 megabytes of fame."

—M. G. Sriram

Although 85% of dieters do lose weight, only 15% keep it off for longer than two years.

MYTH-CONCEPTIONS

"Common knowledge" is frequently wrong. Here are some examples.

MYTH: Cockroaches would survive a nuclear holocaust.
TRUTH: Some scientists say that cockroach bodies contain very little water, which might protect them from radiation damage (although their offspring would be genetically mutated). But on an episode of *MythBusters*, 50 cockroaches were exposed to post-nuclear levels of radiation...and they all died within 24 hours.

MYTH: If you think someone is an undercover cop, ask them. If they are, they have to tell you.
TRUTH: It's a common scene in movies: The criminal asks a suspicious character if he's a cop and avoids entrapment. No such law exists. Undercover cops are allowed to lie to protect themselves.

MYTH: Whatever else was said about Benito Mussolini, the fascist dictator of Italy, at least he made the trains run on time.
TRUTH: Pure propaganda. Italy's railway system was upgraded between World War I and when Mussolini took office in 1922, so whatever improvements had been made weren't his doing. Even so, the claim that the trains in Italy were always on time was an exaggeration.

MYTH: Singer-songwriter Robert Zimmerman changed his name to Bob Dylan in order to honor one of his idols, Welsh poet Dylan Thomas.
TRUTH: The name is an homage, but not to Thomas. Dylan had a favorite uncle named Dillon and was also a big fan of the TV western *Gunsmoke*, which featured a character—a U.S. Marshal—named Matt Dillon.

MYTH: When you're hungry, your stomach rumbles.
TRUTH: It's not your stomach making the noise—it's actually your small intestine. The small intestine is what's behind your belly button; most of your stomach sits behind the lower ribs.

MAN'S BEST FRIEND

...or worst nightmare?

BOUNCY DOG. A family in York, England, reported their bull terrier Harvey missing. At first, they had no idea how he'd escaped—there were no signs of him digging his way under the fence or finding a hole in it. They finally figured out that Harvey had bounced onto the trampoline in the backyard, over the backyard fence, into the neighbor's yard, and away.

STICKY DOG. One day, Pamela Panting was playing fetch with Hector, her Great Dane puppy. The game ended when Hector lost sight of the two-foot-long tree branch Panting had thrown. The next morning, Hector wouldn't eat and was drooling excessively, so Panting took him to a veterinarian. An X-ray revealed the problem: Hector hadn't lost the two-foot-long stick, he'd swallowed it. Cost to remove the branch: $4,000.

CRIME DOG. In Waukesha, Wisconsin, a drug-sniffing German Shepherd police dog named Officer Nutz broke out of his kennel, ran to a nearby supermarket, went through the automatic doors, grabbed a package of prime rib, and ran back outside, where he attacked the raw meat. Officer Nutz was captured on store security cameras; the police department placed him on administrative leave.

EMBARRASSING DOG. The Milner family of Dorset, England, was playing around with Google Earth, an Internet service that displays satellite photos of nearly any location on the planet. They looked up their home and saw a mysterious brown blob on their front lawn. The Milners finally came to realize what that brown lump was: Boris, their bull mastiff. At 200 pounds, the dog was so overweight that he could be seen from outer space.

TRAITOR DOGS. Police in Marion Oaks, Florida, went to the home of Wayne Huff to arrest him on wire fraud charges. Huff came to the door with his two dogs and resisted arrest, so the police used force. The struggle continued as the cops dragged Huff into his front yard. Both of Huff's dogs then attacked him, biting him on his arm, back, leg, and ear. The bites subdued him enough to be peaceably taken away by the police.

FOUNDING FATHERS

You know the names. Here's a look at the people behind them.

CHARLES WALGREEN

In 1896, 23-year-old Walgreen lost a finger in an accident at the Galesburg, Illinois, shoe factory where he worked. Suddenly unemployed and disabled, Walgreen took the advice of his doctor, who suggested he become a pharmacist. Walgreen got his license and in 1901 moved to Chicago to work for a pharmacist named Issac Blood. Upon Blood's retirement, Walgreen bought Blood's store and changed its name to Walgreen's. He began to acquire other stores and eventually built one of the country's first pharmacy chains. Among Walgreen's other innovations were adding lunch counters, soda fountains, and grocery and household items to his pharmacies. By 1927 there were 110 Walgreen's stores. Today, there are more than 6,000.

HENRY MARTYN ROBERT

In 1863 Robert, an army major, was asked to preside over an organizational meeting at his church in New Bedford, Massachusetts. Because the attendees were from different parts of the country, and all were familiar with different rules for how to conduct a meeting, Robert came up with his own rules: a call to order, roll call, reading of last meeting's minutes, officers' reports, committee reports, important new business, unfinished business, announcements, and adjournment. He thought the idea would have universal appeal, but nobody would publish *Robert's Rules of Order*. So in 1876, he paid for the first printing himself. It sold out in four months. Since then, the book has sold more than 4.5 million copies, and Robert's system is the universal standard for how meetings are conducted.

LANE BRYANT

In 1895, 18-year-old Lithuanian orphan Lena Himmelstein moved to New York and found work in a sweatshop for a dollar a week. In 1899 she married a man named David Bryant. When he died five years later Lena Bryant borrowed $300 from her brother-in-law and opened a dressmaking business. The bank misspelled

The Speaker of the U.K. House of Commons is supposed to show extreme reluctance on taking office.

"Lena" as "Lane," but she liked the way it sounded so she called her business Lane Bryant and opened a store in Manhattan (she lived in the back). Bryant found a niche when, at the request of a pregnant customer, she made a dress fitted with an elastic waistband and an accordion skirt. Maternity wear was her specialty until 1914, when she discovered another ignored demographic: plus-size women. Sold via catalog (to "respect privacy"), Lane Bryant had annual sales of $5 million by 1923. When Bryant died in 1951, it was a $200 million company.

JENNY CRAIG

Craig worked for a series of fitness clubs, ultimately becoming an executive at Body Contour, a chain in the South. In 1982 she presented a weight-loss program based on nutrition, one-on-one counseling, and individualized menu plans to her bosses at Body Contour. They turned her down, so she started her own company. Because of a non-compete clause in her contract, Craig opened her first 12 Jenny Craig Weight Loss Centers in Australia. By 1985 the noncompete clause had expired, so Craig expanded to the U.S., opening 12 centers in Los Angeles. There was competition (Nutri-System, Weight Watchers), but Craig's centers offered something others didn't: frozen diet meals sold on the premises. Five years later, the company was national with annual revenues of $350 million. Craig sold the company in 2002; today it's owned by Nestle.

WILBERT GORE

In 1944, 32-year-old chemical engineer Wilbert Gore got a job with DuPont Labs. In 1957 clients from the fledgling computer industry asked DuPont to develop cables insulated with a water-resistant and heat-maintaining substance called polytetrafluororoethylene (PTFE), better known as Teflon. DuPont declined, so Gore quit his job and started W.L. Gore & Associates in the basement of his house to make the cable. Gore landed many lucrative cable-making contracts, including one with NASA, but he developed more than 2,000 other products out of PFTE as well, including artificial blood vessels and a windproof fabric he called Gore-Tex. The first Gore-Tex product: a tent in 1976. It's now used for shirts, jackets, pants, and other outdoor gear. An outdoorsman himself, Gore died at the age of 74 in 1986 while backpacking in Wyoming.

WHATEVER HAPPENED TO...

Giant corporations are as much a part of our culture as movies, music, and sports. Many become household names and then, one day...they're gone.

BEATRICE FOODS

The Rise: In 1894 two Nebraska businessmen formed the Beatrice Creamery, a wholesaler of milk, eggs, and butter purchased from local farmers. By 1910 Beatrice controlled nine Midwestern creameries and shipped their products nationwide. By 1930 the company had 32 dairy plants that churned out 27 million gallons of Meadow Gold brand milk each year. In the 1950s, the company—now called Beatrice Foods—aggressively expanded by purchasing other established food brands, including Jolly Rancher candy, Dannon yogurt, Tropicana orange juice, Clark Bars, Butterball, and Wesson vegetable oil. In the 1970s, Beatrice expanded beyond food, purchasing Avis Rent-a-Car, Playtex, Airstream, and Samsonite. By 1984 the company had annual sales of $12 billion.

The Fall: Beatrice was so successful that others wanted a piece of the business. In 1984 a private equity firm called Kohlberg Kravis Roberts began buying up large chunks of Beatrice stock, so much that KKR was able to place its representatives on Beatrice's corporate board, which then helped direct the company's "future path." In other words, KKR staged a hostile takeover. By 1986 KKR owned all of Beatrice and had paid a total of only $8.7 billion for it. Over the next four years, KKR dismantled and sold off every individual division, product, and brand Beatrice once controlled. The majority of it was sold to Beatrice's biggest competitor, ConAgra Foods.

AMERICAN MOTORS CORPORATION

The Rise: Nash Motors, makers of the classic Roadster, purchased the Kelvinator Appliance Company in 1937. The resulting company, Nash-Kelvinator, bought the Hudson Motor Car Company in 1954 and became American Motors Corporation. The new company was valued at $198 million and was, at the time, the biggest merger in history. Nash CEO George Mason thought consolidation of smaller brands was the only way to compete with the "Big

CompuQuiz: Who invented the floppy disk? Dr. Yoshiro Nakamatsu. (He holds...

Three" car companies—GM, Ford, and Chrysler. In its first decade, AMC's biggest seller was an old Nash model: the Rambler. They added the Rambler American in the late '50s and the sporty AMX and the Javelin in the early '60s. But in 1970 the company decided the best way to carve out a niche was differentiation. Since the Big Three made big gas-guzzlers, AMC made fuel-efficient compacts. Tiny AMC hatchbacks like the Gremlin, Hornet, and Pacer, while ugly and prone to mechanical problems, sold well enough to become icons of the 1970s. Attractive to consumers during the '70s gas shortage, more than 700,000 Gremlins and 900,000 Hornets were sold during the decade. AMC also purchased Jeep from Kaiser Motors in 1970, and the popularity of that brand helped keep the company afloat—just barely—into the 1980s. But for all their efforts, AMC never climbed out of fourth place.

The Fall: Around 1979, Japanese carmakers such as Toyota and Datsun flooded the American market with cheaper, better-built cars that cut into AMC's sales. In 1982 the company was purchased by the French carmaker Renault, which in turn was purchased by Chrysler in 1987. What became of AMC? Chrysler retired all the AMC brand names with two exceptions: Jeep and Eagle.

KENNER TOYS

The Rise: Founded in 1947 by the Steiner brothers (Albert, Philip, Joseph) on Kenner Street in Cincinnati, Kenner Toys' first products were battery-powered bubble blowers. They were an instant hit: By 1950 more than a million Bubble Rockets had sold. In the 1950s and '60s, Kenner produced a long line of classic toys, including the Easy-Bake Oven, Spiro-Graph, and Baby Alive. Kenner was the third-largest toy company in the world (trailing Hasbro and Mattel) when it was purchased by General Mills in 1967. Kenner continued with more popular toys in the 1970s and 1980s, including Play-Doh, Stretch Armstrong, Strawberry Shortcake, and Care Bears. In 1975 filmmaker George Lucas approached Kenner (after rival Mego Toys declined) with a deal for them to make toys based on his upcoming *Star Wars* movie. Smart move: *Star Wars* toys ultimately earned more than $1 billion for Kenner. (Other successful movie tie-ins for Kenner: *RoboCop*, *Ghostbusters*, *Raiders of the Lost Ark*, and *Batman*.)

The Fall: The company vanished in a series of corporate mergers.

...over 2,300 patents, more than twice the 1,093 held by Thomas Edison.)

In 1987 General Mills decided to go back to focusing on food products so it sold Kenner to Tonka Toys (makers of toy cars and trucks). Just four years after that, Tonka Toys, including Kenner, was sold to Hasbro, the world's largest toy company. By 1994 Hasbro had assumed production on all toys once made by Kenner and eliminated the brand name entirely.

EASTERN AIR LINES

The Rise: In 1929 Clement Keys of North American Aviation purchased Pitcairn Aviation. Pitcairn owned just one propeller plane but held a lucrative government contract to fly mail between New York and Atlanta. In 1930 Keys renamed the company Eastern, bought five new planes, and expanded to include passenger flights out of New York, Atlanta, Miami, Boston, and Richmond. Keys's strategy was to let the other airlines do coast-to-coast flights—Eastern would do short hops between large East Coast cities. It worked. Until the end of the 1930s, Eastern was the only airline that flew from New York to Boston and Miami. Former astronaut Frank Borman became CEO in 1975 and aggressively modernized the company. Eastern was the first airline with an all-jet fleet, a computerized reservation system, and a "shuttle service"—hourly flights from New York to Washington, D.C.

The Fall: Congress passed the Airline Deregulation Act in 1978, which ended government price controls of flights. No-frills, low-cost carriers like People Express entered the marketplace, forcing big airlines like Eastern into competitive pricing, often at a loss. By 1985 Eastern served more passengers than any other airline, but was losing $700,000 a day and was $3.5 billion in debt. It was bought out for $615 million by Texas Air Corporation, which also owned Continental Airlines. TAC chief executive Frank Lorenzo stripped many of Eastern's assets and transferred them to his other airlines—six Eastern planes went to Continental and the computer system went to Texas Air. Lorenzo also cut pay and eliminated benefits to Eastern's mechanics and ground crews, leading to a strike by Eastern mechanics, pilots, and flight attendants in 1989. All flights were cancelled, and the loss of revenue was the final blow. Eastern filed for bankruptcy in 1989 but continued to operate, all the while laying off workers and selling off planes (they sold the shuttle service to Donald Trump). In January 1991, Eastern finally ran out of cash and became grounded forever.

SACRIFICE ON THE SOFTBALL FIELD

What has three heads, five good legs, and is one of the most inspiring sports stories we've ever heard? Read on.

BATTER UP!

It was the second inning of a 2008 NCAA Division II women's softball game. The Western Oregon University Wolves were visiting the Central Washington University Wildcats. It was the last game of the season, and both teams were vying for a spot in the NCAA Tournament. Up to the plate walked WOU's 5'2" outfielder, Sara Tucholsky. Some CWU home fans were heckling her about her short stature, but Tucholsky paid them no mind—she was focused on a personal goal: Her softball career would soon be over, and she wanted to hit a home run, a feat she had never accomplished in her eight years of organized ball. In fact, Tucholsky only had three hits in 34 at-bats that season. But now, with two runners on base and no score in the game, here was her chance to redeem herself. First pitch: called strike. Undeterred, Tucholsky dug in on the second pitch and swung as hard as she could...and knew immediately that she had gotten all of it. In her excitement, as she watched the ball sail over the center field fence, she completely missed tagging first base. So a few steps into her turn toward second, she stopped and spun around to go back.

But then...*SNAP!* Her elation turned into agony.

Something had ripped inside Tucholsky's right knee and she collapsed onto the dirt. As she lay there, the umpire informed WOU Head Coach Pam Knox that Tucholsky had to touch every base in order for the home run to count—otherwise a pinch runner would have to take first base, giving her only a single. And her teammates could not assist her, or she'd be out. Seeing no other option, Coach Knox called for the pinch runner.

TOUCH 'EM ALL

That's when CWU's star player, Mallory Holtman, stepped in. The Wildcats' first baseman was the career home run leader in the

Every year about $303,000 in loose change is left at U.S. airport metal detectors.

Great Northwest Athletic Conference but had never made it to the NCAA Tournament. And if her team lost, her collegiate softball career would be over. But none of that mattered as she saw her opponent writhing in agony. Holtman asked the umpire, "Excuse me, would it be OK if we carried her around and she touched each bag?" The ump said that there was no rule against someone from the other team helping her, so Holtman and Shortstop Liz Wallace ran over and gently lifted Tucholsky off the field.

Thus began one of the strangest home run trots in the history of the game. "I don't know what it looked like to observers," recalled Holtman, "but it was kind of funny because Liz and I were carrying her on both sides, and we'd get to a base and gently, barely tap her left foot." For Tucholsky's part, she doesn't remember too much—she was more focused on the pain. The only words she spoke were, "Thank you guys so much."

HOME AT LAST

When Tucholsky's left foot finally touched home plate, the crowd was giving the girls a standing ovation. Many in the stadium were in tears as Holtman and Wallace placed her in a chair. The girls' sacrifice for a player they didn't even know ended up costing their team the game—the Wolves won, 4–2. But afterward, few were talking about the final score. Said Coach Knox, "It's moments like that that you respect that it's just a game. I hope it's a lesson my players will never forget. I certainly won't."

Thanks to Tucholsky's homer, the Wolves earned a spot in the NCAA Tournament, where they came in second place. Tucholsky didn't play, though—she'd torn her ACL. Her last career at-bat turned out to be her only home run. When asked about the incident, Tucholsky maintains that Holtman and Wallace were the real heroes. And they've been pretty humble as well. "In the end," said Holtman, "it's not about winning and losing so much—it was about this girl. She hit it over the fence, and she deserved a home run."

Postscript: It turned out that the umpire was wrong: Because the ball had cleared the fence, the runner was automatically awarded all four bases, so a pinch runner *could* have come in and finished running for Tucholsky. But if the umpire *had* known the correct rule, the world would have been denied an incredible act of sportsmanship.

The average stay for a prisoner on Alcatraz was five years.

UNCLE JOHN'S PAGE OF LISTS

Some random bits from the BRI's bottomless trivia files.

5 MOST WIDELY ASSIGNED BOOKS IN HIGH SCHOOLS

1. *The Adventures of Huckleberry Finn*
2. *The Scarlet Letter*
3. *To Kill a Mockingbird*
4. *Lord of the Flies*
5. *The Great Gatsby*

6 FLAVORS OF KIT-KAT BARS SOLD IN JAPAN

1. Green tea
2. Red bean
3. Yubari melon
4. Cherry blossom
5. Wine
6. Blood Orange

6 MOST COMMONLY MISSPELLED U.S. CITIES

1. Pittsburgh, PA
2. Tucson, AZ
3. Cincinnati, OH
4. Albuquerque, NM
5. Culpeper, VA
6. Asheville, NC

4 WORDS FOR "FART"

1. *Lu-suzi* (Bantu)
2. *Furz* (German)
3. *He* (Japanese)
4. *Prout* (French)

5 PEOPLE ON NIXON'S 1968 "ENEMIES LIST"

1. Tony Randall
2. Joe Namath
3. Paul Newman
4. Steve McQueen
5. Bill Cosby

4 THINGS THAT CONTAIN FORMALDEHYDE

1. Particleboard
2. Lipstick
3. Carpet
4. Draft beer

6 DEFUNCT DEPARTMENT STORE CHAINS

1. May
2. Gimbel's
3. Wanamaker's
4. The Bon Marché
5. Marshall Field's
6. Montgomery Ward

7 HIGHEST TEMPERATURES RECORDED ON EACH CONTINENT

1. Africa: 136°F
2. N. America: 134°F
3. Asia: 129°F
4. Australia: 128°F
5. Europe: 122°F
6. S. America: 120°F
7. Antarctica: 59°F

5 THINGS INVENTED BY MONKS

1. Mechanical clocks
2. Pretzels
3. Roulette
4. The @ sign
5. Munster cheese

7 ANIMALS THAT MATE FOR LIFE

1. Beaver
2. Orangutan
3. Fox
4. Stork
5. Penguin
6. Vulture
7. Pigeon

According to a British study, hospital admissions rise by up to 52% on Friday the 13th.

MAKING A MOVIE, PART I

One of Uncle John's secret dreams is to write, direct, produce, and star in a big-budget Hollywood movie...plus compose the music, choreograph the stunts, design the costumes, program the special effects, cook for the crew, distribute the film....Hold on there, Uncle John! You may need some help.

LIGHTS...CAMERA...ACTION!

Making a big-budget Hollywood movie takes hundreds—even *thousands*—of dedicated people. You've read their names in the closing credits of every feature film you've ever seen. But what do they all do? How does a film actually get made? This article only scratches the surface of what goes into making a movie, but you'll get a good idea of how all of these skilled people work toward the same goal...and what can happen when the goals of some don't match the goals of others. It doesn't take much to turn what could have been a good movie into a bad one, and vice versa. Yet there's one thing that all movies have in common: Whoever comes up with the idea believes it'll be a *great* one.

STAGE ONE: CONCEPT AND DEVELOPMENT

Movies usually come from one of two places: A screenwriter may pen an original story and then find a producer or director who wants to make it, or a producer may come up with the idea—possibly to adapt a book, play, TV show, or an earlier film. The producer will then work up a very rough budget and pitch the concept to a movie studio or other financial backer. If approved, the producer will then *option* the story from the screenwriter or whoever owns the rights to the story or characters. This is a contractual agreement stating that the movie rights can only be sold to that particular studio.

Next, a general outline called a *treatment* is made while a somewhat more refined budget estimate is calculated. After those are done, the studio will make a final decision as to whether or not to put up the funds to make the movie. There are more factors in play than simply whether the film will be *good* or not. These days a big-budget movie must find more ways to recoup its high cost: sequel potential, merchandising opportunities, and DVD sales. Studios are more likely to finance a familiar story with well-known stars that already have a proven track record, thus guaranteeing a better return on their investment. This explains why so many films are sequels or remakes. For most studios, originality is too big a risk.

If the treatment is approved, the project is *green-lighted.* At this point the film is officially *in development.* But that's no guarantee that it will get made. Snags in the process due to creative differences, budget or location disagreements, or scheduling conflicts with the director or lead actor can send the project into "development hell," a condition from which many proposed movies never recover. (See page 71.) But if all goes well, the next steps are to put together a production department and finalize a workable shooting script.

THE MODERN SCREENPLAY: MOVIE BY COMMITTEE

In recent years, the number of people who get writing credits on a single movie has grown significantly. Why? Unless a movie is written and directed by the same person, the screenplay is at the mercy of many people: a producer (often under pressure by the studio) may want to add more action or more romance to make the film more marketable, a big-name actor may demand changes to his or her character, or the director may want to put his or her own stamp on the work. In those cases, *script doctors* are called in. Here are three movies that underwent major changes from conception to release.

CHARLIE'S ANGELS **(2000).** Based on the 1970s TV show, the screenplay reportedly went through 30 revisions and had 18 different writers. The movie didn't even have an ending when filming began. One major change: star Drew Barrymore (who also served as a producer) decided that only the bad guys would use guns; the Angels would rely solely on their martial arts skills.

Did it work? Yes and no. *Charlie's Angels* was critically panned, but the combination of three well-known female leads and a familiar premise helped the film earn over $256 million worldwide, more than recouping its $93 million budget.

I, ROBOT **(2004).** In 1995 screenwriter Jeff Zintar wrote a *spec* *script* called *Hardwired* about a robot who murders a man. Studio after studio optioned it and then dropped it. After spending years in development hell, the project almost died completely until 20th Century Fox obtained the rights to Isaac Asimov's classic *I, Robot* short stories. The studio commissioned Zintar to rewrite his script adopting Asimov's themes—but they *still* wouldn't approve it because it was going to cost too much to make. When Will Smith became interested in the project, everything changed. Fox agreed to a bigger budget if *I, Robot* became a "Will Smith movie." So Smith brought in his favorite screenwriter, Akiva Goldsman, to rewrite the script to match the star's on-screen persona, changing it from a "talky mystery" into an action thriller.

Did it work? Yes. Although *I, Robot* received only mediocre reviews, the combination of Will Smith + sci-fi blockbuster + summer release = a critic-proof movie. It made $345 million worldwide, more than twice its budget.

***GROUNDHOG DAY* (1993).** Danny Rubin's original screenplay about Phil Connors (Bill Murray), a bitter weatherman who finds himself living the same day over and over…and over…until he finally figures out what's really important in life, was altered significantly by director Harold Ramis. Rubin's version began with Phil already stuck in the time loop. Ramis changed it so that Phil enters the time loop *after* the film begins—and the audience has to figure it out along with him. And in Rubin's script, one of Phil's ex-girlfriends wanted to teach him a lesson so she placed a voodoo curse on him. Ramis left the cause unknown and also shortened the time Phil was stuck in the loop from thousands of years to what he estimates is "about ten years." Ramis also put more emphasis on the love story.

Did it work? Yes. Rubin was reportedly upset about the changes, but they paid off: *Groundhog Day* made $70 million domestically (it cost less than $15 million to make) and has been included on many "Top Comedies of All-time" lists.

The lesson: No screenplay is safe in the Hollywood system. Still, a working draft must be completed before the rest of the pieces can be added.

What are the rest of the pieces?
Turn to Part II on page 232.

BAD NEWS BARED

Is being a professional journalist so competitive and fast-paced that writers sometimes make up stories? Here are some real-life journalism scandals.

Busted: Stephen Glass, the *New Republic*
Scoop: In May 1998, the *New Republic* published "Hack Heaven," Glass's dramatic story of Ian Restil, a 15-year-old computer hacker. According to the story, Restil landed a job as a consultant with Jukt Micronics, a company whose databases he'd broken into and sabotaged. The article included an interview with Restil and a first-person account of a "hacking convention" in Maryland. Forbes.com technology reporter Adam Penenberg read the article and thought the details didn't add up. Penenberg did some research and discovered that not only had there been no hacking conference, but Ian Restil and Jukt Micronics didn't even exist. When called out by his superiors at the *New Republic* for making up a news article, Glass fabricated elaborate evidence to cover his tracks. He created phony Jukt voice-mail accounts, business cards, and a Web site. Then he gave his editor, Charles Lane, a Palo Alto, California, phone number for "George Sims," a Jukt executive. Bad idea. Lane knew that Glass had a brother at Stanford (located in Palo Alto), realized it was a ruse and fired Glass. An internal review later determined that of the 41 stories Glass had written for the *New Republic*, 27 contained falsified material.
Aftermath: In 2003 Glass decided to write fiction. His first novel: *The Fabulist*, the story of an ambitious reporter who gets caught making up stories. Today Glass works as a paralegal.

Busted: Janet Cooke, the *Washington Post*
Scoop: In September 1980, the *Post* ran "Jimmy's World," Cooke's harrowing account of violence, poverty, and the heroin trade in an unnamed Washington, D.C., ghetto. At the center of the piece was "Jimmy," an eight-year-old third-generation heroin addict whose ambition was to be a drug dealer when he grew up. The story sickened and saddened readers and city officials, who wanted Cooke to tell them where the boy lived so he could be helped. Cooke refused, claiming that her sources were drug dealers and if

she revealed them, they'd kill her. The city launched a massive search for Jimmy, but couldn't find him, fueling rumors about whether Jimmy was even real. The *Post* addressed—and denied—the rumors in print. Cooke won the 1981 Pulitzer Prize for "Jimmy's World," but the rumors continued, so two days after the Pulitzer win, *Post* editors demanded that Cooke provide evidence of Jimmy's existence. She couldn't—she had made the whole thing up. Jimmy, the eight-year-old heroin addict, didn't exist.

Aftermath: Cooke returned her Pulitzer and became a store clerk in Michigan. Her explanation: The *Post* was a high-stress environment and she was under a lot of pressure from her editors to produce a major story. During an interview with drug dealers and homeless people, she'd heard about a child heroin addict. She couldn't locate him, so she made him up. In 1996 Cooke sold the movie rights to her story for $1.5 million. (The movie was never made.)

Busted: Jack Kelley, *USA Today*

Scoop: Kelley had been a foreign correspondent for *USA Today* since 1991, filing reports from war zones around the world. In 2003 executive editor Brian Gallagher received an anonymous tip that Kelley had "embellished" a story filed from Belgrade, Yugoslavia, in 1999. Gallagher assigned staffer Mark Memmott to investigate. Kelley's main source for the article was "army documents." He told Memmott that he saw the documents in a room with a single translator present, but then changed the story, saying he'd gotten them in an interview with a human rights activist in which two translators were present. The activist had no recollection of Kelley; the first translator denied the participation of a second translator. And then, suddenly, Kelley found the second translator. Memmott became suspicious when her account matched Kelley's word for word, and she called from Texas, not from eastern Europe. It turned out that the "translator" was actually an old friend of Kelley's. In 2003 *USA Today* editors told Kelley they knew about the hoax. Kelley confessed and, a few months later, resigned.

Aftermath: Another internal investigation revealed that Kelley had made up at least part of more than 20 stories. He'd never really found the diaries of dead Iraqi soldiers, witnessed an attack on Palestinians in Israel, trekked through the mountains with a Kosovar rebellion group, or interviewed Elian Gonzales's father in Cuba.

Of all the Beatles autographs in circulation, only about 6% are believed to be authentic.

RANDOM ORIGINS

Once again, the BRI asks—and answers—the question: Where does all this stuff come from?

WATERBEDS

The waterbed has actually been developed—unsuccessfully—numerous times. The first was more than 3,000 years ago, when Persians filled goat skins with water, sealed them with tar, and left them out in the sun to warm the water. The next time was in 1832, when Scottish doctor Neil Arnott filled a rubber-coated, mattress-sized piece of canvas with water, hoping to prevent bedsores. It wasn't a big seller (even in hospitals), nor was it when English doctor James Paget copied the design in 1873. The main reasons: The beds leaked, and they were cold. But in 1926, scientists at B.F. Goodrich came up with a synthetic material that could make waterbeds both leakproof and warm: vinyl. Sold via mail order, they were, once again, a commercial disappointment. Then in 1968, a San Francisco State University student named Charles Hall was trying to create an ultra-soft piece of furniture. After rejecting a gigantic vinyl bag filled with Jell-O, he tried filling it with water (he'd never heard of Arnott, Paget, or Persian goatskin-and-tar beds). Hall called his creation the Pleasure Pit and patented it. Waterbeds finally caught on, at least with Bay Area hippies. They became a national fad in the early 1980s.

NATIONAL GEOGRAPHIC

In January 1888, thirty-three men (including world-renowned explorers, military officers, academics, bankers, and mapmakers) met at the Cosmos Club in Washington, D.C., to organize a group whose mission was to "increase geographical knowledge." Bylaws were written up, and two weeks later the National Geographic Society was officially established. As a first step toward fulfilling their mission, the Society decided to publish a monthly journal, beginning with the first issue of *National Geographic Magazine* in October 1888. It was a dry, academic journal in its early days, but still attracted readers thanks to photographs from exotic places as well as maps and archaeology reports. It didn't become the magazine it is

Straws were used by ancient Egyptian brewers to taste test beer without disturbing the sediment.

today until Alexander Graham Bell was named president of the Society in 1897. Among Bell's innovations: He had the magazine printed on thick paper so it felt more like a book, devised the yellow-trimmed photographic cover, and solicited rollicking firsthand accounts from explorers like Robert Peary and Ernest Shackleton. He also realized that the magazine's strength was showcasing photos from around the world. By 1908 photos took up half of the magazine, and even more than that after 1910 when *National Geographic* ran color images for the first time. By 1950 it was one of the top 10 most-read magazines in the world. It's now published in 32 languages, and reaches more than 50 million readers every month.

TARTAR SAUCE

Before there was tartar sauce, there was *steak tartare*, a French dish that consists of chopped and seasoned raw beef topped with onions and capers. Whoever invented it (that person is lost to history) named it after the Tatars, a nomadic Turkic group who lived in Russia in the medieval era and, according to legend, were known for eating raw meat. *Sauce de tartare* was created in France the 18th century to accompany the entree. It consisted of mayonnaise, pickles, capers, onions, and tarragon. The thick, goopy sauce made its way to England in the late 19th century, where *tartare* was anglicized to *tartar* and was served alongside a distinctively English dish: fried fish.

RADIATION BLOCKING SUNGLASSES

In the early 1980s, NASA developed original coatings to protect their cameras and telescopes from the sun's heat and radiation while in space. Scientists at the Jet Propulsion Laboratories (at California Institute of Technology) thought the concept might have commercial applications, so they leased the technology from NASA. They adapted the basic scientific principles of the coatings to create a product: a welding mask that blocked more of the harmful, blinding UV light given off in welding than conventional masks did. When NASA heard about it, they made their own improvements, making the coatings lighter and more flexible. In turn, JPL took that technology and created sunglasses that block UV rays. Most famous radiation-blocking sunglasses: Blue Blockers, sold via TV infomercials.

If the Milky Way galaxy were the size of Asia, our solar system would be the size of a penny.

COWS ON THE RUN

Where else can you find a bunch of rampaging-bovine stories—each complete with its own pithy Beatles-related title? Only in Uncle John's Bathroom Reader!

BLACK COW RUNNING IN THE DEAD OF NIGHT

Moo-Cow (described by police as "fat") escaped from her pasture in Grafton, Massachusetts, in the middle of the night in February 2007 and ran five miles down Route 140. "She was mad," said resident Paula Tripp. A local rancher lassoed Moo-Cow, but then "the man let go of the rope," said Tripp, "and I grabbed it and got dragged up the street. There was no stopping this thing." In the end, the numerous cops and residents in the posse just had to wait for the Scottish Highlander to get tired and take a rest. As dawn approached, Moo-Cow finally gave up and was returned home. (The following day, the barbed-wire fence around her pasture was fortified.)

DAY TRIPPERS

The hills were alive with the sound of moo-sic in July 2005 when 10 members of a Bavarian family were attacked by a herd of 40 cows. The family members (who ranged from infant to elderly) were crossing a meadow in the foothills of the Austrian Alps when one of the children tried to pet a calf. Bad idea: The protective mother cow interpreted it as an attack and charged the family. Then her bovine companions charged, too—sending picnic supplies flying and the family scattering. An elderly member of the family suffered a heart attack, a seven-year-old was seriously injured, and many other scrapes and bruises were reported, but, thankfully, no one was killed.

I'M SO TIRED

After a cow escaped from a livestock market in Visalia, California, in 2008, she wandered into a nearby tire shop. "It seemed like a nice cow at first," said employee Mario Sanchez, "but I knew something was wrong when it kept coming at me." The cow picked up Sanchez and tossed him onto the tire changing

Cow terminology: A *heifer* is a female cow who has not yet birthed a calf.

machine. Then another employee, Frank Bautista, tried to lure her away. "Come here, Betsy," he said. But then she charged Bautista, too. He scrambled out of the way, and the cow ran back outside and head-butted a car. By that point, workers from the market had caught up and captured her as she trotted down Main Street. Neither of the tire shop employees were seriously injured, and the cow was later sold at an auction.

HEIFER SKELTER

"I worked on a farm when I was a youngster and always told people that cows never attacked," said 50-year-old British police inspector Chris Poole. But apparently he forgot to tell the cows. In 2007 Poole was walking his dog on a well-traveled footpath through a cow pasture. "All of a sudden, we were surrounded," he recalled. "I wasn't scared and waved and shooed them away." But the cows wouldn't be shooed. "I felt this cow butt me hard in the back. I fell to the ground and there were hooves all around me and I was being repeatedly head-butted." Poole suffered four broken ribs, a punctured lung, and a gash on his head. Adding insult to injury: "One cow stood on my arm and broke my watch." Poole recovered, but will now warn people to give cows a "wide berth."

RUN FOR YOUR LIFE IF YOU CAN, BIG GIRL

On the morning of her scheduled execution in January 2006, a 1,200-pound heifer made a break from the slaughterhouse line at Mickey's Packing Plant in Great Falls, Montana. "I watched her do things that are just not possible for a cow," said plant manager Del Morris. After jumping a five-foot fence, Molly (Morris's name for the cow) led police and plant workers on a six-hour chase in which she nearly got hit by an SUV and a tractor trailer, darted across the tracks just in front of an oncoming train, and barreled through a fence when her pursuers cornered her. Even three tranquilizer darts failed to slow Molly down. But it was when she traversed the strong currents to the other side of the icy Missouri River that Morris realized this cow was too special to end up on a dinner plate. After Molly was finally coaxed into a trailer, Morris let Great Falls residents decide her fate. Their choice: a fenced-in field just out of town, where Molly will live out her days.

LEAVE READY ZAGROMYHAT TO US!

Next time you're really bored, try this: Go to an Internet translation page, type a phrase in English and translate it into another language. Then translate the new phrase into another language and then back to English. The results can be quite amusing.

English: "Uncle John's Bathroom Reader."
Greek→English: "Divine John, Reader of Baths."

English: "I've fallen and I can't get up!"
Russian→Japanese→English: "I described and I have upadenny stand up!"

English: "Who let the dogs out?"
Chinese→English: "Who bleeds off the dog?"

English: "Antidepressants may cause dry mouth due to decreased saliva, possibly contributing to the development of tooth decay."
Greek→Japanese→English: "You disagree the medicine with cause, for drying saliou reduction of the mouth contributes to the development of possibility, it is carious tooth."

English: "Rolling on the floor laughing."
Russian→English: "To roll up on to laugh above the sexes."

English: "Mama said knock you out."
Spanish→English: "The breast said eliminates to him."

English: "Let's get ready to rumble!"
Russian→German→English: "Leave ready zagromyhat to us!"

English: "Rarely is the question asked, is our children learning?"
Spanish→French→Dutch→English: "He is seldom the done question, he is our education of the children."

Hold the fries! Until the late 18th century, the French believed that potatoes caused leprosy.

English: "I'd like to buy a vowel, Pat."
Russain→Danish→Japanese→English: "It is to like to do the vowel which purchases, but it is the pad."

English: "You want fries with that?"
Japanese→Hindi→English: "I desire to fritter?"

English: "It was the best of times, it was the worst of times."
Japanese→Korean→Greek→English: "It is time the waistcoat was ugliest when."

English: "I can't believe I ate the whole thing."
Japanese→Swedish→English: "I am all for I ate them all, it is possible to believe what is not."

English: "Don't mess with Texas."
Japanese→Bulgarian→Polish→Korean→English: "Texas which goes round and is confused."

English: "Pardon me, sir, but do you have any Grey Poupon?"
French→German→Chinese→English: "Please forgive me, Mr. Chairman, but have you established your gray poupon?"

English: "To boldly go where no man has gone before."
Korean→English: "Makes boldmakes bold and also anyone man not going before where in order to go."

English: "Frankly, my dear, I don't give a damn."
German→French→English: "Sincerely, my expensive, I do not give swore."

English: "Rubber Ducky, you're my very best friend, it's true!"
Russian→Korean→Swedish→Japanese→English: "Duck of rubber make, as for you my very bosom buddy, as for that truth!"

English: "Elvis has left the building."
Dutch→French→Chinese→English: "The electronic export license material system departed the construction."

FAST FOOD FLOPS

Fast food is such a huge industry that there's bound to be a flop or two. Here are some of the weirdest business decisions in fast food history.

HAVE IT OUR WAY

To stand out from the competition, in 1992 Burger King briefly converted its restaurants from fast food into sit-down restaurants with table service, but only during dinner hours. Customers would continue to order at the counter, but after placing their order they would find a table, and then an employee would bring them their food—up to 15 minutes later (to help customers pass the time while they were waiting for their food, there was a free basket of popcorn on every table...right next to the burning candle). Special "dinner baskets" offered new items such as fried shrimp, fried chicken, fried clams, and baked potatoes. Many locations even put out white tablecloths. The concept was a complete disaster. It slowed down Burger King's customer turnover rate so much that the company estimates that in the two months it tried table service, it lost $10 million.

ARTERY-LICKIN' GOOD

Fried chicken may be delicious, but like anything that's deep-fried, it's loaded with fat, which makes it pretty unhealthy to eat. But that's never stopped Kentucky Fried Chicken from trying to convince the public (several times) that *its* fried chicken is healthier than other fried chicken.

• In 1991 the restaurant introduced Lite N' Crispy—fried chicken without the skin. But it was still breaded and fried, so it had almost the same amount of fat as its Original Recipe chicken. (A Lite N' Crispy breast had 22 grams of fat; an Original Recipe breast has 27.) Lite? Hardly. The FDA quickly levied a $25,000 fine against Kentucky Fried Chicken for misleading the public... which led to the chain's renaming the product "Skinfree Crispy." A few months later, it was gone from the menu.

• At the same time, the chain changed its name to "KFC" to downplay the word "fried." In 2004 the chain began an ad campaign that claimed the "F" in KFC stood for "fresh." Neither plan worked—sales were flat.

YOU DON'T KNOW JACK

Ralston Purina, the corporate parent of Jack in the Box, wasn't satisfied that they were only the fifth most popular hamburger chain in the United States, and decided that the way to carve out a larger niche was to appeal to an underserved audience: adults who don't eat fast food because they see it as "too juvenile." So in 1985 the chain was renamed Monterey Jack's. More than 800 locations were remodeled at a cost of $3 million each, the majority of which was paid for by franchisees. Brightly colored restaurants were repainted stark white, and the burgers and chicken nuggets were replaced with "higher-quality" fare like steak sandwiches and fajitas. It didn't work. Most stores actually *lost* business. And within a year, all the Monterey Jack's were converted back into Jack in the Boxes. In 1986 Ralston Purina sold Jack in the Box to an investment group for $450 million. (Before the Monterey Jack's conversion, the chain had been valued at $500 million.)

McPIZZA

In 1989 pizza was a $21 billion business and growing at a rate of 10% per year, but sales at McDonald's were stagnant, especially in the dinner hours. McSolution: Sell pizza. McDonald's invented a special fast-cook oven that used superhot air streams to cook a pizza in just over five minutes. Then it spent millions to remodel test restaurants—fitting kitchens with the new ovens and expanding drive-through windows so they were large enough for a pizza box to pass through. In 1990 they began the test, selling 14" pizzas (four styles: cheese, pepperoni, sausage, and deluxe) in Evansville, Indiana. The pizzas cost from $6 to $9.50, making them the most expensive items on the McDonald's menu, and the same price as Pizza Hut or Dominos. And while it took only five minutes to cook a pizza, it took more than 10 minutes for it to get to the customer's table—not bad for a pizza, but too slow for superfast McDonald's. Pizza flopped in Evansville. Was that the end? No. McDonald's had made such a huge investment in developing the ovens (reportedly more than $10 million), that they continued to test market pizza in the U.S. and Canada as late as 1997. It never caught on.

It's against the law to play bridge in a hotel in Alabama.

UNCLE JOHN'S CREATIVE TEACHING AWARDS

For outstanding performance in teaching our children to be strange and unusual people.

SUBJECT: Human development
WINNER: Paul Tappan
CREATIVE TEACHING: In May 2008, science teacher Paul Tappan of Anderson High School in Indiana wrote a disciplinary referral for one of his students. It read: "No need for her to come back to my class. Please banish her from the human race and exile accordingly." Not surprisingly, the student's parents were upset. "Why," the student's mother asked, "do we have a teacher in the school system who has that much anger?" Tappan apologized, saying that he'd had a bad day.

SUBJECT: Sex education
WINNER: A teacher in Odawara, Japan
CREATIVE TEACHING: What do you do when some of your sixth-grade boys try to sneak into the girls' locker room? According to this teacher (who went unnamed in press reports), you pick one student, pin a note to his back, and make him wear it in class all day. The note: "I tried but failed to sneak into the girls' changing room. I am an idiot." The upset student refused to come to school for a month afterward. What's more, it turned out that the teacher was wrong—a later investigation found that the student wasn't one of the guilty boys. The teacher apologized, and was transferred to a different school.

SUBJECT: Religion
WINNER: Michael Seymour
CREATIVE TEACHING: Mr. Seymour was teaching at a Sydney, Australia, high school in 2006 when he got into an argument with one of his students, a 16-year-old Muslim boy of Lebanese descent named Wagih Fares. At a heated moment, Seymour cut

The larva of the polyphemus moth consumes 86,000 times its own weight in its first 56 days.

the boy off and said, "I'm not negotiating with a terrorist." The outraged young man ran out of the classroom and left the school, quickly followed by an apologetic Seymour, who immediately realized what he'd done. The incident set off a firestorm of protest in the city's large Muslim community. Seymour was required to take a multicultural sensitivity course, but he was allowed to remain in the school (which set off an even greater firestorm of protest).

SUBJECT: Phys ed
WINNER: Peter Porath
CREATIVE TEACHING: In 2005 the wrestling team at a high school in Woodburn, Oregon, thought it would be funny to play a prank on their wrestling coach, Mr. Porath. According to an Oregon Teacher Commission investigation, here's what happened: "Six wrestlers, weighing between 180 and 215 pounds each, came up to Mr. Porath from behind in an attempt to give him a 'wedgie.' In the process of getting the boys off of him, Mr. Porath bit the inside of a wrestler's leg, leaving distinct teeth marks." Porath was forced to complete a class on "appropriate behavior," and had to write a formal apology to the students. (He later became a baseball coach.)

SUBJECT: Biology
WINNER: Jerick Hutchinson
CREATIVE TEACHING: In November 2007, Jerick Hutchinson, an agriculture teacher at Huntsville High in Arkansas, asked a parent of a student to bring a dead raccoon to the school...so he could teach the kids how to skin it. That's kind of weird, but it got even weirder when the parent brought in a *live* raccoon (it had been caught in a trap) instead of a dead one. Hutchinson, who the school later said had once worked at a slaughterhouse, took the animal out to his truck—and killed it with a nail gun. Then he brought it back in and skinned it for the class. Superintendent Alvin Lievsay said school officials later talked with Hutchinson, telling him not to kill animals on school grounds. "He does a great job," Lievsay told reporters. "The kids love him."

The modern language that most closely resembles ancient Sanskrit: Lithuanian.

ASSASSINATED!

A look at the details involving some infamous murders of prominent political figures, starting in 1584.

VICTIM: William I, Prince of Orange (1533–1584)

BACKGROUND: In the Netherlands he's known as the "Father of the Fatherland," having led the initial stages of the Protestant Dutch revolt against Catholic Spanish rulers that eventually led to independence. King Philip II of Spain (and of the Netherlands) wasn't particularly pleased with that, and offered a substantial reward for William's murder.

THE KILLER: In 1582 a radical French Roman Catholic named Balthasar Gérard heard about the reward. He planned and plotted for two years, and then on July 10, 1584, snuck into William's house in Delft, Holland, and shot him in the chest three times. Gérard was quickly captured and taken to local officials. He was tortured for three days, then tried (he proudly confessed) and convicted. The sentence: He was disemboweled alive and quartered by horses, his heart was cut out and thrown in his face, and then his head was cut off. King Philip gave Gérard's family three large country estates as thanks for their kin's murderous actions.

EXTRA: Gérard remains a hero to some Catholics, and in the tiny village of Vuillafans in eastern France, where he was born, there is a street called Rue Gérard, which is said to be named for him. As for William I, he has the dubious honor of being the first head of state known to have been assassinated with a handgun.

VICTIM: Michael Collins

BACKGROUND: Collins was an Irish Republican Army leader during the 1919–1922 Irish War of Independence. The war ended in a treaty with England that established the Irish Free State (which eventually became the Republic of Ireland). Many in Ireland opposed the treaty, and the dispute led to the brutal 10-month Irish Civil War. Collins had helped negotiate the treaty, supported it, and became commander in chief of the Irish Free State army. On the evening of August 22, 1922, while driving into Cork (his hometown), his army convoy was ambushed near Béal na mBláth, or "Mouth of Flowers." After a confused 20-minute firefight between an estimated 50 men with rifles and at least three machine guns, only one man was dead: Collins, killed by a bullet to the head. Nobody claimed to have taken the shot, and nobody claimed to have seen him go down. He was 31.

THE KILLERS: The subject of who killed Collins remains controversial in Ireland. Two of the most popular theories:

• Éamon de Valera was the president of Sinn Fein, the IRA's political arm, and was a longtime close confidant of Collins. But the two men bitterly split over the treaty. De Valera had been a leading antitreaty figure during the civil war, and was in the area when Collins was killed. He got a report, the theory says, that Collins would be driving into Cork, so he ordered the ambush. De Valera's many supporters still vehemently deny this. He remained a top figure in Irish politics until the 1970s, even serving for 14 years as the president of the Irish Republic.

• Jock McPeak was a Scotsman who fought on the side of the Irish for years. A personal friend of Collins, he was manning a machine gun in the convoy when it was attacked. He wasn't brought under suspicion in the killing until later in 1922, when he was smuggled out of Ireland to Scotland by anti-treaty IRA members. Some people believe he took a moment in the confusion to kill Collins—though nobody seems to know why he would have.

VICTIM: Mohandas Gandhi

BACKGROUND: At 5:10 p.m. on January 30, 1948, the leader of the Indian independence movement was walking the grounds of the Birla House, his home in New Delhi, with several followers when he was shot three times in the chest at point blank range.

THE KILLERS: Shooter Nathuram Godse, 39, surrendered immediately, saying, "No one should think that Gandhi was killed by a madman." Godse was a member of a Hindu nationalist organization known as Hindu Mahasabha (roughly "Hindu Council") that was opposed to Gandhi's cooperation with Muslims and had made at least two other attempts on his life. Godse was hanged on November 15, 1949. Though vilified by the majority of Indians, he is still a hero to many Hindu nationalists.

• Eleven other members of Hindu Mahasabha were also charged in the assassination. Narayan Apte, 37, was with Godse at the time of the murder and was the only other man executed. Several others were found guilty and served sentences of varying lengths.

• Vinayak Damodar Savarkar, 66, was the founder of modern Hindu nationalism in India and a frequent and vocal critic of Gandhi. Charged with being behind the assassination, he was acquitted for lack of evidence. A 1965 inquiry into the murder, however, found new evidence that most experts say would have gotten him convicted. He died in 1966.

OTHER ASSASSINATIONS

Victor Jara. A popular Chilean songwriter and activist in the 1960s, he is credited with aiding the 1970 election of socialist Salvador Allende. On September 11, 1973, a United States-backed coup saw Allende killed and dictator Augusto Pinochet installed. During the coup Jara, 38, was arrested and taken with thousands of others to Chile Stadium in Santiago. Over the next four days, he was beaten, tortured, and finally machine-gunned to death. His body was found four days later in a Santiago slum. In 2008 a new inquest was opened into his murder. It is still ongoing.

John Paul Newman. A member of the parliament of the state of New South Wales, Australia, he had long worked to stop gang activity in his home city of Cabramatta. On September 5, 1994, he was shot and killed in front of his home. In 2001 Phuong Ngo, a local club owner believed to be involved in Vietnamese gangs, was convicted of the murder. Newman's is believed to be the only political assassination in Australian history.

Alexander Valterovich Litvinenko. A former KGB officer, writer, and vocal critic of Russian president Vladimir Putin, he was arrested three times in the late 1990s and finally fled to the U.K. in 2000. In November 2006, he became mysteriously ill, and on November 23 he died. It was later determined that Litvinenko had been poisoned with the radioactive element polonium-210. Investigators were able to track "radiation trails" to two men: Andrei Lugovoi and Dmitry Kovtun, both former KGB agents who met with Litvinenko in the days before his death. Lugovi has been charged by British authorities, but Russian authorities refuse to extradite him. Kovtun was hospitalized in Moscow in 2006 (with radiation poisoning) but managed to recover.

BASKETBALL TEAM NAME ORIGINS

Ever wonder how a team from Utah came to be called the Jazz? Here's how NBA teams got their nicknames.

DALLAS MAVERICKS. Although it makes sense that a Texas-based team would have a western-themed name, it was actually chosen because one of the team's original owners was actor James Garner, star of the TV western show *Maverick*.

DENVER NUGGETS. The Denver Rockets entered the NBA when the American Basketball Association folded in 1976. There was already a team called the Rockets, so Denver executives chose Nuggets after Colorado's gold-mining history.

SAN ANTONIO SPURS. They were formerly the Dallas Chapparals in the American Basketball Association, but team execs wanted a cowboy-themed name when they relocated to San Antonio in 1973.

MINNESOTA TIMBERWOLVES. Minnesota has the largest population of timberwolves in the lower 48 states. The name was suggested by 17 different people in a name-the-team contest.

CHICAGO BULLS. Original owner Richard Klein thought bulls were tough, and so was his team. The name also pays tribute to the city's stockyards and meatpacking industry.

PORTLAND TRAILBLAZERS. A contest was held to allow the public to suggest names. More than 10,000 entries were received, with Pioneers receiving the most votes. But the team decided against it because Portland's Lewis and Clark College used it as *their* nickname. The second-most popular entry, Trailblazers, was used instead.

CLEVELAND CAVALIERS. Team executives let fans vote on the name from five suggestions: the Presidents, the Jays, the Foresters, the Towers, and the Cavaliers.

Donald Trump, take note: The Raritan Indians sold Staten Island to six different groups of settlers.

NEW ORLEANS HORNETS. Until they moved to New Orleans in 2002, they were the Charlotte Hornets. The city of Charlotte resisted British occupation during the American Revolution. British general Lord Cornwallis reportedly called the city "a veritable nest of hornets."

MEMPHIS GRIZZLIES. There are no grizzly bears in Tennessee, but there are in Vancouver, Canada, where the team started in 1995. (The team first picked the Mounties but was forced to change it when the Royal Canadian Mounted Police objected.)

MIAMI HEAT. More than 5,000 entries were received in a team naming contest in 1987. Among the suggestions were the Palm Trees, Beaches, Suntan, and Shade. Team owners picked the Heat.

BOSTON CELTICS. Original owner Walter Brown named them after an older basketball team, the New York Celtics, in honor of the large Irish (also known as Celtic) population in Boston.

WASHINGTON WIZARDS. They were the Washington Bullets (formerly the Baltimore Bullets) until 1995, when owner Abe Pollin decided that "Bullets" was too violent, especially since Washington, D.C., was experiencing higher than normal murder rates. A fan contest was held, and Wizards won out over Dragons, Express, Stallions, and Sea Dogs.

PHILADELPHIA 76ERS. Named for 1776, the year the Declaration of Independence was signed (in Philadelphia).

ORLANDO MAGIC. Magic beat Heat, Tropics, and Juice in a newspaper contest. (It references nearby Disney World, also known as the "Magic Kingdom.")

UTAH JAZZ. Prior to 1979, the team was based in New Orleans, where jazz music originated.

TORONTO RAPTORS. Team executives wanted to use the name Huskies, but when they saw an early logo prototype, they realized it was too similar to the Minnesota Timberwolves' logo. A contest to name the team was held, and Raptors won. Velociraptors were vicious dinosaurs made famous in the movie *Jurassic Park*, which was released just before Toronto got its basketball team.

Michigan has more than 11,000 inland lakes and over 36,000 miles of streams.

UNCLE JOHN'S STALL OF FAME

Uncle John is amazed—and pleased—by the creative ways people get involved with bathrooms, toilets, toilet paper, and so on. That's why he created the "Stall of Fame."

Honoree: Petey P. Cup

Notable Achievement: Becoming the first and only (so far) mascot shaped like a urine sample container

True Story: He's nearly seven feet tall, he walks on two legs, and his body is a giant jar of pee. The yellow spokescup (with blue lid) was created by HealthPartners, a Minnesota-based nonprofit health-care organization. Petey's goal: to "humanize" the company and promote same-day results for urine tests. The campaign is targeted toward "a younger demographic that understands irony, YouTube, and social networking." (Petey has a Facebook page.) In 2008 HealthPartners announced that Petey would be getting a sidekick—Pokey the Syringe.

Honoree: Brad Feld, a venture capitalist from Boulder, Colorado

Notable Achievement: Making a "charitable donation" in a college restroom

True Story: Feld recently gave $25,000 to the University of Colorado. Now the second floor men's room in the technology building displays a plaque bearing his name. Underneath is printed this piece of advice: "The best ideas often come at inconvenient times. Don't ever close your mind to them." Feld's first choice was a restroom at Massachusetts Institute of Technology, his alma mater, but the school declined. The University of Colorado jumped at the chance and would like to remind people that the women's room adjacent to Feld's is still up for grabs.

Honoree: Sim Jae-duck, a.k.a. "Mr. Toilet," a South Korean lawmaker and president of the World Toilet Association

Notable Achievement: Making the best seat in the house into the *entire* house

Postal-carrier quiz: Which dog breed is most prone to biting humans? A: German Shepherd.

True Story: In the town of Suwon, South Korea, Sim tore down his house and in its place built a 24-foot-tall, toilet-shaped building. It's made of steel, and it's painted white to resemble porcelain. Even bigger than the toilet house is the reason it was built: to serve as the "headquarters" for the World Toilet Association (not to be confused with the much larger World Toilet Organization), which is dedicated to improving sanitary conditions for the 2.5 billion people who lack access to clean water and bathrooms. Formed in 2007, the WTA held its inaugural meeting at Sim's toilet house—whose official name is *Haewoojae*, Korean for "a place of sanctuary where one can solve one's worries."

Honoree: Thelma Brittingham, a resident at the Holiday Retirement Village in Evansville, Indiana

Notable Achievement: Having a birthday party for toilet paper

True Story: Trying to bring some fun to the home's senior citizens, Brittingham decided to research the history of toilet paper in the hopes of tracing it back to its date of birth. Her findings: TP was first used in Europe on August 26, 580 A.D. (No word on how she determined that.) So now, each year the retirees put on a birthday party on the special day. Brittingham says, "When some people heard we were celebrating toilet paper's birthday, they asked me, 'Have you lost your mind?'" She assured them that she hadn't.

Honoree: The city of Wuhan, in China's Hubei province

Notable Achievement: Starting a low-cost service for visitors desperately in need of a pit stop

True Story: For tourists wandering through the crowded city of nearly 10 million people, finding a public restroom can be difficult. But now, they can look for a "toilet guide," distinguishable by his red arm band. For only 3 *jiao* (3.8 cents), a guide will escort you to the nearest restroom. The city employs 10 guides who are paid a daily salary of 10 *yuan* ($1.29).

Honoree: Gerardine Botte, director of Ohio University's Electrochemical Engineering Research Laboratory

Notable Achievement: Turning pee into power

True Story: Urine contains ammonia, and ammonia can be bro-

A $100 bill lasts an average of 8.5 years. (That's about 3.2¢ per day.)

ken down into hydrogen and nitrogen, which can provide energy. So why do the millions of tons of ammonia made by humans and farm animals each year just evaporate in waste treatment plants and in ponds on farms? That's the question asked—and answered—by Botte and the science whizzes at OU. After a long process of trial and error, the team is perfecting a device called an *electrolyzer* that uses electric current to break down the ammonia into its component parts, which can then be turned into fuel. Within a few years, many waste treatment plants and farm waste ponds may be converted into power plants with an endless supply of raw fuel. The technology may even lead to pee-powered automobiles. One of the most beneficial aspects of ammonia energy: it creates no greenhouse gases, effectively turning one of our dirtiest byproducts into one of our cleanest forms of energy.

* * *

NEVER

"Never ascribe to malice that which can be explained by incompetence."

—Napoleon

"Never impose your language on people you wish to reach."

—Abbie Hoffman

"Never hold discussions with the monkey when the organ grinder is in the room."

—Winston Churchill

"It's always a bad practice to say 'always' or 'never.'"

—Barack Obama

"Never throw mud. You may miss the mark, and you'll have dirty hands."

—Joseph Parker

"Rule #1: Never lose money. Rule #2: Never forget rule #1."

—Warren Buffett

Licorice gets its flavoring from a Mediterranean herb called *glycyrrhiza glabra.*

THE DA VINCI OF DETROIT

Harley Earl is considered one of the three most important figures in the history of the American auto industry (Henry Ford and GM head Alfred Sloan are the other two). Yet other than car buffs, few people have heard of him.

THE HOLLYWOOD KID

In 1925 the General Motors Corporation made plans to begin manufacturing a car called the LaSalle. It would be sold by Cadillac dealerships, but for a price slightly lower than the least expensive Cadillac. Larry Fisher, Cadillac's general manager, was looking for someone to design it and found his man working in the custom body shop of the Cadillac dealer in Los Angeles: Harley Earl, the son of a Hollywood coach builder who started out building horse-drawn vehicles—actual *coaches*—before switching to automobile bodies in 1908.

Earl, in his early 30s, had acquired a reputation for building one-of-a-kind autos for rich Hollywood movie stars. His car for cowboy star Tom Mix, for example, was painted with stars emblazoned with Mix's "TM" logo and had a leather saddle on the roof. His car for comedian Fatty Arbuckle, while much more sedate and elegant, cost Arbuckle an incredible $28,000—at a time when a new Ford Model T sold for less than $300.

QUICK AND DIRTY

What really impressed Fisher about Harley Earl wasn't so much his cars for the stars as it was his method for designing them: Before he built the final product, Earl made full-sized mock-ups of his vehicles using modeling clay. Unlike working with sheet metal or wood, the common technique of other coach builders, clay was quicker and easier to work with. If Earl wasn't happy with the shape of a door he'd made, for example, instead of spending hours making a new one out of wood or pounding one out by hand from sheet metal, all he had to do was add a little more clay or scrape a little off, repeating the process as often as necessary until he got exactly the look he wanted. The ease of using clay allowed Earl to be very ambitious and creative in his designs, and just as importantly, it allowed him to think of the

First in-flight meal: turkey and vegetables, served aboard the zeppelin *Ilia Mouriametz* in 1914.

car as a single, integrated unit, not a bunch of mechanical components bolted together.

When Earl arrived in Detroit, he set to work designing four different versions of the La Salle: a coupe, a roadster, a sedan, and a touring car. He borrowed heavily from the Hispano-Suiza, a popular European luxury car of the day, and then implemented what would become a lifelong design principle: Longer, lower cars were more appealing to the eye than shorter cars with high rooflines.

SOMETHING TO SEE

Fisher and his boss, GM head Alfred Sloan, were impressed with all four of Earl's designs and ordered them all into production for the 1927 model year. Those 1927 LaSalles were the very first high-volume, mass-produced cars that had ever been designed by what would become known as a *stylist,* someone who cared as much about how the car looked as he did about how it ran.

Remember, the auto industry was barely 20 years old in 1927, and it had taken all that time just to advance the state of the art to the point where cars were dependable, affordable, and could be mass produced by the hundreds of thousands with no loss of quality. The engineers who had made all of this possible weren't concerned with what the cars looked like: If buyers wanted a car that looked good on top of everything else, that was what the custom coach builders were for. Cadillac still sold a lot of unfinished cars to these companies—chassis, engine, power train, wheels, radiator, etc., but no body—and coach building firms could spend as much time as they wanted crafting beautiful, luxurious auto bodies by hand.

Those 1927 LaSalles were special cars indeed—they outshone many of the Cadillacs that were supposed to outshine them. Was it their long, low-slung look? Was it their two-tone paint jobs—unheard of in mass-produced cars, which were still mostly available in only dark blue or black? Was it the "Flying Wing" fenders that did it? Those LaSalles flew off the car lots, so impressing GM head Alfred Sloan that he created an entirely new department, the Art and Color Division, to bring GM's design work in-house, and he brought Harley Earl out from California to run it.

The American auto industry would never be the same again.

Part II of our story is on page 269.

DUMB CROOKS

Proof that crime doesn't pay.

HANGING OUT

In Aachen, Germany, a sales clerk at a clothing store noticed a man with a pronounced triangle-shaped bulge protruding from underneath the back of his coat. "Do you need any help, sir?" she asked. "No," he told her. "I won't be buying anything today." The clerk quickly alerted security, who caught the man with a stolen suit...still on its clothes hanger. "Only a sign saying 'Stop me, I'm a thief!' would have made him look more unprofessional," said the arresting officer.

CALL ME

In 2008 an 18-year-old man burst into a muffler shop in Chicago wildly waving a gun and demanding money. When informed that only the boss could open the safe, the robber gave the employees his cell phone number and ordered them to call him when the boss returned. Instead, the workers called the police, who sent over a plain clothes officer. *He* called the robber and told him the manager was there. Sure enough, the man returned, again waving his gun around, and the officer shot him in the leg. The robber was arrested, treated for his wound, and sent to jail.

CELLULAR BLOCKHEAD

Not wanting to miss his early morning court appearance in Peterborough, Ontario, Donald Baker called the police department the night before and requested a wake-up call. The police were reportedly "amused" that the 51-year-old man would even *think* that was a service they offered. So they decided to run a records check on Baker...and discovered an arrest warrant out on him that they hadn't known about. When he showed up for court the next morning, he was put in jail instead.

DOPE DOPES

Three men from New Orleans, all in their early 30s, wrapped up more than two pounds of marijuana in plastic bags and T-shirts

The metal prong on a buckle is called the *chape*.

and hid the loot under the hood of their car…right on top of the engine block. When police caught up with the trio in a gas station parking lot, one was using a hose to try to put out an engine fire, one was under the car trying to retrieve a flaming bag of pot, and one was throwing another flaming bag of pot into a garbage can. Reportedly, the whole parking lot smelled like marijuana. All three were arrested on drug and reckless endangerment charges.

HERE I AM!

A 40-year-old man from Janesville, Wisconsin, named Lem Lom was walking down a neighborhood street one day in September 2003 when he saw a fancy electronic device about the size of a brick on a front doorstep. Unaware that it was a $2,500 GPS transmitter that served as a "base" to an ankle monitor (worn by a woman under house arrest), Lom snuck up, stole the box, and then took it to his apartment. A short time later, the police were knocking on his door. "Apparently he didn't know what he had because he'd have to be awfully stupid to steal a tracking device," said correctional officer Thomas Roth.

GONE IN 60 SECONDS

On a Saturday morning at around 11:40 a.m. in March 2008, Christopher Koch parked his car in a bank parking lot in Liberty, Pennsylvania. It took him 20 minutes to get up the nerve to rob it—at 12:01 p.m. he burst out of his car wielding a shotgun and wearing an orange ski mask and gloves. Unfortunately for Koch, the bank closed at noon. He banged on the door, got frustrated, and left, never having seen the employees inside. But they saw him and wrote down the license number of his car. Police quickly caught up with Koch and arrested him for attempted armed robbery.

SIGNED, SEALED, DELIVERED

In 2008 convicted burglar Eric Livers, 20, was a fugitive. He was living in New Hampshire after having recently escaped from a halfway house in Wyoming. All he had to do was keep a low profile, which he did…until he called his former boss in Wyoming to request that his final paycheck be mailed to him. His boss called the police instead, who arrested Livers.

"We cannot do everything at once, but we can do something at once." —Calvin Coolidge

COMICAL COMICS

You're probably familiar with Superman, the X-Men, and Archie, but have you ever read about the exciting adventures of Paulina Porizkova?

JAY LENO & SPIDER-MAN: ONE NIGHT ONLY. Released as a tie-in with the 2002 *Spider-Man* movie, although it's unclear why Marvel Comics decided to team Spidey with the 52-year-old talk show host. The plot: Spider-Man and Leno meet to film a commercial for General Motors (the company paid for the product placement), but get attacked by ninjas. Using kung fu and a samurai sword, Leno helps defeat the ninjas.

DRACULA. In 1966 Dell Comics tried to capitalize on the popularity of Batman by reimagining the classic vampire as a superhero. Instead of sucking blood and terrorizing people, Dracula is independently wealthy, lives in a secret cave, has a female sidekick, and devotes his time to exposing phony psychics. Along the way he teams up with Frankenstein's monster, who also has a new image as "the world's strongest hero."

SUPERGIRL, IN COOPERATION WITH THE NATIONAL SAFETY BELT CAMPAIGN. Plot: Supergirl (Superman's cousin) transports her mind into another dimension to retrieve the soul of a man who's in a coma after being in a car crash while not wearing a seat belt. The 1984 comic also includes a note from Secretary of Transportation Elizabeth Dole urging kids to buckle up. The whole thing was paid for by Honda and was distributed to schools by the U.S. Department of Transportation.

SUPERMAN VS. MUHAMMAD ALI. In this 1978 comic, Clark Kent interviews Ali while he's teaching a bunch of kids how to play basketball. Suddenly an evil alien invades Earth, challenging Superman to a death match. Ali wants to be the one to battle the alien and defend Earth, so he challenges Superman to a fight. That match-up never happens—Ali's cornerman disguises himself as Superman and fights (and loses to) Ali, so the real Superman, dressed up as Ali's cornerman (in blackface) can go vanquish the alien.

In an average year, six British anglers die of electrocution from fishing too close to power lines.

***PERSONALITY COMICS PRESENTS PAULINA* PORIZKOVA.** Personality Comics was a publisher with a novel idea: celebrity biographies, presented as comic books. It might have worked, too, except that for their first issue (in 1991) they chose model Paulina Porizkova, who was not exactly a household name. Another problem: The poorly drawn, black-and-white pictures looked nothing like Porizkova. There was no second issue.

CAPTAIN BIO ENCOUNTERS A BRAINSTORM. Novartis Pharmaceuticals, the makers of the epilepsy drug Tegretol, commissioned this comic in 1994. It's about the brilliant Dr. Mark Phillips, who is working on a brainwave-reading invention called the Bio-Meter when he gets struck by lightning. Transformed into Captain Bio, he goes inside a human brain to show the reader how epileptic seizures happen...and how Tegretol fights them off.

CONTINGENCY MANAGEMENT. Michigan textbook publisher Behaviordelia Inc. was looking for a way to appeal to youth culture. So in 1973 they released this psychology book on "behavioral analysis and contingency management," rendered entirely in comic book form. Somehow they forgot that professors, not students, choose textbooks; *Contingency Management* flopped.

POPEYE AND ENVIRONMENTAL CAREERS. Popeye the Sailor Man debuted in the 1920s. What did he have to do with the environment or job training? Nothing. But in 1973 he was used in this comic book to convince kids to go into careers like river cleanup and trash disposal. As Popeye says on the cover, "Hey kids, you can help make this country a better place to live, and get paid well for doing it!"

DI ANOTHER DAY. *X-Statix* is Marvel Comics' British equivalent of *X-Men*, both dealing with teams of crime-fighting superheroes. In 2003 head writer Peter Milligan announced that a new superhero would join the X-Statix team: a zombie Princess Diana. In a story called "Di Another Day," Diana fends off assassination attempts from both the royal family and X-Statix, who gets jealous when the new member gets all the media attention. After complaints from the real royal family, Diana was replaced by "Henrietta Hunter," a fictional pop star (who looked just like Princess Diana).

Roughly 44% of junk mail is thrown away unopened.

UNCLE JOHN CLEANS YOUR KITCHEN

The BRI library boasts a huge collection of odd cleaning tips. Here are a few tricks that even the cleanest of our clean-freak readers may not have heard about.

IN THE KITCHEN

• **Cleaning the Microwave:** Fill a spray bottle with water and spritz the inside of the microwave. Then run the microwave for five to seven seconds. (No more than that!) This will heat the water enough to loosen the stains on the walls, floor, and ceiling of the microwave, making cleanup easier.

• **Dirty Blenders and Garbage Disposals:** You can clean any residual goo off the blades of these appliances with ice—just toss some cubes into the blender or disposal and run it until the ice is crushed. To further clean the garbage disposal, pour a large pot of boiling water down it while it's running, follow up with some liquid soap mixed with lemon juice, and rinse with a second round of boiling water. This should improve the disposal's performance... and its smell.

• **Coffee or Tea Stains in Your Favorite Cup or Mug:** Mix baking soda with a little salt and water to create a paste; then use a sponge to scour the inside of the mug with the mixture. You'll be surprised (we hope!) how quickly those stubborn stains disappear.

• **Burnt Food in a Pot or Frying Pan:** A baking soda paste—this time without salt—can work wonders here, too. Rub the paste onto the stain and let sit for at least three hours (overnight is even better). Then try scrubbing the stain out. If you still can't get it all up, mix two tablespoons of baking soda and a 1/2 cup of vinegar with a cup of water, doubling or tripling the formula, if necessary, to immerse the burnt section of the pan. Bring to a boil and keep it there for 10–15 minutes. If that doesn't get out the scorched food, nothing will.

• **Removing Fish and Other Smells From Cutting Boards:** Cut a fresh lemon in half and rub vigorously with the grain. The acid in

Benjamin Franklin once advised a general that guns would never be as effective as bows and arrows.

the lemon will help to break down the offensive odors, leaving nothing behind but the smell of the lemon.

• **Smelly Refrigerators:** Just about everybody knows that an open box of baking soda helps to remove odors from a smelly fridge, but did you know that it's not just the baking soda? The cardboard box has odor-absorbing properties, too. If you're in the habit of pouring the powdery stuff into a prettier container before you put it in the refrigerator, don't! It probably isn't worth the trouble.

• **Smelly Kitchens in General:** If you've got 1) company coming and 2) an orange and some cloves handy, poke as many cloves as you can into the unpeeled orange and set it on a plate. The clovey orange will give your kitchen a tantalizing scent that will probably last longer than your guests' visit.

AROUND THE HOUSE

• **Wax-Encrusted Candleholders:** You've got two choices with this one: Start by placing the candleholders under hot running water to melt off the wax. If that doesn't work, put the candleholder in the freezer and leave it there for at least two hours. The frozen, hardened wax will be much easier to remove.

• **Ink Stains in the Carpet:** Spray the stain with alcohol-based hair spray. (Sounds risky, but experts swear by it.) While it's drying, soak a clean cloth in a solution of three parts water to one part white vinegar. (Don't even *think* of using red-wine vinegar!) When the hair spray is dry, wring out the cloth and use it to wipe up the ink. (This method also works on fabrics and clothing, too).

• **Rocking Chair Marks on Wooden Floors:** The next time you're cleaning or polishing your floors, turn your rocker on its side and apply furniture polish to the parts of the rocker that contact the floor when the chair is in motion.

• **Dog-doo on the Carpet:** Clean up as much as the mess as you can with paper towels, then spray the area with shaving cream and let sit for 5–10 minutes before wiping up with an old sponge. Next, pour some club soda on the soiled area, let it fizz, then mop it up. Dab the area with a sponge rinsed in cold water; repeat if necessary.

• **Cleaning Ashes From the Fireplace:** Ashes can be a surprisingly effective fireplace-glass cleaner. If you have glass screens or doors on the fireplace, before you remove the ashes, dip a damp cloth in them and use the cloth to wipe down the glass. Then wipe off the glass with a *clean* damp cloth. Then use a spritzer bottle filled with clean water to spray down the rest of the ashes before you shovel them out of the fireplace—this will help keep the dust down during this dirty task.

- **Algae in Gravity-Fed Water Dishes:** Do you have one of those pet water dishes that holds several days' worth of water in an upright container that flows into a dish? If you use it outside, algae can grow inside it. The next time you change the water, dump a handful of uncooked rice into the vessel and fill it about 1/3 full with water. Using the palm of your hand to seal the vessel, shake it vigorously up and down. The grains of rice will scour the algae off the inside of the container. When you're finished, empty out the water and rice and refill with clean, fresh water. Your pet will thank you.
- **Ornate, Carved Wooden Furniture That Collects a Lot of Dust:** Forget ordinary dust cloths—they don't work fast enough. Take a brand new paintbrush with soft bristles, spray it with dust-collecting spray and brush the dust away. Brushing won't take nearly as long as dusting.
- **Make Wooden Tabletops Shine:** Why settle for anything less than a mirror finish? Pick up one of those electric shoe-polish buffers and use it instead of an ordinary rag the next time you're applying furniture polish to the table.

*　　*　　*

HOLY JOKE

An elderly woman had just returned home from church and found a burglar in her home. "Stop! Acts 2:38!" she yelled at him. The burglar stopped in his tracks and sat down, allowing the woman to call the police. When the cops arrived to collect the man, one of the officers asked the burglar, "Why did you just stand there? All the old lady did was yell a scripture at you." "Scripture?" replied the burglar. "She said she had an axe and two .38s!"

Count 'em yourself: Your heart beats approximately 4,000 times an hour.

REALITY BITES

We offer these dumb and bizarre quotes from reality TV shows to save you the trouble of having to watch them yourself. You're welcome.

"I've got eyes and ears in the back of my head."

—Jo, *The Apprentice 2 (U.K.)*

"The monkfish wasn't technically raw because only a little part of it was raw."

—Matt, *Hell's Kitchen*

"Simon gave me advice—he always refers to a fortune cookie and says the moth who finds the melon…finds the cornflake always finds the melon, and one of you didn't pick the right fortune."

—Paula Abdul, *American Idol*

"Is there chicken in chick peas?"

—Helen, *Celebrity Big Brother 2 (U.K.)*

"I'm just trying to take in everything you've done, and then pepper it with a little Stevie B."

—Stephen Baldwin, *Celebrity Apprentice*

"I'm not willing to alienate Giselle, because she's the only one with a straightening iron."

—Elyse, *America's Next Top Model*

"Shut up! I really mean that, from the bottom of my heart."

—Chef Ramsay, *Hell's Kitchen*

"I think I'm pretty smart. My IQ's probably about…500!"

—Lauren, *Beauty and the Geek*

"I'm so angry, I'm fuming! I'm fumigating!"

—Nadia, *Celebrity Big Brother*

"I backstabbed and lied a lot, but I feel like I've accomplished so much, and I'm so proud."

—Todd, winner of *Survivor: China*

The word "fruit" is derived from the Latin word for "enjoy."

GOVERN-MENTAL

Five-time presidential candidate Eugene McCarthy said, "The only thing that saves us from the bureaucracy is inefficiency. An efficient bureaucracy is the greatest threat to liberty." (Looks like our liberty is safe.)

SECRET TREASURE

Did you receive a piece of junk mail in the spring of 2008, addressed to "Resident" and labeled "National Household Travel Survey"? Don't remember? Then you probably threw it away, as did thousands of others who received the mailer from the Department of Transportation requesting that you take part in a survey about your travel habits. If you'd opened the mailer, you would've found a crisp $5 bill inside (a "token of appreciation"). Had the DOT sent out *checks* for $5, they could have tracked how many people cashed them and cancelled all the checks that weren't cashed. But because they sent out cash, there was no way to trace how many people got the money...or how many $5 bills ended up in the trash.

GATOR AID

According to the book *Great Government Goofs*, compiled by Leland Gregory, "Members of the Georgia State Game Commission were fiercely debating the pros and cons of regulating 'alligator rides' when one alert member noticed a typographical error on the agenda—the commission was actually supposed to be discussing whether or not they should regulate 'alligator hides.'"

KICKED THE BUCKET

From 1999 to 2005, the USDA awarded more than $1 billion to farmers who were no longer living. Farm families are eligible to receive money for two years after the head of the household dies in an effort to help them get back on their feet. After an investigation, however, the Government Accountability Office discovered that the USDA has no steps in place to *stop* the payments—families continue receiving payments until an heir of the deceased farmer informs the USDA to stop. According to the GAO's findings, few of the dead farmers' families have contacted the USDA...so most continue receiving checks to this day.

Tougher than you are: Bacteria can live in temperatures as extreme as 176°F and –4°F.

GOING POSTAL

As part of the 2008 economic stimulus package, the IRS decided to inform citizens that their checks were coming, so they sent out letters to 130 million taxpayers. Cost of sending the letters: $42 million. A few weeks later the IRS spent that amount again to send the real checks.

ME ME ME!

In 2007 Rep. Charlie Rangel (D-NY) requested funds for three construction projects at City College of New York. They include the "Charles B. Rangel Center for Public Service," the "Rangel Conference Center," and the "Charles Rangel Library." Cost to taxpayers: $2 million. When freshman Congressman John Campbell (R-CA) railed against the politician for naming buildings after himself while still in office, Rangel, who's been in Congress since 1971, responded, "I would have a problem if you did it, because I don't think that you've been around long enough to inspire a building." The library, incidentally, will only display memorabilia that pertains to Rangel. According to a CBS news report, "It's kind of like a presidential library, but without a president."

NAMING WRONGS

As president, Ronald Reagan preached smaller government and less spending. So why not name one of the biggest and most expensive projects in government history after him? The Ronald Reagan Building and International Trade Center opened in Washington, D.C., in 1998, and it's the largest federal building in the District. (The only larger federal building is the Pentagon, located in Virginia). And at the time, the Ronald Reagan Building boasted the heftiest price tag for a single structure in U.S. government history: $768 million. (Another ironic naming fact: In 1981 the nation's air traffic controllers went on strike—and President Reagan fired them all. In 1998 National Airport in Washington was renamed...Ronald Reagan National Airport.)

LONG-DISTANCE TAXI SERVICE

In 2008 an accused thief named Mark Bailey was being arraigned in Northampton, England. After a brief hearing, the judge ordered that Bailey be sent to the magistrate's courtroom—located in a building across the street—to plead his case. One problem: The prisoner transport van wasn't available (it had "gone on to do other things"). So police officers offered to escort Bailey to the courthouse, about 200 yards away, on foot. Court officials said that the public walk would "violate Bailey's human rights," so they were forced to call for another van…the closest one being in Cambridge, nearly 60 *miles away*. Two and a half hours later, the van showed up, and Bailey took the 30-second trip to the courthouse. The van then drove the 60 miles back to Cambridge. "I've never heard such nonsense," said Conservative MP Brian Binley. "Why we should have to suffer such ludicrous incompetence, and pay for it, is beyond me."

THE TIP OF THE ICE CUBE

In the aftermath of Hurricane Katrina in 2005, the Federal Emergency Management Agency (FEMA) purchased 112,000 tons of ice for $24 million. Unfortunately, they were unable to distribute all of it to those in need, so they stored the unused ice in cold warehouses. Two years later, the ice was still in storage—and the cost to keep it cold all that time totaled more than $11 million, nearly half of what it cost to purchase. Even more embarrassing, it was announced that because FEMA didn't know the "shelf life" for ice, the stockpile couldn't be reused and had to be melted. The cost of the melting operation: another $3.4 million. (FEMA subsequently announced that they are no longer in the business of buying and storing ice for disasters.)

*   *   *

HIGHEST-PAID ATHLETES, BY SPORT (2007)

Golf: Tiger Woods, $127.9 million

Basketball: LeBron James, $40.5 million

Boxing: Floyd Mayweather, $40.3 million

Baseball: Alex Rodriguez, $35 million

Football: Peyton Manning, $30.5 million

NASCAR: Dale Earnhardt, Jr., $27.2 million

…in his *Peanuts* comic strip each August 5th. (She's his daughter.)

WHAT A WAY TO GO

You never know when you're about to breathe your last. Here are some strange tales of folks who died in bizarre ways.

I'VE GOT A LOT OF LIVER TO DO

The pufferfish, or *fugu*, is a well-known ingredient in Japanese sushi. But trained chefs must be very careful to cut it just right so as not to serve the liver, which is full of deadly neurotoxins. In 1975 Mitsugoro Bando VIII, one of Japan's most famous kabuki actors and a man officially designated as one of Japan's "living national treasures," went to a sushi bar with friends and demanded to be served *four* whole fugu livers, which he promptly ate, believing himself immune to the poison. He wasn't (he died), and the sushi chef who knowingly served poison to a living national treasure wasn't immune to losing his restaurant license, either.

IT HAPPENS EVERY FALL

Garry Hoy was a lawyer who had an office in the Dominion Centre, an upscale, state-of-the-art office complex in Toronto. In 1993 Hoy set out to impress some visiting law students by throwing himself with great force against the "unbreakable" windows of his 24-floor office, a trick he'd performed repeatedly at office parties and after-hours drinking sessions in the past. On this occasion he demonstrated the stunt twice: The first attempt went off without a hitch, and it was during was the second attempt that Hoy learned the hard way that "unbreakable" does not necessarily mean "the pane of glass won't pop out of its frame if you throw yourself against it with great force." Hoy, who until that moment was considered to be one of the "best and brightest" members of his firm, was 38.

GOING BY THE BOOK (CASE)

In 2006 Mariesa Weber of St. Petersburg, Florida, was reported missing by her family, who feared she'd been kidnapped from the house they shared. As it turned out, she'd never even left the house. Two weeks after she disappeared, Weber's sister spotted a foot sticking out from behind a bookcase in Mariesa's bedroom,

About 75,600,000 pumpkin pies are baked each winter holiday season in the United States.

which somehow had gone unnoticed the entire two weeks. (And that funny smell coming from the bedroom? The family attributed it to rats.) Authorities speculate Weber was standing on a dresser next to the bookcase to adjust a TV plug when she fell behind the bookcase and died.

BAAAAAD LUCK

Betty Stobbs operated a sheep farm in Durham, England. She didn't have a tractor, so to feed her sheep she carried bales of hay on the back of her all-terrain vehicle. One day in 1999, the hungry flock was so excited to see her (or the food) that they charged, shoving Stobbs and her ATV off a 100' cliff.

WATER WAY TO GO

After the 1985 summer season, the New Orleans Recreation Department threw a party for the city's lifeguards to celebrate the fact that there had been no deaths at any of the city's public swimming pools all summer. More than 100 lifeguards attended the pool party, and it was only when the party was winding down that someone noticed the body of 31-year-old Jerome Moody at the bottom of the pool. Somehow he'd managed to drown without being noticed either by the scores of lifeguards who were in the pool with him, or by the four lifeguards who were on duty at the time.

GAME OVER

Former NFL football coach George Allen came out of retirement to coach Long Beach State, and in 1990 he led the team to a season-ending victory over rival Las Vegas at the end of the 1990 season. In keeping with football tradition, Allen's players dumped a cooler of ice water on him. ("We couldn't afford Gatorade," the 72-year-old Allen joked after the incident.) For more than an hour after the game, Allen braved low temperatures and gusting winds in his soaking-wet clothes to talk with reporters; then he jumped on the team bus and rode all the way back to Long Beach without changing out of them. Big mistake: Allen's health deteriorated rapidly in the days that followed; he contracted pneumonia and died of heart failure only a month after the game.

First Internet character balloon in the Macy's Thanksgiving Day parade: Jeeves (from Askjeeves.com).

STEERED WRONG

The satellite navigation tool known as Global Positioning System, or GPS, is handy for helping lost drivers find their destinations. Just don't rely on your GPS too much...or you'll end up like these folks.

• In 2008 a bus carrying high school students became wedged under a bridge in Seattle, Washington. The driver had been looking at his GPS display instead of the road and missed the big, yellow sign that read "CLEARANCE 9 FEET." (The bus was 11'9".)

• A Czech truck driver followed his GPS and it led him deep into a hedgerow (a narrow alley of trees) in rural England. After the truck got wedged between two trees, the driver left it there for three days because he "didn't want to pay for a costly weekend rescue."

• A California man named Bo Bai got lost in his rental car in Bedford Hills, New York, in 2008. His GPS ordered him to take the next right, so he did...onto train tracks...as a commuter train was speeding toward him. Bai, a computer technician, tried to back out but his tires were stuck. So he jumped out of the car and started waving for the train to stop. It didn't. The collision totaled the car and delayed 10,000 New York-area travelers.

• In England in 2008, a cab driver—dutifully following his GPS—ignored detour signs and drove directly into a river.

• In 2004 a 70-year-old French driver on an 80-mph highway missed the exit for his hotel. When the GPS ordered him to "make a U-Turn immediately," he did...causing a multi-car accident that backed up traffic for hours.

• Edna Wickens lives on a narrow alley in Kent, England. Her house had never been hit by a truck...until truck drivers started using GPS. Since then, her house has been bumped and scraped numerous times, causing more than £20,000 ($37,000) in damage. In fact, the number of GPS-related mishaps has become so high in England—around 30,000—that in 2008 new signs were erected on some roads, reading: "Do Not Follow GPS Very Narrow Road." (Now, whether the truck drivers will actually *see* the signs...)

A lot of hot dogs: More than 50,000,000 people go to Major League baseball games each year.

THE LAST DOUBLE EAGLE, PART I

Think coin collecting is boring? Well, here's the story of the rarest, most valuable coin in American history, a story that takes us through back-alley coin-dealing shops to the royal palace of Egypt and the World Trade Center.

TO COIN A COIN

Ever wonder what happened to the gold that was mined in the California gold rush? Much of it was purchased by the United States government. Following one particularly massive purchase of gold ore in 1850, the U.S. Mint in Philadelphia began production of $20 gold coins. Earlier $10 coins had eagles on them, so because they were twice the value, the new $20 coins were called "Double Eagles." (The name didn't mean the coin has eagles on both sides; there was an eagle on the back and a profile of Lady Liberty on the front.)

These $20 Double Eagles were produced until 1907, when President Theodore Roosevelt commissioned sculptor Augustus St. Gaudens to redesign all the nation's coins. One side of St. Gaudens' new Double Eagle depicted a full-length image of Lady Liberty surrounded by rays of light, holding an olive branch in one hand and a torch in the other. The other side featured a bald eagle soaring across a setting sun. Coin collectors cite the St. Gaudens Double Eagle as one of the most beautiful coins ever made.

THE GOLDEN AGE COMES TO AN END

In 1932, at the height of the Great Depression, Franklin Roosevelt was elected president. As one of his first acts upon taking office in March 1933, Roosevelt moved quickly to protect the U.S. economy. One of his measures was to retain government control over the circulation of gold by banning its export, ending the production of gold coins, and making it illegal for regular citizens to own gold coins or gold bullion. (They could exchange their gold for currency.)

A total of 445,500 Double Eagles were produced in early 1933, just a few days before Roosevelt's order to stop issuing gold coins came down. Here's what happened to them.

• 445,034 were sealed in a vault at the Philadelphia Mint.

• 466 were sent away for testing, and 437 came back to the Mint (29 were destroyed in the testing).

• Those 437 were locked in a safe in the office of the Mint cashier, which could be opened only with two keys, both of which were in the possession of the cashier, George McCann.

• Two of the 437 were sent to the American coins collection at the Smithsonian Institute in Washington, D.C. Those were the only two 1933 gold Double Eagles ever to leave the Mint.

• After Roosevelt's order, the 445,034 in the vault and the 435 remaining in the cashier's safe were, according to Mint records, melted back down into gold bullion in March 1937.

MINT CONDITION

In the 1930s, Philadelphia was a major gold-trading center. An entire district around the Mint was dedicated to gold, including the stores and offices of jewelers, coin dealers, and scrap gold merchants. One of the most prominent gold men was a jeweler named Israel Switt. He had lots of friends and business associates who worked at the Mint, including the cashier, George McCann. And Switt and McCann had something in common: Both men had criminal records. In 1934 Switt had been arrested for trying to sell gold bullion. McCann was arrested (and fired from his job at the Mint) for trying to help steal $10,000 in scrap gold.

But their biggest crime would go undetected for years. Sometime in the early 1930s, McCann stole a handful of 1933 gold Double Eagle coins. It was relatively easy, since he had access to the safe where they were kept. A few days before they were scheduled to be melted down, he smuggled some out and sold them to Switt. Switt, in turn, sold five of the coins to a dealer named James MacAllister in 1937. Price: Three for $300 each and two for $350 each. (In today's dollars, that's about $4,400 and $5,100, respectively.) Switt sold four more Double Eagles to other coin dealers, who resold them to private collectors.

Officials at the U.S. Mint had no idea that any of the coins were missing—they thought all 1933 Double Eagles had been destroyed.

ILLEGAL EAGLE

One of Switt's coins was quietly sold to a Fort Worth, Texas, coin dealer named B. Max Mehl. In 1944 Mehl sold the coin to a very high-profile buyer: King Farouk of Egypt. Farouk liked to collect very expensive things, including rare stamps, jewels, art, Faberge eggs, and, especially, gold coins, of which he possessed more than 8,500. Despite the fact that he frequently dipped into Egypt's treasury to buy such collectibles for himself, Farouk liked to keep his transactions legal. So when he found a 1933 Double Eagle in the United States, Farouk sent a delegation to Forth Worth to obtain the coin from Mehl, and then, in accordance with United States law, applied to the Treasury Department for an export license for the Double Eagle. Unaware that it was an incredibly rare, incredibly valuable, and incredibly *illegal* coin, a low-level bureaucrat in the Treasury approved the export license on February 29, 1944. The coin returned with the delegation to King Farouk in Egypt.

A FEDERAL CASE

Just a few days later, in early March, *New York Herald Tribune* stamps and coins columnist Ernest Kehr was writing an article on the sale of a collection by Stack's, a rare-coin house in New York. The last item listed in the auction: a 1933 Double Eagle. "Excessively rare," read the listing, "the first one that ever came up in any public auction." To find out just *how* rare, Kehr wrote to a friend who would know: the acting director of the U.S. Mint, Leland Howard. Howard did some digging and found out how rare the 1933 Double Eagle was: It was so rare that none were technically supposed to exist outside of the Smithsonian.

Howard immediately notified the Secret Service, which, like the Mint, is a branch of the Treasury Department, and let them know that at least one 1933 Double Eagle coin was being illegally circulated. The Secret Service seized the coin from the Stack's auction, and the agent in charge of the investigation, Harry Strang, quickly assembled a team of agents to look into the possibility of there being more Double Eagles in circulation, and to get them back. (Why did the government want the coins back? It was a security issue—it was the middle of World War II, and the theft of coins pointed out holes in United States government security.)

Amphibians see no color; they perceive only black and white.

Strang started poking around both legitimate and underground coin dealing circles, and that quickly led him to jeweler Israel Switt and former Mint cashier George McCann. After discovering the gold-related criminal records of both men, Strang concluded that McCann must have swiped multiple 1933 Double Eagles from the vault in his office and passed them on to Switt. Strang presented his case to the Department of Justice, expecting to get arrest warrants. But Strang couldn't arrest either man. Why? Eleven years had passed since the theft, and the statute of limitations on the crime had expired.

LOST AND FOUND

Strang and his field agents concluded that there were a total of nine stolen 1933 Double Eagles in circulation. By the end of 1945, the Secret Service had found and seized three; four more were turned in voluntarily. That left two: One was still unaccounted for, and the other was in the possession of King Farouk of Egypt.

Strang lobbied his bosses to try and get the Egyptian coin back to the United States, but the Treasury's lawyers decided that, despite the tremendous effort to recover all the other Double Eagles, Farouk owning one really didn't "present a problem." In other words, trying to get back a coin from a sovereign head of a foreign country was a potential diplomatic nightmare and could create an international incident, an especially unsavory scenario in the middle of World War II. (In 1949—after the war was over—the Treasury Department changed its position and asked the State Department to help them get the coin back via diplomatic channels. The State Department refused, calling the idea "politically inadvisable.")

NUMBER NINE DREAM

The owner of the ninth coin, a collector named L. G. Barnard, came forward in late 1945. He had a Double Eagle...but he refused to give it up. He bought the coin legally from a reputable dealer, he said, and neither he nor that dealer had known it was stolen. So what did the government do? They sued Barnard for it. And they won: In 1947 a federal judge ruled that the Double Eagle was still the property of the government because it had left the Mint via theft. Later that year, with possession of eight Double Eagles, the Treasury Department melted them down.

TWO TO GO

That was about the end of the story—eight Double Eagles had been located, seized, and safely destroyed, and the last one was never going to leave King Farouk's palace. Except that Strang's investigation team had made a mistake: Israel Switt had stolen and resold *10* Double Eagles, not 9. The owner of the 10th coin, a collector named Louis Eliasberg, came forward out of the blue in 1952—three years after the case had been closed—and surrendered the coin to the Treasury Department. It was immediately melted down.

But the Double Eagle saga still wasn't over. In 1952 the Egyptian army staged a coup, took over the country, and deposed King Farouk (due in some part due to his frequent raiding of the treasury to buy himself expensive trinkets). Farouk had to leave behind many of his most valuable possessions, and so in 1954 the Egyptian government, under former general Gamal-Abdel Nasser, announced that King Farouk's collection of more than 8,500 gold coins would be sold at auction. The event would be handled by the New York office of Sotheby's, who predicted the auction would "rival the great sales of the past and will take its place in the bibliography of numismatics."

LOT 185

Officials at the Treasury Department, who had been keeping tabs on all high-end coin auctions since the sudden surrender of the Eliasberg Double Eagle, obtained a catalog for the Farouk auction. Sure enough, one lot interested them: lot 185—it consisted solely of a 1933 Double Eagle. The Treasury contacted the Egyptian government and requested that lot 185 be removed from the auction and immediately returned to the United States. Egyptian officials (and Sotheby's) complied, and the coin was not included in the nine-day auction. That's because the coin, the only remaining 1933 Double Eagle at large, had disappeared.

Did the 1933 Double Eagle ever resurface? To find out, turn to Part II of the story on page 301.

LIKE, TOTALLY '80s SLOGANS!

You probably remember these 1980s catchphrases and slogans because at the time, they were inescapable on T-shirts, TV, and the radio. But do you know where they came from?

Slogan: "Choose Life"
Story: In 1983 fashion designer Katharine Hamnett created a line of political protest T-shirts, all of them white with simple slogans printed in huge black letters: "Worldwide Nuclear Ban Now," "Preserve the Rainforests," "Save the Whales," "Save the World," and the best seller, "Choose Life." The phrase wasn't anti-abortion or anti-capital punishment. Inspired by the Buddhist principle that all life is sacred, Hamnett specifically meant the shirts to protest nuclear proliferation. More than 100,000 "Choose Life" shirts sold in 1984, helped immensely by George Michael when he wore one in the Wham! video for "Wake Me Up Before You Go-Go."

Slogan: "Frankie Say Relax"
Story: In late 1984, "Relax," the debut single by the English pop group Frankie Goes to Hollywood, began climbing the British and American record charts. To market the band and the song, Paul Morley of ZTT, the group's record label, cashed in on the "Choose Life" T-shirt fad by printing "Frankie Say Relax" in large black letters on white T-shirts. Morley created other "Frankie" shirts, such as "Frankie Say Arm the Unemployed" and "Frankie Say War." But the "Relax" shirts were the most popular, helping the song reach #1 in England and the top 10 in the United States. Sales figures are unknown, but Morley claims that ZTT actually made more money off of the shirts than it did from the group's music.

Slogan: "Just Say No"
Story: During a visit to an Oakland elementary school in 1982, a student asked First Lady Nancy Reagan what to do if offered drugs. Reagan's reply: "Just say no." That event inspired the First Lady to

make youth drug prevention her signature cause. With help from a $1 billion federal grant, more than 1,700 schools around the United States formed "Just Say No" clubs. Reagan gave hundreds of speeches, appeared at the 1983 Super Bowl, helped La Toya Jackson record a "Just Say No" theme song, and even guest-starred on a 1983 episode of *Diff'rent Strokes*, all to help kids learn that to reject drugs all they had to do was say "no." Critics said it was overly simplistic; 1960s hippie icon Abbie Hoffman called it "the equivalent of telling manic depressives to 'just cheer up.'" But it may have done some good: according to the National Institutes of Health, teenage drug use in the mid-1980s declined.

Slogan: "Just Do It"
Story: In 1988 Dan Wieden of the Wieden+Kennedy advertising agency was trying to come up with a slogan for the Nike shoe company. One day, while expressing his genuine admiration for the can-do attitude of the Nike team, Wieden said, "You Nike guys, you just do it." He immediately realized that he'd come up with the slogan—if you want to play a sport, just go out and do it. Wieden+Kennedy designed 12 proactively themed commercials for Nike, including the "Bo knows" ads, featuring sports star Bo Jackson ("Bo knows hockey," "Bo knows bicycle racing"). Nike credits the ads with allowing it to reclaim the #1 position in the athletic shoe market from Reebok.

Slogan: "Take a Bite out of Crime"
Story: In 1980 the nonprofit National Crime Prevention Council hired ad agency Saatchi & Saatchi to create a kid-friendly mascot and slogan. Copywriter John Keil considered a lion who "roars at crime" and an elephant who "stomps out crime" but finally opted for a dog who "takes a bite out of crime." Inspired by TV's Columbo, artists drew the dog as a grizzled gumshoe in a trench coat. The character appeared in public service announcements (Keil provided the voice), urging kids to report *any* crime they witnessed, from bullying to drug dealing. The dog wasn't named until a 1982 contest—a New Orleans police officer suggested McGruff the Crime Dog (runner-up: Sherlock Bones). The NCPC says that 75 percent of American children today recognize and trust McGruff... and know the slogan.

...Twinkies, and a CD of the human genome.

A BRIEF LIFE

In 2008 Salon *magazine asked its readers to sum up their lives (or their philosophy of life) in six words or less. Here are some of our favorites.*

Quite often confused; was never satisfied.

Frankly, it is all about me.

Failure was apparently an option here.

I chased him, he caught me.

The greatest underachiever in the world.

Possibility is always better than actuality.

Haven't lived up to my potential.

Jump right in and play.

Don't even try to plan it.

I wanted to be a contender.

Restless, fearful, hopeless, hopeful, joyful, thankful.

Just kept doing the next thing.

Found my path. Walked it fearlessly.

Crawl, step, run, step, crawl, lay.

Didn't do what I should have.

It makes more sense looking back.

Child, adult, wife, mom, widow, me.

Half over but feels like new.

Too much hair, then not enough.

Learned it, used it, forgot it.

Skipped the present pursuing the future.

Not as bad as I expected.

Shout, give; repeat as necessary.

Not what I expected but fun.

Questioned and answered, helped when possible.

Astonished I've made it this far.

Too young for life's great questions.

It's really none of your business.

Never do silly things like this.

Um...what was the question again?

There are 34 "Reindeer" place names in the U.S. Most of them are in Alaska.

COCKTAIL PARTY

Cocktails have a certain glamour—they show up all the time in movies and TV shows and have become part of American culture. But if you're like us, you've probably wondered what's in them and where they came from. Here are the (often murky) origins of a few famous ones.

DRINK: Long Island Ice Tea
HOW IT'S MADE: Stir together a mixture of clear spirits (vodka, gin, light rum, and tequila). Then add triple sec, a splash of sour mix, and a splash of cola, pour it all over ice in a tall glass, and garnish with a lemon slice.
HISTORY: Food writer John Mariani quotes a bartender from the Oak Beach Inn in Long Island, New York, who said he was "fooling around with some drinks" in 1976, put this combo together, and "the thing tasted just like iced tea." Another story is that the drink was invented during Prohibition by a moonshiner in an area of Tennessee called Long Island, so that if the Feds raided him it would look as if his customers were drinking iced tea. A third story: Long Island housewives in the 1950s mixed together a little from each bottle in the liquor cabinet (presumably so that no one would notice any was missing), and added cola to make it look like iced tea.

DRINK: Daiquiri
HOW IT'S MADE: The purist's daiquiri is a combination of white rum, lime juice, and sugar, poured over ice, then strained into a chilled glass. The other kind of daiquiri—the slushy frozen variety—is made in a blender with the same ingredients plus fruit (peaches, bananas, or strawberries), retaining the ice.
HISTORY: After the Spanish-American War (1898), many American engineers lived in the Cuban town of Daiquirí, where they ran the local mines. It was their habit to go to the Venus Hotel to relax on weekends, and Chief Engineer Jennings Cox is credited with "inventing" the daiquiri there. Of course, Cubans had been mixing rum, lime, and sugar for a very long time, but it wasn't until Cox named the cocktail and Admiral Lucius Johnson, a navy medical officer, took it back to the Army and Navy Club

If you're average, you'll flex your finger joints 25 million times during your lifetime.

in Washington, D.C., in 1909, that it gained a following in the United States. F. Scott Fitzgerald mentions the drink in his 1920 novel *This Side of Paradise*, and it's said that the daiquiri was one of Ernest Hemingway's preferred drinks. (The frozen daiquiri is rumored to have been developed much later, at La Florida Bar in Havana, a favorite hangout of Americans.) During World War II, when wartime rationing made it hard to get other spirits, rum from Central and South America was still plentiful, and the daiquiri became very popular. Later, the daiquiri was President John F. Kennedy's favorite drink, an odd fact considering that it originated in Cuba—and Cuba was the site of the ill-fated Bay of Pigs invasion, a low point in the Kennedy administration. (Kennedy also loved Cuban cigars.)

DRINK: Harvey Wallbanger

HOW IT'S MADE: Mix together vodka, orange juice, and Galliano—an Italian liqueur with flavors of vanilla and anise. A Hillary Wallbanger substitutes white wine for the vodka.

HISTORY: The story goes that after losing a big surfing contest in the late 1950s, a surfer named Tom Harvey went to Duke's Blackwatch Bar (or possibly Pancho's Bar—stories vary) in Manhattan Beach, California, and slugged down a few Galliano-spiked screwdrivers. He tried to walk a straight line to the door, but the walls kept getting in his way, earning him the nickname "Harvey the Wallbanger"—and the cocktail he drank that night got the same name. A less-romantic theory is that the Galliano company launched an ad campaign featuring a clumsy cartoon character called Harvey, and the drink got its name from him. The Wallbanger was popular in the 1970s, but it's gone out of favor since then.

DRINK: Manhattan

HOW IT'S MADE: This classic drink begins with a base of rye, blended whiskey, or bourbon. Then add sweet vermouth and a dash of bitters, stir briefly with ice, immediately strain it all into a lowball glass, and garnish with a cherry. A Manhattan made with scotch is called a Rob Roy.

HISTORY: Again, there's more than one possible origin story. Some believe it was first served in New York City's Manhattan

The second and third Academy Awards ceremonies were both held in 1930.

Club at an 1874 banquet given by Lady Randolph Churchill (Winston Churchill's mother) to celebrate the election of Samuel Tilden as New York's governor. But other historians claim that the Manhattan Club bartender invented it for Supreme Court Justice Charles Henry Truax in 1890, when the judge's doctor ordered him to stop drinking martinis.

DRINK: Tom Collins

HOW IT'S MADE: Combine dry gin, sugar, lemon juice, club soda, a lemon or orange slice, and a cherry in an extra-tall glass that's now known generically as a Collins glass. A Ron Collins substitutes rum for gin (*ron* is the Spanish word for rum); a José Collins is made with tequila.

HISTORY: The drink, a variation on the gin fizz, is said to date back to the mid-19th century. It was invented either by a bartender named Tom Collins who worked at the Whitehouse Bar in New York City, or by a headwaiter named *John* Collins who worked at a London hotel. In fact, some experts say it was originally known as a "John Collins," and the name changed when bars started making it with a sweetened gin called Old Tom. Later, during the shortages of World War II, some soldiers were forced to make the drink with aftershave because they couldn't get gin... and called it an Aqua Velva Collins.

DRINK: Cosmopolitan

HOW IT'S MADE: Stir together vodka, triple sec, lime juice, and cranberry juice, and serve in a martini glass with a garnish of lime wedge.

HISTORY: The "Cosmo" had already been fairly popular for two decades when it made its first appearance on *Sex and the City* on July 18, 1999. (Samantha orders one at a wedding reception.) That skyrocketed the Cosmopolitan to fame. Who invented it? No one's quite sure—it may have come from Provincetown, Massachusetts, or San Francisco in the 1970s. But wherever it came from, New Yorkers soon started drinking them, and the rest of the country followed suit. Cosmos are sweet, but they can pack a punch, which is why they're sometimes called "pink kamikazes" or "stealth martinis."

The Massachusetts state horse is the Morgan. State dessert: Boston cream pie.

OL' JAY'S BRAINTEASERS

Uh-oh. Looks like Jay has written the BRI team into a another batch of puzzles. Let's see how we do. Answers are on page 539.

1. HUNGRY BOOKWORM

Kait is the newest member of the BRI team. To test out whether we were really as smart as she's heard (we're not), she asked us a math question that even her 11-year-old son, C. J., answered correctly: "Three *Bathroom Readers* are stacked vertically next to each other on a bookshelf, with their spines facing out. The covers of the books each measure 1/8". The pages of each book measure 2". If the bookworm starts eating at page one of the book on the left, then eats through the books in a straight line until he gets to the last page of the book on the right, how many inches of book will he have eaten?"

2. THE 5TH CONDITION

Uncle John strolled into the office and announced, "Civics quiz, everybody!" After we whined a bit, he asked a question that sounded tough, but he assured us it was not. "According to the U.S. Constitution," he said, "five conditions must be met in order for a candidate to become president. He or she must: 1) be born in the United States, 2) be 35 years old or more, 3) be an American citizen, and 4) have resided in the U.S. for the last 14 years. What's the fifth condition? You may think you don't know it, but you do."

3. SURROUNDED

Julia is riding a horse. Directly to her left is a hippo traveling at the same speed. In front of her is an elephant, also traveling at the same speed. Following behind her—at the same speed—is a lion. And to her right is a ledge. How will Julia make it to safety?

4. BUILDER BLUNDER

JoAnn, Melinda, and Monica each purchased a new home in

Porcelain Estates, an exclusive community consisting of nine shiny houses. But the builders forgot to add an important part to the houses, forcing the three new homeowners to buy the part at the hardware store. One thousand would have cost $4.00. Fifty would have cost $2.00. But JoAnn, Melinda, and Monica needed only one each and paid a combined total of $3.00. What did the builders forget to add?

5. THE RUNAROUND

Two-eff Jeff was sitting in a chair in the middle of the room. One-eff Jef walked up and said, "I'll bet you a dollar that before I run around your chair three times, you'll get up. And I promise I won't push you or throw things at you. When you get up, it will be by choice." Two-eff Jeff took the bet, thinking he'd make an easy dollar. But it was soon obvious that One-eff Jef had won. Why?

6. A MOTHER'S GIFT

Amy challenged us with this classic riddle:

Black as night I'll always be,
Until my mother smothers me.
Then clear as ice I will become
In the rough. Thank you, Mum!
What am I?

7. FEELING FLAT

Thom drove all the way from Crappo, Maryland, to Flushing, New York, without realizing his car had a flat tire, but arrived safely with four fully inflated tires. How?

8. COFFEE DELIVERY!

Trying to figure out the answers to these questions tired us out, but then along came Angie with a large pot of freshly brewed coffee. Yay! "I can give you one gallon," she said. "But you'll have to measure it out yourselves." Then she handed us a three-gallon bucket and a five-gallon bucket. As we were sitting there dumfounded, Maggie told us not to worry—she'd do it. How?

...wore them to protect against reporters' flashbulbs.

BASED ON A "TRUE" STORY

While telling a true story, Hollywood often strays from the truth, embellishing some facts while omitting others. Here are some inconsistencies we found in major motion pictures.

Movie: *The Pursuit of Happyness* (2006)
Reel Story: Homeless father Chris Gardner (played by Will Smith) is trying to turn his life around. He wows an employee of a stockbrokerage by solving a Rubik's Cube in a few seconds, earning a place in the company's prestigious training program. As he goes through the program, Gardner and his nine-year-old son sleep in churches and the subway. After he nearly misses his big final interview because of too many outstanding parking tickets, Gardner finally lands the stockbroker job.
Real Story: Gardner is a real person and he was indeed homeless while in the training program, but he never had his son with him—he didn't even know where the boy was (he was with his mother). The Rubik's Cube incident was pure Hollywood invention, and while Gardner actually was arrested right before his final interview, it wasn't for parking tickets. It was for spousal abuse.

Movie: *Good Morning, Vietnam* (1987)
Reel Story: Deejay Adrian Cronauer (Robin Williams) is drafted into the Army and sent to serve in Vietnam. He is put to work as a disc jockey on Armed Forces Radio, where he delivers long antiwar and antiestablishment (but funny) rants in between songs, ultimately leading to a dishonorable discharge.
Real Story: Only the basics of Cronauer's story were used—he was a deejay sent to Vietnam, where he worked as a deejay. The zany, antiwar diatribes were added by screenwriters to suit the comic style of Robin Williams. Cronauer says he never performed any humorous or political monologues because 1) it would have gotten him court-martialed, and 2) he wasn't antiwar. He was never kicked out of the Army—he merely returned home to Pennsylvania when his tour of duty in Vietnam ended. Cronauer calls himself a life-

How about you? One in every 10 people in the world lives on an island.

long Republican and he even served on President Bush's 2004 reelection campaign.

Movie: *Mask* (1985)

Reel Story: Rocky Dennis (Eric Stoltz) is a teenager with a fatal genetic disorder called *craniodiaphyseal dysplasia.* Calcium buildup in his skull makes his head twice the normal size and causes extreme facial disfigurement. Toward the end of the movie, Dennis gets a job as a counselor at a camp for the blind. He falls in love with a blind girl (Laura Dern) and, having experienced love, dies peacefully.

Real Story: Sadly, the most romantic part of the film is pure fabrication. Dennis never worked at a camp for blind kids and never fell in love with a blind girl. In fact, as a result of his condition, Dennis himself was legally blind from the age of six.

Movie: *Capote* (2005)

Reel Story: This portrayal of Truman Capote (Philip Seymour Hoffman) details Capote's writing of *In Cold Blood*, a book about a brutal murder in Kansas. The title card at the end of the film states that "*In Cold Blood* made Truman Capote the most famous writer in America. He never finished another book."

Real Story: While it's debatable that Capote was the "most famous writer in America," the statement that he never finished another book is simply false. In addition to short stories, newspaper articles, and several anthologies, Capote published several short novels after *In Cold Blood.*

Movie: *Rudy* (1993)

Reel Story: Daniel "Rudy" Ruettiger (Sean Astin) dreams of playing football for Notre Dame. Despite his small stature he makes it onto the team in his senior year. But the coach who let him on the team is replaced by Dan Devine (Chelcie Ross), who won't let Rudy play. In the last game of the year, the rest of the team refuses to play unless Rudy gets to play, too. Rudy plays, Rudy sacks the quarterback, Notre Dame wins.

Real Story: Notre Dame players never staged a protest—Devine actually insisted that Rudy play in that last game.

Who was Adriaen van der Donck? The first and only lawyer in New York City in 1653.

OPEN WIDE

We bet you'll cover your mouth at least once while reading these disturbing dentist stories.

In February 2007, police were called to an Ossining, New York, apartment, and after busting down the door found a dental chair, lights, drills, syringes, painkillers, and even a schedule book (but no sterilization equipment). The tenant of the apartment, Alfonso Ruiz-Molina, 40, who is not a dentist—but played one on actual patients in the apartment—was arrested.

• Dr. George Trusty of Syracuse, New York, was working in his office one day in late 2004 when a song he liked came on the radio. He started dancing. Bad idea: He was drilling into 31-year-old Brandy Fanning's teeth at the time. The drill bit broke and flew into Fanning's upper mouth and into her sinus, lodging near her eye socket. She needed emergency surgery to remove the bit before it could blind her. She sued Dr. Trusty for $600,000.

• In 2007 Roger Bean, 60, of West Palm Beach, Florida, was arrested for running a denture-making business...in his garage, which police described as "filthy." "Shame on me for doing what I do," Bean said, "but I always felt like I was born with the gift to do it." Police said they later received several calls from people who "wanted their teeth back," including one man who had only two real teeth and said he couldn't eat without his dentures.

• By April 2007, Dr. Alan Hutchinson had been practicing dentistry in London, England, for more than 28 years. And during that time, according to a police report, Hutchinson did not regularly wash his hands—and often worked without gloves. It gets worse: The 51-year-old routinely used dental tools to clean his fingernails and ears. And worse: A dental nurse who worked for him for 16 years said she had, on more than one occasion, caught him urinating in his dental sink. She said that she never said anything because she was too embarrassed. Hutchinson was banned from ever practicing medicine in the U.K. again.

The on-board toilet was introduced by Russian Airlines in 1913.

KNOW YOUR KNUCKLES

All your knuckle kneeds met right here—at KnuckleMart.

KNUCKLE SCIENCE

Do your knuckles actually "crack"? Not really. Here's what's going on: Your knuckles, like all the joints in your body, are surrounded by a sac of thick, clear *synovial fluid*. When you stretch the bones of a joint apart, as you do when you crack your knuckles, the sac is stretched. That reduces the pressure in the sac, which causes bubbles to be formed. Stretch it far enough, and the pressure drops low enough for the bubbles to burst—resulting in the loud "pop."

• You've probably noticed that once you've cracked a knuckle, you can't do it again for some time afterward. That's because it takes time for the bubbles to dissolve back into the fluid...usually about a half hour. (According to experts, you can crack them as often as you want—the notion that it is harmful to your joints is an old wives' tale.)

• "Knuckle-walking" is the name for a type of locomotion used by some animals, such as gorillas and chimpanzees. It's a form of *quadrupedalism*, or walking on four limbs (as opposed to our two-legged *bipedalism)*, and involves putting weight on the knuckles of the front limbs when walking. Other animals that use it include the giant anteater and the platypus.

KNUCKLE WORDS

The origin of the word *knuckle* goes back more than 2,000 years to Proto-Germanic, the precursor of all Germanic languages, and the word *knoke*, meaning "bone." Somewhere along the line, the German word *knöchel* came to mean "little bone" and in the 1300s migrated to the English language as *knokel*, or *knuckle*, referring specifically to the finger joints.

• To "knuckle down," meaning to apply oneself earnestly, entered the dictionary in 1864 and is believed to have come from the game of marbles, where shooting required one's knuckles to be on the ground.

The first recorded revolution took place around 2800 B.C. in Sumeria.

• To "knuckle under," meaning to submit or admit defeat, first appeared in 1869 and most likely was derived from the image of a person bent or kneeling with their knuckles on the ground.

• "Knuckleballs" showed up in baseball around 1910. They're so-called because the ball is held in a bent-fingered, knuckle grip when thrown, making it fly with very little or no spin and therefore erratically.

• The word "knucklehead," meaning a not very bright person, was coined in 1942...by the Three Stooges. It's also the nickname of a Harley-Davidson motorcycle style, known by its distinctive ribbed and knobby engine heads, which someone apparently thought looked like knuckles.

KNUCKLE ENTERTAINMENT

• Knucklehead Smiff was the name of the knuckleheaded dummy used by ventriloquist Paul Winchell in his 1950s and '60s TV shows.

• *Knuckle* is the name of both a 1975 TV movie starring Eileen Brennan and a 1989 BBC film starring Emma Thompson and Tim Roth.

• A "white knuckle" experience, or a white knuckle thrill ride or film, is one that has you gripping the arms of your seat so tightly that the blood leaves your knuckles and they look white. The exact origin of the phrase is unknown.

• The British expression "near the knuckle" refers to anything that is more than a little sexually suggestive or risqué. For example, "I thought his jokes were a bit near the knuckle, considering that the audience was mostly five-year-olds."

KNUCKLEANNEOUS

• "Pork knuckles" aren't knuckles. They're the pig's forefeet and ankles (along with the meat around them, of course). "Beef knuckles" actually come from the hind legs, above the kneecap.

• Are the joints of your toes called "toe knuckles"? They are by some people, and since they don't have a nickname like the finger joints do, we here at the Bathroom Readers' Institute say, "Why not? 'Toe knuckles' it is."

The oldest existing manuscript of the Bible is the *Codex Vaticanus*, from the 4th century.

IT'S A CONSPIRACY!

If you know anybody who believes in these wacky theories, please send them our way. We have an invisible bridge we'd like to sell them.

George W. Bush was the inspiration for Curious George!

Conspiracy Theory: George W. Bush was a curious child who was constantly getting into trouble. Margret and H. A. Rey, friends of Bush's parents, wrote a series of books about a mischievous monkey who they named *Curious George* after young Bush. The books were immensely popular, but Bush didn't learn that he was the inspiration for the character until 2006, when he was already president of the United States (his father told him). Facing low approval ratings and a public perception of being dim-witted, Bush was embarrassed and outraged. To prevent the information from leaking out, he ordered the Reys killed. When he found out they'd both been dead for years, Bush ordered the murder of Alan Shalleck, owner of the movie rights to *Curious George* and producer of the 2006 *Curious George* film.

The Truth: It's impossible for Bush to have been the inspiration for *Curious George*. The Reys never met the Bush family, and they wrote their first book in 1939, seven years before Bush was born. Alan Shalleck was a real person: He wrote several episodes of a *Curious George* TV series in the 1980s, but he wasn't a producer on the *Curious George* movie. And he was murdered, but not by Bush. He was found dead in his Florida home in February 2006, the victim of a botched robbery.

The Smurfs cartoon show was a Communist-propaganda project!

Conspiracy Theory: The Smurfs, a race of tiny blue people who lived in mushroom-shaped houses, were invented by Belgian cartoonist Peyo in 1958. They were popular throughout Europe for decades in comic strips and movies and came to the United States in the 1980s as a Saturday morning cartoon show. But American academics started to notice numerous "questionable" elements in the show: The Smurfs lived in a commune and did everything they were told by their leader, Papa Smurf—who wore a red hat (a color associated with Communism) and had a long white beard

Wonder Woman was the pupil of a Chinese martial-arts master named I Ching.

(making him look like Karl Marx). And their enemy was Gargamel, an "evil capitalist" who wanted to trap the magical Smurfs so he could sell them and get rich. In fact, the word "Smurf" is an acronym for "Soviet Men Under Red Father."

The Truth: The theory may have started with the movie *Slacker* (1991), in which one character says that *The Smurfs* is pro-Hindu, preparing children for the coming of the blue-skinned god Krishna by getting them used to seeing blue people. It was only a joke, but the rumor spread. The word "Smurf" is a nonsense word—it couldn't be an anagram for "Soviet Men Under Red Father" because it comes from the original French-language name for the comic: *Les Schtroumpfs*. Peyo didn't put any socialist propaganda in the cartoon series because he wasn't involved in its production. He didn't even create Gargamel, the "evil capitalist" villain—that was written by the show's writers specifically for the American cartoon. Oddly, *The Smurfs* actually contained an element of *anti*-totalitarianism: most of the Smurfs wore white hats, called Phrygian caps, a symbol of liberty worn by anti-monarchists during the French Revolution.

As a POW during the Vietnam War, Sen. John McCain was brainwashed by the Viet Cong. They can "flip the switch" in his brain and turn him into a spy, or worse...anytime they want!

Conspiracy Theory: McCain, a naval pilot, was shot down over Saigon in 1967 and was held captive in a military prison for six years, subject to physical and psychological torture. The Vietnamese hypnotized him, brainwashed him, and implanted a chip in his brain. McCain was released in 1973, but the Vietnamese used the chip to make him run for the U.S. Senate and eventually president. As president, McCain would be the helpless puppet of the Communist government of Vietnam.

The Truth: Sound familiar? It's the plot of the book (and movie) *The Manchurian Candidate*—conspiracy theorists just modernized it by adding "the chip," which they borrowed from UFO conspiracy theories. The theory probably stems from McCain's controversial efforts to normalize diplomatic relations with Vietnam in the 1980s. This enraged veterans and prisoner of war groups, who felt that Vietnam was still the enemy. From there the rumors took off, first turning McCain into a collaborator and then into someone with a chip in his head.

There is zero gravity at the center of the Earth.

WOW! THAT'S DUMB!

Breathtaking stupidity can be very funny...but only when it's happening to someone else, of course. (While you're chuckling at these folks, remember that it could have been you.)

MEAT THE PARENTS

A shoplifter in Kerkrade, Holland, grabbed a package of meat off a supermarket shelf and ran out the door. Employees immediately called the police, and when they arrived, showed them the evidence the robber had left behind: his 12-year-old son. The boy led police to his father.

AND YOU CAN TAKE THAT TO THE BANK

In December 2007, Jeremy Clarkson, host of the popular British TV show *Top Gear*, published a column in the *Sun* newspaper, scoffing at news that the government had lost two computer discs containing the personal information of about 25 million people. It was a fuss about nothing, he said, and to prove it he gave all the details of his personal Barclays bank account. "All you'll be able to do with them is put money into my account, not take it out," he wrote. Shortly thereafter someone withdrew $1,000 from his account. "I was wrong," Clarkson said, "and I have been punished for my mistake." (The money had been sent to a charity.)

PET PEEVE

In Bridgeport, Connecticut, police were called to a domestic disturbance in June 2008 and found Victor Rodriguez arguing with his girlfriend while holding a 9-foot-long python. Rodriguez ordered the snake to attack the police. It didn't. He was arrested.

ASK A SILLY QUESTION

A February 2008 poll found that 23 percent of Brits think that Winston Churchill—probably the most famous British Prime Minister in history—was a fictional character. And 58 percent believe that Sherlock Holmes was a real person.

OH, JUST SKIP IT

In June 2007, a 70-year-old woman in Nanjing, China, started skipping rope at midnight every night to annoy the person who lived below her. She was mad because they had broken a plumbing pipe, leaving her without a toilet. But after a week of the annoying rope-skipping, she had to stop: All that exercise had caused her blood pressure to shoot up to dangerously high levels, and she had to be taken to the hospital.

A WAKE-UP CALL

Franz Zimmerman, 67, of Lathen, Germany, got drunk and fell asleep...between some train tracks. A train rolled over him, with the brakes on (the engineer had seen him), the wheels screaming, and sparks flying. But Zimmerman was *so* drunk that he didn't even wake up. "He was sleeping like a baby," the engineer said. "He didn't notice there was a train on top of him." Zimmerman was arrested—after being woken up—for endangering public safety.

SOMEBODY CALL THE COPS

Police in Largo, Florida, were called to investigate a disturbance outside a bar in July 2007. They found Dana Farrell Shelton, 38, who appeared to be drunk but wasn't causing any apparent disturbance. They asked him to move along and left the scene. Shelton immediately called 911 to report that he was "surrounded by cops" and needed help. The cops went back to the bar and arrested him.

GO KART

A 24-year-old Russian man stole a car from a repair shop in Moscow in June 2008. Witnesses watched him zoom away, go straight through a red light, and smash into a parked car. It turned out that the car was in the shop because it had no brakes.

BEHIND IN HIS WORK

Daniel Everett, 38, walked into a crowded St. Louis County Courthouse in Missouri in 2001, found a public photocopying machine, dropped his drawers, hopped onto the machine, and proceeded to make photocopies of his butt. As police officers approached Everett, who was already holding two copies, he asked them, "What'd I do?"

A snail has two pairs of antennae: one pair for seeing and one for smelling.

CELEBRITY EATS

Country singer and TV star Jimmy Dean is probably best known today for the sausage company he started in 1969—one of the first celebrities to develop and brand his own food product. Here are some more examples.

• **James Brown Cookeez.** In 1994 the Godfather of Soul lent his name and image to a line of mini-cookies. Flavors included Banana Peanut Butter Creameez and Chocolate Chip Feel Goodeez, and one percent of the proceeds from each bag sold benefited anti-domestic violence charities, a crime for which Brown had been arrested five times.

• **Rap Snacks.** Labeling its product "the Official Snack of Hip-Hop," the company is owned by teenage rapper Lil' Romeo. Rap Snacks are potato chips, corn chips, and cheese puffs in 17 different flavors, "each with a different rapper on the wrapper."

• **San Diego Chicken Gum.** The guy in a giant chicken suit became famous for goofing around at San Diego Padres games in the 1970s. That led to a line of Chicken chewing gum. The pieces were shaped like chicken...but they were bubblegum flavored.

• **Jeff Foxworthy Jerky.** It's standard beef jerky, endorsed by the "you might be a redneck if..." comedian and sold almost exclusively at truck stops and Wal-Mart.

• **Mr. T Gold Chain Bubblegum.** The star of *The A-Team* and *Rocky III* was such an '80s cultural phenomenon that someone came out with Mr. T chewing gum—gold-colored "chains" meant to look like the ones Mr. T was famous for wearing.

• **Kiss Coffeehouse.** The rock band Kiss is as famous for its merchandising as it is for its music—maybe more. They've licensed the name and image for comic books, action figures, and even a line of caskets. In 2006 the first of many planned Kiss Coffeehouses opened in Myrtle Beach, South Carolina. It's a standard Starbucks-style coffee shop but with Kiss memorabilia on the walls and rock music–themed coffee beverages, including Rocket Ride Espresso and Rockuccino. (The decaf is called "Unplugged.")

The first Ford cars had Dodge engines.

"PROBABLY WIFE #2"

The Newlywed Game *has been around for decades, making newlywed couples answer leading questions designed to embarrass them...and entertain us.*

Bob Eubanks: What is your husband's favorite condiment?
Contestant: His pool table.

Eubanks: What will your husband say is the last flavor you used too much of in one of your dishes?
Contestant: Burnt.

Eubanks: What is your favorite thing to buy by the foot?
Contestant: Shoes.

Eubanks: What is your favorite wind instrument?
Contestant: The guitar.

Eubanks: What will your husband say is his favorite rodent?
Contestant: His saxophone.

Eubanks: Who is your favorite classical composer?
Contestant: Elton John. (Her husband predicted she'd say Barry Manilow.)

Eubanks: Where was the busiest place you and your husband ever "made whoopee?"
Contestant: My apartment.

Eubanks: "My husband is a closet..."
Contestant: Queen.

Eubanks: In what country will your husband say the last foreign car he drove was manufactured?
Contestant: Texas.

Eubanks: What vowel does your husband most resemble when he sleeps?
Contestant: An R.

Eubanks: What one thing is the city in which you were born best known for?
Contestant: City hall.

Eubanks: What is your favorite crustacean?
Contestant: The stuff in your eyes.

Eubanks: What is your favorite part of our *Newlywed Game* set?
Husband #3: Probably wife #2.

Eubanks: Who will your husband say is his favorite anchorman?
Contestant: Elvis.

Lettuce is 97% water, tomatoes 95%, carrots 90%, and bread 30%.

PLUG AND PLAY

These days, every computer has a USB port (short for Universal Serial Bus), a universal plug for any device you need, like a mouse, keyboard, or printer. But there are a lot more USB-ready devices than you can plug in.

GHOST RADAR. Made by Japanese company Solid Alliance, this device (which looks like a tiny mouse pad dotted with little pink light bulbs) scans the immediate area, analyzes Moon cycles, and takes into account the user's "biometric feedback" to determine if there are any ghosts in the room.

iSHARPENER. Plugged into a PC, it utilizes the computer's power to sharpen pencils, using less energy than a battery-powered or electric pencil sharpener. (Although it's unclear why, if you're sitting at a computer, you would need a pencil.) Other appliances available include a rechargeable shaver, a humidifier, and a USB version of the George Foreman Grill.

PLASMA BALL. It's a black orb that glows with flashes of pink light when plugged in. If you touch it, the pink lights turn blue.

DISCO BALL. This spinning ball projects multicolor flashing lights onto the walls, turning your cubicle into a miniature dance club. The device is also available in a spinning mirrored, non-lighted version.

SNOWBOT. It's a 4"-tall plastic snowman, but instead of eyes, it has a visor where the computer powers a blue light. More USB holiday items: Drumming Santa (plays the drums to *Silent Night* and *Jingle Bells*), a fiber-optic Christmas tree, and a musical Christmas moose.

USB BEVERAGE COOLER. Resembling a retro 1950s gas station soda cooler, this 8"-tall device holds—and chills—one can of soda. (If you prefer hot beverages, there's the USB Mug Warmer that keeps your coffee at 176°F and doubles as a four-port USB hub.)

Credit-card debt is the second major cause of personal bankruptcy. First is unemployment.

USB HEATING SLIPPERS. Made of brown fake fur (with white trim), these slippers heat up and keep your feet extra-toasty, as long as you're sitting within the three-foot cord range of the computer. Also available: heated gloves and an electric blanket.

USB CHIMP. It's a rearview mirror for your computer that sends an image of what's going on behind you onto your screen (so you can hide the video game you're playing if the boss is coming).

USB ROCKET LAUNCHER. It's a triple-barreled cannon that uses compressed air to shoot 3" foam darts from your computer at your cubicle mates up to 20 feet away. (There's also a version that looks like a mini circus cannon.)

USB CELL. It's a AA battery, but inside is a USB plug. Hook this $10 device up to your computer, and five hours later, it's a near-fully charged AA battery usable in any battery-operated device. (Or you could go buy a new AA battery for $1 or so at the store across the street.)

QX5 USB MICROSCOPE. Your computer powers a 200x magnifying lens. It also takes photos and videos of your specimens and saves them to your computer.

USB TURNTABLE. Combining yesterday's music technology with today's, this is a record player that plugs into your computer. You can then play your old records (or your parents') on it and convert the songs into digital MP3 files saved onto the computer.

USB PAPER SHREDDER. This desktop shredder is only about 6" long, so before you can let it shred your sensitive documents into tiny pieces, you have to tear your sensitive documents into tiny pieces.

ARMAGEDDON HUB. Possibly the most useless gadget available. It's a small metal box with two switches, a key, and a red "ultimate destruction" button. Turning the switches and the key and pressing the button, evidently, induces international nuclear war. (Actually, all the Armageddon Hub does when "activated" is make some siren noises.)

The little thumbnail indention on the blade of a pocket knife is called a *choil*.

DUSTBIN OF HISTORY: MASABUMI HOSONO

We all know the story of the Titanic*—we've seen the movies (there have been several), watched the TV specials, and even read the books and magazine articles. But as we at the BRI have discovered over the years, there's always something new to learn about even the best-known stories.*

THE LONG TRIP HOME

In 1910 Japan's Transportation Ministry sent an official named Masabumi Hosono to Russia to study that country's railroad system. Hosono finished his assignment in early 1912 and, following a brief stop in London, began the next leg of his trip home by embarking across the Atlantic on the RMS *Titanic*. Needless to say, *that* leg of the trip didn't go quite as planned. On April 14, at 11:40 p.m., just four days into its maiden voyage, the *Titanic* struck an iceberg while traveling near top speed and began taking on water.

RUDE AWAKENING

It's doubtful that anyone on the *Titanic*, which had been advertised by the White Star Line as being "practically unsinkable," realized at first that the ship had suffered a mortal blow. There were plenty of people on board who didn't even know the ship had hit anything. Many of those who noticed felt only a slight shudder followed by the sound of the engines coming to a stop.

Hosono apparently slept through the entire thing. The first he learned of it was shortly after midnight, 25 or 30 minutes after the collision, when he was awakened by a knock at the door of his second-class cabin and told to put on his life vest.

Three times when he tried to make his way to the lifeboats, he was turned away by the ship's officers, who ordered him to return to the lower levels of the ship. They likely assumed that, as a Japanese person, he must have been traveling in third class, or "steerage." On his third attempt Hosono managed to slip past a guard and make his way to the lifeboats.

There are more than seven million millionaires in the world.

IN THE DARK

Was the *Titanic* sinking, or was it just floating dead in the water, waiting to be assisted by the ocean liner *Carpathia* or one of the half a dozen other ships who'd received her distress calls and were already steaming to her aid?

We know the answer today, of course, but on that fateful night only three men on the *Titanic* did—Edward J. Smith, the captain; Thomas Andrews, the chief designer; and J. Bruce Ismay, the president of the White Star Line. They knew not only that the *Titanic* would sink, but also that it would sink well before help arrived. And they kept the information to themselves, fearing a panic that would cause the passengers to stampede the lifeboats, which when filled to capacity could carry only 1,178 of the more than 2,200 people on board. Even the officers ordered to organize the loading of the lifeboats had no idea the *Titanic* was going down.

THANKS...BUT NO THANKS

Withholding this information did help to keep the loading of the lifeboats orderly, but probably at the cost of hundreds of needless deaths. Many passengers and even many crew members, not suspecting the gravity of the situation, preferred to remain on board rather than risk climbing into the lifeboats. If you had booked passage on a ship that was said to be unsinkable, would you be willing to leave its warm, dry, and seemingly safe environs to climb into a tiny, swinging lifeboat in the middle of the night, and be lowered on pulleys 65 feet straight down into the freezing, iceberg-filled Atlantic? Even the captain's order to load women and children first must have cost some passengers their lives, because it meant that married women were being asked to separate from their husbands, which many refused to do.

Besides, what was the rush? As far as the crew members loading the boats knew, the *Titanic* wasn't sinking. The lifeboats were simply going to ferry passengers to the rescue ships when they arrived, and that was still hours away. There would be plenty of time to load more people into the lifeboats later, if they didn't want to go now. The crew members filled the boats with as many people as wanted to get in, and then lowered them into the water. In the end, only three of the *Titanic*'s 20 lifeboats were filled to capacity when they set down in the Atlantic.

Nothing to snicker at: 71% of office workers surveyed agreed...

Hosono must have sensed what was happening earlier than many of the passengers did, because as he stood next to Lifeboat No. 10 as it was being loaded, he was already steeling himself for the end. "I tried to prepare myself for the last moment with no agitation, making up my mind not to leave anything disgraceful as a Japanese," he explained in a letter to his wife. "But still I found myself looking for and waiting for any possible chance to survive."

That chance came moments later, when the officer loading No. 10 could not coax any more women or children into the boat. "Room for two more!" the officer called out. Hosono watched as another man jumped into the boat.

"I myself was deep in desolate thought that I would no more be able to see my beloved wife and children, since there was no alternative for me than to share the same destiny as the *Titanic*," he wrote. "But the example of the first man making a jump led me to take this last chance." Hosono hopped in, and at 1:20 a.m. he and 34 other people were lowered to safety in a boat built to hold 65.

FINAL MOMENTS

The *Titanic*, by now sitting very low in the water, had just one hour left to live. Eight of the 20 lifeboats had already launched and only one of them—Hosono's No. 10—was filled even *halfway* to capacity. (Lifeboat No. 1 launched with only 12 passengers out of a possible 40.) Many of the passengers still aboard the *Titanic* were just beginning to realize that the "unsinkable" ship might really be sinking.

When the *Titanic* finally slipped beneath the waves at 2:20 a.m., Hosono watched from Lifeboat No. 10. He described the experience in his letter to his wife, which he wrote on board the *Carpathia* as it brought the survivors to New York. "What had been a tangible, graceful sight was now reduced to a mere void. And how I thought about the inevitable vicissitudes of life!"

AFTERMATH

Of the more than 2,200 passengers and crew aboard the *Titanic*, just over 700 survived, including 316 of the 425 women and 56 of 109 children. Even if every woman and child *had* been accommodated in the lifeboats, there still would have been enough room for nearly 700 of the 1,690 men, yet only 338 men survived. Not everyone who perished did so because they declined an opportunity to climb into a lifeboat, not by a long shot. But this must surely have been the cause of many deaths.

In the shock and horror that followed one of the worst peacetime disasters in maritime history, many of these subtle details were lost on the newspaper-reading public. As they counted up the 162 dead women and children, many readers wondered how 338 men had managed to find their way into the lifeboats, "displacing" those helpless victims. Hosono received some of the harshest criticism of all. Not from the American newspapers, who expected chivalrous self-sacrifice from well-bred gentlemen of the middle and upper classes, but were dismissive of foreigners and the rabble traveling in steerage. Few American papers even took an interest in Hosono's story. One that did celebrated the good fortune of the "lucky Japanese boy."

SAVED...AND CONDEMNED

No, the harshest attacks against Hosono came from his own countrymen. For in surviving the *Titanic* disaster, he had broken two cultural taboos. Not only had Hosono chosen ignominious life over an honorable death, he had done so *in public*—on a European passenger liner with the eyes of the world upon him.

Hosono was denounced as a coward by Japanese newspapers and fired from his job with the Transportation Ministry. The ministry hired him back a few weeks later, but his career never recovered. College professors denounced him as immoral, and he was written up in Japanese textbooks as a man who had disgraced his country. There were even public calls for him to commit *hara-kiri* —ritual suicide—as a means of saving face.

Hosono never did kill himself, but there must have been times when he wished he'd died on the *Titanic*. He never spoke of the experience again, and forbade any mention of it in his home. After he died in 1939, a broken and forgotten man, his letter to his wife, written on what is believed to be the only surviving piece of *Titanic* stationery, sat in a drawer until 1997, when the blockbuster film *Titanic* staged its Tokyo premiere. Then the Japanese public's interest in the doomed liner's lone Japanese passenger was renewed again, this time with much more sympathy.

There are about 550 hairs in one of your eyebrows.

THE LAST MEAL

On April 14, 1912, the Titanic *struck an iceberg and sank, killing more than 1,500 people. This is the lavish meal served that night to the ship's first-class passengers...which, for many, would turn out to be their last.*

First Course

Various hors d'oeuvres, oysters

Second Course

Consommé Olga (beef broth, port, celery, leeks, carrots, gherkins)

Cream of Barley Soup

Third Course

Poached Salmon with Mousseline Sauce (hollandaise with whipped cream) and Cucumbers

Fourth Course

Filet Mignon Lili (steak served on baked potato slices and topped with artichoke pieces, foie gras, truffle slices, and a veal reduction sauce)

Sauté of Chicken Lyonnaise (an onion, white wine, and veal sauce)

Vegetable Marrow Farci (stuffed squash)

Fifth Course

Lamb with Mint Sauce, Roast Duckling with Apple Sauce

Sirloin of Beef with Château Potatoes (potato nuggets cooked in butter)

Green Peas, Creamed Carrots, Boiled Rice, or Parmentier (potato soup)

Sixth Course

Punch Romaine (white wine, rum, sugar syrup, and citrus juices)

Seventh Course

Roast Squab (young pigeon) and Cress

Eighth Course

Cold Asparagus Vinaigrette

Ninth Course

Pâté de foie gras with celery

Tenth Course

Waldorf Pudding, Peaches in Chartreuse Jelly, Chocolate and Vanilla Eclairs, or French Ice Cream

All the treasures of earth cannot bring back one lost moment. —French Proverb

BIZARRE BRAZIL

South America's largest country turns out to have some of the world's strangest news items.

UP, UP, AND AWAY

In April 2008, Father Adelier Antonio di Carli, a Catholic priest, took off from the coastal city of Paranagua in a specially designed chair strapped to 1,000 helium-filled party balloons. Although he had a parachute, a GPS device, and plenty of food and water...he was never seen again. The eccentric priest was trying to raise money for a "spiritual rest stop for truckers."

A MODEST PROPOSAL

Mayor Elcio Berti of Bocaiuva do Sul banned the sale of condoms in any of the town's stores in 1998 because, he said, he was concerned that the availability of birth control might result in the town suffering a reduction in population. The law was struck down as unconstitutional, so Berti did something that he thought would counteract condom sales—he spent $35,000 of his own money on Viagra and gave it away to any men in the city who wanted it.

A CUT ABOVE THE REST

Brazilian supermodel Angela Bismarchi danced in, well, nothing, basically, at the head of a 300-person samba ensemble in 2008's Carnival celebration in Rio. She did it to celebrate her latest cosmetic surgery operation—which put a slant in her eyes to fit with the Carnival's theme: the celebration of 100 years of Japanese immigration to the country. It was Ms. Bismarchi's 42nd plastic surgery operation, putting her just five off the world record of 47, held by American "living doll" Cindy Jackson. "I was always vain," said Bismarchi.

MOMS DO THE DARNEDEST THINGS

Claudia Michelle de Brito and her husband tried for four years to have kids, with no luck. They finally opted for a surrogate, but Brazilian law states that only close relatives can be surrogate mothers; de Brito is an only child and none of her female cousins were willing. So her mom volunteered. In 2007 Rosinete Serrao, 51, had four of her daughter's eggs (fertilized by her son-in-law) implanted in her uterus. In September she delivered twin boys, making her one of the few women ever to give birth to her own grandchildren.

THE HORSE-PITAL

The Jockey Club is a Rio de Janeiro medical facility for horses, with extra-large versions of human hospital equipment, such as X-ray and MRI machines. And if you're an obese person in Rio and you need such a test—that's probably where you'll go. Hospitals there started using the horse facility for extra-large people in 2007.

THERE'S NO PLACE LIKE HOME

In June 2008, Sao Paulo police raided the home of a known murderer and found two guns, a gym set, a plasma-screen TV, and $173,000 in cash. All of that might have been fine, but the "home" where he and the contraband were found was a prison cell in a federal penitentiary. An investigation into how the convict managed his posh (and armed) life in a prison is underway.

FANG YOU VERY MUCH

In July 2008, Gabriel Almeida, an 11-year-old Sao Paulo boy, was playing in his back yard when he was attacked by his uncle's pit bull. The dog bit the boy's left arm, at which point the boy responded by sinking his teeth into the dog's neck. Some nearby bricklayers chased the dog off before it could attack again. And Gabriel bit the dog so hard that he lost a tooth…a canine tooth. The boy—and the tooth—made television news all over Brazil.

I AM BARACK OBAMA

In August 2008, Alexandre Jacinto decided to run for a seat on the town council in Petrolina, Brazil—but not under his own name. Brazilian election law says candidates can use any name they want, so Jacinto ran as "Barack Obama." "I read a book about Obama's rise," Jacinto said, "a poor, simple man who became a senator. My aim too is to get to the top—the presidency." He wasn't the only one: Five other candidates around the country also chose the name. So who knows? There just may be a "President Barack Obama" of Brazil someday.

Does yours? 41% of American homes have three or more television sets.

DOING BUSINESS

A new paradigm of core values is emerging from executive team leaders who think outside the box and are able to facilitate synergistic business models by empowering their people-based commodities. Translation: Some people in big business have shown flashes of common sense.

"All of us believe that the product we produce is important. But 99.9% of your customers couldn't care less about your product or service. You are not that important in their universe. And that's almost impossible to accept."

—Peter Drucker

"There's no genius behind it. It's persistence and listening to people."

—Craig Newmark, founder of Craigslist

"Failures in business are caused by self-centeredness, treating business as a short-sighted profit-making endeavor, and clinging to outmoded practices."

—Konosuke Matsushita, founder of Panasonic

"Sales are vanity; profits are sanity."

—Silas Chou

"Risk comes from not knowing what you're doing."

—Warren Buffett

"It doesn't make any difference whether the product is cars or cosmetics. A company is only as good as the people it keeps."

—Mary Kay Ash

"Just because your ratings are bigger doesn't mean you're better."

—Ted Turner

"There is only one boss. The customer. And he can fire everybody in the company from the chairman on down, simply by spending his money somewhere else."

—Sam Walton

"Business opportunities are like buses: there's always another one coming."

—Richard Branson

"Being the richest man in the cemetery doesn't matter to me. Going to bed at night saying we've done something wonderful—that's what matters."

—Steve Jobs

Leading cause of death in China: respiratory disease.

VIDEO TREASURES

Ever been in a video store with no idea what to rent? It happens to us all the time. So we decided to offer a few recommendations.

AMERICAN HEART (1992) *Drama*
Review: "Jack is a suspicious ex-con, newly released from prison, with few prospects and little hope. He also has a teenage son he barely remembers but who desperately wants to have his father back in his life. Hard-boiled, poignant, and powerful." (*Videohound's Golden Movie Retriever*) *Stars:* Jeff Bridges, Edward Furlong. *Director:* Martin Bell.

THE STORY OF THE WEEPING CAMEL (2004) *Documentary*
Review: "A rare white camel calf is born among the herd of a family in the Gobi Desert. The calf struggles for survival after its mother, traumatized by the difficult labor, refuses to allow it to suckle. How this family deals with this small crisis is an unguessable miracle that will delight children and adults alike." (*Decent Films Guide*) *Directors:* Luigi Falorni and Byambasuren Davaa.

KENNY (2006) *Comedy*
Review: "This Australian charmer of a mockumentary about a hardworking, jovial employee for a portable toilet company is a low-key study of underdog pride rather than a bodily function jokefest. Droll about the perceived embarrassment of his trade, Kenny is a barrel-chested, kind-eyed Aussie king in the standalone outhouse business, proud of his sewage-handling capabilities. Reminds us of what's winning about lovable lugs." (*Los Angeles Times*) *Star:* Shane Jacobson. *Director:* Clayton Jacobson.

LAST NIGHT (1998) *Drama/Science-Fiction*
Review: "A film about the end of the world that paints a bittersweet picture. The world will end at midnight precisely and we meet a small group of people as they try to face the end with a certain grace and dignity. As the final hour approaches for the characters, there are moments of startling poignancy." (*Roger Ebert's Movie Yearbook*) *Stars:* Don McKellar, Sandra Oh. *Director:* Don McKellar.

Minimum salary of an NBA rookie in 2008: $442,000. (Maximum for a WNBA player: $90,000.)

THE ORPHANAGE (2007) *Horror/Foreign*

Review: "Young orphan Laura spent her formative years at a large orphanage located by the Spanish seaside. Thirty years later, she returns to the dilapidated institution with her husband and seven-year-old son to reopen it as a facility for disabled children. However, something ominous haunts the darkened hallways of this silent, stately manor." *(All Movie Guide) Director:* Juan Antonio Bayona.

PUCKER UP (2005) *Documentary*

Review: "Five diverse whistlers head to North Carolina to see who will become the champ at the National Whistling Competition. Inherently funny and entertaining simply due to its subject matter. These people take their whistling very seriously." (*Film Threat* magazine) *Directors:* Kate Davis and David Heilbroner.

THE FOUNTAIN (2006) *Science-Fiction*

Review: "A present-day medical researcher works on a cure for cancer. Meanwhile, a 15th century conquistador searches out the Tree Of Life. Finally, in 2500, a man tries to regenerate the Tree in the heart of a star. At heart, this is a simple fable about love and death, but keeps viewers enthralled from Mayan temples to space nebulae. A complex and gorgeous mini-epic." (*Empire* magazine) *Stars:* Hugh Jackman, Rachel Weisz. *Director:* Darren Aronofsky.

A PERFECT WORLD (1993) *Drama*

Review: "A father-son relationship develops between an escaped convict and the seven-year-old boy he takes as a hostage. A very American mix of male bonding, road movie, and thriller that reveals a few signs of originality." (*Halliwell's Film and Video Guide*) *Stars:* Kevin Costner, Laura Dern. *Director:* Clint Eastwood.

GOD IS BRAZILIAN (2003) *Family/Foreign*

Review: "God has reached the end of his tether with the human race and has decided to take a well-earned vacation. But he needs to find someone to fill in for him while he's away. Perusing his list of Saints, he travels to Brazil, where he stumbles across Taoca, a sprightly young man with a verve for life that inspires God to rethink some of his ideas about the human race. Funny, touching, and unique." (Yahoo! Movies) *Director:* Carlos Diegues.

When Magellan prepared to sail around the world in 1519, he spent more on sherry than on weapons.

LEADING LEDES

The lede *is the first sentence of a news story which is supposed to give the "who, what, where, when, why, and how" that will be fleshed out in the article. As these actual ledes show, sometimes you don't have to read any further.*

Fresno police have arrested a high school student accused of stabbing her friend in what the two girls described as a friendship bonding rite." (*San Francisco Chronicle*)

• "A bank robber got as far as a nearby pawn shop before a dye pack, inserted in his wad of stolen cash, exploded in his pants, authorities said." (Associated Press)

• "One of Canada's leading cinema chains has stopped handing out Christmas wrapping paper to its patrons after parents complained it featured angels fondling each other suggestively, newspapers reported on Tuesday." (Reuters)

• "A carpenter who keeps his clothes clean by working in the nude was arrested after a client returned home early and found him building bookcases in the buff." (MSNBC)

• "A woman has been admonished after she admitted feeding her estranged husband a curry containing dog excrement." (BBC)

• "Belgrade: A Serbian man was found dead and half-eaten in the bear cage of Belgrade Zoo at the weekend, during the city's annual beer festival." (GulfNews.com)

• "Indian police forced a thief to gobble down 40 bananas in a few hours, hoping they would force him to excrete a gold necklace he had snatched and swallowed." (Reuters, U.K.)

• "A man faces five years in jail after being accused of assaulting a teenager with a hedgehog." (*Daily Mail*)

• "Fort Hays State University has fired its debate coach for losing his temper at a tournament, engaging in a videotaped shouting match that included pulling down his shorts to expose his underwear." (Associated Press)

The seeds of an Indian Lotus tree remain viable for 300 to 400 years.

WOODSTOCK, Y'ALL

Here's a forgotten piece of modern music history.

THE EVENT

It was 1972, and the Austin, Texas, music scene, which blended country and rock 'n' roll, was beginning to get national attention. *Time* and *Rolling Stone* had written about it, even predicting that Austin's premiere music venue, Armadillo World Headquarters, would be as much of a mecca to country music as San Francisco's Fillmore Auditorium had been to rock. A few ambitious concert promoters decided to take advantage of the hoopla, and organized a three-day day music event near Dripping Springs, a small town west of Austin. The idea was to promote the Austin music style...and cash in along the way.

The lineup for the "Dripping Springs Reunion," held that March, included country music legends Loretta Lynn, Bill Monroe, Hank Snow, Tex Ritter, Tom T. Hall, Charlie Rich, Charlie Pride, and Roy Acuff. But it also included country music's rock-influenced "outlaws," who were leading the Austin scene: Merle Haggard, Kris Kristofferson, Waylon Jennings, Billy Joe Shaver, and Willie Nelson. The promoters dubbed it "Country Music's Woodstock."

THE RESULT

It was a flop. Among the numerous organizing goofs: not providing enough parking spots, camping places, or Porta-Potties. Add to that the fact that the event was poorly advertised—about 200,000 people were expected, but only 60,000 showed up—and it was a financial disaster. But the Dripping Springs Reunion was a success in at least two ways: It was the first time traditional country and "outlaw" country music had been combined at such a large festival; and the appearance of the established artists helped legitimize the lesser-known artists, making the event pivotal in the development of modern country music. It was also an inspiration for Willie Nelson, who decided to hold his first annual "4th of July Picnic" at the same site a year later. Though it's changed locations over the years, that event is still referred to by many as "Willie's Woodstock." And it's still going on today, more than 30 years later.

Thomas Jefferson first proposed the decimal currency system that we use today.

BATHROOM FENG SHUI

It's been a while since we've written about Feng Shui, *the traditional Chinese art of arranging living spaces and the objects within them. Here are some new tips on how you can apply Feng Shui principles to the most important room in your house.*

FENG SHUI 101

Feng Shui ("wind" and "water") refers to the natural forces that Chinese culture credits with bringing good luck, prosperity, and even good health when the life-force energy, called *ch'i,* is flowing properly. They're also said to bring bad luck, poverty, and sickness when the forces are blocked, disrupted, or dissipated in a poorly designed, poorly organized home or workplace.

Having good Feng Shui in the bathroom may seem frivolous or silly to westerners, but it's taken quite seriously in China because so many personal health and sanitation needs are centered in the bathroom. Even if you aren't familiar with Feng Shui (or you don't believe in it), it can still be fun to see how your commode stacks up.

LOCATION, LOCATION, LOCATION

• Your bathroom should not be visible from the front door of your home. This is thought to be bad for your health and the health of your guests as well.

• Your bathroom shouldn't be located at the end of a long hallway, either. This placement can cause the *ch'i* to flow right out of the house, almost as if it were being poured down a drainpipe instead of circulating smoothly through the rooms. Using such a bathroom, Feng Shui adherents say, is like sitting in the middle of a very swift current. And like the bathroom that can be seen from the front door, it can be harmful to your health...and even your pocketbook, since disrupting the proper flow of *ch'i* can cause money to flow out of your house right along with your health.

• Wherever your bathroom is located, the toilet should never sit directly opposite the bathroom door. It should be off to one side or the other, so that it's not the first thing you see when you look inside the bathroom.

Lon Chaney Sr.'s spirit is said to haunt Sound Stage 28 at Universal Studios.

MIRRORS

If you do have a toilet that's directly opposite the bathroom door in a bathroom down a long hallway that can be seen from the front door, take heart: You don't have to tear down your house or move away before your bathroom bankrupts or kills you. All you need to do is put up some mirrors. Mirrors are the duct tape of the Feng Shui world: They can fix just about anything. Their reflective power is said to pull good forces into the house and break up bad or stagnant Feng Shui. They can even push bad spirits out of the house.

• If your bathroom can be seen from the front door, simply keeping the door closed and hanging a mirror on the outside of the door is enough to fix the problem. For a bathroom at the end of a long hallway, a mobile, a wind chime, or a beaded curtain in front of the door will provide extra protection.

• Always be careful to hang mirrors in such a way that even the tallest person in the family can see the top of their head when looking in the mirror. If the mirror can be seen from the toilet, it must be large enough and hung so that even the tallest person can see his entire head while standing near or sitting on the toilet. Any member of the household whose head is even partially cut off when they look in the mirror will suffer from frequent headaches.

• Mirrors that break up or distort an image, such as mirrored tiles, should not be used in the bathroom, for the same reason.

• Placing mirrors on opposite walls so that they create an "infinity" effect can cause ch'i to dissipate and should be avoided.

PLANTS

Plants are considered a source of ch'i and can have either a positive or a negative influence on your bathroom's Feng Shui, depending on where they are placed. They can disrupt the flow of ch'i if they are placed in the middle of the bathroom. But when placed in a corner, they can work wonders, breaking up pockets of stagnant ch'i and causing it to circulate through the house. If you have a corner that protrudes into the bathroom, placing a plant in front of the corner will soften its edges and prevent it from damaging the ch'i of people who use the bathroom.

For more fascinating Feng Shui facts, turn to Page 361.

In the United States, six tubs of Cool Whip are purchased every second.

UNAMUSED

Amusement parks are a billion-dollar industry. The success of Disney World or Six Flags makes would-be entrepreneurs drool, but it's not so easy to get a theme park built. Here are some theme parks that were never even constructed.

THEME PARK: Veda Land

BIG IDEA: Attractions based on Transcendental Meditation

STORY: In the 1970s, illusionist Doug Henning revived the magic show as a popular form of entertainment and starred in an NBC television special called *Doug Henning's World of Magic*, which was seen by 50 million viewers. Also popular in the late 1970s: Transcendental Meditation, a Hinduism-based practice that claims to bring relaxation and inner peace to its followers. Henning was an avid follower of TM and became convinced that his life's mission was to spread the practice. So he began work on a TM-based theme park called Veda Land. Using "astonishing visual and sensory effects, state-of-the-art 3D imagery, and ultra-high-tech entertainment technology," the park would look like an authentic Himalayan mountain village. Proposed attractions included rides based on "the deepest secrets of the universe," a building that seemingly levitated over a lake, and a simulation of life inside a flower. After he was unable to buy land in India or near Orlando, Florida, Henning bought 700 acres near Niagara Falls, Ontario, and set about trying to raise the money he needed to build Veda Land—an astounding $1 billion. He never succeeded. When he died of cancer in 2000 at age 52, he'd been trying to get the project going for nearly 15 years.

THEME PARK: Majestic Kingdom

BIG IDEA: Rides centered around Michael Jackson's hit songs

STORY: In a move to increase tourism in 1998, the city of Detroit solicited applications for the rights to build a casino. Don Barden, owner of a local cable company, applied, but he wanted to build more than just a casino. He and his business partner, pop star Michael Jackson, wanted to build a sprawling theme park called Majestic Kingdom featuring a casino, a hotel, restaurants, nightclubs, and the Michael Jackson Thriller Theme Park. The centerpiece would be a roller coaster enclosed in a weatherproof glass bubble, allowing for year-round use. Despite promising 6,000 new jobs, the project was deemed too large and the Detroit City Council denied Barden's casino license, ending plans for the entire operation. But Jackson didn't give up—in 2006 he announced he was trying to raise $600 million to build a leprechaun-themed amusement park in Ireland.

THEME PARK: Dracula Land
BIG IDEA: Disneyland, but with vampires
STORY: In 2001 the Romanian Ministry of Tourism proposed opening a theme park based upon Romania's most famous historical figure: Vlad the Impaler, the murderous lord who served as the inspiration for Count Dracula. At a cost of $35 million, the park would be built in the Transylvanian village of Sighisoara, where Vlad was born in 1431. The ministry drew up plans for attractions, including underground tunnels, castles, fake caves full of live bats, a replica medieval town, a demonstration of how Vlad cut people's heads off, an "International Dracula Center," and a golf course. Despite the allure of 3,000 new jobs, Sighisoara fought the construction of the park. Led by a local minister, the townspeople claimed that glamorizing Vlad, who is believed to have killed more than 80,000 people, was "an attack on Christian values."

THEME PARK: Disney's America
BIG IDEA: An American history-themed amusement park
STORY: In 1993 Disney announced plans to open Disney's America in Haymarket, Virginia. Like other Disney parks, it would be split into different areas: Native American Village, Civil War Fort, Ellis Island, State Fair, and Family Farm. Individual attractions included a recreation of the Battle of the *Monitor* and the *Merrimack*, and a roller coaster called the Industrial Revolution. But the park's designers had a hard time striking a balance between thrill rides and educational exhibits, and local residents argued that the park was a crass commercial endeavor that tarnished the history it claimed to celebrate. Another problem: Disney wanted to build the park on—and thereby destroy—Civil War battlefields. Bowing to the pressure, in 1994 Disney scrapped plans to build the park.

One percent of Greenland's entire population lives in a single apartment building named Blok P.

STATE QUARTERS

Have you been collecting the state quarters?
Here's what's on the backs of all of them.

BACKGROUND

In 1999 the United States Mint began its nine-year plan to release 50 commemorative quarters, one for each of the states. The quarters had two purposes: to celebrate American history at the dawn of the 21st century, and to generate new interest in coin collecting. The quarters were released, one every few months, between January 1999 and fall 2008, beginning with the 13 original states, and then according to the order in which the states entered the Union. Each state decided what would go on the back of its quarter, be it a local monument, state icon, historical event, or important figure. Here's what they chose, in order of their release.

• **Delaware.** A portrait of Caesar Rodney on horseback. A delegate to the Continental Congress, Rodney rode 80 miles to Philadelphia in a thunderstorm (while suffering from asthma and cancer) to cast the deciding vote that made the colonies send the Declaration of Independence to England.

• **Pennsylvania.** *Commonwealth*, the statue atop the state capitol building. Her right arm extends as a gesture of kindness and her left hand holds a ribbon to symbolize justice.

• **New Jersey.** A rendering of Emmanuel Leutze's 1851 painting *Washington Crossing the Delaware*. In 1776 Washington and his troops crossed that icy New Jersey river to surprise (and defeat) British troops stationed in Trenton.

• **Georgia.** The live oak (the state tree) and the Georgia peach (the state fruit).

• **Connecticut.** In 1687 King James II of England revoked the state's charter. A colonist hid it for safekeeping in the hollow of a giant oak tree, now known as the Charter Oak, which adorns the coin.

• **Massachusetts.** *The Minuteman*, a statue commemorating Revolutionary War soldiers in Minuteman National Historic Park in Concord.

By walking an extra 20 minutes every day, an average person will burn off 7 lb. of body fat per year.

• **Maryland.** The dome of the Maryland State House, built in 1772 and still used by the state legislature. The United States Congress met there from 1783 to 1784.

• **South Carolina.** The yellow jessamine (state flower), the palmetto (state tree), and the Carolina wren (state bird).

• **New Hampshire.** The state emblem, a rock formation on Cannon Mountain called the Old Man of the Mountain. Until it collapsed in 2003, it looked like an old man's face.

• **Virginia.** The three ships—the *Susan Constant*, *Godspeed*, and *Discovery*—that in 1607 brought the first settlers to Jamestown, the first permanent English settlement in the New World.

• **New York.** The Statue of Liberty.

• **North Carolina.** A rendering of the Wright brothers' first airplane flight in 1903 at Kitty Hawk, North Carolina.

• **Rhode Island.** A sailboat (representing the state's most popular sport) on Narragansett Bay.

• **Vermont.** A man tapping trees to get raw maple syrup, with Camel's Hump Mountain in the background.

• **Kentucky.** The state is known for horse racing, so a horse is shown. (Ironically, it's a Thoroughbred, not a Quarter Horse.)

• **Tennessee.** The state's musical heritage is depicted with a fiddle to represent Appalachian music, a trumpet for the blues, and a guitar for country music.

• **Ohio.** With the caption "the Birthplace of Aviation Pioneers," an early wooden airplane (the Wright brothers were born in Ohio) and an astronaut in full space suit (Neil Armstrong and John Glenn are both from Ohio).

• **Louisiana.** An outline of the 1803 Louisiana Purchase (it doubled the size of the United States), the state bird (the pelican), and a trumpet (to represent the state as the birthplace of jazz).

• **Indiana.** A race car, as Indiana is home to the Indianapolis 500.

• **Mississippi.** The state flower, the magnolia.

• **Illinois.** Abraham Lincoln, who grew up and practiced law in the state.

• **Alabama.** A portrait of native Helen Keller sitting in a chair, reading a braille book.

The U.S. flag is always flown at half-staff at Arlington Cemetery,...

• **Maine.** Pemaquid Point lighthouse (built in 1826) guiding a ship safely into harbor.

• **Missouri.** Lewis and Clark are seen returning from their Western expedition in a riverboat on the Missouri River (they returned in 1806), going through St. Louis' Gateway Arch (built in 1965).

• **Arkansas.** Reflecting its major industries, Arkansas's quarter shows rice stalks, a diamond, and a duck.

• **Michigan.** A map of the state with the Great Lakes highlighted.

• **Florida.** On the left is a Spanish galleon (Spain explored and settled Florida in the 1500s); on the right is the Space Shuttle (it launches from Florida's Kennedy Space Center).

• **Texas.** A map of Texas with a large star, referencing its nickname "the Lone Star State," which comes from the Texas flag—red, white, and blue with a single star—designed when it was an independent republic in the 1840s.

• **Iowa.** A one-room schoolhouse with students outside planting a tree. It's a rendering of the painting *Arbor Day* by Iowan artist Grant Wood.

• **Wisconsin.** Three of the state's biggest commodities: a cow, a wheel of cheese, and an ear of corn.

• **California.** As 19th-century naturalist John Muir gazes at Yosemite National Park's granite Half Dome monolith, a California condor soars overhead.

• **Minnesota.** A lake (Minnesota is the "land of 10,000 lakes").

• **Oregon.** Crater Lake, a crystal-blue body of water that sits in a caldera (a volcanic crater) and is the nation's deepest lake.

• **Kansas.** A buffalo (the state animal) and a sunflower (the state flower).

• **West Virginia.** The quarter depicts the state's 3,030-foot long, 876-foot high New River Gorge Bridge—one of the longest and highest steel-span bridges in the world.

• **Nevada.** Three mustangs running free. Nevada is home to more than half of the country's wild horses.

• **Nebraska.** Passing by landmark Chimney Rock is a family in a covered wagon headed west on the Oregon Trail.

• **Colorado.** The Rocky Mountains.

...the Tomb of the Unknown Soldier, and Pearl Harbor.

• **North Dakota.** In 1906 President Roosevelt signed the Antiquities Act, which set aside the state's Badlands as a nature preserve for endangered bison. Today, 400 bison roam the area (and two of them are on the quarter).

• **South Dakota.** Mount Rushmore and a ring-necked pheasant.

• **Montana.** A bison skull, which is both a Western icon and a symbol of the state's Native American heritage.

• **Washington.** A leaping salmon and Mount Rainier.

• **Idaho.** The peregrine falcon, once endangered but now abundant in Idaho.

• **Wyoming.** A bucking horse and a rider, symbolizing the Wild West.

• **Utah.** Two trains and a railroad spike. In 1869 the Union Pacific and Central Pacific railway lines were joined in Promontory, Utah, completing the transcontinental railroad.

• **Oklahoma.** The state bird, the scissortail flycatcher, flying over a field of wildflowers, and the state flower, the Indian blanket.

• **New Mexico.** Over a topographical map of the state is the sun symbol of the Zia Pueblo tribe. Emanating from a circle are four points, which represent the four directions, the four seasons, and the four ages of man (childhood, youth, middle age, old age).

• **Arizona.** The Grand Canyon and a saguaro cactus.

• **Alaska.** A grizzly bear eating a salmon.

• **Hawaii.** A portrait of 19th-century Hawaiian king Kamehameha I, who united the islands into one kingdom.

* * *

EXTREME PUN-ISHMENT

A lion, a hawk, and a skunk were arguing in a clearing. "I am the strongest," said the lion, "because every animal fears me!" "No, *I* am the strongest," said the hawk, "because only I can hunt from the air!" "No, *I* am the strongest," replied the skunk, "because my stench could keep both of you away!"

And then a fisherman walked out into the clearing and easily captured all three animals—hawk, lion, and stinker.

SUITS SUCK

T-shirts are like bumper stickers, only for people, not cars. (Duh.) Here are some real T-shirts sent in by BRI stalwart Megan Todd.

Y2K *Survivor*

Volunteering: It Doesn't Pay

Kenya Dig It?

Practice Safe Lunch: Use a Condiment

Canada: America's hat

Mexico: America's beard

OBSCURE BAND YOU'VE NEVER HEARD OF

Without me, It's Just Awso

SOUTH KOREA'S GOT SEOUL

Beards: They Grow On You

You're handsome

Earthquakes: Not My Fault

Prague: Czech It Out

Sex: Do It for the Kids

Missouri Loves Company

I Got This Shirt at a Thrift Store

EVERYBODY LOVES RAMEN

Attention Ladies: I Enjoy *Grey's Anatomy*

I (blank) Mad Libs

Hyperbole Is the Best Thing Ever!

Suits Suck

Kinetic Energy: Pass It On

Pavlov: The Name That Rings a Bell

Club Sandwiches, Not Seals

I Went T-Shirt Shopping and All I Got Was This Lousy T-Shirt

It's Okay, Pluto. I'm Not a Planet, Either

The Police Never Think It's as Funny As You Do

Ask Me About My Ability to Annoy Complete Strangers

WITH A SHIRT LIKE THIS, WHO NEEDS PANTS?

The last land battle of the U.S. Civil War was fought in Texas.

HYPERMILING 101

Some people call it "ecodriving," others call it penny-pinching. Whether you're doing it out of environmental conscience or financial necessity, saving gas has become a way of life. Here are some tips from the experts.

MOTOR MISERS

For as long as people have been driving cars, there have been a dedicated few motorists who try to squeeze as many miles as they can out of a single tank of gas. During good times, when gas was plentiful and cheap, they did it for the fun of the challenge, or just for the principle of preserving a limited natural resource. In harder times, such as World War II, when gasoline was strictly rationed, or during the oil crisis of 1973, when gas cost more than ever before, people couldn't afford *not* to save gas.

Lucky for us they did do it, because over the years they've developed a lot of gas-saving techniques that we can use today. Many involve nothing more than common sense, and you may be surprised how many of these "secrets" you knew already without even realizing it. Now all you have to do is put them into practice.

FIRST THINGS FIRST: FIGURING FUEL ECONOMY

Many cars now come equipped with onboard computers that track fuel mileage continuously and give an estimate of how much fuel a car is consuming at any given moment. If your car has such a computer, all you have to do is follow the instructions in your owner's manual that tell you how to get the computer to display continuous mpg. Aftermarket computers are also available; they work on most vehicles made after 1996 and sell for under $200.

For those who drive older cars or don't have $200 to spend, calculating a car's mpg at any given moment won't be possible. But it's still possible to calculate the average miles per gallon for each tank of gas using the trip odometer. You probably know this, but just in case...

- The next time you gas up, remember to reset your trip odometer to zero. Then, after you've used up that tank of gas, make a note of how many miles you've driven and how many gallons of

The average North American car contains 300 pounds of plastics.

gas it takes to fill back up. Divide the miles by the number of gallons to get your average mpg. (Remember to reset your trip odometer to zero, so that you can calculate average mpg again the next time you fill up.) If you drove 300 miles and had to buy 12.5 gallons of gas, for example, your average miles per gallon on that tank of gas were roughly 300/12.5=24 mpg.

• If your car doesn't have a trip odometer, it will still have an ordinary odometer that tells you how many miles the car has been driven over its lifetime. Make a note of the odometer reading every time you buy gas, and subtract the previous reading to calculate the number of miles you drove on your last tank of gas.

• However you calculate your car's average mpg, it helps to keep track of the information in a notepad or pocket calendar, so that you can measure how your fuel economy improves over time as you put hypermiling tips into practice.

YOUR FIX-IT CHECKLIST

• **Repairs.** If you aren't already in the habit of keeping your car properly tuned up and fixing mechanical problems as they arise, start now. Just by doing so, you can improve your car's fuel efficiency by anywhere from 4% to 40%, depending on the severity of the problems that need to be fixed.

• **Tires.** Keeping your tires inflated to the proper pressure (listed in the owner's manual and on the inside edge of the driver's side door) can increase fuel economy as much as 3%. Tires that are underinflated require more energy to move because more of their surface area touches the road, increasing friction or what's known as "rolling resistance," which harms fuel economy. Keeping your tires properly inflated saves additional money by reducing wear and extending the life of your tires.

• **Oil.** Be sure to use the correct grade of motor oil; using the wrong grade can reduce your mileage by as much as 2%. Change the oil as often as the auto manufacturer suggests: the longer the oil is in your car, the thicker it becomes with dirt and grime. And the thicker it gets, the more energy is required to push it through the engine.

SLOW AND STEADY WINS THE RACE

The good news: you can save gas in a car that's already tuned up.

In 1989 the Space Shuttle *Discovery* carried 32 fertilized chicken eggs into orbit.

The bad news: you do it by *slowing down*. If you drive 65-75 mph on the highway, the biggest step you can take toward increasing your car's mpg is slowing to 55 mph. Most passenger cars are most economical at between 40 and 55 mph. Then fuel economy drops rapidly as speed increases above 60 mph, due to the fact that aerodynamic drag increases exponentially as speed increases. At high speeds, more than half the gas your car burns is spent overcoming wind resistance. And your lead foot may cost you more than you realize: The Department of Energy estimates that when gas is priced at $4.08 a gallon, every 5 mph you drive over 60 is the same as paying an extra 30 cents per gallon of gas.

In a test conducted by *Consumer Reports* magazine, simply decreasing the speed of a Toyota Camry from 75 to 55 mph resulted in a nearly 30% increase in fuel economy, from 30 up to 40 mpg. And if 55 mph is asking too much, when the Camry slowed from 75 to 65 mph, fuel economy still increased from 30 to 35 mpg.

MELLOW OUT

• If you have aggressive driving habits, such as rapid acceleration and frequent braking, back off a little. Don't accelerate hard just to brake again a short time later; it uses extra gas and wears out your brake pads. It's better to try to maintain a constant speed, with no unnecessary acceleration.

• When you do need to accelerate, do so gently—slow acceleration uses less gas than rapid acceleration. One simple trick for moderating your rate of acceleration is to use the resume/accelerate switch on the cruise control to speed up, instead of stepping on the gas. Cruise control is designed to accelerate at a slow rate, and when you accelerate slowly you use less gas. (Study your owner's manual first if you don't know all the ins and outs of your cruise control system.)

• By eliminating unnecessary acceleration and applying the gas a little more moderately when you need to speed up, you could save an additional 2 to 3 miles per gallon—that's 30 additional miles for every 10 gallons of gas in your tank.

Want more tips on hypermiling? Drive over to page 294.
(But please try to keep your speed under 55 mph.)

SIMPLE SUCCESS STORIES

Inspiring tales of everyday entrepreneurs.

PRODUCT: The Slug-X slug trap
BACKGROUND: In 1999 Inge Beaumont, a 77-year-old retiree and longtime gardener, set out to solve a common gardening problem: how to get rid of slugs...without using poison. Over the next year she tried several different trap designs, and finally came up with a one that worked: a box the size and shape of a cigar box, with a lift-off lid that covers three small wells. What do you put in the wells? Beer—slugs love it. Openings in the side of the trap allow slugs into the wells, where they drink...and drown. "Quite a pleasant way to die," Beaumont said.
SUCCESS STORY: She knew the traps were so good that she had several hundred manufactured and set up an online company, Westfield Products, to sell them. "We had problems to begin with," she said, "as I had never used a computer before." It didn't matter: As word of the traps spread, orders started pouring in from gardeners—and garden centers—all over the world. By the end of 2000, they'd sold sold more than $140,000 worth. But that was nothing: In 2001 they brought in more than $1.5 million.

PRODUCT: Privacy Strips
BACKGROUND: Attorney Jennifer Sloane of Winter Park, Florida, was tired of "shirt gap"—the openings between blouse buttons near the bustline. "It's frustrating when you're trying to project the image of a professional woman," she told the *Orlando Business Journal*, "but your blouse becomes a distraction." She decided to do something about it. In 2005, after a lot of experimentation with different glues, she came up with Privacy Strips, double-sided adhesive strips that you can stick to the inside of a blouse to invisibly hold the edges in place.
SUCCESS STORY: Sloane convinced a local dry-cleaning chain to carry the products, then got national distributors interested and started a Web site that she handles at night after work. She sells Privacy Strips in packs of 10 for $2.99, and since starting out in 2005, she's sold more than 100,000 packages.

66% of American home-based businesses are owned by women.

PRODUCT: Angel Guard

BACKGROUND: In 2006, after Patricia Mandarino's three-year-old daughter, Marilyn, managed to unbuckle the safety belt holding her child safety seat in place, the whole thing tumbled over when the car made a left turn. "I freaked out," said the Spring Hill, Florida, mother. "I had no idea she could do that." Mandarino couldn't find a product designed to keep a toddler's hands off seatbelts, so she decided to make one herself. A year later she came up with Angel Guard, a simple plastic device that fits over the seatbelt buckle to prevent child access to the release button, but still comes off easily for adults.

SUCCESS STORY: Angel Guards went on sale in February 2007, and the simple invention made newspapers all over the country. In 2008 Target stores started carrying them, and Angel Guards became a huge financial—and safety—success.

PRODUCT: The MuSmate

BACKGROUND: One afternoon in 2006, Ken and Anne Armitage of Devon, England, were walking as fast as they could, trying to get to a pub on time. One problem: Anne has multiple sclerosis (MS), which makes walking difficult. (The disease makes it hard for her to lift one of her feet.) Ken, a geophysicist and part-time inventor, had an idea: He tied a strap around the shoe on Anne's weak foot, tied a bungee cord from the shoe to her backpack—and off they went. The cord helped lift Anne's foot with every step and made walking a lot easier. "I covered the last two kilometers and got there in time for tea," she told reporters.

SUCCESS STORY: Wanting to share their discovery, Anne and Ken invented the "MuSmate," short for "muscle mate." The user wears a shoulder harness (it can go on under a shirt) with an elastic cord that runs to a connector attached to their shoe. It improves walking distances for some people by up to 600%. The device has received glowing endorsements from MS treatment centers in England, and is now sold across the country. The FDA approved it in 2008, and the Armitages are attempting to market it worldwide, believing it can help people with MS, cerebral palsy, and stroke symptoms. "If my husband hadn't invented this," Anne says, "I would probably be using a wheelchair by now."

PABLO AND THE PUMPKIN

We can't verify the scientific accuracy of this story… but it's a pretty entertaining Mexican folktale.

LAZY BOY

Once there lived a boy named Pablo. His home was in a deep valley near a tall mountain. Long, long before, the mountain had erupted and had spouted forth something magical on the land below, and because of this, crops grew fast on the farm where Pablo lived. If his father planted corn, the full-grown ears were ripe in a week. If pumpkin seeds were planted, the pumpkins had to be picked in a few days, otherwise they would become too heavy to carry. As for weeds—they were knee-high an hour after they had sprouted.

With things growing so fast, much work was necessary. But Pablo was very lazy. He liked to sleep, and he hated being out in the hot sun. Many times his father had to scold him before he would do any work. One hot afternoon he had to shake the boy hard in order to rouse him.

"You will get no supper until the hoeing is done!" he told Pablo.

So Pablo yawned and stretched, and went out to hoe the field. For an hour he did very well…but then he started to grow tired and sleepy. Sitting in the shade of a cornstalk with his hoe and weeding knife at his side, he rested his head on a pumpkin. And in two minutes Pablo was asleep.

A WHOLE NEW WORLD

Pablo slept…and slept…and slept. And the cornstalk and pumpkin grew and grew. As the corn grew taller, the pumpkin vine became tangled around it and the pumpkin was lifted off the ground along with Pablo and the hoe and knife. But still Pablo slept.

The cornstalk grew taller and taller until no tree in the world could equal its height. It had produced many ears, and the seeds from some of them had sprouted and made still more ears of corn. Meanwhile, the pumpkin had become many miles thick.

After a long time Pablo rubbed his eyes and sat up. What kind of world was this, he wondered. The ground was hard and yellow like a pumpkin. Corn was growing all around. He looked about him. His home was nowhere in sight. He couldn't understand this, for it had been in plain view from the field.

He looked at his feet and saw that his trousers reached only to his knees. He couldn't understand it—when he had put them on, they had come down to his ankles. His shirtsleeves were short, too. His hair had grown down to his shoulders. Poor Pablo! He didn't know what to think or do!

"How long have I been here?" Pablo asked himself.

MR. SPACEMAN

He was hungry, so he ate some corn. He cut off a piece of the ground, and it tasted like pumpkin! He was fond of both corn and pumpkin, so his hunger was satisfied. Then he began to grow cold. In his pocket he had a piece of flint rock; with it he started a fire, using some dried cornstalks.

A long, long distance away, down on the Earth, a little girl stood in front of her home. It was dark, and she was gazing at something high above her. "Mother! Mother! she cried. "There is a round, shining ball in the sky! Come and look at it!" Her mother came, and the two watched the strange sight.

GROUND CONTROL

"Why, there is somebody on it!" exclaimed the mother. "I can see his face! He has a stick in his hand!"

"Yes," replied the girl. "He is building a fire. I hope he does it every night."

"We must not expect too much, Daughter," the woman said. "Some nights he may need only a small fire and on others no fire at all. On those nights there won't be much light in the sky, or perhaps none at all."

"But I am glad to see the nice light," said the girl. "It will make the nights brighter."

"Suppose we give our new sky-friend a name and look for him tomorrow night," suggested the mother. "What name shall it be?"

After the girl thought a minute, she answered, "Let's call him the Moon!" And so it has been called ever since.

It would take 20 new midsize cars to generate the same pollution as one midsize 1960s car.

SPOTTED DICK WITH A SIDE OF NEEPS

Why were the British roaming the Earth for centuries in search of empire? Maybe they were just searching for a decent meal. Here's a taste of what they might have been running away from.

BUBBLE-AND-SQUEAK. A mix of mashed potatoes and chopped cooked cabbage flattened into a layer in a hot skillet and cooked until browned. Supposedly gets its name from the bubbling and squeaking noises it makes while cooking.

COCK-A-LEEKIE: Chicken soup made with leeks and a pound of prunes.

JELLIED EELS. Eels that are cut up and cooked for a short time; the juices exuded during and after cooking become gelatinous as they cool. Served with vinegar.

CHIP BUTTIE: It's basically a french fry sandwich: well-salted "chips" drenched in malt vinegar (or brown sauce or tomato sauce) in between two slices of buttered white bread. Close relatives: the bacon buttie (strips of bacon with dollops of ketchup or brown sauce between slices of buttered toast) and the sugar buttie (white bread spread with salted butter and white sugar).

STEAK-AND-KIDNEY PIE. A substantial dish of lean beef, veal kidneys, onions, mushrooms, and seasonings topped with a beef suet pastry crust, steamed in a pudding bowl. It's usually served with Brussels sprouts and new potatoes. (Suet is solid white fat.)

BEANS ON TOAST: Canned baked beans heated and poured over buttered white toast. Close relative: spaghetti on toast—canned spaghetti served hot on white toast.

TOAD-IN-THE-HOLE: Fried sausages in Yorkshire pudding batter, baked until the batter puffs up.

PEASE PORRIDGE. Dried split peas cooked until soft, then pureed with butter and eggs and steamed in a pudding bowl. It

The last letter George Harrison wrote was to Mike Myers, asking for a "Mini-Me" doll.

thickens as it cools, so leftovers can be sliced and fried in more butter. This dish has been eaten in England since the 1500s.

STOTTY CAKE: Flat, round yeast bread with a firm crust and a dense texture, usually split in half and filled with eggs and bacon or ham, or with pease porridge. *Stott* means "throw." According to legend, bakers would toss the baked breads onto the floor, and if they didn't bounce too much, they were done.

STARGAZY PIE: A Cornish tradition, in which small whole fishes are arranged in a pie as if they were the spokes of a wheel—tails in the center and heads sticking out of the top crust all around the rim, presumably to gaze up at the stars.

NEEPS AND TATTIES: Mashed turnips and creamed potatoes, traditionally served as side dishes with haggis. Mashed turnips are also called bashed neeps. Neep bree is cooked turnips, butter, and ginger pureed with milk.

SPOTTED DICK. A dessert pudding made of flour, beef suet, currants or raisins (those are the spots), sugar, spices, and either water or milk. The doughy mixture is shaped into a cylinder, tied into a pudding cloth, and boiled for a couple of hours. Served with custard sauce.

PLUM PUDDING: There are no plums in this Christmas treat—it's raisins, beef suet, candied fruit, breadcrumbs, almonds, and spices. It's often served with brandy butter (butter, sugar, and brandy, spooned onto the warm pudding, where it melts).

JAM ROLY-POLY: Another dessert pudding. It starts with a dough made of flour, shredded suet, and milk; rolled out; spread with jam; and rolled up like a jelly roll. It's then wrapped in cloth or foil and steamed for an hour. Nickname: "dead man's arm."

* * *

REALITY CHECK

Gas prices topped $4 a gallon in 2008, but on a per-gallon basis, it's relatively cheap. Printer ink costs about $2,700 per gallon. A gallon of Chanel No. 5 perfume costs $48,640. And antivenom, used to treat snake bites, costs $567,000 per gallon.

Q: What was the Addams Family's address? A: 0001 Cemetery Lane.

BANNED BOOKS

As publishers of books that are usually exiled to a certain room in the house, we have a keen interest in other books that have been shunned.

My Friend Flicka, by Mary O'Hara. The 1941 novel about a boy and his horse, set on a Wyoming ranch, was taken off the sixth grade reading list in Clay County, Florida, in 1990 because it contained the word "bitch," even though it was used correctly—in reference to a female dog.

A Light in the Attic, by Shel Silverstein. Cunningham Elementary School in Beloit, Wisconsin, took this humorous poetry collection for children off the shelves in 1985 because one poem jokingly "encourages children to break dishes so they won't have to dry them."

To Kill a Mockingbird, by Harper Lee. The powerful antiracism tale was banned from advanced placement English courses in Lindale, Texas, in 1996 because, for some reason, it "conflicted with the values of the community."

The Rolling Stone Illustrated History of Rock and Roll. A parents' group in Jefferson, Kentucky, wanted it taken out of school libraries in 1982 because all felt that stories about rock music could "cause our children to become immoral and indecent." (The state board refused to remove it.)

Twelfth Night, by William Shakespeare. Like many of Shakespeare's plays, *Twelfth Night* utilizes crossdressing for comedic effect. Because of that, a Merrimack, New Hampshire, English class was prohibited from reading it in 1996. The play, said authorities, "supports homosexuality as a positive lifestyle alternative." (It was written in 1601.)

Uncle Tom's Cabin, by Harriet Beecher Stowe. Written in 1852, *Uncle Tom's Cabin* was the bestselling novel of the 19th century, and its harsh depiction and critique of slavery was a catalyst for

The telephone was originally called a *harmonic telegraph.*

the abolitionist movement in the 1850s and 1860s. Nevertheless, the Waukegan, Illinois, School District tried to ban it in 1984. Why? It uses the "n-word."

The Lorax, by Dr. Seuss. The children's book about animals who die when their forest is destroyed was challenged by the Laytonville (California) School District in 1989 because it "criminalizes the foresting industry."

Blubber, by Judy Blume. This children's novel provides a valuable lesson with a story about a girl who participates in the constant torment of a classmate, only to have the tables turned. In 1990 a parent in Louisville, Kentucky, lobbied to have it removed from her child's elementary school library because some characters in the book "behaved unkindly."

A Wrinkle in Time, by Madeline L'Engle. This 1962 fantasy novel was challenged in Anniston, Alabama, in 1990. A father objected to the book's inclusion of Jesus Christ on a list of people who defended the Earth against the forces of evil.

Black Beauty, by Anna Sewell. Even though this classic novel is about a horse, in 1955 the apartheid government of South Africa banned the book because they thought the title alone might instill pride in black South Africans.

The Grapes of Wrath, by John Steinbeck. The plot: During the Great Depression, a family flees drought and hard times in their native Oklahoma only to find backbreaking work picking crops for meager wages in Kern County, California. In 1939, just weeks after the novel was published, the real Kern County removed the book from its schools and libraries because it was a "smear" on the area.

Brave New World, by Aldous Huxley. The science-fiction book is set in a dystopian future in which people are controlled with mind-altering drugs and mindlessly engage in promiscuous sex. It was taken off of the high school reading list in Miller, Missouri, in 1980 because it made sex "look like fun."

On New Year's Day, German children wear a pretzel around their necks for good luck.

THE MERCENARIES

In July 2008, former British Army officer and admitted mercenary Simon Mann was sentenced to 34 years in prison for attempting to overthrow the government of the African nation of Equatorial Guinea. It made us want to know more about mercenaries in general—and this is what we found.

BACKGROUND

Mercenaries—foreign soldiers who fight for money rather than for a moral or legal attachment to a country or cause—have been employed by warring governments for thousands of years. History's best-known wars, from ancient Greece and Rome to World War I and every war since, have seen "soldiers of fortune" on both sides—the practice was commonplace. It wasn't until modern times that fighting and killing for nothing more than money—and the corollary, paying people to fight—has come to be seen as something immoral. The word "mercenary" itself has negative connotations. Most countries today have banned the use of mercenaries, but they do, of course, still exist. The following is a rundown of just some of history's most intriguing and infamous soldiers of fortune, starting more than 4,000 years ago.

THE MEDJAI

Weni the Elder was one of ancient Egypt's most renowned military commanders. Serving under Pharaoh Pepi I (2283 B.C.), he instituted many changes that affected Egyptian—and regional—armies for millennia. One of them: hiring foreign fighters to bolster his forces. Many were from Nubia, to Egypt's south, and among them were the *Medjai*, seminomadic desert people revered for their fighting skills and their courage. Numerous sculptures, paintings, and engravings depict these distinctive fighters: dark-skinned Africans wearing short, skirtlike garments and carrying bows and arrows. For more than 1,500 years, the Medjai culture interwove with the Egyptian, so much so that during times of peace the Medjai stayed in Egypt, working as bodyguards for royalty. The word "medjai" itself even later became associated with a police force within Egypt itself. If you've seen the 1999 film *The Mummy* you've heard of the Medjai. They're depicted as warriors that have

A single silkworm cocoon can contain 360 yards of silk fiber—enough to cross 3 football fields.

been guarding the mummy's tomb for millennia, since the ancient Egyptians first hired them to do so. (Except in the film...they're Caucasian.)

JEWS FOR PERSIA

In the late 1800s, several ancient writings were discovered on the Nile River island of Elephantine in the south of Egypt. The "Elephantine Papyri," as they're known, were written in the 5th century B.C., when the Persians ruled Egypt. They tell of a community of Jewish mercenaries—and their families—living on the island. Exactly when they first got there is unknown. Some historians believe they may have been loaned to an Egyptian Pharaoh by an earlier king of Judea (part of modern-day Israel), perhaps as early as 700 B.C., and that they later remained as mercenary soldiers when the Persians conquered Egypt in 525 B.C. Several generations of the foreign fighters lived on Elephantine for at least 200 years as a well-established and respected class of citizen.

THE CELTS

Most people are probably familiar with the Carthaginian general Hannibal, who led an army and several elephants across the Alps around 210 B.C. and almost conquered the Romans. What you probably don't know is that at least 3,000 of his soldiers were Celts, better known today as ancestors of the British. Celtic people actually settled in numerous regions throughout Europe and Asia Minor starting in the 600s B.C. And wherever they went, it seems, they earned a reputation as some of the fiercest and wildest fighters in history. When they weren't fighting for themselves they were often fighting for someone else for pay. That included ancient Egyptians, Syrians, and Palestinians in the Middle East; the Spartans, Macedonians, and other Greek city states before the Romans conquests of 146 B.C.; and very often the Romans (who, remember, they also fought against), until the Roman Empire fell, around 400 A.D.

THE CELTS, AGAIN

In 1259 Aed O'Connor, prince of Connaught in the West of Ireland, married a princess from the Hebrides islands of Scotland. She arrived in Ireland accompanied by 160 Scottish warriors who

Illinois is the only state that allows you to pay tollbooth fare in pennies.

became known as the *Galloglaich* (pronounced "galloglas"), meaning "foreign young warriors" in Irish Gaelic. Organized, experienced, well equipped, and brutal, they and their descendants became a large and vital part of Irish armies that fought the English for the next 350 years. By the 1500s, more than 5,000 Galloglaich were fighting in Ireland. They were well respected *and* well paid: Records show that each soldier got 12 cattle per year, as well as food in the form of butter and grain. Commanders got even more, often including land, and many became wealthy and lived as Scottish lords on Irish soil. By the late 1500s, however, methods of warfare were changing drastically: Muskets and cannons were becoming more common, and the hand-to-hand combat the Galloglaich specialized in became obsolete.

THE *REISLÄUFER* OF SWITZERLAND

It's ironic that the nation now known as a permanently neutral bastion of peace once bred some of the most organized and brutal mercenaries in history. From the 1300s through the 1500s, if you had a war to fight in Europe, you called the Swiss. Local *cantons*, now Swiss counties but then controlled by regional lords, kept large contingents of *Reisläufer*—"ones who go to war"—ready to rape and pillage for the right price. Hire them, and your enemy would encounter a massive and deep column of men with *pikes* (thick, long, pointed sticks) and *halberds* (a combination pike and axe) who would put their heads down and rush into battle, slaughtering everything in their path. In 1515 the Swiss began their famous tradition of neutrality, and the days of the Reisläufer were over.

THE HESSIANS

Whom did the Americans fight during the Revolutionary War? The British, of course. And the Germans. King George III made deals with German lords to have German soldiers shipped to America to help fight the rebels. An estimated 30,000 German soliders made the trip, the majority from the region of Hesse, hence the name. One of the war's most famous battles, in fact—the Battle of Trenton—involved Hessians: When General George Washington led his troops across the Delaware River on Christmas night 1776 (picture the painting), on a sneak attack of a gar-

It was just after the 1660s that the phrase "soldier of fortune" was born.

rison in New Jersey, the soldiers he met were Germans—1,400 of them, commanded by Colonel Johann Gottlieb Rall. Washington's men won in a rout and more than 900 Hessians were captured. (The famous "Headless Horseman" from Washington Irving's 1820 tale, *The Legend of Sleepy Hollow*, was based on the tale of a ghost of a Hessian soldier from the Revolutionary War.)

MODERN TIMES: "MAD MIKE" HOARE

Thomas Michael Hoare was an Irishman, born in 1920, who served the British in North Africa during World War II. After the war he moved to South Africa, where he became one of the most notorious mercenaries in modern history. He lived the high life in South Africa in between stints leading his "Wild Geese" mercenary troops in wars in the Congo, Angola, and South Africa from 1961 though the 1970s. (They were the inspiration for the 1978 film *The Wild Geese* starring Richard Burton, Richard Harris, and Roger Moore.) Hoare's downfall came in 1981 when he and a force of 43 soldiers made a botched attempt to overthrow the government of the island nation of the Seychelles in the Indian Ocean. They ended up hijacking a plane to get back to South Africa, where all of them were arrested. Hoare served four years in a South African prison—not for attempting to overthrow a government, but for the hijacking. An inquiry later found that South African Defense Force officials, and possibly French and American intelligence officials as well, were involved in the planning and financing of the attempted coup.

EXECUTIVE OUTCOMES

If you are in need of some hired killers with a respectable corporate feel—these are your guys. EO was incorporated as a "private military company" around 1990, just after the fall of the apartheid regime in South Africa. The first leader of the group: Eeben Barlow, former leader of South Africa's eerily-named Civil Cooperation Bureau (CCB), a covert group whose job it had been to perform "black ops" against black South African organizations. EO didn't just have a few mercenaries to offer: they claimed to have more than 3,000 highly-trained soldiers, plus weaponry including guns, anti-aircraft missiles, tanks, planes—you name it. They were a war waiting to happen...for a price. In the 1990s, they fought

Super Bowl XXVI, in 1992, was the first Super Bowl at which the National Anthem...

battles in Angola, Sierra Leone, and Indonesia, to name just a few. They were also hired by multinational corporations for "security," including—allegedly—De Beers, to protect diamond mines, and Chevron and Texaco, to protect oil drilling operations in Africa. EO disbanded in 1999 (maybe).

SIMON MANN

Mann was born in 1952 and, like Mike Hoare, was a former British military officer. He became involved in Executive Outcomes in the 1990s, then started his own mercenary outfit, called Sandline International, in 1996. Sandline mostly fought rebel groups in African countries, but became well known internationally when an attempt to put down a rebellion in Papua New Guinea—for which Sandline charged $36 million—went awry and led to the toppling of the nation's government. Things went awry again in 2004 when Mann and 69 mercenary troops attempted to take over Equatorial Guinea in Central Africa. At the behest of a group supporting exiled ex-president Severo Moto, they were arrested on the way there—in Zimbabwe—and after years of legal wrangling, Mann was sentenced to 34 years in prison in Equatorial Guinea. Mann claimed the coup was planned and financed by a reclusive London oil tycoon (Equatorial Guinea has *a lot* of oil) named Ely Calil. Mann said the goal of the operation was to install exiled opposition leader Severo Moto, who was living in Madrid, as president. Calil admitted involvement, but said he thought Mann and his mercenaries were simply going to provide Moto with security for a trip to Equatorial Guinea. Calil was never charged with a crime. Mann also named Mark Thatcher, son of former British Prime Minister Margaret Thatcher, as a financier and member of the "management team" of the coup plot. In 2005 Thatcher pleaded guilty to being "unwittingly" involved, and was fined $500,000 and given a four-year prison sentence (suspended).

* * *

ACTUAL NEWS ITEM

"An Australian Army vehicle worth $74,000 has gone missing after being painted with camouflage."

IT'S A WEIRD, WEIRD WORLD

Proof that truth is stranger than fiction.

SEX, VIOLENCE, BUTTER PECAN

Leon Kass is President George W. Bush's Morals and Ethics advisor. In 1994 he published an essay about what he believed to be the worst moral menace threatening human dignity today: ice cream. "Licking an ice cream cone," Kass wrote, "is a catlike activity that has been made acceptable in informal America, but that still offends those who know eating in public is offensive."

THE STRONG, SILENT TYPE

Eija-Riitta Eklöf of Sweden saw film footage of the Berlin Wall on TV when she was a child. It began a lifelong love affair that, in 1979, culminated in "marriage." Eklöf threw a wedding ceremony at the Wall in front of a group of friends and changed her last name to Berliner-Mauer ("Berlin wall" in German). She claims to have had a loving (and physical) relationship with the Wall until it was torn down in 1989 (in what Berliner-Mauer calls "frenzied attacks by a mob"). Now, after two decades of widowhood, Berliner-Mauer says she's still not ready to begin dating again. "The Great Wall of China is attractive, but he's too thick," she told a London newspaper. "My husband was sexier."

PAWS BETWEEN EACH COMPRESSION

In 2008 German medical student Janine Bauer took her year-old son to the zoo in the city of Halle. While looking at the tigers, Bauer noticed that one of the baby tigers was choking on a piece of meat. Zookeepers came to the aid of the tiger and got the meat out of its throat, but it still passed out. So Bauer, a medical student, offered to help. She performed mouth-to-mouth resuscitation and chest compressions, and after about four minutes, the tiger regained consciousness. The grateful zoo named the tiger Johann, after Bauer's son.

That comes to about...12 lattes? In 2007 Starbucks sold $26 million worth of coffee every day.

LAND SHARK

Sam Hawthorne, a 14-year-old from Dudley, England, was attacked by a small shark in 2008. His mother saved him—she heard the boy's screams and pried the shark, which had clamped down on his cheek, off her blood-covered son. Hawthorne escaped with just a small scar. The weird part: The shark had been dead for years and was mounted on a wall in Sam's bedroom. While sleepwalking, he ran into it and knocked it off the wall. Its teeth dug into his cheek for 15 minutes before he woke up.

NOT THEIR TYPE

In December 2007, authorities in Sarasota, Florida, responded to a call about a suspicious package found under a stairwell in a parking garage. Police closed off several blocks and called in the bomb squad, who prepared to detonate the device. At the last moment they realized that the strange-looking contraption wasn't a bomb—it was an old-fashioned manual typewriter.

HOLY INSULTING TRADE, BATMAN!

In professional sports, players sign contracts and basically become the property of their team. When they're traded, it's generally done in exchange for other players, money, or draft picks. But not always. At the beginning of the 2008 baseball season, pitcher John Odom was traded from the minor league Calgary Vipers to the Laredo Broncos. In exchange for Odom, the Vipers got 10 baseball bats, worth about $650. (Odom reports that umpires, players, and coaches now relentlessly call him "Batman.") It's not the first odd deal the Vipers have made. While renovating their stadium in 2004, the team traded a pitcher for 1,500 new seats.

A SHOT IN THE DARK

A 35-year-old man was walking to his car in a parking lot in Guelph, Ontario, when he suddenly felt a sharp pain in his leg. He went to the hospital, where doctors discovered a bullet wound. But the man had been alone and hadn't heard any shots, so where'd the bullet come from? Police believe a man taking target practice on his property in Waterloo, more than a mile away from Guelph, was the culprit. The stray bullet had traveled through "several acres and a tree-lined area" en route to the unlucky victim.

The average American household gets 104 TV stations, but watches only about 16 of them.

THE TAPEWORM DIET

And a few other odd ways people try to lose those extra pounds they've been lugging around.

NAME: The Original Grapefruit Diet

BACKGROUND: The granddaddy of modern fad diets, it was known as the Hollywood Diet when it first caught on back in the 1930s. How'd it work? Through the supposed fat-burning power of the enzymes in grapefruit.

DESCRIPTION: Breakfast was half a grapefruit and tea or coffee. Coffee drinking was encouraged, probably to pep up the food-deprived dieter, who was allowed very few calories—only 800 per day in some versions of the diet (the typical person eats about 2,000 calories per day). Every lunch and dinner started with half a grapefruit and ended with either coffee or tea. The rest of lunch might be two eggs, a tomato salad with vinegar and herbs (no oil), and a piece of melba toast. Dinner, after the grapefruit, might be six ounces of chicken or lean meat and half a head of lettuce with a tomato. The diet lasted for 12 days. Strangely, the rapid weight loss caused by the diet was attributed to the magic of grapefruit...rather than to the lack of food.

NAME: The Cabbage Soup Diet

BACKGROUND: The exact origin of this fad diet is unknown, but it became popular in the 1980s when it was passed around via fax machines (much like similar e-mail fads today).

DESCRIPTION: A seven-day diet (and it's so boring that seven days is probably all anyone could stand). It consists of homemade cabbage soup—as much of it as you like on any day of the diet. There are numerous recipes in circulation, but here's the basic one: cabbage (and other fresh vegetables), canned tomatoes, onion soup mix, and V8 juice. On Day 1 you eat cabbage soup, plus any fruit except bananas. Day 2: same soup, vegetables (no bananas), baked potato with butter. Day 3: more soup, fruits and vegetables (no potatoes, no bananas). Day 4: still more soup, as many as six bananas, fat-free milk. Well, you get the idea. The obvious drawback of the cabbage diet: flatulence.

San Francisco has more dogs (120,000) than children under 14 (93,000).

NAME: The Caveman Diet

BACKGROUND: Also called the Stone Age Diet, the Paleolithic Diet, or the Hunter-Gatherer Diet. Proponents are a little vague about the actual time frame to which it refers, but the idea is that cavemen were thin and healthy from eating the animals and plants they hunted and gathered. So if we emulate their diet, we'll avoid modern illnesses like heart disease and diabetes.

DESCRIPTION: Lean meats, eggs, and seafood are a big part of the Caveman Diet, as are raw fruits and vegetables (although you're allowed to cook the vegetables). But you can't have any grains (or grain products, like pasta), legumes, potatoes, dairy products, yeast, vinegar, sugar, salt. Good news for Neanderthals: Some paleo diets allow diet soda, coffee, wine, and beer. (Yee-ha!)

NAME: The Cookie Diet

BACKGROUND: The 1975 brainchild of Dr. Sanford Siegal, the Cookie Diet *sounds* as if you're going to get to eat cookies—and you are...but not just any cookies.

DESCRIPTION: You eat six of Dr. Siegal's special cookies—"made under his personal supervision in his private bakery"—followed by a high-protein, low-carb dinner of six ounces of meat or fish and one cup of green vegetables. That's it for the day, a total of about 800 calories. The cookies, with a "secret protein blend" that supposedly suppresses hunger, come in five flavors: chocolate, oatmeal raisin, coconut, blueberry, and banana. The Cookie Diet made big news when Madonna complained that while her husband Guy Ritchie was on the diet he lost interest in sex.

NAME: Tapeworm Diet Pills

BACKGROUND: This one almost lands in the "urban legend" category. But it's true, and it goes back to the craze for quack-diets between 1900 and 1920.

DESCRIPTION: The pills contained live tapeworms, which, according to the plan, would infest your gut (just as they do when dogs get them) and mess with your intestines, making you lose weight. There are a number of problems: Tapeworm infestation causes, among other things, abdominal pain, vomiting, diarrhea, flatulence, nausea...and pieces of worm passing through your system. (Ewww!)

The track of oil left on the surface of water by a fast-swimming whale is called *glip*.

THE COMSTOCK LODE, PART II

Here's the second installment of our story on one of the most famous mining strikes in American history. *(Part I is on page 47.)*

GET A LODE OF THIS

When you're pulling gold out of the earth by the pound, word of what you're doing has a way of getting out. In June 1850, a rancher named B. A. Harrison, living in Truckee Meadows, about 10 miles away from the Comstock mine, learned of the strike and went to see it for himself. He collected some samples and brought them to the town of Grass Valley, where he gave pieces to friends. One of them, a local judge (and a miner) named James Walsh, had the ore "assayed," or analyzed, to see what was in it and how much it was worth.

The assayer estimated that an average ton of the ore would yield about $969 worth of gold. No surprise there; Harrison and Walsh knew there was plenty of gold in the ore. But what really stunned everybody—including the assayer, who was so incredulous that he tested the ore a second time—was that each ton would also yield nearly $3,000 worth of *silver.*

Silver? What silver? The assayer explained to Harrison and Walsh that the blue dirt that had proved so frustrating to the prospectors was actually *silver sulfide*, or silver ore, and a very rich deposit of it at that. It was, according to the experts, "an almost solid mass of silver." As Harrison had seen with his own eyes, the exasperated prospectors had already dug up tons and tons of the blue ore and were dumping it in huge waste piles all over the place. They had absolutely no idea what they had stumbled onto.

SHHH!

That night, Harrison, Walsh, and a few other associates made plans to sneak out of town the following morning without attracting attention, so that they could stake their own claims next to the existing ones and maybe even buy out the original claims if they could. But who could keep that big a secret? If you won the lottery on Monday evening, could you really keep it to yourself until Tuesday morning? At least one person must have talked, because by the time the men were ready to leave the following morning, Grass Valley was buzzing with news of the discovery.

SEEING IS BELIEVING

It took just days for word of the strike to spread from Grass Valley to the California gold country. Soon miners who'd been unlucky there began abandoning their existing claims and heading east. But the real rush didn't begin until after Judge Walsh had shipped nearly 40 tons of the ore to San Francisco in fall of 1859, where it yielded more than $118,000 worth of gold and silver.

Many of San Francisco's leading citizens were men who had struck it rich during the gold rush of 1849 and had managed to hang onto their money since then. They weren't the kind of fellows who took to the hills chasing every rumor of a new strike. But seeing the newly minted bullion in the offices of Walsh's bankers made believers out of everyone, and soon they, too, were on their way over the Sierra Nevadas. By the first week of November, when snowfall blocked the mountain passes for the rest of the winter, several hundred people—from the wealthiest speculators to the lowliest prospectors—had made their way to the area and were riding out the winter in tents or whatever shelter they could improvise.

DOWN...AND OUT

Mining the surface gold and silver out of a deposit like the Comstock Lode is easy enough: the ore was so soft, in fact, that it could be mined with just a shovel. But once all the surface ore is gone and prospectors have to start digging deeper into the earth to get at the rest, mining becomes a much more dangerous and expensive proposition. And who knew how long the rich deposit would hold out? Each time the prospectors lifted a spadeful of ore, they faced the very real prospect of finding nothing but worthless dirt or rock underneath.

The thinking among experienced prospectors was that the best way to profit from a lucky strike was to sell out *before* the limits of the strike had been discovered—hopefully at top dollar to feverish

The computer acronym TWAIN stands for "Technology Without An Interesting Name."

investors foolish enough to think the good times would last forever. So when the big money boys from San Francisco rolled into camp, many of the original claim holders sold out for what must have seemed like obscene profits at the time and happily went on their way.

FINDERS, WEEPERS

Pat McLaughlin sold his claim for $3,500. His partner, Peter O'Reilly, held out the longest of all the original stakeholders, eventually selling out for $40,000, after collecting about $5,000 in dividends.

Henry Comstock sold his claim to Judge Walsh for $11,000 and used the money to open mercantile stores in Carson City and Silver City, both of which he hoped would profit from the mining trade he'd helped create. No such luck—both stores failed. Comstock spent the rest of his life roaming the American West, looking for a second mother lode. No luck there, either. In September 1870, Comstock—by now broke, broken, and mentally deranged—committed suicide in Bozeman, Montana.

NAMING RIGHTS

Old Virginny, the man who made the first discovery, was also one of the very first to sell out, reportedly surrendering his interest in the mine for "an old horse, worth about $40, and a few dollars in cash." Another version of the story says he got a couple of blankets and a bottle of whiskey in the bargain as well. It didn't make much difference either way—Old Virginny wouldn't have lived long enough to enjoy his riches even if he'd gotten any. In the summer of 1861, he was thrown from a bucking mustang while drunk and died from head injuries a few hours later.

But Old Virginny does have another claim to fame. According to local legend, in an earlier drunken escapade he fell down and shattered a whiskey bottle. As he watched the contents soak into the dirt, he rose to his feet and proclaimed, "I baptize this ground Virginny." And the town that grew up around and on top of the Comstock Lode was named Virginia City in his honor.

Part III of the rags-to-riches-to-rags-to-riches-to-rags story of the Comstock Lode is on page 338.

THE (ALMOST) COLONY

From the Dustbin of History, the story of an American colony that didn't quite make it, brought to you by BRI historian and master spy Jeff Cheek.

YOU CAN'T GET THERE FROM HERE

Most American students are taught that the first two permanent English colonies in America were Jamestown, Virginia, founded in 1607, and Plymouth, Massachusetts, established in 1620. They're also taught that Jamestown and Plymouth became the nucleii of the first two of the thirteen original British colonies. Their hardy pioneers survived famine, disease, and conflicts with the Native Americans to found what eventually became the United States of America.

Few students (and possibly only the most dedicated American-history buffs) are aware that another successful colony—the Popham Colony—was established in Maine *before* Plymouth. Its demise is difficult to understand, since the colony was fairly well managed, safe, and well-supplied. The other two defied all logic by hanging on; Popham didn't. The reason? Popham's boss got a better offer.

SIR JOHN'S STOCKADE

In May 1607, as Jamestown was being settled, two ships carrying 120 colonists sailed from England, headed for Maine's Kennebec River. The *Gift of God* arrived on August 13, the *Mary and John* three days later. Leading the expedition was an aging nobleman, Governor George Popham, nephew of Sir John Popham, Lord Chief Justice of England and one of the mission's chief financiers. Second in command was a naval officer named Raleigh Gilbert (nephew of famed explorer Sir Walter Raleigh), described by historians as ambitious, brash, and arrogant—and just 25 years old.

Within two months of their arrival they had built Fort St. George, a large walled fort, inside of which were no fewer than 18 buildings, including a storehouse for supplies, a governor's house, a blacksmith's shop, and homes for colonists. Land was cleared and planted. Shipwrights even used local timber to construct a 50-foot ship called the *Virginia*—the first English-built ship in the New World. Popham was a thriving colony with a bright future.

All look up: Elvis Presley believed that he could move clouds with his mind.

WINTER BLUES

Many of the Popham settlers were English gentlemen who had simply come along for the adventure. When the *Gift of God* sailed back to England in December, almost half the colonists went home—a comfortable English estate was preferable to a bitter Maine winter in a stockade. But all those who remained made it through to spring…except Popham himself, who died in February 1608. Compare that to Jamestown, where more than half of the 104 settlers died before the first winter had passed.

Popham's death made Raleigh the colony's new governor…and he did a pretty good job. He used the *Virginia* to fish for cod and to map the rocky coastline, established at least some trade with the local Abenaki tribe, shipped the goods back to England (the whole point of establishing colonies), and reportedly kept the colonists in high spirits through the summer and in the face of winter's return. Then, in September, another ship arrived…and the news it brought was the death knell for Popham Colony.

POP GOES THE COLONY

Gilbert was notified that his elder brother, John, had died, leaving him an enormous estate—including a castle—in Devonshire, England. He had a choice: He could stay in Maine and develop the colony, or return home as Sir Raleigh, Lord of the Manor. He chose the latter, and the colonists, having lost two leaders in one year, had apparently had enough. They decided to go back to England, too. With that, Popham Colony was done…and was soon forgotten. If they'd held on—who knows—American students just may have been told the story of "the original 14 colonies."

Epilogue: In 1990 archaeologist Dr. Jeffrey Brain heard about Popham colony for the first time in his 40-year career. Using the only surviving document from the colony, a map showing the fort, buildings, and some coastline, he searched the Maine coast for the next seven years…and found the lost colony. Excavation is ongoing, but the remains of the fort and several buildings have been found, as well as artifacts such as glass beads, a clay pipe, nails, pottery, and armor. If you're ever up on the Maine coast—go take a look at some forgotten American history.

Mary, Queen of Scots played billiards while awaiting her execution.

POP CULTURE ANAGRAMS

An anagram is a rearrangement of the letters in a word or phrase to get a new word or phrase. Sometimes the new phrase is even a pretty fitting commentary on the original. Here are anagrams of the names of some popular TV shows, books, musicians, songs, and movies.

BUFFY THE VAMPIRE SLAYER becomes... **PITHY FEMALE BRAVES FURY**

THE ROLLING STONES becomes... **HELL! SING SO ROTTEN!**

BEAUTY AND THE BEAST becomes... **A STUD BENEATH, YA BET!**

GREY'S ANATOMY becomes... **AGONY MASTERY**

THE WONDER YEARS becomes... **DREARY TEEN SHOW**

STAR WARS EPISODE ONE: THE PHANTOM MENACE becomes... **REMADE PHENOMENON IS CATASTROPHE, WASTE**

DESPERATE HOUSEWIVES becomes... **WE ARE DEVIOUS SHE-PETS**

A CLOCKWORK ORANGE becomes... **KOOK CREW GO CARNAL**

GOLDILOCKS AND THE THREE BEARS *becomes...* **GIRL HAD CEREALS, THEN TOOK BEDS**

THE SOPRANOS becomes... **A PERSON SHOT**

CHARLIE AND THE CHOCOLATE FACTORY becomes... **THE TALE OF CANDY-O-HOLIC CHARACTER**

HOW THE WEST WAS WON becomes... **WHAT WE SHOT WE OWNS**

SOUTH PARK becomes... **OK, TRASH UP**

BEST IN SHOW becomes... **WHITE SNOBS**

ETERNAL SUNSHINE OF THE SPOTLESS MIND becomes... **ELEMENT SHUTS RELATIONSHIP FONDNESS**

"GOOD VIBRATIONS" *becomes...* **AVOIDING ROBOTS**

One inch of rain, falling over an area of one acre, weighs one ton.

THE COMPLAINT DESK

The best part about living in a free society is that you can complain about anything that bothers you. We all do it, but some people do it loudly and in public...which sometimes makes the rest of us laugh.

ROOTS AND SUITS

The Blue Parrot diner in Louisville, Colorado, was founded in 1919 by two Italian immigrants. Their signature sandwich is "the Wopburger." The offensive name never received a single complaint...until 2007, when an Italian-American tourist objected and threatened a lawsuit. The restaurant's owners changed the name to the "Italian Burger," but after even more people complained about *that*, they changed it back to the Wopburger.

IT'S SO NOT FAIR

For six years, the Wilson County Fair in Tennessee has offered a $2 "religious" discount off admission to anyone who brought a church bulletin. In 2008 an atheist organization called Secular Life protested the discount, claiming it unfairly "promoted Christianity." Fair organizers responded by extending the discount to customers who brought a printout from any atheist Web site.

I SCREAM

In 2008 noise complaints led the city of Worcester in England to place restrictions on ice cream truck music. Music may no longer be played before noon or after 7:00 p.m., may last only four seconds, and may be played only once every three minutes.

PLAY ON WORDS

The Atlantic Theater in Atlantic Beach, Florida, staged Eve Ensler's female-empowerment play *The Vagina Monologues* in February 2007. A woman drove by the theater with her school-age niece, who read the marquee and asked her what a vagina was. The woman complained to the theater, which is ordinarily a comedy club, so they rebilled the play on the marquee as *The Hoohah Monologues*. "We decided we would just use child slang for it," said Atlantic's director Bryce Pfanenstiel.

The first TV series in which every episode was shot in color: *Bonanza* (1959–'73).

PIGGING OUT

For decades one of the traditional activities at the annual St. Patrick Catholic Church Roundup in Stephensville, Wisconsin, was a pig-wrestling contest. It was recently discontinued when some attendees complained that the pigs squealed too much. "Some city folks come out here and don't understand," said a St. Patrick spokesman.

NEGATIVE RESPONSE

In November 2007, England introduced a new scratch-off lottery game called Cool Cash. The game had a weather theme: The player won money if the temperature they scratched off was lower than the one printed on the card. Cool Cash was pulled from stores after officials received complaints from angry players who apparently didn't understand how negative numbers work (such as how –6° is a colder temperature than –5°).

OUT CLUBBING

The Hopwood Unionist Club is a social club in Manchester, England. In 2003 it ended its 100-year tradition as a men-only organization and began admitting women. But in 2008, while a group of men and women were playing bingo and cards in the club's sports room, golf was on the TV set and a woman asked if they could change it to a music channel. The response: Not only did golf stay on, but Hopwood leaders voted to ban women from the sports room. Club secretary Peter Burt said, "There was more to it than the TV channel thing."

BOO HOO

In 2006 Wall Street executives and brokers enjoyed record-high, multimillion-dollar annual bonuses. In a *New York Times* article on the subject, one anonymous broker complained that New York City didn't have a decent selection of $20 million properties for sale.

* * *

"While others may argue about whether the world ends with a bang or a whimper, I just want to make sure mine doesn't end with a whine."

—Barbara Gordon

THE COMMANDER GUY

This marks the end of an era—our final George W. Bush quote page during his presidency. (Please lower the toilet paper to half-mast.)

"And Karen is with us—a West Texas girl, just like me!"

"My job is a decision-making job. And as a result, I make a lot of decisions."

"See, in my line of work you got to keep repeating things over and over again for the truth to sink in, to kind of catapult the propaganda."

"Reading is the basics for all learning."

"I think that the vice president is a person reflecting a half-glass-full mentality."

"It would be a mistake for the United States Senate to allow any kind of human cloning to come out of that chamber."

"As you know, my position is clear—I'm the Commander Guy."

"The public education system...is where children from all over America learn to be responsible citizens and learn to have the skills necessary to take advantage of our fantastic opportunistic society."

"I think if you know what you believe, it makes it a lot easier to answer questions. I'm not gonna answer your question."

"You know, there are all these conspiracy theories that Dick Cheney runs the country, or Karl Rove runs the country. Why aren't there any conspiracy theories that I run the country? Really ticks me off."

"I just want you to know that, when we talk about war, we're really talking about peace."

"I would still invade Iraq even if Iraq never existed."

"Well, I think if you say you're going to do something and don't do it, that's trustworthiness."

"More than two decades later, it is hard to imagine the Revolutionary War coming out any other way."

"I promise you I will listen to what has been said here, even though I wasn't here."

"It'll take time to restore chaos."

In 1940 U.S. paratroopers watched the movie *Geronimo*...

BLOKUS, ANYONE?

Monopoly, Risk, and Uno are classics, but what board games do board game enthusiasts play? We asked our friend, Merry Vediner at funagain.com, *to recommend some, and here's what she came up with.*

BLOKUS (Mensa's Best Mind Game 2003). The players take turns placing their colored tiles on the 400-square board, beginning with their home corner. Every piece set down has to touch at least one other piece of the same color. The goal: dominate the board with your color.

TICKET TO RIDE (Germany's Game of the Year 2004). This game simulates the 19th-century railway boom. Players draw cards that give them longer trains and claims to train routes connecting cities. Points are awarded by connecting two distant cities and for the longest continuous railway.

LOST CITIES (International Gamers Awards, Best Two-Player Game 2000). In this two-player card game, players draw cards to determine what "lost cities" (including "Neptune's Realm" or the Brazilian Rain Forest) they will explore. On the adventures, players draw cards that reveal resources and obstacles.

BUYWORD (*Games Magazine*'s Game of the Year, 2005). In this cross between Monopoly and SCRABBLE, players "purchase" letter tiles, each with a monetary value, which are used to spell words. (Hard-to-use letters like Q, X, and Z are worth the most.) The player who makes the most money wins.

PUERTO RICO (International Gamers Awards, Best Strategy Game 2003). Each player assumes the role of Settler, Builder, Mayor, Prospector, or Trader as they compete to build buildings, grow plantations, and amass wealth in 1540s Puerto Rico.

THROUGH THE DESERT (*Games Magazine*'s Best Family Strategy Game Runner-Up, 1999). Each player is a nomadic tribe (represented by a camel game-piece), fighting for the control of a desert. Players gain points by establishing caravans and taking control of oases and food sources.

...before their first jump. They've been shouting it ever since.

MAKING A MOVIE, PART II: THE PRODUCERS

Now we focus our attention on the plethora of producers and their many tasks—including the most important one: divvying up the money. *(Part I is on page 116.)*

FROM ASSOCIATES TO EXECUTIVES

Once the shooting script is finalized, the producer begins putting together the production department. That includes producers, executive producers, associate producers, co-producers, and line producers. But what do all of these people actually *do*? Their tasks often overlap on the same project, but not only that—people with the same title on another project often have completely different duties. For this reason, the Producers Guild of America (PGA) is currently working to streamline these terms and make the duties more consistent.

• **Producer.** A movie will have several producers; the one in charge of all the others is simply called "producer." Although he or she wears many hats, the primary duties consist of staying with the film from development to release, making sure that every department has everything they need in order to complete their jobs. For a more technical definition, the PGA states: "A producer initiates, coordinates, supervises, and controls all aspects of the motion-picture production process, including creative, financial, technological, and administrative." More and more big-name directors and actors want to be producers as well, allowing them more control (but not all) over how the story will be told.

• **Executive producer.** He or she oversees all the business and legal aspects of the film—negotiating contracts, securing rights, insuring the picture, hiring the core filmmaking team, and sometimes even financing the movie. The creative work can't be started until this process is complete. On some projects, the writer/creator is given an executive producer credit, even though they didn't do a lot of work on the actual film. In other cases, the studio heads who secured rights and approved financing of a film may be given executive producer credits.

• **Associate producer.** He or she works at the producer's side, doing the legwork that the producer doesn't have time for. A mentor/student relationship often results, as most associate producers are working to become full-fledged producers themselves. This is also one of the most common "gift" credits given out as favors to stars or financiers who in reality performed no producer duties at all.

• **Co-producer.** Another confusing term, this title is often awarded for different duties depending on the project and is mostly used in television. On a big-budget film, however, a co-producer credit may be given to a team of production executives who act as liaisons between the producer and the cast and crew.

• **Line producer/unit production manager.** These two terms are often used to describe the same job, depending on the project. What they have in common is that each is the keeper of the budget. If a film is financed for $40 million, the line producer will read the script and then figure out how to divvy up the money—line by line on a 100-page budget—so that every department will have the funds to carry out their duties. After that, it becomes the unit production manager's job to tell the director that there isn't enough money for, say, shooting at an exotic location. If the director insists, the line producer will break down the budget a second time and try to free up money from other departments to fund the location shoot. Compromises such as this are the norm. For example, if the visual effects look weak, it's often because the studio had to pay the star more money than the initial budget could afford.

REEL-LIFE EXAMPLE: *SPIDER-MAN 2*

Here's a very simplified version of how the money was spent on the 2004 superhero movie, one of the most expensive—it had a $200 million budget—and highest-grossing movies of all time.

Story rights: $20 million. Marvel Comics owns the character and charged a hefty price to Sony, the studio that made the film. Marvel has since opened its own film division.

Screenplay: $10 million. *Spider-Man 2* went through many of the same kinds of story changes documented in the section on screenplays. In the end, the money was divided between the men who created the character, Stan Lee and Steve Ditko, plus a host of other screenwriters who wrote drafts. The bulk of the money, however, went to Alvin Sargent who (along with director Sam Raimi) finalized the script and was given the sole writing credit.

Producers: $15 million. That's only the "up front" money. According to Archie Thomas, the movie writer who compiled much of this information for *The Guardian* in 2004, "including performance-related bonuses, or 'bumps' from *Spider-Man* reaching box-office targets, producer Laura Ziskin is rumored to have pocketed over $30 million. The escalating fees paid to actors are often reported, but the producers are among the richest people on the set."

Director: $10 million. Bringing in Sam Raimi to direct the first *Spider-Man* movie was a risk, as he had directed mostly low-budget horror movies, but it paid off big-time...and he was able to negotiate for a much higher salary for the sequel.

Casting: $30 million. (Tobey Maguire: $17 million, Kirsten Dunst: $7 million, Alfred Molina: $3 million, the rest of the cast: $3 million.) Negotiating these deals is often intense. Maguire—earning more than four times his salary from the first film—was reportedly fired during preproduction after showing up with a nonchalant attitude and complaining of a hurt back. When producers offered the part to Jake Gyllenhaal, Maguire's reps had to convince the producers that Maguire was indeed ready for the role and would submit to medical tests to prove it. And along with their salaries, the main stars receive such "perks" as personal assistants, trainers, chefs, first-class travel and accommodations, and anything else their clout can get them. All of the expenses so far are what's called *above-the-line*, paid to actors, writers, producers, and the director.

Production costs: $45 million. Called *below-the-line*, this is the money that goes into paying and feeding the crew, renting the equipment, fees for location shooting, and all the raw materials needed for building the sets. This is the money that the line producer/unit production manager must divvy up. (On smaller films, this is also where the most corners are cut, starting with food and housing for the crew.)

Visual effects: $65 million. Not only can this be the most expen-

One in 10 men grind their teeth while sleeping.

sive part of big-budget movies, it's usually the one that causes projects to go over budget. It takes an army of highly skilled programmers months to create, animate, render, and fuse the digital effects into the film. The more complex the shots, the more they cost. For example, one scene in 2007's *Spider-Man 3*—when Sandman is "born"—took three years to complete and cost nearly as much as the *entire* effects budget for *Spider-Man 2*.

Music: $5 million. Danny Elfman wrote most of the score, but after disagreements with director Sam Raimi, Christopher Young and John Debney were brought in to write additional themes. This is actually quite common. In addition to paying the composers, they had to pay an orchestra to perform the score. In addition to that, part of this budget goes to purchasing rights to songs used in the soundtrack.

Marketing and Distribution: These costs aren't usually added into the film's budget—the studios take care of this and won't disclose how much money is spent on promos and corporate tie-ins, but it's usually in the tens of millions of dollars. The cost for "prints and advertising" on *Spider-Man 2* was reportedly around $75 million.

EXTRA HELP

A recent trend is to get advertisers to pay for a share of the movie in return for product placement. The modern era of product placement began in 1982 when sales of Reese's Pieces skyrocketed after appearing in *E.T.: The Extra-Terrestrial.* A company will now pay millions if the product is displayed prominently and in a good light. There's even a new practice of tailoring the product to the country in which the movie is being shown. In *Spider-Man 2*, North American audiences saw a Dr Pepper logo behind Peter Parker when he got fired from his job; in Europe the logo was digitally replaced with Mirinda, a popular European fruit drink that's also distributed by Pepsico.

But no matter who provides the money, all of the expenses must be budgeted and divvied up before the real work on the movie can begin.

For Part III, go to page 330.

Product most commonly used to clean elephants: Murphy's Oil Soap.

EXERCISE YOUR BRAIN

Given a little time and a modicum of mental strength, you should be able to solve these. (But in case you can't, the answers are on page 540.)

1. Name the only U.S. state that has four consecutive consonants in its name.

2. This special number is in order: **8,549,176,320**. What kind of order?

3. What letter does not occur in any U.S. state name?

4. Name the only number that, when spelled out, has the same number of letters as its value.

5. What do these five words have in common?

adam buoy claim gall ramp

6. Name the only two U.S. states that contain three consecutive vowels in their name.

7. What nine-letter word can be made by unscrambling these letters?

A C C E H I M N S

8. This U.S. state name is made up of three words—in order. The first and the third words have opposite meanings, and the middle word is very egotistical. (*Hint:* It's not a two-word state name.)

9. What's the minimum number of playing cards in a hand that can consist of one king, two clubs, three jacks, and four hearts?

10. Think of the only 9-letter word that contains one vowel. (If your brain isn't too weak.)

11. Think of a dangerous five-letter reptile. Remove the letter "o" and rearrange the remaining letters to form a four-letter crustacean that's not nearly as dangerous.

12. One of these animals does not begin with something that the other three do. What?

pigeon donkey beetle bullfrog

13. Name exactly 100 words that do not contain the letters **a**, **b**, **c**, or **d**. (Hint: They're all connected...and they keep getting bigger.)

14. What's special about the word "swims"?

15. In what well-known word do these six consecutive consonants appear?

tchphr

Bug hussies: Aphids are *born* pregnant.

44 THINGS YOU CAN DO WITH A COCONUT

From the edible white stuff to the husk to the fibrous coating to the leaves to the oil, nearly every part of a coconut plant has dozens of uses. The coconut is truly the plant kingdom's buffalo.

BACKGROUND

The palm tree and its fruit, what we call the coconut, are native to tropical regions, and probably originated in what is now Indonesia. The coconut (technically a seed, not a nut) got its name from Spanish explorers who called it *coco*, a colloquialism that means "grinning face," because the three holes on the side of a coconut husk resemble a face. Coconuts have been common in the West only since the 1800s, but people who know the tropics also know that the coconut tree can provide a vast number of necessities.

1. **Drink the coconut water**, which contains antioxidants, fiber, minerals, and high amounts of potassium, magnesium, protein, and iron.

2. **Make coconut milk.** It's not the same thing as coconut water. To get "milk," grate coconut meat into water, let it soak, then squeeze and remove the pulp.

3. **Make *ruku raa***, a drink from the Maldives, by extracting the nectar from the young buds. This creates a sweet syrup and creamy sugar, useful in cooking or desserts.

4. **Eat the white meat.** Dry or freeze it to keep it longer.

5. **Ferment the nectar** of the flower clusters to make *toddy*, also called *tuba*, palm wine, or "Guam's moonshine."

6. **Eat the cream** that rises to the top of coconut milk.

7. **Make a gelatinlike dessert** called *nata de coco* ("cream of coconut").

8. **Make a coconut-scented** food or fragrance.

9. **Eat the young fruit buds,** but be aware that harvesting them kills the entire tree. (In Asia, they're served in expensive "millionaire's salads.")

10. **Feed your livestock** with the husk fiber.

11. Eat the fluffy, super-sweet substance in a young coconut that will separate into the meat and water.

12. Wrap rice in coconut palm leaves for cooking and storage, like the Filipinos do.

13. Make candy from the sap.

14. Make dye from the roots.

15. Weave the fibrous husk, called the *coir*, into mats or lace it into ropes. You can also use it to make boat caulking, potting compost, yarn, car seat covers, flowerpots, gardening mulch, insulation, brushes, bristles, mattresses, hats, rugs, carpet, bedding, decorations, and even a microporous aquarium filter.

16. Carve shirt buttons from the shells, like they do in Hawaii.

17. Create brushes, brooms, cooking skewers, and arrows from the stiff ribs of the palm leaves.

18. Weave the leaves into thatched roofs, baskets, or mats.

19. Fray a piece of the root and use it as a toothbrush; then make toothpaste out of the coconut oil.

20. Make mouthwash from ground-up roots mixed with water.

21. Buff floors with dried coconut half shells.

22. Make folk music with half shells like the Filipinos, Chinese, and Vietnamese do.

23. Make a bra out of two half shells, even if just for a laugh.

24. Carve the shells into bowls, spoons, ladles, serving trays, bangles, earrings, necklaces, and pendants.

25. Make bags out of the leaves.

26. Make a hamster bed out of a hollowed-out shell.

27. Make a bird feeder out of a cleaned-out half shell.

28. Build furniture or even structures (like Manila's Coconut Palace) with the tree trunks.

29. Build small, salt-resistant bridges out of the trunks.

30. Treat snakebites with coconut oil, like they do in Pakistan.

31. Make shampoo and soaps out of coconut oil.

32. Drink the water of a young coconut to relieve fever, headache, upset stomach, diarrhea, and dysentery. Well, that's what some say it can do. It's also reputed to strengthen the heart and restore energy if you're sick—pregnant women drink lots of it because they believe it gives babies strength and vitality.

33. Prevent fogging on snorkeling goggles by rubbing a fresh, inner coconut husk on the lens.

34. Use the fibers as ground fill to prevent topsoil erosion.

35. Rub coconut oil on your scalp and skin for healthy hair and complexion, or to help ward off infection. It's said to reduce symptoms of skin conditions such as dermatitis, eczema, and psoriasis and aids in immune system function. It also appears to assist with constipation, digestion problems, and weight control.

36. Make a short-term intravenous hydration fluid out of coconut water. Really.

37. Simulate a horse's hoofbeats by banging coconut halves together. This method is often used for sound effects in theater and movies.

38. Make containers, drums, and small canoes out of the hollowed-out trunks like the Hawaiians once did.

39. Use coconut oil for its antibacterial, antiaging, and antiviral properties. It's also been shown to fight off measles, influenza, yeast infections, and fungal infections. A study conducted in the Yucatan has shown that those using coconut oil daily had higher metabolisms, and women didn't suffer typical menopause symptoms.

40. Try coconut oil as an emergency replacement for diesel fuel. Filipino troops used it during World War II.

41. Burn the husks and shells as firewood.

42. Make bombs out of coconut shells filled with gunpowder. (But don't.)

43. Make switches out of the leaf branches for use in corporal punishment. (Don't do that, either.)

44. Inscribe a message on a coconut shell. The crew of *PT-109* did it when they were shipwrecked in 1943. John F. Kennedy commanded that boat, and the coconut later sat on his desk. (It's now in his presidential library.)

...he'd let his daughters stay up late to watch.

MUSICAL NOTES

Pssst! Here's some rumors and idle talk to go with your iPod. Pass it on!

KNIGHTLY NEWS

When the Beatles were invested in the Order of the British Empire in a 1965 ceremony at Buckingham Palace, they were so intimidated by the thought of meeting the Queen that they snuck into a palace restroom for a few minutes to "compose" themselves. At the ceremony "we were giggling like crazy," John Lennon remembered, "because we had just smoked a joint in the loo of Buckingham Palace, we were so nervous. We had nothing to say." (George Harrison swore they only smoked *cigarettes*.)

BURNED

In the 1980s, Pete Burns found fame as the lead singer of Dead or Alive, whose song "You Spin Me Round (Like a Record)," topped the pop charts in 1985. Today he's better known for botched plastic surgery: When a 2000 procedure to remove lip implants went horribly awry, Burns spent his entire fortune on more than 100 surgeries to repair the damage. Ironically, the notoriety revived his career: In 2006 he was cast in the British reality show *Celebrity Big Brother* and hosted the TV special *Cosmetic Surgery Nightmares*.

A BETTE BY ANY OTHER NAME

Bette Midler, whose song "The Rose" hit #3 on the U.S. pop charts in 1979, is named after Bette Davis. So why is her name pronounced "Bet" instead of "Betty?" It's a mistake—Midler's mother thought that was how Davis pronounced *her* name.

SHOCK AND AW(FUL)

During the Second Gulf War in 2003, the U.S. military needed a way to get Saddam Hussein's Ba'ath loyalists to reveal sensitive information, such as where the dictator was hiding. One of the techniques they came up with: forcing the loyalists to listen to heavy metal music—Metallica's "Enter Sandman" was a favorite—interspersed with children's songs like the theme to *Sesame Street* and songs by Barney the Dinosaur. "Trust me, it works," one American official told *Newsweek* magazine.

Hank Williams and John Mellencamp were born with *spina bifida*, a birth defect of the spinal cord.

A HOLE IN THE HEAD

If you've ever said, "I need that like I need a hole in my head," you might want to read this article to find out what you're missing.

THE HOLE STORY

There's actually a term to describe the practice of purposely boring a hole into the human skull for "medical" purposes. It's called *trepanning*, and it dates back at least 7,000 years—archaeologists have discovered Neanderthal skulls that had nickel-size holes in them. During the Middle Ages, the procedure was used to release the "demons," which were believed to be the cause of mental illness. By the 19th century, trepanning was still commonplace, although it was believed to cure mental illness by relieving pressure on the brain, not by exorcising evil spirits. The surgery fell out of favor in the early 20th century, when doctors realized the primitive procedure was ineffective (and dangerous).

In 1962 a Dutch self-help guru named Bart Huges tried to spearhead a modern-day trepanning comeback. While searching for a way to expand his consciousness and increase his brainpower, he somehow concluded that the key was in somehow opening up the skull. His "reasoning": Children are fast learners and have creative minds because their skulls are not yet fully formed or fully enclosed, and their high levels of creativity are due to higher levels of blood flow (and oxygen) to the brain. Huges decided that with trepanning, he could mimic the open skull and reap the rewards of increased blood flow. Using a surgical drill, Huges performed the procedure on himself (and then stitched up the skin over the borehole...himself).

DRILL BITS

For the record, there is absolutely no scientific evidence that drilling a hole in the head results in anything other than putting a person at serious risk of injury or death. But despite being committed to a mental institution after he extolled the virtues of trepanning to reporters, Huges served as a model for many latter-day trepanning advocates. (One more warning: *Do not try this at home*.)

Luke Skywalker's lightsaber sold at auction for $206,600. (Darth Vader's fetched only $118,000.)

• In 2000 Heather Perry of England suffered from chronic fatigue syndrome, of which the major symptom is...chronic fatigue. After doing some research, she decided that the only way to cure the condition was to relieve the pressure on her brain by drilling a dime-size hole in her skull. Doctors refused to do it, so Perry did it herself. She stood in front of a mirror, made an incision in her scalp, and drilled. There was no damage (although she was a few millimeters away from piercing her brain) and, according to Perry, her exhaustion is now gone.

• Peter Halvorson and William Lyons of Utah both received trepanning surgeries and touted the benefits of the cranial pressure-relieving procedure on the Internet. Despite the fact that neither man was a licensed physician, a British woman so believed in the surgery that in 2002 she hired them to drill a hole in her head and increase her "brain blood volume." The patient survived, but Halvorson and Lyons were arrested and convicted of practicing medicine without a license. (They received three years probation.)

• In 1995 Jenny Gathorne-Hardy of London read an article about trepanning and was intrigued by the claim that a skull hole could enhance brain function by increasing blood flow. So she put a local anesthetic on the side of her head and drilled a hole. Gathorne-Hardy later told reporters that she feels "calmer, and that the mental exhaustion I became so used to has gone."

• In the mid-1960s, English painter Joey Mellen wanted a hole drilled in his head, believing it would get him "permanently high." His girlfriend, Amanda Feilding, had successfully trepanned herself (and experienced euphoric highs), but it took a bit more work to accomplish Mellen's goal. Feilding unsuccessfully drilled his head once; the hole wasn't deep enough. Then Feilding took over. She botched the second attempt and Mellen lost a lot of blood—enough to require medical attention. But that didn't stop him. After recovering in a hospital (under psychiatric watch), Mellen went home and drilled the hole himself. When he heard what he later called "an ominous sounding 'schlurp' and the sound of bubbling,"—he knew he'd successfully bored through his skull (but *unsuccessfully* drilled into his own brain).

Donald Trump has *chirophobia,* a fear of shaking hands.

UNLIKELY BENEFACTORS

When people die—or even before—they don't always give their money or assets to their friends and family. Sometimes, often through roundabout circumstances, it ends up in some very unlikely places.

MARGARET WISE BROWN AND *GOODNIGHT MOON*

Margaret Wise Brown wrote more than 100 children's books. The most famous is *Goodnight Moon*, a bedtime story in which "goodnight" is said to all the objects in a room. It's sold 11 million copies, making it one of the most popular children's books ever. Brown died of an embolism while visiting France in 1952 at the age of 42. Her will gave all royalties from future sales of *Goodnight Moon* (at the time, it had sold only about 3,000 copies) to Albert Clarke, a nine-year-old boy whose family lived in the apartment next-door to hers in New York City. Sales of the book slowly grew, and by the time Clarke got access to his inheritance at age 21, there was $75,000 waiting for him, which he blew on a new car and expensive clothes. His lawyer put him on a weekly allowance, but it was still enough to allow Clarke to wander around the United States, spending the money on drugs, cars, bad real estate deals, and legal fees (he was arrested dozens of times on various charges). Over the past 50 years, Clarke accumulated more than $5 million in royalties from the sales of *Goodnight Moon*. When a reporter tracked him down in 2000, he had only a few thousand dollars left.

MARILYN MONROE

At the time of Monroe's death in 1962 at age 36, her estate was worth about $1.6 million. She willed it to the two people she trusted most: her acting teacher, Lee Strasberg (75 percent), and her psychiatrist, Dr. Marianne Kris (25 percent). When Kris died in 1980, her portion of the Monroe estate—which had grown substantially in the past two decades due to merchandising Monroe's image and the enduring popularity of her movies—went to the Anna Freud Centre, a children's psychiatric research hospital in London. It earns about $500,000 a year from the Monroe estate.

Some butterflies have ears on their wings.

IKEA FURNITURE

Ingvar Kamprad founded IKEA in Sweden in 1943 as a mail-order consumer goods business and began opening stores a few years later. Today, Kamprad is worth $30 billion. In 1982 he donated his ownership stake in the IKEA stores to a Dutch charity called the Stichting Ingka Foundation, which operates them through a for-profit subsidiary. With annual profits in the billions, the foundation is technically the world's richest charity. Its goal is to "promote and support innovation in architectural and interior design," but it distributes less than 1% of its earnings to colleges and other institutions...because it's not really a charity. The Foundation is run by a five-member board, headed by Kamprad, who still makes millions of dollars each year because the Foundation only owns IKEA stores, not the IKEA trademark or concept (they're still owned by Kamprad). Every IKEA store in the world pays Kamprad a franchise fee, totaling about $631 million a year. The whole system was set up so that IKEA was protected against a hostile takeover and so Kamprad could pay less in taxes. For example, in 2004 IKEA made a profit of 1.4 billion euros, but paid only 19 million euros in taxes.

YANKEE STADIUM AND RICE UNIVERSITY

In 1955 businessman John Cox acquired all the stock of the Yankee Stadium Holding Company, making him the sole owner of Yankee Stadium and allowing him to lease the stadium back to the team at a lucrative rate. Seven years later, Cox died, leaving Yankee Stadium to his alma mater, Rice University in Houston, Texas. In 1971 New York City invoked the right of eminent domain and forced the university to sell them Yankee Stadium for a $2.5 million "condemnation fee." (The university had a partner: the land under the stadium was owned at the time by the Knights of Columbus. It had been sold to them by its previous owner, John Cox.)

J. M. BARRIE'S *PETER PAN*

In 1929, eight years before he died, Scottish writer J. M. Barrie gave the copyright to his most famous work—his original 1904 stage version of *Peter Pan*—to the Great Ormond Street Hospital. The millions in royalties they've earned since then on productions of the play have enabled the London institution to become England's top children's hospital.

According to statistics, approximately 40,000 Americans are injured by toilets every year.

BEDTIME STORIES

We won't be offended if you doze off while reading this page.

• Studies show that 41 percent of people sleep in the fetal position, 28 percent on their side, 13 on their back, 7 on their stomach, and the rest in two or more positions.

• Mark Twain wrote most of *The Adventures of Tom Sawyer* and *The Adventures of Huckleberry Finn* in bed. Another author who wrote in bed: Robert Louis Stevenson.

• 64 percent of women sleep on the left side of the bed.

• King Louis XI of France received visiting dignitaries in his bed, which he called the Bed of Justice. At one point, he owned 413 beds.

• Tip: The handles on the side of a mattress aren't for moving it—that stretches it out. The handles are only supposed to be used to rotate or flip the mattress on the box springs.

• More than 600,000 Americans are injured by beds every year (mostly by falling out of them or bumping their heads on headboards).

• World record for making a bed: Wendy Wall of Sydney, Australia, made one in 28.2 seconds (1978).

• Queen and king-size beds weren't available until the 1950s. The Simmons company invented them in 1958.

• Sleep experts say that people who sleep on their right side have better digestion.

• The word "mattress" comes from the Arabic *matrah*, for "where something is thrown."

• Two adults sleeping in a double bed have less personal space than a baby in a crib.

• Sleep law: in Tallinn, Estonia, couples are not allowed to play chess in bed.

• 40 percent of men snore, and 30 percent of women do.

• Now *that's* a king-sized bed: the Great Bed of Ware, built in the 1590s in the town of Ware, England. On display at the Victoria and Albert Museum in London, it measures 10 by 11 feet and could sleep as many as 15 people.

Hans Christian Andersen died by falling out of bed. (Odds of this happening: one in 2 million.)

LIFE IMITATES BART

The Simpsons is loaded with references to cultural moments, historical people, and current events. But occasionally things happen on The Simpsons first...and then they happen in real life.

ON *THE SIMPSONS*: In the 2001 episode "HOMR," Homer Simpson earns extra money as a medical test subject. Doctors discover a crayon that's been lodged in his brain since childhood and when it's removed, Homer's IQ doubles.
IN REAL LIFE: In August 2007, 59-year-old Margret Wegner of Germany underwent surgery to cure the chronic headaches and nosebleeds she'd suffered since the age of four. Surgeons discovered—and removed—the cause of the problems: a pencil. Wegner remembers how it happened: As a four-year-old child, she was holding a pencil and tripped, jamming the pencil through her cheek and, apparently, into her brain. After the pencil was removed, Wegner's symptoms instantly disappeared.

ON *THE SIMPSONS*: In the 1993 episode "$pringfield," a casino opens in town. The entertainment there is a flamboyantly dressed German duo named Gunter and Ernst who perform magic and stunts with big cats. Their show ends prematurely when their white tiger Anastasia viciously mauls both Gunter and Ernst.
IN REAL LIFE: Gunter and Ernst were an obvious parody of the Las Vegas magic-and-animals act Siegfried and Roy. While performing at a Las Vegas casino in 2003, Roy Horn was attacked and bitten on the neck by a white tiger named Montecore. It ruptured several nerves and only after nearly three years of rehabilitation could Horn walk again.

ON *THE SIMPSONS*: In "Bart's Friend Falls in Love" (1992), Homer hungrily drools over a new kind of fast-food hamburger called the "Good Morning Burger." The recipe: "We take 18 ounces of sizzling ground beef and soak it in rich, creamery butter, then we top it off with bacon, ham, and a fried egg." The joke is that the sandwich is so disgustingly fattening that only Homer Simpson would ever eat it.

Insignificant, but interesting: 3.8 million pens are purchased by Walt Disney World each year.

IN REAL LIFE: Turns out that Homer isn't the only one who'll eat those monstrosities. Since around 2003, gigantic thousand-plus-calorie burgers have become standard fare on fast-food menus. Wendy's now offers a burger topped with six pieces of bacon, Burger King has a quadruple-patty bacon cheeseburger, and Carl's Jr. makes a burger with a half-pound beef patty topped with a quarter pound of sliced prime rib. And in 2008 a New York chain called Good Burger came out with an actual "Good Morning Burger," topped with a fried egg.

ON *THE SIMPSONS*: In the 1995 episode "Barts Sells His Soul," Bart sells his soul to his friend Milhouse to prove that souls don't really exist (and to pocket an easy five bucks). Bart has an anxiety attack, fearing that perhaps souls do exist...and that now he doesn't have one. He tries to get his soul back, only to discover that Milhouse traded it to the Comic Book Guy for *Alf* pogs.

IN REAL LIFE: In July 2008, New Zealander Walter Scott put his soul up for sale on TradeMe, an auction Web site. The listing stipulated that the winning buyer would receive a framed certificate of soul ownership, but wouldn't be able to control Scott in any way. Ultimately, Scott's soul was sent to Hell. Hell Pizza, a New Zealand chain, bought it for $3,800 directly from Scott after TradeMe cancelled the auction because they thought it was in poor taste. "The soul belongs to Hell. There is simply no better place for it," a Hell spokesman told reporters.

ON *THE SIMPSONS*: In the 1999 episode "They Saved Lisa's Brain," Lisa leads a group of intellectuals to take over the city of Springfield. Among the collective is world-famous astrophysicist Stephen Hawking, who tells Homer that "your idea of a donut-shaped universe intrigues me. I may have to steal it."

IN REAL LIFE: In May 2008, researchers at Ulm University in Germany announced that after five years of study, they found evidence that the universe is small and finite (56 billion light years wide), in direct contradiction of conventional wisdom, which suggests it's infinite. More specifically, the scientists say that temperature fluctuations indicate that the universe is round and tubular... or in other words, it's shaped "like a donut."

An African cicada can produce a 106.7-decibel sound—louder than a subway train.

30 PEOPLE YOU DIDN'T KNOW WERE CANADIAN

...or did you? If you didn't, well, now you know.

1. **Paul Anka,** singer/composer ("Diana" and "My Way")

2. **Norma Shearer,** Oscar-winning actress (*The Divorcée*)

3. **Bat Masterson,** Old West lawman

4. **Frank Gehry,** architect

5. **Fay Wray,** star of the original 1933 *King Kong*

6. **Peter Jennings,** ABC news anchor

7. **Christopher Plummer,** star of *The Sound of Music*

8. **Leslie McFarlane,** writer of the first *Hardy Boys* books

9. **Robert Goulet,** singer/actor

10. **Lennox Lewis,** heavyweight boxing champion

11. (and **12.**) **Scott Abbott** and **Chris Haney,** inventors of Trivial Pursuit

13. **Steve Nash,** two-time NBA most valuable player

14. **Conrad Bain,** played the father on *Diff'rent Strokes*

15. **Mary Pickford,** silent-film actress nicknamed "America's Sweetheart"

16. **Wolverine,** fictional superhero from the X-Men

17. **Tommy Chong,** of Cheech and Chong

18. **Art Linkletter,** TV host

19. **Kim Cattrall,** actress from *Sex and the City*

20. **Jack Warner,** founder of Warner Bros. Studios

21. **Louis B. Mayer,** founder of MGM Studios

22. **James Naismith,** inventor of basketball

23. **John Kricfalusi,** creator of *Ren and Stimpy*

24. **Seth Rogen,** actor/writer (*Knocked Up, Superbad*)

25. **Joe Shuster,** co-creator of Superman

26. **Morley Safer,** journalist from *60 Minutes*

27. **Linda Evangelista,** supermodel

28. **Frederick Banting,** scientist who discovered insulin

29. **Neil Young,** rock star

30. **Monty Hall,** host of *Let's Make a Deal*

According to experts, there are 6,670,903,752,021,072,936,960 possible different sudoku boards.

BUTT...BUTT...

What's so funny about that particular part of the human anatomy? We don't know—it's one of the mysteries of nature...like the rings around Uranus.

GOODNIGHT, MOON

"Utrecht police say a 21-year-old Dutch man is recovering after a 'mooning' that went horribly wrong. The report says a 21-year-old man and two friends were running down a street in Utrecht with their pants pulled down in the back 'for a joke.' At one point the man 'pushed his behind against the window of a restaurant.' The glass broke and resulted in 'deep wounds to his derriere.' Police detained the three men after the incident, but the cafe owner decided not to press charges after the men agreed to pay for the broken window."

—Yahoo! News

OFFICER HANDY

"A Denver sheriff's deputy has been slapped with a 45-day suspension for slapping another deputy's buttocks, which prompted the co-worker to quit. While Deputy Francisco Hernandez reportedly resigned after having his rear-end whacked, attorney Derek Cole called Deputy Bobby Rogers' subsequent suspension an over-reaction. 'It's gross overkill,' Cole said. 'It's like executing somebody for blowing their nose and not washing their hands.' The incident occurred Aug. 30, 2007, when Hernandez bent to pick up some keys only to be 'slapped hard on the buttocks' by Rogers. 'If you're going to stick it out, I'm going to hit it,' Rogers allegedly said after the hit, according to city documents."

—United Press International

TOUCHÉ

"As revenge attacks go, it was pretty cheeky. A 'cheating' husband is having to see 200 photos of his naked bottom plastered on walls, lampposts and bus stops all over his home town. Pasha Cummings believes the posters, which show him posing at a barbecue, are the work of ex-wife Carol—who coincidentally emi-

In the 1860s, the Kansas Pacific Railroad often stopped to allow passengers to shoot at buffalo.

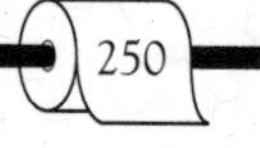

grated to Cyprus the day after they appeared. Beneath the 'glamour shot' the posters read: 'Pasha Cummings: lying, cheating, two-timing arse! Sandra Beckworth is no better.' Cummings recently split with his wife after six years together. He claims he did not start seeing Ms. Beckworth—his boss at the care home where he works—until two months later. But his wife believed otherwise. 'Carol was very bitter when I left her,' Cummings said."

—***The Metro* (U.K.)**

TAKE A SEAT FOR ART

"Stephen Murmer, a popular art teacher at Monacan High School in Virginia, has been placed on administrative leave because of his private 'artwork.' Working under the pseudonym 'Stan Murmur,' he produced pictures by smearing his undercarriage with paint and then sitting on canvas. Far more than your typical 'pressed hams' though, Murmer created images of flowers, including 'Tulip Butts,' with higher-end pieces selling for as much as $900. Things seemed to be going fine until an interview of 'Stan Murmur' wearing only a Speedo, a fake nose, glasses and a towel on his head found its way onto YouTube. According to Chesterfield County schools, 'teachers are expected to set an example for students through their personal conduct,' and apparently painting with your backside is not the example they had in mind."

—***Washington Post***

KICK START

"Engineers in Idaho have developed an interesting new device designed to motivate employees—the World Famous Manually Self-Operated Butt-Kicking Machine. Creator J. Reese Leavitt says the Butt-Kicking Machine came out of a brainstorming meeting when he and his co-workers were talking about raising employee productivity. How does it work? Just sit firmly on your fanny, fasten the seat belt, apply pressure, and a size-9 Chuck Taylor shoe will hit your hindquarters. 'That, by the way, is the most expensive part of the machine,' said Leavitt. 'The shoe cost us about $40.' (The total cost is $250.) Leavitt and his associates plan on renting out the machine for fundraisers."

—NBC-5, Dallas

Area code of Cape Canaveral, where the Space Shuttle launches: 321.

THE FIRST WAR GAME

If you've ever played Risk, Diplomacy, Axis & Allies, Dungeons & Dragons, World of Warcraft, or any other game that lets you conquer the world, here's the war game that started it all—the most influential game you've never heard of.

INSTANT REPLAY

For as long as armies have gone to war, there's been a need to remember lessons learned in battle. The losers want to know what went wrong, so that it doesn't happen again; the winners want to understand why they won, so that they can repeat their success. But how do you pass these lessons on to the next generation of military officers before they've even been in combat?

Card games and chess have both been played in Europe since the 1500s, and over the centuries numerous attempts were made to use them for strategy games that would teach young officers the lessons of war. But no matter how many variations were tried—replacing the jacks, kings, queens, and aces with captains, majors, colonels, and generals, or giving chess more pieces, more players, or a larger or more varied game board—these attempts never came close to recreating the battlefield experience. Their value as an instructional tool for young officers was limited at best.

THE SANDMAN

Then in the early 1800s, Baron George von Reisswitz, a Prussian civil servant and military-history buff, decided to create a war game entirely from scratch:

- Why limit yourself to a chessboard? Von Reisswitz thought it made more sense to play on a surface with real topographical features. He built a box several feet square and filled it with sand that could be used to model the hills, valleys, rivers, roads, and bridges that a Prussian soldier might encounter on a real battlefield.
- He made the playing surface large enough, and the square blocks that represented soldiers small enough, so that the blocks approximated the size of actual soldiers on a battlefield landscape. This allowed von Reisswitz to incorporate the concepts of time and distance into the game, something that had not been a part of card- and chess-based games.

• Troops on the march can only travel a certain number of paces per minute. By setting the scale of the game at 3 centimeters = 100 paces, it was possible to measure the distance between opposing groups of soldiers to calculate where and when they would meet on the battlefield. And since the range of rifles, cannons, and other weapons was also known, it was possible to tell when a group of soldiers would come within range of enemy fire.

Although von Reisswitz discarded playing cards and chess, he retained a third popular game of the era—dice—which he used to incorporate the important and often decisive role that random chance—or "friction," as it's sometimes called—can play in warfare. Is the weather too hot? Too cold? Too wet? Do rain or ice or snow make the roads impassable? Is troop morale unusually high? Abysmally low? Were they sleeping when the enemy attacked? Did their drinking water give them dysentery? Von Reisswitz understood that having more soldiers and a superior position on the battlefield can only go so far in determining the outcome of a battle. He incorporated rolls of the dice to account for anything and everything else.

THE MIDDLEMAN

But von Reisswitz's most interesting and valuable innovation was his decision to deny his players knowledge of everything that was happening on the battlefield.

• In chess, both players see the entire board at all times and know where all the pieces are at any point in the game. In warfare things are very different, of course. The commanders' knowledge is limited to what they and their troops can see with their own eyes. The location and deployment of the enemy, the size of its forces, and the direction in which they are moving are anyone's guess.

• Von Reisswitz wanted to replicate this important concept of limited knowledge, so he created the position of a game master or "umpire," who would host the game and be the only person with full knowledge of everything that was happening.

• At the start of the game, the umpire would explain the battlefield scenario to the commanders of opposing armies, and then these commanders would go off into separate corners or even separate rooms to prepare written orders. Each commander would give their plan to the umpire; neither commander would know what the other's troops were doing.

• Then, as the game progressed, the umpire would reveal this information to the commanders only as quickly as they would have learned it on an actual battlefield. If one side's troops were hiding in a forest, for example, the umpire wouldn't reveal their position on the sand table until the other side's troops got close enough to spot the hidden soldiers themselves.

• As the umpire revealed information to the players, they would use it to issue new written orders. This in turn caused the umpire to reveal still more information, which would prompt yet another set of orders. The process continued this way until one side won the battle.

• Having the umpire implement the orders of both sides at the same time allowed both armies to act simultaneously, just as they would in a real war, instead of having one side sit still while the other side made its move, as was the case in cards or chess.

FRIENDS IN HIGH PLACES

Kriegsspiel, or "Wargame," as the game came to be known, might have remained an obscure hobby had the captain of cadets at the Berlin Military Academy not learned of the game and mentioned it during a lecture in 1811. Two of his students—Prince Friedrich and Prince Wilhelm of Prussia, the teenage sons of King Friedrich Wilhelm III—wanted to play. They arranged for von Reisswitz to umpire a game at Berlin Castle, with the princes commanding their own armies. They enjoyed the experience and told the King about it. He, too, was soon hooked on the game.

Another early player of Kriegsspiel was Baron von Reisswitz's own son, George von Reisswitz the Younger. By the early 1820s, he was an officer stationed in Berlin, and while there he and several friends played regularly. When they didn't like something about the game, they changed it. For example, they abandoned sand tables in favor of maps, which were much more portable, and they changed the scale of the game to allow for larger battles fought with entire brigades (3,000 to 4,000 men) of soldiers.

George's improvements must have been impressive, because when Prince Wilhelm played the new version, he saw to it that it was demonstrated to the entire Prussian general staff. "Gentlemen," the chief of the general staff exclaimed to the group, "this is not a game; this is a war exercise! I must recommend it to the whole army!"

TODAY, PRUSSIA—TOMORROW, THE WORLD

Soon the entire Prussian officer corps was playing Kriegsspiel. Then, after Prussia won wars against Austria in 1866 and France in 1871, other countries began to take an interest in the training methods of the Prussian officer corps, including Kriegsspiel. Interest in the game spread throughout Europe and the United States. By the turn of the century, even civilians were playing, too, with clubs springing up in England and elsewhere. Just as George von Reisswitz the Younger had set to work changing parts of the game he didn't like, the new hobbyists made their own changes.

Many were inspired to create entirely new games of their own:

• In 1913 H. G. Wells, author of *The War of the Worlds*, got in on the act: He wrote *Little Wars*, a set of rules for combat with toy soldiers and spring-loaded cannons.

• In the 1950s, an American war game enthusiast named Charles S. Roberts founded a game company called Avalon Hill, which remained the dominant war game publisher into the 1970s.

• Then in 1971, two war gamers named Gary Gygax and Dave Arneson came up with a game of their own that, if anything, was even more revolutionary than Kriegsspiel.

Even if you've never heard of Gary Gygax and Dave Arneson, you've almost certainly heard of the game they invented. Who knows—maybe you even played it. ***That story begins on page 318.***

* * *

LE JUGHEAD

Remember Jughead, the character from Archie comics who wears a cardboard crown and loves to eat cheeseburgers? In the French version of the comic he's called *Doudingue*, in Spanish he's *Torombolo* and in German he's *Knallkopf* (literally "bang head").

Most expensive video game ever: Grand Theft Auto IV, which cost $100 million to develop.

THE FUNNY PAGES

Great bathroom reading from real newspaper ads.

WANT ADS

Painting Job This Summer? Call for Free Estimates. If I'm not at home, arrange a date with my wife.

Wanted: Widower with school-age children requires person to assume general housekeeping duties. Must be capable of contributing to growth of family.

Cleaner Required, must be contentious.

Wanted: Free Furniture. Full bed, end table, working lamp, and a working floor model TV. You've got to haul it.

FOR SALE

One pair hardly used dentures, only two teeth missing.

American flag, 60 stars. Pole included, $100.

For sale. Three canaries of undermined sex.

Toaster: Great fun for the whole family. Automatically burns toast.

Wedding Dress. Worn once by mistake. Call Stephanie.

15"-diameter, 3-speed fan. It will oscillate if you walk in a circle around it.

Complete set of Encyclopaedia Britannica. Excellent condition. No longer needed. Got married last month. Wife knows everything.

Solid oak funeral handmade casket in good condition. Only used once.

Tombstone: Standard gray. A good buy for someone named Grady.

FROM THE AD PAGE

Open house. Body Shapers toning salon. Free coffee and donuts.

Sheer stockings. Designed for fancy dress, but so serviceable that lots of women wear nothing else.

The hotel has bowling alleys, tennis courts, comfortable beds, and other athletic facilities.

Auto Repair Service. Free pick-up and delivery. Try us once, and you'll never go anywhere again.

In 1961 A&W's Teen Burger became the first fast-food burger to be topped with bacon.

GREAT FOOD DEALS

BLT—$1.85 (lettuce and tomato $.10 extra)

Sliced bologna, regular or tasty, save 30 cents on 2

I Can Believe It's Not Butter! 8 oz. $1.38

Super G String Cheese, $1.49

THE PERSONALS

SWM into chainsaws and hockey masks seeks likeminded SWF. No weirdos, please.

Don't call me if you are uneducated; unemployed; unhealthy smoker; felon; under 30 years old, 5'10"; over 40 years old, 6'8", 230 pounds; like cats, channel surfing; make less than $30,000 annually; or have body parts pierced. Others feel free.

Me—trying to sleep on the bus station bench, pleading with you to give me a cigarette; you—choking on my odor, tripping over your purse trying to get away; at the last moment, our eyes meeting. Yours were blue. Can I have a dollar?

Good-looking, athletic, Notting Hill-based movie star, millionaire, seeks gullible stunner.

Hideous-looking, obese, smelly, ill-tempered, lazy, cowardly, chronic, and a complete liar seeks total opposite.

Minimalist seeks woman.

I am spitting kitty. Ftt Fttttttt. I am angry bear. Grrrrr. I am large watermelon seed stuck in your nose. Zermmmmmmmm. I am small biting spider in your underwear. Yub yub yub. No mimes.

RESTAURANT ADS

Mattie's Restaurant and Yogurt Palace: An Alternative to Good Eating

Bring in this coupon and receive a FREE medium coffee for the price of a small.

Bogie's Child's Menu
Children 12 & under
driver's license required

It takes many ingredients to make Burger King great…but the secret ingredient is our people!

*   *   *

"If you consider the contribution of plumbing to human life, the other sciences fade into insignificance."

—**James Gorman**

THE INTERNUTS

A small sampling of some of the many odd things you can find on the Internet.

I Hate Cilantro. If you really dislike the herb cilantro and you feel the need to share with others, go to *ihatecilantro.com*. This anti-cilantro community of more than 1,700 members write about how much they hate "the most offensive food known to man." ("It tastes like dish soap.")

Ice Chewers Bulletin Board. There are a lot of people out there who like to chew ice, apparently. If you're one of them, *icechewing.iswhaticrave.com* is where you can share your ice-chewing stories, your favorite ice-chewing recipes, or anything at all related to ice chewing, and join the community of more than 3,400 members.

Lasagna Cat. You're familiar with the *Garfield* comic strip. Well, *lasagnacat.com* has a few dozen videos of three people—one playing John, one in a dog costume playing Odie, and one in a cat costume playing Garfield—acting out actual *Garfield* comics as they appeared in newspapers. They even give the dates on which the comics originally appeared.

Nothing. *Blanksite.com* has absolutely nothing on it. It's just a blank white screen. (Its companion site, *Something.com*, does have something on it—the word "something." That's all.)

Men's Long Hair Hyperboard. This site (*mlhh.org*) is a forum for long-haired men about long hair on men. Does your long hair cause friction at work? How do you handle your long hair while riding a motorcycle? How many inches has your hair grown since your last post? If you feel like chatting about it, this is the place for you.

Gooooooooooooooooooooooooooooooooooooooooooooooooooooooooooooogle.com. This works just like google. Really. (But it has to have exactly 59 *o*'s in it.)

The Big Button That Doesn't Do Anything. It's a Web site with a really big button on it. It doesn't do anything. It hasn't done anything for the millions of people that have pushed it since 1994. Go ahead: Go to *pixelscapes.com/spatulacity/button.htm*...and push the button. We did. (It didn't do anything.)

Average annual salary of a Major League Baseball mascot: $40,000.

SEVEN (UNDERWATER) PLACES TO SEE BEFORE YOU DIE

Grab your snorkel and flippers and get yourself to these amazing subaquatic locations before you slip and slide off this mortal coil.

1. THE GREAT BLUE HOLE. It's off the coast of Belize in the Caribbean Sea. If you fly over it what you'll see is the Caribbean's emerald-green water interrupted by a narrow, ring-shaped blue "island." Inside the ring is an almost perfectly circular, darker blue spot, more than 1,000 feet in diameter. It's a sinkhole, and it's about 400 feet deep. During the last ice age, when sea levels were much lower than they are today, it was a dry, limestone cave system. When the water level rose, the cave filled and its roof collapsed, creating the hole. Put on your flippers and you can explore the tunnels below the surface. Jacques Cousteau studied the site in the 1970s, and called it one of the 10 best places on the planet to go scuba diving.

2. THE GALAPAGOS ISLANDS. These islands in the Pacific Ocean, 600 miles off the coast of Ecuador in South America, are remarkable for many reasons, high among them the fact that for millions of years they were isolated from other areas on the planet. Result: The Galapagos Islands are home to some of the most diverse and unique animal life in the world. Aside from the more than 450 species of fish, about 20% of which are found nowhere else, it's the only place in the world where you can see the marine iguana (the world's only oceangoing lizard), Pacific green sea turtles, Galapagos sharks, and Galapagos penguins, the northernmost of the penguin species. You might even see whale sharks, the largest fish in the ocean, which grow up to 40 feet long and can weigh more than 40,000 pounds. (Don't be afraid: They eat plankton.) You may also find yourself in the middle of a school of hundreds of hammerhead sharks. (Go ahead, be afraid now.) Hammerheads can be dangerous to humans, but

Each year, Hostess bakeries produce 500 million Twinkies.

attacks are rare and no human deaths from hammerheads have occurred in recorded history. The best time to go is from December to June, when warm ocean currents keep the water between 75° and 80°F.

3. THE YONGALA. On March 23, 1911, a 350-foot passenger ship sailing from Melbourne to Cairns, Australia, ran into a cyclone off the coast of Queensland. It sank, and all 122 people aboard perished. The ship was the SS *Yongala*, and its wreckage was discovered in 1958 about 13 miles off the coast, resting about 100 feet below the surface. It's now officially part of the largest coral reef system in the world, the Great Barrier Reef. The ship is remarkably intact—and is considered by many expert divers to be the best place to go diving in the world today. It is described as "like swimming in a huge aquarium," with the ship itself being encrusted in many kinds of very colorful soft and hard coral species. On any given dive you may encounter bull sharks, tiger sharks, dolphins, giant groupers (weighing hundreds of pounds), sea turtles, octopi, manta rays, sea snakes, and much, much more. And the water's warm, from 70° to 80°F.
Warning: Do not go inside the ship! It's a protected heritage site, and you can be arrested and heavily fined for disturbing it.

4. THE BIMINI ROAD. It's Atlantis! Well, that's what some people say, anyway. It's actually a half-mile-long succession of large, rectangular limestone rocks configured in an almost rectangular shape about 20 feet beneath the ocean's surface near North Bimini Island in the Bahamas. The shape and layout of the rocks lead many people to believe they're the remains of a manmade structure, possibly a wall, a foundation, or a road. It was discovered only recently, in 1968, by pilots flying over the area, and has since been studied intensely. Most geologists and archaeologists believe it's a naturally occurring, if unique, phenomenon, but others disagree. In any case, you can snorkel or scuba dive in the clear, blue-green waters and check out the sight for yourself.
Bonus trivia: The final scene of *The Silence of the Lambs*, in which Hannibal Lecter says to Agent Starling over the phone, "I'm having a friend for dinner," was filmed at an airstrip on tiny North Bimini Island.

California was an independent republic for 25 days in 1846.

5. BARRACUDA POINT. Located off Sipadan Island in Malaysia, Barracuda Point has many colorful coral and fish species and other amazing flora and fauna, and the water's warm and clear, so you can see it all. But the most amazing thing about this dive locale is that at any moment you may find yourself in the middle of what is called a "barracuda tornado": thousands of the slender, frightening-looking fish, some up to six feet long, forming huge hollow cylindrical towers, swimming in a seemingly choreographed procession. It is considered one of the most exhilarating events in diving. (Luckily, barracudas rarely attack humans.)

6. THE *HISPANIA*. The SS *Hispania* was a 236-foot Swedish steamship that attempted to pass through the treacherous Sound of Mull between the Isle of Mull and the west Scottish coast during a brutal storm in 1954. She ran aground on a reef known as *Sgeir More*, or Big Rock, and sank to the bottom about 85 feet down. (The crew survived; the skipper refused to leave the ship and was last seen standing in the bridge, his hand raised in a salute, as it went down.) The spookily intact ship still stands where it landed, almost upright, covered in orange and white sea anemones. Experienced divers can swim into it and below decks to encounter fish and other marine life that have made the ship their home.

7. BLUE SHARK ISLAND. This is a dive site near Catalina Island, a small, rocky island off the coast of California, south of Los Angeles. For a reasonable price, you can go out on a small boat with experienced divers. Then you can help them cut up some fish. And then you can throw the fish parts (called *chum*) into the water…and help lower the dive cage. *Then* you can climb inside the dive cage and get up close and personal with large blue sharks! And if you want to, you're free to jump in the water *outside* the cage and get even more up-close to the sharks…along with the fish parts and blood and all that. Along with blues, the area is also home to mako, soupfin, and leopard sharks, and if you're lucky you might spot the rare, raylike angel shark. And if you're *really* lucky—or really *un*lucky—you might see a great white shark. They're not uncommon, with specimens approaching 20 feet long seen in the area. To a shark that big, you'd be just another piece of fish parts. So good luck, chum!

Haptodysphoria is the odd sensation some people get when touching peaches or other fuzzy surfaces.

STRANGE LAWSUITS

These days it seems that people will sue each other over practically anything. Here are some real-life examples of unusual legal battles.

THE PLAINTIFF: Caryl Dontfraid
THE DEFENDANT: Binder & Binder, a New York City law firm
THE LAWSUIT: In 2004 Dontfraid, a paralegal at Binder & Binder, told her employer that she suffered from *seasonal affective disorder*, a form of depression triggered by a lack of sunlight in the winter. She asked to work from home, but her request was denied. Ten days later, her department was moved to a different floor, further reducing Dontfraid's access to sunlight. She asked her supervisor for a desk by a window, so he gave her a spot three feet away from one, but she refused it and was fired. Three years later, Dontfraid sued her former employer for $33 million.
THE VERDICT: Pending. But Dontfraid's attorneys probably will have an uphill battle trying to argue their client's disability claim—Binder & Binder specializes in disability claims.

THE PLAINTIFF: Joyce Walker
THE DEFENDANT: Cook County, Illinois
THE LAWSUIT: In 2003, while working as a clerk at Stroger Hospital in Chicago, Walker walked out of the ladies' room and slipped on a banana peel (seriously). She injured her knee, missing 12 weeks of work and requiring injections of anti-inflammatory drugs. She sued Cook County, which ran the hospital, for an undisclosed sum.
THE VERDICT: In 2007 Walker and the county agreed to a settlement. Millions? No, $4,110. "It's the cost of doing business," said county commissioner Liz Gorman.

THE PLAINTIFF: Tomas Delgado
THE DEFENDANT: The family of Enaitz Iriondo
THE LAWSUIT: While driving in Haro, Spain, in 2004, Delgado hit a teenager on a bicycle and dragged him for 340 feet. The bicyclist, 17-year-old Enaitz Iriondo, was killed instantly. A Span-

ish court ruled that although Delgado was speeding, Iriondo was also partially at fault because he wasn't wearing reflective clothing. Delgado's insurance paid $48,500 to Iriondo's parents. Case closed? No. In 2006 Delgado sued Iriondo's family for $30,000—to pay for the damage to his car (plus the cost of a rental while it was being fixed). "It's the only way I have to claim my money back," he told reporters.

THE VERDICT: The case was widely reported by Spanish news media. Result: On the verge of a ruling in 2008, a large mob of angry protesters gathered outside the courthouse where the case was being tried...and Delgado withdrew his suit.

THE PLAINTIFF: Cleanthi Peters

THE DEFENDANT: Universal Studios Florida

THE LAWSUIT: In 1998 Peters, 57, and her 10-year-old granddaughter went though the Halloween Horror Nights haunted house at Universal Studios in Orlando, Florida. Just as they were about to exit the ride, an employee dressed as Leatherface, the masked chainsaw killer from *The Texas Chainsaw Massacre* movies, ran up to Peters and her granddaughter and pretended to attack them. As they ran for the exit they slipped on a wet spot on the ground, and then Leatherface crouched over them with his chainsaw (it was a prop). Two years later, Peters sued Universal for $15,000, claiming to have suffered "extreme fear, emotional distress, and mental anguish."

THE VERDICT: Settled out of court.

THE PLAINTIFF: Macrida Patterson

THE DEFENDANT: Victoria's Secret

THE LAWSUIT: In May 2007, Patterson was putting on a pair of blue Victoria's Secret "Sexy Little Thing" thong underwear when a rhinestone heart that adorned the front of the garment came loose, flew up, and struck her in the eye. It was so painful that she required hospitalization, where tests revealed her cornea was cut in three places. In June 2008, Patterson sued Victoria's Secret for $25,000 for selling her a defective product.

THE VERDICT: Pending, although Patterson's credibility might have been damaged by the fact that she went on *The Today Show* to talk about the lawsuit before she actually filed it.

About 40% of America's population lives within one day's drive of Philadelphia.

THAT'S FUNNY

Comedy quips scientifically proven to make you feel better.

"Laughter is the best medicine…unless you have facial injuries."

—Linda Smith

"I bought a book on hair loss, but the pages kept falling out."

—Jay London

"Another term for balloon is 'bad breath holder.'"

—Demetri Martin

"My credit is so bad I need a cosigner to play Monopoly."

—Joanna Briley

"I saw a truck today with a sign that said 'Driver has no cash.' I'm broke, too. But I don't plaster it all over the side of my car."

—Margaret Smith

"My father always used to say, 'What doesn't kill you, makes you stronger'…until the accident."

—Jimmy Carr

"I've killed so many houseplants. I walked into a nursery once and my face was on a wanted poster."

—Rita Rudner

"Why is there an expiration date on yogurt? It's bad milk with fruit in it. It should say, 'Worse after August 3rd.'"

—Eileen Kelly

"When I told my friends I was going to be a comedian, they laughed at me."

—Carrot Top

"The formula for water is H_2O. Is the formula for an ice cube H_2O squared?"

—Lily Tomlin

"Well, my brother says hello. So, hooray for speech therapy."

—Emo Philips

"My son has a new nickname for me: 'Baldy.' Son, I've got a new word for you: 'Heredity.'"

—Dan Savage

"I used to do drugs. I still do, but I used to, too."

—Mitch Hedberg

"My friends tell me I have intimacy problems, but they don't know me, so who cares what they think?"

—Garry Shandling

A violin bow contains about 150 horsetail hairs.

HIP-HOP NAMEZ

If Uncle John ever became a rapper, he'd call himself "DJ Johnny Outhouzz." Here are some other creative hip-hop names (and they're all real).

- MC Pooh
- Del tha Funkee Homosapien
- Lil' Scrappy
- Fed X
- Beat Bullies
- Chali 2na
- Bazooka Joe Gotti
- Dreddy Kruger
- Coo Coo Cal
- The Boss Hog Barbarians
- Uncle Murda
- Mr. Stinky
- Devastatin' Dave: The Turntable Slave
- Stimuli
- Geologic
- B-Real
- Guccie Mane
- Atoms Family
- Thirstin Howl III
- Rappy McRapperson
- Yak Ballz
- Skull Duggery
- Eargasm
- Futuristic Sex Robotz
- Crunchy Black
- Optimus Rhyme
- Droop-E
- Sweet Tee
- Yo Yo
- Matlock
- Morris Minor & the Majors
- Beelow
- Flobots
- Cool Breeze
- Messy Marv
- Yung Wun
- Tha Alkaholiks
- Metafore
- Big Boi
- Madlib (**M**ind-**A**ltering **D**emented **L**essons **I**n **B**eats)

OWNEY GOES POSTAL

Longtime BRI readers know that we've always had a fondness for dogs. Owney is one of the best ever.

DOG TIRED

One autumn day in 1888, a young, straggly, Terrier-mix mutt snuck into the Albany, New York, post office and went to sleep on top of some empty mailbags. The next morning, postal employees discovered him...and took a liking to him. They decided to let him stay at the office and gave him the name "Owney," although nobody seems to know quite why.

Owney seemed strangely attached to the mail bags. He didn't just like sleeping on them in the office; he sat on top of them in the mail wagons as they were taken to the railroad station to be loaded on mail cars. One day he went a little farther—literally—when he jumped into one of the train cars and made the trip from Albany to New York City, sitting on top of the bags. That, it turned out, was just the beginning.

ON HIS OWNEY

The self-appointed mailbag guard dog started taking longer and longer trips, hopping from mail train to mail train, and would sometimes be away from the Albany office for months at a time. These weren't chaperoned outings—Owney just went wherever he wanted, following the bags on their routes. At some point, the clerks in Albany attached a note to his collar, asking other clerks to look after the dog and to attach baggage tags to his collar so they could keep track of his travels. It quickly became clear that Owney was crisscrossing the entire country, and within a year clerks from New York to California—and even Mexico and Canada—knew him and considered him part of their large, postal family.

By the early 1890s, Owney's exploits were known well enough within the postal community that John Wanamaker, the United States Postmaster General, ordered a special "doggie vest" for the pooch. They needed it to accommodate the growing number of tags on his collar, which were so heavy that Owney could hardly lift his head.

OWNEY OWNS THE WORLD

In 1895 Owney made his way—via dozens of trains—to Tacoma, Washington, where the clerks there decided to put him on a mail ship. Next stop: Kobe, Japan, a trip the dog made officially registered as "Mr. Owney." By this time, he was known around the world and in Japan was issued an imperial passport, leaving him free to travel aboard the trains wherever he liked. From Japan Owney traveled to China, back to Japan, Singapore, the Suez Canal, various stops along the North African coast, and then across the Atlantic to New York City. From there he went by train back to Tacoma, arriving on December 29, 1895, to the cheers of hundreds of fans. Owney had completed the around-the-world trip in just a little more than four months. Not bad for the 1890s...not to mention for a dog.

RETURN TO SENDER

Unfortunately, Owney's heartwarming story has a tragic end. In 1897 he was deemed too old to travel, and the clerks in Albany "retired" him—except that Owney didn't take to the idea. Without the Albany postal employees knowing it, Owney hopped a train and ended up in Toledo, Ohio, where the clerks chained him to a wall in the basement of the postal station. According to the National Postal Museum, "Owney was mistreated while being shown off to a newspaper reporter in Ohio and became so mad that he bit a postal worker." The Toledo postmaster felt he had to do something, so he summoned a police officer, and on July 11, 1897, Owney was shot and killed.

Today, his legend lives on at the Smithsonian National Postal Museum in Washington, D.C., where you can see his stuffed body in a display case. With him are many of the more than 1,100 tags, tokens, hotel room keys, and medals that Owney received in his estimated 143,000 miles of travel as the unofficial mascot of the U.S. Railway Mail Service. In 2008 the *Washington City* paper voted Owney's display the "Best Animal Monument" in all the District. It remains one of the museum's most popular exhibits, especially with children...and postal clerks.

SOLD!

How much would you spend for something you really *wanted? You never know until you get caught up in the bidding frenzy at an auction and end up paying, say, $32,000 for a PEZ dispenser. Here are some record auction prices.*

AN ACTION FIGURE: A 12-inch-tall prototype for the original G.I. Joe line from 1963 was purchased by Baltimore's Geppi Museum in 2003. Price: $200,000.

A YO-YO: Richard Nixon autographed a yo-yo for country star Roy Acuff when the president visited the Grand Ole Opry in 1974. When Acuff died in 1992, the yo-yo sold at auction for $16,000.

A KIDNEY STONE: In 2006 online casino GoldenPalace.com paid actor William Shatner $25,000 for a kidney stone he'd recently passed. (Shatner donated the money to Habitat for Humanity.)

A PEZ DISPENSER: In 1982 PEZ made two prototypes of a dispenser featuring a white-helmeted astronaut. They were shown to the merchandise department of the 1982 World's Fair, but never went into production. That's probably why one of them brought in $32,000 at a collectibles auction in 2006.

A BOTTLE OF WINE: A bottle of Chateau Lafite from 1787, thought to have been owned by Thomas Jefferson (the bottle was engraved with "TH.J"), sold for $160,000 in 1985. It's too old to drink—it was purchased by a Jefferson enthusiast, not a wine collector.

A BOOK: In 1188 King Henry of Brunswick (now part of Germany) commissioned an order of monks to write his political biography, entitled *The Gospels of Henry the Lion.* In 1983 a copy sold at auction for $12 million.

A STAMP: An error at a Swedish printing plant in 1855 resulted in a run of stamps being printed on yellow paper instead of the standard green. Only one of the stamps still exists; it was sold in 1996 for $2.3 million.

A DONUT: To raise money for Hurricane Katrina victims, the "Roula and Ryan" morning radio show in Houston auctioned off a donut on eBay. It pulled in $5,100.

In 2000 Al Capone's toenail clippings were sold at auction for $9,500.

A BASEBALL CARD: There are only six 1909 Honus Wagner "T-206" cards in mint condition known to exist. In 2000 a T-206 once owned by hockey great Wayne Gretzky fetched $1.27 million on eBay.

AN M&M: In 2007 a brown M&M sold for $1,500. What was so special about it? In 2004 the candy had flown on board SpaceShipOne, the first privately funded space flight.

A CAR: Only six Bugatti Type 41 Royale sports cars were ever made, all between 1927 and 1933. Original price: $42,000. One sold at a Japanese auction in 1990. Price: $15 million.

A LETTER: In 1991 a letter written in 1863 by President Abraham Lincoln to Major General John A. McClernand explaining the Emancipation Proclamation sold at auction. Price: $748,000.

A PIANO: A handmade Alma-Tadema model Steinway and Sons piano built in the 1880s was sold to the Sterling and Francine Clark Art Institute in Massachusetts in 1997 for $1.2 million.

A VIOLIN: In February 2008, Russian businessman Maxim Viktorov paid $7 million for a rare 18th-century Stradivarius violin.

A PHOTOGRAPH: Photographer Edward Steichen took a photo of a heavily forested pond in Mamaroneck, New York, in 1904. He titled it "The Pond-Moonlight." In 2008 one of three existing original prints sold for $2.9 million to a private party. (The other two are owned by the Metropolitan Museum of Art and the Museum of Modern Art in New York City.)

A MUSHROOM: An English restaurateur purchased a two-pound Italian white truffle at a charity auction in Tuscany. Price: $28,000.

A PAINTING: Mark Rothko's painting *White Center* sold in 2007 for $72.8 million, an art-auction record.

A PIG: In 1985 Bud Olson and Phil Bonzio bought "Bud the Pig" at a Texas livestock auction for the price of $56,000. Bud was a rare crossbreed barrow. (A "barrow" is a neutered male pig.)

Blah, blah, blah: Studies show that it's usually the more talkative spouse who gets his (or her) way.

THE DA VINCI OF DETROIT, PART II

Harley Earl was a man of many gifts, the most important of which may simply have been good timing. He happened to join GM at a time of profound change in the auto industry when his talents could be put to the most use. *(Part I begins on page 139.)*

MIDEAST MEETS WEST

When Harley Earl arrived in Detroit in the late 1920s, there was no guarantee that his ideas regarding automobile design would prevail. He had the support of Alfred Sloan, the head of General Motors, but the auto industry was still dominated by engineers who were openly hostile to the idea that how a car looked was as important as how well it was built. These engineers were no-nonsense guys and *very* conservative; one designer said they "dressed like detectives and rarely even took their hats off." When Harley Earl from Hollywood rolled into town wearing suede shoes with bronze-colored suits and purple shirts, spinning yarns about the car he'd designed with a saddle on the roof, the engineers dismissed him as a "pretty boy" and a "pantywaist" and probably figured he wasn't going to last very long.

Besides, what was wrong with the way cars looked? They had a certain austere, utilitarian beauty to them, the automotive equivalent of a hammer or an electric drill. Making cars *prettier* made about as much sense to these engineers as putting makeup on a shotgun.

BRAVE NEW WORLD

But the auto industry was changing, and changing quickly. For most of the previous two decades, automakers had sold most of their cars to people who had never owned one before. Henry Ford had won the battle to sell Americans their very first autos; his giant factories could produce them faster, cheaper, and in greater quantities than any of his competitors could. By 1923 the Model T had a 57 percent share of the U.S. automobile market. Half of all the cars in the world were Fords.

By that time, however, just about everyone in the United States who wanted a car had one. Now the trick for automakers was getting customers to replace the cars they already owned—and had already *paid for*—with new ones that cost more money. And the auto companies had to get them to do it long before the old car wore out, because if a company had to wait for the old car to die before they sold the owner a new one, it wouldn't sell enough cars to stay in business.

LIVING IN THE PAST

In the contest to sell Americans their *second* car, Henry Ford was his own worst enemy. Ford was fixated on the Model T and rightly considered it his greatest creation. Yet over the 19 years that it was sold by the company—the *only* automobile sold by the company during that time—he refused to upgrade or improve upon the original design. He dismissed as frivolous "knickknacks" such innovations as speedometers, gas gauges, shock absorbers, hydraulic brakes, accelerators on the floorboard instead of on the steering column, and electric starters in place of hand cranks. Ford fought these improvements year after year, often firing the very capable executives who dared to suggest them. (Many of these executives were snapped up by GM.) On those few occasions when Ford finally did incorporate something new into the Model T design, it was usually long after it had become standard equipment on competing cars.

While Henry Ford kept his foot on the brake, Alfred Sloan of GM kept his mashed down on the accelerator. In addition to continually updating his automobile designs, Sloan invented new ways for people to pay for their cars. Where Ford had always insisted on being paid in cash and in full (banks did not yet offer car loans), Sloan created the General Motors Acceptance Corporation (GMAC) to finance the purchase of GM cars. Even though it was impossible for GM to match Ford on the actual price of the car, GMAC financing actually made GM cars more affordable for many buyers. By 1924, the same year that GM became the first company to accept trade-ins, a third of all GM car purchases were financed by GMAC.

For all the emphasis Sloan put into improving the quality of GM automobiles, he also understood that new technology was

Costco sells a full-sized funeral casket for $924.

very costly to develop, took years to bring to market, and often didn't pan out. But he wanted to maintain the illusion of continual improvement, so in the mid-1920s he introduced the auto industry's first "annual model change." From then on, even when the mechanical components of a car remained the same from one year to the next, the car's appearance would change every year, if only in subtle ways, to keep the public interested in it.

WHAT'S NEW IS OLD...AGAIN

The annual model change would have another effect on consumers: It would cause them to become increasingly dissatisfied with their existing cars from one year to the next, a concept that became known as "planned obsolescence." (Earl preferred to call it "dynamic obsolescence.") With any luck, the planned obsolescence would drive car owners into a car dealership a few years early to trade in older cars that had become shabby and dowdy before their time.

Making annual style changes in all the cars sold by GM's five divisions—Chevrolet, Oakland (later renamed Pontiac), Oldsmobile, Buick, and Cadillac—required a lot of designers, which was why Sloan decided to set up GM's own in-house Art and Color Division. Those conservatively dressed engineers from the Old School may not have wanted to hear it, but guys like Harley Earl, with their suede shoes, loud suits, and purple shirts, were here to stay...and soon they'd be calling the shots.

Putt-putt over to page 415 for Part III of the story.

* * *

REAL (ODD) BOOK TITLES

- *I Was Tortured By the Pygmy Love Queen*
- *Cheese Problems Solved*
- *High Performance Stiffened Structures*
- *Living with Crazy Buttocks*
- *The Joy of Chickens*
- *Greek Rural Postmen and Their Cancellation Numbers*

POLI-TALKS

Public servants often say the strangest things.

"I talk to those who've lost their lives, and they have that sense of duty and mission."

—Sen. Jeff Sessions

"I'm the consul for information, but I don't have any information."

—Ofra Ben Yaacov, Israeli Consul

"Thanks for the question, you little jerk."

—John McCain, when asked by a high school student if he was too old to be president

"Nearly everyone will lie to you given the right circumstances."

—Bill Clinton

"When Newfoundland finally joined with us in Confederation in 1867, it was like a family reunion."

—Stephen Harper, Canadian Prime Minister (Newfoundland joined the Canadian Confederation in 1949)

"You can't just let nature run wild."

—Gov. Walter Hickel, Alaska

"You'll get a chance to ask questions later and make your stupid statements; now let me make mine."

—Karl Rove, to hecklers

"What we have is two important values in conflict: freedom of speech and our desire for a healthy democracy. You can't have both."

—Rep. Dick Gephardt

"PETA is not happy that my dog likes fresh air."

—Mitt Romney, who strapped his dog to the roof of his car

"54."

—Stephen Byers, British Minister for School Standards, after being asked by a BBC interviewer, "What's 8 times 7?"

"We're no longer a superpower, we're a super-duper power."

—Rep. Tom DeLay

"Having plead guilty, I do not believe that I am any different than the vast majority of the members of Congress."

—Rep. Dan Rostenkowski

Sir Walter Scott used the pen name Captain Cuthbert Clutterbuck.

ASHES TO ASHES, WEIRD TO WEIRDER

When it comes to the morbid and the strange, we're the crematorium of the crop!

HANDLE WITH CARE

In May 2007, Leslie Wright of Cambridge, England, died. He was 71 years old. His son, Chris, decided to give him a very special send-off: The elder Wright had owned his own delivery business for decades, and loved his work, so Chris dressed his father in his courier uniform, put him in specially made cardboard coffin marked "Fragile," loaded it up in one of Dad's trucks, and delivered it to a crematorium. "Dad had a fantastic sense of humor," Chris said, "and he would have loved this." And where was "the package" addressed to? "Cloud 9, Peace and Quiet Road, Heaven, Near Scotland."

GHOST IN THE MACHINE

In 2005 Therese Mallik of New South Wales, Australia, testified against the planned expansion of a local crematorium, claiming that, among other things, she had once seen a "ghostlike figure" hovering above the building. When the local *Cessnock Independent* newspaper ran a story with the headline "Witness sees a ghost over Cremator," Mallik sued the paper for making her appear "demented." She lost the suit. (The ghost remains at large.)

UNDERSTANDABLE...BUT GROSS

Employees at a crematorium in Salt Lake City had to call the fire department when the building caught fire in October 2006. Fluids from a burning body had leaked out of the oven and ignited. "Those fluids can be very flammable," fireman Scott Freitag said. "Sort of like a grease fire."

DEAD RINGER

In October 2007, Gina Partington of Manchester, England, called police and told them that her son, 39-year-old Tommy Dennison,

40% of Americans iron their clothes in their underwear or in the nude.

was missing. A few days later the police called with bad news: They had found the body of her son. She went down to the morgue and identified him, and had the remains cremated a day or two after that. Three days later the police called back...and told Partington that her son had been in police custody all along—they'd cremated the wrong man. "I know it sounds unbelievable," the distraught woman said, "but this poor lad was the absolute replica of my son." Police were later able to identify the cremation victim as a 37-year-old homeless man, and notified his family of the mixup. "These circumstances are clearly distressing," a police spokesperson said, "and urgent inquiries are going on to establish how this happened."

THE JOY OF COOKING

When retired pipe fitter Russell Parsons, 67, of Charleston, West Virginia, dies, the people around him will know exactly what to do with him: Parsons, an Army veteran, a cancer survivor, and a widower, has instructions tattooed on his arm. "It's a recipe for cremation," he said. The tattoo reads: "Barlow Bonsall" (the name of the local funeral home) "cook @ 1700-1800 degrees for 2 to 3 hours."

THAT'S HOT!

April 5 is the day of the annual Tombsweeping Festival in China, when people clean the tombs and graves of their ancestors. It's also the day that they burn fake money, which tradition says accumulates as wealth for their ancestors in the afterlife. Apparently the ritual has evolved over the generations. In 2007 Chinese newspapers noted that thousands of people now burn *different* things for the dead...like paper replicas of Viagra pills, to increase the dead's chances for good sex in the afterlife. Pictures of condoms and "bar girls" have also become popular for burnt offerings, the reports said.

* * *

Mixed Messages: In 2008 the Netherlands—which is famous for legalized marijuana smoking in Amsterdam cafes—banned cigarette smoking in all public places. Smoking marijuana remains legal.

The first American railroad ran a distance of 11 miles—between Albany and Schenectady, NY.

OUT, DARN SPOT!

Most of us prefer clean clothes to dirty ones (Uncle John not included). Here are some interesting tips sent to us by neat freak and BRI veteran writer John Dollison to help with problem stains. No guarantee they'll work, but it's fun to see how inventive homemakers can be.

Chewing Gum on Clothes: Throw the article of clothing into a plastic bag, then put the bag into the freezer until the gum is frozen solid—it's a lot easier to remove hardened chewing gum than a soft and sticky glob.

• ***Very* Delicate Delicates:** Here's how to clean lace undies or any other items that are too delicate even for the delicate cycle of your washing machine. Pour some warm water into a gallon jug or similar container and add a little bit of liquid laundry or dish soap. Stir to mix thoroughly, then add the articles of clothing; shake the container, then let soak for half an hour. Rinse the clothing with cool water, wring gently, and hang to dry.

• **Ring Around the Collar:** If you're out of the stuff that's specially designed to remove collar stains, try rubbing some shampoo into the stain. That should work just as well.

• **Speeding Up Hand-Wash Rinsing:** If you do a lot of hand washing in the sink (or in the jug mentioned above), you can speed up the time it takes to rinse out the soap by adding 1/4 cup of white wine vinegar to your rinse water. Just make sure you give your clothes a final rinse in clean water *without* the vinegar.

• **Do-It-Yourself Spot Remover:** If you're tired of paying big money for tiny containers of spot remover, mix one part rubbing alcohol with two parts water and you should find that it removes many kinds of spots just as effectively as the store-bought stuff.

• **Dirty Canvas Shoes:** Using a clean shoe brush—the kind that's used to apply shoe polish—rub some spray-on carpet cleaner into the canvas. Wipe off with a paper towel or a clean piece of cloth and your shoes should look almost like new.

• **Freshen Up a Grubby Old Leather Belt:** Rinse a clean sponge in water and wring it out. Use the sponge to rub cold cream into

Mimes beware: It's against the law in Virginia to call someone and not say anything.

the belt to soften the leather and remove dirt, then wipe the excess cold cream away using a clean cloth.

• **Ink Stains on a Leather Jacket:** If the stain is black ink on a black leather jacket, hang the jacket in a closet and go find something else that *really* needs cleaning. If it's a red ink stain on a white jacket or a blue stain on a red one, or something equally noticeable, lay the jacket on a flat surface, pour some baking soda on the spot and let it sit until the ink is absorbed. (Try it on a small test spot first.) It may take several applications to get the stain up, but with a little effort you should be able to remove it.

MISCELLANEOUS TIPS

• If the sleeve cuffs of an old sweater have gotten too stretched out, soak them in cold water and then dry them with an electric hair dryer set on high, being careful to keep the dryer at least three inches away from the cuffs to prevent burning.

• If you need to dry something quickly on a clothesline before you hang it up, lay the wet piece of clothing on a clean, dry towel, roll the clothing up in the towel, then squeeze the towel so that it soaks up some of the moisture. You should notice a significant improvement in the amount of time it takes the clothing to dry.

• What about the washing machine itself—does *it* ever need washing? Uncle John has his doubts, but Mrs. Uncle John swears by this: Every once in a while she pours half a gallon of white, distilled vinegar into the machine and runs it on the regular cycle without any clothing (the *washing machine* should be free of clothes, not Mrs. Uncle John!).

* * *

UNCLE JOHN'S CREATIVE TEACHING AWARD

Parents of kids at Edgewood Middle School in Trenton, Ohio, complained after learning that a music teacher had the students sing "Weird Al" Yankovic's "The Night Santa Went Crazy" in class. The song features Santa shooting up his workshop...and making sausages out of his reindeer. The teacher was reprimanded (even though the kids probably loved it).

THE COLLECTORS

Uncle John collects postcards. That makes him a deltiologist. *Can you match the collectors on the left with what they collect?* *(Answers on page 540.)*

1. Philographist
2. Bibliophile
3. Numismatist
4. Plangonologist
5. Copoclephilist
6. Conchologist
7. Philatelist
8. Aerophilatelist
9. Arctophile
10. Lepidopterist
11. Vexillologist
12. Brandophilist
13. Cameist
14. Errinophilist
15. Fusilatelist
16. Helixophile
17. Heortologist
18. Iconophile
19. Oologist
20. Phillumenist
21. Phonophile
22. Receptarist
23. Succrologist
24. Vecturist
25. Xylographer

a. bird eggs
b. cameos
c. autographs
d. subway tokens
e. flags
f. coins
g. calling cards
h. sugar packets
i. seashells
j. woodcuts
k. stamps
l. teddy bears
m. religious calendars
n. butterflies
o. tax stamps
p. books
q. matchbook covers
r. keychains
s. airmail stamps
t. corkscrews
u. prints and engravings
v. LPs and 45s
w. cigar bands
x. dolls
y. recipes

THE SUMO WAY

How do sumo wrestlers get so big? They eat...and eat...and then eat some more. But there's more to it than that. (Did we mention they eat?)

BACKGROUND

Sumo wrestling, often called Japan's national sport, is said to date back to prehistoric times, though it only gained popularity as a spectator sport in the early 17th century. The concept is simple: The wrestler (or *rikishi*), wearing only a loincloth, loses the match if any part of his body (other than the soles of his feet) touches the ring painted on the floor, or if his opponent pushes or throws him out of the ring. Other than that, there are few rules in sumo wrestling, and a match can be over in a matter of seconds. One referee calls the match, and five judges must concur.

When they're not competing, the wrestlers live together in *heyas*, or stables, buildings where they sleep, eat, train, and relax. Sumo is hierarchical: The high-ranking, older rikishis are at the top; the younger rikishis serve the older men, study their fighting techniques, and train for several hours a day. Until a wrestler reaches a high rank, he isn't allowed to marry or leave the stable.

Boys who aspire to be rikishis attend after-school sumo classes, join sumo clubs, and participate in junior tournaments. Scouts from the stables tour the clubs looking for likely candidates (the minimum size requirements are 5'7" and 165 pounds), but they don't just choose the biggest, fattest boys—obesity implies a lack of discipline that won't hold up under the difficult training. Instead, the scouts look for sturdy bodies, strong backs, strong grips, speed, agility, and dedication to the sport. Once the boys pass their entrance trials and the medical exams, training begins at age 15.

EARLY TO RISE

The successful sumo wrestler is skilled, strong, and large. The skill and strength come from rigorous training; the bulk comes from rigorous eating. The younger rikishis awake at 5:00 a.m. and begin stretching, followed by foot-stomping, thigh splits, deep squats, and several other exercises. Then they compete in strenuous practice bouts for a few hours until the high-ranking members arrive to instruct—and critique—them. And the young rikishis do all this on an empty stomach. Why? Because eating before exercising would kick-start their metabolisms, thus burning off the pounds they're trying to put on. Only when the senior rikishis begin their own grueling practice do the juniors go off to prepare the huge midday meal. After all the wrestlers have eaten lunch, they take long naps. Exercising before eating keeps their metabolic rate low, which conserves calories and contributes to more weight gain; sleeping after eating encourages the body to store food as weight, instead of using it as energy. But the real key to sumo weight gain is the *amount* of food they eat.

CHANKO VERY MUCH

The sumo wrestler's staple dish is a hearty, high-protein stew called *chanko-nabe*, or *chanko* for short. And just as there are few rules to sumo wrestling, there are even fewer for making chanko. The main ingredient is either meat or fish, but never both. After that, almost anything can be mixed in. The junior rikishis prepare and cook the meat, and then make the broth with chicken bones, kelp (a kind of seaweed), and dried *bonito* (tuna) flakes. The broth is then seasoned with *miso* (soybean paste), soy sauce, *mirin* (rice wine), garlic, ginger, or sesame oil. Once the kettles begin bubbling, they add the solid ingredients: beef, pork, chicken, shrimp and other seafood, and then various combinations of tofu, onions, carrots, *daikon* (a kind of white radish), cabbage, mushrooms, greens, and other vegetables.

The senior rikishis eat first, served by the junior members. These men eat *a lot* of chanko—one wrestler is said to have eaten 29 pounds in a single sitting. They also consume several bowls of rice along with it, all washed down by several pints of beer. Because the senior members take all of the choice bits from the chanko, when the juniors finally get their turn to gorge, the leftovers often aren't as tasty or nourishing, so they add rice, noodles, and eggs.

On tournament days, the preferred chanko meat is chicken. It's considered bad luck to ingest any meat from an animal that's down on all fours—such as pigs or cows—which is where a sumo wrestler does not want to find himself in a match. And fish, which lack arms and legs, are even unluckier.

THE DOWN SIDE

The glory, honor, and fame—not to mention the salary—accorded a champion Japanese sumo wrestler are immense. Grand Champions may earn monthly salaries of about $25,000, plus bonuses paid six times per year based on their career performances to date. They also get prize money (roughly $90,000 for a win in the highest division) and "bout prizes" from sponsors (about $275 per sponsor). But success can come at a high price. Although sumo wrestlers have less actual fat, better reflexes, and more muscle compared to most men of equal height and weight, they face serious health problems that only get worse as they age. The average life expectancy of a Japanese man is 75; for sumo wrestlers it's 65 or less, and many die in their mid-50s. At an average weight of 325 pounds, sumo wrestlers are also prone to the diseases and conditions associated with being overweight: adult-onset diabetes, high cholesterol, high blood pressure, arthritis, gout, and heart attacks. And their excessive alcohol consumption puts them at risk for liver diseases. Plus, most wrestlers suffer from knee and shoulder injuries. (Another problem that has cropped up in recent years: performance-enhancing drugs designed for extreme weight gain, which can put even more strain on a sumo wrestler's heart. Recent allegations of drug abuse prompted Japan's Sumo Association to begin a drug-testing program in 2008.)

MEAT BOMBS AWAY

One sumo wrestler who ate his fair share (and then some) is Konishiki Yasokichi, one of the greatest modern sumo champions. Born Saleva'a Atisano'e in Oahu, Hawaii in 1963, Konishiki is famous for two reasons: He was the first foreign-born wrestler to rise to the second-highest rank in sumo, and he was the heaviest sumo wrestler…ever. At six feet tall, Konishiki's fighting weight maxed out at around 620 pounds. That earned him the nicknames "Meat Bomb" and "Dump Truck."

After Konishiki retired (in the middle of a match) in 1997 just before his 34th birthday, he set his sights on a new goal: enjoying a long, healthy retirement. So far, he's lost 70 pounds, has undergone gastric bypass surgery, and says he feels great. Today Konishiki owns a restaurant in Tokyo. Its most popular dish: chanko-nabe. "We offer three kinds," he says. "The one I eat is low-cal."

WORD ORIGINS

Ever wonder where these words came from?
Here are the stories behind them.

MYSTERY

Meaning: Something unknown or unclear

Origin: "Words like 'mystery' and 'mystify' can sound as if they are connected with 'misty,' since mist can obscure clarity. But the two words are actually quite distinct in origin, with 'mist' being an Old English word, and 'mystery' ultimately deriving from the Greek *mystos*, which means 'remaining silent.'" (From *NTC's Dictionary of Word Origins*, by Adrian Room)

WOMAN

Meaning: An adult, female human

Origin: "Woman does not derive from man. It comes from the Old English *wifmann*, where *wif* meant 'female' and *mann* referred to a person of either sex. Thus, *wifmann* originally equated 'female human.'" (From *Devious Derivations*, by Hugh Rawson)

GROOVY

Meaning: Good, cool, agreeable

Origin: "The term takes you back to the Hippie Sixties, but should actually take you even further back—to the 1930s. In France at that time, American musicians wanted to *groove*, slang for 'make a record.' The highest compliment that could be paid a musician or group was to tell them they were groovy—good enough to be recorded. The term spread to America in the 1950s; by the end of the Sixties, all kinds of things—not just music—were groovy." (From *Abracadabra to Zombie*, by Don and Pam Wulffson)

SNACK

Meaning: A small amount of food eaten between meals

Origin: "A snack is something grabbed in a hurry, from the Dutch *snacken*, meaning to snap at something, although that word was only used for dogs." (From *Word Origins*, by Wilfred Funk)

BLEACHERS

Meaning: Where you sit to watch a sporting event

Origin: "Often said to come from the notion that people sitting in them would be bleached by the sun. (We'll pass over the fact that people would actually tend to get darker by sitting in the sun.) The actual reason was that the benches themselves were bleached from the sun, and were hence also called 'bleaching boards,' referring to the plain boards on which people sat." (From *Jesse's Word of the Day*, by Jesse Sheidlower)

ARENA

Meaning: An indoor stadium

Origin: "This word is now used for a sporting, athletic area, but it derives from the Latin word *arena*, meaning *sand*. How? Sand was sprinkled in the Roman Colosseum to absorb the gladiators' and animal blood spilt during combats." (From *Short Dictionary of Classical Word Origins*, by Harry E. Wedeck)

HARROWING

Meaning: Deeply disturbing

Origin: "A *harrow* is a farm implement—a heavy rake with many teeth, spikes, or discs, used to pulverize and smooth the soil of a plowed field to prepare it for planting. If such a contraption were ever hauled over you, you'd probably understand why *harrowing* is used to describe any frightening or distressing experience." (From *Once Upon a Word*, by Rob Kyff)

BLOCKBUSTER

Meaning: A smash-hit movie

Origin: "The term arose during World War II as Royal Air Force slang for an extremely large bomb, so powerful that it was capable of destroying an entire city block. After the war ended, *blockbuster* was appropriated by the advertising industry." (From *The Word Detective*, by Evan Morris)

The smackdown: 23 U.S. states still allow corporal punishment in schools.

HONK IF YOU LOVE BUMPER STICKERS

We keep thinking that we've seen every clever bumper sticker that exists, but every year readers send us new ones. Have you seen the one that says...

I'll rise, but I won't shine

I would never sell out unless I got a lot of money for it

YOU CAN PICK YOUR NOSE AND PICK YOUR FRIENDS, BUT YOU CAN'T WIPE YOUR FRIENDS ON THE COUCH

CLEAR THE ROAD, I'M 16!

A barrel full of monkeys would not be fun— it would be horrifying

All I want is less to do, more time to do it, and higher pay for not getting it done

When in doubt, mumble

EVERYTHING I NEED TO KNOW I LEARNED IN PRISON

Caution: impending doom

ONE MORE REPO, AND I'LL BE DEBT-FREE!

I do what the bumper stickers tell me to

LEGALLY, IT'S QUESTIONABLE, MORALLY, DISGUSTING. PERSONALLY, I LIKE IT.

Don't call me infantile, you stinkybutt poophead!

When life gives you lemons, shut up and eat your lemons

I *do* work for food

Follow your dreams, except that one where you're at school in your underwear

Shh! I'm listening to a book

C'mon, give me the finger like you mean it

The closer you get, the slower I go

Watch out! I'm late for Drivers' Ed class!

Japanese invention: the Choc-U-Lator, a calculator that looks and smells like a chocolate bar.

IT'S IN THE CARDS

Predicting the future using an ordinary deck of playing cards is a lot like reading your horoscope: Even if you don't take it seriously, it's fun to see what the cards have to say.

DEALER'S CHOICE

Playing cards date back more than 800 years, and it's a safe bet that people have been using them to tell fortunes for almost as long. Because of this, there are more techniques than there are cards in the deck, but here's a pretty good one.

• **Prepare the Deck.** Take an old deck of 52 cards that you don't mind marking up. Mark the bottom of each card with a pen so you can tell whether it's right-side up or upside down when you deal it. Upside-down cards can mean the opposite of what they'd mean if they were right-side up, and in some circumstances they can modify or negate the meaning of cards that are nearby.

Next, discard every deuce, three, four, five, six, and both jokers from the deck. You won't use any of these to tell fortunes; you'll use just the cards with a value of seven or above and the aces.

• **Deal the Cards.** Shuffle the deck thoroughly. The person whose future is being told should cut the cards with their *left* hand (it's closer to their heart). But before they put the two cut sections back together, remove the top card from the bottom pile and the bottom card from the top pile and set them aside. These are the "surprise" cards. Now deal the cards face down into three piles of ten cards each. From left to right, the piles will represent the past, the present, and the future.

Dividing the cards this way may shed light on the accuracy of a particular fortune-telling session: If the Past pile does a good job of describing the subject's past, the Present and Future piles may be just as accurate. If the Past pile describes a past that is nothing like the real thing, you may want to re-shuffle and try again.

• **What About the Surprise Pile?** Does it refer to a surprise that will occur in the present, or in the future? We're not telling (that's part of the surprise).

Hot Christmas toy of 2002 in England: A talking Ozzy Osbourne teddy bear...

COUNTING CARDS

Individual cards, combinations of cards, and whether the cards are right-side up or upside down will all affect how a fortune is read. Here's a look at individual cards, by suit.

♥ HEARTS ♥

Heart cards have a special connection to love and marriage. They can also refer to family, workplace, or social relationships.

♥7 – *Serenity and contentedness*. When the card is upside down, it can mean boredom or weariness brought on by eating too much or by some other form of overconsumption.

♥8 – *Thoughts or dreams of marriage*. They could be the subject's thoughts or those of someone close to them. The card could also represent the affections of a fair-haired or fair-complected person who is, was, or someday will be a part of the subject's life, depending on which pile it's in.

♥9 – *This is the wish card*. It could refer to one of the subject's wishes, or a wish that someone has for them. The card can also represent good luck. When upside down, it can mean a sadness or sorrow that is short in duration.

♥10 – *Can mean happiness or success*. Under certain circumstances, it can cancel out the effect of nearby negative cards. Upside down: a worry that passes quickly.

♥Jack – *Symbolizes a carefree, pleasure-seeking bachelor*. Upside down: a lover in the military, law enforcement, or a similar profession who harbors a grievance or carries a grudge.

♥Queen – *A fair-haired woman*. (No word on whether dyed hair counts as the real thing.) Upside down: an unhappy relationship or love affair with this same woman.

♥King – *A fair-haired man who is generous in nature*. Upside down: the fair-haired man is disappointing in some way.

♥Ace – *A love letter or good news of some kind*. Upside down: a visit from a friend.

♦ DIAMONDS ♦

Diamond cards can refer to relationships or financial matters. They can be positive or negative.

♦**7** – *Cynicism or unfriendly teasing*. Upside down: dishonesty or slander.

♦**8** – *Love*. Upside down: unrequited love.

♦**9** – *Frustration, or barriers in the subject's path*. Upside down: domestic discord or lovers' quarrels.

♦**10** – *Traveling or eviction*. Upside down: Bad luck on a trip.

♦**Jack** – A *subordinate or official of some kind who cannot be trusted*. Upside down: a troublemaker.

♦**Queen** – A *low-class, fair-haired woman who is prone to gossip*. Upside down: A flirtatious and hostile woman.

♦**King** – *A blond or gray-haired man, or a soldier in uniform*. Upside down: a schemer.

♦**Ace** – *Good news of some kind, perhaps in the form of a letter or a proposal of marriage*. Upside down: Bad news.

♣ CLUBS ♣

Clubs are the luckiest cards of all. They can mean anything from material wealth to successful ventures to a happy home life.

♣7 – *Small monetary gains*. Upside down: small money troubles.

♣8 – *The love of a dark-complected man or woman*. Happiness results when the love is returned in kind. Upside down: love and affection from someone who's far more trouble than they're worth.

♣9 – *Money inherited unexpectedly*. Upside down: The receipt of a small gift.

♣**10** – *Luxury and wealth*. Upside down: A voyage over an ocean, either by ship or plane.

♣**Jack** – A *hardworking, passionate, intelligent, funny young man*. Upside down: A flighty, fickle, and irresponsible young man.

♣**Queen** – An *affectionate and passionate dark-complected woman who bears the subject no ill will*. Upside down: The same woman, but very jealous.

♣**King** – A *dark-complected man who is honest and a good friend*. Upside down: Good intentions that do not achieve the desired results.

In 2006 Dublin's River Liffey hosted the world's largest rubber-duck race, with 150,000 ducks.

♣**Ace** – *Letters or e-mails involving money, good luck, or some other pleasing topic*. Upside down: Annoying letters, e-mails, or some other form of correspondence.

♠ SPADES ♠

Who said life was fair? Spade cards, as one fortune-teller puts it, "forebode evil." They can refer to sickness, death, social and familial isolation, and all manner of worries and fears, big and small.

♠**7** – *Run-of-the-mill worries or problems*. Upside down: foolish ideas about existing relationships or ones the subject is trying to start.

♠**8** – *Illness*. Upside down: an engagement that is broken or a proposal that is turned down.

♠**9** – *A bad omen, possibly involving a failure or even death*. Upside down: the death of a loved one.

♠**10** – *Sadness or loss of some kind of freedom*. Upside down: a trouble or sickness that will pass in due course.

♠**Jack** – *A student, perhaps of law or medicine, who lacks social graces and has poor manners*. Upside down: a treacherous person who is scheming against the subject.

♠**Queen** – *A widow or a dark-complected woman*. Upside down: a woman who dislikes the subject and looks for a way to get back at them.

♠**King** – *A widower, a lawyer, or a widower who practices law*. Whoever he is, he makes a poor friend and a dangerous enemy. Upside down: a wish to do evil against others but lacking either the will or the ability.

♠**Ace** – *Happiness*. Upside down: news of a death or some other event that brings great sadness.

...BUT WAIT, THERE'S MORE!

That's how individual cards stack up, but if you think that's all there is to fortune-telling with playing cards, you're not playing with a full deck. What happens when you have two or three kings side by side? Or when the jack, queen, king and ace of spades or one of the other suits are lined up in a row? The answers to these and other mysteries are on page 494.

Medieval Thailand had movable-type printing presses. The type was made from baked ox dung.

OOPS!

Everyone enjoys reading about someone else's blunders.
So go ahead and feel superior for a few moments.

STRADICIDE

In 2008, 26-year-old virtuoso violinist David Garrett had just concluded a concert at the Barbican Centre in London. Nearly as famous as the violinist (who is also a male model and has been compared to David Beckham) is his violin: a 290-year-old Stradivarius valued at millions of dollars. Making his way off of the stage, Garrett slipped. "People said it was as if I'd stepped right on a banana peel," he recalled. "I fell down a flight of steps and on to the case. When I opened it, the violin was in pieces. I couldn't speak and I couldn't get up. I didn't even know if I was hurt...and I didn't care." (While the instrument was being repaired, Garrett was loaned another Stradivarius on which to perform. A three-man security team followed him closely at his concerts to make sure he didn't drop *that* violin.)

HOME TEAM ADVANTAGE

As the two national soccer teams prepared to begin their match, the home team Czech Republic played the Latvian national anthem for the visiting team...which would have been fine if the visiting team was actually Latvia. It was Lithuania. Not only that, stadium officials printed a copy of Latvia's flag in the official game program. Not surprisingly, the Lithuanians were upset, and the Czech Republic's government apologized profusely on behalf of its soccer federation; one federation official resigned and two others were fired. But adding insult to injury, the Czech Republic beat Lithuania, 2–0.

BALLOONATIC

In March 2008, Lefkos Hajji, a 28-year-old contractor from London, devised a romantic scheme to propose to his girlfriend: First, he bought her a $12,000-diamond engagement ring and then took it to a florist. There, he bought a beautiful bouquet of flowers and had the ring placed inside a balloon, which was then filled with

The only planet whose name is from Greek mythology: Uranus. (The rest are Roman.)

helium and attached to a string. Hajji would present the flowers to his love along with a pin; she would pop the balloon as he popped the question. But he never got the chance. Hajji had only gone a few steps away from the flower shop when the string slipped out of his hand. He watched in horror as the balloon—with his ring inside— floated away in the wind. "I felt like such a plonker," he said. "It cost a fortune, and I knew my girlfriend would kill me." He searched frantically for two hours but was unable to find it. After he admitted his goof to his girlfriend, she refused to speak to him until he found or replaced the ring. At last report, it was still gone.

ARE YOU KIDDING?

In 2008 a woman in Orem, Utah, called 911 to report that she was locked *inside* her luxury car. The battery was dead and the key chain's remote control would no longer open her door. When officers arrived, they tried to yell instructions through the closed window but the woman couldn't hear them, so they called her on her cell phone...and explained how to manually slide the locking mechanism located next to her on the door panel.

CONFESSIONS OF A NOT-SO-DANGEROUS MIND

In Louisiana a woman awoke to her phone ringing in the middle of the night. As she placed the receiver against her ear, a man whose voice she didn't recognize exclaimed, "I've killed them all!" The woman immediately put down the phone and called police, who were able to trace the call to a man named Thomas Ballard. They barged into Ballard's apartment and questioned him about his "confession." After a little confusion, Ballard admitted that earlier that evening, he had killed "all the bad guys" in a video game and had intended to call his friend to brag...but accidentally dialed a wrong number.

*   *   *

"If we could sell our experiences for what they cost us, we'd all be millionaires."

—Abigail Van Buren

U.S. city with the highest alcoholism rate: Reno, Nevada. Lowest: Provo, Utah, just one state away.

CHANEL NO. 1

Coco Chanel (1883–1971) was the first celebrity fashion designer. Among her contributions: the little black dress, Chanel No. 5 perfume, and these quotes.

"Elegance is the art of refusal."

"How many cares one loses when one decides not to be something, but to be some*one*."

"Fashion is architecture: It is a matter of proportions."

"Luxury must be comfortable; otherwise it is not luxury."

"Since everything is in our heads, we had better not lose them."

"I invented my life by taking for granted that everything I did not like would have an opposite, which I would like."

"True generosity means accepting ingratitude."

"Nature gives you the face you have at 20; it is up to you to merit the face you have at 50."

"Success is often achieved by those who don't know that failure is inevitable."

"Those who create are rare. Those who cannot are numerous. Therefore, the latter are stronger."

"The most courageous act is still to think for yourself. Aloud."

"There are people who have money...and there are people who are rich."

"A woman who doesn't wear perfume has no future."

"There is no time for cut-and-dried monotony. There is time for work. And time for love. That leaves no other time."

"Fashion is made to become unfashionable."

"A fashion that does not reach the streets is not a fashion."

"If a woman is badly dressed, people will notice her clothes. If she is impeccably dressed, they will notice her."

"One can get used to ugliness, but never to negligence."

"If you were born without wings, do nothing to prevent their growing."

"Fashion fades; only style remains the same."

TOILET TECH

Better living through bathroom technology

ONE-ARMED BANDIT

Inventor: David Muir, Jr., of Centreville, Virginia

Product: The Urinator—a "self-flushing urinal with an integrated gaming and reward system."

How It Works: Designed for public restrooms, the Urinator is a slot machine, except that it's a game of "skill," not luck, and it dispenses reward coupons instead of cash. The customer inserts a coin and then, if he hits the target on the urinal, an LCD screen drops down to provide entertainment while the urinal dispenses a prize. "It is envisioned that the Urinator may provide tickets for free products upon the attainment of certain amounts of a customer urine output coordinated with appropriate accuracy," Muir says.

LITTLE MAN COMPLEX

Company: Weeman of Australia

Product: "The world's first little boy's toilet training urinal"

How It Works: The Weeman is a bucket-like device with a hinged hook that allows it to be hung from the front rim of a standard toilet, creating a urinal small and low enough for even the youngest boys to use. When your son has completed his business, the hinge allows you—or him—to flip the urinal up (*carefully, carefully!*) and pour the contents into the bowl via a "patented, no-splash or drip self-washing design." "Best of all," says the company, "your little boy can enjoy the satisfaction of going to the toilet 'standing up just like Dad!'"

TWO OF A KIND

Inventor: Jo Lapidge of Canberra, Australia

Product: The Litter Kwitter, a toilet training device for cats

How It Works: After you've finished teaching your little boy to shoot straight, why not continue on to the cat? The Litter Kwitter is the latest development in man's eternal struggle to get the cat

Henry Ford never had a driver's license.

to use the toilet, so that man can get out of cleaning the cat box. The method of cat training is similar to the one we described in *Uncle John's Ahh-Inspiring Bathroom Reader* a few years back: Set the special litter box next to the toilet, and after the cat gets accustomed to using it for a few weeks, move it onto the toilet seat. At the bottom of the litter box is an adjustable opening. Over the next two months, gradually increase the size of the hole as the cat gets better at balancing on the toilet seat, until you reach the fully open position and the cat is squatting over the open bowl. (Lapidge says the invention was inspired by the toilet-trained cat in the movie *Meet the Fockers*.)

HARD TO HANDLE

Inventor: Florence Doleac, a French designer

Product: The Poignee Signaletique, or "Identifiable Door Handle"

How It Works: The Identifiable Door Handle addresses the problem of how to direct people who don't speak your language to the nearest restroom. (Uncle John thought the problem had already been solved with the universal man and woman pictograph signs commonly found on restroom doors, but apparently not.) Doleac's solution: a door handle that looks and feels like a bronzed turd. (Really.) The handle on the outside of the door shows foreign guests where the bathroom is; the handle on the inside of the door is there "for inspiration," says the inventor.

MUSICAL CHAIRS

Company: Jammin' Johns

Product: The Jammin' Johns Studio Series "Guitarlet" toilet seat

How It Works: The Guitarlet is a toilet seat with a lid that looks like the face of an acoustic guitar. Jammin' Johns says they are made by an "actual guitar company that manufactures some of the most popular brands of guitars," which chooses to remain anonymous for obvious reasons. Also available: the "Screamer," which looks like an electric guitar, and the "P-ano," which looks like a concert grand. (Jammin' Johns' company slogan: "Music to Your Rear!")

Warning: Guitarlets, Screamers, and P-anos are *not* advised for struggling musicians whose careers are *already* in the toilet.

Big Ben once lost five minutes when a flock of starlings landed on the minute hand.

JUNK FOOD RECIPES

Take packaged snack food...and turn it into something else with one of these weird recipes. (Warning to healthy eaters: DON'T LOOK!)

• **Twinkie Sushi.** Cut Twinkies into inch-long pieces and wrap them in strips of green Fruit Roll-Ups. The result looks like sushi. Serve with dried mango strips (which look like pickled ginger).

• **Pringles Candy.** Mix three cups of crushed Pringles potato chips into a melted package of almond bark. Stir in a cup of Spanish peanuts. Pour onto wax paper; cool, dry, and break into pieces.

• **Kool-Aid Pickles.** Soak some dill pickles in a pitcher filled with equal parts vinegar and cherry or tropical punch-flavored Kool-Aid. The result is a pickle that's sweet, sour...and bright red.

• **Chicken McBigMac.** Not getting enough meat in your diet? Try this: Buy a McDonald's Big Mac and three McChicken sandwiches. Remove the three bun slices on the Big Mac and replace them with the fried McChicken chicken patties.

• **Coke Seafood Au Gratin.** Combine two tablespoons of butter and two of flour. On low heat, add in a cup of milk and a half cup of grated parmesan. As it thickens, add a half cup of Coca-Cola. Pour the sauce over a half pound each of cooked shrimp, crab, lobster, and sole. Top with bread crumbs and bake for 20 minutes.

• **Peppers With Creamy Sauce.** Remove the seeds from six green (or red) bell peppers that have been cut in half. Melt a package of marshmallows. Fill the peppers with the creamy marshmallow sauce and bake until brown.

• **Funyun Onion Rings.** Grind a bag of Funyons in a blender. (Funyuns are made from cornmeal that's formed into rings and heavily seasoned with onion powder.) Dip slices of real onions in the Funyun crumbs, then dip in egg whites and cook in a deep-fryer.

• **Maple Bacon Donut.** If you like bacon with your waffles and you've ever dipped the bacon in maple syrup, you'll love this simple treat: Take a maple bar (a donut with maple frosting, also known as a maple longjohn) and place two strips of extra-crispy bacon on top...and hope you have good health insurance.

Dog breed with the best eyesight: Greyhound.

HYPERMILING 102

A few more tips on how to get the most bang for your buck when you're buying gas for your car. *(Part I is on page 202.)*

DON'T EVEN *THINK* ABOUT IT

A lot of us have dreamed of doing it: One of the most tempting ways to save gas may be to simply shut off the engine anytime you're traveling downhill. Even if you've felt the urge to do it, don't—driving with the engine off can be very dangerous, not to mention illegal in many states, and can even do thousands of dollars of damage to your car. How?

• Many automatic transmissions are lubricated by a pump that is powered by the car's engine. If you turn off the engine while the car is moving, you can severely damage the transmission.

• Power steering and power brakes also rely on the engine for their power. Once the engine has been shut off, your car's steering will become very stiff, and so will the brakes after just a few pumps of the brake pedal. In an older car, you also risk damaging the distributor. So if you're in your car and it's moving, leave the engine on.

AVOID THE DRAFT

Are you old enough to remember the oil crisis of the 1970s, and the fanciful tales of VW Beetles "drafting"—another word for tailgating—so closely behind 18-wheeler trucks that drivers could put their cars in neutral, shut off the engine, and be sucked down the road by the big rigs? This is an urban legend that can get you killed, with the added insult that your gas savings, if any, would be negligible. Don't tailgate big rigs and other large vehicles under *any* circumstances. It's illegal, ineffective, and very dangerous. You'll save a lot more gas just by slowing down, and that increases your safety as well.

The minimum safe distance behind any vehicle is the distance that gives you at least three seconds of reaction time in an emergency. At highway speeds that can be as much as 150 feet. You're probably too close already—stay back!

RUNNING COLD...

• Automobiles that are already warmed up operate more efficiently than cars that are cold, if for no other reason than cars are designed to run on a richer mixture of fuel and air until they are warmed up. Note: this *doesn't* mean you need to let your car sit and idle until it's warm. Warming up in your driveway before starting off can actually be counterproductive. It makes more sense to start driving as soon as the engine is running smoothly, which in most cars, especially newer ones, means almost immediately. The drivetrain (all the parts that transmit the power from the engine to the wheels) also needs to warm up to work efficiently. Believe it or not, so do the tires. The fastest way to warm everything up: Start driving.

• The improved efficiency of warmed-up cars is one of the reasons that stringing all of your errands together into one long trip can save gas. In addition to driving fewer miles by making one big trip instead of several shorter ones, you can save as much as 4 mpg by running the bulk of your errands in a car that's already warmed up rather than one that starts each trip cold.

...AND HOT

Air conditioners get blamed for using a lot of gas. So does rolling down the windows of a car that's traveling at highway speeds, on the theory that a car with its windows rolled down has more aerodynamic drag than one that has them rolled up.

• Turns out there is some truth to the air conditioner claim—in one test by *Consumer Reports* magazine, a Toyota Camry traveling at 65 mph lost about 1 mpg of fuel economy when the air conditioner was turned on.

• But there's no truth to the claim that rolling down your car's windows harms its fuel economy. When *Consumer Reports* rolled down the windows of their test Camry at 65 mph, they didn't notice any change in fuel mileage at all. So roll down your windows to your heart's content, and use the air conditioner if you need to—it's not using as much gas as you might have thought.

IDLE TALK

• Anytime your engine is running and your car isn't moving, you

It's a boy!...again! All shrimp are born male.

are getting 0 mpg. If you expect to be idling for 10 seconds or more, shutting off the engine—provided that it's safe to do so—will save fuel. It also helps to avoid situations where you might spend a lot of time idling, such as at the drive-up window of a fast food restaurant.

• If you drive an automatic, you probably know that when you're stopped and the car is in drive, your foot on the brake is the only thing stopping the engine from slowly pushing the car forward. Whenever you're going to be stopped for more than a few seconds, shift the car into neutral and you'll save a little gas. If you're worried about forgetting to shift back to drive, keeping your hand on the shifter will help you remember.

• Another simple trick: if you're like Uncle John, you're occasionally guilty of the practice of starting your car as soon as you get in it and then spending 30 seconds or more fastening your seat belt, adjusting the mirrors, tuning the radio to your station, and so on. You can save gas by taking care of this stuff *before* starting the car.

LOCATION, LOCATION, LOCATION

• Anytime you have two or more lanes to choose from, figure out which one is the "lane of least resistance" and get in it. The lane of least resistance is the hypermiler's term for the one that requires the least amount of braking or changes in speed, which over time can make a big dent in your fuel economy. On a street where lots of cars are turning right into driveways or parking lots, stay in the left lane. If a lot of cars are stopping in the left lane to make left turns, move into the right lane. On a three-lane street, the lane in the middle is often the clearest.

• Taking back roads, where the speed limits are lower and there are fewer cars around, gives you the flexibility to drive efficiently in ways that aren't possible on busy streets or highways. Just getting out of stop-and-go traffic will improve your gas mileage, and you may save gas even if the backroads route is a little longer.

WEATHER REPORT

• In the winter, any snow on the ground can provide extra rolling resistance to your car, requiring you to use more gas than would be necessary if there were no snow on the road. Because of this, the most fuel-efficient time to drive is right after the road has been plowed, if you can wait until then.

• If your car is covered in snow, clear off as much as you can before you start driving. All that snow can add a lot of weight to the car, and if it's piled up on the roof it can also make the car less aerodynamic. It also cuts down the time you need the electric defroster, which uses a lot of energy.

• Water on the road also increases rolling resistance. For this reason, hypermilers like to practice something known as "ridge riding." If the road has water collecting in tire tracks worn into the road surface, driving just to the left or the right of these ruts—provided the lane is wide enough and it is safe to do so—takes you out of the water onto a part of the road surface that offers less resistance.

ODDS AND ENDS

• If you drive an automatic, when you take your foot off the brake, pause just a second before stepping on the accelerator, to give the transmission a chance to start the car moving. It takes less energy to accelerate your car once it is already moving.

• Coasting in situations where it's appropriate can save gas, too. Keep a close eye on the brake lights of the cars ahead of you as well as the traffic lights in approaching intersections. Anytime you see brake lights flash or a green light turn to yellow, and you know you are going to have to brake soon, it's more fuel efficient for you to take your foot off the accelerator immediately and coast until you need to apply the brakes. Your car uses less gas when your foot is off the accelerator. Once you know you're going to have to stop, it's wasteful to continue accelerating right up to the point where you do need to brake.

• Some fuel-saving techniques that work fine when you're alone on the road or in very light traffic, such as driving below the posted speed limit or coasting slowly up to red lights in the hope that they'll turn green before you come to a complete stop, can be counterproductive on busier roads, even if you don't take road rage and potential collisions into consideration. *You* may be saving gas, but by disrupting the flow of traffic around you, you may also be causing *other* drivers to waste more gas than you're saving.

The weight of insects eaten by spiders every year is greater than the weight of all humans alive.

VIDEO PIRATES

Imagine you're watching TV when suddenly...the screen scrambles and somebody else appears on-screen, hijacking the signal. Despite the technological sophistication of TV broadcasting, it's actually happened quite a few times.

CAPTAIN MIDNIGHT

The Crime: On April 27, 1986, HBO was showing the movie *The Falcon and the Snowman* on the East Coast. Suddenly, the movie disappeared, replaced by a color bar test pattern. Over the color bars was a message in white text that read:

"Good Evening HBO from Captain Midnight. $12.95/month? No way! Showtime/Movie Channel Beware!"

The message remained on-screen for four minutes. Then, just as suddenly as it had appeared, the message went away and *The Falcon and the Snowman* returned. HBO (and the government) had no idea how it could have happened—every person and every piece of equipment in its operations were accounted for—until an anonymous caller contacted the FBI a few weeks later.

The Aftermath: The tipster was calling from a phone booth in Gainesville, Florida, where he'd met a guy named John MacDougall in a local bar and heard him brag about breaking into HBO's feed. MacDougall was promptly arrested...and he confessed. Why'd he do it? MacDougall was a satellite dish salesman frustrated by HBO's requiring satellite owners to buy extra equipment to access its channel, which, along with high subscription fees, hurt his business. So, while working his second job as a satellite uplink supervisor at Central Florida Teleport, he intercepted the HBO signal and broadcast his message. MacDougall was fined $5,000 and sentenced to a year of probation. (He still sells satellite dishes.)

BOOB TUBE

The Crime: East Coast viewers who tuned in to the Playboy Channel on the night of September 6, 1987, didn't get the movie they'd paid for—they got a guilt trip instead. For six minutes, the broadcast was replaced by a black screen with a message in white text that said simply, "Repent your sins."

The Aftermath: Within just a few days of the signal's being hijacked, the FBI determined that the message text was produced with a Knox K50 Character Generator, of which only five were in use in the United States. One of those was located at the Virginia headquarters of the Christian Broadcasting Network, the religious television company that produces *The 700 Club*. Confronted by the FBI, a CBN employee named Thomas Haynie proudly admitted that he was the hijacker. Haynie had access to CBN's satellite, which he used to intercept the Playboy Channel's transmission with the intent to "instill morality." Haynie was fired by CBN, paid a $1,000 fine, and received three years of probation. (When his sentence was up, CBN re-hired him.)

VRILLON OF THE ASHTAR GALACTIC COMMAND

The Crime: On November 26, 1977, the Independent Television News was airing its daily report in southern England when the audio feed suddenly dropped out. Although the image of the newscaster remained intact, what viewers heard was the buzzing, highly distorted voice of someone calling himself "Vrillon of the Ashtar Galactic Command." Vrillon went on to explain that he was from a distant planet and was hijacking the news to warn people that nuclear war was inevitable unless humanity could "learn to live together in peace and goodwill." Vrillon rambled on about peace and understanding for five minutes; then the news returned to normal.

The Aftermath: The identity of the signal hacker was never discovered. But because the highly distorted voice had a clear British accent, authorities are fairly sure that "Vrillon" is not a real alien.

MAX HEADROOM

The Crime: Fifteen minutes into a November 22, 1987, late-night airing of *Doctor Who* on Chicago's PBS affiliate WTTW, the image changed to a shot of a man in a Max Headroom mask (Max Headroom was a character from a short-lived science fiction TV show). In an electronically distorted voice, "Headroom" went on a three-minute, seemingly nonsensical rant. Among his statements: "he's a freaky nerd," "this guy's better than Chuck Swirsky" (a Chicago sportscaster), "they're coming to get me," and "I just made a giant masterpiece printed all over the greatest world newspaper nerds." The man then dropped his pants and mooned the camera as a masked woman slapped his buttocks with a flyswatter. Then the picture turned to static and *Doctor Who* reappeared.

The Aftermath: A joint FBI/ FCC investigation determined that the pirate had extensive knowledge of electronics and broadcasting, because he overtook the *Doctor Who* broadcast by overpowering it with a more powerful signal. This was no small feat, considering that the WTTW antenna was on top of the Sears Tower. According to the FCC, a suitcase-sized device capable of overtaking the WTTW signal could be produced for about $25,000. Agents believe that's what the pirate used, as he beamed his message from a nearby rooftop. But searches of buildings adjacent to the Sears Tower turned up nothing. What was the reason for the signal interruption? It may have been a grudge against Chicago TV station WGN. The same night as the *Doctor Who* interception, the Max Headroom guy cut into WGN's nightly news for a few seconds, and his comment about the "greatest world newspaper nerds" could have been a reference to WGN's call letters, which stand for "world's greatest newspaper" (the station was owned by the *Chicago Tribune)*. But whoever the pirate was, and exactly why he did it, have never been discovered.

*　*　*

TIMELESS TOYS

To date, the National Toy Hall Of Fame, located in Rochester, New York, has honored 39 classic toys and games. They are: alphabet blocks, the Atari 2600, Barbie, the bicycle, Candy Land, checkers, Crayola crayons, the Duncan Yo-Yo, the Easy Bake Oven, the Erector Set, Etch-A-Sketch, the Frisbee, G.I. Joe, the hula hoop, jack-in-the-box, jacks, the jigsaw puzzle, jump rope, the kite, LEGOs, Lincoln Logs, Lionel trains, marbles, Monopoly, Mr. Potato Head, Play-Doh, the Radio Flyer wagon, Raggedy Ann, Raggedy Andy, the rocking horse, roller skates, SCRABBLE, Silly Putty, Slinky, the teddy bear, Tinkertoys, Tonka Trucks, and the View-Master. In 2005 they added perhaps the most timeless toy of them all: the cardboard box.

Q: What is *melanotrichous*? A: Dark-haired.

THE LAST DOUBLE EAGLE, PART II

The exciting conclusion to our story of gold, international intrigue, and the most elusive coin in American history. (Part I is on page 155.)

THE EGYPTIAN CONNECTION

Stephen Fenton was the owner of Knightsbridge Coins, a London coin dealer. In 1994 Fenton and his business partner, Andre de Clermont, began buying rare coins from an Egyptian jeweler. The Egyptian wished to remain anonymous, saying only that he had access to many valuable coins because he was a family friend of a colonel in the ruling Egyptian army of the 1950s. That colonel, it turned out, had "acquired" a number of unsold items from the 1954 King Farouk coin auction, and when the colonel died, his family had sold it to this Egyptian jeweler. Fenton and de Clermont bought several items from him and compared them to the 1954 auction catalog. The coins matched the ones from Farouk's collection.

A year later de Clermont met with the Egyptian at his hotel room to view another coin he was offering for sale. He presented de Clermont with a worn Sotheby's envelope from 1954. Inside was Farouk's 1933 Double Eagle. The Egyptian wanted $325,000 for it, but de Clermont consulted with Fenton and they talked the Egyptian into selling the coin for $220,000. Fenton and de Clermont agreed to split the profits when they resold it.

MOORE INTRIGUE

Fenton started looking for a buyer and through a Kansas City coin dealer named Jasper Parrino he found Jack Moore, who was a high-end coin collector...and a government informant on stolen coins. When Parrino offered Moore a chance to buy a 1933 Double Eagle, Moore told Parrino he was interested, then immediately called the Treasury Department—he knew the entire story of the coin and that if one ever showed up, it was stolen.

Unfortunately, and unlike Moore, Stephen Fenton *didn't* know the whole story of the 1933 Double Eagle. Specifically, he didn't know the part about that coin being stolen federal property that had been missing for more than four decades.

THE STING

The Treasury and the Secret Service talked Moore into helping them stage a sting operation to retrieve the Double Eagle from Fenton. Through Parrino (who was unaware of the sting), Moore told Fenton that he'd buy the Double Eagle for $1.5 million via wire transfer, but that he'd like to receive the coin in person at the Waldorf-Astoria Hotel in New York City. The meeting took place in February 1996. Moore also brought two people with him: a "co-buyer" and a "coin expert"...both of whom were actually undercover Secret Service agents.

Fenton brought the coin to Moore's room, which was rigged with surveillance equipment. As Fenton handed the coin to Moore, Secret Service agents rushed the room, seized the coin, and threw Fenton to the ground. Fenton was arrested and taken into custody at the Manhattan Secret Service offices, where he was charged with conspiring to embezzle and convert to his own use property of the United States. The coin was moved to a Treasury Department vault at the World Trade Center.

DEAL OR NO DEAL

The public defender's office gave Fenton a list of local attorneys, and from it he selected a man named Barry Berke. Berke managed to get Fenton released from custody on the condition that he not leave the city. By April, Berke had convinced a federal judge that Fenton wasn't a criminal and that he'd had no idea he had tried to sell stolen federal property. Fenton was cleared of all criminal charges.

Next to be decided was the issue of ownership of the coin. Berke had to find some way to prove that his client rightfully owned the coin. But the 1947 L. G. Barnard case had established a precedent that the government owned all the 1933 Double Eagles because they had been stolen from the U.S. Mint. In order for Fenton to keep the disputed Double Eagle, Berke would have to prove that this coin was somehow different from Barnard's.

And he did.

FLIPPING A COIN

At a 2000 hearing, Berke argued that since the coin had been purchased through legal channels by Farouk and its export completely cleared by the Treasury Department in 1944, the U.S. government had forfeited its claim to that coin. In July 2001, a federal judge ruled that both Fenton *and* the government had rights to the coin. The judge's solution: The government would retain ownership of the Farouk 1933 Double Eagle, but it would be sold at auction, and the proceeds would be split 50-50 between the Treasury Department and Fenton.

If not for lucky timing, the auction may never have happened at all. In July 2001, the 1933 Double Eagle was removed from a vault in the World Trade Center and transported to Fort Knox. Less than two months later, the World Trade Center was destroyed in the September 11 terrorist attacks.

GOING ONCE...

On July 30, 2002, the world's only 1933 Double Eagle (other than the two in the Smithsonian) was put up for sale at an auction conducted by Sotheby's in conjunction with Stack's coin house. In order to participate, potential buyers had to produce bank records to show they had the ability to pay for the coin, bidding for which would begin at $2.5 million. Coin experts predicted that the final sale price would probably reach around $4.5 million.

Twelve people qualified to take part in the auction, including two phone bidders. Sotheby's vice-chairman David Redden conducted the auction, which began at exactly 6:00 p.m. Within three minutes, bidding topped $4 million. At that point, all but two bidders had dropped out: an anonymous man standing in the back of the room, and a phone bidder for whom a Sotheby's employee acted as a proxy.

When the price reached $6.6 million, the man at the back of the room bowed out. It was all over in nine minutes. The man on the phone had purchased the 1933 Double Eagle for $6.6 million, plus a 15% seller's premium and a $20 fee to the Treasury to "monetize" the coin in order to make it legal currency. Total price: $7,590,020. As agreed, Fenton got half and the Treasury got half (plus the $20). The identity of the buyer remains a secret to this day.

First major American corporation to have a woman on its board of directors: Coca-Cola (1934).

THE ONLY CONSTANT IS CHANGE (GET IT?)

In 2005 Israel Switt, the Philadelphia jeweler whose illegal activities began the Double Eagle saga, died. That August his daughter Joan Langbord was going through his Philadelphia store and made a startling discovery: Those other three coins weren't the only ones in the world after all. In the store's safe were 10 gold 1933 Double Eagle coins. They'd never been sold and had been sitting there for more than 70 years. And what's more startling is that Langbord had no idea of the significance of the coins...until she tried to get them appraised by another coin dealer and found out exactly what these 10 coins were.

The coin dealer had to notify the Secret Service, who then brokered a deal with Langbord. She would turn over the coins to them (she had no choice—they were stolen property) and they'd give her a large cash settlement. How much would she get? No one knows. As of May 2008, Langbord still hadn't received a check and was planning to sue the government for rightful possession of the coins. And what became of the 10 Double Eagles? So far, they remain intact—the Treasury Department has yet to make a decision on whether to melt them down or to display them in a museum.

*　　*　　*

THE ELVIS OF SWIMMING

Olympic swimmer Michael Phelps—the breakout star of the 2008 Games, winning eight gold medals—trains hard, swimming five hours a day, six days a week. All that swimming requires a lot of food. Phelps claims he eats about 12,000 calories a day—six times the requirement of an adult male. Here's his typical menu.

Breakfast: Three fried egg sandwiches with cheese, lettuce, tomatoes, onions, and mayonnaise; a five-egg omelette; a bowl of grits; three slices of French toast; three chocolate chip pancakes; and two cups of coffee.

Lunch: A pound of pasta, two ham and cheese sandwiches with mayonnaise, and 1,000 calories worth of energy drinks.

Dinner: Another pound of pasta, an entire large pizza, and another 1,000 calories worth of energy drinks.

WEIRD ANIMAL NEWS

Strange tales of creatures great and small.

LOUNGING LIZARDS

A rare deep freeze hit the Florida Keys in early 2008 and fooled the native iguana population...into hibernation. Hundreds of the lizards fell out of trees and lied motionless on the ground, prompting concerned Floridians to take the stiff animals into their homes to warm them up. Bad idea: "When they warm up, they go back to being a wild animal," explained a local veterinarian. The iguanas (some as long as five feet) started thrashing about the houses, causing extensive damage and in some cases, they bit people.

BEARLY LEGAL

After a bear repeatedly stole honey from Zoran Kiseloski's bees, the Macedonian beekeeper installed bright lights and a sound system on his farm. For two weeks, he blared the music of Serbian "turbo-funk" star Cera. The tactic worked...until the generator stopped working. Then the bear came back. That prompted Kiseloski to take legal action: He sued the bear. A local judge listened to the beekeeper's testimony and, amazingly, found the bear guilty of theft. However, since the bear wasn't present, the judge ordered the state to compensate Kiseloski 140,000 denars ($3,500) for his losses.

POLLY WANNA %@#$*&!

Shortly after the Warwickshire Animal Sanctuary in Nuneaton, England, took in a parrot named Barney in 2005, they discovered—the hard way—that the bird had learned a few choice phrases from its original owner. When the town's mayor and a female vicar visited, Barney told the mayor to "F*** off!" When the vicar asked if she had heard what she *thought* she'd heard, Barney squawked, "You can f*** off, too!" They thought it was funny, but sanctuary owner Geoff Grewcock didn't. He decided it was time to put the rude bird in a private cage...but not before Barney had taught two other parrots at the sanctuary how to to curse. "It sounds like a construction site, with all the verbal abuse flying about," said Grewcock.

Good news! Only 40% of all heart attacks are fatal.

KISSY FACE

Lipstick manufacturers do whatever they can to stand out. One way to do that is to give the colors weird names. Here are some we came across. (They're real.)

Barbarella
Beautiful Liar
Damage
Jail Bait
Catfight
Funny Face
Hot Voodoo
Suzi Sells Sushi By the Seashore
Manhunt
Promiscuous
Hellbent
Everlasting Rum
Nice Knickers
Mindgame
Heartbreak Heather
Silent Mauvie
Raisin' Cane
Thursday
Melon of Troy
Celebrity Meltdown
But Officer

Gypsy Soiree
St. Pertersburgundy
No Competition
La La Land
Trailer Trash
Cash Flow
Smitten
Woolloomooloo
Electric Banana
Sex Kitten
Sell Out
How to Jamaica Million
Smut
In a Nutshell
Foolish Virgin
Go Fig
Vamp
Crazed
Boiling Point
Hot Pants
Tempt Me
Chai Love You

Box-Office Beige
Plum Plot
Nude Beach
Scorption
Taxi Cab
Toast of the Town
Devil's Claw
Sweet Mama
Marooned
Diva Brown
Mischief
Poppy Dust
Phantom
Sugar and Spice
Wuss
Bambi
Mystery
Marcia Marcia Marcia
Cowboy
Gidget
Metal Glamour
Zsa Zsa

What's the difference between poultry and fowl? Poultry is domesticated fowl.

WE'RE UNDER ATTACK!

Many Bathroom Readers *ago, we wrote about the 1938 radio broadcast of* The War of the Worlds. *Here's what happened when a radio station in Ecuador performed its own version of the drama 11 years later.*

SPECIAL REPORTS

The story of the *War of the Worlds* radio broadcast is well known: In 1938 Orson Welles adapted H.G. Wells's classic science fiction novel into a radio drama told in the form of emergency news broadcasts describing the invasion of Earth by hostile aliens from Mars. Despite the fact that the show was a regularly scheduled installment of Welles's *Mercury Theater On the Air,* and that it was introduced as fiction, many listeners mistakenly believed that Martians had actually landed in New Jersey.

Welles later apologized, insisting that he hadn't intended to fool anyone—it had all been an unfortunate misunderstanding. Six years later, in Santiago, Chile, the radio drama was restaged with similar results. Although the radio station in Santiago advertised the program for a full week before it aired, and made several announcements during the show intended to prevent listeners from becoming alarmed, the broadcast still resulted in mass confusion and was blamed for causing at least one fatal heart attack.

WE INTERRUPT THIS PROGRAM...

Just a few years later, in 1949, a radio station in Quito, Ecuador, decided to produce a new version of *War of the Worlds*, but this one was different: Radio Quito pulled out all the stops in an effort to convince everyone within broadcast range that Ecuador was actually being attacked by invaders from outer space.

Here's how they did it: Weeks before the show was to air, the station began planting fake UFO-sighting stories in the local newspaper. That, producers hoped, would soften up the audience, making them more vulnerable to the suggestion that they were under alien attack. Then they swore all the actors and production staff to complete secrecy and, amazingly, no one leaked the real story to the press. Finally, they began the show by actually interrupting regularly scheduled programming to bring citizens of

Quito—a city of 250,000 people—the "breaking news" that the town of Latacunga, just 20 miles south, was under attack.

At that moment, the only people in Quito who knew it was just a radio play were inside the studio. Simply refusing to let on in any way that the story was fake would have been bad enough, but Radio Quito went a step further, and had one of the actors imitate the voice of Quito's mayor. Women and children, the fake mayor instructed, should run into the jungle and hide. All able-bodied men, meanwhile, were to arm themselves in preparation to mount a defense of the city.

THE SHOW MUST GO OFF

Listeners, meanwhile, had no way of knowing that what they were hearing wasn't real. Skeptics had only to look out their windows to see that *something* was going on. Interviewed a half-century later, one witness to that night's events in Quito recalled his family piling into their car to flee the city. He described complete chaos on the roads, where thousands of residents believed they were fleeing for their lives.

The chaos found its way to the radio station, prompting the actors to stop the performance. That's when things got really ugly: Upon learning that the "invasion" had been a hoax, the frightened crowd transformed into an angry mob—they attacked the building that housed the radio station...and burned it to the ground.

By the time the Ecuadorian army managed to break up the riot, six people had died in the fire and several more had been injured by jumping out of third-floor windows to escape the flames. In the aftermath, the station's artistic director, Leonardo Paez, was deemed responsible for creating the panic. His misguided sense of "entertainment" brought such an angry backlash from the citizens of Quito that Paez was forced to change his name and flee the country. He never returned.

* * *

"No one would have believed..."

—opening line from *The War of the Worlds*

MAKE A WHITE CABBAGE

Every language has colorful expressions that sound normal to a person who uses them every day, but can seem strange when translated into another language. Here are some common French idioms translated into English.

BAISSER LES BRAS
Translation: "Lower the arms"
Meaning: Throw in the towel

BIEN EN CHAIR
Translation: "Good in flesh"
Meaning: Fat

BLAIREAU
Translation: "Shaving brush"
Meaning: A nerd

À PAS DE LOUP
Translation: "As a wolf steps"
Meaning: Quickly

AVOIR DES ANTENNES
Translation: "Have antennae"
Meaning: Have a sixth sense

AVOIR LE CAFARD
Translation: "To have the cockroach"
Meaning: To be depressed

CASSER DU SUCRE SUR LE DOS
Translation: "To break sugar on somebody's back"
Meaning: To talk about someone behind their back

LES DENTS DU FOND QUI BAIGNENT
Translation: "The back teeth are swimming in food"
Meaning: I'm full

CASSER SA PIPE
Translation: "Break the pipe"
Meaning: Kick the bucket

ENTRE QUATRE YEUX
Translation: "Between four eyes"
Meaning: Just between us

FAIRE CHOU BLANC
Translation: "Make a white cabbage"
Meaning: Draw a blank

ACCORDER SES VIOLONS
Translation: "Tune your violins"
Meaning: Get your story straight

MARCHER À CÔTÉ DE SES POMPES
Translation: "To walk next to your shoes"
Meaning: To be out of it

The oldest surviving love poem is written on a clay tablet from around 3500 B.C.

HARLEM GLOBE-TRIVIA

Ever seen the Harlem Globetrotters play? Millions have. With tricks, acrobatics, and amazing basketball skills, they turned sports into entertainment.

• The team began in 1926 as an independent touring team called the Savoy Big Five, named after a Chicago district.

• For their first game, the team wore jerseys that read "New York" because owner Abe Saperstein figured people would believe they were world-class athletes if they were from New York.

• They were renamed the Harlem Globetrotters in 1929—Harlem because most of the team was African American, Globetrotters to create the (false) image of "experience."

• By 1940 they'd played 2,000 games and dominated whatever team they played, including high-school teams, college teams, and semipro squads. Their record that season: 159–8.

• One night in 1939, the Globetrotters were leading their opponent 112 to 5. The crowd was bored, so Globetrotter Inman Jackson started fooling around on the court, doing finger rolls, taking (and making) full and half-court shots, shooting from under his leg, and throwing crazy passes to his teammates. The crowd loved it. Saperstein told the team to do that every night.

• In a February 1948 exhibition, the Globetrotters beat the NBA champion Minneapolis Lakers. The game is credited with leading the NBA to begin admitting black players in 1950.

• By 1953 the Globetrotters were so good that nobody would play them anymore. Saperstein had a friend named Red Klotz who owned a semipro basketball team called the Philadelphia Sphas. He asked Klotz to take the team on the road as the Globetrotters' permanent opponent. The same players took the court every night, but wore different jerseys to create the illusion of different teams, including the Boston Shamrocks, Baltimore Rockets, New York Nationals, Atlantic City Seagulls, New Jersey Reds, and their most famous incarnation, the Washington Generals.

• In 1958 the team was at the peak of its popularity, and four dif-

In the 1st pro basketball league (1898), players got $2.50 for home games and $1.25 for away games.

ferent squads toured the world. (That year Saperstein drafted Wilt Chamberlain, who played with the Globetrotters for a year before leaving to become one of the NBA's all-time greats.)

• During the 1960s civil rights movement, some civil rights leaders criticized the Globetrotters, calling them "Uncle Toms" for pleasing white crowds with "clowning" and "buffoonery." Another civil rights leader, Jesse Jackson, disagreed. "They don't show blacks as stupid," he said. "On the contrary. They show them as superior."

• More than 40 years after the team's formation, the Globetrotters played their first ever game in Harlem, New York, in 1968.

• In the 1970s, the Globetrotters were so popular that they went Hollywood. Team members voiced themselves in two different Saturday morning cartoon shows: *The Harlem Globetrotters* and *Super Globetrotters*. The team played itself in the 1981 live-action made-for-TV movie *The Harlem Globetrotters on Gilligan's Island*.

• The Globetrotters have played in more than 25,000 games—more than any other team in any other sport in history. (All-time record: approximately 22,000 wins and 330 losses.) More than 125 million people in 120 countries have seen a Globetrotters game.

• The Globetrotters' games are all considered exhibition games (they're not in a league and the games don't count), but since the players are paid and the games aren't fixed, the Globetrotters are considered a professional team.

• In 1985 the team signed two women, Olympic gold-medal winners Lynette Woodward and Joyce Walker, making them the first American female professional basketball players.

• In its early barnstorming days, the team lost often. From the 1960s on, losses have been rare. In 1971 the Globetrotters got too wrapped up in the stunts and lost to the New Jersey Reds 100–99. Last loss: by four points in 2006 to a team of college all-stars.

• Memorable Globetrotters: Curly Neal, Meadowlark Lemon, Goose Tatum, Twiggy Sanders, and Sweet Lou Dunbar.

• Famous people that have been made "honorary" Globetrotters: Jackie Joyner-Kersee, Henry Kissinger, Whoopi Goldberg, Kareem-Abdul-Jabbar, Bob Hope, Nelson Mandela, and Pope John Paul II.

Americans buy an estimated 20 million lbs. of candy corn each Halloween (and very little real corn).

THE PLOT AGAINST FDR

Conspiracy theories are fun to read about because they're usually so bizarre that they couldn't possibly be true. What's even more fun is a conspiracy that's not a theory at all. Here's one that actually happened.

ALL THE RAGE IN EUROPE

In the 1930s, many Western countries suffered severe economic depressions. The need to prevent unrest and establish control was so desperate that in Italy, Germany, and Spain, military-backed coups installed fascist governments. In that system a centralized government, led by a sole dictator, holds all the power and the individual citizen has little recourse. Fascist governments readily use force to quell what they perceive as threats, such as labor unions. Notable fascist dictators of the 1930s: Benito Mussolini in Italy, Francisco Franco in Spain, and Adolf Hitler in Germany.

In another country, a fascist coup was attempted not by the military, but by a group of powerful businessmen and politicians. They wanted to overthrow the democratically elected head of state through blackmail and threats of violence and replace him with a puppet dictator who would serve their interests. That country was the United States.

RAW DEAL?

Franklin D. Roosevelt was elected president in 1932 largely on the basis of his New Deal, a far-reaching series of reforms designed to stimulate the economy out of the Great Depression. Roosevelt's plans weren't universally popular—giving control of economic matters to the government instead of business in a free-market economy was viewed by many as communism, especially Social Security, which was perceived as the needy getting "something for nothing."

But the crux of the New Deal was job creation. Roosevelt proposed more than 10 new government agencies such as the Works Progress Administration, the Civilian Conservation Corps, the Civil Works Administration, and the Tennessee Valley Authority, that would oversee construction and beautification projects and generate millions of new jobs.

Speed demon: The giant house spider can travel up to 1.17 miles per hour.

THE PLOT BEGINS

Business leaders were especially opposed to the National Recovery Administration, which set minimum wages and reduced the work week, even in the private sector. Used to paying their workers whatever they wanted (for as much work as they wanted), barons of industry stood to lose millions.

A group of anti-Roosevelt business leaders and politicians (Democrats and Republicans) formed an organization in 1933 called the American Liberty League (ALL), dedicated to "fostering the right to work, earn, save, and acquire property." In other words, they advocated individual wealth-building and villainized welfare. The ALL was so dedicated to that goal that it would do whatever was necessary to secure their wealth. That included staging a militia-backed coup to force Roosevelt out of office and replace him with a pro-business dictator.

BUSINESS CLASS

In June 1933, a number of ALL members met to discuss the specifics of removing Roosevelt. Among those reported to be in attendance were:

- Irénée Du Pont, president of the DuPont chemical company
- Dean Acheson, the undersecretary of the Treasury, a position to which he was appointed by Roosevelt
- Al Smith, the 1928 Democratic presidential candidate
- Grayson Murphy, a board member of several companies, including Goodyear, Bethlehem Steel, and the J. P. Morgan & Co. banking conglomerate
- Robert Clark, one of Wall Street's wealthiest investors
- William Doyle, commander of the Massachusetts department of the American Legion, a veterans' service and political organization. The 300,000 Massachusetts members were almost exclusively veterans of World War I.
- Gerald MacGuire, a bonds investor and commander of the Connecticut department of the American Legion
- Prescott Bush, an influential banker and a board member of several corporations (later, a Republican Senator from Connecticut from 1952 to 1962, father of George H. W. Bush, and grandfather of George W. Bush)

The pressure at the Sun's center is about 700 million tons per sq. inch—enough to smash atoms.

The group concocted a plan to force Roosevelt to create a new cabinet position called the Secretary of General Affairs, which would be filled by a person of the ALL's choosing. Next, they'd force Roosevelt to admit to the public that he had been crippled by polio (not widely known because he was rarely photographed in his wheelchair). The knowledge that the president couldn't walk or even stand without assistance would destroy all trust in his ability to pull the country out of its economic mess, and the backlash would force Roosevelt to shift authority to the Secretary of General Affairs.

In all likelihood, of course, Roosevelt would refuse to meet the ALL's demands to create the new position, confess his condition, and transfer power. Part two of the plan: If Roosevelt refused, Doyle and MacGuire would activate their American Legion brigades to form a militia of more than 500,000 who would then storm Washington, D.C., and take power by force.

THE BUTLER DID IT

For the American people and 500,000 soldiers to go along with a plan to depose a president, the ALL knew that whoever they chose to be the Secretary of General Affairs would have to be popular with both the military and the general public. So, acting on behalf of the plotters, MacGuire approached Smedley Butler, a major general in the Marine Corps and the most decorated Marine in history at that point. Butler was as loved by the military and respected by the general public just as later generals like Dwight Eisenhower, Douglas MacArthur, and Colin Powell would be. That's because in 1932, when World War I veterans marched on Washington to lobby Congress over still-unpaid combat bonuses from 15 years earlier, Butler publicly supported them and even gave a speech encouraging them to fight for what was rightfully theirs.

CLANDESTINE MEETING

MacGuire visited Butler at his home in Newton Square, Pennsylvania, in June 1933. They met for just 30 minutes, but MacGuire gave him the complete details of the plot, including the names of those involved and a promise of $3 million in financial support. Butler asked MacGuire why something as drastic as a coup was necessary. MacGuire said that it was because Roosevelt's social programs proved he was a Communist. "We need a fascist government in this country to save the nation from the Communists who want to tear it down and wreck all that we have built," Butler later said MacGuire told him.

Butler agreed and told MacGuire he was in...except that he really wasn't. What the ALL members hadn't taken into consideration was that the combat bonus protests of the previous summer, which had made Butler beloved among soldiers, ended when President Herbert Hoover sent in the cavalry to break it up. Butler was so appalled by this treatment of the WWI veterans that he renounced Hoover and the Republican party, became a Democrat, and actively campaigned for Roosevelt in the 1932 election.

PLOTLESS

After speaking with MacGuire, Butler promptly reported the meeting and the brewing fascist coup to the McCormack-Dickstein Committee, the congressional committee in charge of investigating threats to the government, such as fascist coups. (In the 1940s, the committee would try to root out Communists under a different name: the House Un-American Activities Committee.)

Butler gave his testimony to the committee between July and November 1934. Nearly all of the conspirators Butler named were asked to testify. But since they weren't subpoenaed, merely asked, they never showed up. The only exception was Gerald MacGuire, and he denied everything. In its final report, the committee officially stated that it believed Butler:

> Your committee received evidence showing that certain persons had made an attempt to establish a fascist government in this country. There is no question that these attempts were discussed, were planned, and might have been placed in execution when and if the financial backers deemed it expedient. This committee received evidence from Maj. Gen. Smedley D. Butler (retired), who testified before the committee as to conversations with one Gerald C. MacGuire in which the latter is alleged to have suggested the formation of a fascist army under the leadership of General Butler.

But the findings—and Butler's credibility—were undercut when the report was released to the public with the names of the conspirators blacked out. The names were never officially released, and no one associated with the "plot" was ever held accountable.

...any other U.S. president. (Grover Cleveland is second, with 584.)

COUP DE-TAH-TAH

So why didn't the federal government prosecute the plotters? At the time, Roosevelt was trying hard to get his New Deal programs passed through Congress. Releasing the names of the government officials and appointees involved would have undermined Roosevelt's authority and made him look like a weak leader. In fact, it may have been Roosevelt himself who suggested that the McCormack-Dickstein Committee withhold the conspirators' names and not pursue charges...provided the plotters agreed to stop speaking out publicly against his social and relief programs.

The compromised report, coupled with the altogether absurd nature of the idea of a fascist coup in America (even if it was true), led to little media coverage. The *New York Times* and *Time* reported on the committee's findings, but dismissed Butler's claims as rumor and hearsay.

How serious were the conspirators? The idea never got past the planning stages, and the conspirators may have met only that once. When news that Butler had turned informant got out, the plot crumbled. But they did have one "backup" plan—shortly after MacGuire met with Butler, MacGuire also approached James Van Zandt, the head of the Veterans of Foreign Wars office, to be the Secretary of General Affairs should Butler decline. After Butler revealed the plot to the congressional committee, Van Zandt told reporters his story, lending Butler's story some credence, but that's as far as it went.

IRONIC POSTSCRIPT

The American Liberty League which, in addition to proposing fascist coups, operated as a legitimate pro-capitalist organization. It folded in 1940. That same year, Franklin Roosevelt was elected to his record third presidential term. Roosevelt was reelected again in 1944, but in the same national election, Republicans took control of Congress from the Democrats, gaining a majority in both the Senate and the House. After Roosevelt's death five months after the election, the conservative government was eager to start anew, and in 1951 passed the 22nd Amendment to the Constitution, which limited future presidents to two terms. Why? Many senators and representatives feared that a president who held office for too long could become a dictator.

INSTANT CLASSIC

In case you don't know, an oxymoron *is a phrase made of two words that appear to be contradictory. Here are some of our newest favorites.*

Cautiously optimistic
Bigger half
Rock opera
Boneless ribs
Resident alien
White chocolate
Global village
Minor crisis
Act naturally
Defensive strike
Slumber party
Oven-fried
Deafening silence
Graduate student
Educated guess
Free trade
Instant classic
Calculated risk
Wilderness management
Vegetarian meatball
Wireless cable
Detailed summary
Fresh from concentrate

Extended deadline
Negative growth
Paid volunteer
Small fortune
Controlled chaos
Doing nothing
Going nowhere
Athletic scholarship
Open-book test
Primitive technology
Audio book
Civil disobedience
Forgotten memories
Virtual reality
Accurate stereotype
Down escalator
Bittersweet
Sharp curve
Unbiased opinion
Alone together
Short distance
Outer core
"The rumors are true"

King Louis XIV of France established the position of "Royal Chocolate Maker to the King."

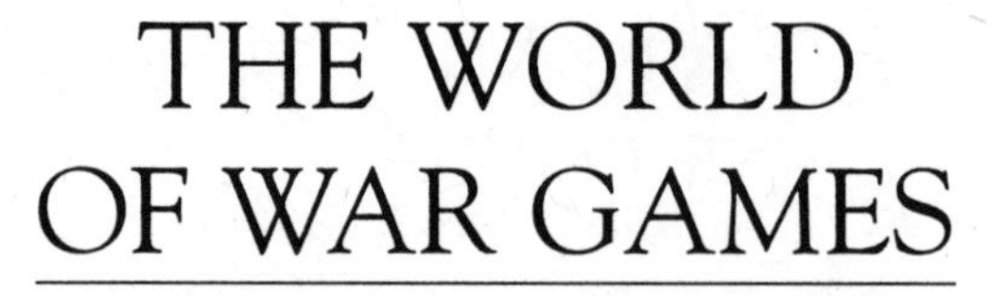

THE WORLD OF WAR GAMES

On page 251, we told you the story of the "most influential game you've never heard of." Well, here's one you have *heard of. And if this one wasn't* the *most influential of all, it certainly comes close.*

ROLL MODEL

More than 30 years after the first edition of Dungeons & Dragons hit store shelves in 1974, the game is still the best-selling "tabletop" or non-computer-based role-playing game of all time. More than 20 million people have played it, and over the years they have purchased more than $1 billion worth of Dungeons & Dragons books, dice, and other merchandise.

Not many games have reached this level of success. Even so, the sales figures alone do not begin to describe the impact that Dungeons & Dragons has had on game-playing culture in the United States and around the world. That's not just because it was the very first role-playing game, but also because it happened to appear at the dawn of the microcomputer revolution.

When Dungeons & Dragons arrived on the scene, only giant corporations and government agencies could afford computers, which cost millions of dollars apiece and filled entire rooms (and they had less computing power than pocket calculators do today). Personal computers were still a few years off, so the only way ordinary people could get access to a computer was by majoring in computer science at a university that had one.

SO MUCH HAS CHANGED

And how did these privileged college students spend their time, once they were granted a few precious hours on one of these rare, multimillion-dollar machines, time that was intended to be used to complete important classroom assignments?

A lot of them created and played computer games.

Many of these early programmers were fans of Dungeons & Dragons, which, because it was based on the roll of the dice, trans-

Captain America's "real" name was Steve Rogers. The Flash's was Britt Reid.

lated easily into computer code. So the programmers did just that. At virtually every point in the evolution of computer games—from single-player games to multiplayer games played on a mainframe computer, to multiple mainframes communicating with each other over the ARPAnet (precursor to the Internet), to personal home computers—these Dungeons & Dragons fans drew directly from their tabletop gaming experience to create one fantasy role-playing game after another.

LOGGING ON

One of the most successful such programmers is Richard Garriot, who wrote his first Dungeons & Dragons–inspired game, Akalabeth, in the summer after he graduated from high school in 1980. When Akalabeth had sold enough copies at $5 a pop to pay for his college education, he followed up with a game called Ultima, which with nine different incarnations over two decades became one of the most successful computer game series of all time. The success of these PC games led to the creation of a "massively multiplayer online role-playing game" (MMORPG) version called Ultima Online, which launched in 1997.

IMAGINARY WORLDS, REAL GOLD

Although it wasn't the first game that enabled hundreds or even thousands of players all over the world to interact in a virtual world over the Internet, Ultima Online demonstrated that such games could make big money by charging players a monthly subscription fee. Its success prompted many other companies to create MMORPGs, and today the games are a *billion-dollar-a-year* industry, with the market leader, World of Warcraft, once again drawing obvious inspiration from Dungeons & Dragons. So even if you've never played the game that started it all, if you've played *any* tabletop or computer role-playing game in the past 30 years, you have the creators of Dungeons & Dragons to thank for it.

And yet for all they contributed to pop culture, outside of gaming circles their names are almost completely unknown.

So who are these people to whom game players owe so much? That part of the story begins on page 393.

Shaquille O'Neal was named Player of the Week his very first week in the NBA.

TROPIC OF MILLER

Observations on the human condition from author Henry Miller, best known for his groundbreaking novel Tropic of Cancer.

"Life has to be given a meaning because of the obvious fact that it has no meaning."

"Man has demonstrated that he is master of everything... except his own nature."

"In expanding the field of knowledge we but increase the horizon of ignorance."

"The moment one gives close attention to any thing, even a blade of grass, it becomes a mysterious, awesome, indescribably magnificent world in itself."

"Fear is something with which we are all so familiar that when a man appears who is without it, we are at once enslaved by him."

"True strength lies in submission, which permits one to dedicate his life, through devotion, to something beyond himself."

"Every moment is a golden one for him who has the vision to recognize it as such."

"The only thing we never get enough of is love; and the only thing we never give enough of is love."

"The frantic desire to live, to live at any cost, is not a result of the life rhythm in us, but of the death rhythm."

"Every man is working out his destiny in his own way and nobody can be of any help except by being kind, generous, and patient."

"Moralities, ethics, laws, customs, beliefs, doctrines—these are of trifling import. All that matters is that the miraculous become the norm."

"The aim of life is to live, and to live means to be aware, joyously, drunkenly, serenely, divinely aware."

"If we have not found heaven within, it is a certainty we will not find it without."

"I have never regretted anything. Regret, like guilt, is a waste of time."

The U.S. Marines' first recruiting station was in a bar.

"STRONGER THAN DIRT"

Time to test your ad-slogan IQ. How many products and brands can you recognize by their slogans? Answers are on page 540.

1. "Live in your world, play in ours."

2. "Because I'm worth it."

3. "You've got questions, we've got answers."

4. "So easy a caveman can do it."

5. "The freshmaker!"

6. "Hello, boys."

7. "Progress is our most important product."

8. "Obey your thirst."

9. "Science for a better life."

10. "The pause that refreshes."

11. "Kid tested. Mother approved."

12. "Quality is job 1."

13. "Let the dance begin."

14. "The cereal that's shot from guns."

15. "Stronger than dirt."

16. "You'll wonder where the yellow went."

17. "Once you pop, you can't stop."

18. "When it rains, it pours."

19. "Australian for Beer."

20. "The Champagne of Beers."

21. "Where do you want to go today?"

22. "Lifts and separates."

23. "Who wears short shorts?"

24. "The toughest job you'll ever love."

25. "It's all inside."

26. "Leave the driving to us."

27. "A mind is a terrible thing to waste."

28. "Zoom-Zoom."

29. "The happiest place on Earth."

30. "Tastes so good cats ask for it by name."

31. "Put a tiger in your tank."

32. "The ultimate driving machine."

33. "We're number two. We try harder."

34. "Be all you can be."

Michael Keaton's costume from *Batman* (1989) weighed 70 pounds.

FAMOUS *AND* SMART

Living proof that not all celebrities are bimbos and bozos.

• **Marcia Cross** (*Desperate Housewives*) was having trouble getting acting work after she left *Melrose Place* in 1997, so she went back to school. Result: She earned a master's degree in psychology from Antioch University.

• Rage Against the Machine guitarist **Tom Morello** graduated Harvard University with honors in 1986. More impressive: He found time to practice guitar for eight hours a day.

• **David Duchovny** (*The X-Files*) has a master's degree in English literature from Yale.

• Guitarist **Jeff "Skunk" Baxter** was a member of the Doobie Brothers and Steely Dan. But while his bandmates spent their free time partying, Baxter was studying missile defense systems. Today he's a freelance defense consultant and chairs a congressional advisory board.

• **Ashley Judd** majored in French at the University of Kentucky, but had four minors: anthropology, theater, art history, and women's studies.

• **Dexter Holland**, lead singer in the punk group the Offspring, has a master's degree (and is halfway to a Ph.D.) in molecular biology.

• **Emeka Okafor,** power forward for the Charlotte Bobcats, joined the NBA in 2004 after three years of college. But he didn't leave school early—it took him only three years to earn his degree (with honors) in finance from the University of Connecticut.

• In 1970 **Brian May** was studying for his Ph.D. in astrophysics at the Imperial College of London by day and playing guitar in the band Queen at night. He quit school in 1971 when the band became successful, but in 2007 he completed his dissertation ("A Survey of Radial Velocities in the Zodiacal Dust Cloud") and was awarded his doctorate.

• **Graham Chapman** earned a medical degree and began a residency at a hospital, but quit to join a comedy troupe formed by some old college friends—Monty Python.

In 2007 Americans threw away or recycled 68 million old TV sets.

WHAT RACE(S) ARE YOU?

White? Black? Cherokee? Chinese? All of the above? Recent DNA studies say you might be surprised.

IT REALLY IS A MELTING POT

In 2006 Professor Peter Fine at Florida Atlantic University asked his class to do a project on their own racial identities, and to submit to DNA tests as part of it. Twelve of the students considered themselves white with European ancestry; one considered himself black and of African descent. Results: Only one of the white students turned out to be completely European, and the black student turned out to have 21% European ancestry. The rest had various degrees of European, African, Native American, and East Asian genes. Professor Fine himself, who considered himself of typical white European stock, found out that he had 25% Native American genes. "I honestly think these tests could have a large effect on American consciousness," Fine told the U.K.'s *Observer* newspaper in 2007. "If Americans recognize themselves as a mixed group of people, that could really change things."

HOW IT WORKS

Recent breakthroughs in the science of genetics have had a huge effect on the world, with applications in medicine, agriculture, law enforcement, and much more. Genetics has also dramatically changed a popular (and growing) pastime: genealogy. Relatively inexpensive DNA tests for *genetic markers* that can reveal familial and ethnic lineages are available to anyone who wants one. And the science behind it, while immensely complex in its details, is basically pretty simple.

Human DNA is alike in every person—but it's not *exactly* alike. Individuals can acquire *mutations* along the way. This can have many different results: Some genetic mutations cause disease, some affect eye or hair color, some do nothing at all. The ones that are used for racial testing are, primarily, ones that have no known effects.

Providence, Rhode Island, has a donut shop for every 4,200 people—6 times the national average.

So...say a guy named Bob acquired such a mutation 1,000 years ago. Bob had 10 kids—and he passed that mutation down to them. They each had 10 kids—and they all got the mutation, too. This kept happening over many generations, and today there are tens of thousands of people with that specific "Bob" mutation. And they're the only ones on Earth that have it. Well, that's exactly what happened countless times in human history.

THE MUTANTS

DNA and fossil evidence suggests that modern *Homo sapiens* (that's us) first appeared in northeastern Africa roughly 200,000 years ago. Their descendants began migrating out of Africa about 60,000 years ago, spreading in different directions at different times. Travel then wasn't as easy as it is today, so those different groups of travelers didn't interact biologically (or in any other way) for very long periods of time. The people who would go on to become the Native Americans, for example, wouldn't interact with the people who went on to become the Europeans for many thousands of years.

In the same way, that long genetic separation resulted in entire groups of peoples acquiring DNA mutations that were unique to them. The people who became the Native Americans acquired mutations long after they got to the Americas. That means the Europeans, naturally, didn't have those mutations—they had unique mutations of their own. This is also true of the many different peoples who were separated for long periods of time over the millennia. When means of travel progressed and those long-separated groups of peoples *did* start interacting, and having children together, those mutations started being shared. And now—we can find them.

THE ODDS

As we said, there are relatively inexpensive tests you can take today that look for these particular genetic markers. One kind of test shows "genetic percentages" of your ethnic heritage. The four very broad ethnic groupings determined by the tests:

African: Peoples of sub-Saharan Africa.

European: This group is much broader than it appears, and includes peoples from Europe, North Africa, the Middle East, India, Pakistan, and Sri Lanka.

Since it began in 1990, the Human Genome Project is estimated to have cost $3 billion.

East Asian: Japanese, Chinese, Mongolian, Korean, Southeast Asian, and Pacific Islander populations.

Native American: Peoples that migrated from Asia to populate North, Central, and South America.

A result of such a test might say that you have 40% European, 40% African, 18% Asian, and 2% Native American heritage. Or it might say 90% Native American and 10% East Asian. It all depends on your ancestors.

THE LOST TREES

Since such tests have become available and affordable to the public, they've been particularly popular among African Americans, whose ancestors came to America as slaves, as they usually have little or nothing in the way of written records to help track their family trees. In 2006 Henry Louis Gates Jr., director of Harvard University's W. E. B. Du Bois Institute for African and African American Studies, produced and hosted a PBS documentary entitled *African American Lives* with just this in mind. "If we could," he said, "trace their family tree back, back beyond slavery, analyze their DNA and tell them where their ancestors came from in Africa, what a great contribution that would be to education."

Gates asked several prominent African Americans, including Oprah Winfrey and actors Chris Tucker and Whoopi Goldberg, to submit to genealogical DNA testing. They all got very interesting results.

THE MIXER

Oprah Winfrey believed she was of Zulu descent (the Zulu people now reside in South Africa). She also believed she had no Native American or European ancestors. She was mostly wrong. The tests showed her to have 89% sub-Saharan African, 8% Native American, 3% East Asian, and 0% European heritage. Regarding her sub-Saharan ancestors, Gates told her that she descends from the Kpella tribe in what is now the West African nation of Liberia; the Bamileke people, in modern-day Cameroon; and the Nkoya people in Zambia.

Chris Tucker guessed he was descended from a tribe in modern-day Ghana. Wrong. His test showed 83% sub-Saharan African,

10% Native American, and 7% European descent. And the African link was to the Mbundu tribe in present-day Angola. Gates said the link was so strong that it was likely that a direct ancestor of Tucker's had been taken into slavery in Angola sometime in the 1700s. (The show featured Tucker going to Angola and meeting with his distant relatives.)

Quincy Jones said that family stories told of Native American ancestry, and thought he had probably a little European blood, too. Result: 66% sub-Saharan African, 34% European, and 0% Native American. His father's line, Jones was shocked to learn, showed *only* European descent, while his mother's showed a connection to the Tikar people of modern Cameroon.

Mae Jemison, the first black female astronaut to go into space, was told she has 84% sub-Saharan African, 13% East Asian, 3% Native American, and 0% European ancestry. She was very surprised to learn about her East Asian heritage, and said it probably stemmed from the fact that in the 1800s many Chinese workers were brought into her family's native Mississippi.

Whoopi Goldberg expressed her frustration at never knowing exactly where her family had come from. "You sit with white folks who say, 'My family goes back to County Cork,' or, 'My family goes back to Sicily,'" she told Gates. "And you say, 'Umm, I don't know, I think Florida.'" Goldberg was told that she had 92% sub-Saharan African, 8% European, and 0% Native American heritage, and that she was related to the Pepel and Bayote people, who live near the Atlantic Coast in the nation of Guinea-Bissau.

The Host: Maybe the most surprising results came for the host of the show. Gates, one of the country's leading African-American scholars, found out that he has 50% sub-Saharan African—and 50% European ancestry. He had no idea. "I'm going to have to give up my job!" he joked. "I'm descended from that African kingdom known as Northern Europe!"

* * *

"It's surprising how much of memory is built around things unnoticed at the time."

—Barbara Kingsolver

Pears, cherries, apricots, and almonds are all members of the rose family.

FOUNDING FOOD-ERS

We tend to take our food products for granted. Turns out there are some pioneers we've never heard of whom we ought to thank.

JULIUS MAGGI

Maggi (1846–1912) owned a flour business in Switzerland and had a lot of opinions about food. For one, he believed people should eat more legumes (such as peas, beans, lentils, chick peas), and for another, he was concerned that women who worked in factories didn't have enough time or money to cook traditional meals for their families. He was so well known for his vociferous opinions that in 1882 the Swiss Public Welfare Society asked him to do a study of the national diet. What he learned led him to invent a convenient—and affordable—powdered pea-and-bean instant soup mix. It was such a success that a few years later he came up with a bigger idea: powdered "bouillon" concentrate (the word comes from the French word for "boil," because that's what you do with bouillon—mix it with boiling water to make instant broth). The bouillon concentrate came in packets or in capsules...until 1906, when Maggi figured out how to compress the concentrate into cubes. Before the invention of bouillon cubes, it took hours of boiling meat, vegetables, and other ingredients to make the broth that was the basis for soup; after the cubes were invented, making a pot of soup was a piece of cake. In fact, the cubes used to be called "pocket soup" or "portable soup." We still use identical bouillon cubes today, and the Maggi company still makes them.

IVAR JEPSON

Jepson emigrated to America from Sweden in 1925 and brought his engineering and inventing skills to the Sunbeam division of the Chicago Flexible Shaft Company. In addition to redesigning toasters and other existing appliances, he came up with a countertop food mixer, dubbed the Sunbeam Mixmaster. It was marketed to the public in 1930, and was an immediate sensation. A complete departure from the few earlier single-beater mechanical mixers, Jepson's design had a motor inside a horizontal housing that extended out over a mixing bowl, with two detachable, interlocking beaters. Sound familiar? His design was so brilliant that it has hardly changed in more than 75 years.

KIKUNAE IKEDA

For centuries, Western scientists identified four basic tastes: sweet, salty, sour, and bitter. In Eastern countries there was a fifth, called *umami*, often described as savory or meaty. In 1908 Professor Kikunae Ikeda, a chemist at Tokyo Imperial University, isolated (from kombu, a kind of seaweed) a white salt called monosodium glutamate, or MSG, which, he discovered, gave that meaty, savory umami flavor to other foods. He called the flavor quality "deliciousness" and named the salt *ajinomoto*—"the essence of taste." Ikeda acquired a patent to produce MSG, and a product called Aji-No-Moto (extracted from wheat gluten instead of seaweed) was first marketed in 1909. Referred to as a "flavor enhancer," it was first produced in the United States in 1934; by 1947 it was on the market as Ac'cent. MSG is still a common flavor enhancer in snack foods, fast foods, condiments, powdered and canned soups, canned vegetables, processed meats, and instant noodles.

Related Fact: At one time "Chinese Restaurant Syndrome"—dizziness, headache, numbness, and other symptoms—was a condition thought to be linked to MSG. Many people were convinced that the syndrome was caused by an overuse of MSG by cooks in Chinese restaurants. However, research has failed to establish any real connection between MSG and the symptoms described by diners.

JOHN L. MASON

In 1858 Mason patented a new and reliable kind of canning jar and lid, known today as the Mason Jar. Until that time, farm families could only depend the limited variety of produce and meat they could store in root cellars, pickle barrels, and smokehouses to get them through the barren winter. The reusable glass Mason jar had a screw-on zinc lid that formed a hermetic seal, making it possible to preserve a much greater variety of fruits, vegetables, jams, relishes, and other foods without risk of spoilage. Unfortunately, Mason's patent expired before he could profit from it. He died a pauper in New York City in 1902.

Henry Ford and Thomas Edison collaborated on an electric-car design.

BACK SIDE STORY

Who among us can honestly say that our career was never in the toilet? Here's a look at a guy who wants it that way.

Artiste: Paul Walker, an Irish director and playwright
Notable Achievement: Writing a play that takes place entirely in a restroom—and actually staging it in one.
Flushed with Success: After writing his award-winning play *Ladies & Gents*, which portrays the dark side of Dublin life in the 1950s as seen from the inside of a restroom (based on a true story), Walker staged the drama as part of the Dublin Fringe Festival. It met with success there, and then toured the restrooms of Europe before Walker brought it to New York's Central Park in March 2008. City Parks & Recreation bureaucrats considered his proposal for more than a year before finally giving him permission to use the facilities near Bethesda Fountain, near the center of the park.
The Play: *Ladies & Gents* is divided into two acts—one in the ladies' room, the other in the men's. (It doesn't matter which one you see first.) During performances, the audience clusters in front of the toilet stalls to watch the action, most of which takes place near the urinals and sinks. One character in the play, a pimp, does sit on a toilet for a time but doesn't actually use it (much to the relief of theatergoers). Audiences aren't allowed to use the facilities, either. But if anyone does have to answer the call of nature, portable toilets are set up outside the restroom during the play's run. The price of admission for the Central Park run (March 19–29, 2008) was $25. Believe it or not, most of the shows sold out.

So what was the hardest part about staging a play in a public restroom in Central Park? Probably the rehearsals, which were conducted *before* the portable toilets were set up. The actors were constantly interrupted by tourists and pushy New Yorkers who cared more about relieving themselves than they did about Art. At least one man refused to look for another restroom or wait for a break in the rehearsals; he just marched right in and took care of business as the actors performed their parts. "He was a bit belligerent, really," said actor John O'Callaghan, who played the pimp. "I guess when you have to go, you have to go."

During the 1950s, both the U.S. and U.S.S.R. had plans to bomb the Moon.

MAKING A MOVIE, PT. III: PREPRODUCTION

Wow, we've already reached the third part of this article and are only now *getting to preproduction? You see, Uncle John? Making a movie does take a lot of work.* *(Part II is on page 232.)*

GATHERING THE TALENT

Now that the script and budget have been approved and the director is onboard, every aspect of the project must be thoroughly planned out in advance. Every film is a "business" in its own right, so first a production company is formed. Then the director (alone or with an illustrator) turns the script into *storyboards*, rough sketches of every planned shot. Those are then sent to each department head so that they can begin the conceptualizing work, such as how the sets and costumes will appear. A rough filming schedule will also be set. Here are the people and departments who start putting it all together.

CASTING

Often a director will have specific actors in mind for the lead parts. It is the *casting director's* job to find and then begin negotiations with those actors. Alternatively, the director may give a detailed description of the roles' requirements. The CD will then advertise the parts in industry trade publications, look at hundreds or even thousands of 8x10 photos, and then schedule auditions, presenting the director with only the best candidates. The CD is usually in sole charge of casting the smaller parts and remains with the production during filming, acting as a liaison between the production company, the actors, and their agents. Sometimes, a CD must get creative to find the perfect person for a role.

Reel-Life Example: When looking for an 11-year-old boy to play the son of Daniel Plainview (Daniel Day-Lewis) in *There Will Be Blood* (2007), casting director Cassandra Kulukundis auditioned hundreds of kids from New York and Los Angeles, but they were all a little too "polished" to play a simple West Texas boy who could shoot a gun. So Director Paul Thomas Anderson sent

Kulukundis to Texas to look for the real thing. There, she found a 6th grader named Dillon Freasier who'd never acted before but otherwise had all of the desired attributes. Kulukundis recorded a screen test in Freasier's living room and sent it to Anderson, who flew out to meet the boy…and knew he was perfect "the minute he laid eyes on him." That's what directors and CDs strive for: the "Eureka!" moment when they know they've found the perfect marriage between actor and role.

Did it work? *There Will Be Blood* made nearly three times its $25 million budget during its theatrical run and went on to receive an Oscar nomination for Best Picture. And critics agreed that Freasier's performance was one of the reasons the film was so powerful.

PRODUCTION DESIGN

The *production designer* is the "architect" of the film, in charge of every object on the screen that isn't an actor. If the screenplay calls for grit and realism, the PD has to make sure that everything in the frame—from the city skyline to the tattered shoes to the trash on the ground—reflects that vision. Reporting to the PD is the *art director*, who oversees the conceptual artists to finalize the film's look. Once the main design elements are approved, a revised set of storyboards is created by the art department that will serve as a guide to setting up lighting, props, and camera angles once filming has started.

Meanwhile, the *property master*—working from an exhaustive list put together by the PD—has already begun the arduous process of finding or creating every object that appears in the movie. A *prop* is any inanimate object that an actor directly interacts with, such as a chair or a gun. A *set dressing* is any object that appears in a scene but that the actors do not touch. The property master searches through catalogs, prop houses, and thrift stores looking for these things. If they can't be found or don't exist, it is up to the art department to build them or modify them from real objects (such as turning an electric razor into a futuristic communicator).

Reel-Life Example: Jeannine Oppewall is a veteran PD with more than 30 films and four Oscar nominations to her credit, one of which was for 1998's *Pleasantville*. The film was especially difficult because it combines a period piece that strives for historical accu-

Medical term for the ring finger: *annulary*.

racy with a fantasy—Oppewall calls this a "hyper-reality." The plot: two modern teenagers are magically transported back to a 1950s TV sitcom town where everything appears in black-and-white and everyone behaves innocently. As the two new teenagers introduce modern values and mores, Pleasantville gradually begins to show color.

On a typical project, Oppewall will spend up to nine months working 14-hour days, researching and drawing up plans. With a period piece, she says, the most important job is taking things out: "air-conditioners, reflectors that run down the middle of the street, cars of the wrong vintage, and satellite dishes." Oppewall supervised the refurbishing of real neighborhood streets plus the creation of a replica of the town on a studio back lot.

Did it work? Yes. *Pleasantville* turned a tidy profit during its theatrical run, taking in nearly $50 million. It also garnered great reviews, most of which acknowledged how convincing the make-believe world was. In her review for the *New York Times*, Janet Maslin wrote, "The film's unsung heroine is Oppewall, who wittily turns the fantasy of Pleasantville into an actual place. Watch the sidewalks crack and the skirts grow less poufy as reality sets in."

FINDING THE LOCATIONS

After reading the script and studying the storyboards, the *location scout* or *manager* travels around to find and photograph potential places to film—a difficult job, as numerous factors must be considered before the director and producers will even go and look at it.

• How much does it cost to film there? Are there permits available? Grand Central Station may be exactly what the film calls for, but will the cost of filming there put the movie over budget?

• How noisy is the location? Nearby construction equipment or an airport can grind a production to a halt. Location scouts must be able to see into the future to know what the conditions will be like when the filming is scheduled.

• How accessible is the location? Is there power available? Only movies with the biggest budgets can afford to send an armada of trucks and helicopters out to the middle of nowhere and power it all up with generators.

If no suitable location can be found, there are options: They can "re-dress" one place to make it look like another, send a film

There have been more than 200 deaths and 12,600 injuries...

crew to the location to get background shots and then digitally add in the actors during postproduction, or re-create the location on a soundstage or a studio back lot.

Reel-Life Example: In the 2000 comedy *Big Momma's House*, Martin Lawrence plays an FBI agent who disguises himself as a matriarchal woman in order to catch a criminal. Production designer Craig Steams knew that "the House" would need to be a character in and of itself, so he sent four location scouts on a search through the southern United States. When the perfect house was finally chosen, producers decided that filming would be much easier in a more controllable environment. So the crew ended up building an exact replica of the house on two stages at Universal Studios.

Did it work? Yes. Martin Lawrence's performance (along with that of the house) may not have won many accolades from critics, but audiences loved it. Made for $33 million, *Big Momma's House* grossed $173 million and spawned a successful sequel.

VISUAL EFFECTS

Because shooting schedules are so tight, the *visual effects coordinator* must read the script and then tell the director what can or can't be filmed on set—and then start figuring out how to do it. There are two kinds of visual effects: those that will be completed in postproduction, and *practical effects*, which will be done on set, such as explosions, gunfire, rain, and...baby cows.

Reel-Life Example: In the 1991 film *City Slickers*, Mitch (Billy Crystal) must help deliver a newborn calf. Because an actual birthing would have been nearly impossible to set up and capture in one take, the visual effects department built an animatronic calf that Crystal "delivered" several times until director Ron Underwood was satisfied.

Did it work? Yes. *City Slickers* was a hit with both critics and audiences. If the birthing scene hadn't been convincing, the story would have suffered. Film critic Roger Ebert apparently didn't notice the ruse. "All of the subplots, like Crystal's love for a baby calf he helps deliver," he wrote, "pay off at the end."

COSTUME DESIGN

Working in conjunction with the art director, based on the PD's

attributed to road rage in the U.S. since 1990.

vision, every single piece of clothing that the actors wear must either be found or created by the *costume designer*.

Reel-Life Example: In a character-driven film such as 2001's *Ocean's Eleven*, the costumes must help tell the story, and director Steven Soderbergh credits much of the movie's success to costume designer Jeffrey Kurland. But the head of an art department can't work in a vacuum; Kurland collaborated with production designer Phil Messina. "We share color schemes and ideas. When I told him that I was going to try to design Terry Benedict (Andy Garcia) with an Asian feeling, Phil designed Benedict's hotel with a distinctively Asian feel. We also talk about color and what he plans to use as upholstery so that the characters don't disappear into his furnishings." This is another job that begins in preproduction and stretches all the way through to the end of filming. "If I remember correctly, George (Clooney) has 26 costume changes, Brad (Pitt) has 24, Elliott (Gould) has 12 or 14. I was constantly making and designing clothes throughout the show." (In movie business lingo, a film project in production is called "the show.")

REHEARSE, REHEARSE, REHEARSE

It's important that the casting be completed as early as possible so the main actors can be brought in to rehearse and train for the various tasks their characters must perform—from stunt work to dancing to foreign accents. An actor may spend a month training for a scene that will take a week to shoot and only takes up a minute of screen time.

Reel-Life Example: When Keanu Reeves, Carrie-Anne Moss, Laurence Fishburne, and Hugo Weaving were cast as the four leads in 1999's futuristic action film, *The Matrix*, they figured training would only last a few weeks. Instead, it took closer to *four months*. Under the tutelage of kung fu choreographer Woo Ping Yuen, they had to learn not only martial arts but how to fight each other while suspended on wires.

Did it work? Yes. *The Matrix* set a new standard for action movies with both its never-before-seen visual effects and complex fight scenes. But it wasn't easy—the film spent four years in development and over a year in preproduction before the first scene was even filmed.

For Part IV, go to page 433.

SUPER BOWL TRIVIA

For our Bathroom Reader *sports fans, a little "bowl" trivia.*

• **City that's hosted the most Super Bowls:** Miami, with 10. Second place: New Orleans, with 9.

• **Only two brothers to be named Super Bowl MVPs:** Peyton Manning of the Indianapolis Colts (2007) and Eli Manning of the New York Giants (2008).

• **Only Super Bowl MVP selected from a losing team:** Chuck Howley of the 1971 Dallas Cowboys.

• **Only team to play the Super Bowl at home:** It's never happened. The closest: the 1985 Super Bowl won by the 49ers at Stanford Stadium, 35 miles from San Francisco.

• **Most Super Bowl appearances without a win:** The Minnesota Vikings and the Buffalo Bills have each been to, and lost, four Super Bowls. The Bills are the only team to lose four in a row (1991–1994).

• **Closest final score:** In 1991 the New York Giants beat the Buffalo Bills by one point, 20–19, thanks to a last-minute field goal.

• **Most Super Bowl wins:** The San Francisco 49ers, Dallas Cowboys, and Pittsburgh Steelers have won five each.

• **Lowest scoring Super Bowl:** Super Bowl VII (1973); Miami beat Washington 14–7. Highest scoring Super Bowl: Super Bowl XXIX (1995). The 49ers beat the San Diego Chargers 49–26, for a combined total of 75 points.

• **Most points scored by one team:** The San Francisco 49ers scored 55 in 1990 to beat the Denver Broncos 55–10. It was the biggest blowout in Super Bowl history.

• **Most-watched Super Bowl:** The 2008 game between the NY Giants and New England Patriots was seen by 97.5 million American TV viewers. With the population at 300 million, that means that about one out of every three U.S. residents watched the game.

• **TV shows that premiered immediately after Super Bowl broadcasts:** *The A-Team, The Wonder Years, Family Guy,* and *Homicide: Life on the Street.*

To date, the year 1888 requires the most Roman numerals: MDCCCLXXXVIII.

CAUGHT IN THE ACT

More tales of dishonest people getting their comeuppance.

CULPRIT: Nigel Hardman, a.k.a. "Prince Razaq," of Warton, England

GRAND SCHEME: After a number of civil servant jobs—mail sorter, meter reader, and accident insurance advisor—Hardman was ready for something different. His chance came after a 2002 car accident, when he applied for disability payments and housing assistance, claiming he was "too ill to work." Now, with a supplemental income, Hardman started training to be a magician. After he recovered, he stuck with his act...but kept on receiving government payments. Donning a turban, long robes, curly-toed sandals, and the name "Prince Razaq," he appeared on the British TV show *The Big Breakfast* (he escaped from a straight jacket while standing on a bed of nails), and his career took off. With newfound fame, Hardman started living in lavish style, even purchasing a 31-foot-long stretch limousine so he could, according to the *Guardian*, "drive stag and hen party guests around Blackpool."

EXPOSED! British fraud investigators, it turned out, had also seen the talent show and soon learned that the man who was "too ill to work" was moonlighting as a death-defying daredevil who swallowed swords and tamed lions. In 2008 Hardman, 40, pleaded guilty to 11 counts of fraud—in all, he bilked £18,000 ($35,000) from the British benefits system. (He was also nearly bankrupt.)

OUTCOME: Hardman was tagged for six months, which means he can't leave his home from 7 p.m. to 7 a.m. If he does, the magistrate warned him, the court will come down on him "like a ton of bricks."

CULPRIT: Martino Garibaldi, a 45-year-old shop owner from Montecalvo, Italy

GRAND SCHEME: Garibaldi's wife (first name not released) thought her marriage was fine...until one day in 2007, when she discovered that all of her money—37,000 euros ($73,000)—was missing from her bank account. And Martino was missing, too. Did he run off? Was he kidnapped? Mrs. Garibaldi hired a private

Snowmelt from Montana's Triple Divide Peak can end up in 3 oceans: Pacific, Atlantic, and Arctic.

investigator to track down her husband, but the search yielded nothing. Her husband and her money were both gone.

EXPOSED! A few months later, in early 2008, Mrs. Garibaldi received a call from one of her friends: watch the new movie, *Natale in Crociera* (*Christmas on a Cruise*), said the friend, and pay close attention to the background people. Mrs. Garibaldi watched it, and sure enough, there was Martino—along with his mistress—sitting at a table enjoying themselves in the background of a scene that was filmed in the Dominican Republic.

OUTCOME: Thanks to the new evidence, Mrs. Garibaldi was able to track Martino down and has since served him with divorce papers…and is suing him to get all of her money back.

CULPRIT: Michael Cosmi, a 29-year-old man from Wayne, New Jersey

GRAND SCHEME: From December 2005 to February 2006, Cosmi would routinely wander around New York City's JFK Airport while speaking loudly into his cell phone: "Yes, yes, I've been robbed! And my patient doesn't have much time!" When a concerned citizen showed interest, Cosmi introduced himself as "Dr. Michael Harris" or "Dr. Michael Stanley" and explained that he desperately needed cab fare to get to Brigantine Hospital in New Jersey to perform emergency surgery. "I promise I'll pay you back," he'd say. "It's a matter of life and death!" In all, Cosmi conned ten people out of more than $800, including a flight attendant; a rabbi; a cop's widow; and an off-duty NYPD captain named Bill Tobin, who gave the scam artist $100.

EXPOSED! A week after he'd been unknowingly conned at the airport, Tobin was riding on the LIRR (Long Island Railroad) and heard Cosmi giving the same spiel to an elderly woman. "I wasn't carrying my gun, which was probably good, because I wanted to stick it in his ear," said Tobin, who arrested Cosmi for fraud.

OUTCOME: Authorities were able to track down Cosmi's other victims (he still had all of their names and addresses in his notebook because he'd promised to pay them back). It was later revealed that Cosmi is the son of a New Jersey prosecutor…and that there is no "Brigantine Hospital" in New Jersey or anywhere else. Cosmi was ordered to pay $2,165 in restitution and undergo drug counseling to avoid a jail term.

The naked truth: The first American film to feature nudity was called *Inspiration* (1915).

THE COMSTOCK LODE, PART III

Here's the third installment of our story of one of the biggest mining bonanzas in American history. *(Part II of the story is on page 222.)*

SELLERS' REMORSE

It didn't take long for the discoverers of the Comstock Lode to realize how wrong they'd been to sell out so early. Having thousands of dollars in their pockets, perhaps for the first time in their lives, must have felt wonderful in an age in which the highest paid miners made $4 a day. In the 1850s, $1,000 had more purchasing power than $100,000 does today.

But as the new owners of the Comstock claims dug deeper into the earth, not only did the ore deposit not peter out as the discoverers had expected it would—it grew larger than the most experienced mining engineers had ever seen before. Who knows how many sleepless night were spent by the early sellouts, anguishing over what might have been had they held onto their claims for just a little longer.

WIDE LODE

Normally, such rich deposits of gold and silver are found in narrow cracks in the Earth known as *veins* or *lodes*. They're deposited there by geothermally heated water, which dissolves trace amounts of gold, silver, or other minerals at deeper levels in the Earth's crust. Then, as the water rises through cracks in the crust and gets near the earth's surface, the hot water cools and the minerals come out of suspension and are deposited in high concentrations in the cracks.

Such cracks are *usually* quite narrow—no more than a few feet wide. But not this time: by the time the miners had dug 50 feet down, the vein had grown to 10 to 12 feet wide, and as the miners dug deeper, it grew wider still. When they reached a depth of 180 feet in December 1860, the vein was more than 45 feet across—so wide, in fact, that traditional methods of reinforcing the mine against cave-ins weren't good enough to do the job. A better technique of timbering had to be found, and in late 1860 a mining engineer named Philipp Deidesheimer found one. Instead of just putting posts against each wall and running a horizontal beam across the top to reinforce the ceiling, Deidesheimer used six-foot lengths of heavy timber to build giant cubes that could be stacked like building blocks to any height, width, or depth.

THE MONEY PIT

Once this and a few other engineering challenges were solved, the Comstock Lode began to produce valuable ore faster than the mining companies could process it. Traditional horse-powered ore processing machines called *arrastras* soon gave way to giant steam-powered mills that by the end of 1861 could process more than 1,200 *tons* of ore per day. More than $2.5 million worth of gold and silver bullion was pulled out of the mines that year; the number more than doubled to $6 million in 1862 and doubled again to more than $12.4 million in 1863.

The miners and the mine owners were making plenty of money, but in these early years nobody made out better than the lawyers. When it became evident that the Comstock Lode was one gigantic ore deposit instead of many small ones, the owners of the original mining claims wanted it all. They filed suit against newer operators to drive them out of business. By the time they succeeded in 1865, more than $10 million—the equivalent of $14 *billion* today and nearly 20% of the entire production of the mines up to that point—had been spent on lawsuits.

BOOM TOWN

As the mine roared to life, so did the city being built on top of it. In the winter of 1859, miners who'd lacked the foresight to bring their own tents with them to Virginia City had had to tunnel into the hillsides for shelter or squat in hovels made of stone, mud, and sagebrush. By the following spring, however, more than a dozen prominent stone buildings had already been built, as had dozens more of wood. Hundreds more went up before the year was out.

The presence of so many miners with money to burn and no place to burn it attracted scores of merchants and aspiring businessmen who hoped to profit by providing them with goods and

Hey, Oprah! *Porphyrophobia* is the fear of the color purple.

services. Soon the wagon trains hauling goods and supplies into the city stretched for miles on end. By the end of 1860, the settlement that had looked like a refugee camp just a year earlier boasted hotels, boarding houses, restaurants, butcher shops, bakeries, tailor shops, candy and cigar stores, and doctors' offices. On the seamier side, there were saloons, gambling halls, opium dens, several brothels, and at least one brewery.

That was just in the first year of growth; in the years to come, Virginia City would add paved streets, gas streetlights, schoolhouses, an opera house, an orphanage, five newspapers (26-year-old Samuel Clemens began using the pen name "Mark Twain" while editor of the *Virginia City Enterprise*), half a dozen churches, telegraph and railroad links to the outside world, and the only elevator between Chicago and California. When a lack of drinking water became a barrier to further growth in the early 1870s, the city ran a seven-mile-long iron pipe up into the Sierra Nevada mountains and began siphoning two million gallons of fresh water into the city every day.

ON THE MAP

By the mid-1870s, Virginia City boasted nearly 30,000 residents and in many respects was the most important community between Denver and San Francisco. The wealth of the Comstock Lode remade the map of the American West and provided the impetus in 1861 to create the Nevada Territory, which became the state of Nevada just three years later. It also helped to spur interest in building America's first transcontinental railroad, which broke ground in 1863. The city of Reno, Nevada, 17 miles outside of Virginia City, was just a stop on the railroad when it was founded in 1868.

Most of the goods and supplies that went to Virginia City passed through San Francisco, giving that city a major economic boost. San Francisco's first stock exchange, founded in 1862, was set up to trade Comstock Lode shares. More prominent brick buildings were built in the city in 1861 alone than had been built in all previous years combined, and the pace of development remained high for many years to come.

Feeling unlucky that you missed out on the Comstock Lode? You might be luckier than you think.
Part IV of the story is on page 446.

Five diseases carried by mosquitoes: Malaria, dengue, yellow fever, encephalitis, and filariasis.

THE WORLD'S LARGEST...

One of the best parts about a road trip: visiting wacky tourist attractions and weird local landmarks. Here are a few towns and cities that have made their mark by having the "world's largest" something or other.

TERMITE

Location: Providence, Rhode Island

Details: Sitting on the roof of New England Pest Control, on the southbound side of I-95, is this 58-foot-long blue bug. "Nibbles Woodaway" (named in a local radio contest) was built in 1980 at a cost of $30,000. Nibbles is 928 times the size of an actual termite, which makes it clearly visible from I-95. The company dresses it up like a witch on Halloween and a reindeer on Christmas. Bonus fact: Nibbles is hurricane-proof, and it's made out of fiberglass, so it's termite-proof.

EGG

Location: Winlock, Washington

Details: A 12-foot-long, 1,200 lb. fiberglass egg sits atop a steel pole right in the center of this small town just south of Seattle. In the early 20th century, Winlock was the second-largest egg producer in the United States, and the town built a giant egg to celebrate its claim to fame. The first egg was built out of canvas in 1923. That egg was replaced with a plastic version in 1944, then with a fiberglass one in the 1960s. The local egg industry clucked its last cluck years ago, but the giant egg remains the centerpiece of Winlock's annual Egg Day celebration in June. Since 9/11, the egg has been painted like an American flag.

BALL OF STAMPS

Location: Omaha, Nebraska

Details: Outside of Omaha is Boys Town, the 900-acre orphanage immortalized in the 1938 Spencer Tracy movie of the same name. Boys Town has a stamp museum, which is where visitors can find the Ball. It measures only 32" in diameter, but weighs a whopping 600 pounds, and consists of approximately 4.65 million postage

Finland is rated the cleanest country in the world.

stamps. The Boys Town Stamp Collecting Club started the project in 1953 by sticking stamps on a golf ball. Just two years later, the ball reached its current size. Visitors may touch the ball, as long as they don't remove—or add—any stamps. (No word on why the residents of Boys Town ever started the stamp ball in the first place.)

SCHOOLTEACHER

Location: Rugby, North Dakota

Details: Rugby's town museum, Pioneer Village, has a display showcasing Cliff Thompson, who was 8 feet, 7 inches tall and was born in Rugby (population 2,900) in 1904. Thompson had a teaching degree, but never taught because his height precluded normal work. So he toured the freak-show circuit as "Count Olaf." The Pioneer Village display includes a lifesize replica of Thompson and an outline of his size-22 foot.

LIGHT BULB

Location: Edison, New Jersey

Details: A 13-foot, eight-ton incandescent light bulb tops the Thomas Edison Memorial Tower and Menlo Park Museum. The giant bulb was installed in 1937, made up of 153 individual pieces of glass, each two inches thick. And it actually still works. The concrete tower (and the big bulb) stand on the exact spot where Edison developed his original (much, *much* smaller) light bulb in 1879.

ROTATING GLOBE

Location: Yarmouth, Maine

Details: David DeLorme, Chairman and CEO of DeLorme, a mapping-software company, commissioned the globe for his company headquarters in 1996. At 41 feet across and three stories tall, "Eartha" is the largest reproduction of the Earth ever constructed. Visitors to DeLorme can view the globe, called "Eartha," at three different levels: North Pole, South Pole, and the equator. Eartha actually spins on its axis at a 23.5 degree angle, like the real Earth, and is covered in 792 computer-generated map panels. It makes one complete revolution (equaling a day) in 18 minutes.

Basketball quiz: How far is the free-throw line from the face of the backboard? A: Exactly 15 feet.

NIXONIA

Random trivia about President Richard M. Nixon (1913–94).

• Nixon is the only person in American history to be elected to two terms as vice president and two as president.

• Nixon claimed to have never had a headache.

• At age three, Nixon fell out of a horse-drawn carriage and was run over by a wheel, leaving him with a permanent scar on his forehead.

• During the 1960 U.S. presidential campaign, 43-year-old John F. Kennedy got a lot of attention because he was so young. But Nixon wasn't much older—he was 47.

• Nixon's favorite lunch: cottage cheese with ketchup.

• Nixon's two favorite songs: "Mr. Bojangles" and "The Impossible Dream."

• At Duke University Law School, Nixon had two nicknames: "Gloomy Gus," because he was considered a sourpuss, and "Iron Butt," because he studied so hard.

• His Secret Service codename: Searchlight.

• Nixon left the Navy and successfully ran for Congress in 1946, won a Senate seat in 1950, and was selected to be Dwight Eisenhower's running mate in 1952. That means he was elected vice president of the United States just six years after leaving the Navy.

• Nixon's mother named him after 12th century English king Richard I (the "Lionheart").

• Most requested document at the National Archives: the 1972 photo of Elvis Presley's Oval Office visit with Nixon.

• When he went in for his annual presidential physical, Nixon would wear his hospital gown backward, with the opening in front, then walk down the hallway to startle nurses.

• Nixon's favorite TV show was *Gilligan's Island.*

• Two of his accomplishments as president: he abolished the draft and he created the Environmental Protection Agency.

• Nixon appeared on the cover of *Time* magazine a record 56 times.

American history quiz: Who was Frank Wills? The janitor who discovered the Watergate break-in.

INJURY...MEET INSULT

Sometimes it seems like life can't get any worse...and then it gets worse.

MULTIPLE CHOICE

Bad: In May 2008, Justin Hill, 42, of Rock Island, Tennessee, was making a left turn into his driveway when a car he hadn't seen suddenly smashed into his. His wife heard the crash and ran outside.

Worse: She left the kitchen stove on, and the resulting fire burned down their home. To top it off, Hill was treated and released from a local hospital that night...after police gave him a ticket for failing to yield to oncoming traffic.

HIT ME TWO TIMES

Bad: In July 2006, Ryan Van Brunt, 16, was hit by a car near her home in West Orange, New Jersey. She spent the next ten days in a coma.

Worse: After she woke up, her family informed her that she had to go to court...because one of the cops who responded to the accident had given her a ticket for jaywalking. (When she was finally able to go to court—six months later—the prosecutor apologized and the charge was dismissed.)

THE GASS BILL

Bad: Antonio Moreno of Madrid, Spain, got a telephone call at work one day in December 2007. It was his wife. She told him that the gas bill had come in the mail, and it was a big bill—prices had been skyrocketing at the time.

Worse: The bill wasn't the only problem: It was addressed to "Antonio Gilipollas Caraculo." Translation: Antonio D***head A**face. When Moreno notified the gas company, a customer service representative apologized and later said it had been a prank by a contractor who would be dealt with. Moreno took the insult in stride, saying the publicity created by the story had at least resulted in old friends he hadn't heard from in years calling...several times a day...asking to speak to "Mr. A**face."

The 19th-century seamen's name for an inflamed pimple or a red nose: *grog-blossom.*

HOLLYWOOD'S #1 STAR

For some reason, "answering the call of nature" has worked its way into nearly every Tom Hanks movie.

• ***The Money Pit* (1986):** Beleaguered homeowner Walter Fielding (Hanks) notices a cherub statue in his yard is having trouble "peeing." "Prostate trouble?" he asks. Later, Walter pees on a small tree in his garden and it falls down.

• ***Joe Versus the Volcano* (1990):** Joe pees off of the luggage raft.

• ***A League Of Their Own* (1992):** Washed-up baseball star Jimmy Dugan pees for nearly a minute in the girls' locker room. "Boy, that was some good peein'," comments Mae (Madonna).

• ***Forrest Gump* (1994):** When Forrest meets John F. Kennedy, he informs the president, "I gotta pee."

• ***Apollo 13* (1995):** Astronaut Jim Lovell urinates into a collection tube. "It's too bad we can't show this on TV," he says.

• ***Saving Private Ryan* (1998):** Captain John Miller and Sergeant Horvath (Tom Sizemore) talk about an old war buddy named Vecchio, who would "pee a 'V' on everyone's jacket, for Vecchio, for Victory."

• ***The Green Mile* (1999):** Warden Paul Edgecomb suffers from a painful urinary tract infection that has him "pissing razor blades."

• ***Cast Away* (2000):** Marooned Fed-Ex executive Chuck Noland is peeing on the beach at night when he sees the faint light of a passing ship.

• ***Road to Perdition* (2002):** Mob hit man Michael Sullivan is asked if coffee makes him sweat. His reply: "It also makes me piss."

• ***The Terminal* (2004):** Stranded immigrant Viktor Navorski must hold his pee for hours while waiting for a pay phone call at New York's JFK Airport.

Ironically, one of the few movies that Tom Hanks *doesn't* pee in, or even mention it, is...1984's *Splash.*

29% of Americans surveyed admit they've intentionally stolen something from a store.

A BEETLE BY ANY OTHER NAME

With more than 21 million built from 1938 to 2003, the original VW Beetle was the longest-running, most-produced car in automotive history. Here's what they call it in other countries:

Poland: *Garbus* ("Hunchback")

Indonesia: *Kodok* ("Frog")

Finland: *Skalbagge* ("Beetle") or *Kuplavolkkari* ("Bubble Volkswagen")

Japan: *Kabuto-mushi* ("Drone Beetle")

Romania: *Buburuza* ("Ladybug") or *Broasca* ("Little Frog")

Estonia: *Pornikas* ("Beetle")

Norway: *Boble* ("Bubble")

Swahili: *Mgongo wa Chura* ("Frog Back") or *Mwendo wa Kobe* ("Tortoise Speed")

Dominican Republic: *Cepillo* ("Brush")

Philippines: *Kotseng kuba* ("Hunchback Car")

Mexico: *Vochito* (a friendly shortening of Volkswagen) or *Pulguita* ("Little Flea")

Italy: *Maggiolino* ("Junebug")

Turkey: *Kaplumbaga* ("Turtle")

Pakistan: *Foxy*

Greece: *Scaraveos* ("Scarab")

Bolivia: *Peta* ("Turtle")

Nigeria: *Catch Fire*

Thailand: *Rod Tao* ("Turtle Car")

Israel: *Hipushit* ("Beetle")

China: *Jia Ke Chong* ("Beetle")

Bulgaria: *Kostenurka* ("Turtle") or *Brambar* ("Bug")

Iran: *Folex* ("Frog")

Iraq: *Agroga* ("Froggy")

Guatemala: *Cucaracha* ("Cockroach")

Nepal: *Bhyagute Car* ("Frog Car")

Russia: *Zhuk* ("Bug")

Belgium: *Coccinele* ("Ladybug")

Spain: *Escarabat* ("Beetle")

Denmark: *Boblen* ("Bubble")

SEAFARING FOOD IN THE AGE OF SAIL

Imagine a diet of rock-hard, weevil-infested crackers, oversalted beef, dried peas, slimy water, and watered-down rum. Now imagine that you're expected to climb riggings, swab decks, haul anchors, and fight wars on that diet.

SETTING SAIL

Today we think of the world as a global community—anyone can get almost anywhere within a matter of hours. But until the end of the 16th century, travelers, traders, and explorers could go only as far as their oar-powered ships could take them. These ships did have sails, but their main power source was muscle, not wind. The Battle of Lepanto in 1571 is considered the last great naval battle fought between oar-powered ships (the 200 galleys of the Christian crusaders defeated the 273 galleys of the Turkish fleet). After that, sailing technology advanced rapidly and the "Age of Sail" began. It lasted almost 300 years.

During this period, the European fleets explored, conquered, and colonized the world from North and South America to the Caribbean, to Africa, and around the Cape of Good Hope to Australia and the South Pacific. They opened up trade with India and the Far East and expanded commerce between European nations. The huge sailing ships moved faster, carried more cargo, and armed themselves more heavily than any ships that preceded them. They also stayed at sea longer—voyages could last for months on end. So what did sailors eat? From the start to the end of the Age of Sail, shipboard food changed very little for ordinary sailors of Western navies and merchant fleets. Distinguishing characteristics: poor quality (and it deteriorated even more during the voyage), insufficient quantities...and the same thing, day after day.

ENOUGH TO MAKE YOU SEASICK

Storage space on board was very limited and had to accommodate cargo, guns, equipment, and enough food and water to last as long as the voyage took—and no one could predict how long that might be. To save space (and money), shipowners and naval procurement officials often skimped on provisions. On top of that, the ships were damp, so dry stores of food, such as dried peas, became infested with weevils and other bugs. Beer soured; butter got rancid. Salted meat and fish survived, but they were *too* salty and there wasn't enough fresh water aboard to spare any for soaking the salt out. Fresh fruit and vegetables? Once a ship left port they were virtually unheard of.

Hungry sailors were at the mercy of almost everyone: penny-pinching shipowners whose main concern was to feed them as cheaply as possible, dishonest ship's pursers who supplied bad food or shortrationed the shipowner (and then sold the stolen goods), and unskilled cooks who couldn't have done much with the available supplies even if they'd been great chefs. It's no wonder that sailors looked forward to their daily portion of rum.

FEELING GROGGY

Drunkenness was a major problem among seamen. Until 1687, sailors in England's Royal Navy received an evening ration of one pint of brandy and got drunk on it; after 1687 and the conquest of Jamaica, they switched from a pint of brandy to a pint of rum—and got drunk on that. In an attempt to control the drunkenness in his fleet, British Admiral Edward Vernon ordered that the rum be diluted with water and distributed twice a day, at noon and at 6:00 p.m. The mixture was quickly dubbed *grog*, in honor of Vernon's nickname, "Old Grog," a reference to the kind of fabric his cloak was made of—*grogram*. The grog dilution was always done in the presence of an officer to make sure that sailors got their full allotment and weren't cheated by pursers who added too much water and then sold the extra rum.

SHIP'S BISCUIT AND OTHER DELICACIES

Ship's biscuit, also called *hardtack* or *pilot's bread*, was a crucial part of a sailor's diet. Biscuit was round, oval, or square crackers made of a dough heavy on flour and light on water (without shortening or yeast, and usually without salt), baked until it was so hard and indestructible that it was reputed to be able to last half a century. It was always infested with weevils, and though the sailors hated the bugs, they were still a sort of asset: the weevils ate tunnels into the biscuit, which made the rock-hard crackers easier to break up

Michael Zaslow's claim to fame: He was the first actor ever killed on *Star Trek*...

and eat. Seamen were very dependent on biscuit for filling their stomachs, but eating it plain wasn't a great menu option, so it was often soaked in water or coffee or crumbled and fried with salt pork or bacon grease.

Salt beef and salt pork were the other staples of a sailor's diet in the Age of Sail. Cheap cuts of meat were preserved in brine, or *pickle*, in casks, where they'd last throughout a voyage. *Salt horse* and *salt junk* were seamen's slang for salted beef, "horse" alluding to the toughness of the beef and "junk" referring to the general belief that provisioners threw all the worst parts of several different animals into the casks of brine. Cheap salted fish and dried fish sometimes replaced salt beef and pork; sailors called it "Poor John."

BURGOO KING

Ship's cooks and sailors had so little to work with that they could combine their limited ingredients in only a few different ways.

- **Lobscouse** was a boiled-up stew of salt meat cut in small pieces, broken biscuit, potatoes, and onions.
- **Salmagundi** consisted of salt fish boiled with onions.
- **Skillygalee** was a watery oatmeal gruel.
- **Burgoo** was a thicker oatmeal gruel or porridge seasoned with salt and sugar. It was so easy to prepare (especially in rough weather) that on some ships the cook made it for every evening meal; some shipowners were too cheap to provide anything *but* the ingredients for burgoo.
- **Bully beef** was salt beef from which the cook had boiled away all the fat (and added it to his grease pot—one of the perks of his job), leaving something so tasteless and hard that the sailors often carved it into trinkets instead of eating it.

AVAST, YE SCURVY SEA DOG

You can't talk about seafaring food without talking about scurvy, a disease caused by vitamin C deficiency. It was rampant on ships for most of the Age of Sail because of the lack of fruit, vegetables, and other foods that contain vitamin C. What's worse, ships generally set sail in the spring, when most people were still run-down from a winter diet of preserved foods and nothing fresh. That

...(which marked the first time Dr. McCoy said, "He's dead, Jim.")

means they *began* the trip in poor health, and after six weeks of hardtack and salt pork, many were very sick, even dying.

AVAST, YE SCURVY SEA DOG

The first signs of scurvy were swollen gums, loss of teeth, skin blotches, and lethargy. The gum problems made it hard to eat the tough biscuit and salt meat, so men with scurvy ate less and less and began to starve. Medical science was primitive, so no one even knew exactly what caused the illness. Scientists deduced that food might have something to do with it, but greed and ignorance prevented the shipowners and naval authorities from acting even on what little they knew. They refused to provision the ships with citrus fruits, green vegetables, or even the ginger that the Chinese took aboard ship as early as the 5th century. Some officials thought that less salt would fix the problem, others that more pickles, cider, or sauerkraut would do the trick.

In 1753 Dr. James Lind published his *Treatise of the Scurvy*, in which he proved by a controlled experiment (one of the first in the diet world) that lemons and oranges were an effective cure—without actually understanding the existence of vitamin C (it wasn't discovered until 1912). By the end of the 18th century, when more seamen were dying of scurvy than in warfare, the British Navy finally accepted Lind's thesis and made lemon juice a compulsory daily issue to all sailors. The lemon juice was mixed into the grog ration and, like magic, scurvy disappeared from the navy.

END OF AN ERA

In the mid-19th century, steam power began to replace wind power. A sail-powered Atlantic crossing could take from one to three months; on a steamship it might take as little as seven days. With shorter voyages, food didn't have to last as long, so the sailors' diet of ship's biscuit and salt meat could be more varied. Shorter trips also meant putting into port more often, so dwindling provisions could be replenished with fresh food. Today, even pleasure sailboats have refrigerators, cruise ships are floating feasts, and the United States Navy takes its menus so seriously that it recruits "mess management specialists" and presents annual awards for food service excellence.

"Food is an important part of a balanced diet." —Fran Lebowitz

MANEUVER-ABILITY

Dr. Henry Heimlich stole the show in 1974 with his famous "abdominal thrust" lifesaving technique, but that's not the only "maneuver" out there. Here are a few you may not have heard of.

THE SELLICK MANEUVER

This is used daily by doctors all over the world, primarily during *intubation*—the insertion of a breathing tube down the throat. It involves applying the correct amount of pressure to the outside of the throat at the *cricoid cartilage*, a ring-shaped piece of cartilage that circles the trachea. Done properly (only by trained professionals), it closes off the esophagus but doesn't close off the airway, allowing a tube—whether for oxygen, for anesthesia, or for other purposes—to be safely inserted. The tube also prevents the patient from, to put it plainly, choking on their own vomit. The insertion technique is named after British anesthesiologist Dr. Brian Sellick, who described it in 1961, although it was actually first written about in 1774 by celebrated Scottish anatomist and doctor Alexander Monro, who recommended it for helping resuscitate drowning victims. When Sellick died in 1996, his obituary said the maneuver "has probably saved more lives and reduced pulmonary morbidity worldwide more than any other advance in anaesthetic management."

THE VALSALVA MANEUVER

You've probably done this one yourself. Hold your nose and close your mouth, and then try to forcefully exhale. Hear your ears pop? That's the *Valsalva maneuver*. It's used to equalize the air pressure in the enclosed middle ears with air pressure outside in the atmosphere. Here's how it works: The *eustachian tubes* are slender tubes that run from the middle ears to the back of the throat, where they are normally closed. When pressure outside your ears decreases, as when you're in a rising airplane, the higher pressure inside the ears causes the ear drum to bulge out. When air pressure outside *increases*, as when diving in water, the opposite occurs, pushing the ear drums inward. Both can damage the ear drums. The Valsalva maneuver forces the openings to the eustachian tubes in

They made him an offer he could refuse: Al Pacino turned down the role of Han Solo.

the throat to open, allowing air to escape or pass into the middle ears, equalizing the pressure with the outside. (The same thing often happens when you yawn or chew gum.) The maneuver is named for Italian physician Antonio Maria Valsalva, who first described it in 1704. It had been used by humans long before that, but Valsalva was the first to explain it medically. (Valsalva is also known as the person who named the eustachian tubes, after 16th century Italian doctor Bartolommeo Eustachio.)

THE GASKIN MANEUVER

This is used by obstetricians and midwives when a rare but very serious birthing event known as *shoulder dystocia* occurs. That's when a baby's head makes it out—but the shoulders don't. A bit of birthing background: In a normal birth the baby's head and body are "born" individually, each during its own contraction. The head comes out first (face down about 90% of the time), with the shoulders lying horizontally or in line with the pelvis. Between contractions, the baby rotates 90° to a vertical, or side-facing, position, now with one shoulder behind the pubic bone and one behind the coccyx (tailbone). In shoulder dystocia, the top (or *anterior*) shoulder gets stuck behind the mother's pubic bone. It can be dangerous for the mother and *very* dangerous for the baby, and it must therefore be dealt with quickly. A common first technique is the "McRoberts leg-lift maneuver," in which the mother, on her back, simply lifts her knees to her chest. If that doesn't free the shoulder then the *Gaskin maneuver* is often tried. In this "all-fours" maneuver, the mother rolls over, gets on her hands and knees, and arches her back, allowing gravity to help the baby's shoulder pass. Simple as it sounds, it has proven to be very effective. It was named after American midwife Ina May Gaskin, and is described as "the first obstetrical maneuver to be named after a midwife." Gaskin learned the technique in the 1970s from a Guatemalan midwife, who had learned it from Mayan women, who have apparently been using it for centuries. It has gained popularity since Gaskin started teaching it in 1976, and is now used increasingly by midwives and obstetricians in clinics around the world.

* * *

"Let him who would move the world first move himself." —**Socrates**

The food eaten by the average American in a lifetime is equal to the weight of six adult elephants.

THE BOOB TUBE

Great art or a waste of time? There are as many opinions as there are channels.

"Television is the first truly democratic culture, available to everybody and entirely governed by what the people want. The most terrifying thing is what people do want."
—Clive Barnes

"I consider the television set as the American fireplace, around which the whole family will gather."
—Red Skelton

"There was a point where I felt like, 'Golly, you work so hard, try so hard and the people say they want meaningful television and then Jerry Springer ends up beating you.'"
—Oprah Winfrey

"Television enables you to be entertained in your home by people you wouldn't have in your home."
—David Frost

"Violence and smut are of course everywhere on the airwaves. You cannot turn on your television without seeing them, although sometimes you have to hunt around."
—Dave Barry

"Television is teaching you whether you want it to or not."
—Jim Henson

"Anyone who's afraid of what TV does to the world is probably just afraid of the world."
—Clive James

"Television is America's jester. It has assumed the guise of an idiot while actually accruing power and authority behind the smoke screen of its self-degradation."
—Lawrence Mintz

"Television is the bland leading the bland."
—Murray Schumach

"Television is the literature of the illiterate, the culture of the lowbrow, the wealth of the poor, the privilege of the underprivileged, the exclusive club of the excluded masses."
—Lee Loevinger

"One of the few good things about modern times: If you die horribly on television, you will not have died in vain. You will have entertained us."
—Kurt Vonnegut

The largest great white shark ever caught was 37 feet long and weighed 24,000 pounds.

HOW TO HAVE A YARD SALE

BRI member Viola Rose is our resident yard sale expert. She has them once a year or so, and she always makes a ton of money. So we asked her to share her secrets with us. (And then she bargained on the price.)

A WORD TO THE WISE

Putting on your own yard sale is fun and easy, and the money that rolls in adds up surprisingly—and delightfully—fast. It's amazing how much dough you can rake in for your unwanted doo-dads, what-nots, and junk. Making your sale sail smoothly is all in the prep work. Here's the lowdown:

1. The Round-up. First, gather up everything you want to sell. Scour your house, yard, and garage, and then ask your friends or anyone else who might willing to donate their junk to your cause. Have everything ready a day ahead of time; it's best to have it all displayed at the beginning of the sale instead of adding stuff later in the day or weekend.

2. Location. Weather permitting, an outside sale that's visible from the road will *always* attract more shoppers, but a backyard or indoor sale can do just fine if you mark it with big, outrageous signs.

3. Setup. Give yourself at least two hours to get your sale ready before starting time. Prepare the night before if possible because people always (repeat: *always*) come early. Even if you write "no early birds" in your newspaper ad, they will still come. So it's much less frustrating (and more exciting) if you're ready to go early and can just sit back and rake in the cash. Keep in mind that in the first three hours of the sale, you'll get 75 percent of your customers.

To display your items, tables are better than tarps or blankets on the ground. But use whatever you've got. If you don't have enough tables, then make sure your stuff is well spread out on the ground and arranged nicely. Don't put items in boxes; most people don't like to dig through boxes or piles and will just pass it by thinking it's junk. Also, a "big spread" with objects in view will make your yard sale look large and enticing from the road.

In Italy, the number 17 is considered unlucky.

Now, here's the ultimate yard sale question: To Price or Not to Price? Answer: It's a waste of time to go around putting teensy little price stickers on every single thing. Price items over $5.00 and then have different priced tables or areas that say $2.00, 50 cents, etc. You can also make up a price in the moment when someone asks how much something is—it's fun to do, and you can keep making up a new price until someone buys it.

4. Advertising. There are two crucial parts to advertising your sale. If you're going to put all this effort into actually having a yard sale, you want it to be worth your time, so always use both.

• Place an ad in the local paper. It is definitely worth the cost. Your ad should run the day before your sale. Obsessive, gung-ho yard salers (like Uncle John) get the paper and actually plan out a route to make sure they hit all the sales. Be sure to include the address, date, time, and a few enticing items, but leave out your phone number. Don't use the words "huge," "mega" or "gigantic" unless it actually *is*, as this makes people feel swindled when they see it isn't. Here's another tip: Try to coerce your neighbors or friends to have a sale at the same time. Then you can advertise "multi-family sale" and share the ad cost. The friendly newspaper classifieds telephone operator will help you make sure your ad looks good and includes all the key ingredients. You might also want to put up a sign at your neighborhood supermarket or advertise on a free online posting site, but you don't need to spend money on any advertising other than in your local newspaper—that's the key.

• The other part of advertising is *signage*. If they can't find you, they will not come...or they'll give up if the signs leading to your sale are unclear or confusing. You can get in trouble for posting signs on telephone poles and street signs—it's actually against the law in most places. One sure-fire method: Make signs out of big cardboard boxes. Put heavy rocks inside the boxes and then tape them closed. Stand the boxes up and write your yard sale info on both sides of them. Then place them at pertinent street corners leading to your sale. Also put one that says SALE HERE on top of a parked car right outside of your sale. Your signs should state the date, time, street address of your sale, and of course, the ever-important arrow pointing the way. Do not busy up the signs with extra info—it makes it hard for drivers to read them. Use simple big, bold, readable letters; this is not the place to be artsy. If you really want to embellish, get some helium balloons and attach them to the signs. That'll get people's attention—no one can resist balloons.

Other options: Ask a neighbor at the corner if you can put a sign in their yard. Or recruit your (or someone else's) 10-year-old to dress in a banana costume and stand at the corner, waving a big yard sale sign. This is also effective for drawing in crowds.

5. Be Prepared.

• Get change. This is essential. Go to a bank and get $30 in five-dollar bills and $20 in ones.

• Have a good supply of paper or plastic bags, and newspaper for wrapping glass items.

• Find an apron, hip sack, or over-the-shoulder purse with several pockets you can use for making change and keeping the fast-flying funds organized.

• Make food in advance—there may not be time to make anything to eat once your sale starts.

6. Sale Day. Depending on how much prep you did, you may just need to get up on time and then go put up the street signs that are already in your car. Or maybe you'll be up at 5:30 a.m., scurrying around in the dark. Either way, now it's time to have some fun.

• Bring out a CD player (be sure to put "Not for Sale" on it) and crank up the tunes. (For some reason, disco is always a big hit.)

• Invite the kids next door to put up a lemonade stand, or sell veggies from their garden. And any money they make they'll probably spend at your sale.

• Invite anyone and everyone to your sale. Once the neighbors realize you're having a sale, they might ask if they can bring over a few things and join in. The more, the merrier; that way you can cover each other for bathroom breaks and kitchen runs. Plus, you'll all buy each other's stuff.

• Make it a potluck, or throw in a bake sale.

• Give something away to every tenth customer as a booby prize. If folks are having fun, they will stay and find more treasures they can't live without and your day will fly by.

At the end of the day, count up your cash and BE AMAZED!

The three most popular condiments in German restaurants: mustard, horseradish, and applesauce.

ROLL THE DICE

The next time you find yourself rolling a pair of dice, know that you're tapping into something primordial—keeping alive an ancient tradition that began long before recorded history.

DEM BONES

Archaeologists can't pinpoint the first humans who threw dice, but they do know this: Unlike many customs that started in one place and then spread, dice-throwing appeared independently all across the populated world. The oldest known dice—dating back at least 8,000 years—consisted of found objects such as fruit pits, pebbles, and seashells. But the direct precursors of modern dice were bones: the ankle bones of hoofed animals, such as sheep and oxen. These bones—later called *astragali* by the Greeks—were chosen because they're roughly cube-shaped, with two rounded sides that couldn't be landed on, and four flat ones that could. Which side would be facing up after a toss, or a series of tosses, was as much of a gamble to our ancestors as it is to us today.

The first dice throwers weren't gamers, though—they were religious shamans who used astragali (as well as sticks, rocks, and even animal entrails) for *divination*, the practice of telling the future by interpreting signs from the gods. How did these early dice make their way from the shaman to the layman? According to David Schwartz in *Roll the Bones: The History of Gambling*:

> The line between divination and gambling is blurred. One hunter, for example, might say to another, "If the bones land short side up, we will search for game to the south; if not, we look north," thus using the astragali to plumb the future. But after the hunt, the hunters might cast bones to determine who would go home with the most desirable cuts.

SQUARING OFF

And with that, gambling—and dice gaming—was born, leading to the next big step in dice evolution. Around 7,000 years ago, ancient Mesopotamians carved down the rounded sides of the astragali to make them even more cube-like. Now they could land

In 2004 Americans gambled and lost—via lotteries, casinos, and sports betting—$78 billion.

on one of *six* sides, allowing the outcome to become more complex. As their technology advanced, materials such as ivory, wood, and whalebone were used to make dice. It is believed that the shamans were the first ones to put marks on the sides of the dice, but it didn't take long for them to roll into the rest of society. Dice first appeared in board games in Ur, a city in southern Mesopotamia. Now referred to as the "Royal Game of Ur," this early version of backgammon (circa 3000 B.C.) used four-sided, pyramidal dice.

However, the most common dice, then and now, are six-sided cubic *hexahedrons* with little dots, or *pips*, to denote their values. The pip pattern still in use today—one opposite six, two opposite five, and four opposite three—first appeared in Mesopotamia circa 1300 B.C., centuries *before* the introduction of Arabic numerals.

WHEN IN ROME

In the first millennium B.C., civilizations thrived in Greece, India, and China—and they all threw dice. In Rome, it was common for gamblers to call out the goddess Fortuna's name while rolling a 20-sided die during a game of chance. But they had to do it quietly—dice games were illegal in Rome (except during the winter-solstice festival of Saturnalia). Not that that stopped anybody from playing it: One surviving fresco depicts two quarreling dicers being thrown out of a public house by the proprietor.

• When General Julius Caesar led his army across the Rubicon River to attack Rome in 49 B.C.—which set in motion his rise to power—he knew that there was no turning back, proclaiming, "*Alea iacta est.*" Translation: "The die is cast."

• Later Roman leaders were also dice aficionados, including Mark Antony, Caligula (he was notorious for cheating), Claudius, Nero, and Commodus, who built special dicing rooms in his palace.

ROLLING ALONG

After the fall of the Roman Empire, many of civilization's advancements and inventions fell out of use. Not dice, though—their use continued through the Middle Ages, being one of the few leisure activities affordable to peasants. In the rest of the world, dice played an important role among the tribes and indigenous peoples of Africa and the Americas, for both recreation and divination.

The world's smallest dice, made in Japan,...

And in 12th-century China, a variation of a dice game led to the introduction of dominoes, which are basically flattened-out dice.

But it was in Medieval Europe that the popularity of dice games soared, starting in the 1100s with a game called Hazard that was played by both aristocrats and commoners. "They dance and play at dice both day and night," wrote Chaucer in *The Canterbury Tales*. These games were so popular that over the ensuing centuries dice guilds and schools formed all over western Europe. That didn't stop the Catholic Church from attempting to ban all gambling games, though. Over the next few hundred years, dozens of popes, bishops, and priests instituted bans against dicing games. And just like in Ancient Rome, the bans didn't stop people from playing them.

A CRAPPY ORIGIN

It was inevitable, then, that dice travelled aboard the ships emigrating to the New World (the religious Pilgrims on the *Mayflower* were none too fond of the crewmen's gambling games). In colonial America, the game of Hazard was introduced by the French in New Orleans, who called it *crapaud*, meaning "toad." The game became popular with slaves, who shortened the name to craps, which is still the most popular gambling dice game in the United States. And in the early 20th century, board games like Monopoly became popular, guaranteeing that nearly every American home would have at least one set of dice.

PAIR OF DICE LOST

Where there is gaming, there is cheating. While ancient civilizations may have believed the gods were responsible for the outcome of the roll, many unscrupulous players felt the need to give the gods a little help. Loaded dice—as well as dice with the corners shaved off—were found in the ruins of Pompeii. When wooden dice were common, enterprising gamblers would grow small trees around pebbles; then they'd carve the dice with the weight inside, leaving no visible marks.

Modern cheaters are just as crafty in their methods. One type of trick dice are *trappers*: Drops of mercury are loaded into a center reservoir; by holding the die a certain way and tapping it against a table, the mercury travels down a tunnel to another reservoir, subtly weighting the die. Another trick is to fill a die with wax that melts

...measure .3 x .3 x .3 mm, can be seen only through a microscope, and cost $870.

at just below body temperature: Held in a closed fist, the wax melts, settling to the desired side.

Today casinos spend millions trying to thwart cheaters in a high-tech war of wits using extremely sensitive equipment to detect even the slightest alteration in a pair of suspect dice. And to keep people from bringing their own dice to the craps table, all casino dice have tiny serial numbers. A more radical way of stopping cheaters: virtual dice rolled by a computer. This not only makes loading dice impossible, but also allows the craps player to "roll the bones" from the keypad of a cell phone. But nothing can replace the actual feeling of shaking the dice in your hands and letting them fly.

DICEY VARIATIONS

Dice made from the ankles of sheep are still used in Mongolia today. And they're just one type of thousands that exist. Have you ever rolled a 30-sided die—the highest-numbered symmetrical polyhedron? Or how about the 100-sided die, called the Zocchihedron (invented in the 1980s by a gamer named Lou Zocchi)? There's also the no-sided die—a sphere with a moving internal weight that causes the sphere to stop rolling with one of its six numbers facing up. There are barrel dice (roughly cylindrical, with flat surfaces), letter dice (like in the game Boggle), playing-card dice (often called "poker dice"), six-siders numbered zero through five, three-sided dice, doubling cubes (such as those used in backgammon), asymmetrical polyhedrons, and countless others.

And those are just the varieties used in gaming. Myriad other dice are used in *cleromancy*, the ancient practice of divining with dice. Tibetan Buddhists use a set of three dice made from conch shells to help make daily decisions. Astrologers use a set of 12-sided dice relating to the Zodiac signs. There are I Ching dice with trigrams and yin/yang symbols. And if you've ever shaken a Magic 8-Ball and asked it a question, you've practiced cleromancy: The responses—"Yes," "No," "Ask Again Later," etc.—are printed on a 20-sided icosahedron.

Though rarely used in games since the Roman Empire, noncubical dice have made a resurgence in the past few decades. They were used for teaching arithmetic before they took the world of gaming by storm, most notably in the role-playing game Dungeons & Dragons. For that story, roll your way over to page 318.

"Not only does God play dice, He sometimes throws them where they can't be seen." —Stephen Hawking

BATHROOM FENG SHUI, PART II

Here are more tips on applying the traditional Chinese principles of Feng Shui *to your "reading room." In the East, as in the West, people like to go with the flow (of* ch'i*)!* *(Part I is on page 193.)*

YOU'VE LOST THAT FENG SHUI FEELING

• Your house's history can influence its *Feng Shui.* Was the previous owner a successful person who moved into a nicer house? Or did they lose money, or suffer family problems, illness, or even death? Their experiences—positive or negative—made an impact on the Feng Shui of your house that may linger to this day.

• Feng Shui is a finite resource that can be depleted over time. Were the previous owners of your bathroom blessed with good luck? They may have used it all up, leaving little for you to enjoy.

• If you suspect that your bathroom is down in the dumps, here's a little trick to help freshen things up. Soak nine citrus peels—orange, lemon, and lime peels work well—in a bowl of water overnight. Then pour the water into a spray bottle and give the bathroom a good squirting, paying special attention to the floors. This is the Feng Shui equivalent of a dog marking its territory: Any bad spirits that are lurking in your bathroom will be forced to leave.

• Another technique is to make loud noises in the bathroom (so to speak). This establishes your presence and scares away any ghosts of previous owners who may still be lurking. The Chinese use firecrackers, but banging a metal pot and lid together should work just as well without the risk of burning down the house.

DOORS

• Big doors should be reserved for big rooms. The bathroom door, because it opens onto a smaller room, should be small. The thinking is that if the door is too big, people will be drawn in and will spend too much time in there, either to indulge their vanity in front of the mirror or because the poor Feng Shui is making them ill. Either way, you can't use the bathroom if there's a crowd of

Nova Scotians have been nicknamed "Bluenoses" or "Bluenosers" since the 1700s.

people in there. If you suspect your bathroom door has turned the room into an attractive nuisance, hang a mirror or picture just outside the bathroom to pull visitors back out again.

• Doors that don't get a lot of use—"dead" doors—can be the source of argument in the home. If you have a bathroom closet that's used to store items that are only taken out once in a while, you might want to consider moving the items to another closet and replacing them with items that will be used regularly, such as towels. Hanging a mirror on the unused door is another solution.

• Keep your bathroom door's hinges oiled so the door opens without squeaking, and plane the edge of the door if it sticks. A squeaky door can upset the bathroom's *ch'i*, and the stress of having to force a door open can disturb the user's ch'i, harming the sense of well-being and even damaging their health.

COLORS

• Believe it or not, *white* is the color of mourning in China, and the idea of painting any room in the house the color of death is considered very bad luck—the occupants may be made ill by it. But that doesn't mean you need to repaint or re-tile; just be sure to fill the bathroom with as many bright, colorful objects—towels, shower curtains, bath mats, decorative soaps—as possible.

• If you're planning to repaint your bathroom, colors that are conducive to good Feng Shui are red (the color of happiness, warmth, and strength), green (the color of spring), and yellow (the color of the sun). Blue's not bad...but it's not too good, either.

FENG SHUI THAT PAYS

• The presence of water is thought to attract money, and because of this many companies in China take special care to locate their places of business within view of lakes, rivers, and the sea. Those that are unable to do so often install fish tanks in their offices, and some companies even make a point of assigning employees who deal directly with money to offices next to the restrooms.

• You can put this moneymaking power of Feng Shui to work for you. Where do you pay your bills? Move your table nearer to the bathroom. Do you play poker? Put the poker table as close to the bathroom as you can, and make a point of excusing yourself from the game often to wash your hands.

Calorie counting as a means of losing weight first became popular in 1918.

BRA-VO!

Here's a look at three remarkable bras.

GUN BRA

Inventor: Paxton Quigley, a Beverly Hills security consultant to the stars

Product: The Super-Bra, "the world's first combined brassiere and gun holster."

How it Works: The bra contains two extra compartments, one large enough to hold a .38 caliber snub-nosed revolver, and a second that holds a can of pepper spray for additional protection. "If a woman is attacked, her purse is the first thing taken from her, so she needs a backup," Quigley says. "A good place to conceal a weapon is the chest area. Women like its ease of access."

BULLET BRA

Agency: The *Bundespolizei*, or German federal police force

Product: A "police bra" made to be worn under bulletproof vests

How it Works: The bra isn't notable so much for what it has as for what it lacks: it has no underwire inserts, and no metal or plastic fasteners, either. Why? Because these features can cause bodily harm and even death when worn under a bulletproof vest. When a bullet strikes a vest, it does so with enough force to drive any rigid parts of the bra *into* the wearer's body. The bra recently became standard issue to all 3,000 female federal police officers in Germany.

BAGGY BRA

Company: Triumph International Japan

Product: The *NO! Reji-Bukuro Bra* (No! Shopping Bag Bra)

How it Works: Created in response to a strict new environmental law that discourages the use of disposable plastic shopping bags, the *NO! Reji-Bukuro Bra* is a padded bra with a purpose: the padding in the bra pulls out and can be used to convert the undergarment into a shopping bag. Bonus: The bras are made from polyester fiber recycled from plastic bottles.

First national TV appearance of Ronald McDonald: the 1966 Macy's Thanksgiving Day Parade.

DEATH ON THE SET

Sometimes, tragically, in the middle of shooting a movie, an actor dies. It's actually happened many times. So what's a director to do? Turns out they have quite a few options.

Actor: Oliver Reed
Movie: *Gladiator* (2000)
Story: Reed had a well-earned reputation as an extremely heavy drinker and partygoer, and he died the way he lived. While shooting *Gladiator* on the island of Malta in 1999, he went to a bar and reportedly drank three bottles of rum, eight bottles of beer, and several shots of whiskey. At the end of the night, Reed, 61, dropped dead from a heart attack. Most of his scenes had been shot, but for the few that weren't, director Ridley Scott used a body double and then, using digital technology, placed Reed's face on the stand-in's body (they were fight scenes). Cost of the re-creation: $3 million. *Gladiator* was released in 2000 and won the Academy Award for Best Picture.

Actor: Frank Morgan
Movie: *Annie Get Your Gun* (1950)
Story: Morgan (best known as the Wizard in *The Wizard of Oz*) was cast as Wild West legend Buffalo Bill Cody in the screen version of this Broadway musical. Just days into filming, Morgan died and was replaced by Louis Calhern. But in the scene where Buffalo Bill first rides into town, when the audience sees Cody from a distance, the actor on horseback is Morgan. The actor in the close-up—and from then on—is Calhern.

Actor: Heath Ledger
Movie: *The Imaginarium of Doctor Parnassus* (2009)
Story: Ledger died at the age of 28 in 2008, under the influence of a range of sleeping pills and antidepressants. At the time, he was on a break from shooting *The Imaginarium of Doctor Parnassus*, a fantasy about a magical traveling theater show. Director Terry Gilliam decided to keep going. The movie's premise, in which Ledger's character travels through different worlds, was adapted so

It takes the average American 129 workdays to earn enough money...

that the character's *appearance* could change as well. Ledger's friends Johnny Depp, Jude Law, and Colin Farrell split the role between them (and donated their salaries to Ledger's three-year-old daughter, Matilda).

Actor: John Candy
Movie: *Wagons East!* (1994)
Story: While filming the comic western in March 1994, the 43-year-old actor suffered a heart attack and died in his sleep in a hotel in Mexico. Almost all of Candy's scenes had been completed, so director Peter Markle used a body double for the remaining footage. *Wagons East!* was released later that year and bombed with critics and audiences.

Actor: Bela Lugosi
Movie: *Plan 9 From Outer Space* (1959)
Story: *Plan 9* is often called the worst film ever made, but Director Ed Wood was able to hire horror movie icon Bela Lugosi because the actor was 73, past his prime, addicted to morphine, and up for anything that paid. Wood cast Lugosi as "the Ghoul Man." After compiling just a few minutes of footage (with no dialogue because Wood hadn't actually written the script yet), Lugosi died of a heart attack. Not wanting to lose out on the publicity from having a recently departed screen legend in his film, Wood shot the rest of *Plan 9* with Tom Mason, a Los Angeles chiropractor, standing in for Lugosi. To account for the two men looking nothing alike, in all of his scenes, Mason held a black cape over his face.

Actor: River Phoenix
Movie: *Dark Blood*
Story: In the fall of 1993, Phoenix (*Stand By Me*, *My Own Private Idaho*) was shooting *Dark Blood*, portraying a man who lived alone on a nuclear testing site and spent his time making strange dolls. With 11 days left to go on the production, Phoenix, then 23 years old, overdosed on cocaine and heroin, and died on the sidewalk outside The Viper Room, a Los Angeles nightclub. There were too many pivotal scenes left to shoot, so producers completely scrapped the movie.

...to pay federal, state, and local taxes for the year.

Actor: Vic Morrow

Movie: *Twilight Zone: The Movie* (1983)

Story: In a horrific morality tale, Morrow played a vicious racist who has the tables turned on him and suddenly finds himself in the jungles of Vietnam, being hunted down by American soldiers. While filming a scene involving gunfire and a helicopter, the pyrotechnics used for the gunfire exploded prematurely, causing the helicopter to crash. The helicopter's blades decapitated Morrow, 53, and also killed two extras, both of whom were children. The movie was released anyway, but it didn't do as well as expected at the box office—probably due to distaste over the accident. Director John Landis was later charged (but acquitted) with involuntary manslaughter and child endangerment.

Actress: Natalie Wood

Movie: *Brainstorm* (1983)

Story: Wood, a star in her childhood and early adulthood with films like *Miracle on 34th Street*, *Splendor in the Grass*, and *West Side Story*, died in 1981 while filming the virtual reality–themed *Brainstorm*. While partying on a yacht off Catalina Island with her husband Robert Wagner and *Brainstorm* co-star Christopher Walken, Wood disappeared. It was later discovered that she had tried to leave the yacht on a dinghy but fell into the water and drowned. She had one scene left to shoot in *Brainstorm*. Paramount Pictures debated for nearly two years about what to do, ultimately completing Wood's final scene with a body double and dubbed dialogue. *Brainstorm* was quietly released in 1983.

* * *

CAN-DO GUY

Dr. Fredric J. Baur was a "food storage technician" for Proctor & Gamble for nearly half a century. His proudest achievement: the cylindrical Pringles potato chip can, which he patented in 1970. How proud was he? He wanted to be buried in one. And when he died in June 2008 at the age of 89, his children honored the request, putting as much of his ashes as would fit into a Pringles can and the remainder in an urn. The two containers were buried side by side.

A cat will almost never meow at another cat. (They save that sound for humans.)

GREAT SCOTT

F. Scott Fitzgerald (1896–1940) was one of the literary giants of the 20th century. Here's why.

"At eighteen our convictions are hills from which we look; at forty-five they are caves in which we hide."

"Genius is the ability to put into effect what is on your mind."

"A sentimental person thinks things will last; a romantic person hopes against hope that they won't."

"Action is character."

"The extraordinary thing is not that people turn out worse or better than we had prophesied. The extraordinary thing is how people keep their levels, fulfill their promises, and seem actually buoyed up by an inevitable destiny."

"Never confuse a single defeat with a final defeat."

"It's not a slam at you when people are rude, it's a slam at the people they've met before."

"Personality is an unbroken series of successful gestures."

"The test of a first-rate intelligence is the ability to hold two opposed ideas in mind and still retain the ability to function."

"Show me a hero and I will write you a tragedy."

"The kiss originated when the first male reptile licked the first female reptile, implying in a subtle, complimentary way that she was as succulent as the small reptile he had for dinner the night before."

"A great social success is a pretty girl who plays her cards as carefully as if she were plain."

"It is sadder to find the past again and find it inadequate than it is to have it elude you and remain forever a harmonious conception of memory."

"The world only exists in your eyes. You can make it as big or as small as you want."

"What people are ashamed of usually makes a good story."

The Earth's gravity makes it impossible for mountains to be taller than 49,213 feet.

WEIRD VIDEO GAMES

Pac-Man *concerned a tiny, pie-shaped creature who ate power pills so that he could catch ghosts. An odd premise, but nothing compared to these.*

• **SOCKS THE CAT ROCKS THE HILL** (1992). Socks, the pet cat of President Bill Clinton, must get to the Oval Office to warn the president about a stolen nuclear bomb. To do that, he must defeat villains including Russian spies, the press corps, and former presidents Richard Nixon and George H. W. Bush.

• **CHAOS IN THE WINDY CITY** (1994). Basketball superstar Michael Jordan battles an army of basketball-headed zombies that has invaded Chicago. To defeat them, he uses an arsenal of magic basketballs (including fiery-hot basketballs and ice-block basketballs).

• **TOOBIN'** (1988). At the beginning of the game, the player floats down a backwoods river in a inner-tube race. Things suddenly take a turn for the worse as the player is chased by dinosaurs, ancient Inca warriors, and angry hillbillies.

• **BILL LAIMBEER'S COMBAT BASKETBALL** (1991). Basketball is supposed to be a noncontact sport. Not the way Laimbeer played it. As a Detroit Piston in the 1980s, he was well-known for frequent flagrant fouls and starting fights on the court. His notoriety led to this futuristic basketball game in which players punch, kick, push, and throw bombs at each other.

• **COOL SPOT** (1993). In the early 1990s, 7-Up created a mascot—an anthropomorphic dot (with arms, legs, and sunglasses) based on the red dot in the 7-Up logo. The Spot was licensed for this game, which was essentially one long 7-Up ad in which the character wanders around a beach firing soda bubbles at enemies.

• **MICHAEL JACKSON'S MOONWALKER** (1990). A drug dealer named Mr. Big has kidnapped some children and takes them to the Moon, where he plans to use a laser cannon to destroy the Earth. As Michael Jackson, you have to defeat Mr. Big and his cronies by using dance moves that shoot "magic rays."

The average age of Forbes's 400 wealthiest individuals is 63.

• **THE TYPING OF THE DEAD** (2000). This semi-educational game is supposed to teach kids to type and spell. In order to fend off hungry zombies, you have to accurately type words. Get them right, the zombies leave you alone. Misspell, and the zombies will eat your `b-r-a-i-n`.

• **EXODUS** (1991). After solving some difficult logic puzzles, you have to answer questions about the Bible. Get those right, and you get to control Moses. The goal is to spread the word of God by shooting large *W*s (for "word of God") at ancient Israelites.

• **THE FANTASTIC ADVENTURES OF DIZZY** (1991). A walking egg named Dizzy must save his family from an evil wizard by solving puzzles. One of the puzzles: Dizzy must pick certain plants and mix them in a bottle to make a medicine for his sick grandpa egg.

• **DRUM MASTER** (2006). In the game Guitar Hero, you get a plastic guitar and play along with well-known rock songs. Drum Master is made for the handheld Nintendo DS—you get to drum along with popular songs with two toothpick-sized sticks.

• **JOHN DEERE'S HARVEST IN THE HEARTLAND** (2007). Using various John Deere tractors and farm implements, you have to plant crops, fertilize crops, harvest crops, and milk cows. (And it's one giant ad for John Deere.)

• **FACE TRAINING** (2007). Using a small camera that attaches to the TV, you have to copy the facial expressions the game tells you to make.

• **PRINCESS TOMATO IN THE SALAD KINGDOM** (1991). On a mission from the dying King Broccoli, the noble knight Sir Cucumber has to rescue Princess Tomato from her captor, Minister Pumpkin. Sir Cucumber is assisted by Percy, a baby persimmon.

• **TOILET KIDS** (1992). A little kid gets up in the middle of the night to use the bathroom and is sucked through the toilet into another dimension populated by creatures who look like bathroom fixtures. The Toilet Kid must then do battle with tough toilet bodyguards and an evil giant urinal.

One in four Americans fall asleep with the TV on at least three nights a week.

THE CONSTELLATIONS

Mrs. Uncle John loves to call Uncle John out of the house (guess where he usually is at the time) to look at the stars. But he's always amazed at the beauty and wonder of the sky. Turns out he's not the only one.

STARGAZERS

When ancient humans looked up at the night sky, why did they start making conceptual pictures based on the pattern of stars? Were they bored? Were they simply being creative? No, at least not all of them. According to historians, they were charting the stars primarily as a way to keep time—as important a thing in ancient times as it is today. Ancient peoples knew for many thousands of years how to keep time generally. They could, of course, keep track of passing days, seasonal changes, and lunar phases. But more precise measurements weren't made until they discovered something that they could measure more precisely: the stars.

FOR THE BIRDS

An example: The Australian aboriginal *Boorong* people noticed at some point that a particular group of stars disappeared for a long portion of the year—and that their reappearance happened to coincide with the beginning of the nesting season of the *neilloan*, a bird known today as the mallefowl. The eggs of the neilloan were an important food source for the Boorong, so charting the movement of those stars also became important. They began to associate the stars with the bird, which had a very practical effect: What better way to remember them than to draw a mental picture (of a bird) based on their configurations and to tell stories and develop traditions based on it?

That's exactly what they did. The constellation *Neilloan* became one of many (including ones for a possum, an eagle, and an evil emu) in a system that was passed down by word of mouth for...who knows how long? The Boorong had no writing system, so no records exist, but some people think it may have been many thousands of years, longer than any other culture in the world. (*Neilloan* corresponds to our constellation *Lyra*, and it becomes visible in the Southern Hemisphere in March, which is still when the mallefowl begin nesting.)

GIVE THEM A BELT

In many parts of the world the emergence of farming and permanent settlements brought about serious star study and hence, the creation of more constellations. Ancient farmers all over the world noted, for example, that when three particularly bright stars rose above a particular point on the horizon, it was time to harvest the crops. Those three bright stars became central in constellations in virtually every part of the world, and are the "warrior's belt" on the constellation we know as *Orion*.

The history of our modern constellations goes back to the writings of Greek scholar Claudius Ptolemy, who in the second century wrote *The Almagest*, or "The Great Book." In it he catalogued 1,022 stars and the 48 constellations that held them, including Cancer, Cassiopeia, Gemini, and Leo. *The Almagest* would be the foundation of Western astronomy for more than a thousand years. Hundreds of constellations were added over the centuries, including many by sailors, who used them for navigation. But not all of them lasted: Here are a few notable "extinct" constellations that can be found on some early 19th century star maps:

★ ***The Battery of Volta.*** Created in 1806 in honor of Alessandro Volta, inventor of the first electric battery.

★ ***Globus Aerostaticus.*** Latin for "hot air balloon," created in 1810 in honor of French ballooning pioneers, the Montgolfier brothers

★ ***Marmor Sculptile.*** Latin for "marble sculpture," it represented a sculpted bust of Christopher Columbus.

★ ***Officina Typographica.*** It means "printing office," and was created in 1810 in honor of the printing press.

THE MODERN AGE

In 1922 the International Astronomical Union (IAU), formed that year for the purpose of standardizing the science of astronomy, threw out most of the newer constellations, took Ptolemy's 48 (with some alterations) and added 40 more recent ones to come up with 88 constellations that cover the entire sky. They are still the only ones officially recognized by astronomers today. A few highlights:

★ An odd one that made it in was *Antlia*. Its original name was *Antlia pneumatica*, which is Latin for "air pump," and so named in honor of the air pump's inventor, French physicist Denis Papin.

★ How many stars are there in a given constellation? Traditionally constellations were made up of a relatively small number of stars—seven in Taurus, nine in Virgo, etc. But scientifically each constellation contains all the stars within its boundary—even the ones we can only see with the most powerful telescopes. That means that there are *trillions* of stars in each constellation.

★ The largest constellation: *Hydra*, a long, snaky region of stars named after the Greek's many-headed serpent that covers approximately 4 percent—of the entire sky. The smallest: *Crux*, the "Southern Cross," seen only in the Southern Hemisphere and covering just .016 percent.

★ There have been some curious coincidences concerning constellations: Ancient Greek stargazers looked at at particular group of stars and saw...a bear. The Micmac people in Eastern Canada looked at that same group and saw...a bear.

★ That group of stars is of course the constellation *Ursa Major*, "Great Bear" in Latin. It is best known for containing seven very distinctive stars that we know as the "Big Dipper." The seven stars of the Big Dipper were interpreted in many different ways around the world: as a plough, a coffin, a chariot—and a hog's jaw—just to name a few.

★ Terminology lesson: The Big Dipper is an an *asterism*, a recognizable grouping of stars that are not an actual constellation. Orion's Belt is another.

★ Some cultures had constellations with no stars in them. The ancient Incas, who lived high in the Andes Mountains, saw an especially brilliant display of stars. They constructed most of their constellations within or near the Milky Way. Some were for dark, splotchy areas of the Milky Way caused by clouds of space dust (the Incas didn't know that, of course), and included the Shepherd, the Toad, the Serpent, and the Llama.

* * *

Even a small star shines in the darkness. —**Finnish proverb**

THERE'S NO PLACE LIKE ZAMUNDA

Match the imaginary place with the book, movie, or TV show it's from. *(Answers on page 541.)*

1. Freedonia

2. Bacteria

3. Mypos

4. San Marcos

5. Shangri-La

6. Skull Island

7. Zamunda

8. United States of Earth

9. Duloc

10. Lower Slobbovia

11. Loompaland

12. Grand Fenwick

13. Florin

14. Barataria

15. Eastasia

16. Taka-Tuka Land

17. Lilliput

18. Vulgaria

a) *Don Quixote*

b) *King Kong*

c) *Duck Soup*

d) *Bananas*

e) *Pippi Longstocking*

f) *Nineteen Eighty-Four*

g) *Chitty Chitty Bang Bang*

h) *Charlie and the Chocolate Factory*

i) *Li'l Abner*

j) *Futurama*

k) *The Great Dictator*

l) *Perfect Strangers*

m) *Coming to America*

n) *The Princess Bride*

o) *The Mouse That Roared*

p) *Gulliver's Travels*

q) *Lost Horizon*

r) *Shrek*

Chemical name for caffeine: 1,3,7-trimethylzanthine.

ESCAPE FROM AMERICA

Why would anyone want to escape America? These folks had their reasons.

THE SEEKERS

The concept of *political asylum*—granting protection to foreigners being persecuted for political reasons—has been around for millennia. One of the earliest known cases: In the 13th century B.C., the deposed ruler of the Hittite Empire, Mursili III, fled to Egypt to escape execution. Ramses II, Egypt's pharaoh, refused Hittite demands that he be sent back. The situation was eventually resolved, leading to history's first known peace treaty, and rules for *extradition*—the process by which one state asks another to surrender a criminal back to the state in which the crime was committed. Similar cases have occurred throughout history all over the world. In more modern times, the United States is the most popular destination for asylum-seekers, but sometimes it happens the other way around: Some Americans actually flee the United States.

ELDRIDGE CLEAVER

Cleaver was a prominent American civil rights leader and the author of the extremely influential 1968 book on "black power," *Soul on Ice*. That same year Cleaver, then the spokesman for the radical Black Panther Party, was charged with attempted murder after being wounded in a shootout with police in Oakland, California. Facing a substantial prison sentence, Cleaver secretly applied for asylum in communist Cuba, claiming he and the Black Panthers were being persecuted by the FBI (an argument many believe to this day). Cuban leader Fidel Castro, whether because he truly supported the Black Panthers as a "liberation movement," or simply because he liked annoying the Americans, granted it, allowing Cleaver to live there as a free man. Cleaver soon felt restricted by the Cuban government and in early 1969 applied for asylum in Algeria. The Soviet-backed African nation happily accepted, and Cleaver ran a Black Panther "embassy" there until 1972, by which time he had sufficiently annoyed the Algerian government. From there he went to Paris and in 1975, after having converted to Christianity, returned to the United States and renounced his Black Panther past. He spent eight months doing

Of all countries, Brazil has the most plant species, with more than 56,000.

community service to clear up his legal troubles and eventually became a Mormon, a conservative Republican, a Ronald Reagan supporter, a crack cocaine addict, and a radio talk-show host. He died in 1998 at the age of 63.

WILLIAM LEE BRENT

In 1968 Brent—another prominent Black Panther Party member—and two other men robbed a San Francisco gas station and got into a shootout with police in which two officers were severely wounded. Brent and the others were arrested. Like Cleaver, Brent jumped bail and headed for Cuba. Unlike Cleaver, he got there by hijacking a TWA flight from Oakland to New York and ordering the pilot to fly to Havana. Brent was granted asylum by the Cubans—and spent the next 37 years there, during which time he went to college, taught high school English, became a disc jockey, and married American travel writer Jane McManus, who moved to the island nation in 1969. In 1996 Brent wrote an autobiography, *Long Time Gone: A Black Panther's True-Life Story of His Hijacking and 25 Years in Cuba.* He died in Havana in 2006 at the age of 75.

HOLLY ANN COLLINS

Not all cases are politically based: In June 1994, Collins, from Minneapolis, Minnesota, picked up her two young children from her ex-husband's house and took them to the Netherlands. She had been hoping to get to New Zealand but was stopped by customs officials in Amsterdam because she didn't have the proper papers. When they said they were going to send her back to America, she told them she wanted asylum...to protect her children from the harm they'd face in the United States. Her ex-husband had been granted custody of the children, she said, but he had physically abused them (charges the husband denies). The case was in the Dutch court system for three years, and in 1997 the three were granted refugee status. That's not the same as asylum—it doesn't protect against extradition, and Collins was now wanted by the FBI for "International Parental Kidnapping." So they lived in secret in the Netherlands for the next 10 years. Then, in 2007 a neighbor recognized her from an FBI "wanted" poster and turned her in. At that point, she filed for asylum, and in 2008, to almost everyone's surprise, got it. Collins is currently working to get her charges dropped in the U.S. so she can come home.

There are over 100 billion known galaxies. How many unknown galaxies there are is not known.

THE JOY OF COOKBOOKS

Cookbooks are the single most popular segment of the book business. Hundreds of new ones are introduced each year; tens of millions are sold. (Hey, we've all got to eat, don't we?) BRI food-editor-at-large Lorraine Bodger sent us the origins of these classics.

THE JOY OF COOKING, by Irma S. Rombauer (1931)

In 1931 Rombauer was a newly widowed 54-year-old socialite and homemaker from St. Louis. She was *not* a professional writer nor even much of a cook. That's probably why her family and friends were astonished when she decided to take the $3,000 left to her by her husband and self-publish a cookbook. She called it *The Joy of Cooking*. In the more than 75 years since its first printing, *Joy* has gone through eight editions, sold more than 18 million copies, and become one of America's all-time most beloved and relied-upon cookbooks.

Rombauer's innovation was first to sweep aside the prevailing approaches to cooking—that it was laborious, exacting, an art, a science, and a challenge to the ordinary housewife. The chatty tone of her writing welcomed readers and reminded them that food was supposed to be a *joy*, not a burden. At the same time, she was down to earth: she specified precise weights and measures and correct pan sizes for baking, and used readily available ingredients. She cared about the ordinary homemaker's food budget and recognized that women cooked both to feed their families and to entertain their friends. They needed simple, speedy recipes (such as applesauce and creamed chicken) as well as fancy ones. And she wrote for everyone: There are recipes for squirrel, porcupine, raccoon, and armadillo, as well as recipes for sachertorte, soufflé Grand Marnier, and lobster thermidor. Third, she had an original approach to recipe instructions: She integrated the ingredients into the recipe steps and made the process of preparation as clear and straightforward as possible. Rombauer spoke to women as they actually were, not as some hoity-toity chef thought they should be. Women loved her book.

Napoleon was only 26 years old when he took command of the French Army in Italy.

The Joy of Cooking was a family business. Rombauer's daughter, Marion Rombauer Becker, illustrated the first edition and joined her mother in the production of later editions. After Rombauer died in 1962, Becker took over the next few *Joys*, including the 1975 edition—the most popular ever. After Becker died in 1976, there was no new edition of the book...until 1997's *All New, All Purpose Joy of Cooking*. For that one, the publisher and the supervising editor made substantial changes to the original, generating a storm of criticism over what had been eliminated (whole chapters on ice cream and pickling) and how the book had lost its unique character. Marion's son Ethan Becker was reportedly very unhappy with the 1997 edition, but got the chance to repair the damage in 2006: The 75th-anniversary edition (based on the 1975 edition) restored traditional recipes...and popular approval.

THE MOOSEWOOD COOKBOOK, by Mollie Katzen (1977)
Ithaca, New York, is the home of the Moosewood Restaurant, started in 1973 by the Moosewood Collective, a group of idealistic friends who wanted to create imaginative vegetarian meals using natural ingredients. Mollie Katzen was one of the founding members. Vegetarianism was a new and intriguing concept to many Americans, and when the restaurant prospered (even in that small college town), Katzen began to compile and adapt its recipes for home cooks. The first edition of *The Moosewood Cookbook*, hand-lettered and illustrated by Katzen, was privately published in 1974; in 1977 a small publisher, Ten-Speed Press, brought out the next edition—and had the good sense to keep the hand-lettering and illustrations that gave the book its uniqueness. Suddenly this "new" kind of cooking was accessible and even fun (not to mention health-oriented and Earth-friendly), and Katzen was largely responsible for making "vegetarian" a household word. *Moosewood* was followed by *The Enchanted Broccoli Forest*, and somewhere along the way Katzen had to fight a legal battle with the Moosewood Collective for the right to use the Moosewood name. (They wound up with the right to use the name too; they don't sell her books at the restaurant or on their Web site). But Mollie Katzen isn't complaining: she has more than six million books in print, she's been host of several PBS TV cooking series, and in 2007 *The Moosewood Cookbook* was inducted into the James Beard Cookbook Hall of Fame.

The average disposable diaper can hold up to 7 pounds of liquid.

MASTERING THE ART OF FRENCH COOKING, by Julia Child, Louisette Bertholle, and Simone Beck (1961)

Almost everyone knows Julia Child. But how did she get to be a culinary icon? In 1948 Julia and Paul Child went to live in Paris when Paul was posted to the American Embassy there, and Julia fell passionately in love with French food. She started taking classes at Le Cordon Bleu, the world's premier cooking school, and spent her days mastering the recipes that comprised the basics of classic French cuisine. It seemed to her and her two close friends, Simone Beck and Louisette Bertholle, that they could write a cookbook that would demystify French cooking for Americans. Convinced that they had a valuable contribution to make, they tested recipes repeatedly, refined techniques, wrote extensive information on equipment and fresh ingredients, and suggested menus and appropriate wines. The huge manuscript took 10 years to complete.

The three women had many difficulties with prospective publishers until the manuscript reached the hands of Judith Jones, a young editor at Alfred A. Knopf, who "got it." At a time when popular American cookbooks were mostly of the *Betty Crocker's Picture Cookbook* variety and the use of convenience foods (canned, frozen, and packaged) was standard practice, Jones felt that Americans might be ready for this groundbreaking book. She threw her full support behind it, and it was finally published in 1961. Jones was right. The first printing sold out immediately; within a year there were 100,000 copies in print.

A year after the book's publication, Child became public television's *French Chef*—giving her (eventually) national exposure and a dedicated following. She wrote 16 more cookbooks, won Emmy awards, and received the French Legion of Honor and the Presidential Medal of Freedom. Declaring Child a "national treasure," the Smithsonian Institution transported her entire Cambridge, Massachusetts, kitchen to Washington, D.C., and reassembled it in the National Museum of American History.

THE I HATE TO COOK BOOK, by Peg Bracken (1960)

When advertising copywriter Peg Bracken showed her husband (also a writer) the manuscript of *The I Hate to Cook Book*, he said, "It stinks." Their marriage didn't last, but the book did—and went on to sell more than three million copies.

The Declaration of Independence, Constitution, and Bill of Rights...

It all started in the 1950s, when Bracken and a group of Portland, Oregon, women friends who called themselves "The Hags" used to meet after work to down martinis and do a little griping about their lives. "At that time," she wrote, "we were all unusually bored with what we had been cooking and, therefore, eating. For variety's sake, we decided to pool our ignorance, tell each other our shabby little secrets, and toss into the pot the recipes we swear by instead of at." What struck people most about about *The I Hate to Cook Book* was that it was witty, funny, and totally irreverent about the sacred subject of cooking. Bracken hated spending time in the kitchen and wasn't afraid to say so—and it turned out that thousands of other women felt the same way. The recipes relied on the use of convenience foods (her recipe for "Sweep Steak," for example, was pot roast cooked with a can of cream of mushroom soup), avoided complicated techniques, and took very little preparation time. She told women—in a tone both friendly and unapologetic—that it was time to stop feeling guilty about dinner and get on with their lives. *That* was revolutionary for the 1960s. Sales of *The I Hate to Cook Book* topped 3 million copies, which encouraged Bracken to write other books, including the equally irreverent *I Hate to Housekeep Book* (1962) and *I Try to Behave Myself* (1964), an etiquette manual. And in keeping with her motto of "keep it simple" she became the spokeswoman for Birds-Eye frozen vegetables in the late 1960s.

* * *

NIGHT AT THE MUSEUM

One night in May 2008, two security cameras suddenly stopped working at the Museum of Anthropology in Vancouver, British Columbia. Shortly after that, the security guard received a call from the alarm company informing him that there was a problem with the security system and to ignore any automated alarms that may occur...which he did. Bad move: The next morning, the guard discovered that 15 art pieces, worth $2 million, were gone. And the alarm company had no records of any calls leaving their headquarters.

...were secretly stored in Fort Knox to keep them safe during World War II.

REEL DUMB

Each year the Golden Raspberry Foundation "honors" the year's worst movies. Here are some memorable lines from Worst Picture winners.

Tom Green: Are you okay?
Marisa Coughlan: I'd be a lot better if you beat my legs with these bamboo reeds.

—*Freddy Got Fingered*

"That's such a good name. 'Tom Lone' rhymes with cone, bone, phone. Not that rhyming's all that important."

—Alex Borstein, *Catwoman*

"I feel like a dolphin who's never tasted melted snow. What does the color blue taste like?"

—Andie MacDowell, *Hudson Hawk*

"We may have lost the war, but we haven't lost our sense of humor—even when we lose a lung, a spleen, a bladder, 35 feet of small intestine, two legs, and our ability to reproduce."

—Kenneth Branagh, *Wild Wild West*

"In the way of love, we're kindergarten toddlers."

—Bo Derek, *Bolero*

Prince: I must have that disease, what's the name of it?
Kristin Scott Thomas: It's called stupid.

—*Under the Cherry Moon*

"I am going to make you as happy as a baby Psychlo on a straight diet of kerbango."

—Kelly Preston, *Battlefield Earth*

Opening title card: "This is not a documentary of the war in Korea but a dramatized study of the effect of war on a group of people. Where dramatic license has been deemed necessary, the authors have taken advantage of this license to dramatize the subject."

—*Inchon*

"How much mail can a dead postman deliver?"

—Kevin Costner, *The Postman*

"I'm so terrifical, I have my own toll-free number: 1-800-UNBELIEVABLE."

—Andrew "Dice" Clay, *The Adventures of Ford Fairlane*

Mole rats are the only mammals that live in colonies, like ants, with a single fertile queen.

OOPS!

Life is full of little slips-ups. Here are a few more tales of seemingly simple things that went very, very wrong.

YOU NAME IT

A computer's spell-checking program only works when there's a human around to double-check that it's not turning people's names into words. Otherwise it could lead to a mishap like the 2008 Middletown Area (Pennsylvania) High School Yearbook. Only four pages were affected, but that came as no relief to Kathy Airbag (Carbaugh), Max Supernova (Zupanovic), and Alexandria Impolite (Ippolito), who said, "It was kind of funny but kind of rude at the same time." The printing company sent out little stickers printed with the correct names, reassuring the students that "this kind of thing happens all the time."

GUNPLAY

In 2007 Robert Glasser and Joey Acosta, two friends from Chaparral, New Mexico, wanted to get matching gun tattoos. For an added touch of realism, the 22-year-olds decided to trace the patterns onto each other's arms using a .357 Magnum. Bad idea: The gun was loaded. It fired as Glasser was tracing the trigger; the bullet travelled through his hand and then hit Acosta's arm. Both men survived. (No word on whether they ever got the tattoos.)

THROW IN THE TOWEL

A 49-year-old Japanese man (name not released) went to his doctor complaining of abdominal pain. After an MRI, he was informed that he had a large tumor that had to be removed immediately. When the surgeons went in, they did find a large lump in his abdomen, but it wasn't a tumor. It was a surgical towel. The doctors described it as "greenish blue, although we are not sure about its original color." It turned out that the towel had been in the man's gut for 25 years—doctors treating him for an ulcer in 1983 accidentally left it there. Officials from the hospital that performed the 1983 surgery apologized for the goof and promised to pay all of the man's medical bills. Amazingly, he isn't suing.

MORE LOST ARTS

On page 44 we told about works of drama and film that were lost to the ravages of time. But they aren't the only artworks that have vanished. Tragically, books, paintings—and even classic TV programs—sometimes suffer the same fate.

TELEVISION

Programs from television's early years, the 1940s and 1950s, weren't saved...because there were few ways to preserve them. Videotape was introduced in 1956, but it was so expensive that networks recycled tapes dozens of times. (A show would be recorded on the tape in the studio, the show was broadcast, then the tape was erased and reused.) Sometimes a process called kinescoping or telerecording was used in order to save shows for later broadcast—a video monitor was filmed by a 35mm camera—but many early shows are gone for good. Here are some notable losses:

• ***The Tonight Show.*** The first 10 years of Johnny Carson's tenure as host of the classic late-night show (1962–1972) were recorded and aired using recycled videotapes. Result: Just a handful of segments—Carson's personal favorites, saved only at his request—survive. The rest of the entire 10 years is gone.

• ***Beulah.*** This sitcom aired on ABC from 1950 to 1953. It was the first television show to star an African-American performer. Of the 87 episodes, 80 are lost.

• **DuMont shows.** When the DuMont Network, one of the first broadcasters, went out of business in 1956, ABC took over many of its facilities. Needing warehouse space, ABC employees dumped hundreds of DuMont kinescopes—nearly its entire 1947–1956 output—into Upper New York Bay in the early 1970s, forever losing footage of early TV shows such as *Your Show of Shows* with Sid Caesar, and *Captain Video*, which was the first science-fiction program. The network produced more than 300 episodes of *Mary Kay and Johnny*, considered by historians to be the first TV sitcom, but only a few minutes of footage survive.

• **Soap operas.** Networks didn't begin to save soap episodes until the late 1970s, believing there was zero replay value in serialized

The day of the week on which Americans are least likely to eat out: Monday.

dramas. For example, only the 1982–1986 episodes of *Search For Tomorrow* were saved—the episodes from 1951 to the early '80s are long gone.

• **Game shows.** The networks didn't think game shows had any replay value, either. Only a few episodes each of the original black-and-white runs of *To Tell the Truth*, *Concentration*, *Match Game*, and *The Price is Right* still exist. ABC's *$10,000* (later *$20,000*) *Pyramid* ran from 1973 to 1980, but just 15 episodes survive. At least three game shows from the '60s and '70s are entirely gone, with not even a pilot episode surviving: *Split Second*, *Second Chance*, and *Snap Judgment* (hosted by Ed McMahon).

• ***Jeopardy!*** Videotapes were used over and over to capture each day's broadcast of the original run of *Jeopardy!*, hosted by Art Fleming in the 1960s and 1970s. Only four episodes are still around.

• ***Doctor Who.*** In 1975 the BBC needed to make room in its vault, so it removed and erased thousands of tapes. Network executives realized they'd made a mistake in 1980, when the BBC science-fiction series *Doctor Who* became a hit on American public television. In trying to round up the show's earliest episodes from 1963 (so as to sell them to PBS), the BBC found out they'd taped over 108 episodes of *Doctor Who*.

• **News and sports.** The BBC's coverage of the 1969 Moon landing was taped over. CBS and NBC both broadcast Super Bowl I, and neither kept the tape. Parts of nearly all World Series broadcasts between 1947 (when they began) and 1974 are missing. For example, only the first few innings of one game of the 1955 Series remains, and the 1947–1949 broadcasts are gone entirely.

BOOKS

• **Sylvia Plath.** Plath was primarily a poet but is best known for *The Bell Jar*, a thinly veiled fictionalization of her descent into severe depression. Plath committed suicide a month after *The Bell Jar* was published in 1963. After her death, the manuscript for her unpublished second novel, *Double Take*, disappeared.

• **James Joyce.** The Irish author (*Ulysses*, *Finnegans Wake*) wrote a play called *A Brilliant Career*. He hated it, his publisher hated it, and so Joyce burned it.

• **T. E. Lawrence.** Lawrence (the real-life "Lawrence of Arabia") wrote a 10-volume memoir called *Seven Pillars of Wisdom* about his time fighting in the Arab Revolt of 1916–1918. In 1919 Lawrence accidentally left his only copy on a bench in a train station in Reading, England, and had to rewrite it from memory.

• **Herman Melville.** Now it's a classic, but Melville's *Moby-Dick* was not well received during the author's lifetime. In fact, Harper & Brothers, Melville's publisher, rejected his follow-up novel, *Isle of the Cross*, in 1853. It has since been lost.

• **Ernest Hemingway.** In 1922 Hemingway's wife, Elizabeth Richardson, was traveling with a suitcase carrying all of Hemingway's unpublished fiction to that point: 20 short stories and a nearly finished novel about World War I. The suitcase was stolen and never recovered.

ART AND SCULPTURE

• ***Le Peintre*** (1963). This Picasso painting was in the cargo bay of Swissair Flight 111 when it crashed into the Atlantic Ocean near Nova Scotia in September 1998. *Le Peintre* was never recovered.

• ***Still Life: Vase with Five Sunflowers*** (1888). Vincent Van Gogh painted a series of six still lifes depicting various numbers of sunflowers in vases. This one is gone. Once in the collection of a Japanese art collector, it burned up in an American air raid during World War II. Around the same time, Van Gogh's *The Painter on His Way to Work* and *The Park at Arles with the Entrance Seen Through Trees* were also destroyed in World War II bombing raids in Berlin.

• ***The Buddhas of Bamyan*** (6th Century A.D.). Carved in what is now Afghanistan, the two sandstone statues were gigantic representations of the Buddha measuring 180 and 121 feet tall. They were destroyed with dynamite in 2001 by the ruling Taliban government, which felt the statues were idols and were therefore forbidden under Muslim law.

* * *

"When you step on the brakes, your life is in your foot's hands."

—**George Carlin**

BATHROOM NEWS

Here are a few fascinating bits of bathroom trivia that we've flushed out from around the world.

POT O' GOLD

In July 2008, an employee of the St. Louis County Justice Center paid a visit to the restroom and found a lot more than sweet relief: When he reached for some toilet paper, he discovered stacks of $50 and $100 bills hidden behind the tissue dispenser. Total: $55,000. Because the bathroom is used by prisoners who are being booked into the jail, it's likely that a prisoner hid the money there. But none of the inmates would admit to knowing anything about the money. So does the employee who found it get to keep it? Doubtful. At last report, the city attorney was still figuring out what to do with it.

DINNER AND A SHOW

Cafe 52 owner Steve Bothwell was probably happy when the Aberdeen, Scotland, city council made plans to set up five portable, open-air urinals around the historic district known as The Green as part of a campaign to eliminate "weekend anti-social behavior." Happy, that is, until the city council plopped one of the urinals down right next to his club's brand-new $80,000 outdoor dining area. Bothwell was so mad that he had the urinal hauled to the city council offices...but a few days later it was back. "Imagine a young family sitting down to have dinner," Bothwell told Scotland's *The Mirror* newspaper, "then seeing a bunch of guys urinating right beside them." Says a spokesperson for the city council: "We are meeting with Mr. Bothwell and hope to find a solution."

STALL OF SHAME

The Minneapolis-St. Paul International Airport got a brand-new tourist attraction in 2007, not that they were very happy about it. The men's room off the food court, near the statue of Snoopy and Woodstock, is the one where Senator Larry Craig of Idaho was arrested on charges of lewd conduct, a scandal that forced him to announce his retirement. (Craig, who pleaded guilty to the

Some Cambodian trains are built entirely out of bamboo and spare parts.

charge, insists he's innocent.) "Where is the Larry Craig bathroom" has become one of the most-asked questions in the airport, and Craig's stall (second from the end) has become one of the most-photographed spots in the terminal.

IT'S NOT UNUSUAL

Some careers end in the men's room; others begin there. In the summer of 2008, Christie's auction house in London made plans to sell what is believed to be the first songs ever recorded by singer Tom Jones, who belted out a four-song demo tape in the men's room of the Pontypridd, Wales, YMCA in 1962. Why record in the men's room? For the same reason you sing in the shower. "He believed it had the best acoustics in the building," said Liz Williams, current president of the Pontypridd YMCA. The tape sold for just under $5,000.

IT'S NOT WHAT YOU THINK

British actor Michael Caine makes a point of booking a hotel suite with *two* bedrooms whenever he travels with his wife of 35 years, Shakira Caine. He says it's the secret to remaining happily married for so long. Here's his reasoning: When he books a suite with two bedrooms, he also gets two *bathrooms*. "Never share a bathroom with a woman," he says. "We book into hotels and ask for two bedrooms and you see them thinking that our marriage is on the rocks, but I'm just trying to get another bathroom."

ANOTHER "LUCKY" FIND

Spanish workers renovating a bathroom in a resort on the Costa Blanca town of Torrevieja in January 2008 are still celebrating their good fortune, of sorts. While tearing out the old false ceiling, one of the workers found a pipe sitting atop one of the ceiling tiles and picked it up. Then, perhaps remembering that resorts in Costa Blanca had been targeted by Basque terrorists, the worker gently set the pipe down again and called the police, who sent over the bomb squad. Sure enough, the object was a pipe bomb, one with a detonator (defective) and 10 ounces of dynamite. The bomb had been sitting there since 1991, when a three-bomb threat was phoned into the authorities, but only two of the bombs went off. The bomb was disposed of safely.

The planet Uranus was originally named Georgium Sidus, and was also briefly known as Herschel.

THE TRUTH ABOUT FOOD ALLERGIES

You hear about this more and more, it seems. Grandma can't drink milk, your next-door neighbor's son can't eat peanut butter, and your best friend breaks out in hives if he even looks at a lobster. What's up with that?

GUESS WHO'S COMING TO DINNER

You just ate dinner and now you're not feeling very well. Your mouth is tingling, you feel nauseated. Maybe you have stomach cramps, or you have to make an emergency pit stop in the nearest bathroom. Food poisoning? Maybe so. Or maybe you've developed a food allergy.

A true food allergy is when your immune system has an abnormal overreaction to a normally harmless food. Your immune system decides that part of what you just ate (usually a food protein) is an *allergen* and harmful to your body, and it overreacts to the food by producing *immunoglobin E* antibodies. (Antibodies fight off bacteria, viruses, and other foreign substances in the blood.) The next time you eat that particular food, the antibodies sense its presence and signal the immune system to send *histamines* and other chemicals into your bloodstream. These chemicals then produce any of a range of allergic symptoms that can run from bothersome to life-threatening.

THE (UN)USUAL SUSPECTS

The majority of true food allergies are triggered by eight foods: peanuts, eggs, fish, soy, tree nuts (like walnuts and pecans), shellfish (usually shrimp, crab, or lobster), cow's milk, and wheat. But there are some surprising twists and turns, too.

- People who are allergic to cow's milk often have no problem eating beef.
- People who are allergic to eggs can usually eat chicken.
- People with shrimp, lobster, or crab allergies often have no difficulties eating clams or oysters.

It's estimated that about 2% of adults and 8% of children have one or more food allergies. The most common food allergies in children: cow's milk, wheat, and soy. Although some allergies can last a lifetime, children typically outgrow their food allergies as their digestive systems mature (as we age, our bodies are less likely to absorb food allergens). But food allergies can start at any time. You may have eaten a food hundreds of times and never had an allergic reaction...and then suddenly you become allergic.

AH-CHOO!

Allergic symptoms typically range from annoying (runny nose, itchy eyes, coughing, scratchy throat) to uncomfortable (nausea, diarrhea, stomach cramps, bloating, hives, rashes, wheezing, asthma). But some people can be so severely allergic to a specific food that ingesting it will cause *anaphylaxis*, a systemic reaction that can be drastic or, in extreme cases, lethal. At first it feels like an ordinary allergic reaction—tingly mouth, itchy rash, a sneezing fit. Then symptoms suddenly escalate: The throat may swell, making breathing difficult, followed by dizziness and even loss of consciousness. The pulse rate shoots up and blood pressure drops, sending the victim into anaphylactic shock. Symptoms this severe can be fatal if the victim doesn't receive immediate emergency medical treatment.

FOOD INTOLERANCE?

There's another kind of food overreaction that has many of the symptoms of a food allergy, but it's not a true allergy: food *intolerance*. The difference is significant: Allergies involve the immune system; intolerances don't. If you're intolerant of a particular food, you might even be able to eat some of it without consequences. But if you have a true food allergy, the symptoms can be triggered by even the smallest amount of the culprit food.

Food intolerances usually result from a deficiency of an enzyme needed for digesting a particular food. People with lactose intolerance, for example, lack the enzyme *lactase*. Your body needs the lactase to break down a sugar called *lactose* that's present in cow's milk. If you drink milk and your body doesn't have enough lactase to break it down, the lactose moves to the large intestine, where it is metabolized by bacteria, producing the uncomfortable (for you) and unpleasant (for those around you) gases—methane, carbon dioxide, and hydrogen.

The Bureau of Alcohol, Tobacco and Firearms prohibits the use of the word...

There are other kinds of food intolerances as well. You might have a bad reaction to a flavoring agent like monosodium glutamate, to aspartame, to food dyes, or to chemical preservatives such as sulfites and nitrite. Some people can't tolerate caffeine; others get headaches from very ripe cheese or red wine.

RANDOM FACTS

• Some people feel sick every time they see, smell, or even think of a particular food. No one knows how or why this happens, but according to scientists, it is a genuine form of food intolerance.

• The odds that you will develop a food allergy are greater if someone in your family has allergies.

• It used to be thought that chocolate was a major food allergen, but studies now show that chocolate allergy is extremely rare.

• People with food allergies and intolerances have always had difficulty shopping in supermarkets—they need to know exactly what's in the products they buy so they can avoid the foods that make them sick. Until recently, manufacturers didn't have to disclose whether their products contained any of the top eight allergens (milk, eggs, fish, shellfish, peanuts, nuts, wheat, and soy). But thanks to the Food Allergen Labeling and Consumer Protection Act of 2004, now they do.

• Number of deaths in the United States caused by allergic reactions to food: about 200 per year.

• Children are more likely to outgrow milk and soy allergies, but less likely to outgrow allergies to fish, shellfish, or peanuts.

• Some ingredients have names that may be unfamiliar when you see them on food labels. For instance, even if a food product says "nondairy," it could have casein or whey, which contain milk proteins—something the lactose-intolerant might want to avoid.

• A British 12-year-old boy named Tyler Savage eats "chicken or tuna with carrots and potatoes and maybe some grapes or an apple." And that's *all* he eats. Why? Because he has a rare condition called *eosinophillic enteropathy*—he's allergic to wheat, gluten, dairy products, eggs, and soy products. "I'm a little bored eating the same food all the time," said Tyler, but he knows he's fortunate that doctors were able to pinpoint his condition before it killed him.

NOT-SO-EASY RIDERS

A rider *is a the part of a performer's contract that includes a list of the artist's backstage demands. The promoter must provide these items, or else the performer might not go on. Here are some real excerpts from real riders.*

Foo Fighters: Among the food items requested by the alternative rock band are "stinky cheese" and a vegetarian soup, because "meaty soups make roadies fart."

Cher: The singer requires a separate room, adjacent to her dressing room, for her wigs.

Clay Aiken: Nuts, shellfish, mushrooms, coffee, chocolate, and mint are banned from all backstage areas. The singer is severely allergic to them.

Metallica: Their 24-page rider states that it's "very important that bacon be available at every meal and during the day."

Prince: The artist demands that all items in his dressing room be covered by clear plastic wrap, which may be removed by nobody other than Prince himself.

Coldplay: This British rock group won't perform unless there are eight "stamped, local postcards" in their dressing room.

Poison: Apparently, this hard rock band played a little too loud in the 1980s, because on recent tours, they've asked for a sign language interpreter to accompany them onstage.

50 Cent: A box of Cuban cigars—which are illegal.

The Wallflowers: In no press materials is singer Jakob Dylan (Bob Dylan's son) to be referred to as "Bob Dylan's son."

Ted Nugent: His dressing room must be stocked with tropical-fruit-flavored Slim-Fast.

K.C. and the Sunshine Band: No strobe lights may be used during the band's performance. Why? A member of the group has epilepsy. If strobes are used, he could have a seizure, in which case the blame—and the hospital bills—would be given to the promoter.

Burt Bacharach: He requires a bottle of "first-class" red wine and some peanut butter.

Dionne Warwick: Most singers want to be picked up at the airport in a limo. Warwick demands a station wagon.

John Mayer: The singer requires several boxes of sugared cereal from which to choose… and four toothbrushes.

Razorlight: This British band requires a plate of cornbread and a selection of music magazines that feature articles about themselves.

Peter Gabriel: He requires promoters to provide a female masseuse to give him a massage, "hippie style."

Billy Idol: Backstage caterers must provide one large tub of I Can't Believe It's Not Butter.

Boy George: The 1980s pop star's performance requires a "crack oil machine," a primitive fog machine used in British theaters in the 19th century.

Iggy Pop: "No toy robots."

Johnny Cash: Not surprisingly, the late singer required a large American flag to wave while he was on stage.

Janet Jackson: Beverages for the singer are to be presented in "fresh, clean, crushed, or cubed ice," and never in "fish ice" (whatever that is).

Nine Inch Nails: Lead singer Trent Reznor needs two boxes of cornstarch (to help him squeeze into a tight pair of leather pants).

*   *   *

HAVE YOU SEEN THIS GIANT?

On wanted posters in New Zealand, the law forbids police from displaying pictures of suspects under 18 years of age. In the town of Christchurch, police found an interesting way to get around the law. They noticed that a teenager suspected in a string of burglaries looked a little like Scottish-born actor Robbie Coltrane, best known for playing Hagrid, the friendly giant in the *Harry Potter* movies. So the cops put the actor's face on the wanted poster. Underneath the photo was written: "Robbie Coltrane is not the burglar, but imagine him aged 16 with lank greasy hair and you have the picture."

FIRST LADY FIRSTS

Just being the spouse of the President of the United States is historic in its own right. But these women made history in other ways.

First to live in the White House: Abigail Adams (1797). First to *not* live in the White House: Anna Harrison, wife of William Henry Harrison. She did not accompany her husband to his inauguration in 1841 because she was ill. President Harrison died a month later; his wife never set foot in the White House.

First to enjoy indoor plumbing at the White House: Abigail Fillmore (1850).

First to be related to her husband (by blood): Eleanor Roosevelt was a fifth cousin, once removed, of Franklin Roosevelt.

First to be the mother of a president: Abigail Adams, wife of John Adams, and mother of John Quincy Adams. (Barbara Bush was the second.)

First to serve in a presidential administration: Sarah Polk was the official secretary of President James K. Polk (1845).

First to make a cameo appearance on a sitcom: In 1975 Betty Ford guest-starred on an episode of *The Mary Tyler Moore Show*.

First to have her own Secret Service agent: Florence Harding (1921).

First to have a monument erected in her honor: Lady Bird Johnson. In 1969 a grove in the Redwood National Forest was named for her.

First to be foreign-born: Louisa Adams (wife of John Quincy Adams) was born in London in 1775. She's the only First Lady born outside of the United States.

First to be honored by *Outlaw Biker* magazine: In 1995 the publication named Barbara Bush "First Lady of the Century."

First to have her own press secretary: Jacqueline Kennedy. In 1962 Kennedy performed another first: She was the first First Lady to give a televised tour of the White House.

THE ORIGINAL DUNGEON MASTERS

When one of the inventors of Dungeons & Dragons died in 2008, Uncle John was surprised that his name wasn't more familiar. That made him wonder: how many other people have never heard this story?

ROLLING THE DICE

Gary Gygax (pronounced GHEE-Gax) was an insurance underwriter living in Lake Geneva, Wisconsin, in the late 1960s. He made his living calculating the probabilities that an individual seeking to buy insurance would become sick or disabled or die, and he used these estimates to set the premiums and payouts on the policies he reviewed. Every policy was like a roll of the dice: If Gygax calculated correctly, the individual received sufficient coverage at a fair price, and the insurance company had a good shot at earning a fair profit. If he was incorrect, either the individual or the insurance company would lose.

In Gygax's free time, he loved to roll dice of a different sort: He played war games in his home with fellow members of a club called the Lake Geneva Tactical Studies Association. There, on a giant table in the basement—just as war gamers had done since the invention of *Kriegsspiel* in the early 1800s (see page 251)—Gygax and his friends re-created famous battles such as Gettysburg or the D-day landings of World War II and fought them all over again in miniature, devoting countless hours to killing each other's soldiers with one roll of the dice after another.

THE LONG MARCH

Participating in these games could be a war of attrition in its own right: Mapping out the battlefield took time, and so did setting up dozens and dozens of miniature soldiers just as they would have been positioned in the real battle. War gamers prided themselves on historical accuracy, and this meant that while the main campaign was being fought across the tabletop, countless other battles raged around it as players bickered over one arcane historical point after another, often brandishing military histories and biographies as they argued. Add to this the fact that a single military campaign might drag on for months, with war gamers meeting every weekend in Gygax's basement until final victory was achieved, and it's easy to understand why the hobby was popular with only a limited number of people.

SPELLBOUND

Just as they had since the invention of Kriegsspiel, gamers were constantly writing new rules for existing games as well as inventing new ones. Gygax was no exception: In 1968 he took four pages of rules that a friend had written for a game set in the Middle Ages called Siege of Bodenberg and expanded them to 16 pages, creating a new game called Chainmail. Each player still had a dozen or more plastic soldiers, but instead of each figure representing up to 20 men as had been standard in other games, Gygax had each figure represent only one soldier.

Chainmail was an interesting departure from other war games, but after several weekends it started to get boring and attendance at the gaming sessions began to drop off. One afternoon Gygax decided to try something new: He grabbed a plastic dinosaur off a shelf and declared it to be a fire-breathing dragon. Then he took an oversized figure of a Viking warrior and said it was a giant. And then he created a wizard who could throw fireballs and lightning bolts and a "hero" character that had four times the strength of an ordinary character. This fantasy element alienated many of the most orthodox war gamers, but plenty of other people liked it—soon Gygax's basement wasn't big enough to hold all the players who wanted to play in his games. He wrote a fantasy supplement to the standard Chainmail rules and published it in 1971.

NEW(ER) AND IMPROVED

One of the early players of Chainmail was a 21-year-old University of Minnesota student named Dave Arneson. He and his wargaming friends began experimenting with Chainmail, keeping what they liked about it and discarding much of the rest. In the process, they created a new game that Arneson named Blackmoor:

• **Armies turn into single characters.** Chainmail had been a game of combat, with the soldiers controlled by one "general" attacking some strategic point held by monsters or another player's soldiers. But Arneson's players got tired of just tackling one military objective after another, so in Blackmoor he got rid of the large armies and had each player assume the identity of a single character. The players rolled dice to determine their characters' attributes: strength, wisdom, charisma, etc. Then the characters went on decidedly *non*military missions, such as sneaking past monsters to steal their treasure or other valuable items that they could sell on the black market. Again, the players rolled dice during each encounter to determine whether or not the mission was successful.

• **The birth of role-playing.** Placing the emphasis on a single character caused players to identify with their characters in a way that they hadn't when they were commanding legions of troops. They gave the characters names, invented personalities, and even began to imagine themselves in the role. The players became so attached to their characters that they didn't want them to die, certainly not during a game—not even after it ended.

• **Die hards.** Arneson responded by revising the rules of Blackmoor to make the characters harder to kill. In Chainmail, a single roll of the dice determined whether a player died in combat. This made sense when there were dozens of soldiers on the board and the action had to be quick, but it didn't when each player had only one character—and one life. So Arneson took an idea from Ironclads, a Civil War naval game he'd written. In that game, he used "hit points" to determine how much damage a warship received from cannon fire. It took numerous hits to sink a warship, and the stronger its armor, the more hits were needed.

Arneson applied the same concept to the characters in Blackmoor. It would take many successful rolls of the dice to accumulate enough hit points to kill a character; if the character was wearing armor, he was even harder to kill. And since each player had only one character instead of dozens, it was easy to keep track of the hit points.

• **You've been promoted.** Arneson also allowed characters to advance to higher levels after surviving difficult ordeals. The characters grew in strength, wisdom, and other qualities, just like human beings. When one game ended, they carried their points over to the next game.

In Tororo, Uganda, it thunders about 251 days of the year.

THE UNDERGROUND

After a few weeks of playing scenarios in conventional landscapes, Arneson decided to try something different. When his players showed up to play the next session, he told them they were going "underground," into the dungeon of an old castle. Not only was it an interesting change of pace from the usual outdoor scenario, but Arneson also found that it was easier to draw a finite number of tunnels and rooms than it was to map out an entire countryside. Moving the action to subterranean tunnels also limited the avenues of escape—instead of scattering in every direction in a "crisis," the players pretty much had to face whatever Arneson threw at them.

ADDITION...AND SUBTRACTION

In the process of inserting all of these interesting elements into the game, Arneson also removed many of the annoying elements of traditional war games. Limited numbers of characters and simplified play reduced the setup time to almost nothing and sped up the pace of the action dramatically. Debates over arcane historical points came to an end—how can you argue about the historical accuracy of stealing gold from a troll?

The role of the game's host—or "umpire," to use a word from Kriegsspiel—expanded significantly. He was no longer just a referee responsible for interpreting the rulebook during reenactments of historical battles. The host became the *creative* master of the game as well, part storyteller, part guide, responsible for designing the dungeon and filling it with monsters and treasures to the limit of his own imagination. He became the Dungeon Master.

After more than six months of developing Blackmoor, in late 1971 Arneson and some friends took the game to Gary Gygax's house in Lake Geneva and hosted a game in which the players tried to sneak into Castle Blackmoor to open a gate from inside. Gygax was impressed with Blackmoor and especially liked the dungeon idea—as a kid, he had often played hooky from school to wander the tunnels beneath an abandoned sanatorium overlooking Lake Geneva. He sensed that, with more organization and development, Blackmoor might have commercial potential.

So how did an obscure fantasy game grow into a worldwide phenomenon? Part II of the story is on page 477.

WEIRD ATTRACTIONS

Not all museums are stuffy, pretentious marble-floored buildings. There's a museum for everything—even dummies.

Attraction: Presidential Pet Museum
Location: Williamsburg, Virginia
Details: Most presidential pet-related treasures are in the presidential libraries, but curator Claire McLean managed to get her hands on some curious mementos of the presidents' pets. For example, she's got a cowbell worn by President Taft's pet cow, Pauline, who grazed on the White House lawn
Be Sure to See...A bronze statue of Barney, George W. Bush's Scottish Terrier, and a portrait of Ronald Reagan's dog Lucky made out of Lucky's actual hair.

Attraction: Center for Urologic History
Location: Linthicum, Maryland
Details: Located in the headquarters of the American Urological Association, this museum is dedicated to the history and science of the human bladder, genitals, and other private matters. Among the displays of various medical devices are one exhibit on the history of male sexuality and dysfunction, and another on 1800s medical quackery.
Be Sure to See... The pineapple-size kidney stone.

Attraction: Vent Haven, the Ventriloquist Museum
Location: Fort Mitchell, Kentucky
Details: In a suburban home outside of Cincinnati, Ohio, lurk hundreds of ventriloquist's dummies. The house is filled to the rafters with dummies, dummy heads, dummies in costumes, dummies that look like famous people (Adolf Hitler, Jimmy Carter, Ronald Reagan), and dummies with names like "Cecil Wigglenose" and "Tommy Baloney." There are exhibits on the history of ventriloquism and on famous ventriloquists, including Edgar Bergen and Waylon Flowers.
Be Sure to See... The "dummy school"—an entire room made to

Portland, Oregon, is home to Casa Diablo, the world's first (and probably only) vegan strip club.

look like a classroom, with dummies filling all but one chair... which remains empty so you can have your picture taken with them.

Attraction: Leila's Hair Museum

Location: Independence, Missouri

Details: Leila Cohoon became a hairdresser in 1949 and shortly thereafter started collecting art made from human hair. Originally a room in Cohoon's cosmetology school, the Hair Museum now occupies a two-room office in a business park. Most of the exhibits come from the Victorian era, when hair was braided into wreaths, framed, and put on the wall as decoration. Cohoon has hundreds of braids and lots of hair art, including jewelry, bookmarks, and buttons, all made out of hair.

Be Sure to See... Celebrity hair—strands that once adorned the heads of Marilyn Monroe and Abraham Lincoln.

Attraction: Moon Museum

Location: The Moon

Details: According to artist Frosty Myers, astronauts on the 1969 *Apollo 12* mission unwittingly took a tiny "Moon Museum" with them to the lunar surface. Myers (with the help of an anonymous Grumman engineer) claims to have secretly put a ¾" by ½" iridium-plated ceramic tablet in a leg of the lunar landing module *Intrepid.* Etched on the tablet are six miniature drawings by major artists of the day—Myers, John Chamberlain, David Novros, Robert Rauschenberg, Claes Oldenburg, and Andy Warhol. Is it really there? No one knows, because NASA didn't sanction the project. But the *Intrepid* is still there, so maybe someday...

* * *

CONE HEAD

Police in Cullompton, England, were called in October 2007 to help a 3-year-old boy: he'd gotten a traffic cone stuck on his head. His parents said he was trying to imitate his hero, Harry Potter. "We shouldn't have laughed," his mother said, "but he looked so comical." It took police 30 minutes to get the boy's head free.

THE RUNNINGMAN, PT. I

You know that scene in Forrest Gump *when he runs across the United States? A British man decided to do that in real life...except around the* world. *Turns out it's a lot harder than it looks in the movies.*

THINKING OUTSIDE THE BOOK

Robert Garside's big idea began as a whim. The 28-year-old London University student was halfheartedly studying in the school's library in 1995 when he came across an edition of *Guinness World Records*. Flipping through it, Garside noticed records for cycling and even walking around the world, but none for *running*. Garside liked to run, so he decided then and there that he would be first human to run across every continent. "I just thought it would be cool to set a world record," he said.

BORN TO...?

You'd think that a quest of that magnitude would require extensive planning, but Garside didn't have that kind of discipline—he took the same casual approach that he'd taken to the rest of his life: Born in Stockport, England, in 1967, he ran away from home at age 17 and then had 80 different jobs over the next decade (including a stint as a cop) before going to college...where he dropped out to start his long run.

Something else that Garside lacked: long-distance running experience. He figured his record attempt would be like "going for a jog every day and not going back home." His laid-back attitude would eventually haunt him, but at least he found out Guinness's requirements to make the attempt official: He must run the length of at least four continents, covering a distance of 18,000 miles; he must cross the equator once and finish at the same longitude from which he began. He had to run from place to place—he could not walk or use any other means of transportation, save for a plane to take him from land mass to land mass, but there was no time limit. And he'd need both visual proof and documented records of his journey.

So Garside stuffed his small video camera into his backpack along with his passport, visas, maps, a water bottle, and his diary. Then, sporting a brand-new pair of running shoes, he set out from

London's Piccadilly Circus on December 7, 1996, with £20 in his pocket. The plan: Run between 25 and 75 miles a day—more if the terrain was flat—and rely on handouts for food, water, and shelter. The night before he left, he watched *Forrest Gump* for inspiration.

THE FIRST LEG

He ran to the English Channel, then crossed into France by boat and ran through Switzerland, Germany, Austria, Slovakia (where he visited his parents), and Poland. He hoped that as his journey progressed, the publicity would increase and he'd land sponsorship deals to pay for meals, accommodations, or, more importantly, airfare to the next continent. But in the early days of the run, Garside relied solely on his charm—he'd spark up conversations with curious onlookers and explain what he was attempting to do... hoping they'd offer up some food, water, or a bed to sleep in. "The gift of gab gets you through," he later said. (It didn't hurt that Garside is tall, thin, and handsome, with a friendly smile.) And every 20 minutes, he turned on his video camera to show where he was. Whenever possible, he convinced police and town officials to sign a document confirming he had run (not walked) into their town.

So what would you think about if you ran the equivalent of two to three marathons every single day through unfamiliar surroundings with no one by your side (most of the time)? "I philosophize while I run," explained Garside, "taking in the local color and trying to interact with the people." Every so often a bicyclist or a pretty girl would join him for small stretches. In France, a dog ran by his side for about 20 miles. "It's like the time-travel show *Quantum Leap*," he said, "but instead of jumping, I'm running from one experience to the next."

NOT SO FAST

As Garside left the familiarity of western Europe, the road turned dangerous. He wrote in his diary about being shot at by gypsies in Russia. Then, when reports of war in Afghanistan reached him, he decided the risk was too great and skipped the country altogether. In Pakistan in September 1997, he wrote: "I was robbed, my tent slashed with a knife, and all my contents taken. I have only my clothes on my back and my passport." But having already run across most of Europe, and now fit enough to feel confident, Garside wasn't about to give up. So he tried again, this time with a little money (thanks to a few private donations) and a laptop computer so he could post updates on a Web site. Calling himself "The Runningman," in October 1997, Garside started anew from underneath the arches of India Gate in New Delhi.

The journey was fraught with peril: A mob in a small Indian town pelted him with rocks, and in another town he was chased by ax-wielding farmers. In March 1998, he ran straight into the harshness of the Tibetan winter. In the Himalayas he met a runner from Spain, who joined him for a stretch—on a few occasions they had to sleep in the snow, but most of the time, people helped them. "A monk I encountered took us back to his monastery," he wrote, "where we got a bed for the night and feasted on a dinner of roasted barley, roasted sheep's fat, and yak tea." From there, Garside headed alone into China.

INCARCERATED

Travel through China was even less hospitable than his path from India. In Huzhou, after evading Chinese police for three months because he didn't have the proper papers, Garside was arrested and sentenced to 30 days in jail, followed by deportation. Again, Garside used his gift of gab to talk his way out of trouble. After three days of annoying his cell mates by running in place to stay in shape, "I begged to be allowed to finish my run and finally, they gave me one day to get out of the country. I had to cover 158 kilometers (98 miles) in that one day. I ran through the night but I did it."

After receiving a donation from a Hong Kong businessman, Garside flew to Japan in late 1998. The Japanese press was very interested in his quest, and he was able to secure more donations after giving interviews. That got him to Australia for the next leg, but in the desolation of the Outback in January 1999, Garside found himself destitute once again. "I arrived in a small town in New South Wales called Violet Town, a guy came out of the pub and said, 'You're that mad Pommie bastard I've seen on TV who's running around the world.' He bought me a beer and introduced me to a wealthy farmer friend, who gave me $1,000 because he was so impressed with what I was doing."

Only Beatles song in which no Beatle plays an instrument: "Eleanor Rigby."

ACROSS THE ATLANTIC

In mid-1999, Garside flew to South America. By this point, his run was well publicized and the hits to his Web site kept increasing. "My original idea was just to see the world. But as I was going through with it I realized I could make myself a future. I have created my own sport—and I am the only practitioner. So I have a monopoly on it," Garside told a reporter in Rio de Janeiro (who bought his dinner and board for the night). And then the runner was off again. In his journal entries, Garside wrote about being threatened at gunpoint in Panama and again just outside of Acapulco—both times he was able to escape by running into heavy traffic. For protection at night, he slept at police stations.

In Venezuela, Garside met 23-year-old Endrina Perez in a Caracas shopping mall. Though they spoke different languages, they developed a deep connection. Perez became Garside's running partner; he gave her the name "Runningwoman." (Perez wasn't the first girl that Garside "befriended" on his journey—there are reports that he'd had at least five girlfriends up to that point, including one woman who followed him on a bicycle for 500 miles through Australia.) Garside and Perez then ran northward through Central America, reportedly making it from Mexico City to the United States—through mostly mountainous terrain—in just 10 days.

COAST TO COAST

In September 2000, they crossed the California border from Tijuana. Suddenly, thanks to an article in *Sports Illustrated*, the Runningman was a minor celebrity. Through his Web site, Garside had been offered sponsorships (Odor-Eaters picked him up for a while) and places to stay. The biggest boost came from a car dealer who provided Team Runningman with a support van that Perez drove while Garside ran.

Like the fictional Forrest Gump, Garside was joined on his journey through the U.S. by other runners, cyclists, and curious onlookers. A skateboarder pledged to follow Garside from San Francisco all the way across the country, but didn't actually make it very far. In fact, no one could keep up with Garside's amazing stamina. But the demanding journey was starting to take a toll on the 34-year-old runner's mind and body. When Garside arrived in New York, he told reporters, "I'm desperate to finish now. I've had enough. I'm missing things like never having more than one pair of shoes or set of clothes. And I'm dying to get a decent cup of tea."

THE HOME STRETCH

Exhausted, Garside decided to skip Africa and Antarctica, having already more than met the four-continent minimum that the record required. But he still had to get back to where he started, so he resumed the trip in Europe. His journey ended in June 2003 in the same place where it officially began: New Delhi, under the India Gate. All told, Garside's run lasted five years and eight months, took him through 29 countries for a total distance of over 30,000 miles, and exhausted 50 pairs of running shoes. Through donations, Garside made and spent a total of £170,000 ($300,000). After arriving home in England, all that was left to do was wait for the Guinness people to examine the proof and declare him the world record holder.

But a shadow was hanging over the Runningman's quest, threatening not only the record, but Garside's reputation as well. Did he really *run* the entire distance? Did all of those amazing adventures really happen to him? There were many who claimed that he cheated and lied his way across the world...and they had evidence to back it up.

For Part II of the Runningman's story,
jog on over to page 512.

* * *

FAMOUS DADS OF FAMOUS PEOPLE

• Uma Thurman's father was the first American to be ordained a Buddhist monk.

• Rachel Weisz's father invented the artificial respirator.

• Ron Laurie, father of Hugh Laurie (*House*) won the gold medal for Rowing in the 1948 Olympics.

• Liv Tyler, the daughter of Steven Tyler of Aerosmith, didn't meet her real father until she was a teenager. She grew up thinking her father was the man that helped raise her, who was also a 1970s rock star: Todd Rundgren.

First president's wife to be known as the First Lady: Dolley Madison, after her death.

PROJECT ORION

Back in the 1940s and '50s, it seemed that someday everything—cars, houses, ships, planes, you name it—would be powered by atomic energy. That never happened, of course, but here's an example of what might have been.

THE NEXT BIG THING

Even before the Manhattan Project produced the world's first atomic bomb in 1945, many of the scientists assigned to the project were already thinking about how they could harness the power of the atom—and the atom bomb—for other purposes. The long-term effects of radiation were not yet completely understood, and the scientists were eagerly looking for peacetime applications. A number of them wanted to find a way to use it to power rockets, but nuclear energy's greatest asset, its enormous power, also presented the biggest challenge. Nuclear fuel contains about *10 million* times as much energy as the equivalent amount of rocket fuel, but nuclear reactors generate so much heat that they would melt even the sturdiest rocket engines. And besides—atomic bombs would have destroyed any combustion chamber built to contain them.

THINKING OUTSIDE THE BOX

Nuclear-powered rocketry didn't appear to show much promise until a scientist named Stanislaw Ulam, formerly of the Manhattan Project, came up with the idea of detonating atom bombs *behind* a spacecraft instead of inside of one. The idea may sound silly, kind of like throwing sticks of dynamite out of the trunk of a car to propel it down the road, but Ulam thought it would work.

In a secret paper published in 1955, he and another scientist, Cornelius Everett, proposed building a spacecraft that looked kind of like a pogo stick mounted atop a trash can lid: Atom bombs would be ejected out the rear of the spacecraft to a distance of 100 to 200 feet away and then detonated. The force of the blast would strike the trash can lid (Ulam and Everett called it the "pusher plate"), giving the spacecraft a sharp, powerful shove. Shock absorbers in the pogo stick section would absorb the force of the blow, protecting the crew and the ship from damage. This process

FM radio waves can leave Earth's atmosphere. AM radio waves cannot.

would be repeated over and over again during launch or whenever the spacecraft was accelerating or decelerating, with an average detonation rate of one atom bomb per second. Like a pogo stick, the spacecraft would *boing! boing! boing!* its way through space. Ulam and Everett called their idea "nuclear pulse propulsion."

Nuclear pulse propulsion might have remained the stuff of science fiction, had the Soviet Union not beaten the United States into space by launching the world's first artificial satellite, Sputnik, in October 1957. Suddenly America was interested in any idea, no matter how loony, that might help it win the space race against the Russians. In 1958 a government agency called the Advanced Research Products Agency (ARPA) awarded the General Atomic company of San Diego a $1 million-a-year contract to develop the idea. The program was code-named Project Orion.

NOT EXACTLY ROCKET SCIENCE

When the rocket fuel you're using has limitless power, there's no need to make the spacecraft small and light, as was the case with the Apollo and Space Shuttle programs. A lot of the money spent on those programs was used to figure out how to reduce the weight of the items needed for a mission, so they could all be crammed aboard a single vehicle with very limited cargo capacity.

With the Project Orion spacecraft, the opposite was true—bigger really *was* better, because an enormous amount of mass was needed to absorb both the physical shock and the radiation produced by all those exploding atom bombs. The Project Orion craft would be built from plate steel or similarly strong materials and would be as sturdy as a submarine or a battleship. It might even be built in a shipyard, or at least built by workers skilled in shipbuilding.

That was the beauty of Project Orion, not to mention one of its strongest selling points: Very little of the design depended on technology that still needed to be developed. (Even the device that ejected the bombs out the back of the ship was existing technology—it was taken from Coca-Cola vending machines.) The United States had learned how to build atom bombs, and it had long known how to build ships. All that remained to be done was to build a ship sturdy enough to be blasted straight up in the air and into outer space.

Project Orion missions would have been cheap, too: It was estimated that the cost of lifting one pound of cargo into orbit with atomic bombs would have been as little as 1% the cost of launching it aboard a rocket powered by conventional fuel.

HIGH-RISE

One plan produced by Project Orion called for a ship that was as tall as a 15-story building, weighing about 200 times as much as the space shuttle (the pusher plate alone would have weighed 1,000 tons). Two stages of shock absorbers separating the pusher plate from the rest of the spacecraft would have stood several stories tall. The crew quarters would also have been enormous, with enough room for the essentials—a galley, sleeping quarters, and so on—and plenty left over for things like a library, an exercise room...and a bomb shelter.

The radiation emitted when the atom bombs were being detonated would have been so intense that the crew would have had to retreat into an especially protective room—probably deep in the center of the spacecraft, surrounded on all sides by storage tanks and supplies—and then wait there until the bombs had stopped. Time spent in the bomb shelter would have been minimal; the scientists estimated that five minutes' worth of atom bombs (about 800 bombs) were enough to launch the ship into Earth's orbit, and another minute or two of detonations in orbit (about 200 bombs) were enough to send it to the Moon.

TO THE MOON AND BEYOND

The cargo capacity of the ship was so great that it could have carried enough equipment to establish a permanent base on the very first trip to the Moon. And that was just the beginning: The ship was designed to carry 2,600 nukes, enough to take it to another planet and back, so after an inaugural trip to the Moon it could have remained in Earth's orbit until NASA was ready to send it on a much longer trip. Interplanetary travel would not have been far off. The program's motto: "Mars by 1965, Saturn by 1970."

There was almost no limit to how big such ships could be or how ambitious their missions were. Project Orion even contemplated the possibility of building a city-sized, 8 million-ton "interstellar ark" capable of traveling at 10% the speed of light, which would enable it to reach Proxima Centauri, the star closest to the Sun, in less than 50 years. And all it would have needed to get there was 1,080 giant atomic bombs weighing three tons apiece.

THANKS...BUT NO THANKS

As ambitious as Project Orion was, it never did win acceptance from the highest levels of government—how many public officials would have been willing to sign off on a spacecraft that set off hundreds of atomic bombs in the atmosphere as it blasted its way into space? Even the most optimistic estimates conceded that every time an Orion spacecraft left the launch pad, it would release enough radiation to kill 10 people from cancer and sicken thousands more even if the ship blasted off from the Nevada desert or some other location many miles from civilian population centers. And that was the kill ratio for a *successful* mission. How many people might have been killed by a disaster similar to the Challenger explosion if the shuttle had been carrying 2,600 atom bombs?

Even if Project Orion was technologically possible, politically it was dead on arrival. After NASA was created in 1958, the federal government began divvying up existing space programs between NASA, which took over the civilian projects, and the Air Force, which took over anything with a military application. Neither of them wanted Orion. NASA didn't want to touch nuclear-powered programs, not even after General Atomic downsized its design for use as the second stage of the Saturn V rockets that would soon take astronauts to the Moon. As few as three Saturn V rockets could have carried the materials to assemble an Orion vehicle in orbit, a vehicle that could take astronauts all the way to Mars in as little as 125 days. But NASA still said no.

THE NAME'S FAMILIAR

Project Orion sputtered along until 1963, when the signing of the Limited Nuclear Test Ban Treaty, which outlawed the exploding of atomic bombs in the atmosphere, killed it for good. About the only part of the program that survives is the name, and that's only a coincidence: When NASA began designing a new generation of spacecraft to replace the space shuttle when it retires in 2010, they named the new spacecraft Orion—but in honor of the *constellation*, not the forgotten atom bomb spaceship.

Largest joint in the human body: the knee.

WHERE'D THEY GO?

Remember when a milkman dropped off a quart each morning? Did a TV repairman ever come to the house to fix your set? Today a lot of once-common jobs are just distant memories.

TV REPAIRMEN. Before TV there was radio...and radio repairmen. When TV replaced radio as the dominant form of entertainment in the early 1950s, many radio fixers switched over to TVs. Like early radios, TVs were expensive and made up of a lot of tubes, wires, and other parts that could be replaced, but fixing one was specialized work that had to be done by trained professionals. As the average household income increased (from $4,100 in 1955 to $30,000 in 1990), the price of TVs went down (factoring in inflation, a TV cost half as much in 1990 as it did in 1955). By the 1990s, it no longer made sense to pay someone to fix a TV set. If a repairman charged $20 an hour (plus the cost of parts), even a minor repair could cost at least $60. It made more sense to do what most people do today: throw it away and buy a new one. In 1978 there were more than 20,000 TV repair facilities in the United States. Today, there are fewer than 5,000. That number will continue to dwindle as more and more Americans replace their old, difficult- and expensive-to-fix tube-based TVs with stable, tubeless high-definition televisions.

CHANDLERS. Ancient Romans created wicked candles from papyrus rolled in melted beeswax or animal fat. As the only source of artificial light for centuries, candles became a major commodity in western Europe, where guilds of candle makers (also called chandlers) handcrafted their candles and sold them door to door. As a profession, candle-making began to die out in the 1830s, when inventor Joseph Morgan devised an automated candle-making machine (a piston ejected candles out of a mold as they solidified) that could produce 1,500 in an hour. Then came the death knell: the light bulb, introduced in 1879, which quickly made chandlers obsolete.

MILKMEN. According to the Department of Agriculture, more than half of the milk sold in the United States in 1950 (along with eggs, ice cream, and butter) was delivered to homes by milkmen, all employed by independent local dairies. By 1963 deliveries had dropped to a third of all milk sold. As of 2001, the last year statistics are available, it's less than 0.4%. Milkmen began to disappear in the late 1960s when dairies were operated by large national franchises and 98% of American homes had refrigerators, reducing the need for daily milk delivery. But the real milkman killer was probably the supermarket. Stores use milk as a "loss leader"; for instance, milk can cost as much as $4 per gallon wholesale, but they sell it for as little as $2, making up the difference with the profit on other items. That's an economic system with which small dairies can't compete.

BRICK MAKERS. Brick-making began in ancient Persia, and the process remained virtually the same for centuries. Brick makers dug for clay and left it exposed to the elements over winter, allowing the freeze-thaw-freeze-thaw cycle to tenderize the clay. In the spring, they ground the clay into a powder, placed it in a soaking pit with water to get it to the right consistency, then mixed it by hand. Next, a chunk of clay was rolled in sand, placed in a mold, left to dry in the sun for two weeks, then fired in a wood- or coal-burning kiln. As it did with candle-making, the Industrial Revolution of the 19th century ended artisan brick-making. Ever since, bricks have been made in factories with temperature control and other processes that make all bricks uniform.

COBBLERS. Also known as shoemakers, cobblers arrived in the Americas with the first English colonists that settled at Jamestown (the voyage was funded in part by a London shoemaker's guild). They were fully established by 1616, and cobblers went door to door soliciting made-to-order shoes. It wasn't until the 1750s that shoemakers abandoned to-order shoemaking and simply made whatever shoes they wanted to (in various sizes) and offered them for sale. And up until the 1840s, all shoes were made by hand with roughly the same tools used for centuries—knives to cut the leather, pliers to stretch it, awls to punch holes in it, and a needle and thread to stitch it into a shoe. The trade survives today, but only for repairs. Most shoemaking has been mechanized since 1846—the year Elias Howe invented the sewing machine.

A group of ferrets is a *business*, a group of gerbils is a *horde*, and a group of hedgehogs is a *prickle*.

FOUNDING FOOD-ERS

This article is the best thing since sliced bread.

OTTO ROHWEDDER

Rohwedder—a jeweler from Davenport, Iowa—was convinced that the world needed evenly sliced bread, and in 1912 started working on plans and prototypes for his first bread slicer. Bad news: they were lost in a fire in 1917. Good news: since he had to start over, this time he addressed bakers' complaints that presliced bread would dry out and consumers wouldn't want to buy it. So in 1928 he came up with a new machine that would slice *and wrap* each loaf of bread. The following year, the stock market crashed, sending the country into the Great Depression. Rohwedder had to sell his invention to the Micro-Westco Company, but they hired him as a VP to work in the newly formed Rohwedder Bakery Machine Division. The concept of sliced bread still didn't hit...until the Wonder Bread Company began nationwide sales of sliced, packaged bread in 1930 (using its own version of Rohwedder's machine). Sliced bread suddenly began to catch on in a big way—along with the pop-up toaster, which had been invented in 1926, but wasn't a very popular consumer item until presliced bread came along. During World War II, the federal government banned sliced bread, claiming that the use of waxed paper for wrapping it was wasteful. But the no-slicing ban lasted just three months: Public outcry was so loud that it forced the government to remove the ban (and anyway, the savings turned out to be minimal). Want to see the original model of Rohwedder's 1928 bread slicer? It's in the Smithsonian Institution in Washington, D.C.

STEPHEN F. WHITMAN

In 1842 Whitman opened a small shop in Philadelphia, where he made and sold fine candy. The company grew as Whitman made innovation after innovation. (For example, in 1856 he introduced the first confection ever packaged in a printed box.) But their biggest contribution to candy culture: the Whitman's Sampler, introduced in 1912. Executives and designers worked long and hard to arrive at exactly the right image for the sampler

Phobos, the larger of the two Martian moons, is only about 15 miles across.

box: an embroidery-look logo that suggested a "sampler" of chocolates. (It was also the first candy box to be wrapped in cellophane.) Within three years the sampler was Whitman's biggest seller and the nation's most popular box of chocolate. The design changed over the years—brighter colors, an overhanging "French" edge, a hinged lid—but it remains basically the same. According to the company, someone buys a Whitman's Sampler box every 1.5 seconds.

DUNCAN HINES

Before Internet searches and the hundreds of travel books that are now available, how did travelers know where to eat and sleep in a city or town they'd never been to? There were only two reliable sources: *Adventures in Good Eating: a Guidebook to the Best Restaurants along America's Highways* (1936) and *Lodging for a Night* (1938), both by Duncan Hines.

In the 1930s, Hines, a salesman for a Chicago printer, traveled the country by car with his wife Florence, keeping detailed notes about every place they visited—the cleanliness, safety, atmosphere, service, value, and quality of the food. For Christmas in 1935, instead of holiday cards Hines sent his friends a list of his favorite eating spots—167 restaurants in 30 states and the District of Columbia. So many people asked for copies of the list that he decided to write *Adventures in Good Eating*. His opinion was considered completely trustworthy because he always paid for his own meals and lodging and allowed no advertising in his books. Later in his career, he created "Recommended by Duncan Hines" signs and charged restaurants and inns a small fee for the privilege of displaying them (which he monitored and controlled carefully). The presence, absence, or removal of a sign could make or break an establishment: many thousands of travelers ate and slept *only* at places approved by Duncan Hines.

Respect for Hines was so great that in 1950 an entrepreneur named Roy Park came up with the idea of making Duncan Hines a "name brand," and licensed a line of products that included ice cream, pickles, dinnerware, cookbooks, and most famously, cake mixes. Park sold it to Proctor & Gamble in 1956; when Hines died in 1959, the line had expanded to more than 100 products.

The tokay gecko uses its tongue to clean its eyes.

IRONIC, ISN'T IT?

There's nothing like a good dose of irony to put the problems of day-to-day life into proper perspective.

YIELD TO ONCOMING IRONY

• While driving the WDJT news van out to Wisconsin's Big Muskego Lake on a Sunday afternoon in January 2007, 27-year-old Susan Wronsky *thought* she was traveling on an icy road. She was actually driving on top of an iced-over channel that ran parallel to the road. The vehicle broke through the ice and came to rest in the mud on the bottom of the five-foot-deep waterway. The van was totaled, but Wronsky escaped without injury. At the time of the accident, she was covering a story on how to drive safely in icy conditions.

• In the early 1990s, in an effort to convince people to drive safely, British transportation officials placed dozens of signs along the notoriously dangerous A1 highway, displaying the number of road casualties over the previous year. In 2008 the signs were removed. Why? They were distracting drivers and—according to some officials—leading to more road casualties.

CUT-AND-PASTE IRONY

In 2008 University of Texas at San Antonio (UTSA) student Akshay Thusu was assigned to help write the school's new honor code. After it was posted on the Internet for review, many people pointed out that a few key sections of the honor code had been plagiarized—they were exact replicas of honor codes from other schools. (Even the definition of "plagiarism" was plagiarized.) Thusu blamed the goof on an "oversight."

ENVIRONMENTAL IRONY

Richard Treanor and Carolynn Bissett, a married couple in Sunnyvale, California, are concerned about the environment. They point to the grove of eight redwood trees they planted in their backyard as proof. Their neighbor, Mark Vargas, is also concerned about the environment. He installed solar panels on his roof. One problem: Treanor and Bissett's redwoods have grown so tall that they block the sun from hitting Vargas's roof, rendering his expensive solar panels nearly useless. After asking the couple several times to cut down the trees (they refused), Vargas contacted Santa Clara County officials, who cited "California's Solar Shade Control Act," which protects solar panels from shade. Treanor and Bissett were informed that they must remove their trees because, according to the Act, the redwoods have become an "environmental hazard."

FILESHARING IRONY

The Recording Industry Association of America (RIAA) has claimed that music filesharing Internet sites violate the copyrights of musicians, thus cutting into their royalties. After numerous legal battles, the RIAA was awarded nearly $400 million in damages from people who ran the file sharing sites. Yet so far none of that money has been paid to the artists whose copyrights were violated in the first place. So some of these acts (such as the Rolling Stones, Van Halen, and Christina Aguilera) have threatened legal action, but the RIAA says it doesn't have the money—they used it to pay their massive legal bills.

UNSINKABLE IRONY

In 2008 a water main broke in Pittsburgh, Pennsylvania, sending a deluge into the SportsWorks building, which was hosting a high-profile museum exhibit. The water didn't harm the exhibit (thanks to the building's sloped floors), although it did shut it down for a few days. What was the exhibit that proved unsinkable? A collection of artifacts from the *Titanic*.

* * *

SHINY UNHAPPY PEOPLE

Ian Down, 42, of London, England, took some pictures of himself in a photo booth and handed them in with the necessary paperwork when he applied for a passport. The passport clerk looked at the photos...and refused to accept them. Why? Because the glare from Down's bald head was too shiny. The clerk instructed Down that he had to get a new set of photos made, and they had to be glare-free. "It was a little embarrassing," said Down.

Greek philosopher Pliny the Elder believed that the souls of the dead resided in beans.

ODD SUPERHEROES

But are they really any odder than a guy who wears his red underwear over his blue tights or a guy who shoots goo out of his wrists?

BOUNCING BOY. First appearing in a 1961 Action comic, Chuck Taine drank what he thought was a bottle of soda, but it was really a "super-plastic fluid" that gives him the ability to turn into a gigantic bouncing ball. He even gets to join the Legion of Superheroes (sidekicks of Superboy) along with other uniquely powered characters, such as Matter-Eater Lad (his superpower: he can eat anything).

ZSAZSA ZATURNNAH. By day, Ada is the meek owner of a beauty salon in a small town in the Philippines (where the comic originates). At night, he eats a piece of magic rock and transforms himself into Zsazsa, a muscular, curvaceous, crime-fighting woman.

SUPER PRESIDENT. On this 1967 cartoon show, American President James Norcross gets caught in a "cosmic storm" and gains the ability to turn himself into steel, water, stone, or electricity.

SUPERDUPONT. Satirizing French stereotypes, this 1972 French-made superhero is a snooty, mustachioed Frenchman who wears a beret, carries a baguette, drinks red wine, and smokes Gauloise cigarettes. He flies around foiling the schemes of an enemy organization called "Anti-France."

LEECH. His parents abandoned him at birth because he had green skin and hollow eyes. Even his superhero friends (Leech is a minor character in *X-Men* comics) avoid him because his power is to negate the powers of those around him.

AQUANUS. An Indonesian version of Aquaman, he can breathe underwater and communicate with fish. But he can do something Aquaman can't—he can shoot rainbows from his belt.

GENERATION TESLA. In this 1995 Serbian comic, inventor Nikola Tesla transports himself to another dimension and reanimates a bunch of dead people and gives them all superpowers.

About 150 injuries per year are attributed to dustpans.

THE DA VINCI OF DETROIT, PART III

How big an impact did Harley Earl have on car design? Even today, auto stylists in Detroit still utter the phrase, "Our father, who art in styling, Harley be thy name." Here's the final installment of our story. *(Part II is on page 269.)*

REINVENTING THE WHEELS

If there's one person responsible for the evolution of what we think of as an "antique" car into one that begins to resemble what we think of as a modern car today, it's Harley Earl. When he arrived at GM in 1927, mass-produced cars still had a sort of thrown-together look, because that was how they were made: Partially assembled cars rolled along a quickly moving assembly line, and autoworkers raced to attach one component after another—a hood over the engine, fenders and a running board on the frame, headlights on the fenders, and so on, until the car was finished. The trunk of the car was exactly that—little more than a steamer trunk attached behind the passenger compartment.

Earl thought that a car should look like a single, unified whole, not just a bunch of components attached to each other, and he began to impart his vision on GM cars. One by one, the distinguishing features of antique cars began to fall away: Boxy shapes and sharp corners gave way to the curves and smooth, flowing lines of Earl's streamlined bodies. Headlights and fenders were integrated into the bodywork, and so was the trunk—from now on, it would be a trunk in name only. And the spare tire would no longer be bolted to the rear or mounted on one of the running boards (Earl got rid of those, too); it would be hidden *inside* the trunk.

LOW RIDERS

Earl liked to explain that his purpose from the very beginning was to make cars lower and longer, if for no other reason than he thought oblong shapes were more pleasing to the eye than the short, boxy cars that were common when he was starting out. Just as he had with the 1927 LaSalle, Earl began lengthening the

The scientific name for hairs standing on end because of fright is *piloerection*.

wheelbase (the distance between the front and rear wheels) of the cars he worked on. This created enough space between them to lower the passenger compartment so that the occupants were cradled more or less *between* the front and rear wheels instead of on top of them, which is where people had ridden since the horse-and-wagon days. In addition to making the car look nicer, lowering the passenger compartment made for a smoother ride.

WHAT A CONCEPT

The changes that Harley Earl brought to automobiles were dizzying, especially to an auto-buying public that had seen very little change in automobiles since their invention. But Earl was careful to introduce his changes gradually, never making more in a year than he thought customers could adjust to. He had an exquisite sense of just how much he could get away with without alienating potential buyers, and he fine-tuned his judgment by producing the auto industry's first concept cars, which he used to preview his designs with the public and test whether they went too far.

THE HIDEOUT

Earl didn't spend a lot of time at the drafting table himself; instead, he oversaw a network of 17 different design studios, including one for each division of GM and 12 other special studios that made up the Art & Color Division. (Earl renamed it the Style Section in 1937.) He did his thinking in a hidden office he called the "Hatchery," which had blacked-out windows, no telephone, and a phony name on the door so that no one would disturb him there. He came up with the overall strategic vision for his cars, and then worked with the different design studios to bring his ideas to life. An excellent critic of other people's work (which didn't always make him the easiest guy to work with), he pushed and prodded and preached and praised until the designers working under him brought his dreams to life, exactly as he'd envisioned them. (Kind of like Uncle John.)

In the process, Earl oversaw the design of virtually every Chevrolet, Oakland (renamed Pontiac in 1932), Oldsmobile, Buick, and Cadillac designed between 1928 and 1959. The 1949 Cadillac Coupe de Ville, Cadillac's first pillarless hardtop, with no roof support pillar behind the front doors to obstruct the driver's

According to Crayola, American kids between the ages of 2 and 8 spend 28 minutes a day coloring.

vision. The 1953 Cadillac Eldorado and Oldsmobile Fiesta, with the first wraparound windshields. The 1959 Chevy El Camino, General Motors' combination sedan and pickup truck (hey, nobody's perfect), produced in response to the successful Ford Ranchero. All these GM cars, and all the others, too—Harley Earl styled each one.

DREAM MACHINES

A true son of Hollywood, Earl thought of his cars as pieces of entertainment. He wanted people to derive pleasure by looking at them, and he wanted driving them to be a dream. "I try to design a car so that every time you get in it, it's a relief—you have a little vacation for a while," he liked to say.

For all the changes Earl made to his cars, in his early years at GM they still managed to be shaped like cars. But in the 1940s and '50s, his designs became ever bolder, as he drew obvious inspiration from locomotives, airplanes, torpedoes, and eventually even atomic missiles and rocket ships. Airplanes and rockets have tailfins because they *need them*—they'd crash without them. The tailfins (inspired by the Lockheed P-38 Lightning fighter plane) that Earl introduced to automobiles, beginning with the 1948 Cadillac, served no functional purpose at all. Earl couldn't give GM customers a real jet plane or rocket ship to the moon, but he could make them feel like they were flying whenever they got behind the wheel of one of his cars.

Thanks in large part to Earl's influence, the American automobile was no longer just a means of transportation. More than ever, it became a status symbol and an object of desire. People didn't buy cars just because they needed them; they bought them because they *had* to have them, a feeling that lasted until they traded it in on the next model (which they also absolutely had to have).

MR. DETROIT, MR. WORLD

Earl worked for GM for 30 years, from 1927 until his retirement in 1958 after overseeing the development of the 1959 models. If *your* dream car was built by GM in that period—a 1957 Chevy Bel Air convertible, perhaps—you have Earl to thank for it. If your dream car hails from the same era but was built by Ford or Chrysler, or even MG or Citroën, you may *still* have him to thank for it

Have you? 50% of Americans admit they have run a red light.

because his designs proved so successful that virtually every other car company in the world adopted his methods, all the way down to the clay mock-ups he pioneered while he was still building cars for Hollywood film stars. Many of the best-looking cars produced by other automakers were designed by Earl-trained stylists who were lured away from GM.

Few of these designers were able to repeat their mentor's success, and without GM's enormous profits, few of the smaller American auto companies, including Kaiser-Frazer, Hudson, and Nash, could keep up with the pace of annual model changes. They either merged with other struggling companies, or went under. Given GM's problems in recent years, it's easy to forget that by the early 1960s more than half of all cars sold in the United States were made by GM, with Ford and Chrysler divvying up the rest. In those days, GM's biggest fear was being broken up by the federal government for being a monopoly—in that sense, the company was actually selling *too many* cars for its own good.

TOO LITTLE, TOO LATE

On Earl's watch, GM cars became ever bigger, ever longer, ever heavier, ever chrome-ier, and yet toward the end of his career even he apparently began to realize that being bigger, longer, and heavier had its limits. After a trip to a sports car race in 1951, Earl came away so impressed with the enthusiasm that the drivers had for their autos that he talked GM into building the company's first-ever two-seater sports car—the 1953 Corvette, which was substantially smaller than most other GM cars made that year.

By the late 1950s, the story goes, Earl couldn't help but notice as he walked from the parking lot into his office that many of his young designers had taken to driving smaller cars—lots of Corvettes, of course, but also Porsches, Triumphs, Fiats, MGs, and even Volkswagen Beetles, whose most appealing feature to VW buyers was that they weren't anything at all like the cars being sold by Detroit. Small cars were likely to play a big role in the future, Earl thought, and as he approached retirement he pushed GM to begin building more small cars so that fans of these little imports would also have a range of domestic cars to choose from.

Earl succeeded in bringing the Corvette into production, but his theory that smaller cars were the wave of the future did not

The Netherlands has about 10,500 miles of bicycle lanes, complete with their own traffic lights.

win much acceptance at GM. After he retired in 1958, his successors continued grinding out one gas-guzzling land yacht after another, even as the Ford Edsel, described by one historian as the "*Titanic* of Automobiles," flopped in 1957 (taking $250 million of Ford's money with it) and sales of the Volkswagen Beetle—and other small cars like it—continued to climb year after year.

END OF THE ROAD

GM paid (and continues to pay) a heavy price for ignoring Earl's advice and not moving into the small-car business in time to compete with the Japanese automakers. But perhaps the most enduring testimony to Harley Earl's brilliance as a designer is that more than 50 years after he left the company (he died from a stroke in 1969 at the age of 75), his cars are still considered the high-water mark of American automobile design. GM has spent 50 years looking for another designer who could make its buyers feel the same way about brand-new Saturns, Chevys, Pontiacs, Buicks, and Cadillacs as they do about the cars designed during the Earl era. And they haven't found one yet.

* * *

COSMIC QUESTIONS

Why are the elderly called "old people," but children are never called "new people"?

If it's true that we're here to help others, then what are the others here for?

Do all cemetery workers work the graveyard shift?

If they're just stale bread to begin with, why do croutons come in airtight, resealable packages?

How come when asked what things they'd bring to a desert island, no one ever says "a boat"?

When a dog food is "new and improved," how do they know?

If a deaf person goes to court, is it still called a hearing?

How did Noah prevent all those animals from eating each other?

HIGH-TECH UNDERWEAR

Who says underwear should only be clean and comfortable? Here's a look at some strange skivvies with extra built-in features.

PRODUCT: A bra that detects breast cancer
INVENTOR: Professor Elias Siores of the University of Bolton in England
HOW IT WORKS: When tumors form in the breast, they are fed by a large blood supply. Because blood is warm, the tumor is warmer than surrounding tissue. Professor Siores' bra, which is still in development, is fitted with a number of microwave antennae that detect changes in temperature within the breast, a cancer-detecting technique known as thermography. "If we can identify transformations that emanate these heat signatures, we may be able to detect these cancers early," says Siores. He hopes to bring a bra to market sometime after 2012.

PRODUCT: Self-cleaning underwear
INVENTOR: Scientists working for the U.S. Air Force
HOW IT WORKS: Who knew that the largest number of casualties from Operation Desert Storm (1991) would be from bacterial infections? Soldiers in combat don't always have the luxury of being able to change into fresh underwear, if they even *have* a clean pair to change into. Underwear worn day after day in those hot desert conditions turned out to be a significant cause of bacterial infections and discomfort. That prompted the military to take the chemical-repelling techology that it had developed to protect soldiers against biological weapons and apply it to T-shirts and skivvies. The underwear is manufactured by using microwave energy to bond tiny "nanoparticles" to the fibers in the underwear fabric. Then chemicals that repel oil, water, bacteria, and other substances are bonded to the nanoparticles. Result: underwear that is very, very difficult to get dirty, because virtually nothing

will stick to it. And because bacteria never gets established, undergarments made with the stuff can be worn for weeks without washing and without risk to the wearer's health. The materials may soon be used to make sports apparel for civilians.

PRODUCT: Flat-D (for "flatulence-deodorizing") underwear
INVENTOR: Brian Conant, a Postal employee, retired member of the National Guard, and president of Flat-D Innovations
HOW IT WORKS: When Conant was in the National Guard, he participated in a military exercise that required him to wear a suit designed to protect him from chemical weapons. At one point in the exercise Conant ripped a really big one...and was surprised to find that neither he nor anyone else could smell any odor. When he told his wife about it, she replied that she, too, would like to be spared the effects of his toxic gas. So Conant got ahold of an extra chemical suit and experimented with it in his spare time. Result: designs for male and female undergarments, which feature strategically placed, keyhole-shaped activated charcoal pads that absorbs odor. (Conant also sells activated charcoal face masks, for use around people who aren't wearing his underpants.)

PRODUCT: ShotGuard Inner Shorts, which block infrared rays
INVENTOR: Cramer Japan, one of that country's largest sportswear manufacturers
HOW IT WORKS: These undies don't protect against skin cancer, they protect against *hentai* (perverts), who have figured out a way to use camcorders with infrared night vision to "see" through many kinds of fabric, in order to take revealing photographs of unsuspecting women. ShotGuard undies are made with a blend of nylon and polyurethane fabric that are impervious to this kind of photography. Cramer president Takashi Hokazono hopes that "by introducing conditions that make photography more difficult, the number of malicious photographers will decrease."

* * *

"People want economy and they will pay any price to get it."

—Lee Iacocca

LOONEY LAWS

Believe it or not, these laws are real.

• In Providence, Rhode Island, it's illegal to sell toothbrushes on Sundays. (Toothpaste is okay.)

• It's against the law in Washington state to pretend that your parents are rich.

• Women in Corvallis, Oregon, are not legally permitted to drink coffee after 6:00 pm.

• By law, Washington drivers must carry an anchor to be used as an emergency brake.

• In Christiansburg, Virginia, it's a crime to imitate the sound of a police whistle.

• It's against the law in Iowa to charge people to watch a one-armed pianist perform.

• In Missouri, men are legally required to have a permit to shave.

• It's a crime in Long Beach, California, to curse while playing miniature golf.

• It's against the law in Oklahoma to display a hypnotized person in a window.

• In Israel, it's illegal to pick your nose on the Sabbath.

• In Florida, widows may not skydive on Sunday afternoons.

• It's illegal for a woman in Joliet, Illinois, to try on more than six dresses in one store.

• It's okay to wear a fake nose in Aberdeen, Scotland, but only if it doesn't conceal your identity.

• Richmond, Virginia, prohibits anyone from flipping a coin to determine who will pay a restaurant tab.

• A man may not legally wear a strapless evening gown in Miami.

• In Devon, Colorado, it's illegal to walk backwards after sunset.

• In Connecticut, it's against the law to play SCRABBLE while waiting for a politician to speak.

• It's illegal to run a three-legged race for money in British Columbia.

• Eating soup with a fork is against the law in New York.

• It's illegal to sell used confetti in Detroit.

But did they lie to the pollster? According to a survey, 70% of Italians say they tell 7.5 lies per day.

DEATH IN THE RING

While the brutal sport of boxing has existed for thousands of years, historians consider the first modern "boxing match" to be one that took place in England in 1681. Since that era of bare-knuckle fights to today's gloved bouts there have been more than 1,400 documented boxing-related deaths. These are just a few.

GEORGE "THE COACHMAN" STEVENSON. His is one of boxing's earliest recorded deaths, going all the way back to 1741. Stevenson fought Jack Broughton in a bare-knuckle contest that lasted about 40 minutes—with no breaks. Stevenson sustained massive injuries, including several broken ribs and probably bruising to his heart. He died about a month later. The tragedy led Broughton, already a champion for many years and quite wealthy from it (the fight was held in "Broughton's Amphitheater"), to codify rules to make the sport safer, including introducing padded gloves. Broughton is still known as the "Father of Boxing" today.

BILL DAY. Day fought William Tower on November 22, 1784, in London. English sportswriter Pierce Egan described how "Tower caught him in one corner of the stage, and held him fast by one hand, while with the other he nearly annihilated Day." The two fought for about 30 minutes; Day died shortly afterward.

SIMON "THE EMERALD GEM" BYRNE. Irishman Byrne, 27, fought Englishman James "Deaf 'Un" Burke, 24, on May 30, 1833, in Salcey Forest in central England. The two heavyweights fought for more than three hours until the fight was called because Byrne's hands were too damaged for him to continue. He was already near death, but lingered for two more days. The sport was illegal at the time (though wildly popular), so Burke was arrested and charged with murder after the bout, but was later acquitted of the crime.

Karma? Byrne has the dubious distinction of being one of only a few boxers who were on both ends of "death" fights. In 1830 he fought Scotsman Alexander "The Highland Hercules" McKay for

Smallest U.S. city with teams in all four major sports leagues: Denver (population: 2.4 million).

53 minutes, after which McKay died. News of the death caused riots across Scotland, and Byrne was charged with manslaughter. And just as Burke would later be for Byrne's murder, Byrne was acquitted.

CLYDE KAUFMAN. One of only a handful to die after a fight he actually won, Kaufman beat Jerry White on October 3, 1931, in Hollister, California, by a technical knockout in the third round. A short time later he was found unconscious on the ground next to his car. That night he was diagnosed with a concussion; he died the next morning.

BENNY "KID" PARET. Paret, from Cuba, was world welterweight champion when he fought Emile Griffith, an American, on March 24, 1962, in New York City. In the 12th round of the nationally televised fight, Griffith hit Paret a reported 18 times in just six seconds. Paret fell onto the ropes unconscious, and died 10 days later from brain injuries. The death prompted journalist Norman Cousins to pen his now-famous (to boxing aficionados, anyway) essay critical of the sport, "Who Killed Benny Paret," in the May 5, 1962, edition of *Saturday Review*.

DAVEY MOORE. On March 21, 1963, the featherweight champion (and former American Olympic champion) faced Cuban Ultiminio "Sugar" Ramos in Dodger Stadium in Los Angeles. The 29-year-old Moore lost the fight, but he did finish it, and even gave an interview before heading for his dressing room. About 45 minutes later he lapsed into a coma; two days later, he died. Because the fight was nationally televised, his death created a public uproar about the safety of the sport. It got considerably more attention when young folksinger Bob Dylan released a song about the incident, "Who Killed Davey Moore?" just three weeks after the fight.

WILLIE CLASSEN. In October 1979, this 29-year-old New Yorker was knocked out in a fight against legendary British fighter Tony Sibson in London. Just a month later, he fought up-and-coming 21-year-old Wilford Scypion in New York City. Scypion beat him badly, knocking him down a few times, but the fight wasn't stopped. In the 10th round Classen was knocked unconscious. Five days later, on November 28, he was dead.

During soccer's '06 World Cup, Germany's heart attack rate tripled on days the German team played.

DUK-KOO KIM. In one of the modern era's most infamous matches, Korean lightweight Kim, 23, met world champion Ray "Boom Boom" Mancini on November 13, 1982, at Caesar's Palace in Las Vegas. Kim had to lose several pounds shortly before the fight and was reportedly dehydrated. He lasted until the 14th of the scheduled 15 rounds, and collapsed and went into a coma minutes later. Emergency brain surgery was performed that night, but Kim died three days later. The tragedy prompted the World Boxing Council to reduce championship fights from 15 to 12 rounds, and it was the main reason for instituting the standing-8 count—in which the referee stops the fight for eight seconds to determine if a fighter is able to go on. Kim's mother committed suicide in South Korea three months later; the fight's referee, Richard Green, did the same in 1983.

LEAVANDER JOHNSON. Johnson had fought professionally for 16 years when, in 2004, he became the International Boxing Federation lightweight champion at the age of 34. In his first defense, and the biggest fight of his career, he fought Mexico's Jesus Chavez at the MGM Grand in Las Vegas on September 17, 2005. The fight was stopped in the 11th round after Johnson took a number of hard punches to the head. He fell into unconsciousness in the dressing room, was hospitalized with swelling and bleeding on the brain, and died on September 22.

EPILOGUE

The grave of the Scottish boxer Alexander "The Highland Hercules" McKay, who died after a match with Simon Byrne in 1830, lies in an English churchyard not far from where the fight was staged. On it is this inscription:

Strong and athletic was my frame,
Far from my native home I came
And bravely fought with Simon Byrne,
Alas, but never to return.
Stranger, take warning from my fate
Lest you should rue your case too late:
If you have ever fought before,
Determine now to fight no more.

Can't take it? Move to Jersey! There are seven rats for every person in New York City.

UNCLE JOHN'S STALL OF FAME

Here's another in-stall-ment of a Bathroom Reader *favorite.*

Honoree: The town fathers (and mothers) of Chauncy, Ohio

Notable Achievement: Inventing a way to collect taxes in the bathroom

True Story: Don't worry, the program is voluntary...sort of. When the town had trouble coming up with the money to pay its $500-a-month streetlight bill in 2006, rather than pass a mandatory tax increase, the town government decided to try something a little more creative and fun: They got a wooden outhouse, dubbed it the "Redneck Wishing Well," and started putting it on the front lawns of various town residents. When the outhouse landed on someone's lawn, the only way to get the city to haul it away was by tossing a contribution toward the light bill into the "well."

Bonus: After a resident had done their duty, *they* got to pick whose lawn got the outhouse next. In the first two days alone, the wishing well collected $200.

Honoree: The administrators of Frederick Community College in Maryland

Notable Achievement: Standing firm against bathroom blackmail

True Story: In the fall of 2007, someone vandalized one of the men's rooms on campus (even worse, they stole all the toilet paper!) and left a note, threatening to continue trashing toilets until the school rescinded its campuswide ban on smoking. Rather than give in to privvy piracy, the school offered a $500 reward for information leading to the arrest and prosecution of the lavatorial louts.

Update: At last report, the toilet terrorists had struck another dozen times, but the smoking ban is still in effect and the reward is still up for grabs. (Students can still smoke in the parking lot.)

Wild Bill Hickok was buried with his Sharps rifle.

Honoree: Residents of the Po Tin Housing Complex in Tuen Mun, China

Notable Achievement: Refusing to take cramped, substandard bathroom conditions sitting down

True Story: The residents were living in apartments with bathrooms that were barely 2' x 2'. A toilet, sink, and shower were crammed into the tiny space, smaller than a phone booth. "As there is no room in the toilet," one resident explains, "the users need to dry themselves and put on clothes in the dining room after showers. Their family members have to stay on the street until receiving a phone call from home, saying the user is fully dressed." After seven years of waiting for the local housing authority to take action, in October 2007, the fed-up residents staged a protest outside the Legislative Council building, complete with a life-size model bathroom to demonstrate how cramped the facilities are. Did the protest do any good? Hard to say—the Housing Authority admitted that the bathrooms "may not be satisfactory" and promised to consider the residents' request, but at last report the residents were still waiting for action.

Honoree: Adam Baker, an amateur painter from Reno, Nevada

Notable Achievement: Taking life's lemons and making lemonade ...in the bathrooms of every state in the union

True Story: When the 42-year-old Baker learned about a contest to paint the official portrait of Governor Kenny Guinn, Baker poured his heart and soul into a loving depiction of Guinn and sent it off to the state capitol...only to learn that the winner was a painter from *out of state*. Rather than get mad, Baker decided to get even: He took his gubernatorial portrait on an extended road trip to every state capitol building in the country, taking care once he arrived to position Governor Guinn in front of the urinals in the men's room and take a few snapshots. So is his portrait a winner? Look up "Kenny's Big Adventure" on YouTube and decide for yourself. As for the Guinn Administration, a spokesperson says that Baker's tour of restrooms "says a lot of what he thinks about his own work."

Honoree: Hayley Greaves, a 20-year-old fashion and costume craft student at Leicester College in England

Four million embalmed ibises (wading birds) were discovered in a single cemetery in Egypt.

Notable Achievement: Designing a hat with real get-up-and-"go."

True Story: In the summer of 2007, Bathstore, a bathroom retailer, sponsored a contest to design a ladies' hat to be worn at the Ascot Gold Cup in Berkshire, England. The horse race, which is attended by the Queen, is one of the highlights of the British social season. More attention is paid to what people in the Royal Enclosure are wearing than to which horse is winning the race, and there's a dress code that requires that all ladies wear hats. With her sponsor in mind, Greaves came up with a splashy number that featured an entire bathroom—bath, sink, and toilet, plus two walls and a tiled floor—atop the hat…and her creation won first prize. "Hayley's hat was beautifully constructed and eye-catching and just what we were looking for," said a spokesperson for Bathstore. "I'm sure it will turn a few heads at the races."

Honoree: A two-year-old Australian boy, identified only as Seth, who lives in the town of Bendingo

Notable Achievement: His curiosity killed a commode

True Story: When Seth finishes his baths, he likes to stick his fingers down the drain to feel the suction of the water as it drains away. Most of the time, the results are unremarkable, but one afternoon in July 2008 was different—Seth got two fingers stuck in the drain, and his parents couldn't get them out. They called paramedics, but every time they tried to free Seth's fingers, he cried out in pain. The only solution: remove the pipe from the tub. The only problem: To do that, they had to rip out the tub (and the wall) to get at the underside of the pipe. It took six hours, a hacksaw, a trip to the emergency room, and a set of hydraulic spreaders, but in the end the kid escaped mostly unscathed (unlike his parents' bathroom), with no cuts or bruises and just one blister.

* * *

POP CULTURE QUIZ

Q: Who is the only movie character to appear on the American Film Institute's "50 Greatest Heroes" *and* "50 Greatest Villains" lists?

A: The Terminator.

The Purefoods Tender Juicy Giants, a basketball team in the Philippines, is named after a hot dog.

THE MAGNA CARTA

Most people have heard of it—maybe in a ninth-grade history class or on Jeopardy! *last week. But what is it? Answer: a piece of writing that has helped shaped governments for 800 years.*

BACKGROUND

When asked to name the most important documents in Western civilization, historians almost always include the Magna Carta. What's so important about it? Many people assume that this landmark document, written in 1215, helped advance human rights and led directly to the Declaration of Independence and the U.S. Constitution. Not quite. The Magna Carta actually wasn't intended to help the common man, but it did mark the first time in history that written law challenged the absolute power of a monarch, and the first time that governments, even kings, could be held accountable for their actions. Without that, modern democracy would not exist.

STRUGGLE FOR THE THRONE

In 1002 Ethelred II, the Anglo-Saxon king of England, married Emma, the daughter of the duke of Normandy (now a region of northern France). The marriage created a blood alliance between these two kingdoms, designed to unite them against invasion by the Vikings. In 1066 the next king of England, Edward the Confessor (an Anglo-Saxon) died, leaving no heirs. That left the door open for the *Norman* bloodline (the one descended from Emma) to make a claim for the throne of England. William, the duke of Normandy, invaded and conquered England.

When William (known today as William the Conqueror) officially became king of England, he installed a *feudal* system. Norman troops who had fought on William's side were given English lands as a reward for their loyalty, and they became *barons*. According to the feudal system, anyone who lived within the baron's jurisdiction was obliged to pay taxes to the baron and serve in his militia. The barons, in turn, paid taxes to the king.

England operated that way until 1199, when King Richard the Lionheart died and his brother, John, claimed the throne. John, the youngest son in the royal family, actually ranked beneath his nephew, Arthur of Brittany, in the order of succession. So how did he become king? Arthur disappeared and John took the throne by force. This enraged the barons, but what could they do? They couldn't fight the king of England...or could they?

FOOL'S PARADISE

Two incidents ultimately drove the barons to challenge the king.

Royal Error #1: In 1207 John appointed the Bishop of Norwich, John de Gray, Archbishop of Canterbury, the Catholic Church's highest representative in England. Traditionally, the king consulted with the bishops of England before making that appointment... but John didn't do that. The bishops protested to Pope Innocent III, who then put his own man, Stephen Langton, in the position. Infuriated that his power had been usurped, King John banished the council of bishops from England. In retaliation, Pope Innocent III excommunicated John (and, by extension, all of England) from the Church. The barons urged John to make amends, which he did...sort of. The Pope agreed to reinstate King John (and England). His price: England itself. The Church would *own* England and John would be little more than a local governor. In addition, the Church levied a huge tax on England. Where would John get the money? From the barons.

Royal error #2: In 1206 French forces seized the region of Normandy. Because it was their ancestral homeland, the barons demanded John send troops to reclaim it. He delayed for eight years before finally leading the English army into the occupied territories himself. England lost; France kept the land.

REBELLION

Upon hearing of the defeat, the barons became furious. They banded together in 1215 (while John was traveling back from France) and decided it was time to take action against the king. Using as a basis the "Charter of Liberties," a ceremonial document issued by King Henry I at his coronation in 1100, they created a new document—one that would be legally binding. Its essence: The king's power would no longer be absolute. He would be accountable for his actions, and the barons would have a say in decision-making.

John returned to London that June to find that the barons had taken control of the city. There was only one way for the king to get his country back: submit to the barons' 63 written demands. In return, the barons offered to sign a pledge of loyalty to King John. The resultant document—all of it in Latin—was called the "Great Charter," or *Magna Carta.*

THE DOCUMENT

Most of those 63 demands relate very specifically to life in 13th-century England. One, for example, repealed a tax on loans inherited by minors; another opened up royal hunting lands to barons. But two sections had a much broader impact.

- Clause 61 called for a committee of barons that could meet at any time to overrule the king's actions, by force if necessary.
- Clause 39—the only part of the Magna Carta that could be applied to a commoner (it prevented the king from jailing anyone or seizing property without proper cause or a fair trial, also known as *habeas corpus*—translation: "you must have the body").

John wasn't about to surrender authority, even with armed barons breathing down his neck. He signed the Magna Carta just to satisfy them. (The ceremony took place on June 15, 1215, under a tree in Runnymede, a meadow in London not far from Buckingham Palace.) But as soon as the barons relinquished control of England and left London, he renounced the document and then appealed to Pope Innocent III, who technically still ruled England. The Pope declared the Magna Carta null and void.

A NEW HOPE

When the barons learned of John's treachery, they declared civil war. But the conflict was brief: King John died in 1216 and was replaced by his nine-year-old son, Henry III. The barons called a truce when the Magna Carta was reissued under Henry's name, although with sections removed, notably Clause 61, the "committee of barons" rule. In 1225 Henry (now 18 years old) pared it down to only 37 clauses. But since he respected the basics of the charter—staying out of Church and baronial affairs—the relationship between the crown and the barons remained smooth. Over Henry's 56-year reign, the document's principles became part of England's legal tradition, an accepted system of assumed rights and laws commonly referred to as "English common law."

...and have less stress and fewer heart attacks than people who don't have pets.

COMING TO AMERICA

In 1765 England needed money to pay for the troops that protected its American colonies. Parliament decided that the colonies should foot the bill, so it passed the Stamp Act, which placed a tax on written materials sold in the colonies, including newspapers, pamphlets, contracts, licenses, and playing cards. Colonists objected to being taxed by an assembly thousands of miles away in which they didn't even have a representative.

The Massachusetts Assembly declared that taxation without representation violated "the natural rights of Englishmen," by which it meant the Magna Carta, the document which had guided the moral code of governing for more than 500 years. That was the first of several colonial challenges to the throne (culminating in the American Revolution), fueled by the Magna Carta's thesis that leaders are not above the law.

In addition to its philosophical influence, a few clauses of the Magna Carta actually became part of American government. Clause 39, or *habeas corpus*, providing that arrests and trials of citizens must have merit, is found in Article One of the U.S. Constitution. And Clause 61, which called for a committee of barons to oversee the king's actions, inspired the "checks and balances" system by which various branches of U.S. government—executive, judicial, and legislative—have oversight of each other to ensure that none of them becomes too powerful.

LASTING IMPACT

What became of the actual physical document? There never was one "master" Magna Carta—42 copies were made and signed, one for each of the barons and two for the king. Amazingly, four of those 42 copies still exist. One is on display at the Houses of Parliament, one is in the British Library, and one is in a cathedral in Salisbury, England. The fourth copy is usually housed at Lincoln Cathedral in Lincolnshire, but is occasionally loaned out. It was shown at the New York World's Fair in 1939 and in 2007 at the 400th anniversary celebration of Jamestown, the first English colony in North America, where it was presented as a link between the old world of England and the new world of America.

Fort Knox is a classified facility. No visitors are permitted, and no exceptions are made.

MAKING A MOVIE, PT. IV: PHOTOGRAPHY

Our big-budget motion picture is finally ready to begin filming. Here are but a few of the hundreds of people who make it happen. (Part III is on page 330.)

THE VISUAL STORYTELLERS

Filming is actually the quickest aspect of movie-making, usually taking only one to three months of the entire process. Adhering to a strict schedule of "get the shot done and move on to the next," the filmmakers assemble the many pieces that will be put together and cleaned up in postproduction. Yet many successful movies—ones that appeal to both viewers *and* critics—will report having had a close-knit crew. The actors say that this production was "different" and "special." Everyone talks about how much fun it was to shoot. Well, for that to happen, it all starts with the single most important person on any movie set.

THE DIRECTOR

Responsible for the tone, pacing, and overall vision of the film, the director has the job of taking what's in the script and translating it to the screen. While his or her primary duty is assisting the actors in their delivery of lines, the director is also usually the last person to sign off on every aspect of the production, from preproduction to the final sound mix. In many cases, especially within the studio system, the producer or the studio can usurp the director's power in an attempt to make the finished product more marketable and more appealing to a mass audience, which is why many experienced directors prefer to take on the producing duties as well. Still, it is the director—not the producers—whom the actors and crew rely on to keep them all on the same page.

DIRECTOR OF PHOTOGRAPHY

Often the director's closest collaborator, the DP is responsible for the film's composition (how everything appears in the frame), its color palette, and how light or dark each scene is. Some directors are very specific about how they want the film to look, meaning

The 16th-century El Escorial palace of King Phillip II of Spain had 1,200 doors.

that the DP simply executes their orders, while other directors are more focused on the acting and give the DP creative license. Either way, DPs are in charge of making sure that the cameras, lenses, and film stock are available and in working order, and see to it that the film is processed after every scene so that the director can review the *dailies*. (Two terms that are often intertwined are the director of photography and the *cinematographer*. If both are listed in a movie's credits, it is usually the DP who oversees the camera crew and the cinematographer who is in charge of the composition and camera moves for each shot.)

Reel-Life Example: Wanting their 2000 comedy, *O Brother, Where Art Thou?*, to look like a "fable," directors Joel and Ethan Coen charged DP Roger Deakins with the task of creating a sepia-toned look, complete with yellow trees and amber skies. One big problem: they were filming in Mississippi during the summer, when the trees were green and the skies blue. After trying various photo-chemical processes—including bleaching the film—Deakins realized that the look couldn't be achieved through conventional means. Result: *O Brother* marked the first time that an entire film was digitally colored. The process took two months to complete.

Did it work? Yes. Critics and audiences loved the quirky film; Deakins was nominated for an Oscar. More praise: Robert Allen of the International Cinematographers Guild wrote that "historians will look back on *O Brother, Where Art Thou?* as a milestone."

MIDDLE MANAGEMENT

Movie sets are chaotic—hundreds of workers, each in charge of a specific task, work on different scenes simultaneously, often out of sequence, most not even aware of the storyline. Here are those whose job it is to keep the chaos in order.

• **Assistant Director.** If you were to visit a movie set, you might mistake the AD for the director—they're usually the loudest, barking orders and yelling "roll" and "cut" while the director sits quietly in a chair looking at a monitor. That's the AD's job—to let the director stay focused on the story being told. The AD must always stay one step ahead, so when the time comes for the cameras to roll, everyone and everything is ready to go. The AD sets the day's schedule and prepares *call sheets*, a list of which actors are needed for the scenes being shot. In addition, the AD relays instructions

Wide load: In 1970 Americans spent $6 billion on fast food; in 2001 they spent over $110 billion.

from the director to the other department heads, including the *1st AD* and *2nd AD*, who do the same thing for the AD that the AD does for the director. Their most important job is setting up and directing the extras.

• **Production Coordinator.** Responsible for maintaining the schedule and making sure the cast and crew are fed and have accommodations while on location.

• **Location Manager.** When a huge film crew takes over a location such as a small town, a city street, or a tourist attraction, the location manager obtains all required permits, heads up the security department, and keeps the locals happy. (On some productions, the location scout stays on as the location manager; on others a separate person is hired.)

• **Script Supervisor.** Responsible for *continuity*, the script supervisor views every single take of a scene—which can begin on location and continue weeks later on a soundstage—to ensure that the lighting, props, hair, makeup, and costumes don't change drastically between takes. The script supervisor also notes when what's been filmed differs from what's in the script.

• **Costume Supervisor.** In charge of the *costumers*, who see to it that the actors' clothes are always in the desired condition. This sometimes requires "aging" a new garment so it looks worn in. Along with the *hairstylist* and *makeup supervisor*, the costumers are in nearly constant contact with the actors—from seconds before the cameras roll to seconds after they cut. On special effects films that require prosthetics, this can be a very large department with many skilled craftspeople working around the clock.

• **Production Assistant.** Basically, they're gofers, ready to do anything that needs to be done. They may run a broken doorknob back to the prop department, or make sure the producer gets his half-decaf double latté with two sugars and no foam. On big-budget movies, each of the principal cast and crew members gets their own PA.

THE TECHNICAL CREW

This group must work together as if they are a single person, because it only takes one little goof to cause the entire scene to be re-set (extras and all) and the shot done over.

• **Clapper-loader.** Loads the film stock into the camera and also

Some 50,000 Canadians fought in the American Civil War, including about 200 for the South.

claps the *slate* (or *clapboard*) before each take (on larger productions, separate people are hired for these jobs). The original use of the slate was to sync up the audio and visual for editing, but with digital technology this is no longer necessary. Still, the slate remains, mostly as tradition, but it does contain necessary information—the scene and take numbers and the date and time.

• **Camera Operator.** Whether following the action on foot with a steady-cam or perched up in a crane zooming out for a wide shot, the camera operator must have not only extensive technical knowledge of the cameras and lenses but a creative eye as well. Larger productions have multiple camera operators.

• **Focus Puller.** Because a movie is designed to be projected on a very large screen, it is essential that the lenses are focused perfectly. The focus puller sits beside the camera and adjusts the focus, based on predetermined calculations. Along with the AD, they arrive on set early to rehearse the upcoming scene, or *block* it, with stand-ins to determine focus and camera movements.

• **Grips.** Led by the *key grip* and including the *dolly grips*, this crew of strong backs is in charge of setting up and breaking down all of the production equipment, including the cameras, cranes, and *dollies* (small train tracks for shots that require the camera to follow the action). Grips also set up the lighting system, which includes the lights, huge diffusers and reflectors, and heavy fabric used to *tent out* windows to keep out extraneous light.

• **Gaffers.** Working closely with the grips, the gaffers are the on-set electricians. They make sure that the lighting systems, cameras, dollies, cranes, fans, rain and wind machines, and video playback monitors are all wired correctly. Because of the enormous amount of power needed to run the equipment, gaffers must be experts, making sure that no fuses blow, which would delay production.

• **Best Boy.** This can be either gender and is divided into two categories: *best boy grip* and *best boy electric*, working as an assistant to the key grip and gaffer, respectively. Larger productions have multiple best boys. Their duties are often determined by what's needed at any given time, be it unloading equipment from a truck or finding a larger fan because the director wants even *more* wind.

• **Location Mixer.** Although very few sounds (footsteps, breaking glass, traffic, etc.) recorded on set in modern feature films ever make it to the final cut, most of the dialogue does: It must be recorded

Éclair means "lightning" in French.

clearly so that the editors, sound designers, and actors can reference them later in postproduction. The *boom operators* stand just outside of the shooting area holding long microphones over the top of the action while the location mixer monitors the scene with headphones.

• **Second Unit Director.** The *second* unit films any shot in which the principal actors are not needed, such as a close-up of an object, an explosion, crowds, or background scenery. On a larger production, third and even fourth units may be necessary.

• **Leadman.** In charge of the *swing gang*, the construction crew that builds and breaks down the sets. Next come the *set dressers* to add in objects such as furniture and wallpaper, as well as matte paintings (photorealistic murals used to convey distant locations) and green screens (monochrome curtains that will be replaced digitally in postproduction). The swing gang is already gone and working on the next set when the crew arrives to film.

• **Stunt Coordinator.** Not only choreographs the stunt performers for any shot deemed too dangerous for the actors, but must ensure the safety of the actors when they insist on doing their own stunts.

• **Wranglers.** In charge of any nonhuman performers.

• **Still Photographer.** Takes pictures for various purposes: framed photographs that will end up in the movie, promotional photos for advertising, as well as reference pics to aid in continuity.

• **Caterers.** Provide all of the meals for a legion of hungry people.

• **Transportation Coordinator.** In charge of getting the principal actors to and from the set each day as well as assembling a convoy of semitrucks—and sometimes airplanes—to transport the equipment to the location.

For Part V, go to page 531.

*　　*　　*

Reel-Life Wrangling Example: On the set of *The Shawshank Redemption* (1994), animal trainer Scott Hart set up a shot in which Brooks (James Whitmore) feeds a maggot to his pet crow. Per requirement, a Humane Society representative monitored the shoot to see that no animals were harmed—and deemed the scene "cruel" to the maggot. The only solution: They had to wait for the maggot to die of "natural causes" before the shot could be filmed.

"WE'RE LOOKING FOR PEOPLE WHO LIKE TO DRAW"

Most of us are suckers for a sales pitch that promises to make us smarter, slimmer, better-looking, or richer—it's human nature. That's probably why these guys were so successful.

FROM THE COMFORT OF YOUR OWN HOME

In 1948 Albert Dorne, a well-known and highly paid American illustrator and advertising artist at the time, came up with a home-study program to teach wannabe commercial artists to draw, paint, illustrate, and cartoon. He called it the Famous Artists School (FAS) and enlisted eleven other "famous artists" as founders. "We're looking for people who like to draw," they confided in full-page ads in magazines and newspapers. "If you have talent, you can be trained for success and security. Find out with our FREE ART TALENT TEST." And the ads, put together by a high-powered New York advertising agency, showed photos of the FAS's biggest selling points: the twelve famous illustrators who were also the school's principal shareholders, surrounded by the tools of their trade, looking prosperous, contented, and friendly.

THE FOUNDING FATHERS

Dorne was born in poverty in 1904 on New York's Lower East Side. He quit school after the seventh grade to support his mother and three siblings, slaving at menial jobs while longing to become an artist. Working in an artist's studio and teaching himself to draw turned his life around; by the time he was 22, Dorne was earning $500 a week (a huge sum in the 1920s) doing magazine illustration, and he went on to become one of the highest-paid, most sought-after illustrators in America. Throughout his career, he took an interest in younger artists. Art was Dorne's way out of poverty, and he wanted to share it with others. But he also saw that sharing his enthusiasm for his craft could be a way to make money for himself.

The world's first veterinary school was founded in 1762 by King Louis XV of France.

The other eleven founders of the Famous Artists School were Norman Rockwell, Jon Whitcomb, Stevan Dohanos, Robert Fawcett, John Atherton, Ben Stahl, Al Parker, Harold Von Schmidt, Fred Ludekens, Peter Helck, and Austin Briggs. All were commercial artists making substantial incomes as illustrators for magazines, books, and advertising, and all were household names. Their familiar signatures were found on the pages of the top magazines of early and mid-20th-century America: *Saturday Evening Post*, *Life*, *Harper's Monthly*, *Boy's Life*, *Cosmopolitan*, *Esquire*, *Fortune*, *Good Housekeeping*, *McCall's*, and many others. Their success stories proved that anyone with talent and drive could make it in the world of commercial art.

I CAN MAKE YOU A STAR

Dorne promised that he and his very successful colleagues would share the secrets of their studios and the tricks of their trade. For a tuition fee (nonrefundable), the Famous Artists School promised enrollees a set of special textbooks written by the founders, a series of sequential mail-in assignments, and return-mail critiques of the completed work. Here's where things got a little fuzzy: it sounded, from the ads, as if students were going to get evaluations from the famous founding artists. Not true: Instead, less-known and totally *unknown* freelance artists wrote the critiques. The founders periodically dropped by the office to review the *instructors'* work, but aside from those brief visits, their main role was simply to profit hugely from their stockholdings in the school. Dorne himself kept a pristine mahogany drawing board at the school's headquarters in Westport, Connecticut—not to work at, but just to show off to the visiting students who regularly toured the premises.

BUT IS IT ART?

Dorne and his co-founders all worked in realistic style, and he figured that was what students wanted to learn. So the school offered three courses: Painting, Illustration/Design, and Cartooning. Each course comprised 24 lessons. The instruction books began with basic techniques and worked up to more complex ones—the first few lessons, for example, were on materials and their use, simple anatomy and figure drawing, and perspective.

Most widely worshipped Roman god: Mars, the god of war.

These are all subjects a student would find at any fine-art school. But the Famous Artists School was selling fame and fortune—not fine art—so the lessons quickly moved into subjects that reflected their students' interest in the commercial art world: draperies, costumes, animal anatomy, the human figure in motion, one called "Pretty Girls," and another called "Today's Men and Women."

ADMAN WITH A PLAN

The Famous Artists School put a lot of money into magazine ads, each featuring one or more of the famous founders of the school. Dorne's pitch:

> We found that many men and women who should have become artists—didn't. Most of them hesitated to find out how much hidden art talent they had. Others who knew they had talent simply couldn't get topnotch professional art training without leaving home or giving up their jobs. My colleagues and I decided to do something about this.

Dorne was appealing to the timid, the fearful, and the stuck-in-a-rut—exactly what he and the founders had *not* been when they'd launched their own careers. But it worked, not least because the rest of the ad was packed with success stories (undocumented) of FAS "graduates" who had embarked (supposedly) on lucrative careers in ad agencies, art studios, and design departments, or worked as freelancers for greeting card companies, galleries, newspapers, and magazines. The same success stories were repeated, ad after ad, but thousands of people still took the free art talent test to qualify for admission to the school. Rarely was any test-taker revealed to have no talent.

In 1948, the founding year, a two-year course in Painting, Cartooning, or Illustration/Design cost $300, payable in monthly installments (plus an extra $11.50 for art supplies). To an aspiring commercial artist, that would have seemed like a small investment compared to the possible returns, since the ads also claimed that the market for illustrators and designers was wide open, waiting to be tapped. "Never before has there been such a demand for artists to fill high-paid jobs," read an ad from 1954, ostensibly written by Jon Whitcomb, "famous illustrator of glamour girls and faculty member of the Famous Artists Course."

Human lice must feed every 24 hours or they will starve to death. (Eww!)

There's no evidence (other than the dubious endorsements in the ads) that FAS students ever actually found those highly paid jobs.

GET IT IN WRITING

The financial success of the Famous Artists School got Dorne thinking about more ways to make money using the FAS model. Moving from the world of art to the world of writing seemed logical, so in 1961 Dorne and two luminaries from the publishing world, Bennett Cerf (Random House's publisher) and Gordon Carroll (a *Reader's Digest* editor), came up with the Famous Writers School (FWS). This time they had a "guiding faculty" of 15, including Rod Serling (of *Twilight Zone* fame), Bruce Catton (Civil War historian), Faith Baldwin (best-selling romance novelist), Mignon G. Eberhart (best-selling mystery writer), J.D. Ratcliff (nonfiction author), Red Smith (popular sports writer), and others. They offered "an opportunity to have your writing talent tested by a group of America's most successful authors" by taking the Famous Writers Aptitude Test.

"What every creative person should know about writing for money" was the come-on in the ads, and the pitch for the FWS was basically the same as the one for the FAS: Discover your hidden talent, take the home study course, get a great job in the field, and make a bundle of money. The ads assured budding writers that jobs were plentiful, salaries were high, and markets were numerous. And there were the usual success stories "documented" in the ads as well. The only problem: None of it was true.

NAILING THE BAD GUYS

In 1970 muckraking journalist Jessica Mitford wrote a piece titled "Let Us Now Appraise Famous Writers" for the July issue of the *Atlantic Monthly*. She didn't mince words.

"How," she asked, "can Bennett Cerf and his renowned colleagues find time to grade all the thousands of aptitude tests that must come pouring in, and on top of that fulfill their pledge to 'teach you to write successfully at home'? What are the standards for admission to the school? How many graduates actually find their way into the 'huge market that will pay well for pieces of almost any length,' which, says J.D. Ratcliff, exists for the begin-

John Lennon shoplifted the harmonica that he played on the song "Love Me Do."

ning writer? What are the 'secrets of success' that the Famous Fifteen say they have 'poured into a set of specially created textbooks'? And how much does it cost to be initiated into these secrets?"

THE AWFUL TRUTH

The answers to Mitford's questions were shocking, as her research clearly showed. The 15 guiding faculty members had absolutely nothing to do with either grading the aptitude tests or teaching anyone anything about writing. The admission standards were nonexistent beyond an ability to pay for the course, and high-pressure salespeople weren't above coercing gullible would-be writers into forking over their money once they'd passed the "aptitude test." According to an Authors League study, at the time the average freelancer was earning not the big fees promised by the Famous Writers School but roughly $3,000 per year—an income barely above the poverty level. And the cost of one course was $785 ($900 if paid in installments). That may not sound like a lot, but compare it (as Mitford did) with the $35 that the University of California Extension at Berkeley charged for a 15-lesson home study short-story-writing course. Mitford wrote:

> What have the Famous Fifteen to say for themselves about all of this? Precious little, it turns out. Most of those with whom I spoke were quick to disavow any responsibility for the school's day-to-day operating methods and were unable to answer the most rudimentary questions: qualifications for admission, teacher-student ratio, cost of the course. They seemed astonished, even pained to think people might be naïve enough to take the advertising at face value.

In 1969, only a year before Mitford's article came out, the FWS had tuition revenues of $48 million, and the school's stock hit $40 per share. The article was picked up by newspapers and circulated to high schools and had national television shows clamoring to interview Mitford. Result: The Famous Writers School's stock steadily lost value, and in 1972 it filed for bankruptcy.

WHERE ARE THEY NOW?

But only a few years later the school was, Mitford lamented,

People born under the zodiac sign Sagittarius make fewer insurance claims than any other sign.

"creeping back," and in 1981 both the Famous Artists School and the Famous Writers School were acquired by Cortina Learning International, a company that specializes in home study courses for foreign languages. They still offer the instructional textbooks and the critiques by professional artists and writers. But now students who are "stuck or need some answers" can contact their instructors by e-mail, snail mail, or toll-free telephone number. The advertising for each school emphasizes the acquisition of skills rather than the pie-in-the-sky financial success and publication that figured so largely in the advertising of the past. "Unleash your inner artist. Learn the secrets of famous artists; study at your own pace," reads a current online ad for the FAS. Cortina isn't making any unrealistic claims for its courses. There's not a word about jobs, markets, or stardom.

* * *

WHY ARE YOU YELLING AT ME, BILLY MAYS?

Do you know Mays? He's the burly, bearded man in a denim shirt who hawks products on TV commercials, infomercials, and home shopping channels, usually shouting superlatives about the product. Here's a sampling of the stuff Mays has sold:

- HandySwitch: a remote control for a lamp
- Mighty Putty: strong glue
- Steam Buddy: a handheld clothes steamer
- Fix It: a car scratch remover
- Liquid Diamond: car polish
- Samurai Sharp: a knife sharpener
- Engrave It: an engraving tool
- OxiClean: clothing detergent
- Six Shooter: a cordless electric screwdriver
- Lint-B-Gone: a lint removing brush
- Awesome Auger: a hole-digger/weed-wacker
- Zorbeez: super-absorbent towels
- Hercules Hook: a superstrong hook that holds up to 150 pounds
- Turbo Tiger: a vacuum cleaner
- Orange Glo: an all-purpose cleanser made from orange oil
- Kaboom!: tile cleaner

Sound travels 15 times faster through steel than through air.

MORE POLITICAL ANIMALS

A few more "tails" of elected officials who weren't quite human.

BOSTON CURTIS

On September 13, 1938, in the small town of Milton, Washington, 52 citizens voted for Boston Curtis to serve as their Republican precinct committee member. Curtis hadn't bothered to campaign, but since he ran unopposed, he won 52 to 0. When results of the election were announced, the town was shocked to learn that they'd voted for a mule. Milton's mayor, Kenneth "Catsup" Simmons (a Democrat), was the mastermind behind the election. He'd brought Boston to the courthouse, inked one of his hooves, and used the mule's hoofprint as a signature for all the legal documents needed to register a candidate. Boston was registered as "Boston Curtis" because he belonged to Mrs. Charles Curtis, who lived in town. Simmons told the press (including *Time* magazine) that he ran Boston to make a serious point: Primary elections were a problem because voters often didn't even know who they were voting for. But people who knew the mayor claimed that he'd also done it to trick the town's Republicans into voting for an animal that resembled the donkey—the mascot of the Democratic party.

BOSCO

If animals can run for office—and win—what happens when they actually get to serve out their terms? The answer lies in the hamlet of Sunol, a tiny rural community located east of San Francisco. In 1981 two locals were arguing over which of them would make a better mayor and decided to hold an unofficial election to settle the dispute. Another local, Brad Leber, entered his dog Bosco, a Labrador-Rottweiler mutt, who ran as a "Puplican" with the platform of "A bone in every dish, a cat in every tree, and a fire hydrant on every street corner." And when all the votes were counted, Bosco was the new honorary mayor.

In 1981 few people, even in San Francisco, knew much about

Sunol. That changed after Bosco's election made world news. The Chinese newspaper *People's Daily* reported that Bosco was proof that Western democracy was a failed system—it couldn't even distinguish between people and dogs. Sunol residents, now the focus of international controversy, retorted that the newspaper had no sense of humor. Bosco served the community, mainly by being himself. Residents enjoyed "bribing" the mayor with beef jerky or ice cream. Tourists were encouraged to pet him. He made the spotlight again when he appeared on *The Third Degree*, a TV game show where celebrity panelists tried to guess his occupation (they failed). And the national media—including Tom Brokaw of NBC—would sometimes meet with Bosco for an "interview." Bosco was such a success that Sunolians reelected him six times. He was mayor until 1994, when he died at age 15. He is memorialized in the Sunol restaurant Bosco's Bones & Brew, where a life-size replica stands atop the bar and dispenses beer with a lift of its leg.

LLAMAS AND DONKEYS AND GOATS (OH, MY!)

Four-legged mayors have presided over several other communities across the United States.

• Clay Henry III is the third generation of goats to be mayor of Lajitas, Texas. Clay III also reportedly drinks beer—30 or 40 a day. (Really.)

• A donkey named Paco Bell out-campaigned a llama to remain the mayor of Florissant, Colorado.

• A goat named Opie won the 2004 mayoral election in Anza, California. "Opie stands for why so many people moved out here," said one local resident. "We don't want some human sitting on a throne."

• Rabbit Hash, Kentucky, elected a dog named Junior Cochran as its mayor. Twice. (He beat out another dog and a donkey.)

* * *

"Sometimes when you sacrifice something precious, you're not really losing it. You're just passing it on to somebody else."

—Mitch Albom

THE COMSTOCK LODE, PART IV

So you think you'd like to own an interest in a gold and silver mine? Be careful what you wish for. Here's the final installment of our story. *(Part III is on page 338.)*

HAND OVER FIST

In all, more than $320 million worth of gold and silver ore was pulled from the Comstock Lode between 1859 and 1878, the equivalent of between $400 and 480 *billion* today. (By comparison, in 2007 Microsoft Corporation had revenues of $51 billion.) And yet for all the wealth that came out of the mines, the overwhelming majority of investors who bought stock in the mining companies over the years *lost* money in the bargain.

Part of this was due to the fact that the operating costs of the mines were staggering. The mines consumed an enormous amount of resources, including millions of pounds of mercury and other chemicals (used to extract the gold from the ore), more than 600 million board feet of timber, and another 2 million cords of firewood. Wages in Virginia City were some of the highest in the world—compensation for the remote location, the dangers of most mining jobs, and the high cost of living in a community where nearly all of the goods and supplies were brought in from hundreds or thousands of miles away.

IN THE HOLE

As the mine shafts got deeper—the deepest reached nearly ¾ of a mile down—the cost of operating the mines soared higher. At these depths, the mines were constantly at risk of flooding with scalding geothermally heated water. Giant, locomotive-sized water pumps had to be lowered into the shafts to get the water up and out of the mines; the largest of these pumps removed more than a million gallons of water per day. And yet even when the water was removed and cooler fresh air was pumped in from the surface, the temperatures at those depths remained so high that the miners could only work for a few minutes at a stretch before retreating into "cooling-off rooms" to douse themselves with ice water.

THE BUBBLE BARONS

But the biggest reason for the investors' losing their shirts was the fact that the owners of the mines were more interested in manipulating stock prices than they were in running their companies responsibly. Time and again, when a fresh deposit of rich ore was discovered, the owners had it mined and processed into bullion as rapidly as possible, even at the expense of damaging the deposit and losing gold and silver through inefficient processing methods. The owners did this to generate as much hype over new discoveries as possible, causing share prices to soar in a speculative bubble.

Then, when the prices peaked, the owners would unload shares on the market and reap a fortune, and then earn even more money when the price began to drop, through a process known as *short selling*. During one run-up of prices in 1872, the share price of the Belcher mine rose from $300 to $1,575 before crashing back to $108, all in the span of eight months.

Ordinary investors often lost the most money when the mines were the most productive, as speculative mania drove prices so high that no amount of gold or silver recovered could have justified the absurd prices paid for shares. Even when the investors were lucky enough to receive dividends from their shares, many used the money to buy more stock, setting themselves up for even bigger losses when the stock tanked.

HIGH TIMES

So why did investors continue to buy shares in the mines year after year? For the same reason that people buy lottery tickets—even if most people are losing, the fortunes made by the handful of winners were so tantalizing that people gladly took the risk. Besides, money can be made in a rising stock market even if the shares aren't worth what people pay for them. So what if a $1,400 share in a mine is really only worth $140? As long as the investor can find someone willing to pay $1,500 for it, the $100 profit is just as real as if the seller had pulled $100 worth of silver and gold out of the mine. Nobody really minded that the shares weren't worth their asking prices, at least not as long as prices kept rising.

...is greater than its polar circumference (24,859 miles).

The cycles of boom and bust continued for nearly 20 years, thanks to the fact that whenever one deposit of valuable ore seemed about to peter out, a new one would be discovered and the process would repeat itself. Sixteen different major discoveries were made over the years—the last one, called the Consolidated Virginia Bonanza, was uncovered at the 1,200-foot level in 1873. At the peak of its output in 1876, the Consolidated Virginia paid out $1,080,000 in dividends per month. But the good times didn't last for long: When the Consolidated Virginia was excavated down to the 1,650-foot level in 1877, the ore suddenly ran out.

THE END?

Eighteen years and $320 million worth of silver and gold after the first discovery, no one was ready to believe that the Consolidated Virginia might be the end of the Comstock Lode—there had to be another rich deposit of ore somewhere, didn't there? Over the next decade, the mining companies spent another $40 million dollars sinking shafts as deep as 4,000 feet in search of new strikes. At first the companies paid these expenses by withholding dividends from shareholders. Then they levied "assessments" on shareholders, which were the opposite of dividends: If a shareholder wanted to hang onto his stock, he had to cough up a sum of money for every share he owned. If he refused, his shares reverted back to the company and could be sold to new investors.

The assessment system worked while new—but smaller—deposits were being found on a fairly regular basis, but as the years passed with no new discoveries, investors began to give up hope. Instead of paying their assessments, they surrendered their shares to the mining companies, who had trouble selling them even for the price of the unpaid assessments. Between 1875 and 1881, the total value of all the mining company shares on the Comstock Lode dropped from $300 million to less than $7 million.

PENNY STOCKS

By 1884 shares that had once sold for $1,500 or more were trading for a nickel apiece; even at that price, it was difficult to find buyers. By then the mining companies were so broke that they had trouble raising enough cash to operate the giant water pumps that kept the mines from flooding. One by one they were shut off, and

Worldwide, Thailand watches the most TV—an average of 22.4 hours per person per week.

when the last one was shut down in October 1886, the deepest levels of the lode disappeared under the water forever. Some mining companies managed to eke out small profits for another decade by mining low-grade ore close to the surface, but by 1895 even these were played out and the Comstock era came to a close.

FROM BOOMTOWN TO GHOST TOWN

As the mine went, so too went Virginia City. When the mining jobs dried up, the miners left town in search of work elsewhere, and the businesses that had served them for so many years began to close their doors. The newspapers shut down; so did the hospital, the orphanages, and eventually even the schools. As passenger and freight traffic declined to nothing, the railroads ripped up their tracks and used the steel to lay tracks to newer mining towns. Private homes that could not be sold were boarded up and abandoned. In the years to come, it became a common practice for those few residents who stayed behind to buy neighboring homes for back taxes and tear them down for the firewood.

TRADING ONE GAMBLE FOR ANOTHER

Although the Comstock Lode gave up its last high-grade ore more than 130 years ago, the riches it produced encouraged speculators to look for similar riches in other parts of the state. Many discoveries (none of them as impressive as the Comstock Lode) were made, and mining remained an important sector of the Nevada economy into the 1920s. But when the Great Depression sent both the mining and ranching sectors into steep decline, in 1931 the state of Nevada came up with another way to keep money flowing into state coffers: In 1931 they legalized gambling.

At the time, many people thought the measure would be temporary and that gambling would be outlawed again as soon as the economy improved. That wasn't the case, of course. Today Las Vegas, founded in 1905 on land auctioned by a railroad company, is one of the largest gambling destinations in the world. There are plenty of casinos in Reno, too. (And if you get tired of gambling, Virginia City, which has found new life as a tourist attraction, is only 17 miles away. It receives two million visitors a year.) So if you've ever struck it big or lost your shirt in Las Vegas, or Reno, or anyplace else in Nevada, remember: It all started with the Comstock Lode.

The late Wilt Chamberlain still holds nearly 100 NBA records.

13 THINGS ABOUT BOTULISM

A few facts about the toxin that has the power to kill you and to eliminate your wrinkles.

1. Botulism is a rare and serious disease caused by the toxin *botulin*, which is produced by a bacterium called *Clostridium botulinum.* The Center for Disease Control says that about 145 cases are reported in the United States each year, although modern medicine makes deaths rare.

2. Symptoms of botulinum poisoning can begin between six hours and two weeks after eating. They include: double vision, blurred vision, slurred speech, difficulty swallowing, dry mouth, and muscle weakness that starts in the upper body, descends down the arms, down the torso, and then down the legs. Breathing muscles can become paralyzed, and death can occur if emergency medical treatment is not given.

3. C. *botulinum* occurs naturally in soils around the world. Its main activity is the consumption of dead organic material—and the toxin is its "poop." The bacteria and their waste can also contaminate plants, and from there, or from the soil itself, can contaminate birds, fish, and mammals.

4. Bacteria are single-celled organisms and some of the most primitive life forms on Earth. C. *botulinum* has probably been making animals and humans sick for as long as it's existed—and by doing so, it's helped shape their eating habits.

5. In times of stress (such as very cold or very hot weather that causes food shortages), C. *botulinum*, like some other bacteria species, can produce an *endospore*—a protective structure in which it can survive in a dormant state until conditions improve. How long can it stay in that state? Microbiologists have found dormant bacterial spores that were *hundreds of millions of years old.* These ancient spores were able to "wake up" and start eating again.

67% of World War II deaths were civilians.

6. Botulism timeline:

• In the 10th century, Emperor Leo VI of Byzantium bans the manufacture of blood sausage. Historians believe this, as well as many other food regulations passed throughout history, could have been due to botulism outbreaks. (Raw and undercooked meats are common botulism poisoning culprits.)

• In 1735 the first authenticated case of the mysterious disease is recorded in southern Germany, again linked to contaminated sausage.

• Between 1817 and 1822, German doctor Justinus Kerner publishes the first accurate description of botulism and calls the illness "sausage poison." This later led to its scientific name: *botulus* is Latin for "sausage."

• In 1895 the cause of a botulism outbreak in the small Belgian village of Ellezelles is identified: a smoked ham eaten at a funeral dinner. Emile Pierre van Ermengem, professor of bacteriology at the University of Ghent, studies the victims and becomes the first person to isolate and identify C. *botulinum* bacterium.

• In 1944 American Dr. Edward Schantz becomes the first to identify the toxin botulin.

7. There are three main types of botulism:

• ***Foodborne botulism*** makes up about 15% of all cases and occurs when a person ingests food that has already-formed botulin toxin in it.

• ***Infant botulism*** makes up approximately 65% of cases and occurs when spores are ingested by infants. The bacteria colonize the intestines, release the toxin, and poison the child.

• **Wound botulism** makes up the remaining 20% and occurs when wounds are infected with the bacteria and secrete the toxin.

8. Why is honey sold with the warning label, "Do not feed to infants under one year of age"? Botulism. Bees naturally collect the spores when they gather nectar, and they mix the bacteria in their honey. Most adults have strong enough immune systems to handle it, but babies don't, making honey a common cause of infant botulism.

9. C. *botulinum* is *anaerobic*: Oxygen kills it. That's why, if the spores are already in the food, home-canned foods can be particu-

Swedish chemist Svante Arrhenius predicted fossil-fuel-related global warming in 1896.

larly dangerous. The canning process depletes oxygen, and if a high-enough temperature is not maintained for long enough during the cooking and canning process, the spores can survive, and they'll feed on the food until it's eaten...by humans.

10. These bacteria also prefer alkaline environments, so the most common canned-food culprits are low-acid foods such as asparagus, lima beans, green beans, corn, meats, fish, and poultry.

11. Ever seen "swollen" cans of food? Hopefully you threw them away. C. *botulinum* creates gases when it eats, and swollen cans are a sign that the food inside might be infected. (The FDA recommends double-plastic-bagging such cans before disposal.)

12. How toxic is it? A little over a pound of botulin is enough to kill every human on Earth.

13. You've probably heard of Botox. That's the brand name for the drug BTX-A. What's that stand for? "Botulin Toxin Type A." The popular cosmetic treatment is actually made from the bacterial toxin: It paralyzes the face muscles, making them flatten out and appear to be less wrinkled. (It's also used for medical purposes, including treating muscle spasms, clubfoot, and crossed eyes.)

*   *   *

NEWS OF THE STUCK

• On Christmas Day 2007, police in Sydney, Australia, rescued a man in a mini-skirt who'd gotten stuck head-first in a clothing donation bin. Police were able to free the 35-year-old man, who claimed he'd been trying to donate clothes when he became stuck.

• A 63-year-old woman mistook railroad tracks for a road on the evening of November 8, 2007, and her car became stuck on the tracks...with a train speeding straight for her. An off-duty police officer and her husband ran to the car as the train's horn blared. They ripped open the car door, pulled out the woman—who needs crutches to walk—and pulled her to safety seconds before the train smashed into the car, flipped it over, and dragged it more than 100 feet down the tracks. The woman and her courageous rescuers were fine.

Emperor Nero's last words: "Jupiter, what an artist perishes in me!"

THE SNOWMOBILE

It's easy to forget that until very recently in history, families who lived in cold-weather areas were snowbound on their land throughout the long winters. One man dedicated his life to changing that.

AN INVENTIVE KID

Fourteen-year-old Joseph-Armand Bombardier was driving his father crazy by constantly tinkering with everything around the house. Young Armand took apart and then rebuilt clocks, toy trains, even the engine on the family car. It became so maddening that his father bought him a seemingly irreparable Ford Model-T engine just to keep him busy in the garage for a while.

Growing up in the remote town of Valcourt, Quebec, in the 1920s meant long winters and impassable roads. If you needed to travel to the next town—or to a hospital—your only option was a horse-drawn sled. Joseph got the broken down Model-T engine running again, and he had grand plans for it. After working for more than a year in his father's workshop, on New Year's Eve 1921, he emerged driving a very loud contraption. It consisted of the engine mounted on wooden skis, with an airplane propeller on the back. And it drove right over the snow. Dad was impressed, but he had other plans for Joseph: As was the tradition with Catholic families in Quebec, the oldest boy was expected to become a priest. So Joseph went to seminary school.

SNOWBOUND

Bombardier was only one of hundreds of inventors attempting to use an engine to power a vehicle through snow.

• In 1909 Russian inventor Igor Sikorsky invented the Aerosan, which also ran on skis and was powered by a propeller. If the snow was too deep, however, the prop couldn't pull the vehicle's massive weight. (Sikorsky would later be integral to the development of the helicopter.)

• About the same time, a French military engineer named Adolphe Kégresse invented a system that converted a regular car or truck into a snow-worthy half-track vehicle (wheels in the front, "caterpillar" tracks in the back). All that resulted was a car that didn't get stuck as easily—not an all-snow vehicle.

• In 1916 Ray H. Muscott of Waters, Michigan, was issued a patent for a rear-tracked, front-ski vehicle that was used by mail carriers in the Midwest. But like the Aerosan, Muscott's vehicle worked only on dry snow. Quebec, like much of the rest of Canada, has wet, deep snow, and no one could come up with a vehicle that could get through it.

GOING INTO BUSINESS

And that's all Bombardier could think about while he was at seminary. So at 17, he convinced his father to let him drop out and become an apprentice at a garage in Valcourt. After a couple of years of learning everything he could about mechanics, in 1926 he made another request to his father: a loan so he could open his own shop. Seeing his son's potential, dad agreed. Young Bombardier quickly earned a reputation around town as a genius who could fix anything from cars to power tools to agricultural pumps. If he needed a tool that didn't exist, he'd build it himself. He even dammed the creek next to the shop and built a turbine to power it. Bombardier was a pretty good businessman, too: He was able to pay his father back in just three years.

As he entered adulthood, the softspoken, bespectacled inventor steadily grew his business. He married Yvonne Labrecque and the two started a family. At night and on Sundays, Bombardier would retreat to his workshop to tinker with snowmobile designs. He tried making a lighter engine so the vehicle wouldn't sink, but it kept overheating. And despite ridicule from both friends and competitors, Bombardier kept redesigning the track, engine, and sleigh, emptying his bank account in the winter only to refill it the following spring and summer.

And that's the way it went for the next eight years...until tragedy struck. In the winter of 1934, Bombardier's two-year-old son's appendix burst. The boy would die if he didn't get to the hospital, which was 30 miles away. But with the roads snowed in and no working prototype of his snowmobile in the garage, there was nothing that Joseph and Yvonne could do, and their son did die.

BACK ON TRACK

Devastated by the loss, Bombardier knew he could help prevent

Clinophobia is the fear of beds; _reclinophobia_ is the fear of Barcaloungers. (We made up the 2nd one.)

other families from suffering the same fate. So he went back into his workshop and redoubled his efforts. And less than a year later, he'd done it: He'd devised a sprocket-and-track system that finally worked. It consisted of a rubber-and-cotton track that wrapped around toothed wheels in the back, and steerable skis in the front—just like a modern snowmobile, only much bigger and louder, and far less streamlined. After receiving a patent, Bombardier expanded his garage into a year-round production plant, creating much-needed jobs in the little town of Valcourt. Under the banner *L'Auto-Neige Bombardier Limitée* (Snowmobile Bombardier Limited), the inventor was ready for the big time.

His first step: advertise. Driving his seven-passenger model—the B7—Bombardier easily made his way through the deep snows of the Quebec winter, always making sure he parked in front of newspaper offices. Sure enough, word of a working snow machine got out and initial sales enabled him to build a new production facility in 1940, when he introduced the 12-passenger B12. Unlike its predecessors, the wheels were solid instead of spoked, which stopped snow from accumulating and slowing down the vehicle. These early snowmobiles were used to deliver freight, take kids to school, and provide emergency services, giving people security and freedom in the winter months like they'd never had before.

BOMBS AWAY

When Canada entered World War II, the government decreed that only people who absolutely needed a snowmobile could buy one. Instead of panicking, Bombardier went into his workshop and within a few weeks built the prototype for the B11, designed especially for military use. Bombardier's armored transport vehicles proved indispensable in the snowy battlefields during World War II, solidifying his reputation as both a genius inventor *and* a savvy industrialist. But he was still more than a decade away from the invention that would have the greatest impact on society: the personal snowmobile.

Because of the technological limitations of the times, smaller engines couldn't power their way through deep snow without overheating. But by the mid-1950s, engine technology had caught up and Bombardier was able to combine a smaller engine with a continuous track system designed by his eldest son, Germain. In

The world's southernmost city: Ushuaia, Argentina.

1958 the company unveiled the two-person Ski-Dog—so named because Bombardier envisioned it taking the place of the sled dogs that wintertime hunters had relied on for centuries. But a printer's error christened the new snowmobile with an unexpected new name: "Ski-Doo."

JUST DOO IT

Thanks in part to the fun name, people viewed the Ski-Doo in a way that Bombardier hadn't—as a recreational vehicle. But he was reluctant to market it as such, thinking the whimsical name might limit sales. Still, there was no denying it: A new winter sport had been born. Costing $900 each, 8,210 Ski-Doos were sold the first year. And although sales steadily increased, Bombardier didn't push the Ski-Doos as hard as he could have, keeping the company's focus on its all-terrain vehicles used by miners and the forestry service, two things for which he felt there would always be a market.

But whether he realized it or not, Bombardier had opened up a whole new world for winter sports enthusiasts. Sadly, he wouldn't live to see the Ski-Doo's incredible success. On February 18, 1964, he died of cancer at age 56.

WINTER LEGACY

Today, Bombardier is a national hero in Canada. His offspring have kept the company going. Under the name Bombardier Recreational Products, they've branched out with Sea-Doos for the water and a whole array of other outdoor recreational machines. Snowmobiles are still used by the military, of course, as well as by search-and-rescue teams and by indigenous hunters in Canada. But their biggest use by far is for fun, as evidenced by the 3,000 snowmobiling clubs that exist around the world. In the United States and Canada, enthusiasts spend more than $28 billion on snowmobiles and related equipment every year. And a recent focus on environmental concerns aims to make them greener, cleaner, and quieter than ever.

If you're ever in Quebec, it's worth stopping by the Bombardier Museum to see his original garage, where many of his prototypes and custom-built tools still reside. And if the roads are impassable, you can always hop on a snowmobile to get there—and you'll know exactly who to thank for it.

Statistics show: People in all income groups spend about the same amount on Christmas gifts.

LAYERS OF THE ONION

Onions, leeks, scallions, garlic, shallots, and chives are essential ingredients in modern cooking. And they're all part of the same family.

THE ONION'S PEDIGREE

Archeological records suggest that onions have been cultivated for more than 5,000 years. It's believed they originated in Asia, though they may grow wild on every continent. The ancient Egyptians considered them sacred and believed that the round shape and concentric rings symbolized eternity. According to some records, the slave laborers who built the Great Pyramid of Cheops, at Giza 5,000 years ago, were fed mainly chickpeas, onions, and garlic. Ancient Greek athletes ate onions and drank onion juice to give themselves energy. Roman gladiators were rubbed down with onion juice in the belief that it would make their muscles firm. By the Middle Ages, onions were common throughout Europe and were eaten by rich and poor alike (one of the few foods that were).

Onion superstitions are common throughout history: They had the power to absorb poison (every onion was checked before cooking; bad onions were tossed out because it was assumed they'd absorbed poison); they cured colds, headaches, earaches, laryngitis, snakebites, and dog bites; they cleared warts and prevented baldness; if hung in the home, they warded off disease. And onions were good travelers—especially on ships, since they keep for long periods in cool, dark places.

KNOW YOUR ONIONS

Onions are edible bulbs (most bulbs—tulips, for example—are inedible), with leafless stalks that grow at least a couple of feet above ground. Cultivated onions are divided into two categories:

• **Short-day onions**, so called because they require only 11 to 12 hours of daylight (per day) to mature, or "bulb up" in the United States. They're usually grown in the South—if you draw a line from San Francisco to Washington, D.C., short-days are grown below it. Short-day onions are planted in the fall and harvested in spring and early summer. They tend to be thinner-skinned and milder in flavor than their counterparts, the long-day onions. Most are yellow or white, but they can be red, too. Popular short-day varieties: "sweet" onions like Grano, Granex, Vidalia (a type of Granex that can be called "Vidalia" only if it's grown in Georgia), Texas Super Sweet, red and white Bermuda, and red Torpedo.

• **Long-day onions** need 14 to 16 hours of daylight to bulb up, so they're usually grown in the North during the long days of summer and harvested from August through autumn and winter. Long-days tend to be more pungent in flavor, thicker-skinned, and hardier than short-day onions, and can be stored through the winter in cool conditions. They're the ones available year-round at the supermarket, for use when a recipe calls for yellow or white onions. Spanish onions are long-day onions.

THE CRYING GAME

Some raw onions are mild enough to bite into, but others will bite you right back. That strong flavor had a defensive purpose in the evolutionary survival of the onion—it kept animals from eating them. Here's why they're so pungent: The onion plant draws sulfur from the soil, which creates sulfur compounds in its cells. When a raw onion is bitten into (or cut), the cells are crushed and two things happen. First, a pungent odor is released; second, a volatile chemical called a *lacrimator* flies into the air and lands in the eyes and nose of the nearest person (or animal), where it attacks nerve endings and causes pain and tears.

The good news: The sulfur compounds are water soluble and heat sensitive, which means that if you rinse a cut onion in water or cook it, the strong bite will diminish. The milky liquid you see when you chop an onion is the residue of the sulfur compounds, so the more you rinse away, the less you'll cry. Of course, it's hard to chop an onion under cold water, but you can rinse an already-chopped onion in cold water. (Chilling it before cutting helps, too.) And when you cook the onion, it calms down even more. Cooked fast in a hot pan, the onion will lose a little bit of its bite; cooked slowly over low heat, it develops a sweeter, mellower flavor. And that's true of garlic, leeks, shallots, and scallions as well.

Highest quality of life of any city: Vancouver, Canada, and Zurich, Switzerland. (Tied for #1.)

ONION FACTS

• There are more than 1,000 kinds of onions, grown in at least 175 different countries.

• Onions aren't rich in minerals or vitamins (except vitamin C), but they're low in calories and have no fat, cholesterol, or sodium.

• China and India are the leading growers of onions. China harvested 2.2 million acres of onions in 2005; India harvested 1.3 million acres.

• In 2007 the value of the U.S. onion crop was $840 million ($334 million for short-day onions; $506 million for long-day onions). Georgia, Texas, Arizona, and California were the big producers of spring onions; Oregon, California, and Washington were the leaders in storage onions.

• A survey by researchers at Texas A&M University showed that men eat almost 40% more onions than women do.

• Americans eat roughly 20 pounds of onions per person per year.

• What are pearl onions (the ones that people serve in cream sauce at Thanksgiving)? They are simply ordinary white onions harvested when they're still small.

GARLIC FOR EVERYONE

In the first half of the 20th century, garlic was considered low-class in the United States. Immigrant, working-class Southern Italians received most of the scorn: Garlic was called "Italian perfume" and "Bronx vanilla" (because there was a large Southern Italian community in the Bronx in New York City). That may seem unthinkable today, when Americans of every income level, religion, background, *and* ethnicity eat nearly three pounds of garlic per person annually. The shift began in earnest during World War II, when the U.S. government wanted dehydrated garlic to season food for the troops and turned to some California growers to meet the need. A few years later, a California farmer in Monterey County took a chance and grew 10 acres of the plant without anticipating much success in the marketplace. Today California is America's major garlic producer.

Like the onion, garlic has a history at least 5,000 years long, and a lot of it lies in garlic's purported medicinal powers. If you were an ancient-Egyptian bald man or if you had tuberculosis, backaches, gas, and not much sex drive (it's like Uncle John has a twin!), garlic would have been the medication of choice. Over the centuries garlic has also been used to treat arthritis and rheumatism, dysentery and dyspepsia, chicken pox and measles, malaria and typhoid, dandruff, constipation, and the common cold. Eighteenth-century doctors thought it could cure the plague. It can't, but modern medical researchers continue to look into garlic's potential curative powers.

GARLIC FACTS

• What causes garlic breath? According to experts, it's chemicals called *thiols*, which are related to the chemicals in skunk spray. What gets rid of them? Browning enzymes—the same things that make apples or peaches turn brown. Browning enzymes are present in lettuce, mushrooms, basil, and blueberries. So consider finishing off your garlicky meal with a green salad or a fruit salad. That should help with your bad breath.

• China is the world's largest garlic grower (the Chinese produce 75% of world tonnage—an estimated 23 billion pounds annually)—followed by India, South Korea, and the United States.

• Garlic has little nutritional value—its primary value is flavor. (And if you eat too much of it, your skin will smell garlicky.)

TAKE A LEEK (THE REST OF THE ONION FAMILY)

Shallots. Shallots are a prized ingredient in French cooking, especially in sauces, stews, and soups. They look somewhat like garlic (a bunch of small, papery-skinned bulbs clustered on a common base), but their flavor is much subtler, and they're structured in layers, like onions. Shallots originated in Asia, were brought to Europe by the Crusaders, and were introduced to the New World by the Spanish explorer Hernando de Soto in the 16th century.

Scallions. Scallions are immature onions, picked when their tops are green and no bulb has formed underground. They're also known as bunching onions, baby leeks, and green shallots. Whatever you call them, their basic look is this: a slender white stem (with almost no bulb at the base), transitioning into long, straight, tubular green leaves. Both the white and green parts are edible—the white part having a stronger flavor. The green part is often snipped or sliced and used as a garnish.

It takes 300 pounds of pressure per square inch to break a macadamia nut's shell.

Leeks. A leek looks kind of like an oversized scallion, with a sturdy white stalk flaring out into fibrous green leaves at the top. Before cooking, the tough tops of the leaves and the scruffy tuft of roots at the base are cut off, leaving only the central part of the stalk. Then they're generally braised and served as vegetables in their own right or used as the base for soups (vichyssoise and Scottish cock-a-leekie are two good examples). Leeks are more popular in Europe than in the U.S. and have been cultivated in the Mediterranean region for over 4,000 years. Ancient Egyptians grew them (they can be seen in tomb paintings), and they were favorite vegetables of the Greeks and Romans. The emperor Nero believed that leeks would improve his singing voice, and he ate so many of them that he was nicknamed "Porrophagus"—leek eater. It's not known how leeks made their way north to England and Wales (possibly with Phoenician traders or with the Romans), but the Welsh have long claimed the leek as a national symbol. Legend says that in a seventh-century battle against the Saxons, Welsh warriors wore leeks on their hats to identify themselves to each other and prevent friendly fire. Even now, Welsh people wear leeks on March 1, St. David's Day (he's their patron saint) and celebrate by eating leek broth and chicken-and-leek pie.

Chives. With most members of the onion family, we use the bulbs (onions, garlic, shallots) or the stalks (leeks), or the stalks and the leaves (scallions). With chives, which don't form large underground bulbs, the onion flavor is in the hollow leaves, which are used as flavoring in soups, salads, and vegetables. (Their lavender flowers are edible too, and can be added to salads.) The ancient Chinese thought chives could stop bleeding and were an antidote to poison. The Romans used them for telling fortunes, and in the Middle Ages, people hung bunches of chives around the house to protect themselves from illness and evil spirits. Dutch settlers in the New World planted chives in their fields for their cows to munch, in the hope that the cows would give chive-flavored milk. (It worked.)

* * *

Life is an onion and one peels it crying.

—French proverb

The average person will grow 6.5 feet of nose hair in their lifetime.

HIGH-TECH TOY FLOPS

Even if a toy is completely original and built around cutting-edge technology, it doesn't necessarily mean anyone will buy it.

SPORTSTALK

By the late 1980s, kids (and adults) were buying baseball cards not just out of love of the game, but also as an investment. In 1989 LJN Toys tried to cash in on the craze with the Sportstalk—a handheld device, about the size of a Walkman, that "played" electronic baseball cards, each of which had a tiny vinyl record embedded on the back. Through the built-in speaker came two minutes of statistics about the player (voiced by Hall of Famer Joe Torre), along with radio calls of famous plays, and players reminiscing about their biggest moments on the field. It probably failed because it cost too much—$28 for the player and $2 per card. Toys "R" Us ordered half a million Sportstalks and sold fewer than 100,000.

JUICE BOX

In 2004 Mattel introduced the Juice Box, a personal, handheld, candy-colored video player for kids. But the Juice Box didn't play DVDs—kids (or their parents) had to buy the special $10 discs especially made for the device (titles included episodes of *Scooby-Doo* and *SpongeBob SquarePants*). To keep the device affordable (it retailed for $70), Mattel had to scrimp on technology: While regular video runs at 30 frames per second, Juice Box videos ran at 10 frames per second, producing a choppy image on a screen less than three inches wide, and in black and white. Industry experts say that despite its limitations, what ultimately forced the Juice Box off the market within a year of its introduction was the increasing popularity of built-in DVD players in cars and minivans.

VIRTUAL BOY

In the early 1990s, the next big thing in electronics was supposed to be virtual reality. Wearing a special helmet, a person would be able to inhabit lifelike imaginary, computerized worlds. But the only virtual-reality product ever released was a dud: Nintendo's

Virtual Boy video game system. The $180 machine looked like a pair of binoculars perched on a tabletop tripod. There were two problems with the setup. First, it wasn't adjustable, resulting in lots of neck cramps; second, it was impossible to play with eyeglasses on. On top of that, the games weren't in color—that would have pushed the price to more than $500, so they were rendered in a fuzzy black, red, and blue display which created a 3-D effect. The image was so difficult to see that headaches due to eye strain were common (the Virtual Boy had a built-in feature that made it turn off every 15 minutes to give players a chance to rest their eyes). Only 14 games were made for the system, including *Virtual Bowling* and *Virtual Fishing*. Only about 700,000 were sold, making it the biggest flop in Nintendo history.

CAPTAIN POWER

Televideo Interactive debuted in 1987 with Captain Power, the first of what was supposed to be a line of toys that interacted with TV shows. The toys were spaceships and military command centers that kids put in front of the TV during action sequences of *Captain Power and the Soldiers of the Future* broadcasts. The toys fired at the screen, and the screen fired back, causing the spaceship to light up, shake, and make noise. If an "enemy" from TV scored a "hit," it would eject the pilot figure from the spaceship. The show itself was a live-action, high-budget production with lots of special effects...but it was a failure. Why? Because the show was no fun to watch without the toys (which cost upwards of $50), and the toys were no fun without the show, which featured a cast of no-name actors and aired in most markets in a seldom-watched 6:00 a.m. Sunday time slot.

* * *

4 FAMOUS MEN WITH WOMEN'S MIDDLE NAMES

1. Drew Allison Carey
2. Richard Tiffany Gere
3. Jeffrey Lyn Goldblum
4. Quincy Delight Jones

THE *CSI* EFFECT

How real are the TV shows that focus on police and lawyers? A few go all out for accuracy, while others get laughed at by the professions they portray. But they've all had an impact on society...both positive and negative.

FAMILIAR FORMULA

If there were no cops, prosecutors, or defense attorneys, the television airwaves would probably be far less crowded. Over the past 60 years, these professions have dominated primetime schedules. Why? Both offer formulas ready-made for drama: A brand-new conflict is presented to the protagonists each week, promising to be full of mystery, intrigue, and...predictability. Viewers can rely on the fact that near the end of the viewing hour, one crucial piece of evidence will appear and lead to the capture of the elusive killer, or to the acquittal of the wrongly accused defendant. Then comes the philosophical musing that wraps everything up neatly, providing a clean slate for next week's episode.

Real life is rarely so cut-and-dried. And while some may argue that cop and lawyer shows are merely entertainment, actual cops and lawyers claim these shows can make their already-difficult jobs even harder.

JURORS' PRUDENCE

The "*CSI* effect" occurs primarily inside the courtroom. Its first incarnation was referred to as the *Perry Mason* effect, based on the popular fictional defense attorney's trademark ability to clear his client by coercing the guilty party into confessing on the witness stand. During Mason's TV heyday, from the 1950s to the '80s, many prosecutors complained that juries were hesitant to convict defendants without that "Perry Mason moment" of a confession on the stand—which in real life is very, very rare.

After *Perry Mason* went off the air, a new kind of law enforcement program appeared: the scientific police procedural (which started with *Quincy, M.E.*, a drama about a crime-solving medical examiner that aired from 1976 to '83). But few cop shows have

An olive tree can live to be 1,500 years old.

matched the success of *CSI: Crime Scene Investigation*, which debuted in 2000 and has spawned two successful spin-offs. A 2006 TV ratings study in 20 countries named *CSI* "the most watched show in the world."

MYTH-CONCEPTIONS

Along with similar shows such as *NCIS*, *Diagnosis: Murder*, and *Bones*, *CSI* focuses on forensic evidence and lab work as the primary means of catching killers. These dramas may be "ripped from the headlines," but when it comes to telling an entertaining story, certain liberties must be taken by the writers:

- On television shows, detectives work one case at a time; in the real world, they juggle a deep backlog of cases.
- Experts who perform scientific analyses are rarely the same people who do the detective work and make arrests, unlike TV where one team tackles every aspect of the investigation. (And few real forensic scientists ever drive a Hummer to a crime scene.)
- The almost instant turnaround of DNA tests is what TV writers refer to as a "time cheat," a trick necessary to get the story wrapped up. In reality, due to the screening, extraction, and replication processes (not to mention the backlog), DNA tests can take months. And the results are rarely, if ever, 100% conclusive.
- Just about every murder investigation on TV leads to an arrest and conviction. In the real world, less than half of these cases are solved.

"If you really portrayed what crime scene investigators do," said Jay Siegel, a professor of forensic science at Michigan State University, "the show would die after three episodes because it would be so boring."

SHOW ME THE SCIENCE

The main problem caused by the *CSI* effect: Juries now *expect* conclusive forensic evidence. According to Staff Sergeant Peter Abi-Rashed, a homicide detective from Hamilton, Ontario, "Juries are asking, 'Can we convict without DNA evidence?' Of course they can. It's called good, old-fashioned police work and overwhelming circumstantial evidence." In the worst-case scenarios, guilty people may be set free because a jury wasn't impressed with evidence that—as recently as the 1990s—would have led to a conviction.

The Tonle Sap River in Cambodia flows south for eight months and north for the rest of the year.

In fact, many forensic experts find themselves on the stand explaining to a jury why they *don't* have scientific evidence. Some lawyers have even started asking potential jurors if they watch *CSI*. If so, they may have to be reeducated.

Shellie Samuels, the lead prosecutor in the 2005 Robert Blake murder trial, probably wishes that her jury had been asked beforehand if they were *CSI* fans. Samuels tried to convince them that Blake, a former TV cop himself (on *Baretta*), shot and killed his wife in 2001. Samuels illustrated Blake's motive; she presented 70 witnesses who testified against him, including two who stated—under oath—that Blake had asked them to kill his wife. Seems like a lock for a conviction, right? Wrong. "They couldn't put the gun in his hand," said jury foreman Thomas Nicholson, who along with his peers acquitted Blake. "There was no blood spatter. They had nothing." The verdict sent a clear message throughout the legal community: Juries will convict only on solid forensic evidence.

This new trend affects cops, too. *CSI*-watching detectives tend to put unrealistic pressure on crime scene investigators not only to find solid evidence, but also to give them immediate results. Henry Lee, chief emeritus of Connecticut's state crime lab (and perhaps the world's most famous forensics scientist), says that, much to the dismay of the police, his investigators can't provide "miracle proof" just by scattering some "magic dust" on a crime scene. And there is no machine—not even at the best-equipped lab in the country—in which you can place a hair in at one end and pull a picture of a suspect out of the other. "And our type of work always has a backlog," laments Lee, who's witnessed the amount of evidence turned in to his lab rise from about five pieces per crime scene in the 1980s to anywhere from 50 to 400 today.

MIRANDA WRONGS

The *CSI* effect doesn't stop at science—the entire judicial process is being presented in a misleading fashion. Mary Flood, editor of a Web site called The Legal Pad, asked a dozen prominent criminal lawyers to rate the most popular shows. Her findings: "Generally, they hate it when *Law & Order's* Jack McCoy extracts confessions in front of speechless defense lawyers. Not real, they say. They go nuts over the *CSI* premise of the exceedingly well-funded, glamorous lab techs who do a homicide detective's job. Even less real, they say. And they get annoyed when *The Closer's* heroine ignores a suspect's requests for a lawyer. Unconstitutional, they say."

DUMB CROOKS

In the real world, it's usually neither the crusading prosecutor nor the headstrong cop who solves the case. Most criminals, cops admit, are their own worst enemies. Either they don't cover their tracks or they brag to friends about what they did, or both. People tend not to think clearly when they commit crimes. But in the past few years there has appeared a new kind of criminal: the kind that watches *CSI*...and learns.

In December 2005, Jermaine "Maniac" McKinney, a 25-year-old man from Ohio, broke into a house and killed two people. He used bleach to clean his hands as well as the crime scene, then carefully removed all of the evidence and placed blankets in his car before transferring the bodies to an isolated lakeshore at night, where he burned them along with his clothes and cigarette butts—making sure that none of his DNA could be connected to the victims. One thing remained: the murder weapon, a crowbar. McKinney threw it into the lake...which was frozen. He didn't want to risk walking out on the ice to get it, so he left it behind. Big mistake: The weapon was later found—still on the ice—and linked to McKinney, which led to his arrest. When asked why he used bleach to clean his hands, McKinney said that he'd learned that bleach destroys DNA. Where'd he learn that? "On *CSI*."

Using bleach to clean a crime scene was almost unheard of until *CSI* used it as a plot point. Now the practice is occurring more and more often. "Sometimes I believe it may even encourage criminals when they see how simple it is to get away with murder on television," said Captain Ray Peavy, head of the homicide division at the Los Angeles Sheriff's Department. It's difficult enough to investigate a crime scene with the "normal" amount of evidence left behind.

MAYBE DON'T SHOW THEM THE SCIENCE?

So should these shows be censored? Should they tone down the science or, as some have argued, use *fake* science to throw criminals a red herring? "The National District Attorneys Association is deeply concerned about the effect of *CSI*," CBS News consultant and former prosecutor Wendy Murphy reported. "When *CSI* trumps common sense, then you have a systemic problem."

But not everyone agrees. "To argue that *CSI* and similar shows are actually raising the number of acquittals is a staggering claim," argues Simon Cole, professor of criminology at the University of California, Irvine. "And the remarkable thing is that, speaking forensically, there is not a shred of evidence to back it up."

And furthering the debate about whether criminals learn from *CSI*, Paul Wilson, the chair of criminology at Bond University in Australia, stated, "There is no doubt that criminals copy what they see on television. However, I don't believe these shows pose a major problem." Prison, Wilson maintains, is where most of these people learn the tricks of their trade. So while law enforcement officials may agree that cop and lawyer shows do have an effect on modern investigations and trials, the jury is still out on exactly *what* that effect is.

THE SILVER LINING

The shows do have their positive aspects. For one thing, they teach basic science, saving the courts time and money by not having to call in experts to explain such concepts as what DNA evidence actually is. Anthony E. Zuiker, creator of the *CSI* franchise, is quick to point this out. "Jurors can walk in with some preconceived notions of at least what CSI means. And even if there are false expectations, at least jurors aren't walking in blind."

Perhaps most significantly, though, ever since *CSI* became a hit in 2000, student admissions into the forensic field have skyrocketed. So even if Zuiker's show is confusing jurors, misinforming police, and helping to train criminals, at least it's proven to be an effective recruiting tool. "The *CSI* effect is, in my opinion, the most amazing thing that has ever come out of the series," he said. "For the first time in American history, you're not allowed to fool the jury anymore."

And finally, a message from Zuiker to anyone who walks up and points out his shows' inherent flaws: "Folks, it's television."

The average American home creates more pollution than the average American car.

THE YARD SALE SHOPPER'S GUIDE

On page 354, we gave you a step-by-step guide to having the perfect yard sale. So now you've got a wad of cash from your big sale. It's time to go shopping...where else? At a yard sale! Here are some great bargain-hunting tips.

THE ZEN OF YARD SALING

Does it seem like every time you go to a yard sale, all the good stuff is already gone? Maybe that's because all the serious shoppers have already been there. For some people, going to yard sales is a passion—and a science. Here are some tips from the experts (yes, there are experts), starting with how to get started.

• **Chart your course.** Check your local paper and online posting sites the night before and map out a route. It ensures getting the most yard saling in for your time and your gas dollars. It also ensures that you won't miss that "big super sale."

• **Let fate lead you.** Or just head out for a weekend drive and look for signs. It's not the most efficient method, but it's always fun.

ITEMS TO AVOID

• Anything electrical that you can't plug in or put batteries in to try it before buying (unless its really cheap and worth the risk).

• Anything that's falling apart or on its last legs. (You will become a junk collector and—even worse—you'll begin to look like one.)

• Old records, unless you know for sure that they are rare collector's items (or unless you actually still have a record player).

• Expired food. Sounds obvious, but you occasionally come across packaged food or supplements at yard sales. It can be tempting because it's cheap, but be sure to check the expiration date.

• Furniture from cigarette smokers' homes (unless you don't mind the smell).

ITEMS TO LOOK FOR

• Things that you use regularly, even if you already have one. Examples: toaster oven, waffle iron, etc. When your old one finally

Only joint in the human body that can rotate 360°: the shoulder.

goes kaput, you have a spare and won't need to spend a lot of money on a new one.

- Plants. They're usually a good bargain, but do inspect them to be sure they're healthy so you don't spread disease or insects to the house plants you already have.
- Random goofy or fun things for Halloween or costume dress-up.
- Kids'/baby clothes, toys, and gear. If you need them, yard saling is the way to go. (They're barely used.)
- Cool things for friends and family. Everyone loves surprise presents. You'll make people happy and it will only cost you pennies.

GOOD THINGS TO BRING WITH YOU

- Water bottle and snacks (and eat before you head out)
- Small bills and change (it's easier to bargain if you have the exact amount)
- An assortment of batteries for checking appliances
- A list of things you are looking for, including measurements
- Tape measure
- Your checkbook (in case you find an unexpected item you didn't budget for, but suddenly can't live without)
- Rope (in case you buy something large and need to tie it to your car)

PRICES

- Be prepared to bargain; it's part of the fun.
- Rule of thumb: a price that's ¼ of retail or less is a pretty good bargain.
- If prices at a yard sale are too high and the people holding the sale won't bargain, don't fret—just head off to the next sale.

RANDOM ADVICE

- Rummage sales at churches and schools are great. It's like a bunch of yard sales all in one room, and the prices tend to be low.
- A useful over-generalization: A nicer neighborhood and house equals nicer stuff.
- Look inside the box. Make sure that what's inside is what you think it is. This applies to CDs and videocassettes, too.

Most satellites orbit the Earth at a height of 93 miles.

WORLD POLITICS 101

Keeping up with world events can be a full-time job. Those of us who just like to peruse the morning paper over coffee and a donut can find ourselves confused by international news—there is such variety in the different types of government from country to country... what does it all mean? Here are some of the basics.

THE SKY IS FALLING

Imagine waking up one morning to newspaper headlines announcing that the United States government had collapsed and that the president and his entire cabinet were stepping down and calling for new elections. It would be frightening. You'd probably expect chaos and lawlessness to follow. You might even wish you'd listened to your crazy neighbor—the one with the stockpile of ammunition and canned goods.

Well, in parliamentary democracies, governments "collapse" all the time—it happened, for example, in Canada in 2006. All it means is that the dominant political party lost control of the legislature. There are almost 200 countries in the world, and each one of them has a government that is organized at least a little bit differently from all the rest. The terminology that reporters use to describe what is going on in the world doesn't always make sense to people who are familiar with only one system. So, for the discerning bathroom reader, here's a social-studies primer to help simplify the world beat.

TYRANTS AND KINGS

Most countries in the world have some form of representative government, in which voters elect politicians to represent them in a legislative assembly. That doesn't mean that they are always full democracies, just that some kind of political representation is built into the system. The least-representative governments: countries like China, Cuba, Syria, Vietnam, and North Korea, where only a single political party is allowed to participate.

Along with undemocratic, single-party systems, there are still a few absolute monarchies left in the world—among them Saudi Arabia, Qatar, and Swaziland—where a hereditary king (or,

First foreign head of state to address Congress: King Kalakaua of Hawaii (1874).

in Qatar's case, an *emir*) has complete control over the government.

There are also plenty of countries where the mechanisms of representative government are mostly for show and the real power is a military *junta* (Myanmar, Fiji, and Libya), or a president without a strong legislature to check his power (Robert Mugabe in Zimbabwe, for example).

THE FREE WORLD

Representative governments tend to fall into two basic categories: *parliamentary* and *presidential*. The biggest difference between the two has to do with what social-studies textbooks call "separation of powers." Under a presidential system (used in countries as varied as the U.S., Mexico, Brazil, Afghanistan, Cameroon, Sudan, and the Philippines), the executive branch of government is completely separate from the legislative branch. In the U.S., this means that the president holds power independently of Congress.

In a parliamentary government (like those in the U.K., Canada, Australia, Italy, Israel, most of Europe, India, Japan, and Cambodia, among others), the executive and legislative branches are combined. The executive (usually called the prime minister) is the leader of the legislative assembly (parliament). Think of the prime minister as a combination of the president of the United States and the Speaker of the House.

The prime minister is also selected differently from a president. A president is elected directly by the voting public to serve a fixed term in office (in the U.S., four years; in Mexico, six). Under a parliamentary system, citizens don't get to vote for prime minister—not directly, anyway. The voters elect members of Parliament (MPs), and the leader of the party that wins the most seats becomes prime minister.

PARTY TIME

Not only is a prime minister not directly elected by popular vote, he (or she) usually doesn't serve a fixed term in office. No one in a parliamentary system does—general elections aren't held on a fixed schedule. In Canada and the U.K., elections are traditionally held at least once every five years, but there isn't even a written rule that requires it.

Roughly 42% of people in the U.K. snore. (They probably keep the other 58% awake.)

So how does the system work? The head of the dominant political party becomes prime minister, and must then "form a government." To American ears that probably sounds like what the founding fathers did back in the 1780s, but it's actually closer to what a president does during his first weeks in office. Primarily, it involves assigning key cabinet positions to the appropriate politicians.

The tricky part is that it's more difficult to form a government at some times than at others. In the U.K., there are two main political parties (Labour and the Conservative, or Tory, party), and one of them usually wins an absolute majority in Parliament. They are then able to form what is called a "majority government." This means, in effect, that the majority party can run the government however it pleases without too much interference from the opposition.

In Canada, the last two elections have resulted in what is called a "minority government." There are four political parties represented in the Parliament of Canada, but two of them (the Conservatives and the Liberals) hold more than 70% of the seats as of 2008. The Conservatives currently have more seats than the Liberals, but not enough to constitute a majority. Because of this, the government of Prime Minister Stephen Harper must make policy compromises and court the votes of MPs from the other three parties in order to get anything done.

MULTIPARTISAN

Some countries have so many political parties that there's *never* a majority government. The Israeli Knesset (their parliament) is a good example: Israel uses a proportional representation system in which citizens cast their votes for a party rather than for an individual candidate. The parties are then assigned seats in the legislature based on the percentage of the popular vote they received. In Israel, any party that gets at least 2% of the vote gains seats. And in the 2003 and '06 elections, the 120 Knesset seats were divided between 12 parties. (Nineteen more were on the ballot but fell short of the 2% threshold for representation.) The party that "won" the 2006 elections controls less than 25% of the legislature. In a situation like this, government-forming becomes a trickier business. The leader of the party that gets the most votes becomes prime minister, and attempts to form a government by piecing together a coalition of smaller parties. Together, such an association can vote as a majority block, but, not surprisingly, these coalitions can be hard to hold together.

WHEN GOVERNMENTS COLLAPSE

Coalition governments last until the least-satisfied party involved decides to withdraw its support. This usually means that the prime minister no longer controls enough votes to get anything done. When this happens, most parliaments will hold a "vote of no confidence" in the prime minister, and the government is said to have "collapsed." In most cases, this leads to the dissolution of parliament and a new round of general elections.

Several European governments collapsed in 2008. Belgium's prime minister offered to resign when he saw that the five-party coalition government he'd spent nine months building was unable to work together on key issues facing the country. In Austria, an uncomfortable alliance between the two dominant parties ended when one of them pulled out of the governing coalition in a bid to force new elections. And in Italy, the 20-month old Prodi government lost a vote of no confidence and was replaced by a new coalition headed by former prime minister Silvio Berlusconi.

LAME DUCKS AND MIDTERM ELECTIONS

Majority governments are more stable than coalitions and are usually able to call elections at a time that is politically advantageous for them—when they think they stand a good chance of retaining power. Sometimes, a prime minister can even step down and be replaced without new elections being held. This happened recently in the U.K. in 2008, when Tony Blair resigned as head of the Labour Party. Because the party still controlled Parliament, they simply chose a new party leader (Gordon Brown), who then became the new prime minister.

To understand how this differs from a presidential system, compare it with what was going on in the U.S. in 2006: The Democrats took control of Congress—despite the fact that there was still a Republican president in office with two years left in his term. Under a parliamentary system, this couldn't happen, because whoever con-

Lucky or unlucky? March 13, 1998, was a Friday the 13th with a full Moon and a lunar eclipse.

trols the legislative branch of the government (parliament) also controls the executive (the prime minister).

MINISTERIAL VS. PRESIDENTIAL

Both systems have their pros and cons. Advocates of parliamentary democracy point out that it is more responsive to social and economic changes. If a prime minister makes an unpopular decision and loses his base of support, he faces a swift removal from office—unlike the American president, who can lose both popular and congressional support and still serve out the remainder of his term.

On the other hand, in situations where political coalitions are difficult to build and maintain, critics charge that parliamentary governments can be unstable. Italy is the most-common example of this: Since becoming a parliamentary republic at the end of World War II, Italy has had 62 governments in 62 years. To be fair, that doesn't mean that there is no functional government in Italy, just that there is a high turnover rate at the prime minister's office. (They're still a highly developed modern democracy with the seventh-largest economy in the world.)

The relative stability of a fixed-term presidential system is not without its shortcomings, either. In the U.S., five of the last seven presidents have been forced to work with a Congress controlled by the opposition party. Critics complain that partisan bickering in such situations can lead to legislative gridlock—as it did in Washington in 1995, when the Republican-controlled Congress and the Democratic president (Bill Clinton) couldn't agree on a budget and the federal government actually shut down all nonessential services for 26 days.

GOD SAVE THE QUEEN

The boundaries that define president and parliament can get even fuzzier. Some presidential governments also have a prime minister (such as France, Egypt, South Korea, and Russia), and some parliamentary governments also have a president (Germany, India, Italy, Ethiopia, and Bangladesh).

And then there's the Queen of England. The U.K. is a constitutional monarchy, which means that it is has a democratic government that evolved over time out of an absolute monarchy (see

Highest number in the language of the Yancos tribe of the Amazon: 3.

"The Magna Carta," page 429). Over hundreds of years, the kings and queens of England gradually lost their political power to parliament. Today, the queen is a figurehead—she plays the same role in former British colonies like Canada and Australia—though she does so through an appointed *governor-general* who acts as her representative. The emperor of Japan has a similar job in his country.

READ WITH CARE

So when you read the paper or listen to the news, remember that no two governments are exactly alike, and that the word "government" itself can have multiple meanings depending on the political system being described. Kings, queens, presidents, and prime ministers play different roles in different countries, and "democracy" comes in different shades. The easiest way to understand international news stories is to check a current almanac or the Internet for background information on a given country. Give it a try and impress (or annoy) your friends with your informed observations about the state of the world. Oh, and vote for Uncle John for President in 2012.

* * *

MEEP MEEP!

Here are a few of the contraptions that Wile E. Coyote ordered from the ACME company in his futile attempts to capture the Roadrunner.

- ACME Atom Re-Arranger
- ACME Bat-Man's Outfit
- ACME Female Road-Runner Costume
- ACME Invisible Paint
- ACME Iron Bird Seed
- ACME Junior Explosive Kit
- ACME Dehydrated Boulders
- ACME Little Giant Do-It-Yourself Rocket-Sled Kit
- ACME Earthquake Pills
- ACME Super Speed Vitamins
- ACME Giant Rubber Band
- ACME Jet-Propelled Unicycle
- ACME Instant Girl
- ACME Anvil
- ACME Triple Strength Fortified Leg Muscle Vitamins (Family Size)

THE ORIGINAL DUNGEON MASTERS, PART II

Here's the second installment of our story on one of the biggest game fads of the 20th century. *(Part I is on page 393.)*

GETTING ORGANIZED

As much fun as Dave Arneson's game—Blackmoor—was to play, it still wasn't very organized. It would have been difficult for new players to learn to play such a complicated and innovative game, let alone host their own sessions without Arneson there to explain everything. It took Gary Gygax's organizational skill to boil the game down to a coherent set of rules that anyone could follow—complete with lists of monsters, character types (such as fighters, clerics, wizards), weapons, spells, and so on. But what rules! Gygax's first draft was 50 pages long. After sending it out to a few dozen gamers for their input, he revised and expanded it to the *150-page* version that became the first commercial edition of the game.

HIGH ROLLERS

It was at about this time that Gygax finally found a solution to a problem with dice games that had annoyed him for years: When two six-sided dice are rolled together, the odds of getting a 6, 7, or 8 are much greater than the odds of rolling a 2 or a 12. Gygax wanted the odds of getting each number to be the same. In the past, he had accomplished this by having players draw numbered poker chips from a hat. But pulling poker chips out of a hat was a bit clunky for a game that was going to be sold to the public.

Gygax found his solution while flipping through a school supply catalog. The common six-sided die is a *regular polyhedron*—a solid figure with identically shaped and sized sides (in this case, a cube with six sides). When he found 4-, 8-, 12-, and 20-sided regular polyhedrons in the catalog, he decided to use them as dice along with the conventional six-sided dice. (Dungeons & Dragons also uses 10-sided dice, but they're not regular polyhedrons).

DYNAMIC DUO

At this stage, the game was known by the working title "Fantasy Game." Apparently neither Gygax nor Arneson thought "Blackmoor" was descriptive enough or had enough marketing pizzazz to work as the new game's title, so that name was given to a scenario within the game instead. Gygax thought a two-word title would work best, so he wrote up a list of words that described or were related to the game—monster, journey, dragon, adventure, quest, dungeon, treasure, and so on—and paired them in different combinations. Then he asked friends and family members to pick the pairs they like the best. Gygax credited his four-year-old daughter with picking the pair that became the game's official title. "Oh, Daddy," she told him, "I like Dungeons & Dragons the best!"

FOR SALE

Finding a publisher turned out to be a lot more difficult than picking a title. When Gygax pitched Dungeons & Dragons to Avalon Hill, the biggest publisher of war games in the United States, they didn't know what to make of it. A game with no opponents? No real winners and losers? No definitive ending? And what about all those weird dice? Dungeons & Dragons had strayed so far from its military origins that executives at Avalon Hill didn't even recognize the game, let alone understand it. They passed.

Gygax decided that he had no choice but to publish the game himself. Together he and a childhood friend named Don Kaye pooled a few thousand dollars and founded a company called Tactical Studies Rules, or TSR for short. They printed 1,000 copies of the game, which went on sale in January 1974 for $10.00, plus an additional $3.50 for the dice. (Arneson received royalties for co-creating the game but did not join or invest in TSR.)

THE ADVENTURE BEGINS

Dungeons & Dragons caught on with college students first. It spread from school to school by word of mouth—it *had* to spread that way, because after printing the game, TSR didn't have any money left to spend on marketing or publicity. Then it began to trickle down to high school and junior high school students, as the college kids came home and taught the game to their younger siblings.

Think your vote doesn't count? Officially, George W. Bush beat Al Gore by 537 votes in 2000.

The first printing of 1,000 copies sold out in just seven months. When another 5,300 sold in less than a year, TSR ordered another 25,000—this at a time when Avalon Hill's best-selling game ever had sold only 10,000 copies. As impressive as these sales figures were, they represented only a fraction of the total number of people who were playing the game. Bootleg photocopies of Dungeons & Dragons outnumbered official copies by as much as two to one in the early years. While this would have been a problem with other games, TSR didn't mind, because these bootleg dungeon masters were introducing thousands of new players to the games. Many would go on to buy legitimate copies of their own.

SCANDAL!

By 1979 TSR was selling more than $4 million worth of games, dice, and other Dungeons & Dragons accessories a year, and sales were predicted to nearly double over the next 12 months. Then in August of 1979, a troubled Michigan State University student named James Dallas Egbert III disappeared into the steam tunnels underneath the school and was not seen again for weeks. Egbert was a Dungeons & Dragons fan, and rumors began to circulate that he'd gone into the tunnels to have a real-life dungeon experience. He was either still down there living out his fantasy, the story went, or had gotten lost or killed trying to find his way back to the surface.

The truth was more tragic: Egbert was struggling with depression and drug addiction, and he had gone into the tunnels to kill himself with an overdose of sleeping pills. When his attempt failed, he left the tunnels and hid out at a friend's apartment for about a month before letting the police know he was OK.

COULD IT BE...SATAN?

Egbert's disappearance had nothing to do with Dungeons & Dragons, but no one knew this until he reappeared. During the weeks he was missing, his story provided journalists with a tantalizing hook into the game fad that was sweeping the country. Religious groups had warned from the start that any game that featured as many demons and magic spells as this one did had to be the work of the devil, and now with Egbert's disappearance their claims found a national audience.

New Hampshire has an official state Seagull Harasser. His job...

YOU CAN'T BE SERIOUS

Gygax was dumbfounded by their accusations. The spells and demons in the game were as imaginary as the gold and treasure. And to demonstrate the absurdity of his critics' claims, Gygax invited them to try to deposit the loot in their bank accounts.

As silly as the controversy was, it dragged on year after year. In 1982 Egbert's story was dramatized in a fictionalized TV-movie called *Mazes and Monsters*, starring 26-year-old Tom Hanks. In 1983 a woman who blamed her son's suicide on a curse he "received" while playing the game formed an organization called Bothered About Dungeons & Dragons (B.A.D.D.) and spent more than a decade leading a moral crusade against the game. Even *60 Minutes* got in on the act, airing a story in 1985 that questioned whether the game had driven some players to suicide.

But if Gygax worried about the impact of the controversy on the game's sales and popularity, he needn't have. The media attention actually boosted sales: Instead of doubling in 1979 as they'd forecast, sales *quadrupled* to more than $16 million and kept right on growing after that, finally peaking at $29 million in 1985.

THE REAL WORLD BUTTS IN

Ironically, though they had invented the first modern role-playing game, by the mid-1980s both Gygax's and Arneson's own roles had ended. They were no longer involved with TSR and did not participate in the further development of their game.

Arneson, who never did join TSR, was the first to go. He ended his creative contributions to the game in 1976 and three years later filed the first of five lawsuits against Gygax and TSR, alleging that he'd been shortchanged on both creative credit and royalties. The suits were eventually settled out of court, but his relationship with Gygax never fully healed. (Today Arneson is a partner in a gaming company called Zeitgeist Games, which publishes a series of his games that are playable using Dungeons & Dragons rules. He taught game design for several years at Florida's Full Sail University before retiring in 2008.)

When Gygax's business partner and childhood friend Don Kaye died suddenly in 1975, Gygax had to bring in outside investors to raise the money he needed to buy out Kaye's widow. In the process, his stake in the company dropped to 35%; then in

1979 the other investors seized effective control of the company, relegating Gygax to a figurehead position where he had very little say over the running of the company. By 1985, the year that revenues peaked at $29 million, the company had become so bloated and mismanaged that it was actually *losing* about $3 million a year. That year, after Gygax lost a second power struggle, he sold his shares in TSR and severed all ties with the company.

By 1997 TSR was more than $30 million in debt and close to collapse. That year the company was acquired by Wizards of the Coast, makers of the best-selling card game Magic: The Gathering. (Today Wizards of the Coast is owned by Hasbro.)

After ending his involvement with Dungeons & Dragons, Gygax dabbled in fantasy fiction writing and other projects. He even developed another role-playing game, called Lejendary Adventure, which went on sale in 1999. Although the game developed a loyal following, it never approached the popularity of Dungeons & Dragons. After years of declining health, Gygax died in 2008 at the age of 69.

STILL ROLLING ALONG

More than 30 years after it was introduced, Dungeons & Dragons remains the best-selling pen-and-paper, or "tabletop," role playing game of all time. An estimated six million people were still playing the game in 2007, and that number was expected to grow following the release of the fourth edition of the game in the summer of 2008.

Drawing inspiration from the online role-playing games that it inspired, the fourth edition includes an online 3D "tabletop," complete with Internet voice chat and even a social networking site similar to MySpace. These features are intended to make it easier for gamers who've spread far and wide over the past 30 years to gather together and play the game with the same old friends, even if only in cyberspace.

FINAL IRONY

You might think that Gygax was inspired by *The Lord of the Rings*, J. R. R. Tolkien's enormously poplular fantasy novels. While the books no doubt helped the success of Dungeons & Dragons, Gygax hated them. "I'd like to throttle that Frodo," he once said.

Q: What are red-faced shags, horned screamers, and beach thick-knees? A: Species of birds.

BEWARE! TOILET ATTACK!

Proving that even life's most hallowed place can be dangerous.

HOME INVASION. In February 2008 in Frankenmuth, Michigan, the toilets in 20 homes—all on the same block—started spitting up water...and sometimes more than water. The splash-backs were caused by the city public works department, which was cleaning out the main sewer line. Usually, a little gurgling is expected when a high-pressure hose is used to flush out the pipes, but for some unknown reason, the toilets in the affected homes erupted like volcanos—in a few cases making a mess all over the walls and ceiling. The city apologized and promised that in the future, instead of announcing the pipe-flushing in the newspaper, they'll put flyers on people's doors warning them to keep their toilet lids securely closed for the next few days.

DETHRONED. A Christchurch, New Zealand, man (he refused to give his name because he was trying to sell his house) was knocked off of his toilet when his house was hit by a runaway SUV. The vehicle had been parked next door by a construction worker who'd applied the emergency brake only halfway. The brake slipped and the truck rolled backward down a hill and bonked into the man's house (it caused only minor damage). When asked by reporters how he thought the construction worker felt, the homeowner said, "What about me? I got knocked off the toilet! I got a hell of a fright!"

WATCH FOR FALLING PORTA-POTTIES. Morning commuters on a highway near Denver, Colorado, got the scare of a lifetime when a portable toilet tumbled off of a flatbed truck in 2007. The first car swerved around the toilet but hit a pickup truck, which then flipped over a few times onto the grass next to the highway. Then a tractor trailer roared through and ran over the toilet. More cars approached the melee and slammed on their brakes, creating even more confusion. In all, eight vehicles were involved in the accident and traffic was backed up for hours. No serious injuries were reported, but the Porta-Potti was a total loss.

Women metabolize caffeine about 25% faster than men do.

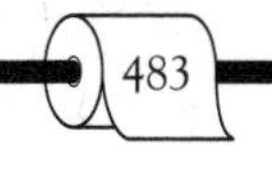

Q&A: ASK THE EXPERTS

Everyone's got a question they'd like answered, like, "Why is the sky blue?" Here are a few of those questions, with answers provided by the nation's leading trivia experts.

TRY TO CONTAIN YOUR EXCITEMENT

Q: *Why is milk sold in rectangular containers, while sodas are sold in round ones?*

A: "Rectangular containers use shelf space more economically than cylindrical ones. So why do soft drink producers stick with round? One reason is that because soft drinks are often consumed directly from the container, the extra cost is justified because they fit more comfortably in the hand." But there's more: "The shelf space that recatangular milk containers save is more valuable than it is for soda containers. Most soft drinks in supermarkets are stored on open shelves, which are cheap and have no operating costs. Milk is stored in refrigerated cabinets, which are both expensive to purchase and costly to operate. Shelf space thus comes at a premium, and hence the added benefit of packaging milk in rectangular containers." (From *The Economic Naturalist*, by Robert H. Frank)

YOU SNOOZE, YOU LOSE

Q: *Why is the snooze on most alarm clocks set to go off after nine minutes instead of 10?*

A: "By setting the snooze time to nine minutes, the alarm clock only needs to watch the last digit of the time. So, if you hit the snooze at 6:45, the alarm goes off again when the last digit equals 4. They couldn't make it 10 minutes, otherwise the alarm would go off right away, or it would take more circuitry. Historically speaking, there's another element to the answer. Clock experts say when snooze alarms were invented, the gears in alarm clocks were standardized. The snooze gear was introduced into the existing mix and its teeth had to mesh with the other gears' teeth. The engineers had to choose between a gear that made the snooze period either 9+ minutes or 10+ minutes. They figured that 'less than 10 minutes' seemed more punctual and marketable than

Sounds fishy: In the U.S., anchovies always rank last on the list of favorite pizza toppings.

sending people back to dreamland for 'more than 10 minutes.' The public became accustomed to this, and clock makers have generally stuck with it." (From *Jewish World Review,* by Jeff Elder)

EXTRA-CRUNCHY PEANUT BUTTER

Q: *Do we eat insects without knowing it?*

A: "We certainly do. It is impossible to totally exclude insects while a food is grown, harvested, and shipped, so most of the foods we eat do contain small quantities of insects or insect fragments. It might be possible to produce, say, a bottle of ketchup that contains not even one insect fragment, but it would take a huge effort that could raise the price to hundreds of dollars. Recognizing this problem, the FDA sets a maximum legal limit on how many insect parts can be contained in a food that is to be sold. For example, peanut butter is allowed to contain up to 30 insect fragments per 100 grams." (From *The Handy Bug Answer Book,* by Dr. Gilbert Waldbauer)

WHERE DID MY CHILDHOOD GO?

Q: *Why can't we remember anything that happened to us when we were babies or toddlers?*

A: "Our memories of past experiences are organized in our brain as narratives. Kids younger than about three don't yet know narrative conventions. They can't tell a story. They don't know how to set the scene. They don't understand time, place, character, or plot. In other words, our memories start at the age when we realize that what we're all trying to do in life is find the moral of the story." (From *Why Things Are & Why Things Aren't,* by Joel Achenbach)

* * *

A RASH DECISION

Factory worker Robert Preston was fired from Phelps Dodge Copper Products in Connecticut and not given a reason, so he sued the company and won nearly $800,000 in damages. But a few weeks later, the judge made Preston pay back the money after the real reason for his termination was discovered. He'd contracted poison ivy and then used a toilet seat at work, which spread the rash to several other employees...including the factory manager.

Q: What brand of toothbrush was carried aboard the *Apollo 11* mission to the Moon? A: Oral-B.

THE PIANO MAN

Everybody loves a good mystery. Like the time Uncle John went to the movies and left Porter the Wonder Dog home alone. When he returned, someone *had eaten three bags of dog food off the kitchen counter. Who did it? (It's a mystery!)*

WASHED ASHORE

On April 7, 2005, police in Sheerness, a coastal town in southeast England, noticed a man wandering the streets. Confused and disoriented, he was wearing a suit and tie and was soaking wet from head to toe. It hadn't been raining, so the police assumed he'd been in the ocean and may have come in from a boat. But he had no ID and no travel papers. Even the tags had been cut out of his clothes. Further complicating matters, the man couldn't—or wouldn't—speak.

The police took him to nearby Medway Maritime Hospital. Doctors, nurses, and social workers spent hours gently trying to persuade the man to talk. He remained completely silent, entirely unresponsive. One doctor was curious if he might have some kind of neurological or other medical condition that prevented him from speaking. So he gave the man a pen and some paper, hoping he'd write down anything—his name or any information that could be used to identify him and notify his family.

The silent man suddenly sprang to life. He grabbed the pen and paper, but he didn't write anything. Instead, he drew an elaborate, detailed sketch of a grand piano. Doctors took him to the hospital chapel, which had a piano. The man sat down and played for more than four hours, nonstop. He played all kinds of music, mostly pieces by Tchaikovsky, as well as other classical music and even a few Beatles songs. And he played them very well. In fact, he played better than that—he played exquisitely, at the level of a virtuoso concert pianist.

So who *was* he?

ENTER THE MEN IN WHITE COATS

The man, whom medical officials called "Mr. X," was admitted to the high-security mental health wing of the West Kent NHS and Social Care Trust. In addition to traditional forms of therapy, doctors tried music therapy and art therapy to get the man to communicate, but to little avail, as therapy requires some kind of interaction. Mr. X barely even ate or drank. Aside from his frequent trips to the piano, the man lived completely inside his own head, with a couple of exceptions. He once drew the Swedish flag in an art therapy session. Another time, he pointed to Oslo, Norway, on a map. A Norwegian interpreter was called in, but could elicit no response from Mr. X.

In an attempt to find his relatives, Mr. X's picture was posted on England's National Missing Persons Helpline Web site. The mysterious circumstances of the case quickly made it front-page news all across Europe. (The media quickly gave Mr. X a new nickname: "the Piano Man.") By mid-May, the Helpline had received more than 500 phone calls and 100 e-mails, which generated 300 "legitimate" leads as to the Piano Man's true identity.

IS YOUR PIANIST MISSING?

Possibilities as to the Piano Man's identities came in from all over the world. Some of the more promising leads:

• A street mime from Rome told Italian police that he recognized the Piano Man as a French street performer named Steven Villa Masson. Reporters from the British newspaper the *Independent* found Masson at his home in Paris, so he wasn't the Piano Man.

• An Italian TV news show uncovered footage of a 2000 music festival that featured a concert pianist who bore a strong resemblance to the Piano Man. His facial structure was similar, and festival participants recalled that he didn't talk much. He also was tracked down and ruled out. He wasn't the Piano Man, either.

• Klaudius Kryspin, a Czech drummer, identified the Piano Man as Tomas Strnad, with whom he had played in a band called Ropotamo in the 1980s. He hadn't seen Strnad since 1996, but when he saw the picture in the newspapers, he said, "I knew it was Tomas." Michael Kocab, the band's lead singer, backed up Kryspin's assertion that the Piano Man looked exactly like Strnad, but it turned out that Kocab had seen the real Strnad on April 10 in Prague, three days *after* the Piano Man had showed up in England, so he couldn't have been the Piano Man.

A diamond heated to 1,400°F will completely vaporize. Not even ashes will remain.

• Susanne Schlippe Steffensen, a Danish politician, told reporters that the Piano Man was her husband, whom she hadn't seen since February when he went to Algeria to visit his family. Steffenson thought he must have wound up in England after a fight with his mother. She went to the West Kent Trust to meet her "husband," but it wasn't him.

• Several Norwegian college students came forward to identify the Piano Man as an Irish exchange student they'd once known. Norwegian newspapers were able to quickly locate the real exchange student. He wasn't the Piano Man.

• Orchestras across Europe were contacted to see if any of them was missing a pianist. Nobody was.

SING US A SONG, PIANO MAN

By August 2005, no leads had panned out and the Piano Man still wasn't speaking, although he was beginning to show signs of having a better rapport with caregivers—for one thing, he was eating and drinking regularly. His social worker Michael Camp told reporters that it was a possibility that they might never learn the man's identity. "If nobody can name this guy, then I don't see how we can possibly find out," he said.

Camp also said that while doctors initially thought the Piano Man must have suffered a highly traumatic event and was in the throes of post-traumatic stress disorder, they were now beginning to think that his extremely withdrawn nature but spectacular piano skill suggested that he must be autistic.

GRAZING IN THE GRASSL

Then, on August 21, just a couple of weeks later, the Piano Man suddenly snapped out of it. According to his doctors at the West Kent Trust (who could reveal only a little information because of doctor-patient confidentiality), he suddenly remembered his name and that he was German. His identity was confirmed with the German embassy, which issued the Piano Man a replacement passport and flew him home.

Three days later, the Piano Man's name was revealed to the public as Andreas Grassl, a 20-year-old student from a farming family in Prosdorf, Germany. How had he wound up in England?

The milk seen in TV commercials is usually a mixture of white paint and turpentine.

In March 2005, Grassl had been working, ironically, as a caregiver in a mental hospital in Saarbrücken, Germany, when he decided to quit his job, move to Paris, and enroll in school there. Grassl called his parents in Prosdorf to let them know he was going to France. After not hearing from him for weeks, they reported him missing to German officials, who told the Grassls there wasn't much they could do—their son was last seen in another country, and he was an adult.

Grassl couldn't enroll in school, he had trouble finding work, and a love affair soured, all leading to a severe depression. He left France and took a train to England, where he decided to commit suicide by drowning himself in the sea at Kent. He actually went into the water but then had second thoughts, and while he was wandering around town in a state of extreme emotional distress, he was discovered by police. Grassl claims that from the day he was picked up and throughout his stay at the hospital, he was under so much emotional stress that he could neither speak nor remember his name.

THE CODA

The "Piano Man" story was the hottest news story in Europe in the summer of 2005. So how could it be that Grassl's worried parents never saw his picture on TV or in a newspaper? "I work hard every day, get up early in the morning to see to the cows, so I hardly ever get to read a paper," Josef Grassl told reporters. "I do watch the news on television, but once I have seen the weather report, I switch it off."

And here's the amazing part: the "Piano Man" who had amazed the mental facility staff with his expert piano playing... hadn't, really. He drew a piano and was allowed to play one, but no one in the media ever witnessed it—reporters merely interviewed hospital staff who had seen him play. Sensationalized news reports exaggerated the claims that he was a concert-level pianist. "The Piano Man" had never received any formal training and had never worked as a professional musician. He was an amateur, at best.

As of 2007, the German pianist who mystified England was studying French literature—not music—at a college in Switzerland.

Those "angelic" rays of sun beaming through clouds are technically called *crepuscular rays*.

eBAY: THE REAL STORY

How one man's hobby became one of the most successful businesses in history.

MYTH-BAY

Here's the legend of how eBay started: One evening in 1995, computer programmer Pierre Omidyar was talking to his fiancée, Pamela Wesley. She mentioned an old hobby, collecting and trading PEZ candy dispensers, and bemoaned the fact that she couldn't find any collectors in her area to trade with. And at that moment eBay was born in Omidyar's mind. The truth: That story was made up by a marketing engineer in 1997 to develop interest in the company. The real story is a bit more complicated...but just as interesting.

Pierre Omidyar was born on June 21, 1967, the only child of French-Iranian parents. At age six, he emigrated with his family from Paris to the United States so that his father could attend a medical residency at John Hopkins University. Young Omidyar was fascinated with computers from the moment he saw them. His first job: writing a program to catalog his school's library (he was 16 and earned $6.00 an hour). "I was your typical nerd in high school," Omidyar recalls. "Or geek—I forget which is the good one."

GO WEST, YOUNG NERD

After graduating from Tufts University in Boston with a degree in computer science in 1988, Omidyar moved to Santa Clara, California, the heart of Silicon Valley and the Hollywood of the Internet Age. He worked as a programmer for a while, but then in 1991 he and some friends started Ink Development Corp., a "pen-based" computer company. (They're the computers you operate by touching the screen with a penlike tool.) Over the next few years he led the company away from that and into what he believed was going to really take off one day: Internet shopping. He also came up with a new company name: "eShop." It wasn't eBay, or even close to it, but it was successful (Microsoft eventually bought it), and in the meantime, Omidyar was thinking up his own project: an Internet auction site.

Why an auction? Because Omidyar liked the idea of a place where professional middlemen and retailers were out of the way and regular people could buy and sell things directly from and to other regular people. And an auction not only gave buyers power that they couldn't get in a store, it added some excitement: Display an item; let people start the bidding; when time runs out, the highest bidder gets the goods. It was the ultimate "free market."

EBOLA-BAY

Over Labor Day weekend in 1995, with the project sufficiently developed in his head, Omidyar stayed home and wrote the programming code for an auction-based Web site. On September 3, "AuctionWeb" was launched. It was, he now admits, ugly, clunky, and awkward. And he didn't even get a specific Internet address for it; he just added it as a page on the site he already had for his Internet-consulting business. The address of that site: ebay.com. Why? The consulting business was called Echo Bay Technology Group. (It wasn't named after a real bay: "It just sounded cool," he later explained.) He had tried to register it as "echobay.com," but that was taken by a Canadian gold-mining company, so he shortened it and ebay.com was born.

At the time he launched the auction site, ebay.com had three different home pages. The first one took you to the consulting business; a link could then connect you to "San Francisco Tufts Alliance," a Tufts University alumni group that his wife headed (he and Pamela had since married); another link then sent you to "Ebola Information"—a tribute to the deadly ebola virus. (Omidyar has a warped sense of humor.) From there you could finally get to AuctionWeb.

No money went into advertising. To generate interest, he relied solely on Internet message boards, where he posted links that simply said "free Web auction." To his surprise, a lot of people clicked on the link—and started buying and selling stuff. First item sold: Omidyar's broken laser pointer. It went for $14.83. By the end of its first year, thousands of auctions had taken place and more than 10,000 bids had been made.

NOT SO FREE MARKET

Despite its early success, AuctionWeb was still a just hobby for

Osama bin Laden, Avril Lavigne, and Tonya Harding have all had a computer virus named for them.

Omidyar—he was still working as program developer—until his Internet service provider forced him to change from a private to a commercial account because of the amount of traffic the site was getting. That increased his overhead from $30 to $250 a month, so he decided to start charging users a small fee. He thought there would be a backlash from his regulars, but, to his surprise, he received few complaints. And soon checks began arriving in the mail, so many of them, in fact, that he had to hire his first employee to handle all the payments. By March 1996, AuctionWeb's monthly revenue was up to $1,000. By April it was $2,500. By May it was $5,000. By June it was $10,000—and Pierre Omidyar quit the last regular job he'd ever have.

SHE-BAY

AuctionWeb's next employee was Jeff Skoll, a computer geek who also had a masters degree in Business Administration from Stanford University. Skoll's first mission: Get rid of the ebola tribute and the other sites, and make AuctionWeb a stand-alone auction site. Omidyar protested, but, luckily for him, Skoll prevailed. Another good idea from the early days: the bulletin board. New users could post questions, which were answered by more experienced users, giving eBay its very own (free) tech support. One of the most popular bulletin board gurus was a man who called himself "Uncle Griff." A curious questioner once asked him what he looked like. He responded, "I'm wearing a lovely flower print dress and I just got done milking the cows," forever etching himself into eBay lore as their "cross-dressing bachelor dairy farmer who likes to answer questions." He was so good and so respected that in the fall of 1996 Skoll asked him (his name was Jim Griffith, and he lived in Vermont) to help answer technical questions directly for eBay while of course keeping his cross-dressing persona alive on the bulletin board. Uncle Griff accepted—and became eBay's first tech-support employee.

THE GLOBAL YARD SALE

Everything about eBay seemed to be right for its time and place. Before eBay, someone who wanted to sell a collectible, antique, or electronic item of value had very few options—especially if they lived in the boondocks—which usually resulted in selling it for much less than it was worth. Omidyar's online auction changed that. It consolidated buyers and sellers into one connected marketplace, making location almost irrelevant (shipping prices notwithstanding). That meant sellers could get top dollar for their items, and collectors and buyers could more easily find the items they wanted. It was a hugely successful formula, and in 1998, just three years after starting the ebola-virus-linked free auction site, the company went public. On the first day the stock price shot up—and eBay was worth more than $2 billion. By 1999 it was worth more than $8 billion...and Omidyar had become one of the wealthiest people on Earth.

SELLING OUT

Lots of companies have good starts, but eBay made sure its success lasted. They constantly updated the site and its tools, making it slicker and easier to use by the month. Some of the most notable upgrades: In 1998 they added the "feedback" feature that allows users to rate sellers and buyers, letting other users know whether they're dealing with a trustworthy person (and encouraging users to police the site at no cost to eBay); in 2002 they purchased the "e-commerce" company PayPal, which allowed for easier Internet payments (eBay gets an additional fee for each transaction); Omidyar and Skoll reached out to companies like Disney, GM, and major airlines to use the site to sell their products. That might seem like it goes against Omidyar's "regular people" model—and it does—but it obviously didn't hurt the auction site, and it made the company many more millions of dollars. On top of that they bought up competing sites—like Half.com and Rent.com—by the dozen.

GIVING BACK

As of 2008, nearly a billion people visit eBay annually, with an average of 12 million items up for sale at any given time. Omidyar himself is worth more than $7 billion. Today he and Pam devote most of their time to the Omidyar Network, a philanthropic organization that helps poor people around the world get into business—and they've pledged to give away all but 1% of their fortune over the next 20 years. "My mother always taught me to treat other people the way I want to be treated and to have respect for other people," he says. "Those are just good basic values to have in a crowded world."

Singapore's highest point, a hill called Bukit Timah, is only 581 feet above sea level.

FINAL THOUGHTS

Some unusual epitaphs and tombstones from the United States and Europe, sent in by our crew of wandering BRI tombstonologists.

In England:
In Memory of Charles Ward
This stone was not erected by
Susan his wife. She erected a
stone to John Salter her second
husband forgetting the affection
of Charles Ward, her husband.

In Massachusetts:
Nearby these grayrocks
Enclosed in a box
Lies Hatter Cox
Who died of smallpox.

In Scotland:
Here lies the body of Sarah,
Wife of John Hayes.
The Lord giveth
And the Lord taketh away
Blessed be the name of the Lord.

In Ireland
Here lie the remains of
John Hall, grocer
The world is not worth a *fig*, &
I have good *raisins* for saying so.

In Illinois:
Anonymous
Cold is my bed, but ah I love it,
For colder are my friends above it.

In Rhode Island:
Thomas Coffin
He's done a-catching cod
And gone to meet his God.

In Scotland:
Here lies John Macpherson
Who was a very peculiar person
He stood six foot two
without his shoe
And was slew
at Waterloo.

In England:
Here lies the wife of
Roger Martin
She was a good wife to
Roger, that's sartin.

In New York:
John Phillips
Accidentally shot as a mark of
affection by his brother.

In Mississippi:
Anonymous
Here lies my wife in earthly mold,
Who when she lived
did naught but scold.
Peace! Wake her not,
for now she's still,
She had; but now I have my will.

In Colorado:
Anonymous
He called Bill Smith a liar.

In Georgia:
Dr. J.J. Subers
Been Here
And Gone
Had a Good Time.

Royale with Cheese: There are more than 1,000 McDonald's restaurants in France.

IT'S IN THE CARDS, PT. II

When Uncle John read his fortune this morning, the ace of spades told him that you'd want more information about telling fortunes with playing cards than we gave you on page 284. We can't fight fate, so here's Part II.

TWO, THREE, AND FOUR OF A KIND

As we told you in Part I, the meaning of an individual card can change if it's dealt upside down. The meaning of different *combinations* of cards in the Past, Present, Future, or Surprise piles will change in proportion to how many of the cards are dealt upside down. For example, in the case of three aces, if only one of the aces is upside down, the right-side-up qualities will predominate over the upside-down qualities. If two of the three aces are upside down, the upside-down qualities will predominate.

SEVENS

Pair of Sevens. Right-side up, two sevens could refer to the love that the subject and another person have for each other. If one or both of the cards are upside down: disloyalty, deceit, or regret.

Three Sevens. Right-side up: sadness brought on by sickness, the loss of friends, or deep remorse. Upside down: a minor ailment, or an unpleasant backlash following a period of great pleasure.

Four Sevens. Right-side up: schemes and traps set by angry, jealous opponents. Upside down: small triumphs over weak enemies.

EIGHTS

Pair of Eights. Right-side up: unexpected developments, which may include passing infatuations or trivial pleasures. Upside down: paying the price for foolishness.

Three Eights. Right-side up: love—the responsible kind—is in the air. Upside down: flirtation, dissipation, and foolishness.

Four Eights. Right-side up: a journey or a new position of responsibility having periods of both success and failure. Upside down: stability and tranquility.

Special Pair Combinations. The eight of diamonds paired with

In the past 75 million years, the Earth's magnetic poles have reversed 171 times.

the eight of hearts symbolizes difficult tasks or a new suit of clothes. Paired with the eight of spades, it indicates sickness; paired with the eight of clubs, it refers to enduring love.

NINES

Pair of Nines. Right-side up: happiness and wealth, or possibly a change of address. Upside down: small problems. If the nine of clubs is paired with the nine of hearts, an inheritance is forthcoming (or was, if it's in the Past pile).

Three Nines. Right-side up: prosperity, happiness, and good health. Upside down: bad judgement, resulting in temporary financial reversals.

Four Nines. An unexpected development is coming. The amount of time that passes before the event takes place is proportionate to how many of the nines are upside down. If all four of them are, don't hold your breath.

Five Nines. Poor eyesight. (There are only *four* nines in a deck.)

TENS

Pair of Tens. Unexpected good luck, perhaps relating to a change of occupation. If one of the tens is upside down, the good luck is not far off. If they're both upside down, be prepared to wait awhile. A ten of diamonds paired with the ten of hearts signifies a wedding in the near future.

Three Tens. Financial ruin resulting from lawsuits. The amount of ruin is proportionate to the number of tens that are upside down.

Four Tens. Great wealth and success resulting from the task at hand. The number of obstacles between the subject and wealth and success is proportionate to the number of upside-down tens.

JACKS

Pair of Jacks. Loss of personal property resulting from schemes. If both jacks are upside down, the loss is imminent; if only one is upside down, you still have a little time to say goodbye to your stuff.

Three Jacks. Right-side up: problems caused by acquaintances

76% of American commuters drive to work alone.

and "friends," possibly involving the smearing of the subjects reputation. Upside down: a physical conflict with a social inferior.

Four Jacks. Wild, noisy parties with plenty of food and drink. The more jacks that are upside down, the less enjoyable the party.

QUEENS

Pair of Queens. Secrets exposed following a confidential meeting between friends. One card upside down: a rivalry forms as a result of the meeting. Both cards upside down: bad behavior—*the subject's*—that does not go unpunished.

Three Queens. A pleasant visit; the visitor could be anyone from a loved one to a perfect stranger. If one or more cards are upside down, you will be the subject of gossip or scandal. If all three cards are upside down, you could be involved in a physical altercation.

Four Queens. A social gathering or occasion of some kind; how *un*happy you are at the event depends on how many of the queens are upside down. If they're all right-side up, you'll have a blast.

KINGS

Pair of Kings. Cooperation, good behavior, and wise decisions in business affairs bring great rewards. The number of obstacles to be overcome is proportionate to the number of upside down cards.

Three Kings. A difficult problem faced head-on. The difficulty of solving it is proportionate to the number of upside-down cards. If all three kings are upside down, the problem will remain unsolved.

Four Kings. Honors, promotions, and special treatment. With every card that is upside down, these goodies diminish in value but will arrive more quickly.

ACES

Pair of Aces. A coming together of some kind. A heart-and-club pair signifies a union entered into for good purposes; a diamond-and-spade pair signifies a union for bad purposes. The other combinations are more neutral. If one or both of the aces are upside down, the goal of the union, be it good or evil, will not be realized.

Three Aces. Personal troubles, perhaps caused by a faithless lover, that are mitigated by the arrival of good news. The extent to

Numbats, marsupials native to Australia, have 52 teeth, more than any other land mammal...

which the subject's problems are their own fault is proportionate to the number of cards that are upside down.

Four Aces. Watch out! Four aces are great in poker...but a disaster in fortune-telling. They could represent physical danger, financial collapse, relationship troubles, even jail time. But there's still hope: The more aces that are upside down, the less serious the trouble.

OTHER COMBINATIONS TO WATCH FOR

Seven of Diamonds with the Queen of Diamonds. A big fight. With the queen of clubs: uncertainty in thought or deed. With the queen of hearts: good news.

Jacks, Queens, and Kings in a Row. Companionship, social enjoyment, festive parties, and other good times.

Nine of Hearts with the King of Hearts. Good luck for lovers.

Seven of Spades with the Jack, Queen, or King of Any Suit. A false friend is exposed.

Queen of Spades with the Jack of Spades. The subject should be wary of a hostile woman who seeks to harm them.

Ten of Diamonds with the Seven of Spades. Delay.

Nine of Diamonds with the Eight of Hearts. A trip.

Ten of Diamonds with the Eight of Clubs. A trip taken for reasons of love or romance.

Five of Spades with the Eight of Spades. Jealousy resulting in offensive, hurtful behavior.

Several Numbered Spades in a Row. Financial setbacks, possibly even bankruptcy, depending on the number of cards.

Seven and Eight of Diamonds. Gossip and innuendo that leads back to the subject.

Ten of Clubs Followed by an Ace. Lots of money. If this combination is in turn followed by an eight and a king, the subject will make or receive a proposition of marriage.

Ace of Diamonds with the Ten of Hearts. Marriage.

Jack, Queen, King, and Ace of the Same Color. Another combination that indicates marriage. If the jack of hearts and the queen of spades are also nearby, there are obstacles to the marriage that must be overcome.

THE GODFATHER OF FITNESS

These days it seems like there's an aerobics studio on every corner, TV ads promise us "washboard abs," and pantries are stocked with granola bars. But 50 years ago, fitness had an entirely different meaning. And then one man—Jack LaLanne—changed it all.

JUMPING JACK

You may remember Jack LaLanne from his television show—a trim, energetic man in a tight jumpsuit, doing jumping jacks in the opening sequence. From the 1950s through the '80s, LaLanne was a part of daily life for millions of Americans—they exercised to his show, read his books, and watched his highly publicized "muscleman stunts." LaLanne brought the American public an amazing number of fitness firsts, including things we still see every day: health clubs targeted at ordinary men and women, sophisticated exercise machines, and televised nutritional tips. What's even more amazing is that in his mid-90s, Jack LaLanne still teaches the value of exercise and good nutrition through the example of his own remarkable health. But for such a health and fitness icon, LaLanne got off to a pretty rough start.

Born in 1914 in San Francisco, he was a thin, sickly child whose mother tried to boost his energy level by feeding him rich desserts. By the age of 15, Jack already had the health troubles of an old man—boils, a bad back, flat feet, and poor eyesight. Worst of all were crippling headaches, so painful that he frequently lost his temper and even contemplated suicide. His moods were so dangerous that on one occasion he tried to burn down the house, and twice tried to kill his brother—once with an axe, and once with a butcher knife.

WORK IT OUT

After numerous doctors failed to diagnose the boy's problem, in 1929 Jack's mother tried a different approach: Instead of taking him to another doctor, she dragged him to the Oakland Woman's City Club for a lecture on health and nutrition. The speaker, Paul

Bragg, preached a gospel of eating only natural foods and getting plenty of exercise. Bragg was also a showman who, to emphasize his own good health, did cartwheels across the stage.

An impressed Jack stayed after the lecture to speak to Bragg. He later recalled, "Dr. Bragg asked me, 'What do you eat for breakfast, lunch, and dinner?' and I told him, 'Cakes, pies, and ice cream.' He said, 'Jack, you are a walking garbage can.'" Bragg explained to him that diet and exercise could cure his headaches and make him strong, athletic…and even attractive. Jack decided to give it a try.

FROM DYING TO DYNAMO

After that day—LaLanne later claimed—he never ate another sweet. He also became a vegetarian (though years later, he added meat back into his diet) and took handfuls of vitamins. He began lifting weights at the local YMCA, and even studied *Gray's Anatomy* to help develop and tone each muscle.

The skinny kid with bad skin, special shoes, and a back brace soon disappeared, along with the headaches and violent episodes, and Jack soon developed the broad-shouldered, narrow-hipped physique that would become his trademark. In high school he excelled in wrestling, football, baseball, swimming, and track. His mother wanted him to become a doctor and missionary, but he wanted to become a missionary of a different sort: Like Paul Bragg, he wanted to promote nutrition and exercise.

At the age of 18, LaLanne started a bakery business, selling whole-grain breads, and converted the family backyard into a gym where he coached local policemen and firemen in exercise and weightlifting. In his spare time, he earned a chiropractic degree.

THE ORIGINAL CULTURE CLUB

In 1936 LaLanne decided to move the gym into a building of its own: the Jack LaLanne Physical Culture Studio in Oakland, California. At a time when private gyms catered mostly to boxers, LaLanne's club opened its doors to everyone, including—and especially—women, kids, and the elderly.

Members of the LaLanne Studio routinely worked out with weights—an idea almost unheard of outside of the boxing community at the time—and got LaLanne's personal assistance and nutritional advice. A blacksmith helped LaLanne invent exercise

Abraham Lincoln's grandfather was also named Abraham, and also died from a gunshot.

equipment, including the world's first leg-extension machines, weight-selector machines, and machines to aid squats. He is credited with designing the first exercise equipment that used pulleys and cables, features standard on weightlifting machines today.

But for all his inventiveness, LaLanne could barely pay the rent during the Studio's early days. And his main obstacle came from an unexpected source—doctors, who called LaLanne a crackpot and told patients that his program was a menace. They claimed that men would become too muscle-bound to raise their arms, women would begin to look like men, and the elderly would get heart attacks. They even warned that LaLanne's methods could lead to hemorrhoids.

In 1936 LaLanne made an unusual offer to attract clients: He invited parents to send their children to his gym, and if he couldn't make them fit and healthy, he'd refund their membership dues. The strategy worked and brought in new customers, including adults. The Studio made a profit throughout the 1930s and '40s, staying open even during World War II while LaLanne served in the Navy. And it was still going strong in the 1950s when he got his big break.

COUCH POTATOES BEWARE

In 1951 a local television station approached LaLanne about hosting an exercise program, the first of its kind in the country. During the audition, LaLanne led a well-dressed TV executive through a series of exercises (all without making the man leave his padded swivel chair). He got the job, and became host of *The Jack LaLanne Show*, an early-morning program that aired on KGO-TV in San Francisco.

On the show LaLanne always wore a jumpsuit that showed off his muscles as he leapt around in ballet slippers. At first he shared a nearly empty studio with nothing but a wooden chair, but eventually he added a white German shepherd named Happy to the cast. Happy did tricks for the kids while Jack led their parents—mostly mothers at that early hour—through calisthenics using chairs and the floor as the primary exercise "equipment."

The show soon became known as much for LaLanne's folksy advice as for the exercising. On diet, he once said, "If man makes it, don't eat it! If it tastes good, spit it out." On exercise: "If your

Dads are less likely than moms to recognize that their child is overweight.

back porch is draggin' and your shoulders are saggin' and you have no pep in your step, it's time for a change!" And on his philosophy of health: "Exercise is king and diet is queen; put them together, and you've got an empire."

At first, TV critics had an even lower opinion of LaLanne than doctors did; they predicted he'd be off the air in weeks. But the show held on and soon began airing in Los Angeles as well.

ESCAPE FROM ALCATRAZ

The success of LaLanne's show didn't quiet his detractors; doctors and sports coaches still called him a fake. "Everyone said I was just a muscle-bound charlatan," he later said. "I had to show them I was an athlete." So in 1954, on his 40th birthday, he set a world record by swimming the length of the San Francisco Golden Gate Bridge underwater…while pulling 140 pounds of equipment behind him.

The stunt gave him some much-needed publicity, so he decided to raise the stakes. In 1955 a handcuffed LaLanne battled strong currents to swim from Alcatraz Island to Fisherman's Wharf in San Francisco—debunking the myth that it was impossible to swim across San Francisco Bay from Alcatraz to the city. Two years later, LaLanne not only swam 6.5 miles through the Golden Gate Channel, he towed a 2,500-pound cabin cruiser behind him. In 1959, at age 45, he did 1,000 pushups and 1,000 chinups in an hour and 22 minutes.

Now a media celebrity, LaLanne willingly shared his workout feats with television audiences, including repeated lifts of 140-pound dumbbells or climbs of a 25-foot rope with 140 pounds of extra weight strapped to his belt. His "health drinks" included hundreds of ground-up supplements as well as liver tablets, kelp, carrot and celery juice, and egg whites. At one point, LaLanne even tried drinking raw cow's blood because he'd learned that the Masai people of East Africa drank it to stay healthy. (A blood clot in his cocktail ended the experiment.)

In 1959 *The Jack LaLanne Show* was nationally syndicated on ABC, and it would continue to run through 1985. Faithful viewers admired LaLanne's stunts as well as the fact that he practiced what he preached: He kept to a strict diet, and his own workouts were so rigorous that he offered a $10,000 prize to any athlete who could match him. Nobody ever collected.

During the Civil War, the Union Army had twice as many deserters as the Confederates.

By the 1960s, millions of Americans were stretching, jumping, and bending with Jack LaLanne. They also listened to his opinions. When he said, "Read every food label, and if you can't pronounce the ingredients, don't buy it," or, "The best part of a doughnut is the hole," they changed their shopping habits. His health club business also expanded, and in the 1980s there were 200 clubs bearing his name. Almost singlehandedly, LaLanne had launched the American health and fitness craze.

THE JUICE IS LOOSE

In the 1980s, the landscape changed. Fitness guru Richard Simmons had a hit daily TV show and Jane Fonda's workout tapes sold millions. After LaLanne's show went off the air in 1985, he became a pitchman for products like home exercise equipment and vitamin supplements.

In 1991 he helped start the home juicing fad with the Jack LaLanne Juice Tiger, a $150 electric juice-making machine. In two years, the company sold more than 600,000, but many were recalled after 14 people suffered eye injuries and facial lacerations when the juicer's grinding mechanism came loose. In 1993 the machine was revamped and re-released as the Jack LaLanne Power Juicer. The 15-year-old infomercial for the Power Juicer still airs regularly on television.

He also keeps performing the feats of strength that helped make him famous. On his 70th birthday in 1984, he swam a mile and a half across Long Beach Harbor in California—with his hands and feet shackled and towing 70 people in 70 rowboats. For his 90th birthday in 2004, he planned to swim 26 miles underwater (with the assistance of oxygen tanks) from Catalina Island to Long Beach Harbor. But he didn't. Reason: His wife, Elaine, pleaded with him not to. "I told him I'd leave him if he tried it," she said.

In 2008 LaLanne turned 94, and he still works out every day for two hours. He's been awarded a star on the Hollywood Walk of Fame, and in 2008 Governor Arnold Schwarzenegger, a longtime fitness advocate himself, inducted LaLanne into the California Hall of Fame. LaLanne plans to keep pushing himself as long as he can, because, as he puts it, "I can't die. It would ruin my image."

Q: What is a *kamalayka*? A: A waterproof shirt made of walrus intestines.

COME SEE THE METEOR SHOWERS

Mark this page and check it now and then. You might get to see several spectacular shows a year...and they're all free.

IT'S A PERSEID! IT'S A LEONID...

Do you know what a *meteoroid* is? It's a small, solid particle traveling through space. How about a *meteor*? It's the streak of light you see in the sky when a meteoroid hits the Earth's atmosphere and burns up. Most meteoroids are smaller than a grain of sand and burn up relatively quickly; some are larger—up to boulder size—and can cause "fireballs" to flare across the sky. Some even make it to the ground, at which point they're referred to as *meteorites*. They're common, but several times a year they become much *more* common, in events known as "meteor showers," or "meteor storms." What's responsible for them? Comets.

Comets are relatively small solid objects in our solar system that, like the planets, orbit our Sun. Unlike the planets, whose orbits are fairly round, comets have *elliptical* orbits (long and narrow), traveling from way out in the solar system to its center at the Sun, which it circles very closely. Comets are made up of ice, dust, and rock, and as they get close to the Sun, some of that ice turns to gas, and some of its dust and rock is ejected. That's what gives comets their big, glowing coronas, and their tails. After many millions of years, the entire orbital path of a comet becomes filled with debris...and then along comes us.

As the Earth makes *its* orbit around the Sun, it passes through several of those debris-filled comet trails. Some of that debris enters our atmosphere—and we see many more meteors than usual. That's how we get those fantastic shows.

THE NAME GAME

Meteor showers are named after constellations, and that causes a lot of confusion, since the meteors have absolutely nothing to do with those constellations. Here's the explanation:

- When you look up into the sky during a meteor shower, you can

An average of two people per year die from flatulence.

can see many seemingly unrelated meteors in a wide swath of the sky, all of them moving in many different directions...but look more closely. If you could draw a line back from all the meteors you see, you'd find that they all go back to one point in the sky.

• All the debris fragments in a comet's path are naturally traveling the same direction, in parallel lines. As we view them as meteors from here on Earth, *perspective* makes those parallel paths appear to recede to a single point in the distance. This point of origin is known as a meteor shower's *radiant*.

• Because it occurs in the sky, the stars become a backdrop, and the radiants of different meteor showers fall "in front" of different constellations. In the case of the *Perseid* meteor shower, for example, which happens every August, its radiant falls within the constellation *Perseus*—hence the name. The radiant of November's *Leonid* meteor shower is located in the constellation *Leo*.

• The confusion comes in because people long ago believed (and many still do) that meteor showers were somehow related to those constellations. They're not: Constellations are made up of stars billions and trillions of miles away; meteor showers actually occur in the Earth's atmosphere—just 50 to 75 miles above your head.

COPY THESE TWO PAGES

There are dozens of noticeable meteor showers during the year. Here's a list of some of the most intense. Put a copy of this page on the refrigerator so you won't miss any of the shows. Check an astronomy book or an online source to find out where the radiant constellations are going to be, dress appropriately—and enjoy.

January: Start off the new year with the *Quadrantids*, seen from about January 1–5. They're named after the constellation *Quadrans Muralis*, which isn't recognized anymore—modern star charts show the Quadrantids emanating from around the constellation *Hercules*. They regularly show as many as 130 meteors an hour (if weather conditions are good).

April: The *Lyrids* are named for the constellation *Lyra*, they peak on April 21 or 22, and can show up to about 30 meteors an hour.

May: The *Eta Aquarids* peak on the night of May 5 and appear to emanate from inside the constellation *Aquarius*. They're relatively

The first American paper currency was a 12-pence note designed by Paul Revere.

mild: In the Northern Hemisphere you can see about 10 meteors an hour, in the Southern Hemisphere about 30—but once in a while those numbers climb. And the comet that left this trail: Halley's Comet, which orbits the Sun every 75.3 years.

June: The *June Boötids* arrive in late June, peaking on June 27—and you never know how many meteors are going to show up. Often it's very few...but sometimes it goes crazy, with more than 100 an hour. Bonus: The particles in this comet trail are moving at about 16 kilometers per second—not very fast in the comet-debris world—making for slow, lazy meteors.

August: The *Perseids* last from around July 20 to August 22, peaking on the night of August 12th, when you can see from 50 to 80 meteors an hour. It's named for the constellation *Perseus*. In 1864 it became the first meteor shower positively associated with a comet —the Swift-Tuttle, which orbits the Sun once every 156 years.

October: In the early evening hours of October 9, 1998, millions of people in Japan looked up—and saw about 500 meteors an hour fill the sky for about two hours. They were the *Dracobinids,* named for the constellation *Draco,* and peak from October 8–10. NASA reports that in some years it can reach as high as *20,000* an hour.

Also in October: The *Orionids* reach their highest output between October 20 and 22 and appear to emanate from the constellation *Orion*. These are some of the fastest meteors, zipping along at about 66 kilometers a second—often producing fireballs.

November: The *Leonids* are associated with *Leo*, and show up every year between November 13 and 21, with the peak generally on the 17th. They're known for their 33-year-cycles—the length of time their comet takes to make one orbit. Some years it causes meteor storms that are downright frightening: On November 12, 1833, an estimated *60,000 meteors an hour* filled the sky above the eastern portion of North America for about four hours before dawn. Many people thought the world was coming to an end.

December: The *Geminids* come between December 12 and 14. Their corresponding constellation is, of course, *Gemini*, and they're known for their multi-colored show—with white, yellow, blue, red, and green meteors—as many as 140 of them per hour—flying across the sky.

THE KITCHEN OLYMPICS

In the world of amateur recipe contests, the Pillsbury Bake-Off is the Nobel Prize, the Oscars, and the Kentucky Derby all rolled into one.

HOMEWARD BOUND

Shortly after World War II, Pillsbury's ad agency was looking for a way to celebrate Pillsbury's 80th anniversary and boost the sales of Pillsbury flour. American women were leaving the jobs they'd held during the war and heading back to the kitchen. So why not hold a recipe contest, with cash prizes big enough to attract the attention of both women and the media? Thus was born the "Grand National Recipe and Baking Contest," held in 1949 at the Waldorf=Astoria Hotel in New York City.

Fifty thousand dollars for the grand prize is a healthy sum, even today, but in 1949 it was a fortune (an additional $20,000 was to be divided among eight other finalists), and contestants flocked to enter what the press dubbed the "Bake-Off Contest"—a nickname that Pillsbury adopted as the contest's official title. Thousands of recipes poured in. A group of home economists read every one and winnowed them down to 100 finalists. The Waldorf's ballroom was transformed into a gigantic kitchen with 100 electric ovens (using power drawn from the New York City subway system), and the 97 women and 3 men went to work. The first grand-prize winner was Mrs. Ralph E. Smafield of Rockford, Illinois. Her winning recipe: No-Knead Water-Rising Twists.

By 1949 standards, the event was expensive to produce, and Pillsbury stockholders were dubious about its value. But research showed that the publicity brought in around 700,000 new customers, so the contest was held annually right up through 1976, when it changed to every other year. The grand prize is now a whopping $1 million.

THE TIMES, THEY ARE A-CHANGIN'

In the booming postwar 1950s, most entries were made-from-scratch cakes, pies, cookies, yeast breads, and quick breads. The labor-intensive entries reflected the belief that women were predominantly homemakers with time to bake fancy cakes (like the

Pope John Paul II once asked Muhammad Ali for an autograph.

1951 winner, Starlight Double-Delight Cake) and homemade breads (like the Ring-a-Ling Rolls that won in 1955).

But by the 1960s, women had begun to work outside the home again, and time-saving and convenience were major issues. So the rules changed: Contestants were allowed to use cake mixes, refrigerated biscuit dough, frozen vegetables, processed cheese, and canned goods, and Pillsbury encouraged recipes for everyday, easy-to-prepare food. The 1963 grand-prize winner, for example, was Hungry Boys' Casserole; the 1967 winner was Muffin Mix Buffet Bread. Tunnel of Fudge Cake, a 1966 finalist, set off a national craze for Bundt pans and Bundt cake mixes.

TRENDS THROUGH THE DECADES

- **1970s.** Entries started showing an international flavor, though the winners generally didn't—judges were still leaning toward old-fashioned baked goods like Pecan Pie Surprise Bars (1971), Banana Crunch Cake (1973), and Whole Wheat Raisin Loaf (1976).
- **1980s.** Entries reflected affluence and an interest in sophisticated entertaining, such as the elegant Chocolate Praline Layer Cake (1988), as well as a swerve toward "healthy" eating—recipes used chicken instead of beef, and more vegetables, like Italian Zucchini Crescent Pie (1980), Broccoli Brunch Braid (1988), and Chick 'N Corn Mini Pies (1984).
- **1990s.** Ethnic recipes like Cheesy Chile Polenta (1998) and Fiesta Chicken Salad (1996) were now firmly entrenched, and the quick-and-easy approach, using more and more convenience foods, was almost taken for granted: In 1998, for example, there was Fresh Pear Salsa made in two steps with only six ingredients, Easy Bruschetta Snacks made in five steps with six ingredients, and Apple Cobbler Cake in four steps with six ingredients.
- **2000s.** Lots of experimentation with unusual combinations of foods and flavors like Papaya-Raisin Steak Rolls in Mojo Sauce (2006), or Raspberry-Chipotle Barbecue Chicken Pizza (2008).

PLAYING BY THE RULES

In the beginning, the only required ingredient for a Bake-Off recipe was ½ cup of Pillsbury flour. After all, if you were proud of your baking, you baked from scratch with basic ingredients like flour, butter, eggs, and sugar. Today it's a different story.

Studies show: Married men change their underwear twice as often as single men.

Modern entrants are required to use at least one ingredient from "List A" (products made by Pillsbury) and another ingredient from "List A" *or* "List B" (mostly products made by that year's Bake-Off co-sponsors). In 2008 List A was a catalog of Pillsbury convenience foods—refrigerated biscuits and rolls, refrigerated pie and pizza crusts, 12 varieties of brownie mix, and Old El Paso taco shells. List B included Green Giant frozen vegetables, Jif peanut butter, Smucker's jams and ice cream toppings, and Crisco oils. Smart contestants have learned to build their recipes around Pillsbury products and work in some co-sponsor products, too.

AND...THEY'RE OFF!

Contestants submit recipes in any of several categories. In 2006 the categories were Cooking for Two, Brand New You (a reference to healthier eating), Dinner Made Easy, Wake Up to Breakfast, and Simple Snacks. In 2008 they were Breakfast & Brunches, Pizza Creations, Entertaining Appetizers, Old El Paso Mexican Favorites, and Sweet Treats. Recipes must be original—anything that's been published or has won a previous cooking contest will be disqualified (and Pillsbury has plenty of researchers checking up). One winner is chosen in each category; the grand-prize winner is chosen from the category winners.

Since 1996 the grand prize has been $1 million, doled out in 20 annual payments of $50,000. But there's more: The grand-prize winner also gets a new GE oven and $7,000 worth of appliances. The winners in each category get $5,000 and a new oven. There are always a few other cash prizes too, like the GE "Imagination at Work" Award, worth $5,000.

WEEDING OUT THE DUDS

Long before the actual Bake-Off, thousands of submitted recipes are scrutinized by an independent judging agency to be sure they meet contest requirements. That eliminates a lot of submissions. Then the recipes are read by home economists, who evaluate them on the basis of taste, appearance, creativity, consumer appeal, and the use of eligible ingredients. More eliminations. The final batch is professionally kitchen-tested for flavor and workability. Eventually the judging agency decides on 100 finalists and 10 alternates, who get the notification phone call around

There are no permanent lakes or rivers in Saudi Arabia.

the end of September. The contest takes place in April of the following year.

LADIES, START YOUR OVENS

Bake-Off day starts with a crack-of-dawn group breakfast (if they're not too nervous to eat) followed by the Grand March (clapping and yelling are required) into the enormous hotel ballroom. Their escorts: the Pillsbury doughboy with George Pillsbury—great-grandson of the company founder—and his wife, Sally. Each contestant is already wearing his or her official contest apron and nametag, and at 8:00 a.m. they sprint for a workstation—one of 100 mini-kitchens sporting an electric range and a 2' x 3' countertop (but no sink). Each is supplied with enough equipment and ingredients to make their recipe three times: The best version goes to the judges, the next best is for photography, and the third is for other contestants and the press to sample. A runner stays nearby to help as needed, but for the next few hours the contestant's total concentration goes into one thing: producing perfection.

And it's not easy. From the moment the baking begins, reporters follow contestants relentlessly, filming them, interviewing them, and possibly even distracting them from the preparation of their recipes. When she's finally got her dish the way she wants it, she places it on a tray and carries it—very carefully—out of the bustling ballroom and down a long, long corridor to the door of the judges' room.

SITTING IN JUDGMENT

At 8:00 a.m. the nine judges are sequestered in a special room set up with tasting tables and a comfortable sitting area. But judging is not a leisurely process, since the first finished dish arrives around 9:00 and the rest follow in a steady stream. And it can become overwhelming as the dishes pour in faster than the judges can cleanse their palates with celery sticks. Each team of judges will taste as many different dishes as there are entrants in their assigned categories, then taste the best ones all over again. When they're done with their own category, they taste the best ones from the other categories in order to arrive at a consensus and declare the winners. Tanya Wenman Steel, a 2008 judge, said, "We repeatedly asked questions like, would people make this in their own homes, did it have an original twist, did it look appetiz-

73% of acne sufferers say they would choose clear skin over winning the lottery.

ing, how easy was it to make, and, most importantly, was it delicious. We were about to award someone $1,000,000 so we took our responsibility very seriously."

Ninety-two women and eight men made it to the finals of the 43rd Pillsbury Bake-Off in 2008. The grand-prize winner: Carolyn Gurtz of Gaithersburg, Maryland, with her recipe for Double-Delight Peanut Butter Cookies (made not from scratch but from a can of Pillsbury refrigerated peanut butter cookie dough). Gurtz was "absolutely shocked. When I looked at *all* the other entries, I don't know how the judges picked just one." Her six-ingredient recipe included one Pillsbury convenience food, four sponsor products...and cinnamon.

CONSPIRACY THEORIES

Who wins the PBO and why is the subject of a lot of conjecture in the amateur recipe contest world, and where there's a prize as big as this one, conspiracy theories are bound to crop up. A few:

- **The Chicken-Sweet Theory:** In 1998 the winner was Salsa Couscous Chicken. In 2000 it was Cream Cheese Brownie Pie; in 2002, Chicken Florentine Panini. In 2004 it was Oats 'n Honey Granola Pie; in 2006, Baked Chicken and Spinach Stuffing; and in 2008, Double-Delight Peanut Butter Cookies. Chicken, sweet, chicken, sweet, chicken, sweet. Coincidence? Not according to conspiracy theorists. They're convinced that the winning recipes always alternate between something with chicken and something sweet. Our advice: do *not* try to win with a chicken recipe in a sweet year (and vice versa).
- **The Crooked-Winner Theory:** Suspicious PBO followers were convinced that Anna Ginsberg, winner of the 2006 grand prize, was not the housewife she claimed to be. A former advertising exec, Ginsberg cleverly plotted her win, they said, by using information she received from someone closely connected to the Bake-Off, then inventing a recipe that used Pillsbury Dunkables—a failing waffle-stick product that Pillsbury was anxious to promote. Ginsberg's winning recipe: Baked Chicken and Spinach Stuffing (2006 was a chicken year). The stuffing was made with Dunkables.
- **The Crooked-Employee Theory:** There's also a good chance, say conspiracy theorists, that corrupt employees of Pillsbury and its

Official state beverage of Alabama: Conecuh Ridge Whiskey...

parent company, General Mills, give preferential treatment or provide inside information to select contestants in exchange for a piece of the pie…uh, cake…uh, winnings.

• **The Men Men Men Theory:** 1996 was a banner year for men in the Bake-Off. Fourteen of them (the most ever) made it to the finals. Coincidentally, that same year the grand prize jumped to $1 million. And who won? A man. Kurt Wait was the first (and so far only) man to win the Pillsbury Bake-Off. But it was no conspiracy—Wait was an experienced cook who had won the grand prize in the Sutter Home Winery's 1994 Build a Better Burger contest with a recipe for Portobello Burgers with Sun-Dried Tomato Mayonnaise. Wait's winning PBO recipe: Macadamia Fudge Torte, made with Pillsbury devil's food cake mix.

HONORABLE MENTION

Inventive recipe titles are a PBO tradition. These not only zing off the weird chart but also make you wonder if you'd actually want to eat them.

Peanut Butter Mole Enchiladas (2008)

South-of-the-Border Sushi Appetizers (2008)

Orange Marmalade–Chorizo Pizza (2008)

Magic Marshmallow Crescent Puffs (1969)

Peacheesy Pie (1964)

Loaded Baked Potato Pizza (2008)

Swaddled Peppers (2004)

Dotted Swiss and Spinach Quiche (1990)

Tropical Crab Rangoon Appetizers (2008)

Granola "Fried" Ice Cream with Red Cinnamon Sauce (2004)

Choco–Peanut Butter–Banana Breakfast Strudel (2008)

Pizza Bubble Ring (2004)

Guess Again Candy Crunch (2000)

Tropical Sunshine Flatcakes with Orange Cream (2008)

Blueberry Burrito Blintzes (2006)

Chicken Manicotti Olé (2002)

Toasted Mexi-Meatball Hoagies (2006)

…Official state beverage of Indiana: water.

THE RUNNINGMAN, PT. II

Part I of Robert Garside's run around the world (page 399) was "man vs. the elements." This time it's "man vs. man." And it's a lot harsher.

THE LYINGMAN

The first person to publicly question Garside's feats was David Blaikie, a former long-distance runner and editor of the magazine *Ultramarathon World.* "I do not believe, based on what he has posted about himself on various Web sites and what has been reported by the media, that he has fully run any of the major sections of the world he has claimed, or even a substantial portion of any section." Only a superhuman, argued Blaikie, could run 50 to 125 miles a day, every day, for days at a time, and then only after months of training and with a support team following close behind. And no one in the ultramarathon community (an ultramarathon is any running race over 26 miles) had even *heard* of this guy before.

Blaikie and others did some digging and found major holes in Garside's story:

• His account of being robbed in Pakistan was a complete fabrication. Garside was actually in London at the time dealing with a "personal crisis" having to do with his ex-girlfriend. In fact, Garside skipped much of that first leg through Europe. *That's* why the official starting point was New Delhi, and not Piccadilly Circus.

• In December 1999, Garside's diary stated that he was "alone and heading up to the Amazon jungle." But several witnesses saw him in Rio de Janeiro at the time, partying with one of Britain's most famous fugitives, train robber Ronnie Biggs.

• Even if Garside had the stamina to do the run himself, there was *no way* that his girlfriend—a student with no long-distance running experience—could have kept up with him through the dangerous jungles of Mexico for 10 straight days. In truth, the couple skipped 800 miles of the run, opting to travel by plane to just south of the United States border.

WAR OF THE WORDS

"Blaikie is my Osama bin Laden," Garside responded. "I've been watching this terrorist every step of the way. This faceless coward is conducting psychological warfare, testing me. You're not supposed to write such things based on theory. You write on evidence." And the evidence, according to Garside, showed overwhelmingly that he accomplished the feat. But the Guinness people were taking their time scrutinizing the hundreds of hours of tapes that Garside gave them, as well as the mounds of credit card receipts, official records, and witness testimonies. "I would never do the things he is saying," said Garside during his run.

So if his run was legitimate, why did he put fictional passages on his Web site? Garside always seemed to have an answer:

- His account of being robbed in Pakistan was a "psychological tactic" designed to fool would-be competitors into thinking that there was no way they could catch up. "As with any competitive sport, there must be tactics. I'm a sportsman, I can do that."
- About partying in Rio when he was supposed to have been running through the Amazon: "At the time I had a representative doing my Web page for me, so I slapped his wrist and it will be changed as soon as I have the time." (It wasn't.)
- Why leave out the part about the plane trip across Mexico? "I didn't think it was interesting. I didn't know people wanted to hear about that."

JUMPING OFF THE BANDWAGON

As more of Garside's lies began to surface, his allies began to abandon him. "Robert has deluded himself into believing that he has not cheated," said journalist Peter Hadfield, who had covered the early part of Garside's attempt. "Every time his fabrications are exposed, he invents a new story and convinces himself it is true. When his cover is blown again, he invents another story and then convinces himself of that."

Even harsher words came from British photo agent Mike Soulsby, who had given Garside more than $10,000 early in the run. But then Soulsby withdrew his support and publicly blacklisted Garside, telling reporters, "I had thought Robert was credible but now realize I have been totally and utterly conned. He's a miserable little two-faced shyster."

As the criticisms kept pouring in and the excuses kept coming out, the war between Garside and Blaikie escalated. Garside claimed Blaikie "sent out the *Ultramarathon World* Taliban posing as journalists" to disrupt his press conferences and taint his name. Blaikie claims that on one night in 2001 Garside made dozens of "abusive phone calls" to his home in Canada. Garside didn't deny it: "I have the moral right to call up this cold, cognitive bastard a million times and keep him up all night and ruin his life. He's ruined mine."

RUNNER'S ENVY

The allegations dogged the final two years of the run. Instead of being celebrated when he arrived in a new city, Garside would have to defend his credibility. "The truth is, my run is too much of an outlandish, wild, wonderful thing to believe. That's why I'm being persecuted. People have been persecuting me my whole life." And why would other long-distance runners be out to get Garside? "They're just jealous that I've done it while they've only talked about it. The hardest thing is to get up day after day after day for over five years and just run, run, run. It's like torture. I have done the run. I have got huge blisters on my left foot to prove it!"

Yet no matter how hard he tried, Garside couldn't run away from the allegations, and each new admission put another dent in his chances of being awarded the record from Guinness. "There's an expression in England," he said, "You can't get anything in life without p*ssing a few people off."

Perhaps the biggest reason that so many runners publicly chided Garside was that had repeatedly turned down requests from actual long-distance runners to join him. Why? What was he hiding?

HARDY-PARDY

In July 2003, only a few weeks after he returned home, Garside was challenged by Britain's Channel Four to run 130 miles around a track in 24 hours...while under observation. That would match the mileage of one of his longest reported days—and, if he succeeded, would put his critics to rest. Garside would have to wear his full pack and carry a bottle of water, just as he did during the actual run. He accepted, writing on his Web site that the challenge would

There are 823 unpaved airport runways in Canada.

be "easy-peasy." It wasn't. According to the ultramarathon runners who monitored the race, Garside's pacing fluctuated throughout and he looked uncommonly winded for someone who claimed to have amazing stamina. Garside gave up after 72 miles, barely halfway through the challenge. Again, he offered an array of excuses: Running on the track was too boring; it was too soon after the world run; he hadn't had enough time to prepare.

NO EXCUSES

Garside's critics pounced. While admitting that 72 miles may be impressive for an amateur, to the ultramarathon runner that distance is "insignificant," so the test confirmed that Garside did not possess the "mental attitude" required to run upwards of 100 miles in a single day over steep terrain in humid conditions while drinking water out of puddles. Still, Garside claimed that in no way did failing the challenge take away from the veracity of his 5½-year run. "That's all that matters," he said.

After that, the press's fascination with Garside faded. In late 2003, he announced plans to swim around the world and to make a movie about his running journey. In 2004 he and Endrina Perez were married, and they later had a child. According to Garside, it took his mind and body two years to fully recover from his run around the world. All he could do was wait for Guinness to finish going over the evidence and make their ruling. That process took nearly four years to complete.

VINDICATION...SORT OF

In March 2007, Guinness finally awarded Garside, by now 40, the official world record. "I am so happy and relieved and I am so grateful to all those people all over the world who helped me throughout the years I was running," Garside beamed to reporters in Piccadilly Circus, where he was honored. But the whispers of "cheater" still lingered, and once again Garside was defending himself. "With good intent, I set out to run around the world...I swear on my mother's life—on Jesus Christ's life—I did it with positive intent and nothing else."

Marco Frigatti, Guinness's head of records, was on hand to present the award...and also found himself on the defensive. "We haven't just asked him what he did and approved him because we liked him," explained Frigatti. "The decision was based on...15 boxes of credit card statements, receipts in Robert's name, and other useful evidence, which supported Robert's presence in all of the 29 countries within the time specified. We also reviewed over 300 time-coded tapes featuring Robert running at different locations during his journey."

So did that finally quiet Garside's critics? Hardly. "I'm stunned, quite frankly," said Ian Champion, the chairman of the U.K. Road Runners Club and a witness to Garside's failed Channel Four Challenge. Champion, along with just about everyone else in the ultramarathon community, refuses to acknowledge Garside's record, maintaining that Guinness's authority "doesn't matter" when it comes to the extreme sport—only sanctioned runs that are monitored by ultramarathon officials would count. So don't expect to see Robert Garside running in any long-distance trials. "He could've achieved so much because his drive and determination are incredibly strong," lamented journalist Peter Hadfield. "Instead, it's his lack of moral character—his readiness to deceive—that's destroyed him."

WHERE IS HE NOW?

After the brief flurry of news stories covering the official record in March 2007, Garside once again slipped out of the limelight. No press reports of his planned swim around the world—or his movie—have surfaced. The various Web sites set up during his run still exist, but they make no mention of the record, the swim, the movie, or even of Garside himself—they just provide links for buying running apparel.

So is Garside living the quiet life? Is he out there right now training in the water? Wait and see, and keep your eyes out for him, because once the Runningman gets going again, who knows where he'll end up...or how he'll get there?

* * *

BIRD WORD

The feather that sticks up from the top of a quail's head is called a *hmuh* (pronounced "h'muh").

Oooh! Ahh! The easiest sounds for the human ear to hear are, in order, "ah," "aw," "eh," and "oo."

THE SECRET RACE TO THE MOON

For nearly 20 years after Neil Armstrong stepped onto the Moon in July 1969, the Soviet Union categorically denied having a manned lunar program of its own. It wasn't until the late 1980s that we began to learn just how close they came to beating the United States to the Moon.

HEARING IS BELIEVING

Not too long after 9:00 p.m. on the evening of April 11, 1961, a United States government listening post off Alaska picked up the sound of human voices speaking in Russian. That wasn't unusual; in the early 1960s, the Cold War was at its height, and the listening post had been set up for the purpose of intercepting Soviet communications.

But as the analysts studied the transmission, they realized that one of the voices was coming from *space*—low-Earth orbit to be exact—and the other voices were transmitting from the Baikonur cosmodrome in Soviet Kazakhstan, headquarters of the USSR's space program. As the entire world would learn in a few hours, the 27-year-old cosmonaut Yuri Gagarin had just become the first human being to fly in space. As was typical with the Soviet space program, the launch had been kept a secret. The signals from space were probably the first inkling the United States had that it had been beaten in the space race once again.

SECOND PLACE

Gagarin had blasted off at 9:07 a.m. Moscow time on the morning of April 12 (Moscow is 12 hours ahead of Alaska). He made just one orbit around the Earth before landing back on Soviet soil at 10:55 a.m. That's not much of a spaceflight by modern standards, but in 1961 it stunned the world. Just as it had when it launched *Sputnik*, the world's first artificial satellite, in October 1957, the Soviet Union had demonstrated that it, not the United States, was leading the way into space. The United States wouldn't be able to send an American astronaut, John Glenn, into orbit until February 1962.

Lady Peseshet of ancient Egypt (about 2400 B.C.) was the world's first known female physician.

JFK'S QUERY

No one felt the sting of second place more than President John F. Kennedy. "Do we have a chance of beating the Soviets by putting a laboratory in space, or by a trip around the Moon, or by a rocket to land on the Moon, or by a rocket to go to the Moon and back with a man?" the president asked in a memo to his vice president, Lyndon Baines Johnson. "Is there any other space program which promises dramatic results in which we could win?"

JFK dispatched Johnson to NASA to get an answer. Wernher von Braun, head of rocket development, suggested that America had a chance at beating the Soviets in a flight *around* the Moon, but that it had an even better chance at being the first country to land a man on the Moon's surface. JFK weighed the options and on May 25, 1961, made his famous speech committing the United States to landing a man on the Moon by the end of the decade.

NO CONTEST?

On July 20, 1969, the United States won the race to the Moon when astronaut Neil A. Armstrong became the first human being to set foot on lunar soil. But had the Soviets contemplated trying to beat the United States to the Moon? For more than two decades after the Moon landing, the official answer was a definitive, categorical "*Nyet!*" The Soviets claimed they skipped the Moon race in favor of the more practical challenge of putting a space station into Earth's orbit. And they succeeded—between 1971 and 1986, they launched seven different space stations into orbit.

The Soviets stuck to their we-didn't-shoot-for-the-Moon story until August 18, 1989, when the government's official newspaper, *Izvestiya*, admitted that the USSR had indeed tried to send a cosmonaut to the Moon, in what was one of the most closely guarded secret programs of the Cold War. They had actually come pretty close to succeeding: Were it not for one large technical challenge that proved insurmountable, the Soviet Union might well have won the race.

When the Soviets were planning their lunar program, they faced the same question NASA had faced: Did they want to go in one large rocket, or did they want to use several launches of smaller rockets to assemble a lunar spacecraft in Earth's orbit

The mascot for the Minnesota Vikings is a purple dinosaur named Vikadontis Rex.

before heading to the Moon? Launching everything aboard one rocket was a quicker option, and since beating America to the Moon was a high priority, that's what the Soviets chose to do. They set to work developing a rocket big enough for the job, called the N-1.

DOWNSIZING

Using one rocket, no matter how big it is, severely limits the options on how to get to the Moon and back, and because of this the Soviets' secret program ended up looking a lot like the Apollo program, which also used one rocket, the Saturn V. But because the N-1 was smaller than the Saturn V, the Soviet mission would be smaller in many respects. It would have less room for cargo, and only two cosmonauts could make the trip, not three as on the Apollo missions. And that meant that only one cosmonaut would get to walk on the Moon, instead of two.

• The Soviet plans called for the N-1 rocket to lift a command ship called the *Lunniy Orbitalny Korabl* (LOK) into Earth's orbit. The command ship would then travel to the Moon and enter lunar orbit. An attached lunar lander, called the *Lunniy Kabina* ("Lunar Cabin," or LK, for short), would then separate from the LOK and descend to the lunar surface with one of the cosmonauts aboard. The other cosmonaut had to remain on the LOK.

• After spending about 24 hours on the surface of the Moon, the cosmonaut would climb back into the LK, launch back into lunar orbit, and dock with the LOK. Once the cosmonaut was safely back aboard the LOK, the LK would be jettisoned, and the LOK would fire its rocket, putting the craft on a return course to Earth. Then, when the LOK arrived in Earth's orbit, the crew compartment would split apart from the rest of the LOK and re-enter the atmosphere with the cosmonauts aboard, parachuting to a landing somewhere inside the Soviet Union. The rest of the LOK would burn up on re-entry.

NOT QUITE APOLLO

For all its similarities with the Apollo program, the Soviet lunar program did have its differences.

• Would you want to land on the Moon all by yourself while wearing an unwieldy spacesuit that's difficult to move around in?

st U.S. coin to feature an African American: the Booker T. Washington Memorial Half Dollar (1946).

What if you fell down—who would help you up? The Soviets were so worried about this possibility that they attached a device to the spacesuit that looked like a hula hoop. If the lone cosmonaut did fall on his back while walking on the Moon, he could use the hula hoop to roll over onto his knees and stand back up.

• The Soviets were also worried about the LK becoming so damaged during landing that it would be unable to blast off from the Moon—landing a man on the Moon just to watch him die there would have been a human tragedy, not to mention a public relations disaster. The Soviets made plans to send a second LK to the Moon in advance of the mission…just in case.

• The second LK would have been useless if the cosmonaut landed too far away from it or couldn't find it after landing on the Moon, so the Soviets also planned to send an unmanned, remote-controlled rover to the Moon in advance of the manned landing. Its job would be to select landing sites for both the primary LK and the unmanned backup, and then to serve as landing beacon for both LKs. The rover would also be equipped with oxygen tanks and a platform for the cosmonaut to stand on, to enable it to ferry the cosmonaut to the backup LK if necessary.

TOO LITTLE, TOO LATE

So why didn't the Soviets make it to the Moon? Part of the problem was that the Soviet leadership didn't take the challenge seriously until it was too late to catch up with the Americans. Premier Nikita Khrushchev endorsed the idea of a lunar program in 1962, but it wasn't until 1964, more than three years after JFK put NASA on a course toward the Moon, that the Soviet leadership started committing resources to the project.

By then it probably would have been too late for them to catch up with the United States even under the best of circumstances, and the Soviets made the situation worse by designing the giant N-1 rocket so that it used 30 smaller rocket motors instead of fewer, more-powerful motors. (NASA's Saturn V used five rocket motors—that's how it got its name.) Getting 30 rocket motors to work together in perfect unison without shaking each other apart is next to impossible, and the Soviets never did pull it off. The N-1 was only test-launched four times—twice before Neil Armstrong landed on the Moon and twice afterward. All four tests

Over 96 billion pounds of edible "surplus" food is thrown away in the U.S. every year.

ended in failure; the rockets either exploded or malfunctioned and had to be destroyed by the Soviet ground control.

SHHH!

Given the open nature of the Apollo program and subsequent NASA missions, it's difficult to absorb just how covert the Soviet Union's manned lunar program was. Launches took place in complete secrecy, although the United States did have an inkling that a Soviet lunar program was underway. The N-1 rockets were nearly 40 stories tall, and once they were rolled out onto their launch pads, it wasn't hard for American spy satellites to find them or for the CIA to guess what rockets that big were designed for.

On a few occasions, the U.S. government was even spooked into thinking they were about to lose the race to the Moon. In September 1968, for example, the U.S. detected the launch of a rocket from Baikonur and tracked its course all the way to the Moon. They even detected the sound of a human voice in a radio signal transmitted from the spacecraft. Was this another Yuri Gagarin moment? This time, NASA got lucky—the voice was only a recording designed to test the spacecraft's radio equipment.

NASA was so concerned about losing the space race that it sped up the pace of its operations. The *Apollo 8* mission (December 21–27, 1968), only the second manned mission of the Apollo program, was originally intended to test equipment in Earth's orbit. But the CIA was so convinced that the USSR was about to send cosmonauts on a flight around the Moon, NASA changed it to a circumlunar mission to keep the Soviets from beating them to the punch. Less than a year later, the Soviets—along with the rest of the world—watched the United States win the race.

NOW WHAT?

With that, the Soviet lunar program lost much of its purpose. For a time, the Soviets considered expanding the program to include a base on the Moon—if they couldn't get there *first*, they reasoned, they could still get there *best*. But the lunar program was canceled in 1974 as the Soviet Union shifted its emphasis to building space stations.

In the early 1970s, NASA began work on a reusable space shuttle. When informed that the United States' shuttle would be

More than 1.6 billion trees are planted in the U.S. every year—about 5 trees for every American.

able to carry military cargo over the Soviet Union, Soviet leader Leonid Brezhnev ordered up a space shuttle of his own. "We are not country bumpkins here!" he is said to have shouted. The first American space shuttle, the *Columbia*, flew on April 12, 1981; the first Soviet space shuttle, named the *Buran*, or "Snowstorm," flew on November 15, 1988. The *Buran* made only a single unmanned flight before the collapse of the Soviet Union in 1991 caused the program to be canceled.

Today the rivalry between the United States and Russian space programs is over, perhaps for good, as they work together with other countries to build the International Space Station.

CABIN FEVER

Not much remains of the Soviet manned lunar program more than 30 years after it was canceled. Remember, it wasn't just canceled; it was officially, categorically denied until the late 1980s, and by then nearly everything that could be recycled or reused by the Soviet space program had long since disappeared. Some parts that couldn't be used for anything else were made into storage sheds, airplane hangars, and even bandstands and children's playgrounds in and around the Baikonur Cosmodrome. Four of the LKs did survive, however. If you ever make it to France, you can see one of them on display at EuroDisney.

* * *

OUR HERO

Fearing that his countrymen weren't living up to their widely held stereotype of habitually burping, sweating, and farting in public, French doctor and author Frédéric Saldmann wrote a book called *Le Grand Ménage* (*Spring Cleaning*). Not allowing your body to release toxins naturally, he explains, causes an unhealthy build-up of "bad air" in your intestines. This can increase the risk of a hiatal hernia, which affects one third of French people. Saldmann's advice: "Dare to fart." And burp. And sweat. (He recommends cutting out antiperspirants.) Among the many benefits of living more naturally, says Saldmann, is that sweating releases pheromones that attract members of the opposite sex.

The Sun shrinks five feet every hour.

ROCK 'N' ROLL LAWSUIT

In the Beatles song "Come Together," John Lennon included a lyric that referenced a Chuck Berry song, an act intended as a tribute to one of the founding fathers of rock 'n' roll. Instead, it got Lennon embroiled in a years-long legal battle with one of the most colorful—and nefarious—characters in the history of the music business.

MEAN MR. LEVY

Morris Levy made a fortune in the music business. From bebop to big-band jazz, from doo-wop to rockabilly and rock 'n' roll, he had his fingers in everything. But he wasn't a music innovator or even a musician—he was known primarily as a wheeler-dealer businessman...and a swindler. Levy started as a tough New York street kid growing up in the Bronx during the Great Depression. He got kicked out of school at 13 for assaulting a teacher, ran away from home, moved to Florida, and hung around nightclubs until he was old enough to join the Navy. Upon his discharge after World War II, he returned to New York and the nightclub scene, and in 1949, with money obtained from his former nightclub bosses—members of the Genovese crime family—Levy opened the legendary jazz club Birdland.

BABY YOU'RE A RICH MAN

One night a representative from the American Society of Composers, Authors and Publishers (ASCAP), the agency that collects publishing royalties for songs performed in public, visited the club. The agent told Levy that he had to pay a monthly fee to cover the songs played by musicians in the club. Levy immediately threw the ASCAP guy out, thinking that it was an extortion ploy from a rival crime family. But after a call to his lawyer confirmed that ASCAP was legitimate, Levy had an inspiration: Owning songs could be lucrative. Anytime a song was played on the radio or performed in public, the owner of its "publishing rights" received a royalty payment.

Levy started a publishing company called Patricia Music (named after his wife) and commissioned the jazz musicians who

Worth the wait? It takes 30 to 45 minutes for gas to pass through your system and become a fart.

worked his nightclubs to compose songs for him, including the standards "Lullaby of Birdland" and "The Yellow Rose of Texas." He began buying up the rights—cheaply—to hundreds of jazz, early rock 'n' roll, and rhythm and blues songs, including "Party Doll" by Buddy Knox, "Honeycomb," by Jimmie Rodgers, and various tunes popularized by jazz greats Dinah Washington, Sarah Vaughan, and Count Basie—and routinely cheated the composers out of royalties.

TAX MAN

In 1957 Levy was named president of the newly formed Roulette Records; within six months he had staged a hostile takeover and owned the label. At Roulette, he quickly found a new way to cheat songwriters: He changed the credits of songs to list *himself* as a songwriter. ASCAP may credit Levy as a songwriter, but he definitely did not help write classic songs like "My Boy Lollipop," "California Sun," or "Why Do Fools Fall in Love?"

Under a corporate umbrella called Big Seven Music, Levy also handled record pressing and distribution for several smaller labels, and was suspected by the government of making secret pirated copies of legitimate albums and selling them to stores (or mob-run music distribution channels) thereby pocketing all the money, without having to pay royalties—or taxes—on any of it.

Any opportunity that Levy could find to make a buck, morally or immorally, legally or illegally, he took it. But when he felt that somebody else had taken advantage of him, Levy utilized the legal system. And Levy didn't care *who* it was—even if it was the most popular musician in the most popular band in the world.

HERE COME OLD FLAT TOP

The first track on the Beatles 1969 *Abbey Road* album is "Come Together," written by John Lennon. The first line: "Here come old flat top, he come grooving up slowly." Shortly after the album's release Lennon admitted to a reporter he'd taken the line from the 1956 Chuck Berry song "You Can't Catch Me," which features the lyric, "Here come old flat top, he was grooving up with me." A few months later, Lennon was sued for copyright infringement, not by Berry, but by the man that owned the copyright to "You Can't Catch Me," Morris Levy.

Levy was probably hoping for a quick settlement, but it looked like the infringement case would ultimately be decided by a judge and jury. Flash forward to 1973. Lennon's life was a mess. In addition to the pending "Come Together" suit, he was facing deportation back to England because of a 1968 marijuana possession charge. His current album, 1972's *Some Time in New York,* had been a bomb, peaking at #48 on the chart due to controversy over the anti-sexism song "Woman is the Ni**er of the World." There was tension in his marriage, too: Lennon wanted to stay in New York; his wife, Yoko Ono, wanted to search for her estranged daughter, Kyoko. In October 1973, Lennon had had enough. He told Ono he was going out to buy a newspaper, but hopped a plane to Los Angeles instead.

IMAGINE ALL THE PEOPLE

Lennon tried to escape his problems by immersing himself in his work. But writing new songs proved to be too emotionally stressful, so he decided that his next album would be cover versions of early rock 'n' roll songs he'd loved as a teenager. He convinced producer Phil Spector to help him make the record (the two had worked together on Lennon's *Imagine* solo album and the Beatles' *Let It Be*).

Spector rented out A&M Studios in Los Angeles and brought in dozens of famous musicians for the project. As many as 30 would be in the studio at one time, including Harry Nilsson, Dr. John, Ringo Starr, and Charlie Watts of the Rolling Stones. Lennon, still trying to forget his problems, drank a lot before, during, and after every session (as did the other musicians, especially Starr and Nilsson). One night, he and Nilsson were so hammered that they got kicked out of the Troubador nightclub for heckling the Smothers Brothers.

GET BACK

Shortly after Lennon started work on what was being called *Oldies but Mouldies*, the suit with Morris Levy over "Come Together" was settled. Terms of the settlement: In exchange for Levy dropping the case, Lennon agreed to record three songs published by Levy's Big Seven Music on his next solo album, with an appropriate portion of proceeds going to Levy. It coincided nicely with Lennon's

Oldies project, and in looking through Levy's catalog, Lennon easily found plenty of his favorite songs; it wouldn't be hard to find three to record.

By the end of 1973, Lennon, Spector, and crew had completed eight tracks for the album: "Bony Maronie" (by Larry Williams), "Sweet Little Sixteen" (Chuck Berry), "Be My Baby," (the Ronettes), "Just Because" (Lloyd Price), "My Baby Left Me" (Elvis Presley), and the three Big Seven songs, "Angel Baby" (Rosie and the Originals), "Ya Ya" (Lee Dorsey), and "You Can't Catch Me"—the Chuck Berry song that had led to Levy's lawsuit.

HAPPINESS IS A WARM GUN

Eight songs was enough for an album, but Lennon wanted to record about 12. And while he was deciding what the final four would be, the recording sessions for *Oldies but Mouldies* came to an abrupt halt. Spector, well known for demanding absolute control in his recording sessions (and also known for a history of mental breakdowns), got so frustrated that the drunken Lennon wasn't taking his direction that he pulled out a handgun, pointed it at Lennon, and fired it into the ceiling. Then he walked out of the studio...with the master tapes. And there wasn't much Lennon or his label, Capitol Records, could do about it. Instead of billing Capitol for the studio time, Spector had paid for it himself, which made the master tapes legally his.

In January 1974, Spector called Lennon and told him he had the tapes and that he'd never give them back. Two months later, Spector was involved in a severe car accident that put him in a coma and required him to have substantial facial reconstructive surgery. The album was definitely off.

HE CAN WORK IT OUT

Lennon grew increasingly depressed. Ono wouldn't take him back, and he couldn't finish the album that the lawsuit settlement agreement required him to do. On top of that, his green-card matter hadn't yet been resolved, so he could feasibly be deported at any time. His heavy drinking wasn't helping either, so Lennon locked himself in his bedroom for a week in spring 1974 and quit drinking, cold turkey.

As the summer began, with Spector out of the picture and the

If you're average, this year you'll walk about 4.5 miles while making your bed.

Oldies but Mouldies tapes still not forthcoming, Lennon moved back to New York City, both to follow up on his immigration case and to find inspiration to write new songs. Over the next few months, he wrote and recorded the songs for the album *Walls and Bridges*, released in October 1974.

Legally, though, he was still bound to record three Morris Levy–owned songs. To get the *Oldies but Mouldies* master tapes back, Capitol Records first threatened to sue Spector, but in the end they just paid him $90,000 in cash. Not wanting to stop his work on *Walls and Bridges*, Lennon waited until after that album was complete before listening to the Spector sessions. The result: Because of his heavy drinking at the time he recorded them, Lennon's voice sounded so bad that only four of the eight *Mouldies* songs were good enough to release, and only one of those ("Angel Baby") was from the Big Seven catalog. But in order to satisfy Levy, he still had to release them. Capitol wouldn't issue them on an EP or as singles; Lennon had no choice but to go back into the studio and finish the album.

DON'T LET ME DOWN

When *Walls and Bridges* was released, Morris Levy was furious. He'd dropped his "Come Together" suit on condition that Lennon's *next* album would contain three songs owned by Big Seven Music; instead, Lennon had made and album of all-new material, except for a section of "Ya Ya," a duet of Lennon on piano and his 11-year-old son, Julian, on drums. (Levy thought that was something of an insult.) Lennon met with Levy and his attorney and explained what had happened with Spector and the missing master tapes, and that Lennon had recorded, but not yet released, the three necessary songs, and would do so on his forthcoming all-covers album (now retitled *Old Hat*). Levy was appeased, and to help Lennon get the album restarted, let him rehearse at Levy's upstate New York farm. Lennon also told Levy he could sell the finished album on Adam VIII, his mail-order label.

Within two weeks, Lennon had recorded nine tracks: "Be-Bop-A-Lula," "Stand By Me," "Reddy Teddy/Rip It Up," "Ain't That a Shame," "Do You Want to Dance," "Slippin' and Slidin'," "Peggy Sue," "Bring It On Home to Me/Send Me Some Lovin'," and "Ya

Ya," which was re-recorded in full. A new title and the album cover art were chosen, too. Graphic artist John Uotomo took a 1961 photo of Lennon standing in a doorway in Hamburg, Germany (the Beatles' early stomping grounds), and put the words "John Lennon: Rock 'n' Roll" above Lennon, rendered to look like a neon sign. Lennon loved the image, and thought *Rock 'n' Roll* was the perfect title.

LET IT BE

In November 1974, Levy asked Lennon to send him a rough mix of the album. Since Levy had a financial interest in it, Lennon agreed, sending him a scratchy, second-generation copy of the tapes—a poor recording, but good enough to listen to in order to get the gist of the album. Lennon didn't think the album was very good; the Spector songs seemed overproduced, while the newly recorded songs felt raw and unfinished. But Capitol Records wouldn't let Lennon shelve it (and neither would Levy), so it was scheduled for release in spring 1975.

That December, Lennon met with his lawyer, Howard Seider, and Levy. Citing a verbal promise Lennon had made to him to let him release *Rock 'n' Roll* on his mail-order Adam VIII label, Levy tried to persuade Seider to get the proper legal clearances from Capitol Records. Seider relayed the request, and Capitol refused outright—not only did Lennon not have the authority to negotiate such deals, but they'd paid $90,000 for the right to make this album. Levy didn't have the legal right to market Lennon's name, image, or recordings.

MIND GAMES, PART 1

Lennon's fortunes improved in early 1975. He and Ono reconciled and moved back in together in New York. His immigration case was dismissed (he was allowed to stay in the United States permanently), and the first single from *Walls and Bridges*, "Whatever Gets You Through The Night," was a #1 hit.

But in February 1975, Levy—unwilling to accept Capitol's refusal to let him market the album—took matters into his own hands. He took the incredibly rough demo that Lennon had sent him a few months earlier and released it as an album through his mail-order label as *John Lennon Sings the Great Rock & Roll Hits:*

In leap years, January always begins on the same day of the week as April and July.

Roots. The cover art was a cheap stock photo of Lennon taken in 1969. When Capitol heard what Levy was doing, it rushed the real version of *Rock 'n' Roll*. They also threatened prosecution against any TV or radio station that advertised Levy's *Roots* album (calling it illegal bootleg material) and legally forced Adam VIII to stop producing the album. Capitol sprung to action so quickly that the commercial for *Roots* had aired for just a few weeks, late at night, in a few East Coast cities. Only 3,000 copies had been pressed, of which 1,270 were sold.

But for some reason, despite the lawsuit, the nearly two years it took to make the album, and the massive headaches they endured while doing so, Lennon and Capitol dropped one of the Levy-owned songs, "Angel Baby," from the final album. That meant he'd released only two Levy-owned songs ("Ya Ya" and "You Can't Catch Me"), not the agreed-upon three, which left the door open for even *more* litigation.

MIND GAMES, PART 2

In 1975 Levy did, in fact, sue Lennon. But not for failure to live up to his end of the bargain. Instead, Levy sued Lennon for $42 million for breach of an oral agreement, because the singer had promised him that he could sell the album on his mail-order label. Lennon countersued for unauthorized use of his name, likeness, and recordings, as well as for damages to his reputation as a recording artist due to the "shoddiness" of *Roots* and its packaging.

United States District Court judge Thomas Griesa heard the case in January 1976. Lennon's attorneys argued that because the master tape Levy used to make *Roots* was an unfinished studio dub, the resulting records could only be of poor quality, and thereby damaging to Lennon's reputation. They also argued that the cover photo of Lennon, a head shot of him with long hair, damaged his credibility, because the photo neither reflected how he looked when the album was made nor evoked the 1950s spirit of the album. To further that point, Lennon showed up for the trial with short hair. William Schurtman, Levy's attorney, badgered Lennon on the witness stand, accusing him of cutting his hair only for the trial. "Rubbish," Lennon replied. "I cut it every 18 months." Everyone in the courtroom, including Judge Griesa, burst into laughter.

Approximately 97% of vegetable varieties grown in 1900 are now extinct.

On February 20, 1976, Judge Griesa issued his 29-page opinion. Griesa believed that Lennon *had* promised Levy the right to issue the oldies album on Adam VIII, but declared the "tentative verbal agreement" void because Lennon had no legal right to negotiate distribution deals—that was Capitol Records' job. After hearing arguments for and against Lennon's countersuit, Griesa ordered Lennon to pay Levy $7,000 for breach of an oral agreement (which, ironically, covered the production costs of *Roots)*, but ordered Levy pay Lennon $110,000 to compensate for the lost income from *Rock 'n' Roll* due to *Roots*, as well as an additional $42,000 in punitive damages for harming his reputation. (Ironic fact: After the decision was read, Levy's attorney, William Schurtman, approached Lennon and asked him to autograph his copy of Lennon's *Two Virgins* LP.)

AND IN THE END

Rock 'n' Roll reached #6 on the British and American album charts. And although it did go Gold over the course of a decade, (more than half a million copies sold), it was ultimately among the lowest-selling studio albums of Lennon's solo career, only slightly edging out his 1972 dud *Some Time in New York City*. But *Rock 'n' Roll* would end up being the last album released during his lifetime.

Shortly after the release of *Rock 'n' Roll*, Yoko Ono announced that she was pregnant with what would be the couple's only child, Sean, born in October 1975 (on Lennon's 35th birthday). Lennon decided to retire from the music business and focus his attention on raising his son. In 1980 he returned to the studio to record a new album, *Double Fantasy*, but he was shot and killed that December at age 40, a month before the album's release to critical acclaim.

Levy's decades of shady business practices did finally catch up with him. Though he'd been under investigation by the FBI off and on since the early 1950s, in 1986 he was finally caught. He was indicted for conspiring with a Genovese boss to extort money from a music wholesaler. He was convicted and sentenced to 10 years in prison, but while the case was on appeal, Levy died of liver cancer in early 1990. He was 62.

MAKING A MOVIE, PT. V: POSTPRODUCTION

Good news, Uncle John: Principal photography has been completed! Bad news: Your movie is only half-done. *(Part IV is on page 433.)*

SHIFTING GEARS

Once filming has wrapped, the number of people working on a movie shrinks from a few hundred to a few dozen. And the workplace shifts from huge soundstages and grand locations to small rooms with computers and video screens. While much of the postproduction work actually begins while the movie is still filming (such as visual effects), most of it isn't completed until a month or two before the movie's release. (That's why movie trailers often have different music, different visual effects, or even different scenes than the final film.)

In charge of the process is the *postproduction supervisor*, who maintains the schedule, hires vendors, brings the actors back if necessary, and keeps the distribution and marketing departments informed of the progress. That way, the director and producer can spend their time looking over the editor's shoulder.

EDITING

Without a highly skilled editor fitting all of the pieces together into a well-paced narrative, the movie wouldn't work. The editor's first task: create an *assembly cut* of the film—nearly every single take from every single scene, put into order according to the script. The director then spends a few days viewing it over and over, marking the best takes for the editor. With that information, the editor makes a *rough cut*. The director then watches *that*, looking for three main things: the order in which the scenes occur, how the shots are cut together within each scene, and which scenes didn't work as planned. With a new set of notes, the editor cuts the movie yet again. This fine-tuning keeps going until everyone is satisfied.

It's said that a good editor will "discover the film" in the cutting room, putting emphasis on an aspect of the movie that the director may not have seen as that important.

Illibilli, Sudan, is the world's longest palindromic place name. Second longest: Nigeria's Uburubu.

Reel-Life Example: The first rough cut of the original *Star Wars* presented to writer/director George Lucas in late 1976 was a mess. The pacing was slow; some shots lingered too long and others ended too quickly. With the film already behind schedule, Lucas fired his editor and brought in three new ones: Paul Hirsch, Richard Chew, and his own wife, Marcia Lucas. One such quick cut was when one of the sandpeople attacked Luke (Mark Hamill) with a staff. At the end of the original shot, the creature raised his staff above his head and then the shot ended abruptly. Hirsch extended the scene by running the film backwards for a brief second just as the creature's arms reached their highest point, then repeated that up-and-down move four times, adding emotional impact.
Did it work? Yes. Lucas has since credited the editing as one of the main reasons for the unparalleled success of *Star Wars*.

ADDITIONAL PHOTOGRAPHY

Why do so many movies have a "typical Hollywood ending?" After the rough cut of the film is finished, the studio will show it to test audiences and focus groups who then answer a series of questions: "Did you understand the plot?" "Did you like the ending?" If the majority of viewers answer "no," the studio will mandate a new ending (often a happier one) and bring the principal actors back in for additional photography, sometimes called *pickups* or *re-shoots*. New sets often have to be built, because movie sets are designed to last only the few days they're needed and are then destroyed.

Another reason for additional photography: Sometimes the director or producer feels something is missing—perhaps a reaction shot that further explains a character's motivation. According to screenwriter John August (*Big Fish*), "In most cases, it's not that you're adding something great, but rather that you're replacing something sucky."

Reel-Life Example: The 2007 horror thriller *The Invasion*, a remake of the classic sci-fi film, *Invasion of the Body Snatchers*, was German director Oliver Hirschbiegel's first English language film. Test audiences (and Warner Bros. execs) found the film too "claustrophobic" and "moody," so producer Joel Silver took the extreme step of bringing in a new director to reshoot much of the film. In fact, he brought in *three* directors—Larry and Andy Wachowski, directors of *The Matrix* trilogy, and their longtime collaborator,

In June 2004, a beauty contest was held in western Croatia...for goats.

James McTeigue—to redo all the action scenes and the ending.

Did it work? No. After arriving in theaters a year and a half after its original announced release date, *The Invasion* was lambasted by critics and bombed at the Box Office.

AUTOMATIC DIALOGUE REPLACEMENT (ADR)

ADR, or lip-synching—also called *looping*—occurs months after filming has wrapped. Although the director would love it if every bit of dialogue recorded during filming was usable, much of it is not—either due to low audible levels, extraneous noises, or performances that didn't quite hit the mark. In addition, naughty words need to be changed so the film can be shown on broadcast television, or if the studio just wants a more family-friendly rating.

Reel-Life Example: In the 1999 comedy *Galaxy Quest*, when Gwen (Sigourney Weaver) sees the "Chompers" that she must run through, the audience hears her say, "Well, screw that!" but her lips are obviously saying...something else.

Did it work? Yes. After the original cut was deemed "too dark," much of the violence and language was toned down in postproduction, making *Galaxy Quest* more accessible to a younger audience that helped it earn more than twice its $45 million budget.

VISUAL EFFECTS

Working against tight deadlines, digital effects artists pore over every layer of every frame, striving to combine digital and traditional shots, often "painting" out green screens and adding in background plates (such as a fake sky)...hoping that the director will approve of their completed shot.

Reel-Life Example: One of the most effects-heavy movies ever made was 2003's *The Return of the King*, the conclusion to the *Lord of the Rings* trilogy. One particularly complex shot featured two giant, elephantlike creatures (called *mûmaks*) crashing into each other, and then tumbling to the ground. After working on the shot for six months, the digital artists were disheartened when director Peter Jackson informed them that it lacked the size, force, and impact that he was looking for. But time was running out—they only had *two days* to redo it. Working nonstop, the effects team was able to match up with Jackson's vision.

Did it work? Yes. Jackson's insistence on perfection in every

President George W. Bush was treated for Lyme disease in August 2006.

aspect of the filmmaking process was rewarded with massive commercial *and* critical success, culminating with eleven Academy Awards, including the Oscar for Best Visual Effects.

SOUND DESIGN

Every scene of a big-budget movie contains dozens of separate and distinct sounds: squeaky floor boards, slamming doors, barking dogs, cars, thunder, coughs, sneezes, crashes, explosions, and so on. Each must either be found or created in post-production. The *sound designer* will first search through vast sound effects libraries (which explains why you've heard the exact same hawk screech in so many movies). What can't be found must be created by *Foley artists*—named after influential Hollywood sound effects man Jack Foley. Working in either a soundproof room or outdoors if required, these technicians pull from a giant bag of tricks.

Reel-Life Example: For the 2008 animated comedy *WALL-E*, in which a discarded robot must save humanity, producer Jim Morris brought in veteran sound designer Ben Burtt, who first made his mark on the *Star Wars* films. Since WALL-E must communicate without words, Burtt used the same technique he used 32 years earlier for R2-D2: he recorded his own voice making kid sounds and then ran those through a synthesizer.

Did it work? Yes. Because the speechless robot was given a human foundation for his vocal utterances, audiences were able to identify with his plight, helping *WALL-E* to become a huge summer hit.

MUSIC

Music is divided into three categories: The *soundtrack* consists of songs played over the top of the scene that help convey mood. These are found by the *music supervisor*, working from a director's wish list. This process is usually started before postproduction begins, as negotiating payments and securing rights can be a lengthy process. The second category is *source music*, sometimes called *incidental music*. This may be the background music played at a restaurant or a carnival ride at a fair. Rights have to be secured for incidental music as well, unless it's in the public domain. The third category is the *score*, original music that a composer creates specifically for the film.

In most cases, the composer isn't brought in until well into

The paper bucket used for chicken by KFC was created by Wendy's founder Dave Thomas.

postproduction. Once on board, he or she will watch the most recent edit of the film—often accompanied by a *temp track* of preexisting music to help convey what the director is looking for. Then it's up to the composer to write the music, and for the music supervisor to hire an orchestra and book studio time to record it. This is also an area where creative differences often occur.

Reel-Life Example: In 1989 Hans Zimmer was hired to score Ridley Scott's action movie, *Black Rain*, starring Michael Douglas as an American cop caught up in the Japanese underworld. Zimmer tried to bring something new to the typical action score by blending in traditional Japanese music. He recalls that producer Stanley Jaffe "hated the score so much that I actually got shouted at after a screening, and I fainted. By the time we got to the dub stage, I was just living in fear. And it's odd because after the Oscars, I went to a private party. Michael Douglas was there, and he said, 'You really saved my a** in *Black Rain*.'"

Did it work? It appears Douglas was right; the movie earned $134 million in worldwide ticket sales. And Zimmer boasts that his ethnically flavored music has had a lasting influence. "*Black Rain* had somehow set up a new way action movies could be scored. Soon everybody was doing the *Black Rain* thing."

TITLE SEQUENCES

Some filmmakers still open their movies with elaborate title sequences. A great deal of work is put into these stand-alone "short films" that, according to Saul Bass, the man who pioneered them in the 1960s, "should create a climate for the story that's about to unfold." The process: The script or the most current cut of the film is sent to a title design company along with the list of credits, a music temp track if one is available, and any instructions concerning the style (animation, computer graphics, and so on). After the designers watch the film, they draw up *style frames* of what the sequence will look like. Once the director approves those, they complete a rough draft of the entire sequence. And it goes back and forth until the director is happy; then the music is mixed in, and the title is ready to go.

Reel-Life Example: Four of the five 2007 Best Picture nominees used a "cold" opening (no title sequence at the beginning). The only one that used a traditional opening title sequence was Jason

Reitman's *Juno*, a comedy starring Ellen Page as a teenager dealing with pregnancy. Reitman hired a small company called Shadowplay to do the sequence, and the process was a bit different than most feature films. Before animating the entire sequence, Gareth Smith, co-founder of Shadowplay, sent style frames—inspired by vintage 1970s punk-rock posters—to Reitman for approval. After that, hundreds of photographs were taken of Page walking on a treadmill carrying a bottle of orange juice. Those were then cut out and hand-animated to create the retro feel. Adding to the whimsy of the sequence was the song, "All I Want Is You," by Barry Louis Polisar, which Reitman had chosen himself. "Title sequences tend to be an afterthought for most films," says Smith. "We prefer to develop ideas early in the filmmaking process, which we think enhances the storytelling of the film."

Did it work? Yes. *Juno* cost $7.5 million and grossed over $228 million worldwide, making it one of the most profitable films of all time...and making Shadowplay a not-so-small company anymore.

PUTTING IT ALL TOGETHER

As the release date looms ever closer, the work intensifies.

• **The final sound mix.** This is the last step in the creative process. Any given shot in a film may contain dozens of sounds. For instance, a bar fight will contain the actors' voices, source music, score music, sound effects of punches landing, windows being broken, and what's known in the industry as *walla* (background murmur noise). Every single one of these sounds needs to be carefully balanced by the sound editor.

• **Locking the picture.** Most of the postproduction tasks have been going on simultaneously, with the director running from one office to another, looking and listening, and signing off on things. But at some point, the work must stop, and that's not often when the filmmakers would prefer. As director Peter Jackson once said, "You never really finish a film; you just keep working on it until they tell you to turn it in." (Just like making a *Bathroom Reader*.)

• **Making prints.** The finished film must be copied up to 2,500 times for distribution to theaters all over the world. This is a highly technical process that takes place in specialized labs. Because making thousands of copies would wear down the master, a series of intermediate prints must be made to copy from: first is the *interposi-*

tive, a low-contrast copy on very fine-grained film stock. From this new master, a set of *internegatives* are made. These contain the separate audio tracks; some will also be given subtitle tracks for foreign markets. The final step is to create the individual copies, which are divided into reels, each holding 2,000 feet of film (on what is technically called a *double reel*). A typical film will comprise five separate reels. Now they're all ready to be sent to theaters—bigger movies will be given fake labels in an effort to curb piracy. Often the final reel won't be sent until the day before the film opens.

MARKETING AND DISTRIBUTION

A separate company, hired by the studio, has been working for months on ways to get the movie shown in as many theaters and to get as much buzz among filmgoers as possible. They negotiate with distributors, film festival organizers, as well as marketing companies that will help promote the film. They send the finished film to *exhibitors*—theater owners who pay for the right to show it and then share in its profits. The latest trend is *viral marketing*, mainly done on the Internet. This consists of getting online users involved in the process while the film is being made, relying on word of mouth to increase the buzz. The more faith a studio has in a film, the more money it's willing to spend to advertise it.

LETTING IT GO

The release date finally arrives. Commercials have been airing; press kits and posters are displayed in theaters; and the stars have promoted the movie on talk shows. Now, the film is completely out of the filmmakers' hands—it is up to the movie-going public to decide whether or not they've succeeded.

But the odds are not in the filmmakers' favor: Out of the roughly 600 movies that get released into U.S. theaters each year (about 2/3 of those are independently made)—only a select few will turn a profit. And less than one percent will become classics. For that to happen, the concept needs to be fresh, the story needs to be well written, the film needs to be well shot, well acted, and well edited; and the timing in the marketplace needs to be right. A misfire in any of these areas results in yet another one of the thousands of movies that you see sitting there see on the video shelf...but never seem to be able to bring yourself to rent.

The only *Brady Bunch* kid to appear in every episode: Bobby.

RANDOM THOUGHTS

We leave you with a few entertaining—and poignant—observations.

"A fine quotation is a diamond on the finger of a witty person, but a pebble in the hands of a fool."

—**John Roux**

"I never knew an early-rising, hard-working, prudent man, careful of his earnings, and strictly honest, who complained of bad luck."

—**Henry Ward Beecher**

"Life is not so bad if you have plenty of luck, a good physique, and not too much imagination."

—**Christopher Isherwood**

"What's right is what's left if you do everything else wrong."

—**Robin Williams**

"I would like to be allowed to admire a man's opinion as I would his dog—without being expected to take it home with me."

—**Frank A. Clark**

"It is a cliche that most clichés are true, but then like most cliches, that cliche is untrue."

—**Stephen Fry**

"Only one man in a thousand is a leader of men. The other 999 follow women."

—**Groucho Marx**

"Natives who beat drums to drive off evil spirits are objects of scorn to smart Americans who blow horns to break up traffic jams."

—**Mary Ellen Kelly**

"There's no better feeling in the world than a warm pizza box on your lap."

—**Kevin James**

"The shortest period of time lies between the minute you put something away for a rainy day and the unexpected arrival of rain."

—**Jane Bryant Quinn**

"The optimist proclaims that we live in the best of all possible worlds, and the pessimist fears this is true."

—**James Branch Cabell**

"I once wanted to save the world. Now I just want to leave the room with some dignity."

—**Lotus Weinstock**

The Welwitschia plant (found only in Southern Africa) can live for 1,000 years.

ANSWER PAGES

OL' JAY'S BRAINTEASERS

(Answers for page 166)

1. HUNGRY BOOKWORM. The bookworm only eats through 2½ inches of book. That's because he started at page 1 of the book on the left (which is facing the right side) and only has to eat through the front cover of book 1, the back cover of book 2, all of the pages of book 2, then through the front cover of book 2, then through the back cover of book 3. At that point he will have reached the last page of book 3 and can stop eating.

2. THE 5TH CONDITION. The person must also be elected.

3. SURROUNDED. Julia will just have to wait until the merry-go-round ride ends…and then dismount.

4. BUILDER BLUNDER. The house address numbers were missing. Each number cost $1.00. So 1000 would have cost $4.00 and 50 would have cost $2.00. But since their new neighborhood only had nine houses, their addresses were each a single number, costing them a total of only $3.00.

5. THE RUNAROUND. One-eff Jef ran around the chair twice and then said, "I'll be back in a week to run around it a third time," knowing that Two-eff Jeff wouldn't be able to sit there for an entire week.

6. A MOTHER'S GIFT. The answer is coal, which starts out black, but becomes a diamond in the rough after Mother Earth "smothers" it for a few million years. Thanks, Mom!

7. FEELING FLAT. The flat tire was Thom's spare tire—in his trunk the whole time.

8. COFFEE DELIVERY! Maggie filled the three-gallon bucket with coffee and then poured it into the five-gallon bucket. Then she filled the three-gallon bucket again and carefully poured it into the five-gallon bucket until it was full, leaving exactly one gallon of coffee in the three-gallon bucket. And then we had coffee!

Film star Jackie Chan's father was a spy for Taiwan.

EXERCISE YOUR BRAIN

(Answers for page 236)

1. New Ha**mpsh**ire.

2. Alphabetical order—if you spell out the numbers.

3. The letter Q.

4. Four.

5. The letters **-ANT** can be added to all of them to form new words.

6. Haw**aii** and L**oui**siana.

7. **Mechanics**, or **mischance**.

8. Connect I cut (Connecticut).

9. Seven.

10. Strengths.

11. Cobra, crab.

12. Donkey—each of the others begins with the name of another animal: **pig**eon, **bee**tle, **bull**frog.

13. Spell each of the numbers from 0 to 99—none contain the letters **a**, **b**, **c**, or **d**.

14. In capital letters, the word has "180-degree rotational symmetry," meaning that if you turn the book upside down, it still says **SWIMS**.

15. Ca**tchphr**ase.

THE COLLECTORS

(Answers for page 277)

1. c **2.** p **3.** f **4.** x **5.** r **6.** i **7.** k **8.** s **9.** l **10.** n **11.** e **12.** w **13.** b **14.** o **15.** g **16.** t **17.** m **18.** u **19.** a **20.** q **21.** v **22.** y **23.** h **24.** d **25.** j

"STRONGER THAN DIRT"

(Answers for page 321)

1. Sony PlayStation (2002)

2. L'Oreal (1967)

3. Radio Shack (2005)

4. GEICO (2004)

5. Mentos (1991)

6. Wonderbra (1994)

7. General Electric (1954)

8. Sprite (1996)

Bubble gum was originally called Blibber-Blubber gum (1906).

9. Bayer (2004)
10. Coca-Cola (1929)
11. Kix (1980)
12. Ford (1972)
13. Viagra (2002)
14. Quaker Puffed Wheat (1920)
15. Ajax Detergent (1962)
16. Pepsodent (1956)
17. Pringles (1990)
18. Morton Salt (1911)
19. Foster's Lager (1992)
20. Miller High Life (1904)
21. Microsoft (1996)
22. Playtex Cross-Your-Heart Bra (1965)
23. Nair (1987)
24. Peace Corps (1961)
25. J.C. Penny (1999)
26. Greyhound (1957)
27. United Negro College Fund (1972)
28. Mazda (2003)
29. Disneyland (1955)
30. Meow Mix (1976)
31. Esso/Exxon (1964)
32. BMW (1975)
33. Avis Rent-a-Car (1962)
34. U.S. Army (1981)

THERE'S NO PLACE LIKE ZAMUNDA

(Answers for page 373)

1. c), 2. k), 3. l), 4. d), 5. q), 6. b), 7. m), 8. j), 9. r), 10. i), 11. h), 12. o), 13. n), 14. a), 15. f), 16. e), 17. p), 18. g)

*   *   *

TOAD AWAY

Australian Cane toads are nearly as big as dinner plates…and poisonous. Their venom has been known to kill large dogs within minutes. That's why Jackson Crews was worried when he saw his dog Bella mistake a cane toad for a pie he was feeding her in his backyard in Bakewell, Australia. "She swallowed it whole," said Crews. He rushed Bella to the vet, where they gave her "an injection to help her vomit." Finally, 40 minutes later, she threw up and out came the toad. And it started hopping around. Amazingly, both animals survived. Vet workers then caught the toad and kept it at their office. They named it Spew.

Uncle John's
LEGENDARY LOST
BATHROOM READER
Our 12th Edition!
Uncle John's
ABSOLUTELY ABSORBING
BATHROOM READER
150 NEW PAGES & ALL YOUR FAVORITES!
the BEST of Uncle John's
Our 15th Bathroom Reader
ALL NEW!
Uncle John's
AHH-INSPIRING
BATHROOM READER
16th
Uncle John's
UNSTOPPABLE
BATHROOM READER
17th
Uncle John's
SLIGHTLY IRREGULAR
BATHROOM READER
ALL NEW!
Uncle John's
GREAT BIG
BATHROOM READER
Uncle John's
CURIOUSLY COMPELLING
BATHROOM READER
by the BATHROOM READERS' INSTITUTE
THE BEST OF THE BEST OF Uncle John's
BATHROOM READER
Uncle John's
TRIUMPHANT
20TH ANNIVERSARY
BATHROOM READER
by the BATHROOM READERS' INSTITUTE
18th
Uncle John's
FAST-ACTING LONG-LASTING
BATHROOM READER
by the BATHROOM READERS' INSTITUTE

THE LAST PAGE

FELLOW BATHROOM READERS:
The fight for good bathroom reading should never be taken loosely—we must do our duty and sit firmly for what we believe in, even while the rest of the world is taking potshots at us.

We'll be brief. Now that we've proven we're not simply a flush-in-the-pan, we invite you to take the plunge: Sit Down and Be Counted! Become a member of the Bathroom Readers' Institute. Log on to *www.bathroomreader.com*, or send a self-addressed, stamped, business-sized envelope to: BRI, PO Box 1117, Ashland, Oregon 97520. You'll receive your free membership card, get discounts when ordering directly through the BRI, and earn a permanent spot on the BRI honor roll!

Well, we're out of space, and when you've gotta go, you've gotta go. Tanks for all your support. Hope to hear from you soon. Meanwhile, remember...

Keep on flushin'!